Intrapartum care

care of healthy women and their babies during childbirth

National Collaborating Centre for Women's and Children's Health

Commissioned by the National Institute for Health and Clinical Excellence

September 2007

RCOG Press

Published by the **RCOG Press** at the Royal College of Obstetricians and Gynaecologists, 27 Sussex Place, Regent's Park, London NW1 4RG

www.rcog.org.uk

Registered charity no. 213280

First published 2007

ISBN 978-1-904752-36-3

RCOG Editor: Andrew Welsh
Original design: FiSH Books, London
Typesetting: Andrew Welsh
Proofreading: Katharine Timberlake (Reedmace Editing)
Index: Jan Ross (Merrall-Ross (Wales) Ltd)
Printed by Henry Ling Ltd, The Dorset Press, Dorchester DT1 1HD

Contents

Guideline Development Group membership and acknowledgements

Guideline Development Group

GDG members

Sara Kenyon	Senior Research Fellow/Guideline Development Group Leader
Tony Ducker	Consultant Neonatologist
Simon Grant	Consultant in Obstetrics and Fetal Medicine
Gill Gyte	Women's Representative (resigned June 2007)
Jayne Jempson	Labour Ward Matron
Carolyn Markham	Women's Representative
Geraldine O'Sullivan	Obstetric Anaesthetist
Julia Sanders	Consultant Midwife
Maureen Treadwell	Women's Representative
Derek Tuffnell	Consultant in Obstetrics
Steve Walkinshaw	Consultant in Obstetrics
Marina Wells	Recruitment and Retention Midwife

National Collaborating Centre for Women's and Children's Health (NCC-WCH) technical team

Martin Whittle	Clinical Co-Director for Women's Health
Martin Dougherty	Executive Director
Rintaro Mori	Research Fellow
Roz Ullman	Senior Research Fellow
Paul Jacklin	Senior Health Economist
Peny Retsa	Health Economist
Debbie Pledge	Senior Information Specialist
Samantha Vahidi	Senior Work Programme Coordinator

Acknowledgements

Additional support was received from Hannah-Rose Douglas, Sjokvist Garcia-Steward, Eva Gautam, Anuradha Sekhri, Rosie Crossley, Paula Broughton-Palmer and Jane Thomas at the NCC-WCH, Wendy Riches, Francoise Cluzeau, Joanne Lord and Phil Alderson at the National Institute for Health and Clinical Excellence (NICE), Sam Richmond at Sunderland Hospital, Peter Brocklehurst and Rona McCandlish at the National Perinatal Epidemiology Unit (NPEU) and Pat Doyle at the London School of Hygiene & Tropical Medicine. We would particularly like to thank Sonja Henderson and the Pregnancy and Childbirth Cochrane Collaboration for access to their reviews prior to publication, Jo Greene and Helen Baston from York and Stavros Petrou from NPEU for their expertise. We also thank the Patient and Public Involvement Programme (PPIP) for NICE whose glossary was adapted for use in this guideline.

Stakeholder organisations

Academic Division of Midwifery, University of Nottingham
Action on Pre-Eclampsia
Addenbrooke's NHS Trust
Airedale General Hospital – Acute Trust

All Wales Birth Centre Group
Alliance Pharmaceuticals Ltd
Anglesey Local Health Board
Association for Continence Advice
Association for Improvements in Maternity Services (AIMS)
Association of Anaesthetists of Great Britain and Ireland
Association of Baby Charities
Association of Chartered Physiotherapists in Women's Health
Association of Clinical Biochemists
Association of Radical Midwives
Association of the British Pharmaceuticals Industry (ABPI)
Baby Lifeline
Barnsley Acute Trust
Barnsley PCT
Bedfordshire & Hertfordshire NHS Strategic Health Authority
Birmingham Women's Hospital
Birth Centre Network UK
Birth Trauma Association
Birthchoice UK
BLISS – the premature baby charity
British Association for Counselling and Psychotherapy (BACP)
British Association of Perinatal Medicine
British Committee for Standards in Haematology
British Dietetic Association
British Maternal and Fetal Medicine Society
British National Formulary (BNF)
British Psychological Society
British Society of Interventional Radiology
Carmarthenshire Acute Trust
CASPE Research
Chartered Society of Physiotherapy (CSP)
CIS'ters
City Hospitals Sunderland NHS Trust
Cochrane Pregnancy & Childbirth Group
Commission for Social Care Inspection
Confidential Enquiry into Maternal and Child Health (CEMACH)
Connecting for Health
Conwy & Denbighshire Acute Trust
Co-operative Pharmacy Association
Cotswold and Vale PCT
County Durham and Darlington Acute Trust
Cymdeithas Tai Hafan
Denbighshire Local Health Board
Department of Health
Depression Alliance
Derbyshire Mental Health Trust
Diabetes UK
Diagnostic Ultrasound (UK) Ltd
Down's Syndrome Association
Dudley Group of Hospitals NHS Trust
Eli Lilly and Company Ltd
English National Forum of LSA Midwifery Officers
Epsom & St Helier University Hospitals NHS Trust
Faculty of Public Health
Ferring Pharmaceuticals Ltd
Fibroid Network Charity
Gloucestershire Acute Trust
Gorlin Syndrome Group
Great Ormond Street Hospital for Children NHS Trust
Group B Strep Support
Guy's and St Thomas' NHS Trust

Health Professions Wales
Healthcare Commission
Heart of England NHS Foundation Trust
Hospital Infection Society
Huntleigh Healthcare
Independent Midwives Association
Infection Control Nurses Association of the British Isles
King's College Acute Trust
La Leche League
Leeds Teaching Hospitals NHS Trust
Liverpool PCT
Liverpool Women's NHS Trust
Luton and Dunstable Hospital NHS Trust
Maidstone and Tunbridge Wells NHS Trust
Maternity Education and Research Group
Maternity Health Links
Medeus Pharma Ltd
Medicines and Healthcare products Regulatory Agency (MHRA)
Medway NHS Trust
Mid and West Regional Maternity Service Liasion Committee (MSLC)
Mid Essex Hospitals NHS Trust
Mid Staffordshire General Hospitals NHS Trust
MIDIRS (Midwives Information & Resource Service)
Midwifery Studies Research Unit
National Childbirth Trust
National Collaborating Centre for Acute Care
National Collaborating Centre for Cancer (NCC-C)
National Collaborating Centre for Chronic Conditions (NCC-CC)
National Collaborating Centre for Mental Health (NCCMH)
National Collaborating Centre for Nursing and Supportive Care (NCC-NSC)
National Collaborating Centre for Primary Care (NCC-PC)
National Collaborating Centre for Women's and Children's Health (NCC-WCH)
National Coordinating Centre for Health Technology Assessment (NCCHTA)
National Council for Disabled People, Black, Minority and Ethnic Community (Equalities)
National Patient Safety Agency
National Perinatal Epidemiology Unit
National Public Health Service – Wales
National Screening Committee
Neoventa Medical
Newcastle Upon Tyne Hospitals NHS Foundation Trust
NHS Direct
NHS Health and Social Care Information Centre
NHS Pathways
NHS Quality Improvement Scotland
NICE – Guidelines HE for information
NICE – Implementation Consultant – Region East
NICE – Implementation Consultant – Region London/SE
NICE – Implementation Consultant – Region SW
NICE – Implementation Consultant – Region NW & NE
NICE – Implementation Consultant – Region West Midlands
NICE – Implementation Co-ordination for information
NICE – R&D for information
NICE – Technical Appraisals (Interventional Procedures) for information
North Middlesex Hospital University Trust
North Tees and Hartlepool Acute Trust
North West London Hospitals NHS Trust
Northern Lincolnshire and Goole NHS Trust
Northwest London Hospitals NHS Trust
Nottingham City PCT
Nutrition Society
Obstetric Anaesthetists Association

OKB Medical Ltd
Patient and Public Involvement Programme for NICE
Pelvic Partnership
PERIGON (formerly The NHS Modernisation Agency)
Pfizer Limited
Princess Alexandra Hospital NHS Trust
PromoCon (Disabled Living)
Queen Charlottes Hospital
Queen Mary's Hospital NHS Trust (Sidcup)
RCM Consultant Midwives Forum
Regional Public Health Group – London
Royal College of Anaesthetists
Royal College of General Practitioners
Royal College of General Practitioners Wales
Royal College of Midwives
Royal College of Nursing
Royal College of Obstetricians and Gynaecologists
Royal College of Paediatrics and Child Health
Royal College of Pathologists
Royal College of Psychiatrists
Royal Devon & Exeter NHS Foundation Trust
Royal Shrewsbury Hospital NHS Trust
Royal Society of Medicine
Royal West Sussex Trust
School of Midwifery
Scottish Executive Health Department
Scottish Intercollegiate Guidelines Network (SIGN)
Sheffield PCT
Sheffield Teaching Acute Trust
Southhampton University Hospitals Trust
St Mary's Acute Trust
Staffordshire Moorlands PCT
Stockport PCT
Sunderland Royal Hospital NHS Trust
Sure Start Ashfield
Sure Start Tamworth
Surrey & Sussex NHS Trust
Survivors Trust
Sussex Ambulance Services NHS Trust
Syner-Med
Tameside and Glossop Acute Trust
Tissue Viability Nurses Association
UK Anaemia
UK Specialised Services Public Health Network
UNICEF UK Baby Friendly Initiative
United Lincolnshire Hospitals NHS Trust
University College London Hospitals (UCLH) Acute Trust
University Hospitals of Leicester
VBAC Information and Support
Welsh Assembly Government
Wirral Hospital Acute Trust
Womens Health Research Group
Worcestershire Acute Hospitals NHS Trust
Worthing Hospital
Yorkshire and Humber Local Supervising Authorities (LSA)
Young Minds

Abbreviations

BIP	Behavioural Index of Pain
BMI	body mass index
BP	blood pressure
CEMACH	Confidential Enquiry into Maternal and Child Health
CI	confidence interval
CS	caesarean section
CSE	combined spinal–epidural
CTG	cardiotocography
DCC	delayed cord clamping
df	degrees of freedom
EAS	external anal sphincter
ECC	early cord clamping
ECG	electrocardiogram
EFM	electronic fetal monitoring
EL	evidence level (level of evidence)
Entonox®	50 : 50 mixture of oxygen and nitrous oxide
EPDS	Edinburgh Postnatal Depression Scale
FBS	fetal blood sampling
FHR	fetal heart rate
GDG	Guideline Development Group
GP	general practitioner
IAS	internal anal sphincter
IM	intramuscular
IPPM	intrapartum-related perinatal mortality
IQR	interquartile range
IV	intravenous
MAS	meconium aspiration syndrome
MBI	Maslach Burnout Inventory
MD	mean difference
MLAC	minimum local analgesic concentration
MSL	meconium-stained liquor
NACS	neurological and adaptive capacity score
NCC-WCH	National Collaborating Centre for Women's and Children's Health
NHS	National Health Service
NICE	National Institute for Health and Clinical Excellence
NICU	neonatal intensive care unit
NS	not significant
NSAIDs	nonsteroidal anti-inflammatory drugs
OASIS	obstetric anal sphincter injuries
PCA	patient-controlled analgesia
PCEA	patient-controlled epidural analgesia
PPH	postpartum haemorrhage
OA	occiput anterior
OP	occiput posterior
OR	odds ratio
OT	occiput transverse
PPI	Present Pain Intensity
PRoM	prelabour rupture of membranes
RCT	randomised controlled trial
RR	relative risk
SCBU	special care baby unit
SD	standard deviation
TENS	transcutaneous electrical nerve stimulation
TRIP	Turning Research into Practice
VAS	visual analogue scale
VE	vaginal examination
WMD	weighted mean difference

Glossary of terms

Absolute risk	Measures the probability of an event or outcome occurring (e.g. an adverse reaction to the drug being tested) in the group of people under study. Studies that compare two or more groups of patients may report results in terms of the **absolute risk reduction**.
Absolute risk reduction (ARR)	The ARR is the difference in the risk of an event occurring between two groups of patients in a study – for example if 6% of patients die after receiving a new experimental drug and 10% of patients die after having the old drug treatment then the ARR is 10% – 6% = 4%. Thus by using the new drug instead of the old drug 4% of patients can be prevented from dying. Here the ARR measures the risk reduction associated with a new treatment. See also **absolute risk**.
Acute sector	Hospital-based health services which are provided on an in-patient, day case or outpatient basis.
Acute trust	A trust is an NHS organisation responsible for providing a group of healthcare services. An acute trust provides hospital services (but not mental health hospital services which are provided by a **mental health trust**).
Advised	A woman should be advised to accept an intervention when the evidence or professional opinion suggests that one particular option is more beneficial than others. See also **offered**, and **supported in their choice**.
Allied health professionals	Healthcare professionals, other than doctors and nurses, directly involved in the provision of healthcare. Includes several groups such as physiotherapists, occupational therapists, dieticians, etc. (Formerly known as professions allied to medicine or PAMs.)
Amniotomy	Amniotomy refers to artificial rupturing of the membranes. This is done during a vaginal examination using an elongated plastic hook, which is used to pierce the membranes, thus releasing the amniotic fluid. This is carried out in the belief that it can stimulate stronger contractions and thus shorten the duration of labour.
Applicability	The extent to which the results of a study or review can be applied to the target population for a clinical guideline.
Appraisal of evidence	Formal assessment of the quality of research evidence and its relevance to the clinical question or guideline under consideration, according to predetermined criteria.
Best available evidence	The strongest research evidence available to support a particular guideline recommendation.
Bias	Influences on a study that can lead to invalid conclusions about a treatment or intervention. Bias in research can make a treatment look better or worse than it really is. Bias can even make it look as if the treatment works when it actually does not. Bias can occur by chance or as a result of **systematic errors** in the design and execution of a study. Bias can occur at different stages in the research process, e.g. in the collection, analysis, interpretation, publication or review of research data. For examples see **selection bias**, **performance bias**, **information bias**, **confounding factor**, **publication bias**.
Blinding or masking	The practice of keeping the investigators or subjects of a study ignorant of the group to which a subject has been assigned. For example, a clinical trial in which the participating patients or their doctors are unaware of whether they (the patients) are taking the experimental drug or a **placebo** (dummy treatment). The purpose of 'blinding' or 'masking' is to protect against **bias**. See also **double-blind study, single-blind study, triple-blind study**.
Case–control study	A study that starts with the identification of a group of individuals sharing the same characteristics (e.g. people with a particular disease) and a suitable comparison (**control**) group (e.g. people without the disease). All subjects are then assessed with respect to things that happened to them in the past, e.g. things that might be related to getting the disease under investigation. Such studies are also called **retrospective** as they look back in time from the outcome to the possible causes.
Case report (or case study)	Detailed report on one patient (or case), usually covering the course of that person's disease and their response to treatment.

Case series	Description of several cases of a given disease, usually covering the course of the disease and the response to treatment. There is no comparison (**control**) group of patients.
Causal relationship	Describes the relationship between two **variables** whenever it can be established that one causes the other. For example there is a causal relationship between a treatment and a disease if it can be shown that the treatment changes the course or outcome of the disease. Usually **randomised controlled trials** are needed to ascertain causality. Proving cause and effect is much more difficult than just showing an association between two variables. For example, if it happened that everyone who had eaten a particular food became sick, and everyone who avoided that food remained well, then the food would clearly be associated with the sickness. However, even if leftovers were found to be contaminated, it could not be proved that the food caused the sickness – unless all other possible causes (e.g. environmental factors) had been ruled out.
Control event rate (CER)	See **event rate**.
Checklist	See **study checklist**.
Clinical audit	A **systematic** process for setting and monitoring standards of clinical care. Whereas 'guidelines' define what the best clinical practice should be, 'audit' investigates whether best practice is being carried out. Clinical audit can be described as a cycle or spiral. Within the cycle there are stages that follow a systematic process of establishing best practice, measuring care against specific criteria, taking action to improve care, and monitoring to sustain improvement. The spiral suggests that as the process continues, each cycle aspires to a higher level of quality.
Clinical effectiveness	The extent to which a specific treatment or intervention, when used under *usual* or *everyday conditions*, has a beneficial effect on the course or outcome of disease compared with no treatment or other routine care. (Clinical trials that assess effectiveness are sometimes called management trials.) Clinical 'effectiveness' is not the same as **efficacy**.
Clinical governance	A framework through which NHS organisations are accountable for both continuously improving the quality of their services and safeguarding high standards of care by creating an environment in which excellence in clinical care will flourish.
Clinical impact	The effect that a guideline recommendation is likely to have on the treatment, or treatment outcomes, of the target population.
Clinical importance	The importance of a particular guideline recommendation to the clinical management of the **target population**.
Clinical question	This term is sometimes used in guideline development work to refer to the questions about treatment and care that are formulated in order to guide the search for research evidence. When a clinical question is formulated in a precise way, it is called a **focused question**.
Clinical trial	A research study conducted with patients which tests out a drug or other intervention to assess its effectiveness and safety. Each trial is designed to answer scientific questions and to find better ways to treat individuals with a specific disease. This general term encompasses **controlled clinical trials** and **randomised controlled trials**.
Clinician	A qualified healthcare professional providing patient care, e.g. doctor, nurse, physiotherapist.
Cluster	A group of patients, rather than an individual, used as the basic unit for investigation. See also **cluster design**, **cluster randomisation**.
Cluster design	Cluster designs are those where research subjects are not sampled or selected independently, but in a group. For example a clinical trial where patients in a general practice are allocated to the same intervention; the general practice forming a cluster. See also **cluster**, **cluster randomisation**.
Cluster randomisation	A study in which groups of individuals (e.g. patients in a GP surgery or on a hospital ward) are randomly allocated to treatment groups. Take, for example, a smoking cessation study of two different interventions – leaflets and teaching sessions. Each GP surgery within the study would be randomly allocated to administer one of the two interventions. See also **cluster**, **cluster design**.
Cochrane Collaboration	An international organisation in which people find, appraise and review specific types of studies called **randomised controlled trials**. The Cochrane Database of Systematic Reviews contains regularly updated reviews on a variety of health issues and is available electronically as part of the **Cochrane Library**.
Cochrane Library	The Cochrane Library consists of a regularly updated collection of evidence-based medicine databases including the Cochrane Database of Systematic Reviews (reviews of **randomised controlled trials** prepared by the **Cochrane Collaboration**). The Cochrane Library is available on CD-ROM and the Internet.
Cohort	A group of people sharing some common characteristic (e.g. patients with the same disease), followed up in a research study for a specified period of time.

Cohort study	An **observational study** that takes a group (cohort) of patients and follows their progress over time in order to measure outcomes such as disease or mortality rates and make comparisons according to the treatments or interventions that patients received. Thus within the study group, subgroups of patients are identified (from information collected about patients) and these groups are compared with respect to outcome, e.g. comparing mortality between one group that received a specific treatment and one group which did not (or between two groups that received different levels of treatment). Cohorts can be assembled in the present and followed into the future (a 'concurrent' or '**prospective**' cohort study) or identified from past records and followed forward from that time up to the present (a 'historical' or '**retrospective**' cohort study). Because patients are not randomly allocated to subgroups, these subgroups may be quite different in their characteristics and some adjustment must be made when analysing the results to ensure that the comparison between groups is as fair as possible.
Combined modality	Use of different treatments in combination (for example surgery, chemotherapy and radiotherapy used together for cancer patients).
Commercial 'in confidence' material	Information (e.g. the findings of a research project) defined as 'confidential' as its public disclosure could have an impact on the commercial interests of a particular company. (Academic 'in confidence' material is information (usually work produced by a research or professional organisation) that is pending publication.)
Co-morbidity	Co-existence of a disease or diseases in the people being studied in addition to the health problem that is the subject of the study.
Confidence interval	A way of expressing certainty about the findings from a study or group of studies, using statistical techniques. A confidence interval describes a range of possible effects (of a treatment or intervention) that are consistent with the results of a study or group of studies. A wide confidence interval indicates a lack of certainty or precision about the true size of the clinical effect and is seen in studies with too few patients. Where confidence intervals are narrow they indicate more precise estimates of effects and a larger sample of patients studied. It is usual to interpret a '95%' confidence interval as the range of effects within which we are 95% confident that the true effect lies.
Confounder or confounding factor	Something that influences a study and can contribute to misleading findings if it is not understood or appropriately dealt with. For example, if a group of people exercising regularly and a group of people who do not exercise have an important age difference then any difference found in outcomes about heart disease could well be due to one group being older than the other rather than due to the exercising. Age is the confounding factor here and the effect of exercising on heart disease cannot be assessed without adjusting for age differences in some way.
Consensus development conference	A technique used for the purpose of reaching an agreement on a particular issue. It involves bringing together a group of about ten people who are presented with evidence by various interest groups or experts who are not part of the decision making group. The group then retires to consider the questions in the light of the evidence presented and attempts to reach a consensus. See also **consensus methods**.
Consensus methods	A variety of techniques that aim to reach an agreement on a particular issue. Formal consensus methods include **Delphi** and **nominal group techniques**, and **consensus development conferences**. In the development of clinical guidelines, consensus methods may be used where there is a lack of strong research evidence on a particular topic.
Consensus statement	A statement of the advised course of action in relation to a particular clinical topic, based on the collective views of a body of experts.
Considered judgement	The application of the collective knowledge of a guideline development group to a body of evidence, to assess its **applicability** to the **target population** and the strength of any recommendation that it would support.
Consistency	The extent to which the conclusions of a collection of studies used to support a guideline recommendation are in agreement with each other. See also **homogeneity**.
Control event rate (CER)	See **event rate**.
Control group	A group of patients recruited into a study that receives no treatment, a treatment of known effect, or a **placebo** (dummy treatment) – in order to provide a comparison for a group receiving an experimental treatment, such as a new drug.
Controlled clinical trial (CCT)	A study testing a specific drug or other treatment involving two (or more) groups of patients with the same disease. One (the experimental group) receives the treatment that is being tested, and the other (the comparison or **control group**) receives an alternative treatment, a **placebo** (dummy treatment) or no treatment. The two groups are followed up to compare differences in outcomes to see how effective the experimental treatment was. A CCT where patients are randomly allocated to treatment and comparison groups is called a **randomised controlled trial**.

Cost–benefit analysis	A type of **economic evaluation** where both costs and benefits of health care treatment are measured in the same monetary units. If benefits exceed costs, the evaluation would recommend providing the treatment.
Cost-effectiveness	Value for money. A specific health care treatment is said to be 'cost-effective' if it gives a greater health gain than could be achieved by using the resources in other ways.
Cost-effectiveness analysis	A type of **economic evaluation** comparing the costs and the effects on health of different treatments. Health effects are measured in 'health-related units', for example, the cost of preventing one additional heart attack.
Cost-utility analysis	A special form of **cost-effectiveness analysis** where health effects are measured in **quality-adjusted life years**. A treatment is assessed in terms of its ability to both extend life and to improve the quality of life.
Crossover study design	A study comparing two or more interventions in which the participants, upon completion of the course of one treatment, are switched to another. For example, for a comparison of treatments A and B, half the participants are randomly allocated to receive them in the order A, B and half to receive them in the order B, A. A problem with this study design is that the effects of the first treatment may carry over into the period when the second is given. Therefore a crossover study should include an adequate 'wash-out' period, which means allowing sufficient time between stopping one treatment and starting another so that the first treatment has time to wash out of the patient's system.
Cross-sectional study	The observation of a defined set of people at a single point in time or time period – a snapshot. (This type of study contrasts with a **longitudinal study**, which follows a set of people over a period of time.)
Data set	A list of required information relating to a specific disease.
Decision analysis	Decision analysis is the study of how people make decisions or how they *should* make decisions. There are several methods that decision analysts use to help people to make better decisions, including **decision trees**.
Decision tree	A decision tree is a method for helping people to make better decisions in situations of uncertainty. It illustrates the decision as a succession of possible actions and outcomes. It consists of the probabilities, costs and health consequences associated with each option. The overall effectiveness or overall cost-effectiveness of different actions can then be compared.
Declaration of interest	A process by which members of a working group or committee 'declare' any personal or professional involvement with a company (or related to a technology) that might affect their objectivity e.g. if their position or department is funded by a pharmaceutical company.
Delphi method	A technique used for the purpose of reaching an agreement on a particular issue, without the participants meeting or interacting directly. It involves sending participants a series of postal questionnaires asking them to record their views. After the first questionnaire, participants are asked to give further views in the light of the group feedback. The judgements of the participants are statistically aggregated, sometimes after weighting for expertise. See also **consensus methods**.
District General Hospital (DGH)	Non-teaching hospital.
Diagnostic study	A study to assess the effectiveness of a test or measurement in terms of its ability to accurately detect or exclude a specific disease.
Dominance	A term used in **health economics** describing when an option for treatment is both less clinically effective and more costly than an alternative option. The less effective and more costly option is said to be 'dominated'.
Double-blind study	A study in which neither the subject (patient) nor the observer (investigator/clinician) is aware of which treatment or intervention the subject is receiving. The purpose of **blinding** is to protect against **bias**.
Economic evaluation	A comparison of alternative courses of action in terms of both their costs and consequences. In **health economic** evaluations the consequences should include health outcomes.
Effectiveness	See **clinical effectiveness**.
Efficacy	The extent to which a specific treatment or intervention, under *ideally controlled conditions*, e.g. in a laboratory), has a beneficial effect on the course or outcome of disease compared with no treatment or other routine care.
Elective	Name for clinical procedures that are regarded as advantageous to the patient but not urgent.
Empirical	Based directly on experience (observation or experiment) rather than on reasoning alone.
Epidemiology	Study of diseases within a population, covering the causes and means of prevention.

Event rate	The proportion of patients in a group for whom a specified health event or outcome is observed. Thus, if out of 100 patients, the event is observed in 27, the event rate is 0.27 or 27%. Control event rate (CER) and experimental event rate (EER) are the terms used in control and experimental groups of patients, respectively.
Evidence based	The process of systematically finding, appraising, and using research findings as the basis for clinical decisions.
Evidence-based clinical practice	Evidence-based clinical practice involves making decisions about the care of individual patients based on the best research evidence available rather than basing decisions on personal opinions or common practice (which may not always be evidence based). Evidence-based clinical practice therefore involves integrating individual clinical expertise and patient preferences with the best available evidence from research
Evidence level	A code (e.g. 1++, 1+) linked to an individual study, indicating where it fits into the **hierarchy of evidence** and how well it has adhered to recognised research principles. Also called level of evidence.
Evidence table	A table summarising the results of a collection of studies which, taken together, represent the evidence supporting a particular recommendation or series of recommendations in a guideline.
Exclusion criteria	See **selection criteria**.
Expectant management	Awaiting events to take their natural course. This would usually include observation of the woman and/or baby's condition.
Experimental event rate (EER)	See **event rate**.
Experimental study	A research study designed to test if a treatment or intervention has an effect on the course or outcome of a condition or disease – where the conditions of testing are to some extent under the control of the investigator. **Controlled clinical trial** and **randomised controlled trial** are examples of experimental studies.
Experimental treatment	A treatment or intervention (e.g. a new drug) being studied to see if it has an effect on the course or outcome of a condition or disease.
External validity	The degree to which the results of a study hold true in non-study situations, e.g. in routine clinical practice. May also be referred to as the **generalisability** of study results to non-study patients or populations.
Extrapolation	The application of research evidence based on studies of a specific population to another population with similar characteristics.
Focus group	A **qualitative research** technique. It is a method of group interview or discussion of between 6–12 people focused around a particular issue or topic. The method explicitly includes and uses the group interaction to generate data.
Focused question	A study question that clearly identifies all aspects of the topic that are to be considered while seeking an answer. Questions are normally expected to identify the patients or population involved, the treatment or intervention to be investigated, what outcomes are to be considered, and any comparisons that are to be made. For example, do insulin pumps (intervention) improve blood sugar control (outcome) in adolescents with type 1 diabetes (population) compared with multiple insulin injections (comparison)? See also **clinical question**.
Forest plot	A graphical display of results from individual studies on a common scale, allowing visual comparison of results and examination of the degree of **heterogeneity** between studies.
Funnel plot	Funnel plots are simple scatter plots on a graph. They show the treatment effects estimated from separate studies on the horizontal axis against a measure of sample size on the vertical axis. **Publication bias** may lead to asymmetry in funnel plots.
Generalisability	The extent to which the results of a study hold true for a population of patients beyond those who participated in the research. See also **external validity**.
Gold standard	A method, procedure or measurement that is widely accepted as being the best available.
Grey literature	Reports that are unpublished or have limited distribution, and are not included in bibliographic retrieval systems.
Guideline	A systematically developed tool that describes aspects of a patient's condition and the care to be given. A good guideline makes recommendations about treatment and care based on the best research available, rather than opinion. It is used to assist clinician and patient decision making about appropriate health care for specific clinical conditions.
Guideline recommendation	Course of action advised by the guideline development group on the basis of their assessment of the supporting evidence.
Health economics	A branch of economics that studies decisions about the use and distribution of health care resources.

Health technology	Health technologies include medicines, medical devices such as artificial hip joints, diagnostic techniques, surgical procedures, health promotion activities (e.g. the role of diet versus medicines in disease management) and other therapeutic interventions.
Health technology appraisal (HTA)	A health technology appraisal, as undertaken by The National Institute for Health and Clinical Excellence (NICE), is the process of determining the clinical and cost-effectiveness of a **health technology**. NICE health technology appraisals are designed to provide patients, health professionals and managers with an authoritative source of advice on new and existing health technologies.
Heterogeneity	Or lack of **homogeneity**. The term is used in **meta-analyses** and **systematic reviews** when the results or estimates of effects of treatment from separate studies seem to be very different – in terms of the size of treatment effects or even to the extent that some indicate beneficial and others suggest adverse treatment effects. Such results may occur as a result of differences between studies in terms of the patient populations, outcome measures, definition of **variables** or duration of follow-up.
Hierarchy of evidence	An established hierarchy of study types, based on the degree of certainty that can be attributed to the conclusions that can be drawn from a well-conducted study. Well-conducted **randomised controlled trials** (RCTs) are at the top of this hierarchy. (Several large statistically significant RCTs which are in agreement represent stronger evidence than say one small RCT.) Well-conducted studies of patients' views and experiences would appear at a lower level in the hierarchy of evidence.
Homogeneity	This means that the results of studies included in a **systematic review** or **meta-analysis** are similar and there is no evidence of **heterogeneity**. Results are usually regarded as homogeneous when differences between studies could reasonably be expected to occur by chance. See also **consistency**.
Inclusion criteria	See **selection criteria**.
In-depth interview	A **qualitative research** technique. It is a face-to-face conversation between a researcher and a respondent with the purpose of exploring issues or topics in detail. Does not use pre-set questions, but is shaped by a defined set of topics or issues.
Information bias	Pertinent to all types of study and can be caused by inadequate questionnaires (e.g. difficult or biased questions), observer or interviewer errors (e.g. lack of **blinding**), response errors (e.g. lack of blinding if patients are aware of the treatment they receive) and measurement error (e.g. a faulty machine).
Intention-to-treat analysis	An analysis of a clinical trial where patients are analysed according to the group to which they were initially randomly allocated, regardless of whether or not they had dropped out, fully complied with the treatment, or crossed over and received the alternative treatment. Intention-to-treat analyses are favoured in assessments of **clinical effectiveness** as they mirror the non-compliance and treatment changes that are likely to occur when the treatment is used in practice.
Internal validity	Refers to the integrity of the study design.
Intervention	Healthcare action intended to benefit the patient, e.g. drug treatment, surgical procedure, psychological therapy, etc.
Interventional procedure	A procedure used for diagnosis or treatment that involves making a cut or hole in the patient's body, entry into a body cavity or using electromagnetic radiation (including X-rays or lasers). The National Institute for Health and Clinical Excellence (NICE) has the task of producing guidance about whether specific interventional procedures are safe enough and work well enough for routine use.
Level of evidence	See **evidence level**.
Literature review	A process of collecting, reading and assessing the quality of published (and unpublished) articles on a given topic.
Longitudinal study	A study of the same group of people at more than one point in time. (This type of study contrasts with a **cross-sectional study**, which observes a defined set of people at a single point in time.)
Masking	See **blinding**.
Mental health trust	A trust is an NHS organisation responsible for providing a group of healthcare services. A mental health trust provides both hospital and community based mental health services.
Meta-analysis	Results from a collection of independent studies (investigating the same treatment) are pooled, using statistical techniques to synthesise their findings into a single estimate of a treatment effect. Where studies are not compatible e.g. because of differences in the study populations or in the outcomes measured, it may be inappropriate or even misleading to statistically pool results in this way. See also **systematic review** and **heterogeneity**.
Methodology	The overall approach of a research project, e.g. the study will be a **randomised controlled trial**, of 200 people, over one year.

Methodological quality	The extent to which a study has conformed to recognised good practice in the design and execution of its research methods.
Multicentre study	A study where subjects were selected from different locations or populations, e.g. a co-operative study between different hospitals; an international collaboration involving patients from more than one country.
Negative predictive value (NPV)	The proportion of people with a negative test result who do not have the disease (where not having the disease is indicated by the 'gold' standard test being negative).
Number needed to harm (NNH)	See **number needed to treat**.
Number needed to treat (NNT)	This measures the impact of a treatment or intervention. It states how many patients need to be treated with the treatment in question in order to prevent an event which would otherwise occur. E.g. if the NNT = 4, then four patients would have to be treated to prevent one bad outcome. The closer the NNT is to 1, the better the treatment is. Analogous to the NNT is the number needed to harm (NNH), which is the number of patients that would need to receive a treatment to cause one additional adverse event. e.g. if the NNH = 4, then four patients would have to be treated for one bad outcome to occur.
Nominal group technique	A technique used for the purpose of reaching an agreement on a particular issue. It uses a variety of postal and direct contact techniques, with individual judgements being aggregated statistically to derive the group judgement. See also **consensus methods**.
Non-experimental study	A study based on subjects selected on the basis of their availability, with no attempt having been made to avoid problems of **bias**.
Non-systematic review	See **review**.
Objective measure	A measurement that follows a standardised procedure that is less open to subjective interpretation by potentially biased observers and study participants.
Observation	Observation is a research technique used to help understand complex situations. It involves watching, listening to and recording behaviours, actions, activities and interactions. The settings are usually natural, but they can be laboratory settings, as in psychological research.
Observational study	In research about diseases or treatments, this refers to a study in which nature is allowed to take its course. Changes or differences in one characteristic (e.g. whether or not people received a specific treatment or intervention) are studied in relation to changes or differences in other(s) (e.g. whether or not they died), without the intervention of the investigator. There is a greater risk of **selection bias** than in **experimental studies**.
Odds ratio (OR)	Odds are a way of representing probability, especially familiar for betting. In recent years odds ratios have become widely used in reports of clinical studies. They provide an estimate (usually with a **confidence interval**) for the effect of a treatment. Odds are used to convey the idea of 'risk' and an odds ratio of 1 between two treatment groups would imply that the risks of an adverse outcome were the same in each group. For rare events the odds ratio and the **relative risk** (which uses actual risks and not odds) will be very similar. See also **relative risk, risk ratio**.
Off-label prescribing	When a drug or device is prescribed outside its **specific indication**, to treat a condition or disease for which it is not specifically licensed.
Offered	A woman should be offered an intervention when the evidence or professional opinion suggests that it is of benefit and there is little risk of harm. See also **advised** and **supported in their choice**.
Outcome	The end result of care and treatment and/or rehabilitation. In other words, the change in health, functional ability, symptoms or situation of a person, which can be used to measure the effectiveness of care/treatment/rehabilitation. Researchers should decide what outcomes to measure before a study begins; outcomes are then assessed at the end of the study.
***P* value**	If a study is done to compare two treatments then the *P* value is the probability of obtaining the results of that study, or something more extreme, if there really was no difference between treatments. (The assumption that there really is no difference between treatments is called the 'null hypothesis'.) Suppose the *P* value was $P = 0.03$. What this means is that if there really was no difference between treatments then there would only be a 3% chance of getting the kind of results obtained. Since this chance seems quite low we should question the validity of the assumption that there really is no difference between treatments. We would conclude that there probably is a difference between treatments. By convention, where the value of *P* is below 0.05 (i.e. less than 5%) the result is seen as statistically significant. Where the value of *P* is 0.001 or less, the result is seen as highly significant. *P* values just tell us whether an effect can be regarded as statistically significant or not. In no way do they relate to how big the effect might be, for which we need the **confidence interval**.

Peer review
Review of a study, service or recommendations by those with similar interests and expertise to the people who produced the study findings or recommendations. Peer reviewers can include professional and/or patient/carer representatives.

Performance bias
Systematic differences in care provided apart from the intervention being evaluated. For example, if study participants know they are in the **control group** they may be more likely to use other forms of care; people who know they are in the experimental group may experience **placebo effects**, and care providers may treat patients differently according to what group they are in. Masking (**blinding**) of both the recipients and providers of care is used to protect against performance bias.

Pilot study
A small scale 'test' of the research instrument. For example, testing out (piloting) a new questionnaire with people who are similar to the population of the study, in order to highlight any problems or areas of concern, which can then be addressed before the full scale study begins.

Placebo
Placebos are fake or inactive treatments received by participants allocated to the **control group** in a clinical trial that are indistinguishable from the active treatments being given in the experimental group. They are used so that participants are ignorant of their treatment allocation in order to be able to quantify the effect of the experimental treatment over and above any **placebo effect** due to receiving care or attention.

Placebo effect
A beneficial (or adverse) effect produced by a **placebo** and not due to any property of the placebo itself.

Point estimate
A best single estimate (taken from research data) for the true value of a treatment effect or other measurement. For example, researchers in one clinical trial take their results as their best estimate of the real treatment effect – this is their estimate at their point in time. The precision or accuracy of the estimate is measured by a **confidence interval**. Another clinical trial of the same treatment will produce a different point estimate of treatment effect.

Positive predictive value (PPV)
The proportion of people with a positive test result who have the disease (where having the disease is indicated by the 'gold' standard test being positive).

Power
See **statistical power**.

Primary care
Healthcare delivered to patients outside hospitals. Primary care covers a range of services provided by GPs, nurses and other healthcare professionals, dentists, pharmacists and opticians.

Primary care trust (PCT)
A primary care trust is an NHS organisation responsible for improving the health of local people, developing services provided by local GPs and their teams (called **primary care**) and making sure that other appropriate health services are in place to meet local people's needs.

Probability
How likely an event is to occur, e.g. how likely a treatment or intervention will alleviate a symptom.

Prognostic factor
Patient or disease characteristics, e.g. age or **co-morbidity**, which influence the course of the disease under study. In a randomised trial to compare two treatments, chance imbalances in **variables** (prognostic factors) that influence patient outcome are possible, especially if the size of the study is fairly small. In terms of analysis these prognostic factors become **confounding factors**. See also **prognostic marker**.

Prognostic marker
A **prognostic factor** used to assign patients to categories for a specified purpose – e.g. for treatment, or as part of a clinical trial, according to the likely progression of the disease. For example, the purpose of randomisation in a clinical trial is to produce similar treatment groups with respect to important prognostic factors. This can often be achieved more efficiently if randomisation takes place within subgroups defined by the most important prognostic factors. Thus if age was very much related to patient outcome then separate randomisation schemes would be used for different age groups. This process is known as stratified random allocation.

Prospective study
A study in which people are entered into the research and then followed up over a period of time with future events recorded as they happen. This contrasts with studies that are **retrospective**.

Protocol
A plan or set of steps that defines appropriate action. A research protocol sets out, in advance of carrying out the study, what question is to be answered and how information will be collected and analysed. Guideline implementation protocols set out how guideline recommendations will be used in practice by the NHS, both at national and local levels.

Publication bias
Studies with statistically significant results are more likely to get published than those with non-significant results. **Meta-analyses** that are exclusively based on published literature may therefore produce biased results. This type of bias can be assessed by a **funnel plot**.

Qualitative research	Qualitative research is used to explore and understand people's beliefs, experiences, attitudes, behaviour and interactions. It generates non-numerical data, e.g. a patient's description of their pain rather than a measure of pain. In health care, qualitative techniques have been commonly used in research documenting the experience of chronic illness and in studies about the functioning of organisations. Qualitative research techniques such as **focus groups** and **in-depth interviews** have been used in one-off projects commissioned by guideline development groups to find out more about the views and experiences of patients and carers.
Quality-adjusted life years (QALYS)	A measure of health outcome that looks at both length of life and quality of life. QALYS are calculated by estimating the years of life remaining for a patient following a particular care pathway and weighting each year with a quality of life score (on a zero to one scale). One QALY is equal to one year of life in perfect health, or two years at 50% health, and so on.
Quantitative research	Research that generates numerical data or data that can be converted into numbers, for example clinical trials or the national Census that counts people and households.
Quasi-experimental study	A study designed to test whether a treatment or intervention has an effect on the course or outcome of disease. It differs from a **controlled clinical trial** and a **randomised controlled trial** in that: • the assignment of patients to treatment and comparison groups is not done randomly, or patients are not given equal probabilities of selection, or • the investigator does not have full control over the allocation and/or timing of the intervention, but nonetheless conducts the study as if it were an experiment, allocating subjects to treatment and comparison groups.
Random allocation or randomisation	A method that uses the play of chance to assign participants to comparison groups in a research study, for example, by using a random numbers table or a computer-generated random sequence. Random allocation implies that each individual (or each unit in the case of **cluster randomisation**) being entered into a study has the same chance of receiving each of the possible interventions.
Randomised controlled trial (RCT)	A study to test a specific drug or other treatment in which people are randomly assigned to two (or more) groups: one (the experimental group) receiving the treatment that is being tested, and the other (the comparison or **control group**) receiving an alternative treatment, a **placebo** (dummy treatment) or no treatment. The two groups are followed up to compare differences in outcomes to see how effective the experimental treatment was. (Through randomisation, the groups should be similar in all aspects apart from the treatment they receive during the study.)
Relative risk (RR)	A summary measure which represents the ratio of the risk of a given event or outcome (e.g. an adverse reaction to the drug being tested) in one group of subjects compared with another group. When the 'risk' of the event is the same in the two groups the relative risk is 1. In a study comparing two treatments, a relative risk of 2 would indicate that patients receiving one of the treatments had twice the risk of an undesirable outcome than those receiving the other treatment. Relative risk is sometimes used as a synonym for **risk ratio**.
Reliability	Reliability refers to a method of measurement that consistently gives the same results. For example someone who has a high score on one occasion tends to have a high score if measured on another occasion very soon afterwards. With physical assessments it is possible for different clinicians to make independent assessments in quick succession – and if their assessments tend to agree then the method of assessment is said to be reliable.
Retrospective study	A retrospective study deals with the present/past and does not involve studying future events. This contrasts with studies that are **prospective**.
Review	Summary of the main points and trends in the research literature on a specified topic. A review is considered non-systematic unless an extensive literature search has been carried out to ensure that all aspects of the topic are covered and an objective appraisal made of the quality of the studies.
Risk ratio	Ratio of the risk of an undesirable event or outcome occurring in a group of patients receiving experimental treatment compared with a comparison (**control**) group. The term **relative risk** is sometimes used as a synonym of risk ratio.
Royal Colleges	In the UK medical world, the term Royal Colleges, as for example in 'The Royal College of ...', refers to organisations which usually combine an educational standards and examination role with the promotion of professional standards. The nursing/midwifery colleges do not have responsibility for standards of training.
Sample	A part of the study's **target population** from which the subjects of the study will be recruited. If subjects are drawn in an unbiased way from a particular population, the results can be generalised from the sample to the population as a whole.
Sampling	Refers to the way participants are selected for inclusion in a study.
Sampling frame	A list or register of names that is used to recruit participants to a study.

Scottish Intercollegiate Guidelines Network (SIGN)	SIGN was established in 1993 to sponsor and support the development of evidence-based clinical guidelines for the NHS in Scotland.
Secondary care	Care provided in hospitals.
Selection bias	Selection bias has occurred if: <ul><li>the characteristics of the **sample** differ from those of the wider population from which the sample has been drawn, or</li><li>there are systematic differences between comparison groups of patients in a study in terms of prognosis or responsiveness to treatment.</li></ul>
Selection criteria	Explicit standards used by guideline development groups to decide which studies should be included and excluded from consideration as potential sources of evidence.
Semi-structured interview	Structured interviews involve asking people pre-set questions. A semi-structured interview allows more flexibility than a structured interview. The interviewer asks a number of open-ended questions, following up areas of interest in response to the information given by the respondent.
Sensitivity	In diagnostic testing, it refers to the chance of having a positive test result given that you have the disease. 100% sensitivity means that all those with the disease will test positive, but this is not the same the other way around. A patient could have a positive test result but not have the disease – this is called a 'false positive'. The sensitivity of a test is also related to its '**negative predictive value'** (true negatives) – a test with a sensitivity of 100% means that all those who get a negative test result do not have the disease. To fully judge the accuracy of a test, its **specificity** must also be considered.
Single-blind study	A study in which *either* the subject (patient/participant) *or* the observer (clinician/investigator) is not aware of which treatment or intervention the subject is receiving.
Specific indication	When a drug or a device has a specific remit to treat a specific condition and is not licensed for use in treating other conditions or diseases.
Specificity	In diagnostic testing, it refers to the chance of having a negative test result given that you do not have the disease. 100% specificity means that all those without the disease will test negative, but this is not the same the other way around. A patient could have a negative test result yet still have the disease – this is called a 'false negative'. The specificity of a test is also related to its '**positive predictive value'** (true positives) – a test with a specificity of 100% means that all those who get a positive test result definitely have the disease. To fully judge the accuracy of a test, its **sensitivity** must also be considered.
Standard deviation	A measure of the spread, scatter or variability of a set of measurements. Usually used with the mean (average) to describe numerical data.
Statistical power	The ability of a study to demonstrate an association or causal relationship between two **variables**, given that an association exists. For example, 80% power in a clinical trial means that the study has a 80% chance of ending up with a *P* **value** of less than 5% in a statistical test (i.e. a statistically significant treatment effect) if there really was an important difference (e.g. 10% versus 5% mortality) between treatments. If the statistical power of a study is low, the study results will be questionable (the study might have been too small to detect any differences). By convention, 80% is an acceptable level of power. See also *P* **value**.
Structured interview	A research technique where the interviewer controls the interview by adhering strictly to a questionnaire or interview schedule with pre-set questions.
Study checklist	A list of questions addressing the key aspects of the research methodology that must be in place if a study is to be accepted as valid. A different checklist is required for each study type. These checklists are used to ensure a degree of consistency in the way that studies are evaluated.
Study population	People who have been identified as the subjects of a study.
Study quality	See **methodological quality**.
Study type	The kind of design used for a study. **Randomised controlled trials, case–control studies**, and **cohort studies** are all examples of study types.
Subject	A person who takes part in an experiment or research study.
Supported in their choice	Where this is a service that will not be routinely provided by the maternity units, women should be able to do so. See also **advised** and **offered**.
Survey	A study in which information is systematically collected from people (usually from a sample within a defined population).
Systematic	Methodical, according to plan; not random.
Systematic error	Refers to the various errors or biases inherent in a study. See also **Bias**.
Systematic review	A review in which evidence from scientific studies has been identified, appraised and synthesised in a methodical way according to predetermined criteria. May or may not include a **meta-analysis**.

Systemic	Involving the whole body.
Target population	The people to whom guideline recommendations are intended to apply. Recommendations may be less valid if applied to a population with different characteristics from the participants in the research study – e.g. in terms of age, disease state, social background.
Tertiary centre	A major medical centre providing complex treatments which receives referrals from both primary and secondary care. Sometimes called a tertiary referral centre. See also **primary care** and **secondary care**.
Triangulation	Use of three or more different research methods in combination; principally used as a check of validity. The more the different methods produce similar results, the more valid the findings.
Triple-blind study	A study in which the statistical analysis is carried out without knowing which treatment patients received, in addition to the patients and investigators/**clinicians** being unaware which treatment patients were getting.
Trust	A trust is an NHS organisation responsible for providing a group of healthcare services. An **acute trust** provides hospital services. A **mental health trust** provides most mental health services. A **primary care trust** buys hospital care on behalf of the local population, as well as being responsible for the provision of community health services.
Validity	Assessment of how well a tool or instrument measures what it is intended to measure. See also **external validity**, **internal validity**.
Variable	A measurement that can vary within a study, e.g. the age of participants. Variability is present when differences can be seen between different people or within the same person over time, with respect to any characteristic or feature that can be assessed or measured.

1 Introduction

Birth is a life-changing event and the care given to women has the potential to affect them both physically and emotionally in the short and longer term.

This guideline covers the care of healthy women in labour at term (37–42 weeks of gestation). About 600 000 women give birth in England and Wales each year, of whom about 40% are having their first baby.[1,2] Most of these women are healthy and have a straightforward pregnancy. Almost 90% of women will give birth to a single baby after 37 weeks of pregnancy with the baby presenting head first. Most women (about two-thirds) go into labour spontaneously. Thus the majority of women giving birth in the UK fall under the scope of this guideline.

More than 90% of births take place in designated consultant wards or combined consultant/GP wards. In England in 2002–2003, 1% of births took place in GP wards, 3% in midwife wards and 2% at home.[3]

An estimated 47% of births were described as 'normal births' in England in 2002–2003. Normal birth is defined as that without surgical intervention, use of instruments, induction, or epidural or general anaesthetic.[3]

In total, 22% of births in England in 2002–2003 were by caesarean section and about 11% were instrumental births, including forceps or ventouse. Instrumental births were associated with a longer hospital stay in England and Wales in 2002–2003.[3]

About one-third of women had an epidural, general or spinal anaesthetic during labour in England in 2002–2003.[3]

The importance of effective communication between women and caregivers during intrapartum care has been identified by the GDG as one of the most important themes that runs through the guideline. To facilitate good practice and the implementation of this issue, the GDG has developed 'recommendations on implementing good communication' at important points within the guideline.

1.1 Aim of the guideline

Clinical guidelines have been defined as 'systematically developed statements which assist clinicians and patients in making decisions about appropriate treatment for specific conditions'.[4] The guideline has been developed with the aim of providing guidance on care of healthy women and their babies during childbirth.

1.2 Areas within the remit of the guideline

1.2.1 Care throughout labour

- Advice on communication between healthcare professionals and women during labour including decision making and consent
- Effect of support on women in labour
- Identification of women and babies who may need additional care, including recognition and referral of serious emergency maternal or fetal complications arising during labour
- Appropriate hygiene measures for vaginal birth, both in and out of water.

1.2.2 Care in the first and second stage of labour

- The diagnosis of the onset of labour and timing of admission or request for midwife visit at home and observations undertaken
- Assessment and management of progress in labour, including 'active management' and identification/management of delay in the first stage of labour
- Assessment of fetal wellbeing including appropriate use of electronic fetal monitoring
- Care of women in labour, including observations, nutrition, fluid balance and bladder care
- Advice on non-invasive birth techniques aimed at promoting the birthing process in the first stage of labour
- Appropriate use and effect of pharmacological and non-pharmacological pain relief
- Appropriate use of and the effects of regional analgesia, and care of women who have had regional analgesia
- Appropriate care during the birth process including the effect of positions and water birth and management of the second stage with regard to pushing techniques
- Appropriate techniques to reduce perineal trauma, including advice for women with previous third- or fourth-degree tears or genital mutilation
- Assessment and management of delay in the second stage of labour, including appropriate criteria for operative vaginal birth using either forceps or ventouse
- Identification and management of women with meconium-stained liquor
- Identification and management of women with prelabour rupture of membranes at term, with particular reference to observations and duration of 'watchful waiting' before induction, factors during prelabour rupture of membranes at term that influence maternal and neonatal outcomes following birth, use of antibiotics before birth, and criteria for antibiotics in healthy newborns.

1.2.3 Care in the third stage of labour

- Definition and indications for management of the third stage
- Identification of women at increased risk of postpartum haemorrhage (PPH) or with PPH, and strategies to reduce this risk
- Management of delay in the third stage and identification of retained placenta.

1.2.4 Immediate care after birth

- Assessment and repair of perineal trauma (vaginal tears or episiotomy)
- Assessment of neonatal wellbeing, facilitation of mother–infant bonding and basic resuscitation techniques immediately after birth
- Assessment of maternal wellbeing immediately after childbirth.

1.2.5 General remark on pharmacological treatments

Advice on treatment options will be based on the best evidence available to the GDG. When referring to pharmacological treatments, the guideline will normally make recommendations within the licensed indications. Exceptionally, and only where the evidence supports it, the guideline may recommend use outside the licensed indications. The guideline will assume that prescribers will use the Summary of Product Characteristics to inform their prescribing decisions for individual consumers.

1.3 Areas outside of the remit of the guideline

- Women or their babies in suspected or confirmed preterm labour (before 37 weeks of gestation); women with an intrauterine fetal death; women with co-existing severe morbidities such as pre-eclampsia (high blood pressure of pregnancy) or diabetes; women who have multiple pregnancies; women with intrauterine growth restriction of the fetus.
- Women who have been covered in other guidelines, for example women who have their labour induced (inherited NICE clinical guideline D, *Induction of Labour*)[5], or women who have caesarean birth or with breech presentation (NICE clinical guideline 13, *Caesarean Section*)[6].
- Techniques for operative birth or repair of third- or fourth-degree perineal trauma; additional care for women with known or suspected infectious co-morbidities such as group B streptococcus, HIV or genital herpes virus.

1.4 For whom is the guideline intended?

This guideline is of relevance to those who work in or use the National Health Service (NHS) in England and Wales, in particular:

- midwives, obstetricians, obstetric anaesthetists, neonatologists, maternity support workers and any healthcare professional involved in care of women during labour and birth in any setting
- those responsible for commissioning and planning healthcare services, including primary care trust and local health board commissioners, Wales commissioners, and public health and trust managers
- pregnant women, their families, birth supporters and other carers.

A version of this guideline for women, their families and the public is available, entitled 'Understanding NICE guidance: Care of women and their babies during labour'. It can be downloaded from the National Institute for Health and Clinical Excellence (NICE) website (www.nice.org.uk/CG055) or ordered via the NHS Response Line (0870 1555 455) quoting reference number N1327.

1.5 Who has developed the guideline?

The guideline was developed by a multi-professional and lay working group (the Guideline Development Group or GDG) convened by the National Collaborating Centre for Women's and Children's Health (NCC-WCH). Membership included a senior research fellow (midwife) as the Guideline Leader, three obstetricians, a neonatologist, an obstetric anaesthetist, three midwives, and three patient/carer/consumer representatives.

Staff from the NCC-WCH provided methodological support for the guideline development process, undertook systematic searches, retrieval and appraisal of the evidence, health economics modelling and, together with the Guideline Leader, wrote successive drafts of the guideline.

All GDG members' interests were recorded on declaration forms provided by NICE. The form covered consultancies, fee-paid work, shareholdings, fellowships, and support from the healthcare industry.

1.6 Other relevant documents

This guideline is intended to complement the maternity section of the Children's National Service Framework (NSF) as well as other existing and proposed works of relevance. It will also link to relevant clinical guidelines issued by the Institute, including:

- *Pregnancy and Childbirth – Induction of Labour* (NICE clinical guideline D, 2001)[5]
- *Infection Control: Prevention of Healthcare-Associated Infection in Primary and Community Care* (NICE clinical guideline 2, 2003)[7]
- *Antenatal Care: Routine Care for the Healthy Pregnant Woman* (NICE clinical guideline 6, 2003)[8]
- *Caesarean Section* (NICE clinical guideline 13, 2004)[6]
- *Postnatal Care: Routine Postnatal Care of Women and Their Babies* (NICE clinical guideline 37, 2006)
- *Antenatal and Postnatal Mental Health: Clinical Management and Service Guidance* (NICE clinical guideline 45, 2007).

This guideline provides an update of *The Use of Electronic Fetal Monitoring: the Use and Interpretation of Cardiotocography in Intrapartum Fetal Surveillance* (inherited clinical guideline C) issued in 2001. Inherited clinical guideline C will be withdrawn upon publication of this new guideline.

1.7 Guideline development methodology

This guideline was commissioned by NICE and developed in accordance with the guideline development process outlined in the NICE technical manual.[9]

1.7.1 Literature search strategy

Initial scoping searches were executed to identify relevant guidelines (local, national and international) produced by other development groups. The reference lists in these guidelines were checked against subsequent searches to identify missing evidence.

Relevant published evidence to inform the guideline development process and answer the clinical questions was identified by systematic search strategies. Additionally, stakeholder organisations were invited to submit evidence for consideration by the GDG provided it was relevant to the clinical questions and of equivalent or better quality than evidence identified by the search strategies.

Systematic searches to answer the clinical questions formulated and agreed by the GDG were executed using the following databases via the OVID platform: MEDLINE (1966 onwards); Embase (1980 onwards); Cumulative Index to Nursing and Allied Health Literature (1982 onwards); British Nursing Index (1985 onwards); PsycINFO (1967 onwards); Cochrane Central Register of Controlled Trials (1st quarter 2006); Cochrane Database of Systematic Reviews (1st quarter 2006); and Database of Abstracts of Reviews of Effects (1st quarter 2006). Other databases utilised were Allied and Complementary Medicine (Datastar platform, 1985 onwards) and MIDIRS (specialist midwifery database).

Search strategies combined relevant controlled vocabulary and natural language in an effort to balance sensitivity and specificity. Unless advised by the GDG, searches were not date specific. Language restrictions were not applied to searches. Both generic and specially developed methodological search filters were used appropriately.

Searches to identify economic studies were undertaken using the above databases, and the NHS Economic Evaluations Database (NHS EED) produced by the Centre for Reviews and Dissemination at the University of York.

There was no systematic attempt to search grey literature (conferences, abstracts, theses and unpublished trials). Hand searching of journals not indexed on the databases was not undertaken.

At the end of the guideline development process, searches were updated and re-executed, thereby including evidence published and included in the databases up to 24 April 2006. Any evidence published after this date was not included. This date should be considered the starting point for searching for new evidence for future updates to this guideline.

Further details of the search strategies, including the methodological filters employed, can be obtained from the NCC-WCH.

1.7.2 Synthesis of clinical effectiveness evidence

Evidence relating to clinical effectiveness was reviewed using established guides[9-16] and classified using the established hierarchical system shown in Table 1.1.[16] This system reflects the susceptibility to bias that is inherent in particular study designs.

Table 1.1 Levels of evidence for intervention studies[15]

Level	Source of evidence
1++	High-quality meta-analyses, systematic reviews of randomised controlled trials (RCTs) or RCTs with a very low risk of bias
1+	Well-conducted meta-analyses, systematic reviews of RCTs or RCTs with a low risk of bias
1−	Meta-analyses, systematic reviews of RCTs or RCTs with a high risk of bias
2++	High-quality systematic reviews of case–control or cohort studies; high-quality case–control or cohort studies with a very low risk of confounding, bias or chance and a high probability that the relationship is causal
2+	Well-conducted case–control or cohort studies with a low risk of confounding, bias or chance and a moderate probability that the relationship is causal
2−	Case–control or cohort studies with a high risk of confounding, bias or chance and a significant risk that the relationship is not causal
3	Non-analytical studies (for example case reports, case series)
4	Expert opinion, formal consensus

The type of clinical question dictates the highest level of evidence that may be sought. In assessing the quality of the evidence, each study receives a quality rating coded as '++', '+' or '−'. For issues of therapy or treatment, the highest possible evidence level (EL) is a well-conducted systematic review or meta-analysis of randomised controlled trials (RCTs) (EL = 1++) or an individual RCT (EL = 1+). Studies of poor quality are rated as '−'. Usually, studies rated as '−' should not be used as a basis for making a recommendation, but they can be used to inform recommendations. For issues of prognosis, the highest possible level of evidence is a cohort study (EL = 2−).

For each clinical question, the highest available level of evidence was selected. Where appropriate, for example, if a systematic review, meta-analysis or RCT existed in relation to a question, studies of a weaker design were not included. Where systematic reviews, meta-analyses and RCTs did not exist, other appropriate experimental or observational studies were sought. For diagnostic tests, test evaluation studies examining the performance of the test were used if the efficacy of the test was required, but, where an evaluation of the effectiveness of the test in the clinical management of patients and the outcome of disease was required, evidence from RCTs or cohort studies was used.

The system described above covers studies of treatment effectiveness. However, it is less appropriate for studies reporting diagnostic tests of accuracy. In the absence of a validated ranking system for this type of test, NICE has developed a hierarchy for evidence of accuracy of diagnostic tests that takes into account the various factors likely to affect the validity of these studies (Table 1.2).[9]

For economic evaluations, no standard system of grading the quality of evidence exists. The search strategies adopted were designed to identify any relevant economic studies. Abstracts of all papers identified were reviewed by the health economists and were discarded if they did not relate to the economic question being considered in the guideline. The relevant papers were retrieved and critically appraised. Potentially relevant references in the bibliographies of the reviewed papers were also identified and reviewed. All papers reviewed were assessed by the health economists against standard quality criteria for economic evaluation.[17]

Evidence was synthesised qualitatively by summarising the content of identified papers in evidence tables and agreeing brief statements that accurately reflected the evidence. Quantitative synthesis (meta-analysis) was performed where appropriate.

Summary results and data are presented in the guideline text. More detailed results and data are presented in the evidence tables on the accompanying CD-ROM. Where possible, dichotomous outcomes are presented as relative risks (RRs) with 95% confidence intervals (CIs), and continuous outcomes are presented as mean differences with 95% CIs or standard deviations (SDs). Meta-analyses based on dichotomous outcomes are presented as pooled odds ratios (ORs) or pooled relative risk (RRs) with 95% CIs, and meta-analyses based on continuous outcomes

Table 1.2   Levels of evidence for studies of the accuracy of diagnostics tests[9]

Level	Type of evidence
Ia	Systematic reviews (with homogeneity)[a] of level-1 studies[b]
Ib	Level-1 studies[b]
II	Level-2 studies[c]; systematic reviews of level-2 studies
III	Level-3 studies[d]; systematic reviews of level-3 studies
IV	Consensus, expert committee reports or opinions and/or clinical experience without explicit critical appraisal; or based on physiology, bench research or 'first principles'

[a] Homogeneity means there are no or minor variations in the directions and degrees of results between individual studies that are included in the systematic review.

[b] Level-1 studies are studies that use a blind comparison of the test with a validated reference standard (gold standard) in a sample of patients that reflects the population to whom the test would apply.

[c] Level-2 studies are studies that have only one of the following:
- narrow population (the sample does not reflect the population to whom the test would apply)
- use a poor reference standard (defined as that where the 'test' is included in the 'reference', or where the 'testing' affects the 'reference')
- the comparison between the test and reference standard is not blind
- case–control studies.

[d] Level-3 studies are studies that have at least two or three of the features listed above.

are presented as weighted mean differences (WMDs) with 95% CIs. Forest plots for new meta-analyses carried out for the guideline are also presented on the accompanying CD-ROM.

1.7.3 Health economics

The aim of the economic input into the guideline was to inform the GDG of potential economic issues relating to intrapartum care.

The health economist helped the GDG by identifying topics within the guideline that might benefit from economic analysis, reviewing the available economic evidence and, where necessary, conducting (or commissioning) economic analysis. Reviews of published health economic evidence are presented alongside the reviews of clinical evidence.

The primary economic focus in this guideline was on place of birth for low-risk women in England and Wales. This included a systematic review of the relevant economic literature. In addition, the health economists developed a decision-analytic cost-effectiveness model supported by the GDG who provided guidance on the data needed to populate the model and on the assumptions required to make the comparisons relevant to the scope of the analysis. A description of the model is presented in Appendix E.

A costing of ST-analysis for intrapartum fetal monitoring was also undertaken as part of this guideline. This was done to assess whether this new technology was potentially cost saving from an NHS perspective when 'downstream' resource use is considered. Further details for this analysis are presented in Appendix F.

The economic evidence resulting from these analyses was considered by the GDG members in drafting the recommendations. Summaries of the economic evidence resulting from these analyses are presented before the recommendations.

1.7.4 Forming and grading recommendations

For each clinical question, recommendations were derived using, and explicitly linked to, the evidence that supported them. In the first instance, informal consensus methods were used by the GDG to agree evidence statements and recommendations. Additionally, in areas where important clinical questions were identified but no substantial evidence existed, formal consensus methods were used to identify current best practice. Shortly before the consultation period, formal consensus methods were used to agree guideline recommendations (modified Delphi technique) and to select 5–10 key priorities for implementation (nominal group technique).

1.7.5 External review

This guideline has been developed in accordance with the NICE guideline development process. This has included giving registered stakeholder organisations the opportunity to comment on the scope of the guideline at the initial stage of development and on the evidence and recommendations at the concluding stage.

1.7.6 Outcome measures used in the guideline

The GDG defined women's and babies' mortality, complications and long-term outcomes, and women's satisfaction as primary outcomes, and labour events (length of labour and interventions), birth events (mode or place of birth, complications of birth, perineal trauma), newborn events (condition at birth, birth injuries, admission to neonatal units), women's assessment of birth experience, and women's mental and psychological health as secondary outcomes. The GDG considered other outcomes when they were relevant to specific questions.

1.8 Schedule for updating the guideline

Clinical guidelines commissioned by NICE are published with a review date 4 years from date of publication. Reviewing may begin earlier than 4 years if significant evidence that affects guideline recommendations is identified sooner. The updated guideline will be available within 2 years of the start of the review process.

2 Summary of recommendations and care pathway

2.1 Key priorities for implementation (key recommendations)

2.1.1 Key practice recommendations

Communication between women and healthcare professionals

All women in labour should be treated with respect and should be in control of and involved in what is happening to them, and the way in which care is given is key to this. To facilitate this, healthcare professionals and other caregivers should establish a rapport with the labouring woman, asking her about her wants and expectations for labour, being aware of the importance of tone and demeanour, and of the actual words they use. This information should be used to support and guide her through her labour.

Support in labour

A woman in established labour should receive supportive one-to-one care.

A woman in established labour should not be left on her own except for short periods or at the woman's request.

Normal labour

Clinical intervention should not be offered or advised where labour is progressing normally and the woman and baby are well.

Planning place of birth

Women should be offered the choice of planning birth at home, in a midwife-led unit or in an obstetric unit. Women should be informed:

- That giving birth is generally very safe for both the woman and her baby.
- That the available information on planning place of birth is not of good quality, but suggests that among women who plan to give birth at home or in a midwife-led unit there is a higher likelihood of a normal birth, with less intervention. We do not have enough information about the possible risks to either the woman or her baby relating to planned place of birth.
- That the obstetric unit provides direct access to obstetricians, anaesthetists, neonatologists and other specialist care including epidural analgesia.
- Of locally available services, the likelihood of being transferred into the obstetric unit and the time this may take.
- That if something does go unexpectedly seriously wrong during labour at home or in a midwife-led unit, the outcome for the woman and baby could be worse than if they were in the obstetric unit with access to specialised care.
- That if she has a pre-existing medical condition or has had a previous complicated birth that makes her at higher risk of developing complications during her next birth, she should be advised to give birth in an obstetric unit.

Clinical governance structures should be implemented in all places of birth (see Boxes 3.1 and 3.2).

Coping with pain

The opportunity to labour in water is recommended for pain relief.

Before choosing epidural analgesia, women should be informed about the risks and benefits, and the implications for their labour.

Perineal care

If genital trauma is identified following birth, further systematic assessment should be carried out, including a rectal examination.

Delay in the first stage of labour

When delay in the established first stage of labour is confirmed in nulliparous women, advice should be sought from an obstetrician and the use of oxytocin should be considered. The woman should be informed that the use of oxytocin following spontaneous or artificial rupture of the membranes will bring forward her time of birth but will not influence the mode of birth or other outcomes.

Instrumental birth

Instrumental birth is an operative procedure that should be undertaken with tested effective anaesthesia.

2.1.2 Key research recommendations

Planning place of birth

The best possible studies comparing different places of birth should be undertaken in the UK. Prospective research to assess clinical outcomes, including safety, for all places of birth should be undertaken, as well as qualitative data collection to assess women's experiences of birth.

Wellbeing of women

Studies are needed that investigate the components affecting a woman's satisfaction with her birth experience, including her emotional and psychological wellbeing. A robust method of assessing a woman's satisfaction is also needed.

Delay in the first stage of labour

Studies are needed that investigate the effectiveness of any strategies to increase spontaneous vaginal birth where diagnosis is made of delay in the first stage of labour.

2.2 Summary of recommendations

Chapter 3 Planning place of birth

3.2 Benefits and risks of planning each place of birth

Women should be offered the choice of planning birth at home, in a midwife-led unit or in an obstetric unit. Women should be informed:

- That giving birth is generally very safe for both the woman and her baby.
- That the available information on planning place of birth is not of good quality, but suggests that among women who plan to give birth at home or in a midwife-led unit there is a higher likelihood of a normal birth, with less intervention. We do not have enough information about the possible risks to either the woman or her baby relating to planned place of birth.
- That the obstetric unit provides direct access to obstetricians, anaesthetists, neonatologists and other specialist care including epidural analgesia.
- Of locally available services, the likelihood of being transferred into the obstetric unit and the time this may take.

- That if something does go unexpectedly seriously wrong during labour at home or in a mid-wife-led unit, the outcome for the woman and baby could be worse than if they were in the obstetric unit with access to specialised care.
- That if she has a pre-existing medical condition or has had a previous complicated birth that makes her at higher risk of developing complications during her next birth, she should be advised to give birth in an obstetric unit.

Clinical governance structures should be implemented in all places of birth (see Boxes 3.1 and 3.2).

Box 3.1   Clinical governance in all settings

- Multidisciplinary clinical governance structures, of which the Labour Ward Forum is an example, should be in place to enable the oversight of all places of birth. These structures should include, as a minimum, midwifery (ideally a supervisor of midwives), obstetric, anaesthetic and neonatal expertise, and adequately supported user representation.
- Rotating staff between obstetric and midwife-led units should be encouraged in order to maintain equivalent competency and experience.
- Clear referral pathways should be in place to enable midwives to inform or seek advice from a supervisor of midwives when caring for a woman who may have risk factors but does not wish to labour in an obstetric unit.
- If an obstetric opinion is sought by either the midwife or the woman on the appropriate place of birth, this should be obtained from a consultant obstetrician.
- All healthcare professionals should document discussions with the woman about her chosen place of birth in the hand-held maternity notes.
- In all places of birth, risk assessment in the antenatal period and when labour commences should be subject to continuous audit.
- Monthly figures of numbers of women booked for, being admitted to, being transferred from and giving birth in each place of birth should be audited. This should include maternal and neonatal outcomes.
- The clinical governance group should be responsible for detailed root-cause analysis of any serious maternal or neonatal adverse outcomes (for example, intrapartum-related perinatal death or seizures in the neonatal period) and consider any 'near misses' identified through risk-management systems. The Confidential Enquiry into Maternal and Child Health (CEMACH) and the National Patient Safety Agency (NPSA)'s 'Seven steps to patient safety' provide a framework for meeting clinical governance and risk-management targets.
- Data must be submitted to the national registries for either intrapartum-related perinatal mortality or neonatal encephalopathy once these are in existence.

Box 3.2   Clinical governance for settings other than an obstetric unit

- Clear pathways and guidelines on the indications for, and the process of transfer to, an obstetric unit should be established. There should be no barriers to rapid transfer in an emergency.
- Clear pathways and guidelines should also be developed for the continued care of women once they have transferred. These pathways should include arrangements for times when the nearest obstetric or neonatal unit is closed to admissions.
- If the emergency is such that transfer is not possible, open access must be given on-site for any appropriate staff to deal with whatever emergency has arisen.
- There should be continuous audit of the appropriateness of, the reason for and speed of transfer. Conversely, audit also needs to consider circumstances in which transfer was indicated but did not occur. Audit should include time taken to see an obstetrician or neonatologist and the time from admission to birth.

A national surveillance scheme which allows appropriate comparisons, including safety and cost-effectiveness, of all places of birth should be established to address the poor quality and lack of coverage of current data.

National registries of the root-cause analysis findings relating to all intrapartum-related deaths over 37 weeks of gestation should be established.

A definition of neonatal encephalopathy should be agreed and a national register commenced. The information collected should also include data on transfer during labour from each of the different birth settings.

3.3 Assessment for choosing place of birth

Tables 3.7 to 3.10 should be used as part of an assessment for choosing place of birth.

Tables 3.7 and 3.8 show medical conditions or situations in which there is increased risk for the woman or baby during or shortly after labour, where care in an obstetric unit would be expected to reduce this risk.

The factors listed in Tables 3.9 and 3.10 are not reasons in themselves for advising birth within an obstetric unit but indicate that further consideration of birth setting may be required.

These risks and the additional care that can be provided in the obstetric unit should be discussed with the woman so that she can make an informed choice about place of birth.

Table 3.7   Medical conditions indicating increased risk suggesting planned birth at an obstetric unit

Disease area	Medical condition
Cardiovascular	Confirmed cardiac disease Hypertensive disorders
Respiratory	Asthma requiring an increase in treatment or hospital treatment Cystic fibrosis
Haematological	Haemoglobinopathies – sickle-cell disease, beta-thalassaemia major History of thromboembolic disorders Immune thrombocytopenia purpura or other platelet disorder or platelet count below 100 000 Von Willebrand's disease Bleeding disorder in the woman or unborn baby Atypical antibodies which carry a risk of haemolytic disease of the newborn
Infective	Risk factors associated with group B streptococcus whereby antibiotics in labour would be recommended Hepatitis B/C with abnormal liver function tests Carrier of/infected with HIV Toxoplasmosis – women receiving treatment Current active infection of chicken pox/rubella/genital herpes in the woman or baby Tuberculosis under treatment
Immune	Systemic lupus erythematosus Scleroderma
Endocrine	Hyperthyroidism Diabetes
Renal	Abnormal renal function Renal disease requiring supervision by a renal specialist
Neurological	Epilepsy Myasthenia gravis Previous cerebrovascular accident
Gastrointestinal	Liver disease associated with current abnormal liver function tests
Psychiatric	Psychiatric disorder requiring current inpatient care

Table 3.8 Other factors indicating increased risk suggesting planned birth at an obstetric unit

Factor	Additional information
Previous complications	Unexplained stillbirth/neonatal death or previous death related to intrapartum difficulty
	Previous baby with neonatal encephalopathy
	Pre-eclampsia requiring preterm birth
	Placental abruption with adverse outcome
	Eclampsia
	Uterine rupture
	Primary postpartum haemorrhage requiring additional treatment or blood transfusion
	Retained placenta requiring manual removal in theatre
	Caesarean section
	Shoulder dystocia
Current pregnancy	Multiple birth
	Placenta praevia
	Pre-eclampsia or pregnancy-induced hypertension
	Preterm labour or preterm prelabour rupture of membranes
	Placental abruption
	Anaemia – haemoglobin less than 8.5 g/dl at onset of labour
	Confirmed intrauterine death
	Induction of labour
	Substance misuse
	Alcohol dependency requiring assessment or treatment
	Onset of gestational diabetes
	Malpresentation – breech or transverse lie
	Body mass index at booking of greater than 35 kg/m^2
	Recurrent antepartum haemorrhage
Fetal indications	Small for gestational age in this pregnancy (less than fifth centile or reduced growth velocity on ultrasound)
	Abnormal fetal heart rate (FHR)/Doppler studies
	Ultrasound diagnosis of oligo-/polyhydramnios
Previous gynaecological history	Myomectomy
	Hysterotomy

Table 3.9 Medical conditions indicating individual assessment when planning place of birth

Disease area	Medical condition
Cardiovascular	Cardiac disease without intrapartum implications
Haematological	Atypical antibodies not putting the baby at risk of haemolytic disease
	Sickle-cell trait
	Thalassaemia trait
	Anaemia – haemoglobin 8.5–10.5 g/dl at onset of labour
Infective	Hepatitis B/C with normal liver function tests
Immune	Non-specific connective tissue disorders
Endocrine	Unstable hypothyroidism such that a change in treatment is required
Skeletal/neurological	Spinal abnormalities
	Previous fractured pelvis
	Neurological deficits
Gastrointestinal	Liver disease without current abnormal liver function
	Crohn's disease
	Ulcerative colitis

Table 3.10 Other factors indicating individual assessment when planning place of birth

Factor	Additional information
Previous complications	Stillbirth/neonatal death with a known non-recurrent cause
	Pre-eclampsia developing at term
	Placental abruption with good outcome
	History of previous baby more than 4.5 kg
	Extensive vaginal, cervical, or third- or fourth-degree perineal trauma
	Previous term baby with jaundice requiring exchange transfusion
Current pregnancy	Antepartum bleeding of unknown origin (single episode after 24 weeks of gestation)
	Body mass index at booking of 30–34 kg/m²
	Blood pressure of 140 mmHg systolic or 90 mmHg diastolic on two occasions
	Clinical or ultrasound suspicion of macrosomia
	Para 6 or more
	Recreational drug use
	Under current outpatient psychiatric care
	Age over 40 at booking
Fetal indications	Fetal abnormality
Previous gynaecological history	Major gynaecological surgery
	Cone biopsy or large loop excision of the transformation zone
	Fibroids

Indications for intrapartum transfer

The following risks and benefits should be assessed when considering transfer to an obstetric unit, bearing in mind the likelihood of birth during the transfer:

- indications for electronic fetal monitoring (EFM) including abnormalities of the fetal heart rate (FHR) on intermittent auscultation
- delay in the first or second stages of labour
- significant meconium-stained liquor
- maternal request for epidural pain relief
- obstetric emergency – antepartum haemorrhage, cord presentation/prolapse, postpartum haemorrhage, maternal collapse or a need for advanced neonatal resuscitation
- retained placenta
- maternal pyrexia in labour (38.0 °C once or 37.5 °C on two occasions 2 hours apart)
- malpresentation or breech presentation diagnosed for the first time at the onset of labour, taking into account imminence of birth
- either raised diastolic blood pressure (over 90 mmHg) or raised systolic blood pressure (over 140 mmHg) on two consecutive readings taken 30 minutes apart
- uncertainty about the presence of a fetal heartbeat
- third- or fourth-degree tear or other complicated perineal trauma requiring suturing.

Chapter 4 Care throughout labour

4.1 Communication between women and healthcare professionals

All women in labour should be treated with respect and should be in control of and involved in what is happening to them, and the way in which care is given is key to this. To facilitate this, healthcare professionals and other caregivers should establish a rapport with the labouring woman, asking her about her wants and expectations for labour, being aware of the importance of tone and demeanour, and of the actual words they use. This information should be used to support and guide her through her labour.

To establish communication with the labouring woman, healthcare professionals should:

- Greet the woman with a smile and a personal welcome, establish her language needs, introduce themselves and explain their role in her care.
- Maintain a calm and confident approach so that their demeanour reassures the woman that all is going well.
- Knock and wait before entering the woman's room, respecting it as her personal space, and ask others to do the same.
- Ask how the woman is feeling and whether there is anything in particular she is worried about.
- If the woman has a written birth plan, read and discuss it with her.
- Assess the woman's knowledge of strategies for coping with pain and provide balanced information to find out which available approaches are acceptable to her.
- Encourage the woman to adapt the environment to meet her individual needs.
- Ask her permission before all procedures and observations, focusing on the woman rather than the technology or the documentation.
- Show the woman and her birth partner how to summon help and reassure her that she may do so whenever and as often as she needs to. When leaving the room, healthcare professionals should let her know when they will return.
- Involve the woman in any handover of care to another professional, either when additional expertise has been brought in or at the end of a shift.

4.2 Mobilisation and position

Women should be encouraged and helped to move and adopt whatever positions they find most comfortable throughout labour.

4.3 Support in labour

A woman in established labour should receive supportive one-to-one care.

A woman in established labour should not be left on her own except for short periods or at the woman's request.

Women should be encouraged to have support by birth partner(s) of their choice.

Team midwifery (defined as a group of midwives providing care and taking shared responsibility for a group of women from the antenatal, through intrapartum to the postnatal period) is not recommended.

4.4 Eating and drinking in labour

Controlling gastric acidity

Neither H2-receptor antagonists nor antacids should be given routinely to low-risk women.

Either H2-receptor antagonists or antacids should be considered for women who receive opioids or who have or develop risk factors that make a general anaesthetic more likely.

Eating and drinking in labour

Women may drink during established labour and be informed that isotonic drinks may be more beneficial than water.

Women may eat a light diet in established labour unless they have received opioids or they develop risk factors that make a general anaesthetic more likely.

4.5 Hygiene measures during labour

Tap water may be used if cleansing is required prior to vaginal examination.

Routine hygiene measures taken by staff caring for women in labour, including standard hand hygiene and single-use non-sterile gloves, are appropriate to reduce cross-contamination between women, babies and healthcare professionals.

Selection of protective equipment should be based on an assessment of the risk of transmission of microorganisms to the woman, and the risk of contamination of the healthcare practitioner's clothing and skin by women's blood, body fluids, secretions or excretions.*

Chapter 5 Coping with pain in labour: non-epidural

5.2 Women's views and experiences of pain and pain relief in childbirth

Healthcare professionals should consider how their own values and beliefs inform their attitude to coping with pain in labour and ensure their care supports the woman's choice.

5.3 Pain-relieving strategies

Women who choose to use breathing and relaxation techniques in labour should be supported in their choice.

Women who choose to use massage techniques in labour that have been taught to birth partners should be supported in their choice.

The opportunity to labour in water is recommended for pain relief.

For women labouring in water, the temperature of the woman and the water should be monitored hourly to ensure that the woman is comfortable and not becoming pyrexial. The temperature of the water should not be above 37.5 °C.

Any bath or birthing pool should be kept clean using a protocol agreed with the microbiology department and, in the case of birthing pools, in accordance with the manufacturer's guidelines.

The use of injected water papules is not recommended.

Acupuncture, acupressure and hypnosis should not be provided, but women who wish to use these techniques should not be prevented from doing so.

The playing of music of the woman's choice in the labour ward should be supported.

5.4 Non-pharmacological analgesia

Transcutaneous electrical nerve stimulation (TENS) should not be offered to women in established labour.

5.5 Inhalational analgesia

Entonox (a 50 : 50 mixture of oxygen and nitrous oxide) should be available in all birth settings as it may reduce pain in labour, but women should be informed that it may make them feel nauseous and light-headed.

5.6 Intravenous and intramuscular use of opioids for labour

Pethidine, diamorphine or other opioids should be available in all birth settings. Women should be informed that these will provide limited pain relief during labour and may have significant side effects for both the woman (drowsiness, nausea and vomiting) and her baby (short-term respiratory depression and drowsiness which may last several days).

Women should be informed that pethidine, diamorphine or other opioids may interfere with breastfeeding.

If an intravenous or intramuscular opioid is used, it should be administered with an antiemetic.

Women should not enter water (a birthing pool or bath) within 2 hours of opioid administration or if they feel drowsy.

---

* This recommendation is from 'Infection control: prevention of healthcare-associated infection in primary and community care' (NICE clinical guideline 2).

Chapter 6 Pain relief in labour: regional analgesia

6.2 Regional analgesia versus other types of analgesia in labour

Before choosing epidural analgesia, women should be informed about the risks and benefits, and the implications for their labour.

This information about choosing epidural analgesia should include the following:

- It is only available in obstetric units.
- It provides more effective pain relief than opioids.
- It is associated with a longer second stage of labour and an increased chance of vaginal instrumental birth.
- It is not associated with long-term backache.
- It is not associated with a longer first stage of labour or an increased chance of caesarean birth.
- It will be accompanied by a more intensive level of monitoring and intravenous access.
- Modern epidural solutions contain opioids and, whatever the route of administration, all opioids cross the placenta and in larger doses (greater than 100 micrograms in total) may cause short-term respiratory depression in the baby and make the baby drowsy.

6.3 Timing of regional analgesia

Women in labour who desire regional analgesia should not be denied it, including women in severe pain in the latent first stage of labour.

6.4 Care and observations for women with regional analgesia in labour

Intravenous access should always be secured prior to commencing regional analgesia.

Preloading and maintenance fluid infusion need not be administered routinely before establishing low-dose epidural analgesia and combined spinal–epidural analgesia.

The following additional observations should be undertaken for women with regional analgesia:

- During establishment of regional analgesia or after further boluses (10 ml or more of low-dose solutions) blood pressure should be measured every 5 minutes for 15 minutes.
- If the woman is not pain free 30 minutes after each administration of local anaesthetic/opioid solution, the anaesthetist should be recalled.
- Hourly assessment of the level of the sensory block should be undertaken.

Women with regional analgesia should be encouraged to move and adopt whatever upright positions they find comfortable throughout labour.

Once established, regional analgesia should be continued until after completion of the third stage of labour and any necessary perineal repair.

Upon confirmation of full cervical dilatation in women with regional analgesia, unless the woman has an urge to push or the baby's head is visible, pushing should be delayed for at least 1 hour and longer if the woman wishes, after which pushing during contractions should be actively encouraged.

Following the diagnosis of full dilatation in a woman with regional analgesia, a plan should be agreed with the woman in order to ensure that birth will have occurred within 4 hours regardless of parity.

Oxytocin should not be used as a matter of routine in the second stage of labour for women with regional analgesia.

Continuous EFM is recommended for at least 30 minutes during establishment of regional analgesia and after administration of each further bolus of 10 ml or more.

6.6–6.8 Establishing and maintaining regional analgesia

Either patient-controlled epidural analgesia or intermittent bolus given by healthcare professionals are the preferred modes of administration for maintenance of epidural analgesia.

Either epidural or combined spinal–epidural analgesia is recommended for establishing regional analgesia in labour.

If rapid analgesia is required, combined spinal–epidural analgesia is recommended.

It is recommended that combined spinal–epidural analgesia is established with bupivacaine and fentanyl.

It is recommended that epidural analgesia is established with a low-concentration local anaesthetic and opioid solution with, for example, 10–15 ml of 0.0625–0.1% bupivacaine with 1–2 micrograms per ml fentanyl. The initial dose of local anaesthetic plus opioid is essentially a test dose and as such should be administered cautiously to ensure that inadvertent intrathecal injection has not occurred.

Low-concentration local anaesthetic and opioid solutions (0.0625–0.1% bupivacaine or equivalent combined with 2.0 micrograms per ml fentanyl) are recommended for maintaining epidural analgesia in labour.

High concentrations of local anaesthetic solutions (0.25% or above of bupivacaine or equivalent) should not be used routinely for either establishing or maintaining epidural analgesia.

Chapter 7 Normal labour: first stage

7.1 Normal labour

Clinical intervention should not be offered or advised where labour is progressing normally and the woman and baby are well.

In all stages of labour, women who have left the normal care pathway due to the development of complications can return to it if/when the complication is resolved.

7.2 Definition of the first stage of labour

For the purposes of this guideline, the following definitions of labour are recommended:

- Latent first stage of labour – a period of time, not necessarily continuous, when:
  ○ there are painful contractions, and
  ○ there is some cervical change, including cervical effacement and dilatation up to 4 cm.
- Established first stage of labour – when:
  ○ there are regular painful contractions, and
  ○ there is progressive cervical dilatation from 4 cm.

7.3 Duration of the first stage of labour

Women should be informed that, while the length of established first stage of labour varies between women, first labours last on average 8 hours and are unlikely to last over 18 hours. Second and subsequent labours last on average 5 hours and are unlikely to last over 12 hours.

Definition of delay in the first stage of labour [repeated from Section 14.1]

A diagnosis of delay in the established first stage of labour needs to take into consideration all aspects of progress in labour and should include:

- cervical dilatation of less than 2 cm in 4 hours for first labours
- cervical dilatation of less than 2 cm in 4 hours or a slowing in the progress of labour for second or subsequent labours
- descent and rotation of the fetal head
- changes in the strength, duration and frequency of uterine contractions.

7.4 Observations on presentation in suspected labour

The initial assessment of a woman by a midwife should include:

- listening to her story, considering her emotional and psychological needs, and reviewing her clinical records
- physical observation – temperature, pulse, blood pressure, urinalysis
- length, strength and frequency of contractions
- abdominal palpation – fundal height, lie, presentation, position and station
- vaginal loss – show, liquor, blood
- assessment of the woman's pain, including her wishes for coping with labour along with the range of options for pain relief.

In addition:

- The FHR should be auscultated for a minimum of 1 minute immediately after a contraction. The maternal pulse should be palpated to differentiate between maternal and FHR.
- If the woman does not appear to be in established labour, after a period of assessment it may be helpful to offer a vaginal examination.
- If the woman appears to be in established labour, a vaginal examination should be offered.

Healthcare professionals who conduct vaginal examinations should :

- be sure that the vaginal examination is really necessary and will add important information to the decision-making process
- be aware that for many women who may already be in pain, highly anxious and in an unfamiliar environment, vaginal examinations can be very distressing
- ensure the woman's consent, privacy, dignity and comfort
- explain the reason for the examination and what will be involved, and
- explain the findings and their impact sensitively to the woman.

Some women have pain without cervical change. Although these women are described as not being in labour, they may well consider themselves 'in labour' by their own definition. Women who seek advice or attend hospital with painful contractions but who are not in established labour should be offered individualised support and occasionally analgesia, and encouraged to remain at or return home.

The use of admission cardiotocography (CTG) in low-risk pregnancy is not recommended in any birth setting.

7.6 Observations during the established first stage of labour

Verbal assessment using a numerical pain score is not recommended routinely.

A pictorial record of labour (partogram) should be used once labour is established.

Where the partogram includes an action line, the World Health Organization recommendation of a 4 hour action line should be used.* [repeated from Section 7.7]

Observations by a midwife during the first stage of labour include:

- 4 hourly temperature and blood pressure
- hourly pulse
- half-hourly documentation of frequency of contractions
- frequency of emptying the bladder
- vaginal examination offered 4 hourly, or where there is concern about progress or in response to the woman's wishes (after abdominal palpation and assessment of vaginal loss).

In addition:

- Intermittent auscultation of the fetal heart after a contraction should occur for at least 1 minute, at least every 15 minutes, and the rate should be recorded as an average. The maternal pulse should be palpated if an FHR abnormality is detected to differentiate the two heart rates. (See recommendations in Section 7.8 for reasons to transfer to continuous EFM.)

---

* Anonymous. World Health Organization partograph in management of labour. World Health Organization Maternal Health and Safe Motherhood Programme. *Lancet* 1994;343(8910):1399–404. See also www.who.int/reproductive-health/impac/Clinical_Principles/Normal_labour_C57_C76.html.

Ongoing consideration should be given to the woman's emotional and psychological needs, including her desire for pain relief.

Women should be encouraged to communicate their need for analgesia at any point during labour.

7.7 Possible routine interventions in first stage of labour

The package known as active management of labour (one-to-one continuous support; strict definition of established labour; early routine amniotomy; routine 2 hourly vaginal examination; oxytocin if labour becomes slow) should not be offered routinely.

Where the partogram includes an action line, the World Health Organization recommendation of a 4 hour action line should be used.*

In normally progressing labour, amniotomy should not be performed routinely.

Combined early amniotomy with use of oxytocin should not be used routinely.

7.8 Fetal heart assessment and reasons for transfer to continuous EFM

Intermittent auscultation of the FHR is recommended for low-risk women in established labour in any birth setting.

Initial auscultation of the fetal heart is recommended at first contact in early labour and at each further assessment undertaken to determine whether labour has become established.

Once a woman is in established labour, intermittent auscultation of the fetal heart after a contraction should be continued as detailed in Section 7.6.

Intermittent auscultation can be undertaken by either Doppler ultrasound or Pinard stethoscope.

Changing from intermittent auscultation to continuous EFM in low-risk women should be advised for the following reasons:

- significant meconium-stained liquor, and this change should also be considered for light meconium-stained liquor (see recommendations in Section 12.1)
- abnormal FHR detected by intermittent auscultation (less than 110 beats per minute [bpm]; greater than 160 bpm; any decelerations after a contraction)
- maternal pyrexia (defined as 38.0 °C once or 37.5 °C on two occasions 2 hours apart)
- fresh bleeding developing in labour
- oxytocin use for augmentation
- the woman's request.

Chapter 8 Normal labour: second stage

8.1 Definition of the second stage of labour

For the purposes of this guideline, the following definitions of labour are recommended:

- Passive second stage of labour:
  - the finding of full dilatation of the cervix prior to or in the absence of involuntary expulsive contractions.
- Onset of the active second stage of labour:
  - the baby is visible
  - expulsive contractions with a finding of full dilatation of the cervix or other signs of full dilatation of the cervix
  - active maternal effort following confirmation of full dilatation of the cervix in the absence of expulsive contractions.

---

* Anonymous. World Health Organization partograph in management of labour. World Health Organization Maternal Health and Safe Motherhood Programme. *Lancet* 1994;343(8910):1399–404. See also www.who.int/reproductive-health/impac/Clinical_Principles/ Normal_labour_C57_C76.html.

8.2 Duration and definition of delay in the second stage of labour

Nulliparous women:

- Birth would be expected to take place within 3 hours of the start of the active second stage in most women.
- A diagnosis of delay in the active second stage should be made when it has lasted 2 hours and women should be referred to a healthcare professional trained to undertake an operative vaginal birth if birth is not imminent.

Parous women:

- Birth would be expected to take place within 2 hours of the start of the active second stage in most women.
- A diagnosis of delay in the active second stage should be made when it has lasted 1 hour and women should be referred to a healthcare professional trained to undertake an operative vaginal birth if birth is not imminent.

If full dilatation of the cervix has been diagnosed in a woman without epidural analgesia, but she does not get an urge to push, further assessment should take place after 1 hour.

8.3 Observations for women and babies in the second stage of labour

All observations should be documented on the partogram. Observations by a midwife of a woman in the second stage of labour include:

- hourly blood pressure and pulse
- continued 4 hourly temperature
- vaginal examination offered hourly in the active second stage or in response to the woman's wishes (after abdominal palpation and assessment of vaginal loss)
- half-hourly documentation of the frequency of contractions
- frequency of emptying the bladder
- ongoing consideration of the woman's emotional and psychological needs.

In addition:

- Assessment of progress should include maternal behaviour, effectiveness of pushing and fetal wellbeing, taking into account fetal position and station at the onset of the second stage. These factors will assist in deciding the timing of further vaginal examination and the need for obstetric review.
- Intermittent auscultation of the fetal heart should occur after a contraction for at least 1 minute, at least every 5 minutes. The maternal pulse should be palpated if there is suspected fetal bradycardia or any other FHR anomaly to differentiate the two heart rates.
- Ongoing consideration should be given to the woman's position, hydration, coping strategies and pain relief throughout the second stage.

8.4 Women's position and pushing in the second stage of labour

Women should be discouraged from lying supine or semi-supine in the second stage of labour and should be encouraged to adopt any other position that they find most comfortable.

Women should be informed that in the second stage they should be guided by their own urge to push.

If pushing is ineffective or if requested by the woman, strategies to assist birth can be used, such as support, change of position, emptying of the bladder and encouragement.

8.5 Intrapartum interventions to reduce perineal trauma

Perineal massage should not be performed by healthcare professionals in the second stage of labour.

Either the 'hands on' (guarding the perineum and flexing the baby's head) or the 'hands poised' (with hands off the perineum and baby's head but in readiness) technique can be used to facilitate spontaneous birth.

Lidocaine spray should not be used to reduce pain in the second stage of labour.

A routine episiotomy should not be carried out during spontaneous vaginal birth.

Where an episiotomy is performed, the recommended technique is a mediolateral episiotomy originating at the vaginal fourchette and usually directed to the right side. The angle to the vertical axis should be between 45 and 60 degrees at the time of the episiotomy.

An episiotomy should be performed if there is a clinical need such as instrumental birth or suspected fetal compromise.

Tested effective analgesia should be provided prior to carrying out an episiotomy, except in an emergency due to acute fetal compromise.

Women with a history of severe perineal trauma should be informed that their risk of repeat severe perineal trauma is not increased in a subsequent birth, compared with women having their first baby.

Episiotomy should not be offered routinely at vaginal birth following previous third- or fourth-degree trauma.

In order for a woman who has had previous third- or fourth-degree trauma to make an informed choice, discussion with her about the future mode of birth should encompass:

- current urgency or incontinence symptoms
- the degree of previous trauma
- risk of recurrence
- the success of the repair undertaken
- the psychological effect of the previous trauma
- management of her labour.

Women with infibulated genital mutilation should be informed of the risks of difficulty with vaginal examination, catheterisation and application of fetal scalp electrodes. They should also be informed of the risks of delay in the second stage and spontaneous laceration together with the need for an anterior episiotomy and the possible need for defibulation in labour.

8.6 Water birth

Women should be informed that there is insufficient high-quality evidence to either support or discourage giving birth in water.

Chapter 9 Normal labour: third stage

9.1 Definition and duration of the third stage of labour

For the purposes of this guideline, the following definitions are recommended:

- The third stage of labour is the time from the birth of the baby to the expulsion of the placenta and membranes.
- Active management of the third stage involves a package of care which includes all of these three components:
  - routine use of uterotonic drugs
  - early clamping and cutting of the cord
  - controlled cord traction.
- Physiological management of the third stage involves a package of care which includes all of these three components:
  - no routine use of uterotonic drugs
  - no clamping of the cord until pulsation has ceased
  - delivery of the placenta by maternal effort.

The third stage of labour is diagnosed as prolonged if not completed within 30 minutes of the birth of the baby with active management and 60 minutes with physiological management.

9.2 Observations in the third stage of labour

Observations by a midwife of a woman in the third stage of labour include:

- her general physical condition, as shown by her colour, respiration and her own report of how she feels
- vaginal blood loss.

In addition, in the presence of haemorrhage, retained placenta or maternal collapse, frequent observations to assess the need for resuscitation are required.

9.3 Physiological and active management of the third stage

Active management of the third stage is recommended, which includes the use of oxytocin (10 international units [IU] by intramuscular injection), followed by early clamping and cutting of the cord and controlled cord traction.*

Women should be informed that active management of the third stage reduces the risk of maternal haemorrhage and shortens the third stage.

Women at low risk of postpartum haemorrhage who request physiological management of the third stage should be supported in their choice.

Changing from physiological management to active management of the third stage is indicated in the case of:

- haemorrhage
- failure to deliver the placenta within 1 hour
- the woman's desire to artificially shorten the third stage.

Pulling the cord or palpating the uterus should only be carried out after administration of oxytocin as part of active management.

In the third stage of labour neither umbilical oxytocin infusion nor prostaglandin should be used routinely.

Chapter 10 Normal labour: care of the baby and woman immediately after birth

10.2 Initial assessment of the newborn baby and mother–infant bonding

The Apgar score at 1 and 5 minutes should be recorded routinely for all births.

If the baby is born in poor condition (the Apgar score at 1 minute is 5 or less), then the time to the onset of regular respirations should be recorded and the cord double-clamped to allow paired cord blood gases to be taken. The Apgar score should continue to be recorded until the baby's condition is stable.

Women should be encouraged to have skin-to-skin contact with their babies as soon as possible after the birth.[†]

In order to keep the baby warm, he or she should be dried and covered with a warm, dry blanket or towel while maintaining skin-to-skin contact with the woman.

Separation of a woman and her baby within the first hour of the birth for routine postnatal procedures, for example weighing, measuring and bathing, should be avoided unless these measures are requested by the woman, or are necessary for the immediate care of the baby.[†]

Initiation of breastfeeding should be encouraged as soon as possible after the birth, ideally within 1 hour.[†]

---

* At the time of publication (September 2007), oxytocin did not have UK marketing authorisation for this indication. Informed consent should be obtained and documented.

† Recommendations relating to immediate postnatal care (within 2 hours of birth) have been extracted from 'Routine postnatal care of women and their babies' (NICE clinical guideline 37). Please see NICE clinical guideline 37 for further guidance on care after birth.

Head circumference, body temperature and birthweight should be recorded soon after the first hour following birth.

An initial examination should be undertaken by a healthcare professional to detect any major physical abnormality and to identify any problems that require referral.

Any examination or treatment of the baby should be undertaken with the consent and in the presence of the parents or, if this is not possible, with their knowledge.

10.3 Initial assessment of the mother following birth

Observations taken following the birth of the baby should include:

- maternal observation – temperature, pulse, blood pressure, uterine contraction, lochia
- examination of placenta and membranes – assessment of their condition, structure, cord vessels and completeness
- early assessment of maternal emotional/psychological condition in response to labour and birth
- successful voiding of the woman's bladder.

10.4 Perineal care

Perineal or genital trauma caused by either tearing or episiotomy should be defined as follows:

- first degree – injury to skin only
- second degree – injury to the perineal muscles but not the anal sphincter
- third degree – injury to the perineum involving the anal sphincter complex:
  - ○ 3a – less than 50% of external anal sphincter thickness torn
  - ○ 3b – more than 50% of external anal sphincter thickness torn
  - ○ 3c – internal anal sphincter torn.
- fourth degree – injury to the perineum involving the anal sphincter complex (external and internal anal sphincter) and anal epithelium.

Before assessing for genital trauma, healthcare professionals should:

- explain to the woman what they plan to do and why
- offer inhalational analgesia
- ensure good lighting
- position the woman so that she is comfortable and so that the genital structures can be seen clearly.

The initial examination should be performed gently and with sensitivity and may be done in the immediate period following birth.

If genital trauma is identified following birth, further systematic assessment should be carried out, including a rectal examination.

Systematic assessment of genital trauma should include:

- further explanation of what the healthcare professional plans to do and why
- confirmation by the woman that tested effective local or regional analgesia is in place
- visual assessment of the extent of perineal trauma to include the structures involved, the apex of the injury and assessment of bleeding
- a rectal examination to assess whether there has been any damage to the external or internal anal sphincter if there is any suspicion that the perineal muscles are damaged.

The timing of this systematic assessment should not interfere with mother–infant bonding unless the woman has bleeding that requires urgent attention.

The woman should usually be in lithotomy to allow adequate visual assessment of the degree of the trauma and for the repair. This position should only be maintained for as long as is necessary for the systematic assessment and repair.

The woman should be referred to a more experienced healthcare professional if uncertainty exists as to the nature or extent of trauma sustained.

The systematic assessment and its results should be fully documented, possibly pictorially.

All relevant healthcare professionals should attend training in perineal/genital assessment and repair, and ensure that they maintain these skills.

Women should be advised that in the case of first-degree trauma, the wound should be sutured in order to improve healing, unless the skin edges are well opposed.

Women should be advised that in the case of second-degree trauma, the muscle should be sutured in order to improve healing.

Repair of the perineum should be undertaken as soon as possible to minimise the risk of infection and blood loss.

Perineal repair should only be undertaken with tested effective analgesia in place using infiltration with up to 20 ml of 1% lidocaine or equivalent, or topping up the epidural (spinal anaesthesia may be necessary).

If the woman reports inadequate pain relief at any point this should immediately be addressed.

If the skin is opposed following suturing of the muscle in second-degree trauma, there is no need to suture it.

Where the skin does require suturing, this should be undertaken using a continuous subcuticular technique.

Perineal repair should be undertaken using a continuous non-locked suturing technique for the vaginal wall and muscle layer.

An absorbable synthetic suture material should be used to suture the perineum.

The following basic principles should be observed when performing perineal repairs:

- Perineal trauma should be repaired using aseptic techniques.
- Equipment should be checked and swabs and needles counted before and after the procedure.
- Good lighting is essential to see and identify the structures involved.
- Difficult trauma should be repaired by an experienced practitioner in theatre under regional or general anaesthesia. An indwelling catheter should be inserted for 24 hours to prevent urinary retention.
- Good anatomical alignment of the wound should be achieved, and consideration given to the cosmetic results.
- Rectal examination should be carried out after completing the repair to ensure that suture material has not been accidentally inserted through the rectal mucosa.
- Following completion of the repair, an accurate detailed account should be documented covering the extent of the trauma, the method of repair and the materials used.
- Information should be given to the woman regarding the extent of the trauma, pain relief, diet, hygiene and the importance of pelvic-floor exercises.

Rectal nonsteroidal anti-inflammatory drugs should be offered routinely following perineal repair of first- and second-degree trauma provided these drugs are not contraindicated.

Chapter 11 Prelabour rupture of membranes at term

11.1 Prelabour rupture of membranes at term

There is no reason to carry out a speculum examination with a certain history of rupture of the membranes at term.

Women with an uncertain history of prelabour rupture of the membranes should be offered a speculum examination to determine whether their membranes have ruptured. Digital vaginal examination in the absence of contractions should be avoided.

Women presenting with prelabour rupture of the membranes at term should be advised that:

- the risk of serious neonatal infection is 1% rather than 0.5% for women with intact membranes

- 60% of women with prelabour rupture of the membranes will go into labour within 24 hours
- induction of labour* is appropriate approximately 24 hours after rupture of the membranes.

Until the induction is commenced or if expectant management beyond 24 hours is chosen by the woman:

- lower vaginal swabs and maternal C-reactive protein should not be offered
- to detect any infection that may be developing women should be advised to record their temperature every 4 hours during waking hours and to report immediately any change in the colour or smell of their vaginal loss
- women should be informed that bathing or showering are not associated with an increase in infection, but that having sexual intercourse may be.

Fetal movement and heart rate should be assessed at initial contact and then every 24 hours following rupture of the membranes while the woman is not in labour, and the woman should be advised to report immediately any decrease in fetal movements.

If labour has not started 24 hours after rupture of the membranes, women should be advised to give birth where there is access to neonatal services and advised to stay in hospital for at least 12 hours following the birth.

If there are no signs of infection in the woman, antibiotics should not be given to either the woman or the baby, even if the membranes have been ruptured for over 24 hours.

If there is evidence of infection in the woman, a full course of broad-spectrum intravenous antibiotics should be prescribed.

Women with prelabour rupture of the membranes should be asked to inform their healthcare professionals immediately of any concerns they have about their baby's wellbeing in the first 5 days following birth, particularly in the first 12 hours when the risk of infection is greatest.

Blood, cerebrospinal fluid and/or surface culture tests should not be performed in an asymptomatic baby.

Asymptomatic term babies born to women with prelabour rupture of the membranes (more than 24 hours before labour) should be closely observed for the first 12 hours of life (at 1 hour, 2 hours and then 2 hourly for 10 hours). These observations should include:

- general wellbeing
- chest movements and nasal flare
- skin colour including perfusion, by testing capillary refill
- feeding
- muscle tone
- temperature
- heart rate and respiration.

A baby with any symptom of possible sepsis, or born to a woman who has evidence of chorioamnionitis, should immediately be referred to a neonatal care specialist.

Chapter 12 Meconium-stained liquor

12.1 Monitoring and treatment of women with meconium-stained liquor

Continuous EFM should be advised for women with significant meconium-stained liquor, which is defined as either dark green or black amniotic fluid that is thick or tenacious, or any meconium-stained amniotic fluid containing lumps of meconium.

Continuous EFM should be considered for women with light meconium-stained liquor depending on a risk assessment which should include as a minimum their stage of labour, volume of liquor, parity, the FHR and, where applicable, transfer pathway.

Amnioinfusion should not be used for the treatment of women with meconium-stained liquor.

---

* Care of women who have their labour induced is covered by 'Induction of labour' (inherited clinical guideline D).

12.2 Resuscitation of babies with meconium-stained liquor

If significant meconium-stained liquor is identified, healthcare professionals trained in FBS should be available in labour and healthcare professionals trained in advanced neonatal life support should be readily available for the birth.

Suctioning of the nasopharynx and oropharynx prior to birth of the shoulders and trunk should not be carried out.

The upper airways should only be suctioned if the baby has thick or tenacious meconium present in the oropharynx.

If the baby has depressed vital signs, laryngoscopy and suction under direct vision should be carried out by a healthcare professional trained in advanced neonatal life support.

If there has been significant meconium staining and the baby is in good condition, the baby should be closely observed for signs of respiratory distress. These observations should be performed at 1 and 2 hours of age and then 2 hourly until 12 hours of age, and should include:

- general wellbeing
- chest movements and nasal flare
- skin colour including perfusion, by testing capillary refill
- feeding
- muscle tone
- temperature
- heart rate and respiration.

If there has been light meconium staining, the baby should be similarly observed by the healthcare professional at 1 and 2 hours and should be reviewed by a neonatologist if the baby's condition causes concern at any time.

Chapter 13 Complicated labour: monitoring babies in labour

13.2 Women's views on fetal monitoring and mobility

Women should be informed that continuous fetal monitoring will restrict their mobility.

13.4 EFM and record-keeping

In order to ensure accurate record-keeping regarding EFM:[*]

- The date and time clocks on the EFM machine should be correctly set.
- Traces should be labelled with the mother's name, date and hospital number.
- Any intrapartum events that may affect the FHR should be noted at the time on the FHR trace, which should be signed and the date and time noted (for example, vaginal examination, FBS or siting of an epidural).
- Any member of staff who is asked to provide an opinion on a trace should note their findings on both the trace and the woman's medical records along with the date, time and signature.
- Following birth, the healthcare professional should sign and note the date, time and mode of birth on the FHR trace.
- The FHR trace should be stored securely with the woman's medical records at the end of the monitoring process.

---

[*] This guideline updates and replaces 'The use of electronic fetal monitoring: The use and interpretation of cardiotocography in intrapartum fetal surveillance' (inherited clinical guideline C), issued in 2001.

13.5 Interpretation of FHR traces

The recommended definitions and classifications of the FHR trace/cardiotocograph produced during EFM are shown in Tables 13.1 and 13.2.

Table 13.1   Definition of normal, suspicious and pathological FHR traces

Category	Definition
Normal	An FHR trace in which all four features are classified as reassuring
Suspicious	An FHR trace with one feature classified as non-reassuring and the remaining features classified as reassuring
Pathological	An FHR trace with two or more features classified as non-reassuring or one or more classified as abnormal

Table 13.2   Classification of FHR trace features

Feature	Baseline (bpm)	Variability (bpm)	Decelerations	Accelerations
Reassuring	110–160	≥ 5	None	Present
Non-reassuring	100–109 161–180	< 5 for 40–90 minutes	Typical variable decelerations with over 50% of contractions, occurring for over 90 minutes Single prolonged deceleration for up to 3 minutes	The absence of accelerations with otherwise normal trace is of uncertain significance
Abnormal	< 100 > 180 Sinusoidal pattern ≥ 10 minutes	< 5 for 90 minutes	Either atypical variable decelerations with over 50% of contractions or late decelerations, both for over 30 minutes Single prolonged deceleration for more than 3 minutes	

Further information about classifying FHR traces is given below.

- If repeated accelerations are present with reduced variability, the FHR trace should be regarded as reassuring.
- True early uniform decelerations are rare and benign, and therefore they are not significant.
- Most decelerations in labour are variable.
- If a bradycardia occurs in the baby for more than 3 minutes, urgent medical aid should be sought and preparations should be made to urgently expedite the birth of the baby, classified as a category 1 birth. This could include moving the woman to theatre if the fetal heart has not recovered by 9 minutes. If the fetal heart recovers within 9 minutes the decision to deliver should be reconsidered in conjunction with the woman if reasonable.
- A tachycardia in the baby of 160–180 bpm, where accelerations are present and no other adverse features appear, should not be regarded as suspicious. However, an increase in the baseline heart rate, even within the normal range, with other non-reassuring or abnormal features should increase concern.

For women having continuous EFM, a documented systematic assessment based on these definitions and classifications should be undertaken every hour.

During episodes of abnormal FHR patterns when the woman is lying supine she should be advised to adopt the left-lateral position.

Prolonged use of maternal facial oxygen therapy may be harmful to the baby and should be avoided. There is no research evidence evaluating the benefits or risks associated with the short-term use of maternal facial oxygen therapy in cases of suspected fetal compromise.

In the presence of abnormal FHR patterns and uterine hypercontractility not secondary to oxytocin infusion, tocolysis should be considered. A suggested regimen is subcutaneous terbutaline 0.25 mg.*

In cases of suspected or confirmed acute fetal compromise, delivery should be accomplished within a time appropriate for the clinical condition.

Continuous EFM in the presence of oxytocin:

- If the FHR trace is normal, oxytocin may be continued until the woman is experiencing 4 or 5 contractions every 10 minutes. Oxytocin should be reduced if contractions occur more frequently than 5 contractions in 10 minutes.
- If the FHR trace is classified as suspicious, this should be reviewed by an obstetrician and the oxytocin dose should only continue to increase to achieve 4 or 5 contractions every 10 minutes.
- If the FHR trace is classified as pathological, oxytocin should be stopped and a full assessment of the fetal condition undertaken by an obstetrician before oxytocin is recommenced.

13.6 Adjuncts to the use of continuous EFM including FBS

Digital stimulation of the fetal scalp by the healthcare professional during a vaginal examination should be considered as an adjunct to continuous EFM.

If fetal death is suspected despite the presence of an apparently recorded FHR, then fetal viability should be confirmed with real-time ultrasound assessment.

FBS should be advised in the presence of a pathological FHR trace, unless there is clear evidence of acute compromise.

Where assisted birth is contemplated because of an abnormal FHR pattern, in cases of suspected fetal acidosis FBS should be undertaken in the absence of technical difficulties or any contraindications.

Where there is clear evidence of acute fetal compromise (for example, prolonged deceleration greater than 3 minutes), FBS should not be undertaken and urgent preparations to expedite birth should be made.

Fetal blood samples should be taken with the woman in the left-lateral position.

The classification of FBS results shown in Table 13.4 is recommended.

Table 13.4   The classification of fetal blood sample results

Fetal blood sample result (pH)	Interpretation of the results
≥ 7.25	Normal FBS result
7.21–7.24	Borderline FBS result
≤ 7.20	Abnormal FBS result

These results should be interpreted taking into account the previous pH measurement, the rate of progress in labour and the clinical features of the woman and baby.

After an abnormal FBS result, consultant obstetric advice should be sought.

After a normal FBS result, sampling should be repeated no more than 1 hour later if the FHR trace remains pathological, or sooner if there are further abnormalities.

After a borderline FBS result, sampling should be repeated no more than 30 minutes later if the FHR trace remains pathological or sooner if there are further abnormalities.

The time taken to take a fetal blood sample needs to be considered when planning repeat samples.

---

* At the time of publication (September 2007), terbutaline did not have UK marketing authorisation for this indication. Informed consent should be obtained and documented.

If the FHR trace remains unchanged and the FBS result is stable after the second test, a third/further sample may be deferred unless additional abnormalities develop on the trace.

Where a third FBS is considered necessary, consultant obstetric opinion should be sought.

Contraindications to FBS include:

- maternal infection (for example, HIV, hepatitis viruses and herpes simplex virus)
- fetal bleeding disorders (for example, haemophilia)
- prematurity (less than 34 weeks).

13.8 Risk management when using continuous EFM in labour

Clinicians should take into account the time that it will take to achieve birth by both instrumental vaginal birth and caesarean section when making decisions regarding concern over fetal well-being during labour.

FHR traces should be kept for 25 years and, where possible, stored electronically.

In cases where there is concern that the baby may suffer developmental delay, FHR traces should be photocopied and stored indefinitely in case of possible adverse outcomes.

Tracer systems should be available for all FHR traces if stored separately from women's records.

Tracer systems should be developed to ensure that FHR traces removed for any purpose (such as risk management or for teaching purposes) can always be located.

Paired cord blood gases do not need to be taken routinely. They should be taken when there has been concern about the baby either in labour or immediately following birth.

An additional clamp to facilitate double-clamping of the cord should be available at all birth settings.

Chapter 14 Complicated labour: first stage

14.1 Definition of delay in the first stage of labour

A diagnosis of delay in the established first stage of labour needs to take into consideration all aspects of progress in labour and should include:

- cervical dilatation of less than 2 cm in 4 hours for first labours
- cervical dilatation of less than 2 cm in 4 hours or a slowing in the progress of labour for second or subsequent labours
- descent and rotation of the fetal head
- changes in the strength, duration and frequency of uterine contractions.

14.2 Interventions for perceived delay in first stage of labour

Where delay in the established first stage is suspected the following should be considered:

- parity
- cervical dilatation and rate of change
- uterine contractions
- station and position of presenting part
- the woman's emotional state
- referral to the appropriate healthcare professional,

and women should be offered support, hydration, and appropriate and effective pain relief.

If delay in the established first stage of labour is suspected, amniotomy should be considered for all women with intact membranes, following explanation of the procedure and advice that it will shorten her labour by about an hour and may increase the strength and pain of her contractions.

Whether or not a woman has agreed to an amniotomy, all women with suspected delay in the established first stage of labour should be advised to have a vaginal examination 2 hours later, and if progress is less than 1 cm a diagnosis of delay is made.

In women with intact membranes in whom delay in the established first stage of labour is confirmed, amniotomy should be advised to the woman, and she should be advised to have a repeat vaginal examination 2 hours later whether her membranes are ruptured or intact.

When delay in the established first stage of labour is confirmed in nulliparous women, advice should be sought from an obstetrician and the use of oxytocin should be considered. The woman should be informed that the use of oxytocin following spontaneous or artificial rupture of the membranes will bring forward her time of birth but will not influence the mode of birth or other outcomes.

Multiparous women with confirmed delay in the first stage should be seen by an obstetrician who should make a full assessment, including an abdominal palpation and vaginal examination, before making a decision about the use of oxytocin.

All women with delay in the established first stage of labour should be offered support and effective pain relief.

Women should be informed that oxytocin will increase the frequency and strength of their contractions and that its use will mean their baby should be monitored continuously. Women should be offered an epidural before oxytocin is started.

Where oxytocin is used, the time between increments of the dose should be no more frequent than every 30 minutes. Oxytocin should be increased until there are 4–5 contractions in 10 minutes. (See also Chapter 13 on monitoring babies in labour.)

The woman should be advised to have a vaginal examination 4 hours after commencing oxytocin in established labour. If there is less than 2 cm progress after 4 hours of oxytocin, further obstetric review is required to consider caesarean section. If there is 2 cm or more progress, vaginal examinations should be advised 4 hourly.

Amniotomy alone for suspected delay in the established first stage of labour is not an indication to commence continuous EFM.

Where a diagnosis of delay in the established first stage of labour is made, continuous EFM should be offered.

Continuous EFM should be used when oxytocin is administered for augmentation.

Chapter 15 Complicated labour: second stage

15.1 Delay in the second stage of labour

Duration and definition of delay in the second stage of labour

Nulliparous women:

- Birth would be expected to take place within 3 hours of the start of the active second stage in most women.
- A diagnosis of delay in the active second stage should be made when it has lasted 2 hours and women should be referred to a healthcare professional trained to undertake an operative vaginal birth if birth is not imminent. [repeated from Section 8.2]

Parous women:

- Birth would be expected to take place within 2 hours of the start of the active second stage in most women.
- A diagnosis of delay in the active second stage should be made when it has lasted 1 hour and women should be referred to a healthcare professional trained to undertake an operative vaginal birth if birth is not imminent. [repeated from Section 8.2]

Where there is delay in the second stage of labour, or if the woman is excessively distressed, support and sensitive encouragement and the woman's need for analgesia/anaesthesia are particularly important.

Consideration should be given to the use of oxytocin, with the offer of regional analgesia, for nulliparous women if contractions are inadequate at the onset of the second stage.

In nulliparous women, if after 1 hour of active second stage progress is inadequate, delay is suspected. Following vaginal examination, amniotomy should be offered if the membranes are intact.

Women with confirmed delay in the second stage should be assessed by an obstetrician but oxytocin should not be started.

Following initial obstetric assessment for women with delay in the second stage of labour, ongoing obstetric review should be maintained every 15–30 minutes.

Instrumental birth

Instrumental birth should be considered if there is concern about fetal wellbeing, or for prolonged second stage.

On rare occasions, the woman's need for help in the second stage may be an indication to assist by offering instrumental birth when supportive care has not helped.

The choice of instrument depends on a balance of clinical circumstance and practitioner experience.

Instrumental birth is an operative procedure that should be undertaken with tested effective anaesthesia.

If a woman declines anaesthesia, a pudendal block combined with local anaesthetic to the perineum can be used during instrumental birth.

Where there is concern about fetal compromise, either tested effective anaesthesia or, if time does not allow this, a pudendal block combined with local anaesthetic to the perineum can be used during instrumental birth.

Caesarean section should be advised if vaginal birth is not possible.[*]

Chapter 16 Complicated labour: immediate care of newborn

16.1 Basic neonatal resuscitation

All relevant healthcare professionals caring for women during birth should attend a course in neonatal resuscitation at least annually, which is consistent with the algorithm adopted in the 'Newborn life support course' developed by the Resuscitation Council (UK).[†]

Basic resuscitation of newborn babies should be initiated with air.

Oxygen should be available for babies who do not respond once adequate ventilation has been established.

Emergency referral pathways for both the woman and the baby should be developed and implemented for all birth settings.

Chapter 17 Complicated labour: third stage

17.1 Definition of delay in the third stage of labour

Prolonged third stage:

The third stage of labour is diagnosed as prolonged if not completed within 30 minutes of the birth of the baby with active management and 60 minutes with physiological management. [repeated from Section 9.1]

---

[*]   See 'Caesarean section' (NICE clinical guideline 13).

[†]   Available from www.resus.org.uk/siteindx.htm.

17.2 Treatment of women with a retained placenta

Intravenous access should always be secured in women with a retained placenta.

Intravenous infusion of oxytocin should not be used to assist the delivery of the placenta.

For women with a retained placenta oxytocin injection into the umbilical vein with 20 IU of oxytocin in 20 ml of saline is recommended, followed by proximal clamping of the cord.

If the placenta is still retained 30 minutes after oxytocin injection, or sooner if there is concern about the woman's condition, women should be offered an assessment of the need to remove the placenta. Women should be informed that this assessment can be painful and they should be advised to have analgesia or even anaesthesia for this assessment.

If a woman reports inadequate pain relief during the assessment, the healthcare professional must immediately stop the examination and address this need.

If manual removal of the placenta is required, this must be carried out under effective regional anaesthesia (or general anaesthesia when necessary).

17.3 Risk factors for postpartum haemorrhage

Women with risk factors for postpartum haemorrhage should be advised to give birth in an obstetric unit where more emergency treatment options are available.

- Antenatal risk factors:
  - previous retained placenta or postpartum haemorrhage
  - maternal haemoglobin level below 8.5 g/dl at onset of labour
  - body mass index greater than 35 kg/m²
  - grand multiparity (parity 4 or more)
  - antepartum haemorrhage
  - overdistention of the uterus (for example, multiple pregnancy, polyhydramnios or macrosomia)
  - existing uterine abnormalities
  - low-lying placenta
  - maternal age (35 years or older).
- Risk factors in labour:
  - induction
  - prolonged first, second or third stage of labour
  - oxytocin use
  - precipitate labour
  - operative birth or caesarean section.

If a woman has risk factors for postpartum haemorrhage, these should be highlighted in her notes and a care plan covering the third stage of labour should be made and discussed with the woman.

The unit should have strategies in place in order to respond quickly and appropriately should a postpartum haemorrhage occur.

17.4 Management of postpartum haemorrhage

Immediate treatment for postpartum haemorrhage should include:

- calling for appropriate help
- uterine massage
- intravenous fluids
- uterotonics.

No particular uterotonic drug can be recommended over another for the treatment of postpartum haemorrhage.

Treatment combinations for postpartum haemorrhage might include repeat bolus of oxytocin (intravenous), ergometrine (intramuscular, or cautiously intravenously), intramuscular oxytocin with ergometrine (Syntometrine), misoprostol,* oxytocin infusion (Syntocinon) or carboprost (intramuscular).

Additional therapeutic options for the treatment of postpartum haemorrhage include tranexamic acid (intravenous) and rarely, in the presence of otherwise normal clotting factors, rFactor VIIa, after seeking advice from a haematologist.*

If possible, a member of the healthcare team should be allocated to remain with the woman and her partner during postpartum haemorrhage to ensure communication and offer support throughout the emergency situation.

No particular surgical procedure can be recommended above another for the treatment of postpartum haemorrhage.

2.3   Research recommendations

Chapter 3 Planning place of birth

The best possible studies comparing different places of birth should be undertaken in the UK. Prospective research to assess clinical outcomes, including safety, for all places of birth should be undertaken, as well as qualitative data collection to assess women's experiences of birth.

There is a need to establish a single generic health-related quality of life index value for the multi-attribute perinatal and maternal outcomes of intrapartum care.

Chapter 4 Care throughout labour

Studies should evaluate the impact of a standardised training programme for maternity care support workers in the intrapartum period. Outcomes should include: maternal and neonatal mortality, adverse outcomes, long-term outcomes, women's satisfaction and costs as outcomes.

Studies are needed that investigate the components affecting a woman's satisfaction with her birth experience, including her emotional and psychological wellbeing. A robust method of assessing a woman's satisfaction is also needed.

There should be studies carried out to investigate the effects of caseload midwifery (defined as one midwife providing care and taking responsibility for a group of women from the antenatal, through intrapartum to the postnatal period) on women, babies and healthcare professionals, including cost-effectiveness and long-term outcomes.

Use of either H2-receptor antagonists or antacids in labour should be evaluated for women who have or develop risk factors, who have opioids or who may need a general anaesthetic.

Hygiene rituals around the time of vaginal examination and birth would benefit from further research.

Chapter 5 Coping with pain in labour: non-epidural

A combination of randomised trials and qualitative research should investigate the effect of a package of care, involving the use of non-invasive techniques throughout labour and birth, on women's birth experiences. This should include studies that explore which aspects of the package of care affect both women's experience and maternal and neonatal outcomes.

An RCT to compare the effect of pethidine [IM] and diamorphine [IM], and to explore optimum doses. Outcomes should encompass analgesic effect, and short- and long-term neonatal outcomes (including breastfeeding).

---

* At the time of publication (September 2007), misoprostol and rFactor VIIa did not have UK marketing authorisation for this indication. Informed consent should be obtained and documented; however, if this is not possible, follow the Department of Health guidelines – 'Reference guide to consent for examination or treatment' (2001) (available from www.dh.gov.uk). It may be appropriate to get consent in the antenatal period.

Chapter 6 Pain relief in labour: regional analgesia

There is a need for studies:

- to optimise the management of labour in women with epidurals to reduce the excess instrumental birth rate, including the routine use of oxytocin in the second stage, in nulliparous women with a low-dose epidural
- to explore the optimum duration of the passive and active second stage of labour, for women with an epidural
- to assess the impact of low-dose epidurals with opioids (fentanyl) on neonatal outcomes, including resuscitation and breastfeeding.

Chapter 7 Normal labour: first stage

A prospective cohort study on impact of length of labour on outcomes is needed.

Studies to examine the clinical efficacy of the initial contact observations/examination

Studies looking at the efficacy of the use of the partogram, and the comparison of a partogram with an action line and one without, should be carried out.

Further studies are required to investigate methods of assessing pain relief, attitudes to pain, effects of labour pain, and long-term outcomes.

Chapter 8 Normal labour: second stage

Studies are needed to investigate strategies to reduce the chance of having perineal trauma.

Chapter 9 Normal labour: third stage

Studies should be carried out to investigate the timing of cord clamping and balance of risk/benefit to both mother and baby.

Chapter 10 Normal labour: care of the baby and woman immediately after birth

Research is needed into the optimum analgesia required during perineal repair.

Chapter 11 Prelabour rupture of membrane at term

A randomised controlled trial to evaluate the effect of routine administration of prophylactic antibiotics on neonatal infection, in women with term prelabour rupture of membranes, over 24 hours.

The investigation and management of babies born with risk factors for infection requires further evaluation.

Chapter 12 Meconium-stained liquor

There is a need for development of a standardised scoring system for degree of meconium staining and association with neonatal outcomes.

Chapter 13 Complicated labour: monitoring babies in labour

A further randomised controlled trial of ST segment analysis should be undertaken.

Further study investigating computerised expert systems should be undertaken.

Chapter 14 Complicated labour: first stage

The start dose of oxytocin for augmentation, and the increments, should be the subject of further research.

Studies are needed that investigate the effectiveness of any strategies to increase spontaneous vaginal birth where diagnosis is made of delay in the first stage of labour.

Chapter 17 Complicated labour: third stage

Further randomised controlled trials investigating the effectiveness of the use of nitro-glycerine in the treatment of retained placenta should be conducted.

Further research should identify the best drug combinations, route and dose for the treatment of postpartum haemorrhage.

2.4 Care pathway

The following care pathway has been developed to outline how the recommendations in this guideline should be applied in clinical practice. The care pathway includes recommendations for both normal labour and complicated labour, and when to exit from and return to the normal care pathway. This care pathway is available in a separate document, the Intrapartum Care Quick Reference Guide, available from NICE and on the NICE website (www.nice.org.uk/ CG055quickrefguide).

Intrapartum care

Normal labour and birth

Key:

OB seek obstetrician advice (transfer to obstetric unit if appropriate)

HT healthcare professional trained in operative vaginal birth

Normal labour and birth

Care throughout labour
Ask the woman about her wants and expectations for labour

Don't intervene if labour is progressing normally

Tell the women that first labour lasts on average 8 hours and second labour lasts on average 5 hours

Ensure supportive one-to-one care

Do not leave the woman on her own

Encourage involvement of birth partner(s)

Encourage the woman to mobilise and adopt comfortable positions

Take routine hygiene measures

Do not give H_2-receptor antagonists or antacids routinely to low-risk women

For coping with pain, see pages 10–11

Vaginal exam
Tap water may be used for cleansing prior to exam

Ensure exam is really necessary

Ensure consent, privacy, dignity and comfort

Explain reason for the exam and what's involved

Explain findings sensitively

Initial assessment
Listen to the woman. Ask about vaginal loss and contractions

Review clinical records

Check temperature, pulse, BP, urinalysis

Observe contractions, fetal heart rate (FHR)

Palpate abdomen

Offer vaginal exam

For coping with pain, see pages 10–11

Women not in established labour
If initial assessment normal, offer individualised support and encourage these women to remain at/return home

For prelabour rupture, see page 14

First stage of labour
Use a partogram once labour is established

If a partogram action line is used, this should be a 4-hour action line

Every 15 min after a contraction check FHR

Every 30 min: document frequency of contractions

Every hour: check pulse

Every 4 hours: check BP, temperature and offer vaginal exam

Regularly: check frequency of bladder emptying

Consider the woman's emotional and psychological needs

For coping with pain, see pages 10–11

Concerns **OB**
Indications for electronic fetal monitoring (EFM) in low-risk women, e.g. significant meconium-stained liquor, abnormal FHR, maternal pyrexia, fresh bleeding; see pages 17 –18

↑ diastolic BP (over 90 mmHg) or ↑ systolic BP (over 140 mmHg) twice, 30 min apart

Uncertainty about the presence of a fetal heartbeat

Suspected delay
Nulliparous: < 2 cm dilatation in 4 hours

Parous: < 2 cm dilatation in 4 hours or slowing in progress

See page 12

see top of page 8

Intrapartum care | Normal labour and birth

Second stage of labour

Every 5 min after a contraction: check FHR

Every 30 min: document frequency of contractions

Every hour: check BP, pulse, offer vaginal exam

Every 4 hours: check temperature

Regularly: check frequency of bladder emptying

Assess progress, including fetal position and station

If woman has full dilatation but no urge to push, assess after 1 hour

Discourage the woman from lying supine/semi-supine

Consider the woman's position, hydration and pain-relief needs. Provide support and encouragement

For coping with pain, see pages 10–11

Concerns OB

Indications for EFM in low-risk women, e.g. meconium-stained liquor, abnormal FHR, maternal pyrexia, fresh bleeding, oxytocin for augmentation, see pages 17–18

Nulliparous: consider oxytocin, with offer of regional analgesia, if contractions inadequate at onset of second stage

Delay

Nulliparous: active second stage 2 hours

Parous: active second stage 1 hour

See page 13

Episiotomy OB / HT

Carry out episiotomy only when there is:

- clinical need such as instrumental birth
- suspected fetal compromise

Do not offer routinely following previous third- or fourth-degree trauma

Use mediolateral technique (between 45° and 60° to right side, originating at vaginal fourchette)

Use tested effective analgesia

Birth

see top of page 9

Key:

OB seek obstetrician advice (transfer to obstetric unit if appropriate)

HT healthcare professional trained in operative vaginal birth

| **Intrapartum care** | Normal labour and birth |

Third stage of labour
Observe physical health

Check vaginal loss

Active management: oxytocin (10 IU IM), early cord clamping/cutting and controlled cord traction; advise that this reduces risk of haemorrhage and shortens third stage

Physiological management: if requested by low-risk woman. No oxytocin/no early cord clamping; delivery by maternal effort. Do not pull cord or palpate uterus

Concerns OB
Retained placenta

Active management: > 30 min

Physiological management: > 1 hour

See page 16

Care after birth
Woman: observe general physical condition, colour, respiration, how she feels; check temperature, pulse, BP, uterine contractions, lochia, bladder voiding. Examine cord, placenta and membranes. Assess maternal emotional/psychological condition

Baby: record Apgar score at 1 and 5 min; keep warm

Encourage skin-to-skin contact between woman and baby as soon as possible

Don't separate the woman and baby in the first hour

Initiate breastfeeding within the first hour

After 1 hour, record baby's head circumference, body temperature and weight

Concerns OB
Suspected postpartum haemorrhage: take emergency action, see page 20

Basic resuscitation of newborn babies should be started with air, see page 19

Perineal care
Carry out systematic assessment of any trauma, including a rectal examination, sensitively. Explain assessment to the woman and confirm analgesia is effective. Document extent and findings

Lithotomy, if required, only to be used for assessment and repair

First-degree trauma: suture skin unless well opposed

Second-degree trauma: suture vaginal wall and muscle for all second-degree tears. Suture skin unless well opposed

Use continuous non-locked technique for suturing vaginal wall and muscle

Use continuous subcuticular technique for suturing skin

Offer rectal NSAIDs following perineal repair

For coping with pain, see pages 10–11

Concerns OB
Refer if uncertain of nature/extent of trauma

Third- or fourth-degree trauma

Intrapartum care

Coping with pain

Supporting women

- Consider your attitude to coping with pain in labour and ensure your care supports the woman's choice.

- Offer support and encouragement.

- Encourage her to ask for analgesia at any point during labour.

Pain-relieving strategies

- Encourage labouring in water to reduce pain.

- Support women's use of breathing/relaxation techniques, massage, music.

- Acupuncture, acupressure and hypnosis should not be provided, but do not prevent women if they wish to use these.

- Do not offer TENS to women in established labour.

Inhalation analgesia and opioids

- Ensure access to Entonox and opioids such as pethidine or diamorphine. Explain that:
  - they provide limited pain relief
  - Entonox may make the woman feel nauseous and light-headed
  - opioids may cause drowsiness, nausea and vomiting in the woman
  - opioids may cause short-term respiratory depression and drowsiness for several days in the baby
  - opioids may interfere with breastfeeding.

- Provide antiemetic if opioids used.

- No birthing pool or bath within 2 hours of opioids or if drowsy.

Before choosing epidural

- Inform women that epidural:
  - is only available in obstetric units
  - provides more effective pain relief than opioids
  - is associated with a longer second stage of labour and an increased chance of vaginal instrumental birth
  - is not associated with long-term backache
  - is not associated with a longer first stage of labour or an increased chance of caesarean birth
  - is accompanied by a more intensive level of monitoring and IV access
  - large amounts of epidural opioid may cause short-term respiratory problems in the baby and make the baby drowsy.
  See page 11.

Intrapartum care

Coping with pain

Regional analgesia

(Regional analgesia is only available in obstetric units, administered by an anaesthetist.)

```
┌─────────────────────────────────────────────────┐
│   Provide for all women who request regional     │
│   analgesia (including those in severe pain in    │
│   latent first stage) after discussion, see      │
│   page 10                                         │
└─────────────────────────────────────────────────┘
                        │
                        ▼
┌─────────────────────────────────────────────────┐
│              Secure IV access                    │
│   Preloading/maintenance fluid infusion not      │
│              needed routinely                    │
└─────────────────────────────────────────────────┘
```

┌──┐   ┌──┐
│ Establishment/after each bolus: measure BP │   │ Epidural or combined spinal–epidural   │
│ every 5 min for 15 min; provide continuous │   │ analgesia is recommended   │
│ EFM for 30 min (see pages 17–18)   │   │   │
│   │   │ Use low-concentration anaesthetic and   │
│ After 30 min: call anaesthetist if the woman │ ───►   │ opioid for establishing and maintaining   │
│ is still in pain   │   │ epidural   │
│   │   │   │
│ Every hour: check level of sensory block   │   │ Do not use high concentrations of local   │
│   │   │ anaesthetics routinely   │
│ No routine use of oxytocin in the second   │   │   │
│ stage   │   │ Use combined spinal–epidural analgesia   │
│   │   │ (bupivacaine and fentanyl) for rapid relief│
│ Encourage and help the woman to adopt   │   │   │
│ any comfortable upright position   │   │ Continue epidural until after completion of│
└──┘   │ the third stage and any perineal repair   │
              │   └──┘
              ▼
┌──┐
│ Fully dilated: delay pushing for at least │
│ 1 hour, unless baby's head is visible or   │
│ woman has urge to push   │
│   │
│ Birth should take place within 4 hours   │
└──┘

Complications

Delay in the first stage

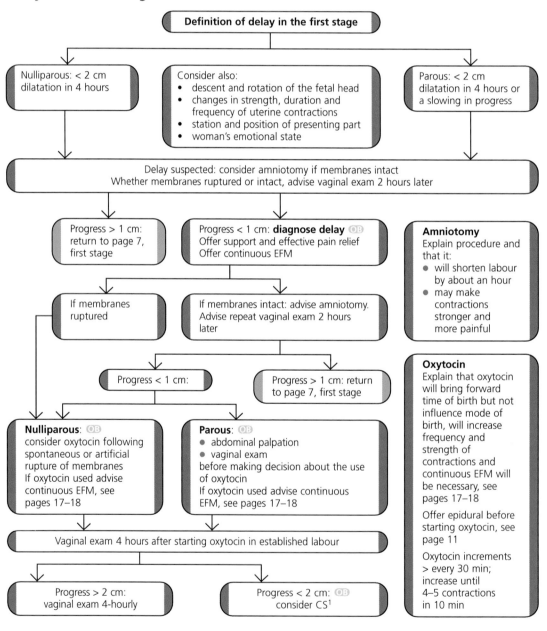

¹ See 'Caesarean section' (NICE clinical guideline 13).

| Intrapartum care | Complications |

Delay in the second stage

Nulliparous: delay suspected if inadequate progress after 1 hour of active second stage

↓

Offer vaginal exam; advise amniotomy if membranes intact

Offer support and encouragement and consider analgesia/anaesthesia

Birth within 1 hour: return to page 9, third stage

No birth within next hour (total active second stage = 2 hours) **HT**

Parous: active second stage = 1 hour **HT**

↓

Diagnosis of delay in the second stage

↓

Assessment and ongoing review every 15–30 min by obstetrician **OB**
Do not start oxytocin

Good progress: return to page 8, second stage

Consider instrumental birth if concern about fetal well-being or for prolonged second stage

Advise CS if vaginal birth not possible

Birth expected to take place within 3 hours of start of active second stage for nulliparous women and within 2 hours for parous women

↓

Instrumental birth **HT**
Choice of instrument depends on balance of clinical circumstance and practitioner experience

Use tested effective anaesthesia

If declined or if concern about fetal compromise, use pudendal block with local anaesthetic to perineum

Birth: return to page 9, third stage

Key:

OB seek obstetrician advice (transfer to obstetric unit if appropriate)

HT healthcare professional trained in operative vaginal birth

Prelabour rupture of the membranes (PROM) at term

```
                                    ┌──────────────────────┐        ┌──────────────────────┐
                                    │   Suspected PROM     │        │  PROM certain history │
                                    └──────────┬───────────┘        └───────────┬───────────┘
┌─────────────────┐                            ↓                                ↓
│ Normal          │                ┌──────────────────────┐        ┌──────────────────────┐
│ progress: return│                │  Offer speculum exam │        │   No speculum exam    │
│ to page 7, first│  ←─────────────│  Avoid digital vaginal│       └───────────┬───────────┘
│ stage           │                │  exam in absence of  │                    │
│ If membranes    │                │  contractions        │                    │
│ intact advise   │                └──────────┬───────────┘                    │
│ woman to        │                           ↓                                │
│ return home     │                                                            │
└─────────────────┘                                                            │
```

PROM – care of the woman
Advise woman that:
- risk of serious neonatal infection is 1% rather than 0.5%
- 60% will go into labour within 24 hours
- induction of labour is appropriate after 24 hours
No antibiotics for woman or baby without signs of infection
If evidence of infection, prescribe full course of broad-spectrum antibiotics

Until induction or if the woman chooses expectant management beyond 24 hours
Do not offer lower vaginal swabs and maternal C-reactive protein

Advise the woman to record her temperature every 4 hours during waking hours and to report immediately any change in the colour or smell of her vaginal loss

Inform her that bathing or showering are not associated with an increase in infection, but that having sexual intercourse may be

Assess fetal movement and heart rate at initial contact and then every 24 hours following membrane rupture while the woman is not in labour

Advise the woman to report immediately any decrease in fetal movements

PROM > 24 hours
Induction of labour[2]

Transfer/access to neonatal care

Stay in hospital at least 12 hours after birth so the baby can be observed

PROM – care of the baby
If no signs of infection do not give antibiotics to the baby

For baby with possible sepsis or born to a woman with evidence of chorioamnionitis: immediately refer to neonatal care

Observe asymptomatic term babies (PROM > 24 hours) for the first 12 hours at 1 hour, 2 hours then 2-hourly for 10 hours:

- general wellbeing
- chest movements and nasal flare
- skin colour (test capillary refill)
- feeding
- muscle tone
- temperature
- heart rate and respiration

No blood, cerebrospinal fluid and/or surface culture tests for asymptomatic baby

Woman to inform immediately of any concerns about the baby in first 5 days

---

[2] Care of women who have their labour induced is covered by 'Induction of labour' (NICE inherited clinical guideline D).

Intrapartum care	Complications

Meconium-stained liquor

```
┌────────────────────────────────────┐        ┌──────────────────────────────────────┐
│  Light meconium-stained liquor      │        │  Significant meconium-stained liquor │
└────────────────────────────────────┘        │  Dark green or black amniotic fluid  │
                  │                             │  that is thick or tenacious, or any  │
                  ▼                             │  meconium-stained fluid containing   │
                                                │  lumps of meconium  OB               │
                                                └──────────────────────────────────────┘
                                                                 │
                                                                 ▼
```

┌────────────────────────────────────┐   ┌──────────────────────────────────────┐
│ Consider continuous EFM based on   │   │ Advise continuous EFM, see pages 17–18│
│ risk assessment: stage of labour,   │   └──────────────────────────────────────┘
│ volume of liquor, parity, FHR,   │   │
│ transfer pathway; see pages 17–18   │   ▼
└────────────────────────────────────┘

┌────────────────────────────────────┐   ┌──────────────────────────────────────┐
│ **Baby in good condition**   │   │ FBS available in labour and advanced │
│ 1 and 2 hours, observe: │   │ neonatal life support available for │
│ ● general wellbeing   │   │ birth   │
│ ● chest movements and nasal flare   │   │   │
│ ● skin colour (test capillary refill)│   │ Do not suction nasopharynx and   │
│ ● feeding   │   │ oropharynx before birth of the   │
│ ● muscle tone   │   │ shoulders and trunk   │
│ ● temperature   │   │   │
│ ● heart rate and respiration   │   │ Suction upper airways only if   │
│   │   │ thick/tenacious meconium in oropharynx│
│ Review by a neonatologist if baby's │   └──────────────────────────────────────┘
│ condition causes concern at any time│   │   │
└────────────────────────────────────┘   ▼   ▼
```

┌─────────────────────────┐   ┌──────────────────────────┐
│ **Baby has depressed**  │   │ **Baby in good condition**│
│ **vital signs**         │   │ 1 hour, 2 hours then      │
│ Laryngoscopy and        │   │ 2-hourly until 12 hours   │
│ suction under direct    │   │ old, observe:             │
│ vision by a healthcare  │   │ ● general wellbeing       │
│ professional trained in │   │ ● chest movements and     │
│ advanced neonatal life  │   │   nasal flare             │
│ support                 │   │ ● skin colour (test       │
└─────────────────────────┘   │   capillary refill)       │
                              │ ● feeding                 │
                              │ ● muscle tone             │
                              │ ● temperature             │
                              │ ● heart rate and          │
                              │   respiration             │
                              └──────────────────────────┘

**Key:**

OB   seek obstetrician advice (transfer to obstetric unit if appropriate)

HT   healthcare professional trained in operative vaginal birth
```

Intrapartum care   Complications

Retained placenta ⓄⒷ

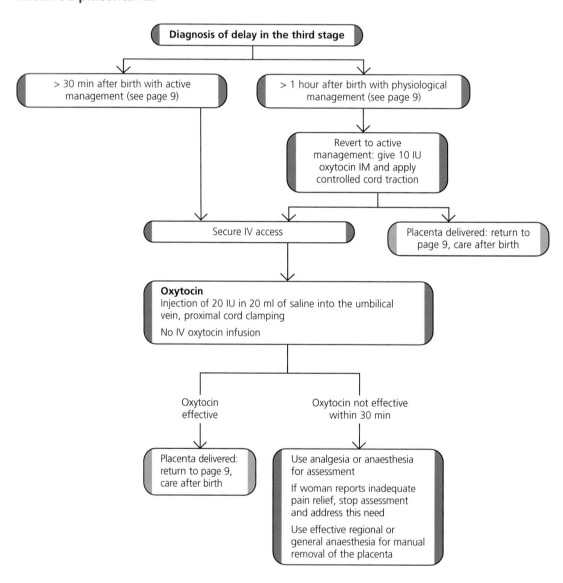

Key:

ⓄⒷ   seek obstetrician advice (transfer to
        obstetric unit if appropriate)

ⒽⓉ   healthcare professional trained in
        operative vaginal birth

| Intrapartum care | Complications |

Continuous EFM

Key:

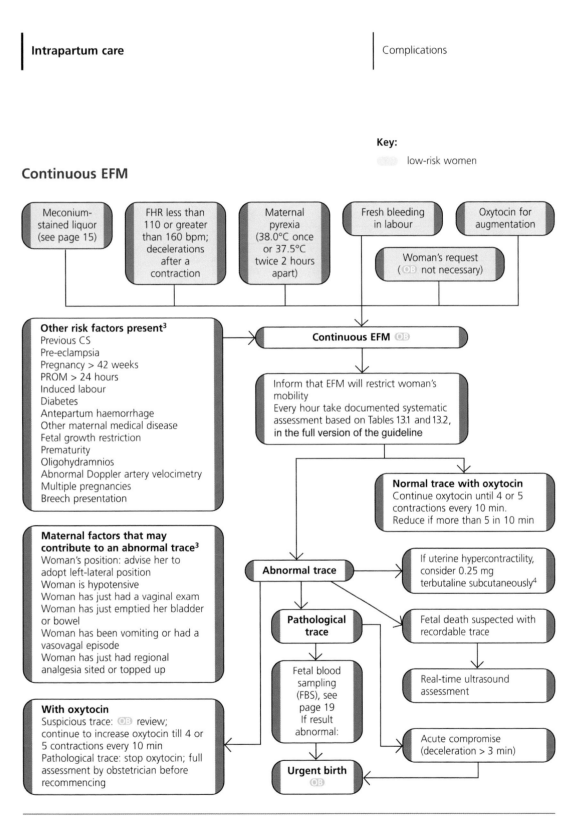

low-risk women

Meconium-stained liquor (see page 15)

FHR less than 110 or greater than 160 bpm; decelerations after a contraction

Maternal pyrexia (38.0°C once or 37.5°C twice 2 hours apart)

Fresh bleeding in labour

Oxytocin for augmentation

Woman's request (OB not necessary)

Other risk factors present[3]
Previous CS
Pre-eclampsia
Pregnancy > 42 weeks
PROM > 24 hours
Induced labour
Diabetes
Antepartum haemorrhage
Other maternal medical disease
Fetal growth restriction
Prematurity
Oligohydramnios
Abnormal Doppler artery velocimetry
Multiple pregnancies
Breech presentation

Continuous EFM OB

Inform that EFM will restrict woman's mobility
Every hour take documented systematic assessment based on Tables 13.1 and 13.2, in the full version of the guideline

Normal trace with oxytocin
Continue oxytocin until 4 or 5 contractions every 10 min.
Reduce if more than 5 in 10 min

Maternal factors that may contribute to an abnormal trace[3]
Woman's position: advise her to adopt left-lateral position
Woman is hypotensive
Woman has just had a vaginal exam
Woman has just emptied her bladder or bowel
Woman has been vomiting or had a vasovagal episode
Woman has just had regional analgesia sited or topped up

Abnormal trace

If uterine hypercontractility, consider 0.25 mg terbutaline subcutaneously[4]

Pathological trace

Fetal death suspected with recordable trace

Fetal blood sampling (FBS), see page 19
If result abnormal:

Real-time ultrasound assessment

With oxytocin
Suspicious trace: OB review; continue to increase oxytocin till 4 or 5 contractions every 10 min
Pathological trace: stop oxytocin; full assessment by obstetrician before recommencing

Acute compromise (deceleration > 3 min)

Urgent birth OB

---

[3] These factors (risk factors for women outside the scope of this guideline and maternal factors that may contribute to an abnormal trace) are from 'Electronic fetal monitoring' (NICE inherited guideline C) which this guideline updates and replaces.
[4] At the time of publication (September 2007), terbutaline did not have UK marketing authorisation for this indication. Informed consent should be obtained and documented.

Fetal blood sampling (FBS)

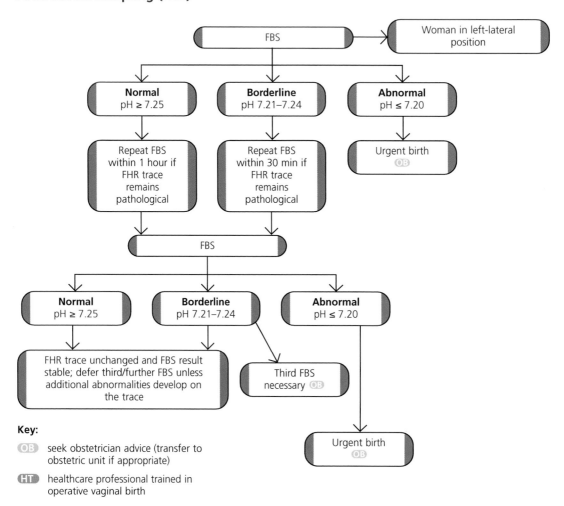

Key:

OB seek obstetrician advice (transfer to obstetric unit if appropriate)

HT healthcare professional trained in operative vaginal birth

Neonatal resuscitation

- Start basic resuscitation of newborn babies with air.

- Use oxygen for babies who do not respond.

- Attend a neonatal resuscitation course at least once a year[5].

---

[5] Consistent with the algorithm adopted in the 'Newborn life support course' developed by the Resuscitation Council (UK), available from www.resus.org.uk/siteindx.htm

Intrapartum care	Complications

Postpartum haemorrhage

Risk factors for postpartum haemorrhage

Antenatal risk factors for which women should be advised to give birth in an obstetric unit:
- previous retained placenta or postpartum haemorrhage
- maternal haemoglobin level below 8.5 g/dl at onset of labour
- increased body mass index
- 4 or more previous babies
- antepartum haemorrhage
- overdistention or abnormalities of the uterus
- low-lying placenta
- woman 35 years or older

Risk factors in labour:
- induction
- prolonged first, second or third stage of labour
- oxytocin use
- precipitate labour
- operative birth or CS

→

Have strategies in place to respond quickly and appropriately to a postpartum haemorrhage
Highlight risk factors in the notes
Plan and discuss care

Managing postpartum haemorrhage

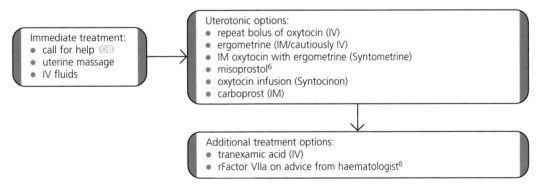

Immediate treatment:
- call for help (OB)
- uterine massage
- IV fluids

→

Uterotonic options:
- repeat bolus of oxytocin (IV)
- ergometrine (IM/cautiously IV)
- IM oxytocin with ergometrine (Syntometrine)
- misoprostol[6]
- oxytocin infusion (Syntocinon)
- carboprost (IM)

↓

Additional treatment options:
- tranexamic acid (IV)
- rFactor VIIa on advice from haematologist[6]

Key:

(OB) seek obstetrician advice (transfer to obstetric unit if appropriate)

(HT) healthcare professional trained in operative vaginal birth

---

[6] At the time of publication (September 2007), misoprostol and rFactor VIIa did not have UK marketing authorisation for this indication. Informed consent should be obtained and documented; however, if this is not possible, follow the Department of Health guidelines 'Reference guide to consent for examination or treatment' (2001) (available from www.dh.gov.uk). It may be appropriate to get consent in the antenatal period.

3 Planning place of birth

3.1 Introduction

Prior to 1945 the majority of births took place at home. The Cranbrook Report of 1959 stated that hospital maternity services were to provide for 70% of births, and hospitalisation of birth accelerated in the 1960s such that by 1970 nearly 90% of births occurred within hospitals.[19,20] The Peel report in 1970 stated that facilities should be provided for all women to give birth in hospital, based largely on findings from the Reports of the Confidential Enquiry into Maternal Deaths and this led rapidly to over 95% of women giving birth in a hospital setting.[21] This provision of care was challenged and a number of initiatives culminated in the publication of the document Changing Childbirth in 1993 which recommended that women should have more choice in their place of birth, and that more choices should be available.[22] In 2004 the National Service Framework (NSF) for Children, Young People and Maternity Services, and Maternity Matters in 2007,[625] actively promoted midwife-led care for women, following appropriate assessment, and recommended that healthcare providers should develop midwife and home birth services to meet the needs of local populations.[23,24] None of these initiatives were supported by strong evidence regarding safety of place of birth.

The configuration and choice of services are currently evolving but more than 90% of births still take place in designated consultant wards (obstetric units) or combined consultant/GP wards.[25] This figure is taken from the Maternity Hospital Episode Statistics but the categories used do not reflect current changes in practice. Also local variation in the availability of different birth settings will affect women's options for choosing their preferred place of birth.

3.2 Benefits and risks of planning each place of birth

Clinical question
What are the outcomes (benefits and harms) and costs related to each birth setting?

Terminology used in the reviews
The terms used to define place of birth in the literature are not consistent and are a source of confusion. Planned place of birth incorporates both *booked* place of birth and *intended* place of birth at the onset of labour. The *booked* place of birth is the place of birth chosen at the first appointment or during pregnancy.

The *actual* place of birth is where the baby is born.

3.2.1 Planned home versus hospital birth

Introduction
The difficulty of conducting a randomised controlled trial (RCT) evaluating effectiveness and safety of planning home birth compared with hospital birth is evident from the lack of papers in the literature. Thus only observational studies were considered in the systematic review below. Predefined criteria were used to assess the validity of the identified studies, some of which were significantly flawed and thus excluded from the systematic review. It should be noted that any systematic review containing only observational data has inherent bias and confounding factors, and the results should be interpreted with great caution.

Previous guideline
Planned home birth was reviewed in the NICE clinical guideline *Caesarean Section*.[6] Two systematic reviews; one cohort study and one case–control study were included. The guideline

recommended that 'during their discussions about options for birth, healthy pregnant women with anticipated uncomplicated pregnancies should be informed that delivering at home reduced the likelihood of CS.'.

Searching the literature
Two systematic reviews[27,28] and 16 studies[26,29-45] were identified from the search. Each of these publications was graded according to a validity (quality) index (see Appendix C) and five studies[29,30,32,35,36,45] were selected for inclusion in this review. Excluded papers and the reasons for their exclusion are presented in Appendix C. An explanation of the methodological reasons for excluding three large studies from the current review is given below.

One of the systematic reviews by Olsen[27] was a Cochrane review which included the only small randomised controlled trial.[26] The trial, rather than the Olsen Cochrane review, was included.

Another systematic review[28] by the same author (Olsen) included six observational studies. This was also excluded because it included studies with significant methodological weakness in the meta-analysis. In particular, although the original study included in the Olsen review did attempt to put the data (raw perinatal mortality data) into a regression analysis, the data were directly included in the meta-analysis in the Olsen review. This makes the analysis invalid.

There was one large population-based UK study[31] conducted in 1994 ($n = 8010$) that compared a planned home birth population with a planned hospital birth population. Although the study matched some of the demographic background of these women, there were over 1000 unmatched women who planned home birth and they were included in the analysis. The inclusion of an excess of women planning home birth who were not matched to women planning hospital birth makes the matching process invalid. Moreover, the study showed significant differences in demographic and obstetric risks between the planned home and hospital groups, and the analysis did not employ any means to control confounding and, following assessment against the pre-defined criteria, this study was, therefore also excluded from this review.

Description of included studies
There are six included studies and that these were published in seven papers. Details of the included papers were given in Appendix C and in the evidence tables.

All were observational studies,[29,30,32,35,36,45] except one pilot randomised controlled trial.[26] Two of the studies were conducted in the UK,[26,45] two in Australia,[30,35,36] one in Switzerland[32] and one in Canada.[29] Three of the studies reported women's outcomes[26,29,32] and two babies' outcomes[30,45] with two reporting both.[35,36]

The Canadian study[29] and one of the Australian studies[30] compared intended places of birth at the onset of labour, while all the others compared booked places of birth.[26,32,35,36,45]

In addition, for the purpose of obtaining transfer rates between planned and actual place of birth, any study conducted in the UK since 1980 reporting transfer rates during labour was selected, so that a point estimate could be obtained. Two UK studies conducted since 1980[31,43] were used to obtain the rates of transfer from the home birth setting to hospital during labour.

Review findings

Mode of birth and other obstetric interventions
Four included studies reported women's outcomes and these are summarised in Table 3.1.

A pilot randomised controlled trial (Dowswell) conducted in the UK in 1994 compared 11 women (planned home birth = 5; planned hospital birth = 6).[26] The study was a pilot and underpowered to show any differences in relevant outcomes. [EL = 1+]

As this study does not give sufficient information, we considered other studies.

A cross-sectional study (Janssen) conducted in Canada between January 1998 and December 1999 compared 862 women who intended a home birth at the onset of labour with a matched control group of 571 women with a planned midwife-led unit birth and 743 women with a planned obstetric unit birth.[29] [EL = 3] Women were matched by age, parity and lone parent status. After controlling for various confounding factors, the comparison of planned home birth

Table 3.1 Summary of women's outcomes on planned home versus hospital birth

Outcome	Dowswell[26]	Janssen[29]	Ackermann-Liebrich[32]	Woodcock[35,36]
Comparisons	Booked place of birth	Intended place of birth at the onset of labour	Booked place of birth	Booked place of birth
Mode of birth and other obstetric interventions				
Mode of birth	Neither instrumental birth (forceps or ventouse) nor CS occurred in the study	CS: adjusted OR 0.31 [95% CI 0.22 to 0.43]	CS: OR 0.45 [95% CI 0.19 to 1.00] Instrumental vaginal birth: OR 0.41 [95% CI 0.14 to 1.04]	Instrumental vaginal birth: adjusted OR 0.14 [95% CI 0.10 to 0.18] Emergency CS: adjusted OR 0.25 [95% CI 0.17 to 0.38] Elective CS: adjusted OR 0.06 [95% CI 0.03 to 0.14]
Analgesia	Use of pethidine: OR 0.16; 95% CI 0.00 to 8.19	Epidural analgesia: adjusted OR 0.20 [95% CI 0.14 to 0.27]	Analgesics: OR 0.16 [95% CI 0.07 to 0.33]	Not reported
Oxytocin	Not reported	Induction of labour: adjusted OR 0.16 [95% CI 0.11 to 0.24] Augmentation of labour: adjusted OR 0.33 [95% CI 0.23 to 0.47]	Induction of labour: OR 0.18 [95% CI 0.06 to 0.43] Use of oxytocin/ demoxytocin during expulsion period: OR 0.34 [95% CI 0.18 to 0.61]	Induction of labour: adjusted OR 0.05 [95% CI 0.03 to 0.08]
Episiotomy	Not reported	Adjusted OR 0.22 [95% CI 0.13 to 0.33]	OR 0.09 [95% CI 0.04 to 0.18]	Not reported
Maternal mortality and other women's complications				
Maternal mortality	Not reported	Not reported	Not reported	Not reported
Maternal infection	Not reported	Adjusted OR 0.23 [95% CI 0.09 to 0.57]	Not reported	Not reported
Perineal tears	Perineal sutures: OR 0.69; 95% CI 0.07 to 6.73	Third- or fourth-degree perineal tear: adjusted OR 0.86 [95% CI 0.45 to 1.63]	Perineal lesion: OR 3.25 [95% CI 1.83 to 6.10] Perineal and vaginal lesion: OR 0.25 [95% CI 0.05 to 2.53] Intact perineum: OR 6.22 [95% CI 3.05 to 14.31]	Third-degree perineal tears: adjusted OR 0.54 [95% CI 0.12 to 2.49]
PPH	Not reported	Adjusted OR 0.91 [95% CI 0.57 to 1.44]	Not reported	Adjusted OR 3.83 [95% CI 2.59 to 5.66]
Duration of labour	Not reported	Not reported	Not reported	Long labour (> 18 hours): adjusted OR 5.57 [95% CI 3.80 to 8.18]
Fetal distress	Not reported	Not reported	Not reported	Adjusted OR 0.38 [95% CI 0.28 to 0.52]
Retained placenta	Not reported	Not reported	Not reported	Adjusted OR 1.96 [95% CI 1.16 to 3.32]
Shoulder dystocia	Not reported	Not reported	Not reported	Adjusted OR 0.45 [95% CI 0.18 to 1.10]

CS = caesarean section; PPH = postpartum haemorrhage.

with planned hospital birth showed evidence that women who planned home birth had less use of epidural analgesia, less induced labour, less augmented labour, less use of episiotomy, and a lower rate of CS.

A cohort study (Ackermann-Liebrich) conducted in Switzerland between 1989 and 1992 comprised 489 women with a booked home birth and 385 women with a booked hospital birth.[32] [EL = 2+] The sample included 214 pairs matched by age, parity, gynaecological/obstetric history, medical history, presence/absence of a partner, social class and nationality. There were no significant differences between matched pairs for birth complications or duration of labour. Women in the booked home birth group had fewer inductions of labour, a lower rate of CS, less analgesic, less use of oxytocin/demoxytocin, fewer instrumental vaginal births, and fewer episiotomies.

A cross-sectional study (Woodcock) conducted in Western Australia between 1981 and 1987 compared 976 women with a booked home birth (all booked home births for that period) with 2928 matched controls (1 : 3), matching by year of birth, parity, previous stillbirth, previous death of liveborn child, maternal age, maternal height, marital status and postcode.[35,36] [EL = 3] Women who booked a home birth were had fewer instrumental births and CS.

Maternal mortality and women's complications
No comparative studies with high or reasonable quality that reported maternal mortality was identified. Other women's complications were reported in the above one small pilot trial and three observational studies.

The pilot randomised trial reported incidence of perineal tears, although the study is underpowered to show any significant difference. [EL = 1+]

The Janssen study showed a lower incidence of women's infection, although there was no evidence of difference in the rate of third- or fourth-degree perineal tear or incidence of postpartum haemorrhage (PPH). [EL = 3]

The Ackermann-Liebrich study showed fewer perineal tears with more women having an intact perineum. [EL = 2+]

In the Woodcock study, women who booked a home birth were more likely to have a long labour (> 18 hours), less fetal distress, with a higher incidence of PPH and of retained placenta. In addition, there was a trend towards reduced incidence of shoulder dystocia. [EL = 2+]

Women's satisfaction and psychological/mental health
No comparative study with high or reasonable quality that reported women's satisfaction and/or other psychological/mental outcomes.

Perinatal mortality that is directly related to intrapartum events and other neonatal complications
Two included studies reported intrapartum-related perinatal mortality (IPPM) and one study reported intrapartum perinatal mortality. Therefore the review did not consider perinatal mortality or other neonatal complications. (See Appendix C for details.) Intrapartum-related perinatal mortality is defined as deaths from intrapartum 'asphyxia', 'anoxia' or 'trauma', derived from the extended Wigglesworth classification 3.[600] This includes stillbirths and death in the first week. The denominator was all births (live births and stillbirths). Intrapartum perinatal mortality is defined as perinatal mortality excluding deaths of low birthweight infants and babies with congenital malformations. The results of the included studies are summarised below and in Table 3.2.

A UK cross-sectional population-based study (NRPMSCG) compared perinatal mortality of booked home births with overall rate in the Northern Region.[45] The intrapartum-related perinatal mortality (IPPM) rate for women who booked home birth in the Northern Region in 1983 was compared with that for all of those who had a birth in the region. [EL = 3] This reported an IPPM rate, of 1.86 per 1000 births (5/2689) for women who booked at home compared with an overall rate of 1.23 per 1000 (642/520 280). The RR was 1.51 [95% CI 0.63 to 3.63]).

A cross-sectional population-based study (Bastian) ($n = 1\,502\,756$) conducted in Australia between 1985 and 1990 [EL = 3] comprised population-based data and included a comparison of intended home birth at the onset of labour with data for the whole country, including details

Table 3.2 Intrapartum perinatal mortality and intrapartum-related perinatal mortality (IPPM) rates for planned home birth compared with planned hospital birth or overall birth

Authors	Year	Country	Notes on study design	Planned home birth	Planned hospital birth or overall births	Summary statistics
NCC-WCH (Appendix D)	1999–2003	UK	<u>Booked place of birth</u> A population-based study in the UK. Internal validity was improved by using IPPM rates to control background risk, but the number of planned home birth was drawn from transfer rates in previous studies. Sensitivity analyses were conducted to examine the uncertainty in the transfer rates.	IPPM rate 1.37/1000; upper 1.58, lower 0.82 *Subgroups:* Completed home birth: IPPM rate 0.50/1000; upper 0.45, lower 0.56 Transferred group: IPPM rate 6.59/1000; upper 9.12, lower 1.31	IPPM rate Overall: 0.68/1000	IPPM rate RR 2.01; upper 2.32, lower 1.21
	1994–1998	UK		IPPM rate 1.18/1000; upper 1.36, lower 0.71 *Subgroups:* Completed home birth: IPPM rate 0.46/1000; upper 0.52, lower 0.41 Transferred group: IPPM rate 5.52/1000; upper 8.67, lower 1.92	IPPM rate Overall: 0.90/1000	IPPM rate RR 1.31; upper 1.51, lower 0.79
NRPMSCG[45]	1981–1994	UK	<u>Booked place of birth</u> A population-based study in the Northern Region on a planned home birth population. Internal validity was improved by using IPPM rates to control background risk.	IPPM rate 1.86/1000 (5/2689)	IPPM rate Overall: 1.23/1000 (642/520 280)	IPPM rate RR 1.51 [95% CI 0.63 to 3.63]
Bastian[30]	1985–1990	Australia	<u>Intended place of birth at the onset of labour</u> A population-based study conducted in Australia on an intended home birth population. Internal validity was improved by using IPPM rates to control background risk. However the intended home birth group included a small number of high-risk women, which may have contributed the excess. It could also be assumed that there was higher proportion of high-risk women in overall birth group.	Intrapartum perinatal mortality rate 2.7/1000 [95% CI 1.5 to 3.9/1000]	Intrapartum perinatal mortality rate Overall: 0.9/1000 [95% CI 0.85 to 0.95/1000]	Intrapartum perinatal mortality rate RR 3.02 [95% CI 1.92 to 4.74]

of perinatal deaths for home births.[30] Excluding perinatal mortality associated with congenital malformation and/or extreme immaturity, the intrapartum perinatal mortality rate was higher for babies born at home (home birth: 2.7 per 1000 live births [95% CI 1.5 to 3.9]; overall: 0.9 per 1000 live births [95% CI 0.85 to 0.95]). Intrapartum asphyxia was responsible for about half (24 out of 50 deaths) of infants dying after an intended home birth at the onset of labour in Australia between 1985 and 1990. The study reported that the two largest contributors to the excess mortality were underestimation of the risks associated with post-term birth, twin pregnancy and breech presentation, and a lack of response to fetal distress. However, it could also be possible that the practice in Australia between 1985 and 1990 was for a higher proportion of high-risk women to give birth at home.

In order to address the GDG's concern about the lack of any relevant UK study, the NCC-WCH conducted an analysis at the request of the GDG to obtain the best estimate of IPPM rate in the UK. The analysis is described in full in Appendix D.

All births in England and Wales, including home births (intended or unintended) occurring between 1994 and 2003 were obtained from National Statistics. All IPPM data were derived from the Confidential Enquiry into Maternal and Child Health (CEMACH). Denominators were derived by using unintended home births and transfer rates from home to hospital, using estimates from previous studies, with sensitivity analyses. It should be noted that the calculated IPPM rates are sensitive to transfer rates, which themselves are particularly uncertain. The overall IPPM rate for England and Wales improved between 1994 and 2003. The IPPM rate for booked home births (1.37 per 1000 births [range 0.72 to 1.78]) appeared to be higher than the overall IPPM rate (0.68 per 1000 births [95% CI 0.65 to 0.71]) in the period 1999–2003 (RR 2.01 [range 1.01 to 2.74]), although there was no evidence of difference in the period 1994–1998 (RR 1.31 [range 0.67 to 1.78]). IPPM rate for subgroups of home birth were also considered. The analysis showed the highest IPPM rate for women who had transferred their care from home to hospital during pregnancy or labour (6.59 per 1000 [range 1.10 to 12.19] between 1999 and 2003). However those who had booked and completed the home birth showed relatively low IPPM rate (0.50 per 1000 [range 0.41 to 0.62] between 1999 and 2003) The details of the method and the results of this analysis are described in Appendix D. [EL = 3]

The IPPM rates of the included studies are summarised in Table 3.2. It was not possible to conduct a meta-analysis of the included studies on IPPM rates, because of heterogeneity in study design, difference in clinical practice in difference countries and different time periods.

Transfer rates
Two studies[31,43] were identified that reported transfer rates and these are summarised in Table 3.3. [EL = 3]

Evidence statement on planned home versus hospital birth
There is a lack of good-quality evidence relating to women's and babies' short- or long-term outcomes for birth at home compared with hospital and there is no evidence on serious maternal morbidity and mortality. Limited low-quality evidence shows less intervention with a planned home birth compared with a planned birth in hospital. Transfer rates between home and hospital settings show great variation.

While only three low-quality studies reported IPPM or intrapartum perinatal mortality rates, the findings suggest that there may be a trend towards higher rates when birth was planned at home.

The unreliability of these data means that these findings should be interpreted with caution. Factors leading to the unreliability of the data include:

- a lack of routine collection of data on place of birth
- the mix of high- and low-risk women in the home-birth studies

Table 3.3 Transfer rates during labour for home birth

Region	Year	Transfer rate during labour
Northern Region[43]	1993	20.9% (nulliparous 56.3%; parous 17.4%)
England and Wales[31]	1994	12.5%

- the majority of women in these studies were self-selected populations, which questions the generalisability of the studies
- inconsistent definitions
- questionable relevance to the UK setting.

3.2.2 Midwife-led unit (birth centre) versus obstetric unit

Introduction
A midwife-led unit (sometimes called a birth centre) was defined as a place that offers care to women with a predefined uncomplicated pregnancy and where midwives are the lead professionals for intrapartum care.

During labour and birth, medical services including obstetric, neonatal and anaesthetic care are available, should they be needed, but they may be in a separate area within the same building (midwife-led unit alongside obstetric unit), or in a separate building (standalone midwife-led unit), which may involve transfer by car or ambulance.

Standard definitions have recently been adopted by the Health Care Commission (2007) for obstetric units, and alongside and standalone midwife-led units.

Previous guideline
Care provided in a midwife-led unit was reviewed in the *Caesarean Section* guideline.[5] Two case series, one systematic review of six RCTs and one cross-sectional study were included. It was recommended that 'during their discussions about options for birth, healthy pregnant women with anticipated uncomplicated pregnancies should be informed that planned childbirth in a midwife-led unit does not reduce the likelihood of CS.'.

Standalone midwife-led unit (standalone unit) versus obstetric unit

Searching the literature
Thirteen studies, all included in recent structured reviews,[46,47] were identified from the search. Each of these publications was graded according to a validity (quality) index (see Appendix C) and five publications were selected for inclusion in this review. Excluded papers and the reasons for their exclusion are presented in Appendix C.

A series of studies by Rooks[48–51] (National Birth Centre Study) were large case series in the USA and did not employ any controlled design and therefore were excluded from the review.

The difficulty of conducting a randomised controlled trial (RCT) evaluating effectiveness and safety of planning standalone unit birth compared with planning obstetric unit birth is also evident from the literature. No RCTs were identified for standalone units. Two structured reviews were identified that evaluated the evidence for midwife-led units including standalone midwife-led units.[46,47] All studies included in the Stewart review[46] as well as in the Walsh review[47] were appraised. However it should also be noted that any systematic review containing only observational data has inherent bias and confounding factors, and therefore the results should be interpreted with great caution.

Description of included studies
A total of five cohort studies, one of which was conducted in the UK,[52] were included in this review. Three studies were conducted in the US[53–55] and the other one was in Germany.[56] [EL = 2+] See Appendix C for further details of studies included in this review. A list of included and excluded studies is also presented in Appendix C. The UK study[52] compared booked places of birth, although all the other included studies compared intended places of birth at the onset of labour.

In addition, for the purpose of obtaining transfer rates, any study conducted in the UK since 1980 reporting transfer rates from all identified studies were selected, so that an estimate could be obtained. Two UK studies[52,627] were used to obtain transfer rates in this way.

Review findings
A summary of the review findings is shown in Table 3.4.

Mode of birth and other obstetric interventions
Analgesia use in standalone midwife-led units was considered by two retrospective cohort studies, one in the USA[53] (*n* = 149) and the other in the UK[52] (*n* = 20 118). Both studies reported that women in the midwife-led unit groups were significantly less likely to use any type of analgesia. In four cohort studies, there was a statistically significant increase in the number of spontaneous vaginal births in standalone units.

Maternal mortality and other women's complications
None of the studies reported maternal mortality. Perineal trauma was considered by four cohort studies. Statistically, there was a significant increase in the proportion of women who had an intact perineum, with planned birth in a standalone midwife-led unit. There was no evidence of difference in blood loss or PPH in two cohort studies.

Women's satisfaction and psychological/mental health
One cohort study reported women's psychosocial outcomes.[52] Of the 248 (52%) women who responded, 88% agreed that the birth centre had considerable advantages over a hospital birth, and 96% said they would recommend the birth centre to a friend. Women commented positively on the home-like environment of the birth centre, on the confidence they had in their midwives, on the fact that they felt they were treated as an individual, and on their sense of control over the labour and birth.

Perinatal mortality that is directly related to intrapartum events and other neonatal complications
None of the included studies reported any form of perinatal mortality. Two studies reported Apgar score of the babies. The German[56] study reported fewer babies with Apgar score less than 7 at 1 minute in the intended standalone unit group, compared with the control group, but no evidence of difference at 5 and 10 minutes. The US study by Feldman[53] showed no evidence of difference in Apgar score between the two groups.

Transfer rates
There were two studies[52,627] identified, one[52] of which was included in the structured review.[46] The reported transfer rate is summarised in Table 3.5. [EL = 3]

Table 3.5 Transfer rates during labour for standalone units

Region	Period	Transfer rate in labour
London[52]	1997–1999	11.8%
All United Kingdom[627]	2001–2002	18.0% (IQR 18.5 to 24.8)

Evidence statement on standalone midwife-led units versus obstetric units
There is a lack of good-quality evidence available on maternal and baby outcomes for standalone midwife-led units. When compared with planned birth in obstetric units, the available data show a reduction in analgesia use and an increase in vaginal birth and intact perineum rates. There is no evidence on serious maternal morbidity or mortality, or perinatal mortality.

The intrapartum transfer rate in two studies was reported as 12% up to 25%.

Midwife-led unit alongside obstetric unit (alongside unit) versus obstetric unit

Description of included studies
One recently published systematic review that included five RCTs and one quasi-controlled trial was identified.[57] [EL = 1+] These six trials involved 8677 women from the UK (three trials), Sweden, Australia and Canada. The structured review[46] cited earlier also reviewed alongside units, and included this systematic review by Hodnet *et al*. The systematic review involved comprehensive searches and was good quality. The included trials varied considerably in the scope of the intervention (some study groups differed solely in intrapartum care whereas in others there were differences in antenatal and/or postnatal care as well as intrapartum care) and the length of time

Table 3.4 Summary of outcomes of women who planned birth at standalone midwife-led units compared with those who planned birth at obstetric units; data from Stewart et al.[46]

	UK Studies	Studies from other countries			
Authors	Saunders[52]	David[56]	Feldman[53]	Scupholme[54]	Stone[55]
Region/country	London/UK	Berlin/Germany	New York City/USA	USA	USA
Study design	Cohort study	Cohort study	Cohort study	Cohort study	Cohort study
Total number of women and characteristics of women	20 118 women: Booked place of birth 589 booked to give birth at standalone midwife-led units and 19 529 who received standard care or had home birth	4072 women Intended place of birth at the onset of labour All women who gave birth in two birth centres between 1992 and 1994, compared with matched sample of women who gave birth in the same area over same time period and who planned to give birth in a standard setting	149 women Intended place of birth at the onset of labour All women booked to give birth in birth centre over a 3-month period in 1981, compared with control group who met same low-risk criteria at 37 weeks and who planned to give birth in a standard setting	500 women Intended place of birth at the onset of labour Women who commenced at birth centre over 15 months period, compared with women who gave birth during the same time period and met same booking criteria and who planned to give birth in standard setting	146 women Intended place of birth at the onset of labour All women met same low-risk birth centre eligibility criteria and had themselves selected either midwifery or obstetric led care
Comparison	Standalone midwife-led let unit vs obstetric unit	Standalone midwife-led unit vs obstetric unit	Standalone midwife-led unit vs obstetric unit	Standalone midwife-led unit vs obstetric unit	Standalone midwife-led unit vs obstetric unit

Mode of birth and other obstetric interventions

Mode of birth	Women in the midwife-led unit group had more vaginal birth (86% vs 72% (difference 13.3% [95% CI 10.2% to 16.2%]), less instrumental (forceps or ventouse) birth (4% vs 15%) and less CS (6% vs 13%)	Not reported	Rate of spontaneous vaginal birth: 91% in the midwife-led unit group, compared with 84% in the hospital group, $P < 0.001$ Rate of CS: 3% vs 5% Rate of instrumental (forceps or ventouse) birth: 5% vs 11% $P < 0.001$	There were no statistically significant differences between rates of vaginal birth (94% for the midwife-led unit group vs 89% for the control group) or CS (7% vs 11%). Women in the midwife-led unit group were statistically less likely to have instrumental (forceps or ventouse) birth (3% vs 10%), $P < 0.001$	Women in the midwife-led unit group were more likely to have vaginal birth (92% vs 83%), less likely to have instrumental (forceps or ventouse) birth (2% vs 3%) and less likely to have CS (6% vs 14%)
Analgesia use	Women in the midwife-led unit group were less likely to use epidural (11% of midwife-led unit group vs 31% of comparison group (difference 19.3% [95% CI 16.5% to 22%]), less likely to use pethidine (8% vs 26% (difference 17.7% [95% CI 15.4% to 20%]), less likely to use Entonox® (53% vs 67% (difference 14.3% [95% CI 10.1% to 18.5%]), and more likely to use TENS (67% vs 4% (difference 2.9% [95% CI 1% to 5%])	Not reported	Not reported	There was a statistically significant difference in the number of women who had an epidural for pain relief: 31% of the midwife-led unit group vs 75% of the control group, $P < 0.01$	Not reported

Maternal mortality and other women's complications

Maternal mortality				
Maternal mortality	Not reported	Not reported	Not reported	Not reported
Perineal trauma	Women in the midwife-led unit group were less likely to have an episiotomy (5% vs 19% in the comparison group, $P < 0.001$), but there were no significant differences in levels of intact perineum, or perineal tears	Women in the midwife-led unit group were significantly more likely to have an intact perineum (25% vs 6% in the standard care group, $P < 0.01$), less likely to have an episiotomy (47% vs 78%, $P < 0.0001$), and more likely to have a tear not involving the anal sphincter (26% vs 6%, $P < 0.01$). There was no significant difference in levels of third- and fourth-degree perineal tears	Not reported	Women in the midwife-led unit group were more likely to have an intact perineum (12/54; 22%) than women receiving standard care (4/52; 8%), $P < 0.01$
Blood loss or PPH	There was no difference in the rate of women who had a PPH (7% in the midwife-led unit group vs 7% in the comparison group)	There was no statistically significant difference in the number of women who had PPH (3% in the midwife-led unit group vs 2% in the standard care group)	Not reported	Not reported

Women's satisfaction and psychological/mental health

Women's satisfaction	248 (52%) women responded: Of these, 88% agreed that the midwife-led unit had considerable advantages over a hospital birth and 96% said they would recommend the midwife-led unit to a friend; women commented positively on the home-like environment of the midwife-led unit, on the confidence they had in their midwives, on the fact that they felt treated as an individual, and on their sense of control over the labour and birth	Not reported	Not reported	Not reported

Perinatal mortality that is directly related to intrapartum events and other neonatal complications

Any form of perinatal mortality	Not reported	Not reported	Not reported	Not reported
Apgar score	Not reported	There were a statistically significant reduced number of babies in the midwife-led unit group with a 1 minute Apgar score < 7 (2% vs 4%, $P = 0.002$). However, Apgar scores at 5 and 10 minutes showed no evidence of differences	There were no statistically significant differences in Apgar scores between the two groups	Not reported

CS = caesarean section; PPH = postpartum haemorrhage.

between randomisation and onset of 'treatment', but all trials shared one common aspect of the intervention: intrapartum care in a home-like setting. Two sets of meta-analyses were conducted by the NCC-WCH, one including all six trials, and one including only the three UK trials[58–60] to examine any difference in effectiveness between UK trials and trials in other countries. Another subgroup analysis conducted in the above Cochrane review stratified the results on the basis of whether the staff in the alongside unit were shared with the main obstetric unit or functioned as a separate team.[57] The Cochrane review included only four outcomes but the NCC-WCH analysed all the outcomes in the original review [EL = 1+]. A summary of results from the meta-analysis of all six included trials, as well as that of three UK trials, is presented below. Two UK RCTs[58,59] and three UK observational studies[61,62,626] were included in the structured review to obtain transfer rates.[46] [EL = 3]

Review findings

Mode of birth and other obstetric interventions
The results in Table 3.6 summarising both meta-analyses comparing planning birth between alongside midwife-led units and obstetric units showed no statistical difference in rates of induction, augmentation, instrumental vaginal birth, and CS. There was a statistically significant reduction in epidural usage, increase in normal vaginal birth, and an increase in women with no analgesia/anaesthesia in the alongside units compared with the obstetric units. There was also a significant reduction in episiotomy.

When stratifying the results on the basis of the staffing arrangements there were statistically significant reductions in use of induction/augmentation, epidural and opioid analgesia, and episiotomy in trials involving units that had separate staffing while in trials which include units that had the same staff between the two settings there was only a statistically significant reduction in episiotomy.

Maternal mortality and other women's complications
None of the studies reported maternal mortality.

The meta-analyses comparing planning birth between alongside midwife-led units and obstetric units showed no statistical difference in incidence of prolonged first stage of labour, prolonged second stage of labour and PPH. There was a significant reduction in vaginal/perineal tears with an increase in the intact perineum rates.

When stratifying the results on the basis of the staffing arrangements there were statistically significant reductions in incidence of perineal tears in trials involving units that had separate staffing, while in trials which include units that had the same staff between the two settings there was no evidence of difference in other complications.

Women's satisfaction and psychological/mental health
One UK trial[59] that had the same staff between the two settings reported women's satisfaction and assessment of birth experience, although these were poorly defined and poorly measured. This showed, with borderline significance, an increase in the proportion of women who felt involved in decisions about care and who rated their intrapartum care highly. One Swedish trial[63,64] that had different staffing between the two settings reported that significantly more women preferred the same setting for birth the next time.

Perinatal mortality directly related to intrapartum events and other neonatal complications
None of the studies reported perinatal mortality directly related to intrapartum events

A meta-analysis[57] that included six trials [EL = 1+] found that there was no statistical difference in the number of babies with an Apgar score less than 7 at either 1 minute or 5 minutes, or in the number of babies admitted to a neonatal unit. There was a tendency (not statistically significant) towards an increase in perinatal mortality, although this included deaths from all causes including stillbirths due to intrauterine death before labour.

When stratifying the results on the basis of the staffing arrangements, there were no statistically significant differences in Apgar scores of the babies in either subgroup. However, in trials from units that had separate staffing between the two settings there was a significant increase in

Table 3.6 Summary of meta-analyses for alongside units compared with obstetric units

Outcome	All trials			UK trials			Separate staff and greater continuity of carer in alongside unit			Same staff and degree of continuity of carer between alongside and obstetric units		
	Number of trials	Pooled RR	95% CI	Number of trials	Pooled RR	95% CI	Number of trials	Pooled RR	95% CI	Number of trials	Pooled RR	95% CI
Mode of birth and other obstetric interventions												
Spontaneous vaginal birth	5	1.03	1.01 to 1.06	2	1.03	1.00 to 1.06	3	1.04	1.01 to 1.06	2	1.03	0.98 to 1.07
Instrumental vaginal birth	5	0.88	0.77 to 1.01	2	0.88	0.76 to 1.02	3	0.87	0.72 to 1.05	2	0.89	0.74 to 1.08
Caesarean section	6	0.85	0.73 to 1.00	3	0.89	0.74 to 1.06	3	0.87	0.72 to 1.06	3	0.83	0.65 to 1.05
Induction	4	0.89	0.72 to 1.09	2	0.97	0.80 to 1.17	3	0.82	0.68 to 0.98	1	1.06	0.90 to 1.24
Augmentation	5	0.81	0.67 to 1.00	3	0.86	0.63 to 1.17	3	0.70	0.62 to 0.79	2	1.02	0.85 to 1.22
Opioid analgesia	5	0.74	0.55 to 1.00	3	0.95	0.80 to 1.14	3	0.81	0.74 to 0.88	2	1.05	0.98 to 1.13
Epidural analgesia	6	0.83	0.75 to 0.92	3	0.84	0.74 to 0.95	3	0.81	0.72 to 0.92	3	0.87	0.72 to 1.04
No analgesia/anaesthesia	4	1.19	1.01 to 1.40	3	1.22	0.95 to 1.57	2	1.13	0.94 to 1.36	2	1.42	0.96 to 2.10
Episiotomy	5	0.85	0.74 to 0.99	2	0.81	0.71 to 0.93	3	0.82	0.73 to 0.91	2	0.86	0.75 to 0.97
Maternal mortality and other women's complications												
Maternal mortality	Not reported			Not reported			Not reported			Not reported		
Prolonged first stage	(Only UK trials)			2	1.11	0.90 to 1.38	1	1.06	0.87 to 1.29	1	1.42	0.86 to 2.34
Prolonged second stage	(Only UK trials)			2	0.95	0.79 to 1.16	1	0.94	0.74 to 1.18	1	0.99	0.71 to 1.40
Vaginal/perineal tears	4	1.08	1.03 to 1.13	2	1.09	0.98 to 1.21	3	1.10	1.04 to 1.16	1	1.03	0.94 to 1.13
Intact perineum	4	1.10	0.91 to 1.33	2	1.14	1.04 to 1.25	2	1.11	0.99 to 1.25	2	1.18	1.01 to 1.39
PPH	(Only trial with separate staff)			1	0.93	0.69 to 1.25	2	0.97	0.80 to 1.18	(No trial with same staffing)		
Women's satisfaction and psychological/mental health												
Women preferred the same setting next time	(Only trial with separate staff)			(No UK trials)			1	1.81	1.65 to 1.98	(No trial with same staffing)		
Women felt involved in decisions about care	(Only UK trials)			1	1.04	1.00 to 1.08	(No trial with separate staffing)			1	1.04	1.00 to 1.08
High rating of the care	(Only UK trials)			1	1.14	1.07 to 1.21	(No trial with separate staffing)			1	1.14	1.07 to 1.21
Perinatal mortality directly related to intrapartum events and other neonatal complications												
Perinatal mortality directly related intrapartum events	Not reported			Not reported			Not reported			Not reported		
Perinatal mortality	5	1.83	0.99 to 3.38	2	1.52	0.77 to 3.00	3	2.38	1.05 to 5.41	2	1.24	0.48 to 3.19
Apgar score less than 7 at 1 minute	(Only trial with the same staff)			(No UK trials)			(No trial with separate staffing)			1	0.35	0.04 to 3.22
Apgar score less than 7 at 5 minutes	(Only trial with separate staff)			(No UK trials)			2	1.19	0.53 to 2.64	(No trial with same staffing)		
Admission to neonatal unit	3	1.00	0.70 to 1.43	1	1.06	0.80 to 1.40	2	1.23	0.94 to 1.63	2	0.76	0.34 to 1.71

PPH = postpartum haemorrhage.

perinatal mortality, while in trials from units that had the same staff between the two settings there was no statistically difference in perinatal mortality.

Transfer rates
Four studies[58,59,61,62] reported transfer rates, as shown in Table 3.7. [EL = 3]

Table 3.7   Transfer rates during labour for alongside units

Region	Period	Transfer rate during labour
Leicester[58]	1989–1990	28.6%
Aberdeen[59]	1991–1992	25.8%
East Dorset[626]	1992–1993	12.4%
Kirkcaldy[61]	1995–1996	26.4% (nulliparous 38.6%; parous 12.8%)
London[62]	2003	30.6%

Evidence statement on alongside midwife-led units versus obstetric units
The quality of evidence for alongside midwife-led units is better than that for other non-obstetric settings because it is derived from RCTs conducted in the early 1990s. Overall, meta-analyses of RCTs showed an increase in the number of women with intact perineum, an increase in the proportion of women without analgesia and an increase in spontaneous vaginal birth, when care in alongside units is compared with obstetric units.

The analysis of data from all five trials was of borderline statistical significance, but suggested a possible increase in overall perinatal mortality in alongside units compared with obstetric units (RR 1.83 [95% CI 0.99 to 3.38], $P = 0.05$). However, none of the trials reported perinatal mortality that is directly related to intrapartum events and analysis of data restricted to the two UK trials did not reveal any statistically significant difference in perinatal mortality rates for babies born in alongside units compared with obstetric units (RR 1.52 [95% CI 0.77 to 3.0]).

Further subgroup analysis of the Cochrane review has suggested that staffing arrangements may influence outcomes. In trials that had the same staff shared between an alongside unit and an obstetric unit, there were no significant differences in women's and babies' outcomes including perinatal mortality. In trials that had separate staff in an alongside unit from an obstetric unit and a team midwifery model, there was evidence of significant reduction in interventions including induction of labour, augmentation of labour, use of opioid and epidural analgesia, rate of episiotomy, and rate of vaginal/perineal tears and increase in spontaneous vaginal birth, but a statistically significant increase in perinatal mortality. There is no indication as to which component or components of care might contribute to this.

Transfer rates to obstetric units within these studies ranged from 12.4% to 31% in labour. When stratified by parity, transfer rates in labour were 38.6% for nulliparous women and 12.8% for parous women.

3.2.3   Economic evaluation of planning place of birth

Searching the literature
One structured review was identified that provided information about the cost-effectiveness of different models of maternity care.[46] The majority of the economic evaluations included in this review are limited by narrow, short-term perspective and incomplete data. This has led to inconclusive or contradictory findings. Given the limitations of this review, a new systematic literature review to identify the best available economic evidence as regards all the existing birth settings was undertaken.

Description of included studies
This review identified two full economic evaluations. Both studies relate to the US healthcare setting and they sought to evaluate which place of birth is the most cost-effective option for low-risk women.

Review findings
One study[65] compared hospital, home and birth centres, in terms of their cost-effectiveness. Outcome data, derived from earlier published studies, were based on women with low-risk pregnancies. However, there is a serious concern that the authors have not adequately controlled for risk, as outcomes for hospital birth are based on post-date pregnancies, which are at a higher level of risk than term pregnancies. Therefore, there may be systematic differences between the pregnancies in the birth setting comparators in this analysis. Costs were based on charges to the mother for a routine birth. Effectiveness was defined as a birth without intrapartum fetal or neonatal mortality. The authors reported that their analysis showed that, in terms of intrapartum fetal and neonatal mortality, home births and birth centres dominate hospital births, meaning that home and birth centre births are both less expensive and safer than hospital births. They also suggested an incremental cost-effectiveness ratio for birth centres relative to home births of $2.3 million per intrapartum and neonatal death avoided. The authors' conclusion that home birth is a cost-effective health care alternative may not be warranted as the comparison of intrapartum and neonatal mortality is being made without adequately controlling for risk between the different birth settings.

The second study[66] used a decision analytic approach in order to assess which place of birth is the most cost-effective. In this paper there were two comparators: hospital, which was regarded as a traditional birth setting; and birth centre. The authors reported that the average cost of delivery at the birth centre ($3,385) was lower than hospital births ($4,673). They also reported that the utility for average low risk was greater in the birth centre than at the hospital (0.92592 and 0.79507 respectively). However, these utilities do not seem to be based on health-related quality of life and it is not clear how they were derived. They may simply reflect the subjective assessment of the authors. The study suggested that the birth centre dominated in this model, being cheaper and more effective than the hospital alternative. A threshold sensitivity analysis suggested that the transfer rates from birth centres to hospital would have to reach an "unrealistic" 62% before birth centres ceased to dominate the hospital setting. Sensitivity analysis also demonstrated that the dominance of birth centres was contingent on lower charges in that setting compared with hospital. However, no sensitivity analysis was undertaken on utilities and given the concerns about how these were derived more generally, the conclusions of this paper may be in doubt.

As is evident from the above commentary, there are a number of limitations with the above studies. Both studies relate to a US setting and results may not be generalisable to the UK. In particular, costs may differ from those faced in the NHS and place of birth comparisons do not reflect current clinical practice in the UK. For the purpose of this guideline we developed a model that would better reflect NHS costs and place of birth settings available in the UK.

Economic modelling
In order to maximise the health gain from scarce healthcare resources, it is important to consider cost-effectiveness. The economic model described in more detail in Appendix E illustrates the decision-analytic approach that could be used to assess the cost-effectiveness of different places of birth from the perspective of the NHS. However, the output from any such model can only be as good as the inputs with which it is populated.

Evidence statement on economic evaluation of planning place of birth
There is at present insufficient evidence to make a like-for-like comparison of place of birth in terms of clinical effectiveness. Therefore, the model cannot currently inform recommendations for place of birth based on cost-effectiveness, and better outcomes data are needed to inform future decision making.

GDG interpretation of the evidence (advantages and disadvantages of planning each place of birth)
The quality of evidence available is not as good as it should be for such an important healthcare issue and most studies do not report complete or consistent outcome data. Of particular concern is the lack of reliable data, relating to relatively rare but serious outcomes such as perinatal mortality that is directly related to intrapartum events or serious maternal morbidity in all places of birth. Uncontrolled confounding and selection bias are particular methodological limitations of most studies.

However, this situation should be improved once the results of a prospective study evaluating outcomes of home births, births in midwife-led units and obstetric units which is currently being undertaken by National Perinatal Epidemiology Unit. Birthplace Study) and following improved collection of data by CEMACH of the place of birth.

Planning birth outside an obstetric unit seems to be associated with an increase in spontaneous vaginal births, an increase in women with an intact perineum and, for home births, improved maternal satisfaction.

The GDG was unable to determine whether planning birth in a non-obstetric setting is as safe as birth in an obstetric unit. This was because the data from the included studies consistently showed a non-significant increase in perinatal mortality (including perinatal mortality that is directly related to intrapartum events) in non-obstetric settings.

Recommendations on planning place of birth

Women should be offered the choice of planning birth at home, in a midwife-led unit or in an obstetric unit. Women should be informed:

- That giving birth is generally very safe for both the woman and her baby.
- That the available information on planning place of birth is not of good quality, but suggests that among women who plan to give birth at home or in a midwife-led unit there is a higher likelihood of a normal birth, with less intervention. We do not have enough information about the possible risks to either the woman or her baby relating to planned place of birth.
- That the obstetric unit provides direct access to obstetricians, anaesthetists, neonatologists and other specialist care including epidural analgesia.
- Of locally available services, the likelihood of being transferred into the obstetric unit and the time this may take.
- That if something does go unexpectedly seriously wrong during labour at home or in a midwife-led unit, the outcome for the woman and baby could be worse than if they were in the obstetric unit with access to specialised care.
- That if she has a pre-existing medical condition or has had a previous complicated birth that makes her at higher risk of developing complications during her next birth, she should be advised to give birth in an obstetric unit.

Clinical governance structures should be implemented in all places of birth (see Boxes 3.1 and 3.2).

Box 3.1 Clinical governance in all settings

- Multidisciplinary clinical governance structures, of which the Labour Ward Forum is an example, should be in place to enable the oversight of all places of birth. These structures should include, as a minimum, midwifery (ideally a supervisor of midwives), obstetric, anaesthetic and neonatal expertise, and adequately supported user representation.
- Rotating staff between obstetric and midwife-led units should be encouraged in order to maintain equivalent competency and experience.
- Clear referral pathways should be in place to enable midwives to inform or seek advice from a supervisor of midwives when caring for a woman who may have risk factors but does not wish to labour in an obstetric unit.
- If an obstetric opinion is sought by either the midwife or the woman on the appropriate place of birth, this should be obtained from a consultant obstetrician.
- All healthcare professionals should document discussions with the woman about her chosen place of birth in the hand-held maternity notes.
- In all places of birth, risk assessment in the antenatal period and when labour commences should be subject to continuous audit.
- Monthly figures of numbers of women booked for, being admitted to, being transferred from and giving birth in each place of birth should be audited. This should include maternal and neonatal outcomes.
- The clinical governance group should be responsible for detailed root-cause analysis of any serious maternal or neonatal adverse outcomes (for example, intrapartum-related perinatal death or seizures in the neonatal period) and consider any 'near misses' identified through risk-management systems. The Confidential Enquiry into Maternal and Child Health (CEMACH) and the National Patient Safety Agency (NPSA)'s 'Seven steps to patient safety' provide a framework for meeting clinical governance and risk-management targets.
- Data must be submitted to the national registries for either intrapartum-related perinatal mortality or neonatal encephalopathy once these are in existence.

> **Box 3.2** Clinical governance for settings other than an obstetric unit
>
> - Clear pathways and guidelines on the indications for, and the process of transfer to, an obstetric unit should be established. There should be no barriers to rapid transfer in an emergency.
> - Clear pathways and guidelines should also be developed for the continued care of women once they have transferred. These pathways should include arrangements for times when the nearest obstetric or neonatal unit is closed to admissions.
> - If the emergency is such that transfer is not possible, open access must be given on-site for any appropriate staff to deal with whatever emergency has arisen.
> - There should be continuous audit of the appropriateness of, the reason for and speed of transfer. Conversely, audit also needs to consider circumstances in which transfer was indicated but did not occur. Audit should include time taken to see an obstetrician or neonatologist and the time from admission to birth.

A national surveillance scheme which allows appropriate comparisons, including safety and cost-effectiveness, of all places of birth should be established to address the poor quality and lack of coverage of current data.

National registries of the root-cause analysis findings relating to all intrapartum-related deaths over 37 weeks of gestation should be established.

A definition of neonatal encephalopathy should be agreed and a national register commenced. The information collected should also include data on transfer during labour from each of the different birth settings.

Research recommendations on planning place of birth

The best possible studies comparing different places of birth should be undertaken in the UK. Prospective research to assess clinical outcomes, including safety, for all places of birth should be undertaken, as well as qualitative data collection to assess women's experiences of birth.

There is a need to establish a single generic health-related quality of life index value for the multi-attribute perinatal and maternal outcomes of intrapartum care.

3.3 Assessment for choosing place of birth

Clinical question
What are the risk factors which should be included in assessment to determine the most appropriate place of birth for women during pregnancy and in labour?

3.3.1 Choosing place of birth

Description of included studies
No high-quality studies were identified that directly addressed this question.

Evidence statement on choosing place of birth
There is no strong evidence on assessment for choosing place of birth and thus the GDG discussed each condition related to place of birth.

GDG interpretation of the evidence on choosing place of birth
The following criteria have been produced by consensus with the aim of providing consistency of advice for women when considering the relative risk associated with where they wish to give birth.

Recommendations on choosing place of birth

Tables 3.7 to 3.10 should be used as part of an assessment for choosing place of birth.

Tables 3.7 and 3.8 show medical conditions or situations in which there is increased risk for the woman or baby during or shortly after labour, where care in an obstetric unit would be expected to reduce this risk.

The factors listed in Tables 3.9 and 3.10 are not reasons in themselves for advising birth within an obstetric unit but indicate that further consideration of birth setting may be required.

These risks and the additional care that can be provided in the obstetric unit should be discussed with the woman so that she can make an informed choice about place of birth.

Table 3.7 Medical conditions indicating increased risk suggesting planned birth at an obstetric unit

Disease area	Medical condition
Cardiovascular	Confirmed cardiac disease
	Hypertensive disorders
Respiratory	Asthma requiring an increase in treatment or hospital treatment
	Cystic fibrosis
Haematological	Haemoglobinopathies – sickle-cell disease, beta-thalassaemia major
	History of thromboembolic disorders
	Immune thrombocytopenia purpura or other platelet disorder or platelet count below 100 000
	Von Willebrand's disease
	Bleeding disorder in the woman or unborn baby
	Atypical antibodies which carry a risk of haemolytic disease of the newborn
Infective	Risk factors associated with group B streptococcus whereby antibiotics in labour would be recommended
	Hepatitis B/C with abnormal liver function tests
	Carrier of/infected with HIV
	Toxoplasmosis – women receiving treatment
	Current active infection of chicken pox/rubella/genital herpes in the woman or baby
	Tuberculosis under treatment
Immune	Systemic lupus erythematosus
	Scleroderma
Endocrine	Hyperthyroidism
	Diabetes
Renal	Abnormal renal function
	Renal disease requiring supervision by a renal specialist
Neurological	Epilepsy
	Myasthenia gravis
	Previous cerebrovascular accident
Gastrointestinal	Liver disease associated with current abnormal liver function tests
Psychiatric	Psychiatric disorder requiring current inpatient care

Table 3.8 Other factors indicating increased risk suggesting planned birth at an obstetric unit

Factor	Additional information
Previous complications	Unexplained stillbirth/neonatal death or previous death related to intrapartum difficulty Previous baby with neonatal encephalopathy Pre-eclampsia requiring preterm birth Placental abruption with adverse outcome Eclampsia Uterine rupture Primary postpartum haemorrhage requiring additional treatment or blood transfusion Retained placenta requiring manual removal in theatre Caesarean section Shoulder dystocia
Current pregnancy	Multiple birth Placenta praevia Pre-eclampsia or pregnancy-induced hypertension Preterm labour or preterm prelabour rupture of membranes Placental abruption Anaemia – haemoglobin less than 8.5 g/dl at onset of labour Confirmed intrauterine death Induction of labour Substance misuse Alcohol dependency requiring assessment or treatment Onset of gestational diabetes Malpresentation – breech or transverse lie Body mass index at booking of greater than 35 kg/m² Recurrent antepartum haemorrhage
Fetal indications	Small for gestational age in this pregnancy (less than fifth centile or reduced growth velocity on ultrasound) Abnormal fetal heart rate (FHR)/Doppler studies Ultrasound diagnosis of oligo-/polyhydramnios
Previous gynaecological history	Myomectomy Hysterotomy

Table 3.9 Medical conditions indicating individual assessment when planning place of birth

Disease area	Medical condition
Cardiovascular	Cardiac disease without intrapartum implications
Haematological	Atypical antibodies not putting the baby at risk of haemolytic disease Sickle-cell trait Thalassaemia trait Anaemia – haemoglobin 8.5–10.5 g/dl at onset of labour
Infective	Hepatitis B/C with normal liver function tests
Immune	Non-specific connective tissue disorders
Endocrine	Unstable hypothyroidism such that a change in treatment is required
Skeletal/neurological	Spinal abnormalities Previous fractured pelvis Neurological deficits
Gastrointestinal	Liver disease without current abnormal liver function Crohn's disease Ulcerative colitis

Table 3.10 Other factors indicating individual assessment when planning place of birth

Factor	Additional information
Previous complications	Stillbirth/neonatal death with a known non-recurrent cause
	Pre-eclampsia developing at term
	Placental abruption with good outcome
	History of previous baby more than 4.5 kg
	Extensive vaginal, cervical, or third- or fourth-degree perineal trauma
	Previous term baby with jaundice requiring exchange transfusion
Current pregnancy	Antepartum bleeding of unknown origin (single episode after 24 weeks of gestation)
	Body mass index at booking of 30–34 kg/m²
	Blood pressure of 140 mmHg systolic or 90 mmHg diastolic on two occasions
	Clinical or ultrasound suspicion of macrosomia
	Para 6 or more
	Recreational drug use
	Under current outpatient psychiatric care
	Age over 40 at booking
Fetal indications	Fetal abnormality
Previous gynaecological history	Major gynaecological surgery
	Cone biopsy or large loop excision of the transformation zone
	Fibroids

Indications for intrapartum transfer

The following risks and benefits should be assessed when considering transfer to an obstetric unit, bearing in mind the likelihood of birth during the transfer:

- indications for electronic fetal monitoring (EFM) including abnormalities of the fetal heart rate (FHR) on intermittent auscultation
- delay in the first or second stages of labour
- significant meconium-stained liquor
- maternal request for epidural pain relief
- obstetric emergency – antepartum haemorrhage, cord presentation/prolapse, postpartum haemorrhage, maternal collapse or a need for advanced neonatal resuscitation
- retained placenta
- maternal pyrexia in labour (38.0 °C once or 37.5 °C on two occasions 2 hours apart)
- malpresentation or breech presentation diagnosed for the first time at the onset of labour, taking into account imminence of birth
- either raised diastolic blood pressure (over 90 mmHg) or raised systolic blood pressure (over 140 mmHg) on two consecutive readings taken 30 minutes apart
- uncertainty about the presence of a fetal heartbeat
- third- or fourth-degree tear or other complicated perineal trauma requiring suturing.

4 Care throughout labour

4.1 Communication between women and healthcare professionals

Introduction
Effective communication in all its forms is a fundamental aspect in today's maternity services. The overall aim of caring for women during labour and birth is to engender a positive experience for the woman and her family, while maintaining their physical and emotional health, preventing complications and responding to emergencies. To successfully achieve this aim, good communication between all those involved in the care of women during the process of childbearing is crucial. Developing a rapport, trust and effective communication between healthcare providers and women is important to a woman's positive childbirth experience. Other factors include involvement in decision making, informed explanations and meeting personal expectations. All these elements have a powerful impact upon women and their childbirth experience. Their influence, as to whether the experience is good or bad, cannot be overestimated.

The views, beliefs and values of the woman, her partner and her family in relation to her care and that of her baby should be sought and respected at all times. Women should be fully involved so that care is flexible and tailored to meet her and her baby's individual needs. Women should have the opportunity to make informed decisions about every aspect of their labour and birth. Women sometimes decline the offer of interventions for numerous reasons including previous unpleasant experiences. Individualised care should be supported by giving evidence-based information and active informed consent should be sought from women before all monitoring procedures, examinations and treatments.

Clinical question
What effect does communication have on a woman's perception of her birth experience?

- Interventions include the effect of control, choice and decision making on psychosocial wellbeing in the medium and long term.
- Outcomes include postnatal depression and post-traumatic stress disorder.

Description of included studies
The search yielded 2615 titles, 182 of which were selected for retrieval. The search did not impose geographical limits, but papers were not included if it was felt that the cultural setting of the research would be unlikely to generalise to women in the UK. Papers were also rejected if they did not have information on caregiver behaviour linked to psychosocial outcomes for women. Within the remaining papers, 19 were selected as key, either because they were methodologically sound empirical studies specifically designed to address the link between caregiver behaviour and psychosocial outcomes for women ($n = 18$) or because they were reviews that highlighted this link ($n = 1$).[67–85]

Review findings
A systematic review of 137 reports of factors influencing women's evaluation of their childbirth experiences was included.[67] [EL = 3] The review identified four factors that were seen as key in shaping women's experience of labour: personal expectations; the amount of support from caregivers; the quality of the caregiver–patient relationship; and the involvement in decision making. It is concluded that the influences of pain, pain relief, and intrapartum interventions on subsequent satisfaction are important but not as powerful as the influences of the attitudes and behaviours of the caregivers.

A Swedish longitudinal cohort study of 2541 women measured women's global experience of labour and birth and obtained information on the possible risk factors during pregnancy and 2 months after birth.[68] [EL = 2+] The following categories of risk factors were identified that were associated with women's experience of labour and birth:

- factors related to unexpected medical problems
- social factors

- factors related to the woman's feelings during labour, such as pain and lack of control
- factors that may be easier for caregivers to influence, such as lack of support in labour and administration of analgesia.

A UK prospective study sent questionnaires to women 1 month before the birth to assess their preferences and expectations, and at 6 weeks after birth to discover their experiences and assess psychological outcomes.[69] [EL = 2+] Findings are based upon data from 1146 women. Parity was found to be strongly associated with feeling in control, with multiparous women feeling more in control than nulliparous women in all cases. In logistic regression analyses, the feeling of being in control associated with staff behaviour was found to relate primarily to being able to get comfortable, the feeling of being treated with respect and as an individual and perceiving staff to be considerate.

As part of a large randomised trial in the UK, which assessed the timing of intervention in prolonged labour, women's views were explored using a specifically designed questionnaire.[70] [EL = 3] Analysis of findings from 412 nulliparous women in response to an open-ended question revealed the following main themes: support, information, intervention, decision making and control, and pain relief. One hundred and eight women said they wanted to participate in decision making but the degree of involvement varied among women.

Secondary analysis of questionnaire survey data, also collected during an RCT, was carried out to explore factors relating to women's experience of birth. Data were collected from women receiving either care in an alongside midwife-led unit or standard hospital care.[71] [EL = 3] The two groups were combined for the purposes of this analysis ($n = 1111$). Logistic regression analysis identified five explanatory variables: involvement in the birth process (perceived control) and midwifery support were predictive of a positive experience; anxiety, pain and having a first baby were predictive of a negative experience.

Findings from a questionnaire survey (Sweden) distributed to women 1 day after giving birth ($n = 295$; response rate = 91%) showed that women usually experienced severe pain and various degrees of anxiety, and most were seized with panic for a short time or for some part of their labour.[72] [EL = 3] Despite these negative feelings, most women felt greatly involved in the birth process, were satisfied with their own achievement and thought they had coped better than expected. Of the 38 variables tested in regression analysis, the six that contributed to explaining women's overall birth experience were: support from the midwife (sensitivity to needs); duration of labour; pain; expectations of the birth; involvement and participation in the birth process; and surgical procedures (emergency caesarean section, vacuum extraction, forceps, episiotomy).

Another questionnaire survey was sent to women 8–9 months after they had given birth (Australia) ($n = 790$; response rate = 71%).[73] [EL = 3] Findings revealed that not having an active say in decisions was associated with a six-fold increase in dissatisfaction among nulliparous women and a 15-fold increase among multiparous women. When adjusted for parity in a logistic regression model, the following factors were highly related to dissatisfaction with intrapartum care: lack of involvement in decision making ($P < 0.001$); insufficient information ($P < 0.001$); a higher score for obstetric interventions ($P < 0.015$); and the perception that caregivers were unhelpful ($P < 0.04$).

A second Australian cross-sectional questionnaire survey returned by 1336 women (response rate = 62.5%) 6–7 months after they had given birth found that, after adjusting for parity, social factors and obstetric care, caregivers perceived as unhelpful and not having an active say in decisions about their care had the greatest impact on women's experience of birth.[74] [EL = 3]

A third Australian prospective descriptive study employed telephone interviews conducted 4–6 weeks after birth to investigate women's experiences ($n = 499$ women).[75] [EL = 3] One in three women identified a traumatic birthing event and reported the presence of at least three trauma signs. Twenty-eight women (5.6%) met DSM-IV criteria for acute post-traumatic stress disorder. The level of obstetric intervention experienced during childbirth together with the perception of inadequate intrapartum care during labour was consistently associated with the development of acute trauma symptoms.

A questionnaire survey of first-time mothers in Finland ($n = 271$; response rate = 83%) investigated women's perceptions of labour and birth.[76] [EL = 3] Regression analysis showed that positive childbirth experiences were associated with the positive characteristics and professional skills of the attending midwife, the positive attitude of the child's father towards the pregnancy and a short labour.

In the USA (early 1990s), there was a convenience sample of 15 women (eight first-time mothers) who told 33 birth stories.[77] [EL = 3] From the findings, the researchers concluded that when decision making was increasingly shared between the women and the caregivers, the women expressed more positive emotions. Professional knowledge and power needs to be supportive, not directive, of the birthing processes.

A Swedish qualitative study using interviews with 18 women (six primiparous) who were 2–4 days post birth investigated women's experiences of labour and birth. The study took place in Sweden in 1994.[78] [EL = 3] Three main themes emerged: the need to be seen as an individual; to have a trusting relationship; and to be supported and guided on one's own terms. These themes were associated with a positive birth experience.

Another small-scale (n = 14) interview-based study conducted in Iceland also explored women's experience of giving birth.[79] [EL = 3] Analysis of the data showed that women have a need for a sense of control as well as a need for caring and understanding. Additionally there was a need for a good relationship with the midwife, which included the women feeling safe and secure. An explanation of events and reassurance regarding progress were also important to women.

A second Icelandic qualitative study sought views and experiences from a purposive sample of ten women who had experienced both caring and uncaring encounters during childbirth in Iceland.[80] [EL = 3] The authors summarised three traits of the caring midwife which were defined as follows:

- competence – has the necessary knowledge and skills needed to coach a woman through the journey of labour and giving birth; is responsible, attentive, deliberate and communicates effectively
- genuine concern and respect for the woman – gives of her or himself, shows solidarity and sharing, is encouraging and supportive, respectful and benevolent
- positive mental attitude – is cheerful and positive, reliable and trustworthy, considerate and understanding.

Similarly the authors summarised three traits of the uncaring midwife:

- lack of competence – being rough when giving care to women, ineffective communication, not taking the initiative when needed and lack of understanding and flexibility
- lack of genuine concern and respect for the woman as a person – being thoughtless, strict on routines and rules, not taking notice of the woman and lacking in cooperation; being indifferent and untouched by the event as such, lack of interest and understanding in general, being non-supportive and insensitive, being hurried and in a rush
- negative character traits – being gloomy and brusque, cold, unkind or harsh.

An interesting US study showed a sample of 20 women videotapes of their births while simultaneously interviewing them.[81] [EL = 3] In separate interviews, the 25 caregivers were also shown the videotapes and interviewed. Although women and caregivers appeared to agree about what information women required and how it should be given, caregiver perceptions were more positive than those of the women. Many women wanted more information and valued detailed information to explain what was happening.

A discussion paper based on a previous paper[82] puts forward an idea that women are of less interest to the caregivers than the equipment, and that lack of information disempowers women. [EL = 3] Caregivers were seen to block women's worries or concerns by silence, changing the subject or by neutral statements such as 'let's see how we go'.

Participant observation of a convenience sample of 12 primiparous women in the second stage of labour examined communication between midwives, student midwives, labouring women and their partners, by analysing videotaped recordings.[83] [EL = 3] Communication was categorised using one of the following: innovation, encouragement, directing, educating, questioning, social and professional. Findings revealed that most communication was categorised as being directing, encouraging or educational, with the latter two categories showing a degree of overlap.

Midwives were found to fall into one of two groups: those that tend to be directing or those that tend to be encouraging and educating. Women preferred the latter type of communication.

The Caring Behaviour Assessment tool has been used on a convenience sample of 31 women following normal birth (USA) to look at women's perceptions of caring behaviour from nurses during childbirth.[84] [EL = 3] Findings showed that the behaviours perceived by women to be most indicative of caring focused on professional competence and monitoring of the woman's condition. The most caring behaviours included knowing what they were doing, treating the woman with respect and as an individual, being kind and considerate and reassuring the patient.

A cross-cultural qualitative study compared responses from semi-structured interviews conducted with ten Chinese women and ten Scottish women (giving birth in Scotland).[85] [EL = 3] In addition, 45 unstructured interviews were undertaken with health workers, relatives and friends. Responses to the birth experience were partly related to the woman's culture, with Chinese women being more accepting of care given, but there were issues that were common across all the women irrespective of cultural background, notably that the feeling of being in control was linked to a better emotional outcome. Caregivers' failure to engage with the woman as a human being was experienced as very traumatic.

Evidence statement

The studies included in this review varied in the methodology that they used as well as the method of analysis undertaken. Nevertheless, a number of strong common themes emerge and it is apparent that the way caregivers relate with the labouring women is hugely influential upon the woman's experience of birth. The first theme highlights that women value being treated as an individual, with respect and care. Secondly, most women need information and interpretation of that information in order to feel guided and supported throughout the birth.

These findings are usefully summarised by the words women use to describe both the midwife and the feelings involved in a positive birth experience. These words include: caring, considerate, understanding, competent, trustworthy, empathic, tender, kind, friendly, calm, alert, peaceful, having professional expertise, unhurried.

Women want to receive information and assistance, to be involved, to feel safe and secure, to feel at ease and to be able to be themselves.

Recommendations on communication

All women in labour should be treated with respect and should be in control of and involved in what is happening to them, and the way in which care is given is key to this. To facilitate this, healthcare professionals and other caregivers should establish a rapport with the labouring woman, asking her about her wants and expectations for labour, being aware of the importance of tone and demeanour, and of the actual words they use. This information should be used to support and guide her through her labour.

To establish communication with the labouring woman, healthcare professionals should:

- Greet the woman with a smile and a personal welcome, establish her language needs, introduce themselves and explain their role in her care.
- Maintain a calm and confident approach so that their demeanour reassures the woman that all is going well.
- Knock and wait before entering the woman's room, respecting it as her personal space, and ask others to do the same.
- Ask how the woman is feeling and whether there is anything in particular she is worried about.
- If the woman has a written birth plan, read and discuss it with her.
- Assess the woman's knowledge of strategies for coping with pain and provide balanced information to find out which available approaches are acceptable to her.
- Encourage the woman to adapt the environment to meet her individual needs.
- Ask her permission before all procedures and observations, focusing on the woman rather than the technology or the documentation.

- Show the woman and her birth partner how to summon help and reassure her that she may do so whenever and as often as she needs to. When leaving the room, healthcare professionals should let her know when they will return.
- Involve the woman in any handover of care to another professional, either when additional expertise has been brought in or at the end of a shift.

4.2 Mobilisation and position

Clinical question
What is the effectiveness of the following interventions or techniques in labour on outcomes?

- mobilisation
- positions including: 'freedom to choose' option; standing; squatting; kneeling; semi-recumbent; lying on back; left lateral; birth stool, etc.

Previous guideline
Mobilisation during labour was reviewed in the *Caesarean Section* guideline.[6] Two RCTs were included. The guideline recommended that women should be informed that walking during labour has not been shown to influence the likelihood of CS.

Description of included studies
Evidence for the effect of different positions and mobilisation during the first stage of labour on labour outcomes is drawn from one systematic review of RCTs[86] and five RCTs.[87–91]

Review findings
A systematic review of maternal positions during the first stage of labour was identified which included 14 RCTs (seven of which used women as their own controls).[86] [EL = 1–] Most trials where women acted as their own controls were small-scale (*n* = 23 or fewer in six of the trials). In the other trials, sample sizes ranged from 40 to 1067, with four of the trials involving over 200 women. The trials of positioning during the first stage of labour compared mobilisation or upright positions with one or more horizontal positions in bed. Outcome measures included pain, comfort, uterine activity and labour progress. In trials where women acted as their own controls, they were requested to alternate between two different positions (e.g. standing, walking or sitting up versus side-lying or supine) during labour for equal periods (usually 30 minutes). Measures were made after each period of reported location and intensity of pain, uterine activity and labour progress. Other trials assigned women to an upright group or a recumbent group for a longer period of time. e.g. active first stage, the whole of the first stage or the duration of labour. The differences in study design, the lack of detail in most papers regarding measures taken to prevent bias, difficulties of compliance and different pain assessment methods undermine the reliability of the findings and prevent pooling of data. The one consistent finding was that none of the women in any of the studies reported greater comfort in the supine position. In addition, it was found that alternating between different pairs of positions has different effects on uterine efficiency. Alternating between supine and sitting seems to reduce the efficiency of uterine activity compared with alternating between supine and standing or side-lying. It was also noted that many women had difficulty in remaining upright and/or mobilising during labour, especially towards the end of the first stage of labour and during the second stage. No conclusion could be drawn regarding the effects of position and mobilisation on reported pain or duration of labour.

A fairly large US randomised trial compared walking in the first stage of labour (*n* = 536) with no walking (usual care) (*n* = 531).[87] [EL = 1+] Women in spontaneous labour following uncomplicated pregnancies were randomised once labour had been established (cervical dilatation of 3–5 cm). Neither group underwent continuous electronic fetal monitoring (EFM) unless a fetal heart rate abnormality was detected using intermittent monitoring, epidural anaesthesia was requested or oxytocin augmentation was required. This then excluded any further ambulation. The amount of time spent walking undertaken by both groups of women was recorded by the attending nurse, and the distance walked was recorded using a pedometer (how the use of this instrument may have impacted upon the comfort of the labouring women is not discussed). Of the women assigned to the walking group, 22% chose not to walk. Of the 420 women who actually walked during labour, the mean walking time was 56 minutes (SD = 46 minutes). The degree of ambulation in the non-walking group was minimal. There were no significant differences between the characteristics of women in the two trial groups. Analysis was on an intention-to-treat basis. No significant differences were found between the two groups in terms of labour outcomes (e.g. length, use of oxytocin for augmentation, use of analgesia), mode of giving birth, maternal or neonatal outcomes. Of those women who walked during labour, 278 were asked if they would do so in a future labour: 99% said that they would.

A prospective Australian RCT was carried out to determine whether there was any advantage or disadvantage to giving women the option to ambulate during labour compared with labouring in the recumbent position.[88] [EL = 1+] All women entering the trial (*n* = 196) underwent continuous EFM using a scalp electrode. This was carried out via telemetry for women in the ambulant group. The demographic and obstetric characteristics of the two trial groups were similar. Analysis was carried out on an intention-to-treat basis. No significant differences were found between the groups in terms of labour outcomes, mode of giving birth, maternal or neonatal outcome. Only 37 of the 96 women allocated to the ambulant group (39%) actually chose to ambulate for 30 minutes or longer. Of those who did ambulate, the mean time spent in an upright position was 1.5 hours (SD 0.8 hours). During the time of recruitment of women into the trial, 389 declined to participate, 46% for fear of losing the option to ambulate during labour.

In a small, older, UK prospective RCT, 68 women in spontaneous labour were allocated to either an ambulant or recumbent group for the first stage of labour.[89] [EL = 1−] Trial participants were recruited from a group of women who had expressed antenatally a desire to be ambulant. Each group comprised 17 nulliparous women and 17 parous women. Continuous EFM was performed for all women with the use of a fetal scalp electrode (via telemetry for the ambulant group) and contractions were monitored using an intrauterine pressure catheter. A number of significant differences were noted between the two groups, all in favour of the ambulant group. Ambulant women were given less analgesia, contractions were less frequent and were of greater amplitude, duration of labour was shorter, there were more normal births and babies' Apgar scores were also higher in the ambulant group. For women in the ambulant group, the mean time spent mobilising was 2.2 hours [range 0.8 to 8.3 hours]. The selection bias inherent in this study needs to be taken into consideration when interpreting these findings.

An RCT conducted in Argentina compared the pain perceptions of two groups of 50 women allocated to adopt alternately a vertical (sitting, standing or walking) or horizontal (lie on side or back) position for periods of 15 minutes throughout the first stage of labour.[90] [EL = 1+] Each woman thus acted as her own control and was asked to adopt a position of her own choosing between the assigned position periods in order to reduce 'carry-over' effects. The participants were all staff connected with the public education sector. Pain levels were measured during each 15 minutes horizontal or vertical position period using two validated pain scales (a Likert-type scale and a 10 cm visual analogue scale (VAS)). Pain scores were reported for each dilatation interval (2–3 cm, 4–5 cm, 6–7 cm and 8–9 cm). During the first half of the first stage (i.e. from 2 to 5 cm cervical dilatation) there was no difference noted in reported pain between the two positions. As labour progressed however, there was a statistically significant difference noted in measured pain levels, both abdominal contraction pain and lumbar pain, with higher levels of pain being associated with horizontal positions.

A small US trial randomly allocated nulliparous women in spontaneous labour to upright (*n* = 20) or recumbent (*n* = 20) groups.[91] [EL = 1+] The recumbent group included the options of supine, lateral or all fours. The upright group included standing, walking, kneeling, sitting or squatting. Outcome measures included the duration of the active phase of labour (defined as 4–9 cm dilatation), uterine contraction pattern and maternal comfort (as measured by a researcher using a standardised tool). Women allocated to the upright group had a significantly shorter active phase of labour (mean difference 90.25 minutes, *P* = 0.003) and had contractions that were longer lasting and more frequent than women in the recumbent group. There was no significant difference in reports of women's physical comfort.

Evidence statement
Surprisingly, there are no trials examining the effect of freedom of movement throughout labour compared with restriction of movement on outcomes such as comfort, labour progress and fetal wellbeing. There is a lack of high-level evidence to suggest that either mobilisation or any particular position in the first stage of labour affects outcomes.

Recommendation on mobilisation and position

Women should be encouraged and helped to move and adopt whatever positions they find most comfortable throughout labour.

4.3 Support in labour

Clinical question
Is there evidence that support in labour for women improves outcomes? interventions include:

- any support from partners
- other birth supporters
- health professionals
- continuity of care.

4.3.1 One-to-one care

Introduction
Traditionally, women have been attended and supported by other women during labour and birth. However, with the movement of the majority of births from home to hospital since the middle of the 20th century, continuous support has become the exception rather than standard care. Women's support needs in labour have been shown to have four dimensions: emotional, information support, physical support and advocacy. Women in the UK today usually labour with their partners present, providing them with physical and emotional commitment, but for some women this may be insufficient to provide them with the level and type of support that they need in the context of a modern institutional birth environment.

Previous guideline
One-to-one care is defined as continuous presence and support either by husband/partners, midwives or other birth supporters during labour and childbirth. One-to-one care was reviewed in the NICE *Caesarean Section* guideline.[6] The guideline reviewed one systematic review and recommended that women should be informed that continuous support during labour from women with or without training reduces the likelihood of CS.

Description of included studies
The updated systematic review was identified during the search for this guideline.[92] The systematic review examined 15 trials including 12 791 women in both high income and low income countries (Australia, Belgium, Botswana, Canada, Finland, France, Greece, Guatemala, Mexico, South Africa and the USA). The impact of one-to-one care was considered different by status of caregivers, so that the review was stratified by the care providers. In eight trials, the support was provided by a member of the hospital staff, e.g. a midwife, student midwife or nurse. In the remaining seven trials, the providers were not members of the hospital staff; they were women with or without special training, a childbirth educator, a retired nurse, or a close female relative, usually the woman's mother. There is no identified trial that investigated the effectiveness of continuous support by husbands or partners. In nine of the trials, hospital policy permitted women to be accompanied by their husbands/partners or other family members during labour, while in the other six trials, no additional support people were allowed. Presence of husbands or partners was considered as usual practice in the UK. [EL = 1+]

Review findings

Labour events
a) Stratified analysis by care-providers

Women supported by a member of the hospital staff were less likely to have analgesia than women receiving standard care (RR 0.97 [95% CI 0.95 to 0.99]). This difference was also apparent if the support was provided by birth attendants other than professionally trained staff (RR 0.83 [95% CI 0.77 to 0.89]).

b) Meta-analysis of all trials

Meta-analysis of findings from nine trials without stratification, which included 10 322 women, showed no significant difference in length of labour (WMD (random) −0.28 hours [95% CI −0.64 to 0.08 hours]).

Birth events
a) Stratified analysis by care-providers

Women supported by a hospital staff member were more likely to have a spontaneous vaginal birth (RR 1.03 [95% CI 1.01 to 1.06]), less likely to have an instrumental vaginal birth (RR 0.92 [95% CI 0.85 to 0.99]) or caesarean section (CS) birth (RR 0.92 [95% CI 0.85 to 0.99]). If support was given by non-hospital staff, the positive impact on spontaneous vaginal birth, instrumental vaginal birth and caesarean birth remained, with RR of 1.12 [95% CI 1.07 to 1.18], 0.59 [95% CI 0.42 to 0.81] and 0.74 [95% CI 0.61 to 0.90], respectively.

b) Meta-analysis of all trials

There appeared to be no difference in the rates of perineal trauma. One trial, which investigated the rate of episiotomy when support was provided from a specially trained nurse, found no significant difference between supported women versus those with standard care (RR 0.97 [95% CI 0.90 to 1.05]). Meta-analysis of two trials, both of which investigated support by a member of hospital staff, showed no significant difference in perineal trauma (RR 0.99 [95% CI 0.95 to 1.03]).

Newborn events
Meta-analysis of trials showed no significant difference in low 5 minute Apgar scores (seven trials, total RR 0.81 [95% CI 0.56 to 1.16]; with support by a member of hospital staff RR 0.83 [95% CI 0.56 to 1.22] and with support by non-hospital staff RR 0.64 [95% CI 0.22 to 1.92]); and admission to neonatal units (four trials RR 0.94 [95% CI 0.82 to 1.09]).

Women's satisfaction and experience of childbirth
Meta-analysis of eight trials showed that there was no significant difference in dissatisfaction and negative experience of childbirth between women supported by a hospital staff member (RR 0.83 [95% CI 0.67 to 1.02]) and women receiving standard care, but there was a significant difference if support was provided by a non-hospital staff member (RR 0.64 [95% CI 0.58 to 0.78]).

Women's mental and psychological health
There was one trial that investigated the incidence of postpartum depression in women given support by a specially trained nurse.[93] There were fewer supported women who reported postpartum depression than those receiving standard care, but this difference was not statistically significant (RR 0.89 [95% CI 0.75 to 1.05]). Another trial investigated the impact of postpartum self-esteem on women given support by a retired nurse.[94] There was no evidence of a difference in the number of women with low postpartum esteem, between supported care and standard care (RR 1.07 [95% CI 0.82 to 1.40]).

Long-term outcomes
One trial investigated the long-term outcomes of support by a specially trained nurse for women in labour. There were no significant differences between the trial groups for poor relationship with partner postpartum (RR 1.00 [95% CI 0.80 to 1.23]), postpartum urinary incontinence (RR 0.93 [95% CI 0.81 to 1.06]) or postpartum faecal incontinence (RR 0.89 [95% CI 0.64 to 1.24]).

Evidence statement
In general, the included studies were of good quality. A range of professionals prividing one-to-one care, including obstetric nurses, was identified within the studies. There is evidence to suggest that women with one-to-one care throughout their labour are significantly less likely to have caesarean section or instrumental vaginal birth, will be more satisfied and will have a positive experience of childbirth. This impact becomes more apparent when non-professional staff members, rather than professional staff members, care for them. The non-professional person

providing one-to-one care in labour within these studies varied in their level of training, background and in the context of care.

There is little evidence on perinatal mortality and the long-term wellbeing of women and their children.

There is also a lack of high-level evidence to suggest that support by partners, other family members or friends affects clinical outcomes.

GDG interpretation of the evidence
Although in the UK midwives usually provide the majority of care during labour and childbirth, there were no studies identified that compared one-to-one support from a midwife with that provided by another professional. The reviewed studies are from a range of countries, some of which are not representative of the UK setting, especially in that partners/support persons were not usually allowed to accompany women during labour. This means it is not possible to extrapolate all these findings regarding support from a non-professional person to the UK. The role of maternity care support workers remains unevaluated in the UK.

Recommendations on one-to-one care

A woman in established labour should receive supportive one-to-one care.

A woman in established labour should not be left on her own except for short periods or at the woman's request.

Women should be encouraged to have support by birth partner(s) of their choice.

Research recommendation on one-to-one care

Studies should evaluate the impact of a standardised training programme for maternity care support workers in the intrapartum period. Outcomes should include: maternal and neonatal mortality, adverse outcomes, long-term outcomes, women's satisfaction and costs as outcomes.

4.3.2 Continuity of care

Introduction
Continuity of care in maternity services refers to both continuity of carer and consistency of care. The former has received most attention both in terms of policy and in research where continuity of care is defined in terms of continuity of carer and describes care provided by a midwife or a small group of midwives, from early pregnancy to the postnatal period. Continuity of carer was highlighted as a key component of good maternity care in the Health Committee Second Report: Maternity Services, vol. 1 (1992) (the Winterton Report),[95] and further endorsed by the Report of the Expert Maternity Group at the Department of Health (the Changing Childbirth Report) (1993),[96] which identified among its ten key indicators of success (page 70) that:

- every woman should know one midwife who ensures continuity of her midwifery care – the named midwife
- every woman should know the lead professional who has a key role in the planning and provision of her care
- at least 75% of women should know the person who cares for them during their birth.

Two main models of midwifery care have evolved as a way of organising services so as to provide continuity of carer in a way that is sustainable within the existing NHS structure, namely team midwifery and caseload midwifery. Team midwifery is a team of midwives looking after a group of women and caseload midwifery aims for a more personal relationship with the woman and involves a small group of midwives. Sizes of team midwifery teams vary greatly, ranging from four midwives to ten or more, with hospital-based teams tending to be larger than community-based teams. The aim of most team midwifery schemes is to increase the chance that women will be cared for in labour by a midwife they have met antenatally, with the focus on intrapartum continuity often taking precedence over antenatal and postnatal continuity. Caseload midwifery describes a system of care whereby one midwife (sometimes referred to as the 'named midwife') is responsible, and provides the majority of the care, for a group of women backed up by a small group of associate midwives (usually two or three). When there is one midwife backing up a named midwife this system is also know as 'one-to-one' care.[97] Team midwifery schemes have usually been hospital based, or integrated across hospital and community settings. Caseload midwifery schemes tend to be community based. These two systems of care will be reviewed separately below. Some studies investigated a package of care which included both care in midwife-led units and continuity of care. This review includes schemes which provide care in a variety of settings, including traditional delivery suite, birthing rooms within a traditional midwifery suite and separate birth units. For the purposes of this review where one midwife has taken responsibility for a group of women this has been categorised as caseload midwifery. Where there has been shared responsibility between a group of midwives this has been categorised as team midwifery.

While much research confirmed that continuity of carer was highly valued by many women, concern has been raised about the effects on midwives of working in systems designed to provide continuity of care, particularly hospital-based team midwifery schemes.[98]

Previous guideline
Continuity of care was reviewed in the NICE 'Antenatal Care' clinical guideline.[99] Two systematic reviews were appraised in the guideline. It was recommended that antenatal care should be provided by a small group of carers with whom the woman feels comfortable and there should be continuity of care throughout the antenatal period. They also recommended that a system of clear referral paths should be established so that pregnant women who require additional care are managed and treated by the appropriate specialist teams when problems are identified.

Team midwifery

Description of included studies
There were two systematic reviews[100,101] and four RCTs[102–108] identified. One systematic review included two trials,[100] and another included seven trials.[101] The trials that were included in the former systematic review were all included in the latter systematic review. A new meta-analysis was conducted by using a total of ten trials.[100–108] [EL = 1+]

Among the ten trials, three were conducted in England, five in Australia, one in Canada, and one in Sweden. A total of 1229 women were involved. The ten trials were all evaluations of team midwifery, with teams ranging in size from four to ten midwives. Six of the ten studies were of community-based teams coming into the hospital or midwife-led unit to provide care during labour and the postnatal period. The review here relates to team midwifery rather than continuity of carer per se.

A cross-sectional study[98,109] with a 5% random sample of midwives in England ($n = 1166$) measured occupational stress, especially burnout, in midwives, comparing those in midwifery teams (hospital-based and community-based) with traditional hospital-based midwives and GP-attached midwives.

Review findings
Details of the included trials on team midwifery care are summarised in Table 4.1.

Labour events
It was not possible to conduct a meta-analysis on the length of labour owing to the different measures used. There were no consistent findings in duration of either the first, second or third stage of labour. Meta-analysis was conducted for interventions related to labour as follows. Induction (nine trials, $n = 10\,341$): RR 0.96 [95% CI 0.88 to 1.05] (test for heterogeneity $P = 0.11$); augmentation (nine trials, $n = 10\,201$): RR 0.83 [95% CI 0.78 to 0.90] (test for heterogeneity $P < 0.0001$); epidural (ten trials, $n = 10\,399$): RR 0.80 [95% CI 0.74 to 0.86] (test for heterogeneity $P = 0.04$); opioid analgesia (nine trials, $n = 10\,146$): RR 0.75 [95% CI 0.75 to 0.84], $P < 0.00001$ (test for heterogeneity $P < 0.00001$). Overall, women receiving care from a team of midwives were less likely to have interventions than women receiving standard maternity care, although there was a significant level of heterogeneity among these trials.

Birth events
Meta-analysis was conducted for interventions related to birth, with findings as follows. CS (ten trials, $n = 10\,622$): RR 0.90 [95% CI 0.80 to 1.00] (test for heterogeneity $P = 0.31$); instrumental vaginal birth (nine trials, $n = 10\,449$): RR 0.85 [95% CI 0.76 to 0.95] (test for heterogeneity $P = 0.52$); episiotomy (ten trials, $n = 9810$): RR 0.79 [95% CI 0.74 to 0.85] (test for heterogeneity $P = 0.02$). Overall, women receiving care from a team of midwives were significantly less likely to have these interventions.

Six trials reported no significant difference in postpartum haemorrhage (PPH) and five trials reported no significant difference in either manual removal of placenta or retained placenta.

Newborn outcomes
Meta-analysis was conducted for interventions related to newborn events with results as follows. Condition at birth (Apgar score less than 7 at 5 minutes) (seven trials, $n = 6135$): RR 1.17 [95% CI 0.81 to 1.680] (test for heterogeneity $P = 0.68$); admission to neonatal units (nine trials, $n = 10\,404$): RR 0.90 [95% CI 0.79 to 1.03] (test for heterogeneity $P = 0.05$); perinatal mortality (nine trials, $n = 10\,423$): RR 1.63 [95% CI 1.04 to 2.56], $P = 0.03$ (test for heterogeneity $P = 0.69$). Although there were no differences between groups regarding Apgar score at 5 minutes or admission to neonatal intensive care, there was a significantly higher perinatal mortality noted for babies born to women cared for within the team midwifery model.

Women's satisfaction and experience of childbirth
Virtually all the trials reported on women's satisfaction and their assessment of the childbirth experience. This was measured using various qualitative methods. All the trials reported that team midwifery systems of care designed to provide intrapartum care by a midwife met antenatally increased women's satisfaction and resulted in more positive experiences of childbirth compared with standard maternity care.

Women's mental and psychological health
One trial reported on the emotional wellbeing of women who were given continual support from a team of midwives. Responses to the Edinburgh Postnatal Depression Scale (EPDS) 2 months after the birth showed that 16% of women in the team midwifery care group and 12% in the standard care group were depressed (EPDS score > 12) – a non-statistically significant difference ($P = 0.19$).

Long-term outcomes
There were no long-term outcomes reported in the relevant articles.

Wellbeing of healthcare professionals
The cross-sectional study[98,109] ($n = 1166$) measured occupational stress, especially burnout, in midwives, comparing those in midwifery teams (hospital-based and community-based) with traditional hospital-based midwives and GP-attached midwives. Burnout was measured using an adaptation of the the Maslach Burnout Inventory (MBI). The study found that burnout was associated with a lack of freedom to make decisions at work, longer contracted hours and low control over work pattern. Findings showed that midwives working in hospital-based teams had the highest reported levels of burnout, followed by traditional hospital-based midwives. No relationship was found between higher levels of burnout and continuity rate, number of nights worked on-call and type of caseload. It would appear, however, that this association is strongly linked with working within the constraints of a hospital-based system where midwives tend to have less autonomy over working pattern and decision making compared with community-based midwives.

Table 4.1 Details of trials of team midwifery care

Trial	Team description	Routine antenatal visits by doctor	Setting for intrapartum care	System for maternal transfer to obstetric team	Maternal transfer to obstetric team in midwife-managed group (%)	Restriction of medication and technology	Postnatal visits at home by team midwives	Control group
Flint et al. (1989) England Reported in Waldenstrom and Turnbull (1998)[101] and Hodnett (1999)[100]	Team of 4 midwives	At booking, 36 and 41 weeks	Traditional hospital	No	Not reported	No	Yes	Hospital antenatal, intrapartum and postnatal care provided by variety of obstetricians and midwives
MacVicar et al. (1993) England Reported in Waldenstrom and Turnbull (1998)[101]	2 midwifery sisters + 8 staff midwives	At 26, 36 and 41 weeks	3 birthing rooms	Yes	Antenatal – 23% first stage of labour – 18% second stage of labour and after birth – 4%	Yes (EFM and epidural)	No	Antenatal shared care by GPs and community midwives, birth within specialist unit by hospital staff
Kenny et al. (1994) Australia Reported in Waldenstrom and Turnbull (1998)[101]	Team of 8 (6.8 full-time midwife equivalents)	At booking, 32 and 40 weeks	Traditional hospital	No	Not reported	No	Yes	Hospital antenatal, intrapartum and postnatal care provided by a variety of doctors and midwives
Rowley et al. (1995) Australia Reported in Waldenstrom and Turnbull (1998)[101] and Hodnett (1999)[100]	Team of 6 midwives	At 12–16, 36 and 41 weeks	Traditional hospital	No	Not reported	No	No	Hospital antenatal, intrapartum and postnatal care provided by a variety of doctors and midwives
Harvey et al. (1996) Canada Reported in Waldenstrom and Turnbull (1998)[101]	Team of 7 midwives	At booking and 36 weeks	1 birthing room	Yes	Antenatal – 1% Intrapartum – 26%	No	Yes	Family physician or obstetrician selected by woman, in hospital care in all city hospitals
Waldenstrom et al. (1997) Sweden Reported in Waldenstrom and Turnbull (1998)[101]	Team of 10 midwives (8.5 full-time equivalents)	On medical indication only	Birth centre	Yes	Antenatal – 13% Intrapartum – 19% Postnatal – 2%	Yes (EFM, epidural, pethidine, nitrous oxide, oxytocin)	Yes	Antenatal care provided by community midwives, 1 or 2 routine visits by doctor, hospital antenatal, intrapartum and postnatal care provided by variety of midwives in close collaboration with obstetricians

Trial	Team description	Routine antenatal visits by doctor	Setting for intrapartum care	System for maternal transfer to obstetric team	Maternal transfer to obstetric team in midwife-managed group (%)	Restriction of medication and technology	Postnatal visits at home by team midwives	Control group
Homer et al. (2001)[103] Australia Homer et al. (2002)[104] Australia	Team of 6 midwives	An obstetrician was available at all antenatal clinic sessions. Details not given as to whether consultations with obstetrician routine or as necessary	Traditional hospital Team midwives worked 12 hour shifts on delivery suite compared with 8 hour shifts for standard care midwives	Not reported	Not reported	No	Yes	Antenatal care provided by a variety of midwives in the antenatal clinic and the woman's GP. Intrapartum and postnatal care provided by a different set of midwives in each clinical area
Biro et al. (2000)[105] Australia Biro et al. (2003)[106] Australia	Team of 7 midwives provided care for low-risk women and high-risk women alongside obstetricians (integrated team)	At 12–16, 28 and 36 weeks or as necessary	Traditional hospital Team midwives worked longer shifts on delivery suite than standard care midwives	Not reported (but not necessary for obstetric reasons as team work with obstetricians)	Not reported (but not necessary for obstetric reasons as team work with obstetricians)	No	No	Care provided by a variety of staff. Antenatally this included obstetricians, GPs, hospital-based midwives and community-based midwives. Cared for by a variety of obstetricians and midwives during labour and postnatally
Waldenstrom et al. (2000)[107] Australia	Team of 8 midwives	Not reported	Traditional hospital Team midwives worked same shift patterns as standard care midwives	Not reported	Overall – 2.2%	No	No	Care provided by a variety of obstetricians and midwives antenatally, often also involved GP. Variety of midwives allocated to delivery suite and postnatal ward provided care in these areas. Comparison group also included option of care at birth centre where care was provided by a small group of midwives throughout antenatal, intrapartum and postnatal period
Hicks et al. (2003)[102] England	Team of 8 midwives	Referred as necessary to a consultant but still had care managed by midwifery team	Traditional hospital delivery suite but working to community midwifery shift patterns with on-calls	Not reported	None	No	Yes	Antenatal care provided mainly by GP and/or community midwives. Intrapartum and postnatal care undertaken by variety of midwives. Also included Domino scheme (care provided by small group of community midwives with care led by one midwife)

EFM = electronic fetal monitoring.

Caseload midwifery

Description of included studies

One UK RCT and one UK cluster RCT were identified for inclusion in this review. The RCT compared women cared for by a named midwife with three associate midwives (*n* = 648) in a hospital-based midwifery development unit (MDU) with women receiving shared care (*n* = 651) (majority of care provided by GP with three or four visits to the obstetrician at the hospital).[110] [EL = 1+] The cluster RCT was randomised on the basis of geographical area, with three areas in each cluster.[97] [EL = 1−] In three areas caseload midwifery care was provided to all low-risk women booked for maternity care (*n* = 770). The caseload model involved each named midwife being allocated 35–40 women to care for, with back-up provided by one or two associate midwives. In the remaining three areas shared care was provided to women (*n* = 735) by the GP and community midwife in the established way, with occasional visits to the hospital to see an obstetrician. Details for each study are presented in Table 4.2.

Review findings

It was not possible to perform a meta-analysis owing to the methodological differences between the two studies.

Labour events

Findings from the (non-cluster) RCT showed that women cared for within the caseload midwifery model had fewer inductions of labour: 199 (33.3%) versus 146 (23.9%); difference 9.4% [95% CI 4.4% to 14.5%]. There was no significant difference found for other labour events including augmentation of labour (difference −3.4%), opioid analgesia (difference 2.5%) and epidural (difference 1.4%). The lower use of epidural analgesia (10% versus 15%) and oxytocin augmentation of labour (46% versus 53%) was also evident in the cluster RCT. No differences in induction of labour were noted, however.

Birth events

Findings from the RCT showed that significantly more women in the caseload midwifery group had an intact perineum following birth: 120 (23.6%) versus 160 30.5%, while fewer had an episiotomy: 173 (34.0%) versus 147 (28.0%) or a first- or second-degree perineal tear: 216 (42.4%) versus 218 (41.5%); test for overall difference *P* = 0.02 (χ^2). No significant differences were found between groups for mode of birth, with the incidence of spontaneous vaginal birth being 73.7% in the shared care group compared with 73.5% in the caseload midwifery group. Findings from the cluster RCT showed no differences between groups for perineal trauma or mode of birth.

Newborn outcomes

Findings from the RCT showed no difference for newborn outcomes between groups, Apgar score 8–10 at 5 minutes: 565 (96.6%) versus 589 (97.8%), difference −1.2% [95% CI −3.1% to 0.6%]; admission to special care baby unit (SCBU) 40 (6.6%) versus 33 (5.4%), difference 1.2% [95% CI −1.4% to 3.9%]. There were nine stillbirths plus neonatal deaths in the shared care group compared with four in the caseload midwifery group (difference 0.4% [95% CI −0.4% to 1.2%]. Findings from the cluster RCT also showed no differences between the groups in newborn outcomes. There were a total of 11 stillbirths plus neonatal deaths (1.5%) in the shared care group and six (0.7%) in the caseload midwifery group (difference 0.8% [95% CI −0.2% to 1.8%]).

Women's satisfaction and experience of childbirth

In the RCT women were found to be significantly more satisfied with their maternity care; antenatal care: difference in mean scores 0.48 [95% CI 0.41 to 0.55]; intrapartum care: 0.28 [95% CI 0.18 to 0.37]; hospital-based postnatal care: 0.57 [95% CI 0.45 to 0.70]; home-based postnatal care: 0.33 [95% CI 0.25 to 0.42].

A basic cost comparison of team midwifery versus conventional midwifery

Rationale

The evidence does not suggest that team midwifery leads to significantly better outcomes. Indeed, a meta-analysis undertaken as part of this guideline suggested that team midwifery resulted in statistically significant increases in perinatal mortality compared with the standard model: RR 1.64 [95% CI 1.04 to 2.58], *P* = 0.03.

Table 4.2 Details of included studies of caseload midwifery model

Trial	Description of caseload midwifery practice	Routine antenatal visits by doctor	Setting for intrapartum care	System for maternal transfer to obstetric team	Maternal transfer to obstetric team in midwife-managed group	Restriction of medication and technology	Postnatal visits at home by caseload midwives	Control group
Turnbull et al. (1996)[110] Scotland	Named midwife responsible for woman's care from booking until discharge to health visitor. Back-up by associate midwife if not available. Implemented within a new midwifery development unit	No. Referred to obstetrician as necessary	Birthing room in midwifery development unit (alongside)	Not described	Overall – 32.8% (permanently transferred)	No	Yes	Shared care provided by GP, a variety of midwives and obstetricians based in antenatal clinic, delivery suite and postnatal ward with community midwives providing postnatal care at home
North Staffordshire Changing Childbirth Research Team (2000)[97] England	One GP-attached community midwife with a caseload of 35–40 women. Caseload midwives worked in pairs or threes to provide 24 hour cover	Scheduled in to the shared care system	Traditional hospital setting, but caseload midwives did provide home assessment for women in early labour	Not described	Not reported	No	Yes	Community midwives part of team providing shared care to women alongside the woman's GP and hospital-based obstetricians and midwives

Anecdotally, a number of providers appear to have ceased providing a team midwifery service on the grounds of cost. Similarly, one reason team midwifery did not become more widely established was because additional funding was not made available for it. This would seem to indicate, at least from the perspective of service providers, that team midwifery is a more costly service than the conventional model. If it is both more expensive and less effective we can say unambiguously that it is not cost-effective, being 'dominated' by the conventional model.

At this stage we do not have the detailed cost data to do a full cost comparison of the two models of care. The only quantitative information we have at this stage comes from a maternity unit in the north of England currently offering a form of team midwifery care. They state that they have an annual midwife to birth ratio of 1 : 26 against a national average of 1 : 33. At this stage we do not know how representative this unit's ratio is of team midwifery models in general but it does at least seem consistent with the perception that team midwifery (TM) is a more resource-intensive service. If we assume that the this service was typical then we could estimate the additional midwife staffing cost per birth as follows:

Annual cost of midwife	$= £40,000$ approximately
Hospital births	$= n$
Additional midwifery staffing in TM model	$= (1/26 - 1/33) \times n = 0.008 \times n$
Additional midwifery staffing cost	$= £40,000 \times 0.008 \times n = £326 \times n$
Additional midwifery cost per birth	$= £326$

Clearly, a full cost comparison would also have to include 'downstream' cost differentials between the two models of care, especially as the meta-analysis undertaken for the guideline found the following intervention differences for team midwifery:

Induction:	pooled OR 0.88 [95% CI 0.80 to 0.98], $P = 0.02$
Augmentation:	pooled OR 0.83 [95% CI 0.76 to 0.91], $P < 0.001$
EFM:	pooled OR 0.30 [95% CI 0.27 to 0.33], $P < 0.001$
Epidural:	pooled OR 0.77 [95% CI 0.71 to 0.85], $P < 0.001$
Narcotics:	pooled OR 0.72 [95% CI 0.66 to 0.78], $P < 0.001$
Caesarean section:	pooled OR 0.91 [95% CI 0.81 to 1.02], $P = 0.12$; NS
Instrumental birth:	pooled OR 0.84 [95% CI 0.75 to 0.95], $P = 0.005$
Episiotomy:	pooled OR 0.73 [95% CI 0.67 to 0.80], $P < 0.001$

This meta-analysis suggests that women receiving care from team midwifery have less intervention and therefore 'downstream' costs may, to some extent, offset higher staffing costs of service provision. The most important of these 'downstream' savings is likely to relate to a lower rate of instrumental vaginal birth and the saving per birth that this might be expect to produce is calculated below.

From NHS Reference Costs (2004) finished consultant episode data:

Normal birth	$= 382\ 669$
Instrumental births	$= 64\ 995$
Caesarean sections	$= 130\ 353$
Total births	$= 578\ 017$

Odds of instrumental$_{\text{conventional birth}}$	$= 64\ 995/513\ 022 = 0.127$
Odds of instrumental$_{\text{TM birth}}$	$= 0.84$ OR from meta-analysis $\times 0.127 = 0.107$
Number of instrumental$_{\text{TM}}$ births	$= 55\ 870$
Reduction in instrumental births due to TM	$= 64\ 995 - 55\ 870 = 9125$

Cost of instrumental vaginal birth	$= £1,263$
Cost of normal vaginal birth	$= £863$

Cost saving of reduction in instrumental births due to TM	$= 9125 \times (£1,263 - £863) = £3.65$ million
Cost saving per birth	$= £3,650,000/578\ 017 \quad = £6.30$

While this is a substantial saving it falls a long way short of what would be required to offset the additional staffing costs of providing a team midwifery service.

This analysis does not constitute a proper costing of the two alternative models of care. However, if its assumptions are accepted it would suggest that a team midwifery model is more expensive than a conventional model of midwifery care. When taken together with some evidence of higher perinatal mortality it could not be recommended on cost-effectiveness grounds.

Evidence statement

Team midwifery
In general, the studies included were of good quality. There was heterogeneity between the studies, particularly in both the settings for intrapartum care and the size of the team, which makes interpretation difficult. There is evidence to support that women cared for by a team of midwives throughout their pregnancy, intrapartum and postnatal period are less likely to have interventions during labour, and that such care is highly valued by women. However, there is an increased perinatal mortality associated with team midwifery care. There was no indication as to which component of care, or combination of components of care, might have contributed to this.

There is some evidence that midwives working in hospital-based teams experience higher levels of burnout than those working in community-based teams.

There is little evidence about its cost-effectiveness.

Caseload midwifery
Findings from two trials show that women cared for in a caseload midwifery system are less likely to receive interventions during labour and that women prefer this system of care compared with traditional shared care. No evidence of difference in other maternal or neonatal outcomes was found.

There is no evidence about its cost-effectiveness.

Recommendation on continuity of care

Team midwifery (defined as a group of midwives providing care and taking shared responsibility for a group of women from the antenatal, through intrapartum to the postnatal period) is not recommended.

Research recommendations on continuity of care

Studies are needed that investigate the components affecting a woman's satisfaction with her birth experience, including her emotional and psychological wellbeing. A robust method of assessing a woman's satisfaction is also needed.

There should be studies carried out to investigate the effects of caseload midwifery (defined as one midwife providing care and taking responsibility for a group of women from the antenatal, through intrapartum to the postnatal period) on women, babies and healthcare professionals, including cost-effectiveness and long-term outcomes.

4.4 Eating and drinking in labour

Clinical question
What is the effectiveness of the following interventions or techniques in labour on outcomes?

• restricting fluids and nutrition.

4.4.1 Reducing gastric aspiration in labour

Routine prophylactic drugs in normal labour for reducing gastric aspiration

Description of included studies
A systematic review identified three randomised controlled trials.[111] [EL = 1+] The intervention was any drug, with any route of administration, in any dosage. The drug categories were particulate and non-particulate antacids, H2-receptor antagonists, dopamine antagonists and proton pump inhibitors, although no trials were identified on proton pump inhibitors. The primary outcome measure was the incidence of gastric aspiration in the woman. The review found none of the trials to be of good quality.

Review findings

There was limited evidence to suggest that antacids may reduce the chance of vomiting in labour when compared with no intervention (one trial, *n* = 578; RR 0.46 [95% CI 0.27 to 0.77]). When individual antacids were compared with each other, when tested in one study, there was no significant difference in incidence of vomiting (Gelusil® versus Maalox® (*n* = 300): RR 0.83 [95% CI 0.39 to 1.75]; Gelusil versus Mylanta II® (*n* = 325): RR 1.32 [95% CI 0.58 to 2.99]); Maalox versus Mylanta II (*n* = 285): RR 1.59 [95% CI 0.69 to 3.65]). There was no significant difference in vomiting (one trial, *n* = 1287; RR 0.96 [95% CI 0.73 to 1.27]); CS (one trial, *n* = 1287; RR 0.93 [95% CI 0.59 to 1.47]); emergency general anaesthetic (one trial, *n* = 1287; RR 0.92 [95% CI 0.62 to 1.35]); PPH (one trial, *n* = 1287; RR 0.83 [95% CI 0.08 to 9.14]) and stillbirth (one trial, *n* = 1287; RR 0.69 [95% CI 0.17 to 2.89]) when H2-receptor antagonists were compared with antacids. Again, the number of participants was too small for the results to be conclusive.

Dopamine antagonists given alongside pethidine may reduce vomiting in labour (one trial, *n* = 584; RR 0.40 [95% CI 0.23 to 0.68]) when compared with placebo or no treatment given alongside pethidine, but the subgroups from the study population were too small to make an assured comment. The trial showed no significant difference in Apgar scores < 7 at 1 minute (RR 1.02 [95% CI 0.62 to 1.69]) or perinatal deaths (RR 1.22 [95% CI 0.24 to 6.21]). When two different dopamine antagonists were compared (metoclopramide versus perphenazine; *n* = 393) there was no significant difference in vomiting (RR 1.45 [95% CI 0.64 to 3.32]), Apgar score < 7 at 1 minute (RR 0.83 [95% CI 0.47 to 1.47]) or perinatal death (RR 0.25 [95% CI 0.03 to 2.23]).

Evidence statement

The studies were too small to assess the incidence of gastric aspiration, Mendelson syndrome and its consequences. There is limited evidence that antacids or dopamine antagonists given alongside pethidine reduce the chance of vomiting in labour. There is also limited evidence that H2-receptor antagonists have no impact on vomiting and other outcomes when compared with antacids.

There were no trials identified on proton pump inhibitors.

Recommendation on reducing gastric aspiration

Neither H2-receptor antagonists nor antacids should be given routinely to low-risk women.

Either H2-receptor antagonists or antacids should be considered for women who receive opioids or who have or develop risk factors that make a general anaesthetic more likely.

Research recommendation on reducing gastric aspiration

Use of either H2-receptor antagonists or antacids in labour should be evaluated for women who have or develop risk factors, who have opioids or who may need a general anaesthetic.

4.4.2 Eating and drinking in labour

Description of included studies

One randomised controlled trial, published in 1999, was identified (eating group = 45; starved group = 43). The study population comprised women in labour at 37 weeks of gestation or greater who had one baby with cephalic presentation. The intervention was a low-residue diet compared with water only.[112] [EL = 1+]

Review findings

The results showed that restriction of food throughout the course of labour results in a significant increase in plasma β-hydroxybutyrate (mean difference (MD) 0.38 mmol/l [95% CI 0.21 to 0.55 mmol/l], *P* < 0.001) and non-esterified fatty acids (MD 0.35 mmol/l [95% CI 0.22 to 0.48 mmol/l], *P* < 0.001) when compared with eating a low-residue diet. There was a significant increase in plasma glucose (MD 0.62 mmol/l [95% CI 0.22 to 1.01 mmol/l], *P* = 0.003) and insulin (MD 15.6 mmol/l [95% CI 2.9 to 28.3 mmol/l], *P* = 0.017) in the eating group when compared with the starved group. Gastric antral cross-sectional areas measured within 1 hour of labour were significantly higher in the eating group (MD 1.85 cm² [95% CI 0.81 to 2.88 cm²], $P = 0.001$) and these women were also twice as likely to vomit at or around giving birth (MD 19% [95% CI 0.8% to 38%], $P = 0.046$). The volumes vomited by the women in the eating group were significantly larger (MD 205 ml [95% CI 99 to 311 ml], $P = 0.001$) than the volumes vomited by women in the starved group. Lactic changes remained similar in both groups (MD −0.29 mmol/l [95% CI −0.71 to 0.12 mmol/l], $P = 0.167$). However, the study showed no significant differences in maternal outcomes (duration of first and second stage of labour, oxytocin requirements, mode of birth) or neonatal outcomes (Apgar scores, umbilical artery and venous blood gases) between the two groups of women (only means reported).

Evidence statement

The limited evidence suggests that a light diet significantly reduces the rise of plasma β-hydroxy-butyrate and the non-esterified fatty acids from which it is derived, while significantly increasing plasma glucose and insulin. However, the significant increase in volumes vomited must be considered, given that there were no significant differences in maternal or neonatal outcomes.

4.4.3 Intervention to prevent ketosis

Carbohydrate solution versus placebo

Description of included studies

Three randomised controlled trials, conducted by the same researchers at the Leyenburg Hospital in the Netherlands, were identified for review. The first study involved 201 nulliparous women randomised at 2–4 cm cervical dilatation (carbohydrate solution $n = 102$; placebo $n = 99$).[115] [EL = 1+] Women were able to consume small standardised amounts of food or drink on specific demand, with total amount of intake of kilojoules calculated for each woman at the end of the study. The second trial involved 202 nulliparous women randomised at 8–10 cm cervical dilatation, (carbohydrate solution $n = 100$; placebo $n = 102$).[113] [EL = 1+] Women were not allowed any other solutions. The final study involved 100 nulliparous women randomised at 8–10 cm cervical dilatation (carbohydrate solution $n = 50$; placebo $n = 50$).[114] Women were only allowed water in addition to the study solutions. [EL = 1+]

Review findings

In the first study, the median intake of study solution was 300 ml [range 17 to 1600 ml] in the placebo group and 400 ml [range 0 to 1600 ml] in the carbohydrate group ($P = 0.04$).[115] Similar proportions of women in both groups had a small additional intake (32% placebo group; 32.5% carbohydrate group). The median total calorific intake by the placebo group during the study was 0 kJ [range 0 to 1086 kJ] and 802 kJ [range 140 to 3618 kJ] for the carbohydrate group ($P < 0.001$). There was no statistically significant difference in the need for augmentation (RR 0.83 [95% CI 0.55 to 1.26]) or in the need for pain-relieving medication (opiates: RR 0.96 [95% CI 0.44 to 2.11]; epidural: RR 1.56 [95% CI 0.89 to 2.73]; Entonox: RR 3.64 [95% CI 0.72 to 15.8]), when women in the carbohydrate group were compared with women in the placebo group. While there was no significant difference between the carbohydrate and placebo groups for spontaneous birth (RR 0.90 [95% CI 0.68 to 1.17]) or for instrumental birth (RR 0.78 [95% CI 0.52 to 1.17]), the number of caesarean sections was significantly higher in the carbohydrate group (RR 2.9 [95% CI 1.29 to 6.54]). There were no significant differences in Apgar scores at 1 minute ($P = 0.17$), Apgar scores at 5 minutes ($P = 0.18$) or the arterial umbilical cord pH ($P = 0.07$) between the carbohydrate and placebo groups.

In the second study, the median intake of study solution was 200 ml [range 15 to 200 ml] in the placebo group and 200 ml (10 ml to 200 ml) in the carbohydrate group ($P = 0.42$).[113] There were no significant differences in spontaneous birth (RR 1.07 [95% CI 0.88 to 1.30]), instrumental birth (RR 1.05 [95% CI 0.69 to 1.60]) or CS (RR 0.15 [95% CI 0.02 to 1.16]) when the carbohydrate group was compared with the placebo group. No significant differences were observed in neonatal outcome: Apgar scores at 1 minute ($P = 0.22$), Apgar scores at 5 minutes ($P = 0.32$) or the arterial umbilical cord pH ($P = 0.80$), when the carbohydrate group was compared with the placebo group. In addition, when the carbohydrate and placebo groups were compared, there were no significant differences in changes in glucose ($P = 1.00$), lactate ($P = 0.07$) or plasma β-hydroxybutyrate ($P = 0.21$). There was a significant decrease in free fatty acid levels ($P = 0.02$), with the carbohydrate group tending to decrease to a higher degree.

In the third study, there were no significant differences in spontaneous birth ($P = 0.30$) or vaginal instrumental birth ($P = 0.84$) when the groups were compared.[114] However, the cohort was too small to draw conclusions. There were four caesarean sections in the placebo group and none in the carbohydrate group, but no statistical calculations were made.

Arterial umbilical cord pH, pCO_2, pO_2, HCO_3 and base excess were similar in both groups, as were venous umbilical cord results. However, no statistical data were presented.

Evidence statement
There is no evidence of difference in mode of birth, or fetal and neonatal acid–base balance between taking carbohydrate solution and placebo during labour.

Isotonic sports drink versus water

Description of included studies
One randomised controlled trial conducted in the UK and published in 2002 was identified.[116] The study involved 60 women at 37 weeks of gestation or greater, with a singleton fetus having cephalic presentation (sports drink group $n = 30$; water group $n = 30$). [EL = 1+]

Review findings
In the sports drink group there was a significant decrease in plasma β-hydroxybutyrate (MD −0.63 [95% CI −0.85 to −0.42]) and non-esterified fatty acids (MD −0.36 [95% CI −0.46 to −0.25]) when compared with the water-only group. Mean plasma glucose remained unchanged in the sports drink group, but decreased significantly in the water-only group (MD 0.76 mmol/l [95% CI 0.22 to 1.3 mmol/l]). The total quantity of liquid consumed was significantly higher ($P = 0.001$) in the sports drink group. The mean calorific intake was also higher for the sports drink group (47 kcal/hour (SD 16 kcal/hour) compared with the water-only group (0 kcal/hour). However, there was no significant difference in gastric antral cross-sectional area (MD −0.63 cm² [95% CI −1.12 to 0.70 cm²]), volume vomited within 1 hour of giving birth (MD 65 ml [95% CI −141 to 271 ml]) or volume vomited throughout labour (MD 66 ml [95% CI −115 to 246 ml]), when the two groups were compared. There was no difference between the two groups with respect to duration of labour, use of oxytocin, mode of giving birth or use of epidural analgesia. The study authors only presented the data as mean (SD) or proportion (%), but noted that all results were non-significant.

Evidence statement
There is a small amount of evidence to demonstrate that ketosis is prevented by relatively small calorific intake provided by isotonic drinks and that these provide an alternative source of nutrition that is rapidly emptied from the stomach and rapidly absorbed by the gastrointestinal tract.

There is limited evidence that labour outcomes were not compromised in either the sports drink group or the water-only group.

GDG interpretation of the evidence (eating and drinking in labour)
The development of ketosis in labour may be associated with nausea, vomiting and headache and may be a feature of exhaustion. Limited evidence suggests that a light diet or fluid carbohydrate intake in labour may reduce ketone body production while maintaining or increasing glucose and insulin. However, the volume of stomach contents may increase, increasing the chances of the woman being sick. There are no differences in any measured outcomes.

Recommendations on eating and drinking in labour

Women may drink during established labour and be informed that isotonic drinks may be more beneficial than water.

Women may eat a light diet in established labour unless they have received opioids or they develop risk factors that make a general anaesthetic more likely.

4.5 Hygiene measures during labour

Introduction
Puerperal sepsis was the leading cause of maternal mortality in the UK up until the early 20th century. Deaths due to sepsis fell dramatically following the widespread availability of antibiotics in the 1940s and the passing of the Abortion Act in 1967, with no deaths from sepsis being reported in the triennium 1982–84. Unfortunately, deaths from sepsis have been reported in each of the subsequent triennial reports, with 13 maternal deaths being directly attributed to sepsis in the 2000–02 report: five women following a vaginal birth, two after giving birth at home. The continued deaths of previously healthy women by overwhelming infection following childbirth and the spread of blood-borne diseases such as HIV highlight the importance of adequate hygiene measures during labour, to protect both the woman and her caregivers. Many women are exposed to invasive procedures during labour, all of which have potential to introduce pathogens into the genital tract. While the rituals of perineal shaving and the administration of enemas, previously performed to reduce contamination of the genital tract during birth, have been discredited, well-established practices of cleansing and draping the vulva prior to vaginal examinations and birth are still commonly practised.

General points
General points in infection control were reviewed in the NICE clinical guideline *Infection Control*, published in June 2003.[7] The guideline reviewed 169 articles for the section relating to general principles of infection control. Twenty-six recommendations were provided for areas of hand hygiene, use of personal protective equipment, and safe use and disposal of sharps. The recommendations below are specific to women in labour; however, they do not override the recommendations in the *Infection Control* guideline.

Clinical question
Are there effective hygiene strategies for vaginal birth out of water to protect both women and babies, and healthcare professionals?

- Strategies include vaginal examination and antisepsis.
- Outcomes include infection control and rates of infection.

4.5.1 Chlorhexidine vaginal douching and perineal cleaning

Chlorhexidine vaginal douching

Description of included studies
There was one systematic review identified. This review included three RCTs (*n* = 3012) in the USA, comparing chlorhexidine vaginal douching during labour with sterile water as a placebo control.[117] [EL = 1++]

Review findings

Women's outcomes
Three trials reported the incidence of chorioamnionitis, including 1514 and 1498 women in the chlorhexidine and placebo groups, respectively. There was no statistically significant difference between the two groups (RR 1.10 [95% CI 0.86 to 1.42]). The same three trials also reported the incidence of postpartum endometritis. Although the data suggested a small reduction in the risk of postpartum endometritis with the use of the chlorhexidine vaginal wash, the difference was not statistically significant (RR 0.83 [95% CI 0.61 to 1.13]). There was no report of other maternal outcomes or side effects of chlorhexidine in these three trials.

Newborn outcomes
Three trials reported on neonatal outcomes, involving 1495 and 1492 neonates in the chlorhexidine and placebo groups, respectively. One trial (*n* = 910 neonates) indicated that there was no significant difference in neonatal pneumonia (RR 0.33 [95% CI 0.01 to 8.09]). For neonatal meningitis, one trial with 508 and 513 neonates in the intervention and control groups, respectively, did not show significant difference (RR 0.34 [95% CI 0.01 to 8.29]). Two trials, involving 1038 and 1039 neonates in the intervention and control groups, respectively, found neither significant difference in blood culture confirming sepsis (RR 0.75 [95% CI 0.17 to 3.35]) nor in perinatal mortality (RR 1.00 [95% CI 0.17 to 5.79]). No significant difference was found for neonatal

sepsis (three trials, *n* = 2987; RR 0.75 [95% CI 0.17 to 3.35]). There was a trend suggesting that the use of vaginal chlorhexidine during labour might lead to a higher tendency for newborns to receive antibiotics, but this association was not statistically significant (RR 1.65 [95% CI 0.73 to 3.74]). No other neonatal outcomes or side effects of chlorhexidine were reported.

Perineal cleaning

Description of included studies
There was one UK controlled study (*n* = 3905) identified which compared cetrimide/chlorhexidine for perineal cleaning during labour with tap water.[118] [EL = 2+] The allocation of intervention/control was by alternate months. The study population included women who had a caesarean birth (17.2% for cetrimide/chlorhexidine and 16.3% for tap water).

Review findings

Women's outcomes
The findings (cetrimide/chlorhexidine group *n* = 1813; tap water group *n* = 2092) showed no evidence of a difference in the number of women who developed fever (temperature > 38 °C) (OR 1.2 [95% CI 0.8 to 1.9]), use of antibiotics (OR 1.02 [95% CI 0.86 to 1.9]), perineal infection (OR 1.4 [95% CI 0.77 to 2.7]), perineal infection (OR 1.4 [95% CI 0.77 to 2.7]), perineal breakdown (OR 5.8 [95% CI 0.3 to 999]) or caesarean wound infection (OR 1.3 [95% CI 0.86 to 1.9]). There was one maternal death in each arm: both were considered to be due to anticardiolipin syndrome.

Newborn outcomes
The results for babies' outcomes showed no difference in eye infection (OR 1.1 [95% CI 0.78 to 1.7]), cord infection (OR 1.3 [95% CI 0.7 to 2.1]), other infections not specified (OR 0.87 [95% CI 0.65 to 1.2]), admission to SCBU (OR 1.1 [95% CI 0.9 to 1.4]), use of antibiotics (OR 0.99 [95% CI 0.82 to 1.2]) or fever (temperature > 38 °C) (OR 1.4 [95% CI 0.66 to 3.0]). There were 27 perinatal deaths reported in the cetrimide/chlorhexidine group (total *n* = 1813) and 21 perinatal deaths reported in the water group (total *n* = 209). The causes of death were reported as one due to uterine rupture and three due to intrapartum asphyxia in the cetrimide/chlorhexidine group, and one due to necrotising enterocolitis and one due to neonatal septicaemia in the water group. Other deaths were considered to be due to either congenital abnormality or birthweight less than 1000 g.

Evidence statement
There is evidence that the use of cetrimide/chlorhexidine is no more effective than water for perineal cleaning.

No evidence exists to provide advice on the use of sterile gowns, sterile packs or vulval cleansing prior to vaginal examination or vaginal birth in reducing maternal or neonatal morbidity.

Recommendations on vaginal douching and perineal cleaning

Tap water may be used if cleansing is required prior to vaginal examination.

4.5.2 Double gloves during episiotomy and other procedures

Double gloves during episiotomy

Description of included studies
There were two RCTs conducted in Thailand comparing the use of double gloves with single gloves while performing an episiotomy. Outcome measures were perforation rates only. The earlier study included 2058 sets of gloves (double-gloving *n* = 1316; single-gloving *n* = 742),[119] and the later study included 300 sets of gloves (double-gloving *n* = 150; single-gloving *n* = 150).[120]

Review findings
The earlier study reported perforation rates of double inner gloves as 2.7% (*P* < 0.05), outer as 5.9%, compared with single gloves as 6.7%. The later study reported perforation rates of double inner gloves as 4.6% (*P* < 0.05), outer as 22.6%, compared with single gloves as 18.0%.

Evidence statement
Wearing two gloves appears to reduce perforation rates in inner gloves compared with single-gloving. However, caution needs to be taken in interpreting these results as there was no concealment.

Arm sleeves

Description of included studies
One case series conducted in the UK (*n* = 80) has evaluated the effectiveness of wearing a sterile arm sleeve on top of the gown to prevent contamination during obstetric procedures.[121] [EL = 3]

Review findings
The contamination of arms and hands was 3.8% and 5%, respectively.

Evidence statement
There is insufficient evidence on the use of a sterile arm sleeves in preventing contamination.

Recommendation on double-gloving

Routine hygiene measures taken by staff caring for women in labour, including standard hand hygiene and single-use non-sterile gloves, are appropriate to reduce cross-contamination between women, babies and healthcare professionals.

Selection of protective equipment should be based on an assessment of the risk of transmission of microorganisms to the woman, and the risk of contamination of the healthcare practitioner's clothing and skin by women's blood, body fluids, secretions or excretions.*

Research recommendation on hygiene measures during labour

Hygiene rituals around the time of vaginal examination and birth would benefit from further research.

4.6   Identification of women and babies who may need additional care

The GDG members decided to use the criteria below (the list is not exhaustive) to identify women and babies who may need additional care, and therefore would need referral to specialist care not covered in this guideline:

- intrapartum haemorrhage
- placental abruption
- ruptured uterus
- 'suspected' amniotic fluid embolus
- 'suspected' pulmonary embolus
- eclampsia and severe pre-eclampsia
- cord prolapse
- PPH
- shoulder dystocia
- massive obstetric haemorrhage
- maternal collapse
- monitoring suggesting fetal compromise
- undiagnosed breech.

---

* This recommendation is from 'Infection control: prevention of healthcare-associated infection in primary and community care' (NICE clinical guideline 2).

5 Coping with pain in labour: non-epidural

5.1 Introduction

A woman's desire for, and choice of, pain relief during labour are influenced by many factors, including her expectations, the complexity of her labour and the severity of her pain. To many women the pain of labour is significant and the majority require some form of pain relief. Flexible expectations and being prepared for labour may influence her psychological wellbeing after birth. Extreme pain can result in psychological trauma for some women, while for others undesirable side effects of analgesia can be detrimental to the birth experience. Effective forms of pain relief are not necessarily associated with greater satisfaction with the birth experience and, conversely, failure of a chosen method can lead to dissatisfaction.

There are two schools of thought around how women might cope with the pain of labour. The first suggests that in the 21st century there is no need to suffer unnecessarily during labour and that effective analgesia is available and should be offered. The second sees pain as part of the experience of birth and advocates that women should be supported and encouraged to 'work with the pain' of labour.

While individual women or carers may identify with either view, the reality for most women is probably somewhere between these two. The challenge for midwives and healthcare professionals is not only to identify where that individual woman lies on the continuum, but also, through good communication, to recognise and respond appropriately to changes in the woman's stance during labour.

Whatever the woman's viewpoint, it is fundamental that she should be treated with respect and as an individual. Women need to be in control of, and involved in, what is happening to them and the manner in which they are supported is key to this. Continuing communication between woman and midwife during the progress of labour about her desire for analgesia is also fundamental, as is the recognition of severe distress.

Clinical question
What is the effectiveness of the following interventions or techniques in labour on outcomes?

- breathing and relaxation
- massage
- complementary therapies
- birth balls
- injected water papules
- water (including temperature regulation).

5.2 Women's views and experiences of pain and pain relief in childbirth

Description of included studies
This systematic review was undertaken to specifically address the outcome of women's views of pain relief and the experience of childbirth in relation to intrapartum analgesia. The included studies involve women in labour at term, entering labour without complications. Outcomes include women's views of pain relief and the overall experience of childbirth (including satisfaction with the childbirth experience).

Review findings

A systematic review of 137 reports of pain and women's satisfaction with childbirth was identified for inclusion.[67] [EL = 2++] The review includes descriptive studies, randomised controlled trials and systematic reviews of intrapartum interventions. Findings were summarised qualitatively. Thirty-five reports of 29 studies met the inclusion criteria for observational studies of childbirth satisfaction. Sample sizes ranged from 16 to 2000 and more than 14 000 women from nine countries were studied. Thirteen reports of five systematic reviews and seven randomised controlled trials were also included. More than 27 000 women were included and the methodology of the studies was generally very good. One systematic review and 20 RCTs met the inclusion criteria for studies of intrapartum pain relief that included a measure of satisfaction as an outcome. The most common method of assessment of satisfaction was a single VAS score, usually made in the immediate postnatal period. The methodological quality of these studies was quite good with generally small sample sizes. The author illustrates the complexity of the relationship between pain, pain relief and women's experiences of childbirth with findings from two population-based surveys (one UK (*n* = 1150) and one Australian (*n* = 1336)). The UK survey found that women who were very anxious about labour pain antenatally were less satisfied after the birth. The most satisfied women postnatally were those who had used no pain-relieving drugs during labour. All effects were independent of parity or demographic variables. In the Australian survey, the odds of dissatisfaction were greater when women rated their caregivers as less than very helpful and when women felt they were not actively involved in decision making. The impact on dissatisfaction was greater than that for ratings of pain relief as unsatisfactory. It is also noted that women's views of pain and of pain relief are not the same thing. In 11 of the 21 trials reported in the review, discrepancies were noted between the ratings of pain compared with ratings of pain relief. Synthesis of evidence from all the reviewed papers led to the conclusion that four factors exist:

- personal expectations
- the amount of support from caregivers
- the quality of the caregiver–patient relationship
- the involvement in decision making.

These factors appear to be so important that they override the influence of age, socio-economic status, ethnicity, childbirth preparation, the physical birth environment, pain, immobility, medical interventions and continuity of care when women evaluate their childbirth experience. The author concluded that the influences of pain, pain relief and intrapartum interventions on subsequent satisfaction are neither as obvious, nor as powerful, as the influences of the attitudes and behaviours of the caregivers.

One RCT was identified that investigated nulliparous women's satisfaction with childbirth and intrapartum pain relief when labouring at term.[122] [EL = 1+] The study conducted in Australia compared epidural and non-epidural analgesia findings and, therefore, are from within the context of a trial. Women were 'surveyed' (presumably by questionnaire, but this is not explicit) approximately 24 hours postnatally and again 6 months postpartum by a mailed questionnaire. Women recruited into the study were randomised into one of two groups – the EPI group who were encouraged to have an epidural as their primary pain relief (*n* = 493), and the CMS group who received one-to-one continuous midwifery support throughout labour and were encouraged to avoid epidural analgesia but instead use Entonox, intramuscular (IM) pethidine and non-pharmacological pain relief (*n* = 499). There was a high crossover rate within the study: 61.3% women crossed over from the CMS group to the EPI group (*n* = 306) and 27.8% crossed over from the EPI group to the CMS group (*n* = 137). Analysis was undertaken on an intention-to-treat basis. Women allocated to the EPI group were significantly more satisfied with their intrapartum pain relief, and the reported pain intensity post-administration was significantly lower for this group. Both groups reported similar and high levels of satisfaction with a degree of midwifery support during labour (median [interquartile range], *P* value obtained using Wilcoxon rank sum test) (CMS 95 mm [IQR 88 to 100] versus EPI 96 mm [IQR 90 to 100], *P* = 0.24); participation in intrapartum decision making (CMS 5 [IQR 4 to 5] versus EPI 5 [IQR 4 to 5], *P* = 0.35); achievement of labour expectations (CMS 3 [IQR 2 to 4] versus EPI 3 [IQR 2 to 4], *P* = 0.32) and achievement of birth expectations (CMS 2 [IQR 2 to 5] versus, EPI 2 [IQR 2 to 5], *P* = 0.54). Despite the difference in satisfaction with pain relief and levels of pain experienced between the two groups, reports of the overall labour experience and overall birth experience were similar for both groups (labour:

CMS 4 [IQR 3 to 4] versus EPI 4 [IQR 3 to 4], $P = 0.74$, birth: CMS 4 [IQR 4 to 5] versus EPI 4 [IQR 3 to 5], $P = 0.60$). Findings obtained from the 6 month follow-up questionnaire ($n = 642$; response rate = 64.7%) showed that women in the CMS group were significantly less likely to plan to use an epidural in a subsequent labour (OR 0.64 [95% CI 0.47 to 0.89]). Despite the high crossover rates and intention-to-treat analysis, the findings from this study are, perhaps, as would be expected, i.e. improved pain relief associated with epidural use. This may be because women allocated to the CMS group delayed requests for an epidural. Unfortunately, this is not discussed in the paper, thus making interpretation of the findings difficult.

A prospective survey undertaken in Finland ($n = 1091$) sought women's expectations for intrapartum pain relief antenatally, measured pain intensity during labour and birth, and followed up women's satisfaction with pain relief on the third day postnatally.[123] [EL = 3] Antenatally, 4% of nulliparous women and 14% of multiparous women felt they would not need any analgesia during labour, with 90% of women overall expressing a wish for intrapartum analgesia. Prior to the administration of any analgesia, 89% of nulliparous women and 84% of multiparous women described their pain during labour as either 'very severe' or 'intolerable'. Twenty percent ($n = 213$) of women, of whom 14% were nulliparous and 86% were multiparous, received no analgesia during labour. The pain scores of these women did not differ significantly from those women who then went on to receive analgesia. After administration of pain relief, 50% of multiparous women and 19% of nulliparous women still reported pain scores of 8–10 on the BS-11. This difference reflects a higher degree of usage of epidural analgesia among the nulliparous women. Eighteen percent of women rated their pain relief as poor, 37% rated it as moderate, and 45% as good. Surprisingly, views of pain relief were not related to parity. Half of all women complained of inadequate pain relief during labour which, in multiparous women, was significantly associated with the second stage of labour. Overall, 95% of women stated that they were satisfied with their care during childbirth. Ratings of overall satisfaction were not related to parity, level of pain experienced or pain relief received. Findings reflect a lack of effective pain relief, particularly for those women who, for whatever reason, do not choose an epidural. Dissatisfaction with childbirth was very low, and was associated with instrumental births, but not with usage of analgesia. Despite an apparent low level of effectiveness of pain relief, most women expressed satisfaction with care during labour. This may reflect low expectations of pain relief in this population and again demonstrates the complexity of the relationships between reported pain, pain relief, satisfaction with pain relief and the experience of childbirth.

One European multicentre study was reviewed which examined nulliparous women's expectations and experiences of intrapartum analgesia.[124] [EL = 3] The study involved over 100 women from each of five countries (Italy, UK, Belgium, Finland and Portugal; total $n = 611$). All women were interviewed during the last month of pregnancy and again approximately 24 hours postnatally. Expectations of pain, pain relief and satisfaction were assessed using a 10 cm VAS. Findings showed that women who expected higher levels of pain were more likely to be satisfied with analgesia (Spearman's rho = 0.15, $P = 0.001$). Women who experienced higher levels of pain following administration of analgesia were less satisfied with pain relief (Spearman's rho = −0.66, $P < 0.0001$). Maternal satisfaction with the overall childbirth experience was positively correlated with pain expectations (Spearman's rho = 0.23, $P < 0.001$) and pain before analgesia (Spearman's rho = 0.16, $P < 0.001$), and negatively correlated with pain after analgesia (Spearman's rho = −0.30, $P < 0.001$). The most satisfied women were those who expected more pain, were satisfied with analgesia received and had good pain relief after analgesia. Pain did not correlate with women's educational level, age or social class. Generally, women's satisfaction with analgesia and the birth experience was high. It should be noted that all hospitals involved in the study were tertiary centres with above average epidural rates. Other components of the birth experience, e.g. involvement in decision making, friendliness and expertise of staff, were not investigated in this study.

Evidence statement

A woman's experience of birth vary enormously and is influenced by many factors including her expectations, degree of preparation, the complexity of her labour, and the severity of the pain she experiences.

The attitude and behaviour of the caregiver is consistently seen to be the most obvious and powerful influence on women's satisfaction. Women are more satisfied with pain relief when their expectations of pain and how they choose to manage it are met.

GDG interpretation of the evidence (advice to clinicians regarding non-epidural pain relief)
This section offers advice to clinicians caring for women in labour regarding non-epidural pain relief, based on the GDG's work and deliberations.

It is important to remember that relatively simple things can make a difference.

Women appreciate having someone whom they know and trust with them in labour, although there is no high-level evidence on the benefits of this.

Women should be able to play music of their own choice and drink and eat a light diet if they want to during labour.

They can choose to walk, move around, find comfortable positions, sit, stand up, or lie down on their sides. However, if they lie on their backs, they are likely to feel the pain more intensely.

We have prioritised the options for analgesia on the basis of the strength of the evidence of their effectiveness:

- The evidence shows that immersion in water provides effective pain relief, so encouraging the woman to get into a warm bath or birthing pool will help reduce the pain of the first stage of labour, and mean they are less likely to need an epidural. As far as we know, this does not adversely affect maternal or neonatal outcomes. Using a bath or a birthing pool for pain relief does not mean that the woman has to remain in it for birth unless she wants to. Women can get out of the water at any time if they do not like it or want to try another method of analgesia.
- Entonox has the advantage that it acts very quickly and rapidly passes out of the system without affecting the baby and it can be used anywhere – even in the bath. It takes the edge off the pain and helps many women. Some women feel dizzy or light-headed when using it but the advantage of Entonox is that if the woman does not like it, it can be stopped and the side effects will also stop.
- Women who choose to use breathing and relaxation techniques or massage, by their birth partner, should be supported. The little evidence available shows that they may significantly reduce the pain and they do help many women in labour and do not adversely affect either maternal or neonatal outcomes.
- Women who choose to use acupuncture or hypnosis should be able to, although they are not provided by the maternity unit. The little evidence available shows that they may reduce the pain of labour and do not appear to adversely affect either maternal or neonatal outcomes.
- Opioids such as pethidine or diamorphine are widely used and the evidence available shows they provide poor analgesia and can make women feel nauseous and drowsy. As pethidine crosses the placenta, it may make the baby sleepy. This means that the baby may suffer respiratory depression at birth and is sleepy and reluctant to feed for several days after birth. Pethidine should always be administered with an anti-emetic. Women can still use the bath or birthing pool as long as they are not drowsy and have not had pethidine in the previous 2 hours.
- There is no evidence on the effectiveness of birth balls for reducing the pain of labour. They may, however, help women find a comfortable position.
- We also know that using a transcutaneous electronic nerve stimulation (TENS) machine does not provide any pain relief once the woman is in established labour, and is therefore not recommended at this stage. There are no trials of its use in latent labour when some women choose to use it.
- All women use some kind of pain-relieving strategies during labour, and many will use several different ones. What is important is that they are able to communicate with you to ensure that as far as possible, they feel in control and confident and that both of you remain flexible about what is wanted.

Recommendation on women's views and experiences of pain and pain relief

Healthcare professionals should consider how their own values and beliefs inform their attitude to coping with pain in labour and ensure their care supports the woman's choice.

5.3 Pain-relieving strategies

Introduction
The evidence regarding pain-relieving strategies is described below and incorporates a wide range of strategies used by many women over the centuries, to help them cope with labour, that do not require professional oversight.

See also Section 4.3.1 on support in labour.

5.3.1 Breathing and relaxation

Description of included studies
One controlled trial of breathing and relaxation techniques was described in a systematic review of complementary therapies used during labour (n = 54 women, but 20 were lost to follow-up).[125] [EL = 1−] Women were randomised into an experimental group who received 'respiratory autogenic training' (progressive muscle relaxation and focused slow breathing) or a control group who attended a 'traditional psychoprophylactic course' (no details are given about the content of this course, but it may also have included a form of relaxation training).

Review findings
Although a significant reduction in reported intrapartum pain was noted for women in the experimental group, this was only found after adjusting for women who were very anxious during pregnancy. Postnatal reports of labour pain and labour experience did not differ significantly between the two groups.

Evidence statement
There is a lack of evidence that breathing and relaxation techniques reduce measured pain in labour or affect any other outcome.

> **Recommendation on breathing and relaxation**
>
> Women who choose to use breathing and relaxation techniques in labour should be supported in their choice.

5.3.2 Touch and massage

Description of included studies
Two systematic reviews were identified which included evaluation of the use of massage or therapeutic touch for pain relief during labour.[85,125] [both EL = 1+] Each review included two controlled trials, with a total of three studies included overall: two RCTs and one prospective cohort study. The two RCTs reviewed were fairly small (n = 24 and n = 60) and conducted in the USA and Taiwan, respectively.

Review findings
Differences between the trials prohibit pooling of the data. In both trials the woman's partner was shown how to carry out massage and this was then performed for set periods of time throughout the first stage of labour (20–30 minutes/hour). In the larger trial, the control group received a 'casual' contact with the researcher for the same periods of time, while in the smaller study the control group received 'usual care' including guidance on breathing and relaxation techniques. In the larger study it is not clear whether the nurse carrying out the pain assessment was blinded, while in the smaller trial, blinding of the nurse assessor was carried out. Pain was also assessed by the women themselves. Both trials showed a significant reduction in labour pain as reported by the nurse observers and the women. No mention was made of other analgesia used during labour, for women in either group.

In the smaller study, a significant reduction in intrapartum stress and anxiety was reported by both the women and the blinded observer. There was also a significant improvement in maternal mood (self-rated using a depression scale) both during labour and postnatally.

A prospective cohort study, conducted in the USA, examined the effect of therapeutic touch during labour ($n = 90$). Women in the experimental group received touch from the midwife (e.g. handholding) for a period of 5–10 seconds after each verbal expression of anxiety. The study was carried out during a 30 minute intervention period at the end of the first stage of labour (8–10 cm dilatation). The control group received 'usual care'. Despite the seemingly short duration of the intervention, maternal anxiety (as measured by blood pressure, verbal expressions of anxiety and anxiety scores reported by mother in the early postnatal period) were found to be reduced significantly ($P < 0.05$) in the experimental group, compared with the control group.

Evidence statement
The limited available evidence suggests that massage and reassuring touch reduces a woman's measured pain and expressed anxieties during labour. There is no high-level evidence that birth outcomes are influenced by massage.

Recommendation on touch and massage

Women who choose to use massage techniques in labour that have been taught to birth partners should be supported in their choice.

5.3.3 Labouring in water

Introduction
The Winterton report recommended that all maternity units should provide women with the option to labour and give birth in water.[95] However, the number of women actually using water during labour is not well reported. A survey between April 1994 and March 1996 identified 0.6% of births in England and Wales occurring in water, 9% of which were home births.[126] There would appear to be a wide variation in the use of water during birth, with one birth centre reporting up to 80% of women using water during labour and up to 79% giving birth in water.[127]

Previous guideline
Water birth was reviewed in the NICE *Caesarean Section* guideline.[6] The guideline reviewed one systematic review, one RCT and some other observational studies and recommended that women should be informed that immersion in water during labour has not been shown to influence the likelihood of CS, although it may affect other outcomes.

Description of included studies
There was one systematic review and one RCT identified for inclusion in the review. The systematic review included eight trials.[128] [EL = 1+] Out of the eight trials, six examined labouring in water in the first stage, one examined labouring in water in the second stage, and one investigated the timing of the use of water in the first stage of labour. An additional RCT examined effectiveness of use of water in the first stage compared with augmentation.[129] [EL = 1–]

There was no relevant study identified that addressed hygiene measures for water birth.

Review findings

Use of water versus other methods

Women's outcomes
Meta-analysis of findings from four trials reported in the systematic review[128] [EL = 1+] showed that the use of water in the first stage of labour reduces the use of epidural/spinal analgesia/anaesthesia (OR 0.84 [95% CI 0.71 to 0.99]). One trial reported significantly reduced reported pain for those women who laboured in water compared with those not labouring in water (OR 0.23 [95% CI 0.08 to 0.63]).

Meta-analysis of four trials in the review showed no evidence of differences on duration of the first and second stages of labour between women who laboured in water and those who did not. Six trials reported on instrumental birth rates and CS. Findings from a meta-analysis of these trials showed that overall there was no evidence of any difference: instrumental vaginal birth rate (OR for use of water 0.83 [95% CI 0.66 to 1.05]) and CS rate (OR for use of water 1.33 [95% CI 0.92 to 1.91]).

There was no evidence of differences on perineal trauma with labouring in water: episiotomy (OR 0.89 [95% CI 0.68 to 1.15]), second-degree tears (OR 0.90 [95% CI 0.66 to 1.23]) or third/fourth-degree tears (OR 1.38 [95% CI 0.85 to 2.24]).[128] [EL = 1+]

Newborn outcomes
Five trials reported on Apgar scores at 5 minutes and there was no difference in the number of babies with a score of less than 7 at 5 minutes (OR 1.59 [95% CI 0.63 to 4.01]). Two trials reported admissions to the neonatal unit and found no evidence of difference (OR 1.05 [95% CI 0.68 to 1.61]). Infection rates were reported in four trials and were found to be very low (6/629 versus 3/633; OR 2.01 [95% CI 0.50 to 8.07]).

Timing of use of water
One trial in the systematic review compared early versus late immersion during the first stage of labour, and found significantly higher epidural analgesia rates in the early group (42/100 versus 19/100; OR 3.09 [95% CI 1.63 to 5.84]) and an increased use of augmentation of labour (57/100 versus 30/100; OR 3.09 [95% CI 1.73 to 5.54]).[130]

Augmentation versus use of water
One trial compared augmentation versus immersion in water during the first stage of labour.[129] [EL = 1−] It showed that use of water reduced rate of augmentation (RR 0.74, $P = 0.001$) and increased some aspects of satisfaction (freedom of movement MD 1.46, $P = 0.001$; privacy MD 1.18, $P = 0.03$; satisfaction with the care MD 1.07, $P = 0.49$). There were more babies admitted to neonatal units with use of water (admission to neonatal unit 6/49 (water), 0/50 (air), $P = 0.01$), but there is no evidence of a difference on cord arterial pH or infection rate (cord arterial pH 7.26 (water), 7.25 (air), $P = 0.97$; infection 8/49 (water), 9/50 (air), $P = 0.78$).

Evidence statement
Labouring in water reduces pain and the use of regional analgesia. There is evidence of no significant differences regarding adverse outcomes when comparing labours with and without the use of water. There is insufficient evidence on timing of use of water in labour.

There is no good-quality evidence regarding hygiene measures for water birth.

Recommendations on labouring in water

The opportunity to labour in water is recommended for pain relief.

For women labouring in water, the temperature of the woman and the water should be monitored hourly to ensure that the woman is comfortable and not becoming pyrexial. The temperature of the water should not be above 37.5 °C.

Any bath or birthing pool should be kept clean using a protocol agreed with the microbiology department and, in the case of birthing pools, in accordance with the manufacturer's guidelines.

5.3.4 Birth balls

Overview of available evidence
No studies were identified which examined the use of birth balls during labour.

Evidence statement
There is no evidence of any effect of birth balls on birth experience or clinical outcomes.

5.3.5 Injected water papules

Description of included studies
Two systematic reviews were identified, both of which reviewed the same four RCTs examining the effectiveness of cutaneous water injections.[85,125] [EL = 1+]

Review findings
The four included trials were of fair to good quality, with sample sizes ranging from 35 to 272. Women in labour reporting back pain or severe back pain were entered into the trials. Three trials described adequate randomisation, three were double-blinded placebo-controlled trials, and three trials were analysed on an intention-to-treat basis. In all cases there were some missing data due to women giving birth before the end point of the trial [range 4% to 30%]. Differences between the trials mean pooling of data is not possible. In all four trials back pain was significantly reduced for 45 to 90 minutes following the intradermal injections of sterile water, as measured by a VAS. In the one trial that compared subcutaneous and intradermal water injections, both were found to be similarly effective compared with the control of subcutaneous saline injections. Despite the pain relief reported, there was no significant difference between experimental and control groups in three of the trials, regarding subsequent use of analgesia. In one trial, use of subsequent analgesia was higher in the experimental group than in the control group where women received massage, baths and were encouraged to mobilise. In this trial, women in the control group were more likely than women in the experimental group to say that they would choose the same pain relief option for a subsequent labour. In the other three trials, women who had received cutaneous water injections were more likely to say they would choose the same option for a future labour. No trial reported the effects of repeated injections.

One of the main disadvantages of this method of pain relief is the intense stinging pain that many women report during the administration of the intradermal injections. An RCT was conducted in Sweden to compare the perceived pain during administration of intradermal versus subcutaneous injections of sterile water.[131] [EL = 1+] The work involved 100 healthy women (not pregnant/in labour) in a blind, controlled trial with a crossover design. Perceived pain was measured using a VAS. The findings showed that intradermal injections were reported as being much more painful than subcutaneous injections (mean 60.8 mm versus 41.3 mm, $P < 0.001$). It is not known, however, whether this finding would apply to women in labour.

Evidence statement
There is a lack of evidence of the benefit of injected water papules on birth experience or clinical outcomes.

Recommendation on injected water papules

The use of injected water papules is not recommended.

5.3.6 Complementary and alternative therapies

Previous guideline
The *Caesarean Section* guideline reviewed the effectiveness and safety of complementary and alternative therapies for women during labour.[6] The guideline included a systematic review comprising seven trials and five observational studies. In the guideline, it was recommended that women should be informed that the effects of complementary therapies used during labour (such as acupuncture, aromatherapy, hypnosis, herbal products, nutritional supplements, homeopathic medicines, and Chinese medicines) on the likelihood of CS have not been properly evaluated, and further research is needed before such interventions can be recommended.

Acupressure and acupuncture

Description of included studies
Four reasonable quality RCTs were identified.[132-135] A Korean trial (intervention $n = 36$; control $n = 39$) compared SP6 acupressure to controls that received touch at the same point.[132] A second trial, conducted in Norway (intervention $n = 106$; control $n = 92$), compared a group of women who received acupuncture with a group who did not receive acupuncture or a placebo.[135] A third study, also conducted in Norway, compared acupuncture with false acupuncture (intervention $n = 106$; control $n = 102$).[134] A Swedish study involving 90 women (intervention $n = 46$; control $n = 44$) was also identified. The control did not receive any form of placebo.[133] While the trial that investigated effectiveness of acupressure in labour reported separately, a new meta-analysis was conducted using these three trials on acupuncture, as they are considered to have reasonable homogeneity. [EL = 1+]

Review findings
There was evidence of reduction in pain score after SP6 acupressure compared with SP6 touch (WMD −1.20 [95% CI −2.04 to −0.36]), but no evidence of difference in use of pharmacological pain relief (RR 0.54 [95% CI 0.20 to 1.43]).

Meta-analysis of the RCTs showed that acupuncture significantly reduced the use of pharmacological pain relief (two trials RR 0.74 [95% CI 0.63 to 0.86]), epidural analgesia (two trials RR 0.45 [95% CI 0.29 to 0.69]) and the need for augmentation of labour with oxytocin (two trials RR 0.58 [95% CI 0.40 to 0.86]). There was no evidence of differences in pain score after acupuncture (one trial MD −0.20 [95% CI −0.80 to 0.40]) or rate of spontaneous vaginal birth (three trials RR 1.03 [95% CI 0.97 to 1.09]). Outcomes such as maternal satisfaction and maternal and neonatal complications were not investigated.

Hypnosis

Description of included studies
A systematic review, published in 2004, involving five RCTs and 14 comparative studies was identified, but only the evidence from the RCTs has been included here.[136] All the RCTs were conducted in either the UK or the USA. [EL = 1+]

Review findings
Meta-analysis of the RCTs showed that hypnosis significantly reduced the use of pharmacological pain relief (three trials RR 0.51 [95% CI 0.28 to 0.98]) and of the need for labour augmentation (two trials RR 0.31 [95% CI 0.18 to 0.52]). No other outcomes were considered.

Aromatherapy

Description of included studies
A systematic review involving one RCT in New Zealand was identified.[137] The study population comprised 22 multiparous women. Women in the intervention group received essential oil of ginger or essential oil of lemongrass in the bath, and they were required to bathe for at least 1 hour. [EL = 1+]

Review findings
There was no evidence of a difference in the use of pharmacological pain relief (RR 2.50 [95% CI 0.31 to 20.45]), rates of spontaneous vaginal birth (RR 0.93 [95% CI 0.67 to 1.28]), instrumental birth (RR 0.83 [95% CI 0.06 to 11.70]) or CS (RR 2.54 [95% CI 0.11 to 56.25]). There were no other outcomes investigated.

Music

Description of included studies
One RCT published in 2003 involving 110 women in labour (intervention $n = 55$; control $n = 55$) provides the evidence for this subsection.[138] Women in the intervention group listened to soft music without lyrics for 3 hours, whereas women in the control group did not listen to music. The trial was conducted in Thailand. [EL = 1+]

Review findings
The trial compared scores made using two VASs, and showed a significant reduction in both the sensation of, and distress from, pain (sensation of pain (pre and 3 hourly post tests undertaken three times): $F(1107) = 18.69$, $P < 0.01$, effect size = 0.15; distress of pain (undertaken as above): $F(1107) = 14.87$, $P < 0.001$, effect size = 0.12). There were no other outcomes investigated.

Audio-analgesia

Description of included studies
Again, one RCT that was included in the systematic review was included.[137] [EL = 1+] This was conducted in the UK and published in 1965. The study population comprised 25 women in labour. Women in the intervention group received audio-analgesia which consisted of 'sea noise' white sound set at 120 decibels, and the control group received sea noise at a maximum of 90 decibels.

Review findings
The trial reported maternal satisfaction about care received, which showed no evidence of a difference (RR 2.00 [95% CI 0.82 to 4.89]). There were no other outcomes available.

Evidence statement
There is some evidence from small studies regarding the use of acupuncture, acupressure and hypnosis for the management of pain in labour. There is a lack of evidence on other outcomes.

Acupuncture seems to be associated with a reduction in the use of pharmacological pain relief and augmentation, but with no reduction in pain scores.

Hypnosis seems to be associated with a reduction in the use of pharmacological pain relief and augmentation. There is a lack of evidence on pain scores.

There is a lack of high-level evidence that music, aromatherapy or audio-analgesia influence women's pain in labour or any other outcome.

Recommendations on complementary therapies

Acupuncture, acupressure and hypnosis should not be provided, but women who wish to use these techniques should not be prevented from doing so.

The playing of music of the woman's choice in the labour ward should be supported.

Research recommendation on non-invasive techniques in labour

A combination of randomised trials and qualitative research should investigate the effect of a package of care, involving the use of non-invasive techniques throughout labour and birth, on women's birth experiences. This should include studies that explore which aspects of the package of care affect both women's experience and maternal and neonatal outcomes.

5.4 Non-pharmacological analgesia

Introduction
This section covers TENS, which once again does not require professional oversight.

Clinical question
Is there evidence that the type, frequency and mode of administration of the following pharmacological and non-pharmacological pain relief and regional analgesia influence outcomes?

- pharmacological pain relief: Entonox®, PCAs, pethidine, diamorphine and meptazinol (Meptid®)
- non-pharmacological pain relief: TENS.

5.4.1 Transcutaneous electrical nerve stimulation (TENS)

Description of included studies
One systematic review conducted in 1997 was identified.[139] (*n* = 877: TENS *n* = 436; controls (sham TENS or no treatment) *n* = 441). The systematic review included ten RCTs, among which three RCTs compared TENS with no TENS, seven RCTs compared TENS with sham TENS and one RCT compared both. Only one RCT achieved an adequate level of blinding. [EL = 1+]

Review findings
Pain outcome measures were reported in ten RCTs. There was no consistency in the method of measuring, but no study recorded any difference in pain intensity or pain relief scores between TENS and controls. The need for additional analgesic interventions was reported in eight RCTs. There was no evidence of difference for this need (combined RR 0.88 [95% CI 0.72 to 1.07]). There were no reports of adverse events in the ten RCTs.

Evidence statement
There is high-level evidence that TENS is not an effective analgesic in established labour. There is no high-level evidence on the analgesic effect of TENS in the latent phase of labour.

> **Recommendation on TENS**
>
> Transcutaneous electrical nerve stimulation (TENS) should not be offered to women in established labour.

5.5 Inhalational analgesia

Introduction
This form of analgesia has been available since 1962 and approved for midwives to administer since 1970. It involves the woman inhaling through a mask or mouthpiece. It has the advantages of rapid action, it is non-accumulative and does not pass across the placenta to affect the baby.

5.5.1 Nitrous oxide

Description of included studies
One systematic review published in 2002 was identified.[140] The study included eight controlled studies and eight observational studies. [EL = 2+] While most studies included use of a 50% nitrous oxide concentration, nine involved comparisons of varying concentrations ranging from 30% to 80%. Owing to the inconsistency of the included methods, the results are summarised descriptively.

Review findings
Analgesic efficacy was adequately reported in 11 studies. Although there was no clear, quantitative, objective evidence, seven studies described significant analgesia with nitrous oxide and two studies reported that women chose to continue using nitrous oxide even after the study period was over.

The effect of nitrous oxide on uterine contractions was reported in one study, and no alteration was observed. Another study found no effect on the progress of labour. Nausea and vomiting was reported as ranging from 5% to 36% with nitrous oxide but there were no proper controls in eight studies. Loss of consciousness was reported in two RCTs, but this was not statistically significant.

Apgar scores were reported in four studies, and there was no evidence of any differences. One study also showed no difference in early neurobehavioural scale.

Evidence statement
There is a moderate level of evidence to support the use of nitrous oxide in labour. Nitrous oxide seems to relieve some pain but can make women feel nauseous and light-headed. There is no evidence of harm to the baby.

> **Recommendation on nitrous oxide**
>
> Entonox (a 50 : 50 mixture of oxygen and nitrous oxide) should be available in all birth settings as it may reduce pain in labour, but women should be informed that it may make them feel nauseous and light-headed.

5.6 Intravenous and intramuscular use of opioids for labour

Introduction
Pethidine is widely used as an analgesic during labour. Its ease of administration and the fact that the Central Midwives' Board approved it in 1950 has probably contributed to its widespread use.

Pethidine did not undergo RCTs prior to its introduction into clinical practice in the UK, and its perceived analgesic efficacy could in part be due to its sedative effects.

5.6.1   Intramuscular use of opioids

Intramuscular (IM) opioids versus placebo

Pethidine versus placebo

Description of included studies
Two double-blind RCTs compared IM pethidine with an IM placebo. The first trial (*n* = 224) was reported in a systematic review.[141,142] [EL = 1+] A second RCT involving 50 women was conducted in Hong Kong.[143] [EL = 1+]

Review findings
An RCT, reported in a systematic review, found significantly more women were dissatisfied with pain relief in the placebo group compared with the group of women who received pethidine when assessed during labour (83% versus 71%, *P* = 0.04) and after giving birth (54% versus 25%, *P* = 0.00004). It should be noted that the number of women dissatisfied with pain relief was high in both groups. Similarly, significantly more caregivers were dissatisfied with the placebo. No other outcomes were investigated.

Results from a second RCT conducted in Hong Kong support these findings.[143] [EL = 1+] A significant reduction in VAS pain score 30 minutes post-administration was found for women in the group who received pethidine (*n* = 25) compared with those who received the placebo (*n* = 25) (pethidine: median change −11 mm; placebo: median change +4 mm, *P* = 0.009). At 30 minutes the median VAS score was significantly lower in the pethidine group compared with the control group (54 versus 78 mm, *P* = 0.01). Eight women in the group who received pethidine required no further analgesia compared with one in the control group (*P* = 0.01). Thirty minutes after administration, women were also asked to rate on a 5-point Likert scale how satisfied they were with the pain relief received. Scores were significantly higher for women in the pethidine group, although neither had very high scores (median 2 for pethidine group and 1 for control group). Eight percent of women in the pethidine group were totally dissatisfied with the pain relief received compared with 60% in the control group.

IM opioids versus IM opioids: different opioids

Description of included studies and review findings

Tramadol versus pethidine
Two systematic reviews include three RCTs of tramadol 100 mg versus pethidine 50–100 mg for analgesia in labour.[141,142] [EL = 1+] The trial sizes ranged from 40 to 60 women, and in total involved 144 women.

Two trials reported women's satisfaction with pain relief 1–2 hours post-administration and both found no significant difference between the two groups (women not satisfied with pain relief: 15/50 versus 13/49; OR 1.18 [95% CI 0.49 to 2.84]). The third trial reported VAS scores following administration of analgesia, which was significantly lower in the group of women who had received pethidine compared with those who received tramadol (mean 66.10 mm [SD 18.34 mm] versus 52.91 mm [SD 22.23 mm]; WMD 13.20 mm [95% CI 0.37 to 26.03 mm]). All trials included measures of nausea/vomiting during labour and meta-analysis of the findings showed no significant difference between the two drugs (6/74 versus 9/70; OR 0.63 [95% CI 0.21 to 1.84]). Similarly, meta-analysis of the findings showed no significant difference in drowsiness/sleepiness between tramadol and pethidine (16/74 versus 22/70; OR 0.61 [95% CI 0.29 to 1.29]). There were no significant differences found for mode of birth. Neonatal outcome was not evaluated.

A more recent RCT conducted in Turkey (*n* = 59) reported greater pain relief with pethidine (100 mg) compared with tramadol (100 mg), although neither provided good analgesia.[144] [EL = 1+] On a 5-point Likert scale of pain intensity, the median score at 1 hour post-administration was 4 for pethidine and 5 for tramadol (*P* < 0.05). Incidence of nausea and fatigue 1 hour following drug administration was also significantly higher in women who were given tramadol (nausea: 1/29 versus 9/30, *P* = 0.004; fatigue: 15/29 versus 23/30, *P* = 0.045). The findings of this study are a little difficult to interpret as it is not clear which statistical tests were applied to any given comparison. The incidence of neonatal respiratory depression was high in this study, occurring in three of the babies born in the pethidine group and seven in the tramadol group. It was reported that all recovered with 'supplementary oxygen therapy in the ICU'. No opiate antagonists were given. Mean Apgar scores at 1 minute were 7.76 (SD 1.06) and 7.13 (SD 1.38), and at 5 minutes 9.28 (SD 0.65) and 9.17 (SD 0.91) in the pethidine and tramadol groups, respectively.

Meptazinol versus pethidine
Evidence for this section is drawn from the two systematic reviews identified in the subsection above and includes the same seven trials that compare pethidine with tramadol.[141,142] [both EL = 1+] In six of the trials, 100 mg meptazinol (Meptid®) was compared with a similar dose of pethidine. In one trial the comparison was between 75 mg meptazinol and 50 mg pethidine. The trials involved a total of 1906 women, with trials ranging in size from 10 to 1035 women.

A variety of outcome measures were used to assess pain relief, e.g. lack of satisfaction with pain relief 1–2 hours post-administration, VAS (0–100), need for additional pain relief during labour and use of epidural analgesia. In these studies, analgesia was found to be similar for the two drugs, with no significant differences between the various outcome measures. Three trials investigated nausea and vomiting. In two of these trials, there were no significant differences but the largest trial ($n = 1035$) showed that pethidine resulted in significantly less nausea and vomiting (184/498 versus 141/507; OR 1.52 [95% CI 1.17 to 1.98]). Meta-analysis of the three trials retains this significant difference owing to the dominant effect of the large trial (OR 1.37 [95% CI 1.09 to 1.72]). The large trial was the only study to investigate drowsiness/sleepiness and found this to be significantly higher in women who had received pethidine compared with those who received meptazinol (202/522 versus 147/513; OR 0.64 [95% CI 0.49 to 0.83]). No significant differences were found regarding mode of birth, fetal distress, Apgar scores, neonatal death or admission to a neonatal unit. Only the large trial reported on naloxone administration as an outcome measure, where a tendency towards higher incidence of naloxone administration was noted for babies born to women in the pethidine group (231/496 versus 198/479; OR 0.81 [95% CI 0.63 to 1.04]). This high incidence of naloxone administration is not commented upon by the authors of the review, although it should be noted that naloxone use is much less frequent in current UK practice following recommendations made by the UK Resuscitation Council.

Diamorphine versus pethidine
One UK RCT compared IM diamorphine ($n = 65$) with IM pethidine ($n = 68$).[145] [EL = 1+] Nulliparous women were randomised to receive either IM pethidine 150 mg or diamorphine 7.5 mg. Multiparous women were randomised to receive either 100 mg pethidine IM or 5 mg diamorphine IM. All participants received the anti-emetic prochlorperazine at the same time as the trial drugs. Two measures of pain relief favoured diamorphine compared with pethidine: VAS score (0–100) 1–2 hours after administration (58 versus 67; WMD −9.00 [95% CI −10.21 to −7.79], $P < 0.0001$) and women not satisfied with pain relief 1–2 hours post-administration (35 versus 56; RR 0.63 [95% CI 0.43 to 0.94], $P = 0.02$). Vomiting during labour was also significantly reduced in the group of women who received diamorphine (11 versus 28; RR 0.39 [95% CI 0.17 to 0.86], $P = 0.02$). No significant difference was found for sleepiness or drowsiness during labour, mode of birth, 5 minute Apgar scores or neonatal death/admission to neonatal intensive care unit (NICU). Time from first drug dose to birth was shorter for women assigned to the pethidine group (4.5 versus 4.9 hours, WMD 0.40 hours [95% CI 0.26 to 0.54 hours]). This represents a difference of 24 minutes, which is not likely to be significant clinically.

Pentazocine versus pethidine
Six double-blind RCTs compared 40–60 mg pentazocine with 100 mg pethidine. Trial sizes ranged from 60 to 180 women, including 678 women in total, and are summarised in two systematic reviews.[141,142] [EL = 1+] Based on a meta-analysis of findings from all six studies, no significant difference was found between the two groups regarding pain relief (measured as women not satisfied with pain relief 1–2 hours after administration): OR 0.99 [95% CI 0.70 to 1.39]. Significantly more women in the pentazocine group required further analgesia (OR 1.95 [95% CI 1.31 to 2.89], data from five studies). There was a trend towards fewer women suffering nausea and vomiting during labour in the pentazocine group, although the numbers involved were small and did not reach statistical significance (OR 0.56 [95% CI 0.30 to 1.07]). No significant differences were noted for drowsiness/sleepiness in labour. Few trials reported on other outcomes and, where they did, the numbers involved were small and differences not statistically significant.

IM opioids versus IM opioids: same opioid, different doses

Description of included studies
Two trials conducted in the 1970s compared a higher and lower dose of pethidine. Both are reported in the two systematic reviews outlined above.[141,142] A total of 173 women were involved in the two studies. One trial reported in both systematic reviews compared tramadol 50 mg (*n* = 30) with 100 mg (*n* = 30).[141,142]

Review findings

Pethidine 40–50 mg versus pethidine 80–100 mg
Each study used a different outcome for the assessment of pain relief. In the larger study, women's satisfaction with pain relief 1–2 hours post-administration was recorded. A high proportion of women in both groups were not satisfied with the pain relief received; 42/55 in the lower dose group and 37/57 in the higher dose group (OR 1.73 [95% CI 0.77 to 3.88]). The smaller study (*n* = 20 in each group) reported numerical pain scores 2 hours after drug administration. Again there was no difference between the two groups (mean numerical pain score): lower dose 1.70 (SD 0.63); higher dose 1.35 (SD 0.45); OR 0.35 [95% CI 0.01 to 0.69]. Both studies reported the need for additional analgesia (other than epidural), which was significantly higher for women in the lower dose group (28/88 versus 10/85; OR 3.74 [95% CI 1.75 to 8.00]). The use of epidural analgesia was not reported, perhaps because these studies were carried out in the 1970s when the use of epidural analgesia was not widespread. The incidence of nausea and vomiting was also investigated by both studies and, although found to be higher for the higher dose in both, this did not reach statistical significance (9/88 versus 17/85; OR 0.46 [95% CI 0.20 to 1.06]. Drowsiness and sleepiness were also more commonly reported by women in the higher dose group, although again this increase did not reach statistical significance (11/68 versus 19/65; OR 0.48 [95% CI 0.21 to 1.07], one study). No other maternal outcomes were reported. Neonatal outcomes were only investigated by the smaller study, where one baby in the higher dose group required resuscitation and one required naloxone, compared with none in the lower dose group.

Tramadol 50 mg versus 100 mg
Findings from this trial showed that more women in the lower dose group were not satisfied with pain relief 1–2 hours after administration (27/30 versus 7/30; OR 14.44 [95% CI 5.24 to 39.74]). Side effects were rare and slightly more prevalent in the higher dose group, but these differences did not reach statistical significance (nausea or vomiting: 1/30 versus 3/30, OR 0.35 [95% CI.005 to 2.61]; drowsiness or sleepiness: 2/30 versus 3/30, OR 0.65 [95% CI 0.11 to 4.00]). There was one instrumental birth and one caesarean birth in each group. No other outcomes were considered.

5.6.2 Intravenous use of opioids

Intravenous (IV) opioids versus placebo

IV pethidine versus IV placebo

Description of included studies
Two RCTs were reviewed that compared IV pethidine with an IV placebo (saline). The first was a double-blind RCT undertaken primarily in order to investigate the effects of pethidine on labour dystocia, looking at analgesic efficacy as a secondary outcome.[146] [EL = 1+] A second RCT, carried out in Thailand, examined the efficacy and side effects of IV pethidine.[147] [EL = 1+]

Review findings
In an RCT involving women in delayed active labour (4–6 cm cervical dilatation, delay diagnosed by attending obstetrician), the women were randomly assigned to receive 100 mg pethidine IV (administered in 50 ml saline over 15 minutes) (*n* = 205) or IV placebo (*n* = 202).[146] [EL = 1+] Pain was assessed using a VAS 15, 30 and 60 minutes after administration. Pain scores, at all times, were significantly lower for women receiving the pethidine (severe pain score (7–10 on VAS): at 15 minutes RR 0.87 [95% CI 0.78 to 0.96]; at 30 minutes RR 0.75 [95% CI 0.66 to 0.84]; at 60 minutes RR 0.74 [95% CI 0.66 to 0.84]; during second stage: RR 0.77 [95% CI 0.69 to 0.86]). However, more than 66% of the women rated their pain scores as severe throughout the first hour

following the administration of pethidine. The incidence of side effects was significantly higher in the women who received pethidine (any adverse effect: RR 1.91 [95% CI 1.44 to 2.53]; nausea: RR 1.60 [95% CI 1.05 to 2.43]; vomiting RR 1.97 [95% CI 1.09 to 3.55]; dizziness RR 4.68 [95% CI 2.59 to 8.46]). The need for augmentation with oxytocin was also significantly higher in the intervention group (RR 2.24 [95% CI 1.13 to 4.43]). Neonatal outcomes were also found to be significantly worse following the administration of pethidine, namely: Apgar < 7 at 1 minute: RR 4.11 [95% CI 1.72 to 9.80]; umbilical cord arterial pH< 7.20: RR 1.55 [95% CI 1.13 to 2.14]; umbilical cord arterial pH< 7.10: RR 3.94 [95% CI 1.76 to 8.82]. There were no significant differences in Apgar scores at 5 minutes: Apgar < 7 at 5 minutes: RR 11.82 [95% CI 0.66 to 210.25].

In a second RCT, women in established labour (3–5 cm cervical dilatation) requesting analgesia were randomly allocated to received IV pethidine (n = 42) (women < 75 kg received 50 mg, women > 75 kg received 75 mg) or IV saline (n = 42) (1.0 or 1.5 ml).[147] [EL = 1+] Women who had nausea and/or vomiting were also given 25 mg promethazine. VAS scores were reported by women 15, 30 and 60 minutes post-administration. These scores were then categorised prior to statistical analysis (0 = no pain; 1–3 = mild pain; 4–7 = moderate pain; 8–10 = severe pain). An observer recorded the woman's vital signs, the fetal heart rate (FHR) and rated level of sedation (on a 5-point Likert scale) at the same intervals. No significant differences were found between the intervention and control group regarding blood pressure (BP), pulse or respiratory rate, or the FHR (described as mean differences, no statistical analysis reported). No significant differences were found between the two groups for median pain scores at each time interval. The means of the pain increment scores for each time interval (i.e. 0–15 minutes, 15–30 minutes, etc.) were significantly higher for the control group throughout the study period. It is questionable, however, whether it is meaningful to calculate and compare means of categorical scores derived from a 0–10 scale. Side effects were more frequent in the intervention group: nausea/vomiting: n = 15 versus n = 2; dizziness: n = 11 versus n = 0. The authors reported no significant differences for mode of birth, Apgar scores or administration of naloxone, but no figures were given. Women's views of pain relief were sought within 24 hours of giving birth. While significantly more women in the intervention group gave positive reports of the effectiveness of pain relief, this figure was only 23.80% compared with 7.10% in the control group.

IV opioids: dose-finding

IV morphine

Description of included studies
A dose-finding study, conducted in Sweden, investigated the analgesic efficacy of IV morphine during the first stage of labour.[148] [EL = 3]

Review findings
IV morphine was given to 17 women (11 nulliparae) in active labour (three contractions every 10 minutes lasting at least 60 seconds and a cervical dilatation of at least 4 cm) and requesting analgesia. Amniotomy was performed if membranes had not ruptured spontaneously. All women were given repeated doses of IV morphine (0.05 mg/kg) after every third contraction, until a total dose of 0.20 mg/kg was reached. Pain intensity and level of sedation were measured using a 10 cm VAS scale. Women were also asked to indicate on a schematic diagram where the pain was located. Pain assessments were performed immediately after the first three contractions following each administration of morphine. Morphine was found to significantly reduce reported pain intensity (initial pain intensity versus pain intensity following four doses of morphine: mean = 85 mm [range 53 to 100 mm] to 70.0 mm [range 46 to 99 mm], z = 2.49, P = 0.01, Wilcoxon test). However, this decrease translates to a reduction from 'unbearable' to 'severe' pain rather than a clinically significant reduction in pain. The number of women experiencing back pain was significantly reduced from 13/14 to 4/14 (P = 0.01) but in 14/17 women there was no reduction in abdominal pain after morphine administration. Following morphine administration, 14/17 women requested and received epidural analgesia. The sedative effects of IV morphine were marked: VAS before versus after morphine administration 0 mm [range 0 to 0 mm] versus 78 mm [range 56.1 to 99.5], P < 0.05. The authors also reported that several women who received the maximum dose of morphine were asleep between contractions, and three could not be given all the dose increments of morphine owing to its severe sedative effects. No difference in neonatal outcome was reported (Apgar scores at 1 and 5 minutes).

IV opioids versus IM opioids

IV pethidine versus IM pethidine

Description of included studies
One Canadian RCT was identified that compared IV pethidine ($n = 19$) with IM pethidine ($n = 20$).[149] [EL = 1+]

Review findings
IM pethidine was administered in 50–100 mg doses every 2 hours as required, up to a maximum dose of 200 mg. The IV group of women received a 25 mg bolus then a background infusion rate of 60 mg/hour, with an additional 25 mg bolus available at hourly intervals if required. The main outcome measure was pain intensity during labour, which was measured using a 10 cm VAS when the analgesia was administered and every 30 minutes thereafter. Other outcome measures included pulse rate, BP, respiratory rate, side effects of medication, levels of sedation (5-point Likert scale), mode of birth and a second or third day postnatal assessment of satisfaction with pain relief. The baby's Apgar scores, vital signs and any required resuscitation interventions were also recorded. No significant differences were found between groups for maternal physiological measurements. The women who received IV pethidine had significantly lower pain scores from times 1.5 hours to 4.0 hours. However, women in the IM group received significantly less pethidine (mean = 82 mg) compared with the IV group (mean = 121 mg). Four women in the IV group received one additional bolus of 25 mg pethidine and one woman received two additional boluses. Eight women in the IM group also used Entonox compared with one in the IV group. Subgroup analysis of findings from women in the IV group who received 100–150 mg pethidine (mean dose 127 mg) ($n = 10$) still showed significantly lower pain scores when compared with women who received 100 mg pethidine IM. No other statistically significant differences were found regarding side effects, infant outcomes or women's satisfaction 2–3 days postnatally.

IV opioids versus IV opioids

Butorphanol versus pethidine versus butorphanol + pethidine

Description of included studies
A recent US RCT compared 1 mg butorphanol, 50 mg pethidine or both drugs in combination (0.5 mg butorphanol + 25 mg pethidine).[150] [EL = 1–] Fifteen women were randomly allocated to each group. Unfortunately, owing to the loss of an undisclosed number of women post-randomisation (including exclusion of women who requested an epidural within seven contractions of IV drug administration), there is a potentially high level of bias within the trial.

Review findings
Level of sedation, pain intensity and nausea were assessed using a 0–10 verbal scale, just before drug administration and between the sixth and seventh contraction post-administration. Women were also asked to choose words from a pain affective magnitude check list to describe the pain of the previous two contractions. All three treatments provided significant, but only moderate, pain relief (verbal scale scores before and after administration (mean): butorphanol: 7.2 (SD 0.6) versus 5.5 (SD 0.8), $P < 0.05$; pethidine: 7.4 (SD 0.4) versus 5.2 (SD 0.5), $P < 0.05$; butorphanol + pethidine: 7.4 (SD 0.4) versus 4.7 (SD 0.8), $P < 0.05$). No significant difference was found between groups regarding degree of pain relief. Unfortunately, the study did not report on the number of women who requested or received additional pain relief (the study ended with the seventh uterine contraction after administration of the study drug). Sedation increased after all drug treatments to a similar degree. Nausea was unaffected by drug treatment. (Exact figures are not reported but the findings are represented graphically.) FHR abnormalities were not significantly different between treatment groups ($n = 5, 3, 5$ butorphanol, pethidine, combination, respectively). Only two babies had Apgar scores of below 8 at 1 minute (one score of 6 in the butorphanol group and one score of 7 in the pethidine group). All babies had Apgar scores of 8 or above at 5 minutes.

IV patient-controlled analgesia (PCA): different opioids

Description of included studies and review findings

IV PCA: remifentanil versus pethidine
Two small UK RCTs provided the evidence for analgesic efficacy of PCA remifentanil compared with PCA pethidine.[151] [EL = 1+] [152] [EL = 1–]

In a recent RCT women received either remifentanil 40 mg with a 2 minute lockout (*n* = 20) or pethidine 15 mg with a 10 minute lockout (*n* = 20).[151] [EL = 1+] Baseline assessments were carried out for pain intensity (10 cm VAS), sedation score (5-point Likert scale), vital signs, nausea and anxiety. These measurements were repeated every 30 minutes following the administration of analgesia along with assessments of women's satisfaction with analgesia (10-point VAS). Continuous pulse oximetry was also carried out, plus 1 hour of continuous FHR monitoring following the commencement of PCA. One protocol violation was noted for a woman in the pethidine group and her data removed from the analysis (i.e. not an intention-to-treat analysis). Eighteen women in the remifentanil group continued to use the PCA up to, and during, birth compared with 14 women in the pethidine group (NS). Almost all women in both groups used Entonox as well as IV PCA. No significant differences were noted for pain intensity scores between the two groups (overall mean (SD) remifentanil: 6.4 cm (1.5 cm); pethidine: 6.9 cm (1.7 cm)). There were also no significant differences noted for levels of nausea, sedation, anxiety or time spent with oxygen saturation < 94% or < 90%. Satisfaction scores at 60 minutes were significantly higher for remifentanil than pethidine (median): 8.0 [IQR 7.5 to 9.0] versus 6.0 [IQR 4.5 to 7.5], *P* = 0.029). No significant differences were noted for classification of FHR tracings, Apgar scores or cord blood pH. Babies in the pethidine group had significantly lower Neurologic Adaptive Capacity Scores 30 minutes after birth, but there was no difference after 120 minutes.

An earlier small-scale double-blind RCT conducted at the same UK hospital also compared PCA remifentanil and PCA pethidine, although with slightly different doses.[152] [EL = 1−] Nine women were randomised to receive an IV bolus of remifentanil 0.5 mg/kg with a lockout period of 2 minutes and eight women were randomised to receive a bolus of 10 mg pethidine with a lockout period of 5 minutes. A 10 cm VAS was used to assess pain, nausea and itching immediately prior to administration of analgesia, at hourly intervals post-administration throughout labour and again 30 minutes after giving birth. Women's vital signs were also recorded along with 1 and 5 minute Apgar scores. At the start of the study, more women in the remifentanil group were receiving oxytocinon compared with women in the pethidine group (6/9 versus 2/8). Despite this, there was no significant difference in the initial baseline mean VAS score for pain (pethidine 47 mm; remifentanil 48 mm). The mean VAS score for pain throughout labour was reported as being significantly lower in the remifentanil group (actual value not given, although hourly mean scores were represented graphically). The post-birth VAS score was also reported to be significantly lower for women in the remifentanil group (again actual value not stated). No significant differences were found for nausea or itching between the two groups. No episodes of maternal hypotension, bradycardia or respiratory rate < 12 were recorded. Median Apgar scores at 1 and 5 minutes were found to be significantly lower in babies born to mothers who had received pethidine (median at 1 minute: remifentanil: 9 [range 9 to 9]; pethidine: 5.5 [range 5 to 8], *P* = 0.01; at 5 minutes: remifentanil: 10 [range 9 to 10]; pethidine: 7.5 [range 6 to 9], *P* = 0.04). One baby in the pethidine group was admitted to the neonatal unit. The trial was terminated early owing to concerns over the neonatal effects noted in the pethidine group.

IV PCA: fentanyl versus alfentanil
A small double-blind RCT conducted in Canada compared fentanyl with alfentanil, both administered as PCA.[153] [EL = 1−] Women in the fentanyl group (*n* = 11) received a loading dose of 50 mg IV. The PCA pump was then programmed to deliver a dose of 100 mg with a lockout of 5 minutes. A background infusion of 100 mg/hour was maintained. Women randomised to receive alfentanil (*n* = 12) were given a loading dose of 500 mg IV. The PCA pump was programmed to deliver a dose of 1 mg with a background infusion of 1 mg/hour. Hourly measurements were made of the drug dose received, total dose, sedation score and side effects. VAS pain scores were recorded every 30 minutes. Neonatal effects were assessed by Apgar scores, umbilical venous and arterial blood gases and neurobehavioural scores recorded at 4 and 24 hours. Two women were withdrawn from the data analysis owing to failure to observe the study protocol (these are not reported in the figures above). The two study groups were similar regarding demographic and obstetric details. No significant differences were found between the two groups for VAS pain scores from 1 to 3 cm cervical dilatation (mean [SD]: fentanyl: 61.0 mm [19.6 mm]; alfentanil: 67.3 mm [29.2 mm]) or 4 to 6 cm cervical dilatation: fentanyl: 54.9 mm [24.9 mm]; alfentanil: 67.7 mm [20.2 mm]). However, the mean VAS pain scores at 7 to 10 cm cervical dilatation were significantly higher in the alfentanil group compared with the fentanyl group (64.6 mm

[12.2 mm] versus 85.7 mm [13.9 mm], $P < 0.01$). No significant differences were observed for VAS scores for sedation, incidence of nausea or incidence of pruritus. Five of the 12 women receiving alfentanil described the pain relief as inadequate compared with one of the nine in the fentanyl group (NS). There were no significant differences in neonatal outcome with regard to Apgar scores, neurobehavioural scores, umbilical venous pH or naloxone requirement.

5.6.3 Patient-controlled administration for IV and IM use of opioids in labour

IV PCA opioids versus IM opioids

Description of included studies
One RCT was identified that compared IM diamorphine with IV PCA diamorphine for analgesia in labour.[154] [EL = 1+] A second small unblinded RCT conducted in the UK compared remifentanil via PCA ($n = 18$) with 100 mg pethidine IM (+ anti-emetic) ($n = 18$) ($n = 13$ primigravid women in each group).[155] [EL = 1–]

Review findings

IV PCA diamorphine versus IM diamorphine
This trial, carried out in Scotland in 2000–2002, assigned women to receive either 5 mg diamorphine IM (multigravid women) or 7.5 mg diamorphine IM (primigravid women), or a loading dose of 1.2 mg diamorphine IV with a PCA pump set to deliver 0.15 mg diamorphine per dose with a 5 minute lockout period (maximum dose 1.8 mg/hour) (IM group $n = 177$; IV PCA group $n = 179$). Primary outcomes were analgesia requirements during labour and women's satisfaction with pain relief. Women's perceptions of pain in labour, side effects and clinical outcomes for the women and babies were also recorded. Pain intensity during labour was measured using a verbal descriptor with pain at four levels and a 10 cm VAS. Pain scores were repeated hourly, between contractions, throughout labour. Findings for primigravid women and multigravid women are reported separately.

In primigravid women, those in the PCA group used significantly less analgesia than those in the IM group (IM mean 3.2 mg/hour; PCA mean 1.7 mg/hour; difference 1.5 mg/hour [95% CI 1.1 to 1.9 mg/hour], $P < 0.001$). Women in the PCA group were more likely to opt for an epidural and less likely to remain in the trial until the baby was born, although these differences did not reach statistical significance. Most women (over 80% in both groups) used additional analgesia, e.g. Entonox or TENS). Findings for multigravid women were similar. Again women in the PCA group used significantly less diamorphine compared with women in the IM group (IM mean 3.1 mg/hour; PCA mean 1.6 mg/hour; difference 1.6 mg/hour [95% CI 1.1 to 2.0 mg/hour], $P < 0.001$). Significantly fewer multigravid women completed their labour using IV PCA diamorphine compared with IM diamorphine (61% versus 79%, RR 0.77 [95% CI 0.61 to 0.97] but the need for an epidural was similar between the two groups, and much lower than in primigravid women (15%). Satisfaction with intrapartum pain relief measured 6 weeks postnatally was lower for women in the PCA group. Primigravid women allocated to the PCA group were significantly more likely to state that they were very dissatisfied with their use of diamorphine compared with women in the IM group (PCA 35% versus IM 7%, RR 5.08 [95% CI 2.22 to 11.61]). Only 34 % of primigravid women in the PCA group reported that they would use diamorphine again compared with 61% of the IM group (RR 0.56 [95% CI 0.40 to 0.79]). Findings for multigravid women were similar with significantly more women saying they were very dissatisfied with PCA diamorphine and significantly fewer in the PCA group stating that they would use it again. In addition, 44% of multigravid women in the PCA group felt they had received pain relief too late in labour, compared with 19% of IM users (RR 2.32 [95% CI 1.21 to 4.49]). The mean VAS score for primigravid women in the IM group was significantly lower than that for the PCA group (6.7 versus 5.3, difference 1.4 [95% CI 0.8 to 2.0]). There was no difference in mean maximum VAS scores. No significant differences were found for multigravid women's reported pain intensity during labour. Clinical outcomes were similar for women and babies in both groups. The authors explained the relatively poor outcomes for PCA diamorphine by stating that women and midwives appeared to lack confidence in the PCA and its ability to relieve intrapartum pain. Most women allocated to the PCA group used only a small proportion of the diamorphine potentially available to them, and quite quickly moved on to other forms of analgesia.

IV PCA remifentanil versus IM pethidine

An unblinded RCT conducted in the UK compared remifentanil via PCA (20 mg bolus over 20 seconds, 3 minute lockout, no background transfusion) (*n* = 18) with 100 mg pethidine (+ anti-emetic) (*n* = 18) (*n* = 13 primigravid women in each group).[155] [EL = 1–] Pain was assessed using a 10 cm VAS. Sedation and anxiety were assessed using a similar scale. Degree of nausea and vital signs were also recorded. All measurements were made prior to administration of analgesia and every 30 minutes thereafter. All women were monitored using continuous pulse oximetry. Pain scores at 60 minutes post-administration and maximum pain score during the first 2 hours post-administration were significantly lower in the PCA remifentanil group (median scores at 1 hour: 72 versus 48, *P* = 0.0004; maximum scores over 2 hours: 82.5 versus 66.5, *P* = 0.009). Women's and midwives' assessment of 'overall effective analgesia' were both significantly higher in the remifentanil group. For two women receiving pethidine and seven receiving remifentanil, haemoglobin saturations of ≤ 94% were recorded. The minimum saturation did not differ significantly between the two groups. There was no significant difference in the minimum recorded ventilatory rates between women in the two groups. There was no significant difference in numbers of women experiencing nausea and vomiting between the two groups (pethidine *n* = 10, remifentanil *n* = 5, *P* = 0.06). Significantly fewer women in the remifentanil group had a spontaneous vaginal birth (11/18 versus 16/17, *P* = 0.04). The authors reported no difference in Apgar scores between the two groups; however, this was based on data from the subgroup of women who did not receive an epidural.

Evidence statement

Parenteral opioids have a limited effect on pain in labour irrespective of the agent, route or method of administration. Tramadol, meptazinol and pentazocine are not widely used in the UK and the evidence to date shows no advantage over pethidine. There is limited evidence that diamorphine (IM) provides more effective analgesia than the other opioids studied, with the fewest side effects for the woman.

There is a lack of evidence on the optimum dose or route of administration, as well as the effect of opioids on infant behaviour in the longer term, particularly feeding.

Recommendations on intravenous/intramuscular opioids

Pethidine, diamorphine or other opioids should be available in all birth settings. Women should be informed that these will provide limited pain relief during labour and may have significant side effects for both the woman (drowsiness, nausea and vomiting) and her baby (short-term respiratory depression and drowsiness which may last several days).

Women should be informed that pethidine, diamorphine or other opioids may interfere with breastfeeding.

If an intravenous or intramuscular opioid is used, it should be administered with an antiemetic.

Women should not enter water (a birthing pool or bath) within 2 hours of opioid administration or if they feel drowsy.

Research recommendation on intravenous/intramuscular opioids

An RCT to compare the effect of pethidine [IM] and diamorphine [IM], and to explore optimum doses. Outcomes should encompass analgesic effect, and short- and long-term neonatal outcomes (including breastfeeding).

6 Pain relief in labour: regional analgesia

6.1 Regional analgesia

Introduction
In the UK, epidural analgesia was first used during labour in the 1960s, and its use became more widespread over the following 10 years. In 1971 the Central Midwives' Board issued a statement stating that they had no objections to an experienced midwife undertaking 'top-ups'.

The advent of neuraxial opioids changed the manner in which epidural analgesia was achieved during labour. Prior to the 1980s, local anaesthetics alone were used to provide regional analgesia in labour. Subsequently, opioids, e.g. fentanyl, were added to the local anaesthetic solutions, thereby allowing a lower concentration of local anaesthetic to be used.

Clinical questions
Is there evidence that the type, frequency and mode of administration of the following pharmacological and non-pharmacological pain relief and regional analgesia influence outcomes?

• analgesia: spinal, combined spinal–epidural, epidural and mobile epidural.

When is use of each of these methods of regional analgesia appropriate?

What observations, above baseline care, should be undertaken on both mother and baby while using regional analgesia?

What IV fluids should be used to maintain blood pressure during labour while using regional analgesia?

What is the most effective use of regional analgesia to minimise instrumental delivery rates and optimise pain relief in the second stage of labour?

6.2 Regional analgesia versus other types of analgesia in labour

6.2.1 Epidural analgesia versus no analgesia

Description of included studies
One RCT (Mexico, 1999), reported in a systematic review[156] and as an English abstract of a Spanish paper,[157] has been conducted which compared epidural analgesia and no analgesia. [EL = 1+] The study involved 129 nulliparous women (epidural $n = 69$; no analgesia $n = 63$) who were recruited into the study 'at the beginning of the active first stage of labour'.

Review findings
The Mexican trial found that the first stage of labour was significantly shorter in women who had epidural analgesia compared with women with no analgesia (WMD −119.00 minutes [95% CI −154.50 to −83.50 minutes]).[156] There was no significant difference in the length of the second stage of labour (WMD −6.03 minutes [95% CI −12.61 to 0.55 minutes]).[156] Labour was described as 'very painful' by 9% of the women with epidural analgesia compared with 100% women with no analgesia.[157] There was no difference in mode of birth between the two groups.

6.2.2 Epidural analgesia compared with non-epidural analgesia

Description of included studies
A recent Cochrane systematic review involving 21 RCTs (*n* = 6664 women) compared epidural (all forms) versus non-epidural or no analgesia.[156] [EL = 1+] Only one trial compared epidural analgesia with no analgesia and is reported above. Three of the included studies were excluded from the current review as the populations involved fell outside the scope of this guideline (namely women with pregnancy-induced hypertension and severe pre-eclampsia), leaving 17 studies involving 5576 women for this meta-analysis. All trials included women in labour at ≥ 36 weeks of pregnancy. One trial included women with induced labour as well as spontaneous onset of labour. All trials compared epidural analgesia with opioid analgesia. Epidural analgesia included pateint-controlled epidural analgesia (PCEA) as well as bolus top-ups with or without background infusions (continuous epidural infusion *n* = 6; intermittent boluses *n* = 5; PCEA *n* = 3; PCA with background infusion *n* = 2; intermittent boluses or continuous infusion *n* = 1).

Review findings
Only two of the included trials investigated women's perceptions of pain relief during the first and second stages of labour and found this was significantly better for women with epidural analgesia (first stage: WMD −15.67 [95% CI −16.98 to −14.35]; second stage: WMD −20.75 [95% CI −22.50 to −19.01], total *n* = 164). The need for additional pain relief was significantly lower in the groups of women who received epidural analgesia (13 trials) (RR 0.05 [95% CI 0.02 to 0.17]. The time of administration of pain relief to time pain relief was satisfactory was significantly lower for women in the epidural groups (one trial) (WMD −6.70 minutes [95% CI −8.02 to −5.38 minutes]). The second stage of labour was significantly longer for women with epidural analgesia (ten trials) (WMD 18.96 minutes [95% CI 10.87 to 27.06 minutes]) and the incidence of instrumental birth was higher for this group compared with women with non-epidural analgesia or no analgesia (15 trials) (RR 1.34 [95% CI 1.20 to 1.50]). Epidural analgesia was also found to be associated with an increased incidence of oxytocin augmentation (ten trials) (RR 1.19 [95% CI 1.02 to 1.38]), maternal hypotension (six trials) (RR 58.49 [95% CI 21.29 to 160.66]), maternal fever > 38 °C (two trials) (RR 4.37 [95% CI 2.99 to 6.38]) and urinary retention (three trials) (RR 17.05 [95% CI 4.82 to 60.39]). There was a significantly lower incidence of naloxone administration to the baby (four trials) (RR 0.15 [95% CI 0.06 to 0.40]) in the epidural groups, but no significant difference for umbilical artery pH < 7.2 (five trials) (RR 0.87 [95% CI 0.71 to 1.07]). There was no significant difference in the CS rate between the epidural and non-epidural groups (17 trials) (RR 1.08 [95% CI 0.92 to 1.26]). No significant difference was found for women's satisfaction with pain relief during labour (five trials) (RR 1.18 [95% CI 0.92 to 1.50]) or satisfaction with the childbirth experience (one trial) (RR 0.95 [95% CI 0.87 to 1.03]). There were also no differences found for: women's perceived feeling of poor control in labour, length of first stage of labour, headache, perineal trauma requiring suturing, long-term backache, Apgar score < 7 at 5 minutes and admission to NICU. No trials reported on serious potential problems such as venous thromboembolic events, respiratory failure or uterine rupture or long-term outcomes including neonatal morbidity, urinary incontinence or breastfeeding duration.

NB. The authors also conducted a sensitivity analysis excluding trials where more than 30% of women did not receive the allocated intervention. Results of this analysis did not differ significantly from the original findings.

A new meta-analysis was undertaken including only trials where low-dose epidural analgesia was used (less than, but not equal to, 0.25% bupivacaine or equivalent). Findings from this meta-analysis showed that low-dose epidural analgesia is associated with an increased risk of instrumental birth (seven trials) (RR 1.31 [95% CI 1.14 to 1.49]), longer second stage of labour (four trials) (WMD 20.89 minutes [95% CI 10.82 to 29.57 minutes]) and an increased risk of oxytocin augmentation (four trials) (RR 1.31 [95% CI 1.03 to 1.67]).

Findings from an earlier systematic review support the findings of the Cochrane review.[158] [EL = 1+] This review included 14 RCTs involving 4324 women. Two of these trials were excluded from the Cochrane review, and one (not mentioned by Cochrane) is noted to have had trial groups that were not well matched. The review also included two prospective studies involving 397 women. The prospective cohort studies were included in order to obtain data on breastfeeding and long-term urinary incontinence, neither of which was available from RCT data. Despite the slight difference in included trials, findings were similar to those for the Cochrane, review with women in epidural groups reporting less pain in the first stage (WMD −40 mm [95% CI −42 to −38 mm], $P < 0.0001$) and second stage of labour (WMD −29 mm [95% CI −38 to −21 mm], $P < 0.001$). This meta-analysis also found women to be more satisfied with epidural pain relief than non-epidural pain relief (OR 0.27 [95% CI 0.19 to 0.38], $P < 0.001$). Again epidural analgesia was not found to be associated with an increase in duration of the first stage of labour but was associated with a significantly lengthened second stage, use of oxytocin post analgesia and instrumental birth. The significant increase in maternal hypotension and fever > 38 °C noted by the Cochrane review was also evident in the findings of this review. Data from one of the prospective cohort studies reviewed showed that epidural use was associated with a significantly higher rate of urinary incontinence in the immediate postpartum period, but this difference was not evident at 3 or 12 months. The other prospective cohort study found no difference between groups regarding breastfeeding 'success' (not defined) at 6 weeks.

One further systematic review has been carried out to assess the effect of epidural versus non-epidural analgesia during labour on funic acid–base status of the baby at birth.[159] [EL = 1+] The review includes eight RCTs involving 2268 women and five non-RCTs involving 185 women. Of the eight RCTs, six were included in the Cochrane review. One was excluded on methodological grounds; the other consists of unpublished data not reported by Cochrane. Based on findings from the RCTs, umbilical artery pH was found to be significantly better for babies born to women in the epidural group (WMD 0.009 [95% CI 0.002 to 0.015], $P = 0.007$) as was base excess (WMD 0.779 mEq/l [95% CI 0.056 to 1.502 mEq/l], $P = 0.035$). The authors conclude that epidural analgesia is associated with improved neonatal acid–base status, suggesting that placental exchange is well preserved during epidural analgesia.

An RCT conducted in the USA investigated the effects of epidural analgesia on maternal fever > 38 °C.[160] [EL = 1+] The study was a secondary analysis of data collected during a trial conducted at one hospital over a 9 month period (1995–96) involving 715 women comparing epidural analgesia with PCA pethidine. Thirty-two per cent ($n = 115$) of the women allocated to the epidural group did not receive epidural analgesia (most owing to rapid progress and birth) and 28% ($n = 98$) of women allocated to receive PCA pethidine did not do so, again most of these owing to rapid progress. Only five women randomised to receive PCA pethidine crossed over and were given an epidural. Tympanic temperature was measured and recorded (frequency of measurements not stated). Incidence of maternal temperature > 38 °C was significantly higher in the epidural group (54/358 (15%) versus PCA 14/357 (4%), $P < 0.001$). When the effects of parity were investigated, it was found that this effect was apparent in nulliparous women but not in multiparous women (nulliparous with epidural 47/197 (24%) versus nulliparous with PCA 9/189 (5%), $P < 0.001$; parous with epidural 7/161 (4%) versus parous with PCA 6/168 (3%), NS). Stepwise logistic regression revealed that the following factors were significantly and independently associated with women's temperature > 38 °C: prolonged labour > 12 hours, internal fetal monitoring and oxytocin augmentation. The authors conclude that nulliparity and dysfunctional labour are significant co-factors in the fever attributed to epidural analgesia. It is also described how approximately 90% of the babies born to women with temperature > 38 °C received screening for neonatal sepsis and antibiotic therapy, even though none were found to have positive blood cultures. The proportion receiving septic screen and antibiotic therapy was the same, irrespective of whether epidural analgesia was used during labour.

A recent prospective cohort study has been undertaken in the USA to evaluate whether epidural analgesia is associated with a higher rate of abnormal fetal head positions at birth compared with non-epidural analgesia or no analgesia.[161] [EL = 2+] Women with spontaneous onset ($n = 698$) and induced labours ($n = 864$) were included in the study. The epidural group was far larger than the non-epidural group: $n = 1439$ and $n = 123$, respectively. Women were enrolled into the study 'as soon as possible' after admission to the delivery suite. Most of the women in spontaneous labour (92%) were enrolled before they had reached 4 cm cervical dilatation. An ultrasound scan was performed to ascertain the position of the fetal head at enrolment. Subsequent ultrasounds were performed at the time of administration of epidural analgesia (immediately before or within 1 hour of commencement), 4 hours after enrolment if an epidural had not been sited and when the woman was near the end of the first stage of labour (> 8 cm cervical dilatation). The position of the baby at birth was ascertained by asking the care provider immediately after the birth. Positions as recorded by ultrasound scans were determined by a single ultrasonographer some time later. For reporting of findings, ultrasound scans were divided into three categories – enrolment, epidural/ 4 hour and late labour. Of the study sample of 1562 women, 1208 (77%) had an interpretable epidural/4 hour ultrasound and 802 (51%) had an interpretable late ultrasound scan. The most common reason for missing data was the ultrasound scan not being performed, either because the woman declined the offer of a scan or the researcher was not available to perform it. Findings showed that changes of position by the unborn baby are common throughout labour, with final fetal position being established close to birth. Consequently, fetal position at enrolment was not a good predictor of fetal position at birth. Of women with a baby in the occiput posterior (OP) at birth, only 31% (59/190) had a baby in the OP position at enrolment in early labour. When comparing epidural with non-epidural groups, it was found that there were no significant differences in the proportion of babies in the OP position at enrolment or at the epidural/4 hour scan (enrolment: 23.4% versus 26.0%, NS; epidural/4 hours: 24.9% versus 28.3%, NS). However, women with an epidural were significantly more likely to have a baby in the OP position at birth (12.9% versus 3.3%, $P = 0.002$). Epidural was not associated with an occiput transverse (OT) position at any stage of labour. Further analysis also revealed that women with an unborn baby in the OP position at enrolment did not report more painful labours than those with an unborn baby in other positions, nor did these women report more severe back pain. There was also no difference in reported labour pain for different fetal positions at birth. Multinomial logistic regression examined association of epidural analgesia with the position of the baby at birth. The model incorporated maternal age, height, BMI, birthweight, gestational age, sex of baby, induction of labour, fetal position on enrolment, length of labour, and placental position. Epidural analgesia was found to be associated with an increase in the risk of OP position at birth compared with an occiput anterior (OA) position at birth (adjusted OR 3.5 [95% CI 1.2 to 9.9]). Epidurals were not associated with increased risk of OT position at birth (adjusted OR 1.3 [95% CI 0.6 to 3.0]). Mode of birth varied according to the position of the baby at birth, with spontaneous births being far more common where the baby was in an OA position (OA 76.2%; OT 13.5%; OP 17.4%, $P < 0.001$).

Another secondary analysis of RCT data reported above[160] was undertaken to examine the effects of epidural analgesia on the Friedman curve.[162] [EL = 1+] The analysis was performed for the subgroup of women who were admitted in labour with cervical dilatation of at least 3 cm and compared women with PCEA ($n = 226$) with women receiving PCA pethidine ($n = 233$). Progress in labour was assessed following the maternity unit's usual protocol, which included vaginal examinations performed at least 2 hourly. The absence of cervical change over 2 hours led to augmentation of labour using oxytocin. There was a low crossover from pethidine to epidural use ($n = 14$). Findings for duration of labour and rate of cervical dilatation showed that epidural analgesia was associated with a significant slowing of cervical dilatation leading to a lengthened active first stage of labour (median [first and third quartiles]): 5.2 hours [3.9, 8.0] versus 4.0 hours [2.7, 7.0], $P < 0.001$. There was no significant difference noted for the second stage of labour. Further subgroup analysis was undertaken in order to compare women who received oxytocin augmentation with those who did not. Findings from this analysis showed that the effects of epidural analgesia were apparent where women laboured without oxytocin, with both first and second stages of labour being significantly longer for women who had epidural analgesia (active first stage of labour: 4.9 hours [3.5, 6.1] versus 3.5 hours [2.0, 5.0], $P < 0.001$; rate of cervical dilatation: 1.2 cm/hour [0.9, 1.6] versus 1.5 cm/hour [1.0, 2.5], $P = 0.001$; second stage: 0.7 hours [0.4, 1.1] versus 0.6 hours [0.3, 0.9], $P = 0.046$; total length of labour: 5.6 hours [4.1, 7.3] versus 4.1 hours [2.7, 5.7], $P < 0.001$). These effects were not evident in women whose labours were augmented with oxytocin. Epidural analgesia was associated with a significantly higher rate of oxytocin augmentation (44% versus 32%, $P = 0.009$), forceps birth (12% versus 3%, $P = 0.003$) and a significantly lower rate of spontaneous births (82% versus 92%, $P = 0.004$). There was no significant difference in CS rate (5% versus 6%, $P = 0.94$).

A recent Canadian prospective cohort study investigated whether epidural analgesia during labour is a risk factor for back pain.[163] [EL = 2+] A group of women who received epidural analgesia for pain relief during labour ($n = 164$) were compared with a group who did not receive epidural analgesia ($n = 165$). Women with back pain prior to pregnancy were excluded from the study. Multivariate logistic regression analysis was used to provide adjusted relative risk estimates for risk factors associated with back pain following birth. Adjustments were made for parity, ethnicity, mode of birth and woman's weight. The frequency of low back pain was highest on day 1 after giving birth, being about 50% for each study group. Measured using a numeric pain scale on day 1 after the birth, there was significantly higher back pain in women who had received epidural analgesia compared with those who had not (median [range]: 1 [0 to 8] versus 0 [0 to 8], $P < 0.05$). For the subset of women who reported no back pain during pregnancy, the incidence of new onset back pain was also higher in the epidural group (adjusted RR 2.05 [95% CI 1.07 to 3.92]). However, these differences were not apparent at 7 days or 6 weeks postpartum (day 7: adjusted RR 1.00 [95% CI 0.54 to 1.86]; 6 weeks: adjusted RR 2.22 [95% CI 0.89 to 5.53]).

One large population-based cohort study was reviewed which examined the association between epidural analgesia and mode of birth.[164] [EL = 3] The study involved all singleton births at term in Sweden during 1998–2000, excluding elective caesarean sections, giving a population sample of 94 217 women. The sample included induced and spontaneous labours. It is inferred that all women are included i.e. those with medical and/or obstetric complications, although this is not made explicit. The study population was drawn from 52 delivery units which were stratified according to epidural rate (20–29%, $n = 5$ units; 30–39%, $n = 11$ units; 40–49%, $n = 20$ units; 50–59%, $n = 13$ units and 60–64%, $n = 3$ units). Fewer than 6% of women gave birth in a unit with an epidural rate below 30%. Most births, 40%, took place in units where 40–49% women received an epidural analgesia for labour ($n = 37 985$). Rates of caesarean birth and instrumental birth were then compared for each category of unit. No association was found between rate of epidural analgesia and non-elective caesarean birth. The lowest proportion of caesarean sections, 9.1%, were performed in units with the lowest epidural rate (20–29%) and the highest epidural rate (60–64%), with an OR 0.84 [95% CI 0.77 to 0.93] and OR 0.85 [95% CI 0.77 to 0.93], respectively (OR calculated to compare values with delivery units performing 40–49% epidurals as the reference group). For delivery units in other categories (30–39%, 40–49% and 50–59%) the CS rate ranged from 10.3% to 10.6%, with no statistical difference. No clear association was seen between epidural rate and rate of instrumental birth. Instrumental births were most common in units with an epidural rate of 50–59%, OR 1.23 [95% CI 1.18 to 1.29] compared with the 40–49% group. The lowest instrumental birth rate, 14.1%, was seen in units where 30–39% women had epidural analgesia for labour, OR 0.88 [95% CI 0.84 to 0.92]. In the other groups the instrumental birth rate varied between 15.3% and 15.7%. Comparison was also made between different levels of maternity care provision (classified as levels I, IIb, IIa and III, with level III representing university hospitals). Again no clear association was found between epidural rates at different levels of maternity unit and mode of birth.

Evidence statement
There is high-level evidence that, compared with non-epidural pharmacological analgesia, epidural analgesia:

- provides more effective pain relief in labour
- is associated with a longer second stage of labour and an increase in instrumental birth, although this effect could be due to the package of care currently practised
- has no evidence of a longer first stage of labour
- has no evidence of an increase in caesarean section
- has a positive effect on neonatal acid–base status.

Recommendations on epidural analgesia versus others

Before choosing epidural analgesia, women should be informed about the risks and benefits, and the implications for their labour.

This information about choosing epidural analgesia should include the following:

- It is only available in obstetric units.
- It provides more effective pain relief than opioids.
- It is associated with a longer second stage of labour and an increased chance of vaginal instrumental birth.
- It is not associated with long-term backache.
- It is not associated with a longer first stage of labour or an increased chance of caesarean birth.
- It will be accompanied by a more intensive level of monitoring and intravenous access.
- Modern epidural solutions contain opioids and, whatever the route of administration, all opioids cross the placenta and in larger doses (greater than 100 micrograms in total) may cause short-term respiratory depression in the baby and make the baby drowsy.

6.3   Timing of regional analgesia

Description of included studies
Six studies which addressed this issue were identified.[165–171] The studies are heterogeneous, thus each study is summarised in a narrative manner below.

Review findings
The study, involving 60 women, was conducted in Italy.[165] [EL = 2+] This was a prospective cohort study with sequential allocation. The study attempted to quantify minimum local analgesic concentration (MLAC) of extradural bupivacaine for women in early labour (median cervical dilatation 2 cm) and for women in late labour (median cervical dilatation 5 cm). There was evidence that MLAC of bupivacaine for women in late labour was higher than that for those in early labour.

Another study, conducted in Taiwan and published in 1999, involved 120 women.[166] [EL = 1+] Women scheduled for induced labour were randomly allocated to receive either 0.0005% fentanyl for epidural analgesia in their early first stage of labour or no epidural analgesia during their early first stage of labour. The early first stage was defined as cervical dilatation equal to or less than 4 cm. Women who received fentanyl in their early first stage seemed to have less pain on the visual analogue pain scale, although there was no evidence of a difference in duration of first and second stage, mode of birth, cord arterial gas or Apgar score.

Another RCT, conducted in the USA and published in 1994, studied 149 women in whom labour was induced with oxytocin and 334 women in spontaneous labour.[167,168] [EL = 1+] The trial compared either epidural bupivacaine analgesia or intravenous nalbuphine during their early first stage of labour (defined as cervix dilated at least 3 cm but less than 5 cm) For both the induction and spontaneous labour cohorts, there was evidence that women in the early epidural group had a lower pain score between 30 and 120 minutes after the randomisation, and an increased incidence of hypotension. In comparison, women in the early IV nalbuphine group had newborns with a lower umbilical arterial and venous pH than the other group. There was no evidence of a difference in the mode of birth or duration of labour, between the cohorts. This derives from two studies (one for induced/augmented labour, the other was spontaneous labour) and therefore needs clarification.

The fourth study was an RCT, conducted in Israel, published in 1998 and involving 60 women.[169] [EL = 1+] The trial compared an early administration group, who received epidural bupivacaine with cervical dilatation less than 4 cm, and a later administration group, who received the same dose of epidural bupivacaine with cervical dilatation equal to or more than 4 cm. There was no evidence of a difference in duration of second stage, mode of birth or Apgar score at 1 and 5 minutes.

The fifth study is an RCT, conducted in the USA, published in 2005.[170] [EL = 1+] The trial compared intrathecal fentanyl and intravenous hydromorphine injection in 750 nulliparous women in spontaneous labour with cervical dilatation of less than 4 cm. Following the intrathecal fentanyl, the women received epidural analgesia (0.625 mg/ml bupivacaine with 2 micrograms/ml fentanyl by patient-controlled epidural analgesia). There is evidence that the women who received intrathecal fentanyl had a shorter duration of labour, lower pain scores and fewer newborn babies with low Apgar scores, while there was no evidence of a difference in mode of birth.

One trial, conducted in Israel involving 449 nulliparous term women in early labour (at less than 3 cm of cervical dilatation), compared either immediate initiation of epidural analgesia at first request ($n = 221$) with delay of epidural until at least 4 cm of cervical dilatation.[171] [EL = 1+] There was no evidence of a difference in CS rate (RR 1.18, $P = 0.77$), the use of oxytocin in the first stage (RR 1.07, $P = 0.57$) or spontaneous vaginal birth (RR 0.91, $P = 0.85$) between the two groups. However, in the late epidural group 78% of women stated that in their next labour they would prefer to be in the early epidural group, 7.0% preferred to be allocated to the other group and 3.2% were undetermined. The differences in preferences between the two groups were statistically significant ($P < 0.001$).

Evidence statement
There is a high level of evidence that intrathecal or epidural analgesia administered during the early first stage of labour does not affect the progress of labour, mode of birth or immediate neonatal condition compared with administration later in labour.

Recommendation on timing of epidural analgesia

Women in labour who desire regional analgesia should not be denied it, including women in severe pain in the latent first stage of labour.

6.4 Care and observations for women with regional analgesia in labour

6.4.1 Preloading with intravenous (IV) infusions for epidural analgesia

Description of included studies
One systematic review published in 2004 was included in this subsection.[172] [EL = 1+] The systematic review included a total of six trials involving 473 women. Among the six trials, two trials used high-dose local anaesthetic, two trials used low-dose anaesthetic with fentanyl and two trials used combined spinal–epidural (CSE), comparing preloading IV infusion with dummy or no preloading as controls.

Review findings

High-dose anaesthetic
In one trial, preloading reduced the incidence of women's hypotension (RR 0.07 [95% CI 0.01 to 0.53]; $n = 102$ women) and fetal heart rate abnormalities (RR 0.36 [95% CI 0.16 to 0.83]; $n = 102$ women), although there was no evidence of differences in other perinatal and maternal outcomes for this trial and another high-dose epidural trial.

Low-dose anaesthetic
Meta-analysis of the two trials using low-dose anaesthetic showed that there was no evidence of differences in women's hypotension (RR 0.73 [95% CI 0.36 to 1.48]; $n = 260$ women) and fetal heart rate abnormalities (RR 0.64 [95% CI 0.39 to 1.05]; $n = 233$ women). No other outcomes were reported.

CSE
There was no evidence of differences reported between the two groups in the CSE trials (spinal/opioid trial: RR for women's hypotension 0.89 [95% CI 0.43 to 1.83]; $n = 40$ women; RR for fetal heart rate abnormalities 0.70 [95% CI 0.36 to 1.37]; $n = 32$ women). There were no reported incidents of hypotension or fetal heart rate abnormalities in the opioid-only study ($n = 30$ women).

Evidence statement
Preloading infusion for high-dose epidural anaesthesia may reduce the incidence of maternal hypotension and fetal heart rate abnormality. There was no evidence of differences in other outcomes.

There was no evidence that IV fluid preloads influenced maternal hypotension and fetal heart rate abnormalities, in women receiving CSE or low-dose epidural analgesia.

Recommendations on preloading for regional analgesia

Intravenous access should always be secured prior to commencing regional analgesia.

Preloading and maintenance fluid infusion need not be administered routinely before establishing low-dose epidural analgesia and combined spinal–epidural analgesia.

6.4.2 Observations for women with epidural in labour

Description of included studies

No evidence was found for the effects upon labour outcomes of carrying out maternal observations. Two systematic reviews are summarised here that provide evidence pertaining to side effects associated with epidural analgesia. One systematic review specifically focused on side effects and co-interventions of epidural analgesia and their implications for the care of women during labour and childbirth.[173] [EL = 1+] The second is the systematic review reported above that compared epidural with non-epidural analgesia.[156] [EL = 1+]

Review findings

A systematic review of 19 RCTs published between 1990 and 2000, involving 2708 women, has been conducted to describe the side effects and co-interventions that accompany epidural analgesia in labour.[173] [EL = 1+] It is not stated whether all trials included only women with term pregnancies. A range of epidural methods was used in the included trials: CSE, traditional bolus epidural, low-dose epidural with opioid and one trial involving PCEA. Seven studies had one trial group where epinephrine was added to the epidural, and two evaluated the use of clonidine. A narrative summary of findings is given. The most commonly investigated side effect was hypotension (16 studies). This was defined as a systolic blood pressure reading below 90–100 mmHg or a 20–30% decrease below baseline. The overall range for the incidence of maternal hypotension was 0–50%, with an average incidence of 10.5% across 44 trial groups (calculated as the mean incidence for all trial groups reporting that outcome). In 16 trial groups, covering a wide range of epidural agents, including opioids, there were no incidents of hypotension. Eight trial groups reported an incidence of hypotension above 20%. Five of these included the use of either sufentanil or clonidine (drugs not currently used in the UK).

Motor power was evaluated in eight studies using the Bromage or a modified Bromage scale to assess leg strength or the rectus abdominus muscle test (ability to rise from the supine position). Reported in terms of no impairment, the range across eight trials was 76–100%, with an overall average incidence at least 87.7% (this imprecise figure comes about owing to one trial reporting the incidence of no impairment as > 80% for all four trial groups). Eight studies also reported the ability of women to walk during labour. The incidence is given as 15.3–100%, although details are missing from the table. It is noted that even in trials where women are encouraged to walk in labour, a large proportion chose not to.

Four studies investigated voiding difficulty as a side effect of epidural analgesia. The ability to micturate 'spontaneously' (three studies) ranged from 0% to 68%, with an average incidence of 27.5%. The need for catheterisation (one study) ranged from 28% to 61% across three study groups, with an average incidence of 41.3%.

Sedation was reported by five studies. A wide range of findings was recorded: 1–56%, with an average incidence of 21%. The highest levels of sedation (32–56%) were found in women who received 5–10 micrograms sufentanil.

Pruritus was investigated by 17 studies. In comparison groups from these 17 studies, in which women were given drug combinations including opioids, the incidence of pruritus ranged from 8% to 100% with an average incidence of 62%. The highest incidences occurred in groups with the highest doses of opioid. The incidence of pruritus occurring in the eight study groups from six trials who did not receive opioids, ranged from 0% to 4%. The duration of itching was not reported by any of the studies, but most did mention that treatment was not required.

Nausea (without vomiting) was investigated by seven studies, with the incidence ranging from 0% to 30% with an average of 7.3%. Nausea and vomiting (five studies) ranged from 0% to 20% with an average of 4.6%.

Shivering as a side effect was only reported by two studies, each of which recorded one case of shivering.

The systematic review reported in the subsection above (epidural versus non-epidural) reported a number of side effects as outcomes.[156] This review is based upon meta-analysis of 18 of the included trials (*n* = 5705 women). All trials included women in labour at ≥ 36 weeks of pregnancy. One trial included women with induced labour as well as spontaneous onset of labour. One trial compared epidural analgesia with no analgesia and the remainder compared epidural analgesia with opioid analgesia. Epidural analgesia included PCEA as well as bolus top-ups with or without background infusions. Findings showed that epidural analgesia was associated with a significant increase in the following side effects compared with non-epidural analgesia: maternal hypotension (six trials): RR 58.49 [95% CI 21.29 to 160.66]; maternal fever > 38 °C (two trials): RR 4.37 [95% CI 2.99 to 6.38]; and urinary retention during labour (three trials): RR 17.05 [95% CI 4.82 to 60.39]. No significant differences were found between groups for nausea and vomiting (seven trials): RR 1.03 [95% CI 0.87 to 1.22] or drowsiness (three trials): RR 1.00 [95% CI 0.12 to 7.99]. Epidural analgesia was also found to be associated with a significant increase in the length of the second stage of labour (ten trials): WMD 16.24 minutes [95% CI 6.71 to 25.78 minutes] and an increased use of oxytocin augmentation (ten trials): RR 1.19 [95% CI 1.02 to 1.38].

Evidence statement

The safety issues involved mean that there is no evidence on the effects of carrying out maternal observations upon clinical outcomes.

Evidence was found on the side effects of epidural analgesia. These were:

- hypotension (mainly derived from studies of high-dose local anaesthetic techniques)
- urinary retention
- pyrexia
- pruritus.

Recommendation on observations for women with regional analgesia

The following additional observations should be undertaken for women with regional analgesia:

- During establishment of regional analgesia or after further boluses (10 ml or more of low-dose solutions) blood pressure should be measured every 5 minutes for 15 minutes.
- If the woman is not pain free 30 minutes after each administration of local anaesthetic/opioid solution, the anaesthetist should be recalled.
- Hourly assessment of the level of the sensory block should be undertaken.

For monitoring babies' wellbeing for women with regional analgesia, refer to Section 6.4.6 later in this chapter. For general observations for women in the first, second and third stages of labour, refer to Sections 7.6, 8.3 and 9.2, respectively.

6.4.3 Positions and mobilisation for women with regional analgesia

Description of included studies

A systematic review has been carried out to determine the effect of first-stage ambulation on mode of birth for women with epidural analgesia.[174] [EL = 1+] The review was of good quality and identified five RCTs for inclusion and meta-analysis (*n* = 1161 women). A second recent systematic review has been conducted in order to assess the effectiveness of maintaining an upright position versus a supine position during the second stage of labour, in order to reduce the number of instrumental births in women choosing epidural analgesia.[175] [EL = 1+] Only two studies of good methodological quality, but involving quite small samples, are included in the review (*n* = 281 women). Finally, a UK RCT was identified which compared lateral position with a sitting position for nulliparous women with epidural analgesia in the second stage of labour.[176] [EL = 1–] The trial is described as a pragmatic RCT, which refers to a trial that is designed to assess the outcomes of interventions as applied in practice (rather than in a trial setting, which is sometimes seen as artificial and not representative of usual practice). The drawback of this pragmatic approach is that sometimes the methodological rigour of the trial is undermined, thus not allowing generalisation of findings. In the trial, women were randomly assigned to the lateral position or upright position for second stage of labour at the first point of consent, antenatally. Women were asked to maintain their allocated trial position during the passive second stage of labour until the onset of active pushing.

Review findings

First stage
The systematic review of ambulation in the first stage of labour for women with epidural analgesia compared ambulatory with non-ambulatory groups. The ambulatory groups also included women who spent time in an upright position (standing or sitting > 45 degrees from the horizontal) but not necessarily walking. The amount of time women were asked to spend walking also varied, ranging from at least 5 minutes in every hour to at least 20 minutes every hour (in one trial the period of time spent walking was not recorded, but all women in the ambulatory group were reported to have walked for at least some of the time). The proportion of women in the ambulatory groups who actually walked during the first stage of labour ranged from 66% to 86%. The amount of walking observed by women in the non-ambulatory groups ranged from none at all to 15% walking for at least some of the time. All included studies had similar inclusion criteria (singleton, cephalic presentation, term, uncomplicated pregnancy). Three included only nulliparous women. Four trials included induced labours as well as those with spontaneous onset. Four trials included ambulation only during the first stage, with the second stage conducted with the women in bed. There was no statistically significant difference in the mode of giving birth when women with an epidural ambulated during the first stage of labour compared with those who remained recumbent: instrumental birth (RR 0.91 [95% CI 0.93 to 1.44]) and caesarean section (RR 0.91 [95% CI 0.70 to 1.19]). There were also no significant differences between the two groups for any of the following outcomes: use of oxytocin augmentation, duration of labour, satisfaction with analgesia, hypotension, FHR abnormalities or Apgar scores. There were no apparent adverse effects associated with ambulation but the incidence of reporting adverse effects was low.

Second stage
A recent systematic review has been conducted in order to assess the effectiveness of maintaining an upright position versus a supine position during the second stage of labour.[175] [EL = 1+] Upright positions included standing, walking, kneeling, squatting or sitting > 60 degrees to the horizontal. There was no significant difference between groups regarding risk of instrumental birth (RR 0.77 [95% CI 0.46 to 1.28]) and caesarean section (RR 0.57 [95% CI 0.28 to 1.16]). Both studies reported a significant reduction in duration of labour associated with upright positions (one study reported duration of second stage and the other total labour duration). Data on other outcomes including perineal trauma, postpartum haemorrhage (PPH), maternal satisfaction and infant wellbeing were insufficient to draw any conclusions.

A UK RCT was also identified which compared lateral position in the second stage of labour with a sitting position.[176] [EL = 1−] Findings from this study showed that women allocated to the lateral position for the passive second stage (n = 49) had a lower rate of instrumental birth than women allocated to the sitting position (n = 58), although this just failed to reach statistical significance (32.7% versus 51.7%, $\chi^2 = 3.9$, degrees of freedom (df) = 1 [95% CI 0.40 to 1.01], with an associated reduction in episiotomy (44.9% versus 63.8%, $\chi^2 = 3.8$, df = 1 [95% CI 0.44 to 1.00]. However, the overall rates of perineal trauma was not significantly different (78% versus 86%, RR 0.75 [95% CI 0.47 to 1.17]). The findings from the study cannot be generalised owing to a number of methodological weaknesses, including an underpowered sample size due to difficulties in recruitment, and a significant difference between the two trial groups in body mass index and rates of induction of labour. It was also noted that the rate of instrumental birth was higher for women included in the trial than expected based on the previous year's data.

6.4.4 Pushing in the second stage for women with regional analgesia

Description of included studies
A recent systematic review including five RCTs, involving a total of 462 women, has been carried out to assess the impact of discontinuing epidural late in labour (> 8 cm cervical dilatation) on mode of birth, women's perceptions of analgesia and satisfaction with care.[177] [EL = 1+] The trials included spontaneous onset and induced labours. Details are not given as to the proportion of induced labours in each trial. A second recent systematic review was identified that aimed to compare the potential benefits and harms of a policy of delayed pushing, among women who had uncomplicated pregnancies, with effective epidural analgesia established in the first stage of labour.[178] [EL = 1+] The primary outcome examined was instrumental birth. Secondary outcomes

included other modes of birth, a range of maternal complications, long-term maternal outcomes and fetal outcomes. Nine trials were included in the review involving 2953 women. Most studies excluded women with medical or obstetric complications. A small, recent US RCT compared immediate (*n* = 22) versus delayed pushing (*n* = 23) in two groups of nulliparous women, in induced labour at term, with effective epidural analgesia.[179] [EL = 1+] Finally, a prospective cohort study conducted in Ireland was identified that also compared delayed pushing with early pushing, in the second stage.[180] [EL = 2+] All women were having their first baby, giving birth at term and were described as similar in terms of height and age. Infant weights were also similar between the two groups. No details were given regarding the unborn baby's position or station at the onset of the second stage.

Review findings
Findings from the meta-analysis of the systematic review carried out to assess impact of discontinuing epidural late in labour showed no difference in instrumental birth rates, i.e. discontinuing an epidural prior to the second stage of labour does not lower the incidence of instrumental births (RR 0.84 [95% CI 0.61 to 1.15]).[177] [EL = 1+] Conversely, no significant difference was found between groups regarding rates of spontaneous birth (RR 1.11 [95% CI 0.95 to 1.30]) or CS (RR 0.98 [95% CI 0.43 to 2.25]). Duration of the second stage was found to be similar between the two groups (three studies) (WMD −5.80 minutes [95% CI −12.91 to 1.30 minutes]). The two studies not included in the meta-analysis also found no significant difference in the length of the second stage. No significant differences were found for fetal outcome: low Apgar score at 1 minute (four studies) (RR 1.55 [95% CI 0.94 to 2.55]) and umbilical artery pH (three studies) (RR 3.92 [95% CI 0.45 to 34.21]). The only significant difference found between the two study groups was a significant increase in women's reports of inadequate analgesia, in groups where the epidural was discontinued late in the first stage of labour (four studies) (RR 3.68 [95% CI 1.99 to 6.80]). Unfortunately, women's views of, or satisfaction with, care during labour were not reported by any of the trials.

The second recent systematic review compared the potential benefits and harms of a policy of delayed pushing, among women with uncomplicated pregnancies and with effective epidural analgesia established in the first stage of labour.[178] [EL = 1+] Eight studies compared immediate pushing at discovery of full dilatation with delayed pushing. One study used early pushing (within 1 hour of discovery of full dilatation) as the control group. The duration of delay until pushing commenced in the experimental group varied between studies, ranging from 1 hour (or earlier if involuntary urge to push) to 3 hours. One study set no time limit on the delay. Management of the active second stage also varied between studies and included techniques for pushing (e.g. breath-holding) and use of oxytocin. The methodological quality of included studies varied, with only one reporting adequate random allocation concealment. Three studies enrolled women before full dilatation was reached, and one of these subsequently excluded 19% of enrolled women on medical grounds or owing to first-stage caesarean section. Meta-analysis of findings showed a small reduction in the incidence of instrumental births which failed to reach statistical significance (RR 0.94 [95% CI 0.84 to 1.01]). Meta-analysis of the five studies which reported mid-pelvic or rotational instrumental births showed a 31% reduction in the delayed pushing group, which was statistically significant (RR 0.69 [95% CI 0.55 to 0.87]). Total duration of the second stage of labour was significantly higher for the delayed pushing groups in seven of the eight studies where this was reported, with an overall increase of 58 minutes (calculated from findings of three trials that reported mean duration with SD) (WMD 58.2 minutes [95% CI 21.51 to 94.84 minutes]). However, duration of the active second stage varied between trials. Meta-analysis of two trials that reported the mean length of the active second stage, with SD, showed no significant difference between the two groups (WMD 1.11 minutes [95% CI −20.19 to 22.40 minutes]). Only two studies reported intrapartum fever. One of these studies found no significant difference between the groups; the other found a significantly higher incidence of maternal fever in the delayed pushing group. None of the other secondary maternal outcomes examined showed any significant difference. Only one study reported pelvic floor morbidity at 3 months postpartum and found no significant differences between the two groups. No study reported on urinary incontinence. Few studies reported infant outcomes and no significant differences were found for any of the outcomes examined.

In the USA, an RCT compared immediate versus delayed pushing.[179] [EL = 1+] Women in the immediate pushing group commenced pushing as soon as full dilatation was reached and were coached to hold their breath and push three to four times for a count of ten, during each contraction. Women in the delayed pushing group were encouraged to wait until they felt an urge to push or until they had been in the second stage for 2 hours (whichever came first). These women were then encouraged to push without holding their breath and for no more than 6–8 seconds for each push, up to three times per contraction. The use of oxytocin enabled the researchers to control the frequency and duration of second-stage contractions. While the two groups of women were similar in terms of most demographic variables, women in the immediate pushing group were significantly younger than those in the delayed pushing group. Second stages were significantly longer in the delayed pushing group (mean duration 38 minutes longer, $P < 0.01$) but the length of active pushing was significantly longer in the immediate pushing group (mean duration 42 minutes longer, $P = 0.002$). Findings showed that while babies in both groups exhibited oxygen desaturation during the second stage, this was significantly greater in the immediate pushing group ($P = 0.001$). There were also significantly more variable fetal heart rate (FHR) decelerations and prolonged decelerations in the immediate pushing group. There were no significant differences between the two groups for other FHR patterns, umbilical cord gases or Apgar scores. There were also no significant differences in caesarean births, instrumental vaginal births, prolonged second stage (> 3 hours) and episiotomies between the two groups. There were, however, significantly more perineal tears in the immediate pushing group ($n = 13$ versus $n = 5$, $\chi^2 = 6.54$, $P = 0.01$). The findings of the study may not however, generalise to multiparous women, women without epidural analgesia or women without oxytocic infusion in the second stage.

A prospective cohort study conducted in Ireland also compared delayed pushing with early pushing in the second stage.[180] [EL = 2+] Women in the delayed group ($n = 194$) were discouraged from pushing until the baby's head was visible or until 3 hours had elapsed since full dilatation of the cervix. Women in the early pushing group ($n = 219$) were encouraged to push as soon as the second stage was diagnosed. No details are given regarding the type of pushing encouraged. Due to a labour ward policy of active management of labour, three-quarters of the women in each group had an oxytocin infusion in progress during the second stage of labour. The second stage was significantly longer for women in the delayed pushing group ($P < 0.001$), despite the fact that it appears from the figures presented that women in the early pushing group waited on average 0.7 hours before commencing pushing, compared with 0.9 hours for women in the delayed pushing group. There was no significant difference in the spontaneous birth rate between the two groups. There was, however, a significant reduction in the use of non-rotational forceps in the delayed pushing group (44.84% versus 54.79%, $P < 0.04$). Abnormal fetal heart patterns and/or the passage of meconium was more common in the delayed pushing group (27.8% versus 3.91%, $P < 0.01$). Admissions to neonatal intensive care unit (NICU) were also higher for babies from the delayed pushing group ($n = 14$ versus $n = 5$, $P = 0.017$). The authors suggest these poorer outcomes may be attributable to the extensive use of oxytocin in the second stage of labour (approximately 75% for each group). Apgar scores and number of babies requiring intubation were similar between the two groups. No differences were reported for episiotomy rates, incidence of third-stage complications or postnatal morbidity. No further details were given.

Evidence statement
There is high-level evidence that epidural analgesia using low-dose local anaesthetic/opioid solutions allow some mobilisation compared with high-dose epidurals.

There is evidence that discontinuing epidural analgesia late in labour does not improve the rate of spontaneous birth, or any other clinical outcome, and can cause distress to the woman.

There is high-level evidence that delaying directed pushing (1 to 3 hours, or earlier if the woman has an involuntary urge to push), compared with directed pushing at diagnosis of second stage, reduces the risk of a mid-pelvic or rotational instrumental birth.

GDG interpretation of the evidence (mobilisation and pushing techniques for women with regional analgesia)
The advantage of mobilisation with low-dose local anaesthetics decreases over time. There is no effect of mobilisation following epidural analgesia on any maternal or neonatal outcomes.

Recommendations on position and pushing with regional analgesia

Women with regional analgesia should be encouraged to move and adopt whatever upright positions they find comfortable throughout labour.

Once established, regional analgesia should be continued until after completion of the third stage of labour and any necessary perineal repair.

Upon confirmation of full cervical dilatation in women with regional analgesia, unless the woman has an urge to push or the baby's head is visible, pushing should be delayed for at least 1 hour and longer if the woman wishes, after which pushing during contractions should be actively encouraged.

Following the diagnosis of full dilatation in a woman with regional analgesia, a plan should be agreed with the woman in order to ensure that birth will have occurred within 4 hours regardless of parity.

For position and pushing for women without regional analgesia, refer to Section 8.4.

6.4.5 Use of oxytocin for women with regional analgesia

Description of included studies
One RCT conducted in the UK was identified.[181] [EL = 1+] The study was published in 1989, and 226 nulliparous women with an epidural were included in the study population, but the intervention was routine use of the infusion of oxytocin (initial 2 mU/minute up to 16 mU/minute) compared with a placebo targeting a normal healthy population.

Review findings
Women with an oxytocin infusion had less non-rotational forceps births than the placebo group, shorter duration of the second stage (MD −17.0 minutes [95% CI −31.4 to −3.8 minutes]), less postpartum blood loss (MD −19.0 ml [95% CI −49.0 to 1.0 ml]), and fewer episiotomies (RR 0.84, $P = 0.04$) compared with women in the placebo group. There is no evidence of reduction in the number of rotational forceps birth performed for the malposition of the occiput. There is no evidence of differences in Apgar scores of the babies (Apgar at 1 minute MD 0.0 [95% CI −0.31 to 0.45]; Apgar at 5 minutes MD 0.0 [95% CI −0.17 to 0.14]).

Evidence statement
There is little evidence on oxytocin infusion for management of the second stage, compared with expectant management.

Limited evidence showed a high-dose oxytocin infusion shortened the duration of the second stage and reduced the rate of non-rotational forceps births.

Recommendation on use of oxytocin with regional analgesia

Oxytocin should not be used as a matter of routine in the second stage of labour for women with regional analgesia.

For other recommendations regarding use of oxytocin in the first and second stage of labour, refer to Sections 14.2.6 and 15.1.2, respectively.

6.4.6 The use of continuous EFM with regional analgesia

Introduction
A new review of continuous EFM and regional analgesia was undertaken considering two comparisons (low-dose and high-dose epidurals).

Epidural versus non-epidural analgesia (low dose: defined as bupivacaine less than 0.25% or equivalent)

Description of included studies
There were two studies identified.[182–184] Both studies were conducted in the USA. The epidural dose was 0.125%[184] or 0.0625%[182,183] bupivacaine with 2 micrograms/ml fentanyl following

0.25% bupivacaine, compared with meperidine 10 mg[184] or 15 mg[182,183] every 10 minutes lock-up following 50 mg meperidine. The trials were of good quality. [EL = 1+]

Review findings
The first trial (*n* = 358 mixed parity) published in 1997 showed no difference in the incidence of non-reassuring FHR tracings (RR 1.07 [95% CI 0.27 to 4.21]). The second trial (*n* = 200 nulliparous) published in 2002 showed that women with epidural analgesia had less beat-to-beat variability of the FHR (RR 0.23 [95% CI 0.15 to 0.30]) and more accelerations of the FHR (RR 1.42 [95% CI 1.24 to 1.63]), although there was no evidence of difference in the incidence of decelerations of the FHR (*P* = 0.353).

Evidence statement
There is no overall evidence of a difference in the incidence of FHR abnormalities when comparing the use of low-dose epidural and meperidine.

Intrathecal opioid with or without local anaesthetic versus no intrathecal opioids

Description of included studies
There was one systematic review identified for intrathecal opioids including 3513 women in 24 trials.[185] [EL = 1+] Three intrathecal opioids were tested (sufentanil, fentanyl and morphine), with or without various doses of intrathecal or epidural bupivacaine. The meta-analysis included all high and low doses of intrathecal opioids.

Review findings
Meta-analyses of the included trials showed that women with intrathecal opioid had a higher incidence of fetal bradycardia within 1 hour of analgesia than the control group, although there was no evidence of an overall difference in the incidence of FHR abnormalities.[185]

Evidence statement
There is an increase in the incidence of fetal bradycardia following the administration of intrathecal opioid, compared with no use of intrathecal opioid.

GDG interpretation of the evidence (monitoring babies for women with regional analgesia)
If fetal heart rate abnormalities are to occur, this is likely to be shortly after administration of doses of analgesic in regional analgesia.

Recommendation on monitoring with regional analgesia

Continuous EFM is recommended for at least 30 minutes during establishment of regional analgesia and after administration of each further bolus of 10 ml or more.

6.5 Effect of epidural fentanyl on breastfeeding

Description of included studies
Two studies were identified which investigated the effects of epidural fentanyl on breastfeeding. A US RCT (2005) assigned women who had previously breastfed a child, and who requested an epidural during labour, to one of three groups: epidural with no fentanyl (*n* = 60), epidural with an intermediate dose of fentanyl (1–150 micrograms) (*n* = 59) and epidural with a high dose of fentanyl (> 150 micrograms) (*n* = 58).[186] [EL = 1+] Demographic and labour characteristics were similar between the two groups. More than 95% in each group had a spontaneous vaginal birth. Differences between umbilical cord concentrations of fentanyl were significantly different in ways which reflected the group allocations. Women were asked to complete a questionnaire within 24 hours of giving birth asking for details of any breastfeeding problems encountered. They were also assessed by a lactation consultant during this period. A follow-up questionnaire survey of breastfeeding was undertaken at 6 weeks postpartum.

A UK cross-sectional study retrospectively examined the medical records of 425 nulliparous women randomly selected from the birth register (year 2000) of one hospital, to investigate the impact of intrapartum fentanyl on infant feeding at hospital discharge.[187] [EL = 3] Exclusion criteria for the study included women who were prescribed drugs for chronic conditions, preterm babies, babies admitted to NICU or babies who were unwell. Findings are reported below.

NB. These studies did not investigate analgesic effect, women's satisfaction or any other outcome other than breastfeeding.

Review findings

Newborn outcomes

Findings from the US RCT showed that within 24 hours of birth there were no significant differences between the three groups, in numbers of women reporting a breastfeeding problem (no-fentanyl group and intermediate-dose fentanyl groups $n = 6$ (10%) versus high-dose fentanyl group $n = 12$ (21%), $P = 0.09$).[186] The proportion of women having some difficulty breastfeeding within the first 24 hours was also assessed by a lactation consultant. Again, the proportion of women assessed as having problems was similar among the three groups. A significant difference was detected in the baby's neurological and adaptive capacity score (NACS), with median scores of 35, 34 and 32 in the no-fentanyl, intermediate-dose fentanyl and high-dose fentanyl groups, respectively, although the authors note that the clinical importance of this is not known. Among the 157 women who responded to the 6 week follow-up questionnaire, 14 (9%) were no longer breastfeeding: one in the no-fentanyl group, three in the intermediate-fentanyl group and ten in the high-dose fentanyl group ($P = 0.002$). If a woman reported a problem within 24 hours of birth, she was more likely to have stopped breastfeeding by 6 weeks than women who reported no problems within the first 24 hours (29% versus 6%, $P = 0.004$). Babies born to women in the high-dose fentanyl group with umbilical cord fentanyl concentration > 200 pg/ml were less likely to be breastfeeding at 6 weeks postpartum than babies with fentanyl concentration < 200 pg/ml ($P = 0.02$).

The UK retrospective cross-sectional study found that the proportion of women bottle-feeding varied with intrapartum analgesia administered: 32% women whose only analgesia was Entonox bottle-fed; 42% women who received only IM opioids plus Entonox bottle-fed; 44% women who received neuraxial analgesia containing only local anaesthetic bottle-fed; and 54% of women who received neuraxial analgesia containing an opioid (fentanyl) bottle-fed.[187] Logistic regression analysis was carried out to identify predictors of bottle-feeding at hospital discharge. The final model contained five variables as follows: caesarean section (OR 0.25 [95% CI 0.13 to 0.47]); woman's occupation (OR 0.63 [95% CI 0.40 to 0.99]); antenatal feeding intention (OR 0.12 [95% CI 0.08 to 0.19]), woman's age (OR 0.90 [95% CI 0.85 to 0.95]); and fentanyl dose (OR 1.0004 [95% CI 1.000 to 1.008] for each microgram administered). The model is predictive of 51.7% of the variation in infant feeding. Bottle-feeding is predicted for 75.3% of cases and breastfeeding for 83.3% of cases.

Evidence statement

There is a moderate level of evidence on the use of fentanyl to reduce the total dose of bupivacaine, which results in less motor block, a longer duration of analgesia but also increases the incidence of pruritus.

Evidence from small studies, of variable quality, suggests a weak association between the dose of fentanyl and the duration and success of breastfeeding.

Research recommendations on breastfeeding and regional analgesia

There is a need for studies:

- to optimise the management of labour in women with epidurals to reduce the excess instrumental birth rate, including the routine use of oxytocin in the second stage, in nulliparous women with a low-dose epidural
- to explore the optimum duration of the passive and active second stage of labour, for women with an epidural
- to assess the impact of low-dose epidurals with opioids (fentanyl) on neonatal outcomes, including resuscitation and breastfeeding.

6.6 Mode of administration

6.6.1 Continuous infusion versus intermittent bolus for epidural analgesia

Description of included studies
Eight trials were identified from the search.[188–195] All trials were compared between intermittent repeated bolus and continuous infusion for epidural analgesia during labour, except one trial that was initiated with combined spinal–epidural (CSE) analgesia and then maintained with epidural analgesia.[188] As for the medications that were used, four trials employed bupivacaine only,[190–193] three used bupivacaine plus fentanyl[189,194,195] and the rest ropivacaine plus fentanyl.[188] All the trials showed reasonable homogeneity and therefore meta-analyses were conducted to summarise the results. [EL = 1+]

Review findings
There was evidence that more local anaesthetic was required in the continuous group than the intermittent group (total dose two trials WMD −5.78 [−7.61 to −3.96]), although there was no evidence of differences in the mode of birth (spontaneous vaginal birth eight trials RR 1.23 [95% CI 0.92 to 1.65], CS eight trials OR 0.95 [95% CI 0.63 to 1.43]); adverse events (including hypotension five trials OR 1.46 [95% CI 0.80 to 2.66], pruritus one trial RR 0.73 [95% CI 0.24 to 2.21], motor block (Bromage score = 0) three trials OR 1.57 [95% CI 0.61 to 4.00], abnormal or non-reassuring FHR trace two trials OR 1.39 [95% CI 0.83 to 2.33]); or Apgar scores (Apgar score less than 7 at 1 minute two trials OR 7.79 [95% CI 0.38 to 157.97], Apgar score less than 7 at 5 minutes two trials OR 5.36 [95% CI 0.25 to 116.76]). Only two trials reported satisfaction. One reported that women with continuous infusion were more satisfied with the pain relief in both the first and second stage than those with intermittent infusion.[192] The other reported no evidence of a difference between the two arms and therefore there was a need to be careful when drawing conclusions. [190]

Evidence statement
Although continuous infusion of epidural analgesia seemed to increase the total amount of required analgesia, compared with intermittent bolus injection, it might also increase women's satisfaction. There was no evidence of differences in other outcomes including mode of birth, adverse events and neonatal outcomes.

6.6.2 Patient-controlled epidural analgesia (PCEA) versus continuous infusion

Description of included studies
There was one systematic review[196] [EL = 1+] and one trial[197] [EL = 1+] identified from the search. Both showed reasonable qualities. The systematic review included nine trials and 640 women, comparing patient-controlled epidural analgesia (PCEA) without background infusion with continuous infusion in labour. All the included trials used ropivacaine or bupivacaine for epidural analgesia.[197]

Review findings

Analgesia outcomes
From the meta-analysis in the systematic review, there were fewer reported anaesthetic interventions in the PCEA group than in the infusion group. The PCEA group seemed to have less local anaesthetic and experience less motor block. There was no evidence of differences in other adverse events including hypotension, high sensory block, shivering, nausea and pruritus.

The new trial showed a similar trend that hourly requirement of local anaesthetic was less in the PECA group than the infusion group, although there was no evidence of a difference in incidence of adverse events including nausea, hypotension and itching.[197]

Women's outcomes
There was no evidence of a difference in the mode of birth or duration of labour between both the two groups found in the meta-analysis and in the new trial.[196,197]

Newborn outcomes
There was no evidence of differences in the incidence of low Apgar scores at both 1 and 5 minutes reported in both the systematic review and the new trial.

Women's satisfaction
There was no evidence of a difference in women's reported satisfaction with the pain relief.

Evidence statement
PCEA seemed to reduce the need to recall the anaesthetists, the total dose of local anaesthetic and women's motor block, compared with continuous epidural infusion. There were no apparent differences in other outcomes.

6.6.3   PCEA versus intermittent bolus by hospital staff

Description of included studies
There were four trials identified comparing PCEA and intermittent bolus given by hospital staff for epidural analgesia during labour.[198–201] The first trial conducted in 1990 included 58 women, and used 12 ml of 0.125% bupivacaine with 1 : 400 000 epinephrine on request from anaesthesiologists, compared with 4 ml increments of the same solution to a maximum 12 ml/hour by PCEA.[198] [EL = 1+] The second trial was conducted in 1991 using bupivacaine–fentanyl. It included 50 women and compared PCEA with bolus administered by midwives. PCEA was commenced with a solution of 0.125% bupivacaine plus fentanyl 2 micrograms/ml and the analgesia was maintained at either a 4 ml/hour constant infusion plus 4 ml bolus on demand (lockout interval: 15 minutes) or 8 ml/hour infusion plus 3 ml bolus.[199] [EL = 1+] The third trial was conducted in 1995, by the same author as the second trial, using bupivacaine-fentanyl (0.125% bupivacaine plus 3 micrograms/ml fentanyl). It included 167 women and compared PCEA with bolus administered by staff.[200] [EL = 1+] The latest trial using bupivacaine–fentanyl, was conducted in 2005, included 187 women, and compared PCEA with staff administration. PCEA (0.08% bupivacaine and 2 micrograms/ml fentanyl 5 ml/hour infusion with a 5 ml bolus and 15 minute lockout interval) was compared with boluses of 20 mg bupivacaine and 75 micrograms of fentanyl in a 15 ml volume.[201] [EL = 1+] All of them were of reasonable quality.

Review findings

Analgesia outcomes
In the first trial, there was no evidence of a difference in the hourly local anaesthetic required or sensory levels.[198] In the second trial, the women in the midwife-administered group showed a lower pain score 2 hours after the analgesia started, although there was no evidence of differences in the incidence of adverse events such as nausea, pruritus, shivering hypotension, or motor block.[199] In the third trial, there was borderline evidence that the women in the staff-administered group showed lower pain scores 2 and 3 hours after the initiation of the epidural analgesia, although there was no evidence of a difference in the median pain scale, incidence of hypotension, shivering, pruritus or vomiting. However, urinary retention for the women was more common in the PCEA group than in the other group.[200] The latest trial showed that women in the PCEA group experience less pain during the first and second stage of labour, but used more bupivacaine than the control group.[201]

Women's outcomes
In the first, second and latest trial, no evidence of a difference was reported in duration of labour and mode of birth.[198,199,201] In the third trial, there was a trend that the women in the PCEA group had less spontaneous vaginal birth ($P = 0.08$) and a longer duration of the second stage of labour ($P = 0.02$).[200]

Newborn outcomes
There was no evidence of a difference in Apgar scores of the newborn babies in all trials.

Women's satisfaction
The former two trials showed that women in the PCEA groups were significantly more satisfied with the pain relief than the other groups, although there was no evidence of a difference in the latter two trials.

Evidence statement
There was a moderate level of clinical evidence on PCEA versus intermittent bolus administration by hospital staff. Although there was no apparent difference in analgesic, obstetric and neonatal outcomes, PCEA might increase a woman's satisfaction.

6.6.4 PCEA different lockout

Description of included studies
There were four trials identified comparing different bolus doses and lockouts for PCEA.[202–205] The first trial was conducted in 1993, comparing five different doses/lockouts for PCEA (2 ml bolus/10 minutes lockout, 3 ml/15 minutes, 4 ml/20 minutes, 6 ml/30 minutes and 8 ml/hour continuous) of bupivacaine–fentanyl with epinephrine and included 68 women.[202] [EL = 1+] The second trial was conducted in 2000, comparing 12 ml bolus/25 minutes lockout and 4 ml bolus/8 minutes lockout of bupivacaine–sufentanil, PCEA and included 203 women.[203] [EL = 1+] The third trial was conducted in 2005 in Lebanon, comparing three different regimens (3 ml bolus/6 minutes lockout, 6 ml/12 minutes and 9 ml/18 minutes) and included 84 women.[204] [EL = 1+] The forth trial, conducted in the USA in 2005, compared 5 minute lockouts with 15 minutes lockouts and included 60 women.[205] [EL = 1+] All trials were of reasonable quality.

Review findings

Analgesia outcomes
In the first trial, there was no evidence of a difference in the pain score among the five different regimens except for the total amount of local anaesthetic used, which was consumed more in the continuous infusion group than in the other four groups.[202] In the second trial, the larger dose group showed a lower pain score but more total amount of anaesthetic consumed than in the smaller dose group.[206] There was no evidence of a difference in severity of hypotension shown in this trial. The third trial showed a trend that women in the largest dose group required less rescue analgesia than the other two groups, although there was no evidence of differences in pain scores, sensory and motor block or total amount of anaesthetic used among the three groups.[204] There was no evidence of differences in pain scores, motor block, sensory block or FHR changes between the 5 and 15 minute lockouts in the latest trial.[205]

Women's outcomes
All trials reported no evidence of a difference in duration of labour and mode of birth.

Newborn outcomes
All trials reported no evidence of a difference in Apgar scores of the newborn babies.

Women's satisfaction
Although the second trial showed that women in the larger dose group rated higher satisfaction with the pain relief than the smaller dose group, there was no evidence of a difference in women's satisfaction with the pain relief in the rest of the trials.[203]

Evidence statement
A larger dose for PCEA might reduce the pain score and increase women's satisfaction, but might result in a higher dose of total analgesic used.

GDG interpretation of the evidence (mode of administration – epidural analgesia)
All modes of administration of epidural analgesia were found to provide effective pain relief. PCEA, when compared with continuous epidural infusion, reduces the total dose of local anaesthetic used, resulting in less motor block. When compared with intermittent bolus injection by hospital staff, PCEA increased women's satisfaction with pain relief.

There is insufficient evidence on obstetric and neonatal outcomes for all modes of administration.

Recommendation on mode of administration (regional analgesia)

Either patient-controlled epidural analgesia or intermittent bolus given by healthcare professionals are the preferred modes of administration for maintenance of epidural analgesia.

6.7 Establishing regional analgesia in labour

6.7.1 Combined spinal–epidural versus epidural analgesia

Description of included studies
This section is informed by one systematic review plus two additional RCTs. The recent systematic review includes 14 RCTs (*n* = 2047 women)[207] [EL = 1+] and was undertaken to assess the relative effects of combined spinal–epidural (CSE) versus epidural analgesia. The review includes the UK COMET trial.

Review findings
The systematic review examined 25 outcomes, although many of the findings from the meta-analysis are based on data drawn from a small subset of included trials.[207] Of the outcomes examined, only three were found to differ significantly between the two trial groups. Time of onset of effective analgesia, following first injection, was found to be significantly shorter for CSE (four trials) (WMD −5.50 minutes [95% CI −6.47 to −4.52 minutes]). The number of women satisfied with their analgesia was found to be significantly higher in the CSE group (three trials) (OR 4.69 [95% CI 1.27 to 17.29]). The only other significant difference found between groups was a higher incidence of pruritus in women with CSE (nine trials) (OR 2.79 [95% CI 1.87 to 4.18]). No significant differences were found between women in the two groups regarding outcomes relating to the clinical procedure, i.e. post-dural puncture headache (PDPH) (nine trials) (OR 1.46 [95% CI 0.37 to 5.71]); known dural tap (six trials) (OR 1.77 [95% CI 0.53 to 5.94]) or the number of women requiring a blood patch for PDPH (six trials) (OR 1.47 [95% CI 0.24 to 8.98]). In addition, no significant differences were found regarding incidence of other side effects, need for augmentation, mode of birth or neonatal outcomes.

A recently published RCT conducted in Saudi Arabia also compared CSE with epidurals.[208] [EL = 1+] Women allocated to the CSE group (*n* = 50) received intrathecal bupivacaine 0.25% 0.5 ml (1.25 mg) with fentanyl 25 micrograms in 0.5 ml. The epidural component consisted of 10 ml bupivacaine 0.0625% with fentanyl 1.5 micrograms/ml, followed by an infusion of 6–10 ml/hour according to the woman's height. The comparison group (*n* = 51) received a low-dose epidural consisting of an initial bolus (10–20 ml) of bupivacaine 0.0625% with fentanyl 1.5 micrograms/ml (volume determined by woman's height). For further analgesia, the same regimen as for CSE was used, i.e. 10 ml bupivacaine 0.0625% plus fentanyl 1.5 micrograms/ml infusion at 6–10 ml/hour. Both groups comprised healthy, nulliparous women at 36 or more weeks of gestation, in the first stage of labour, who requested epidural prior to 4 cm cervical dilatation. All women received the allocated method of analgesia. Findings showed a significantly faster onset of analgesia for women who received CSE. After 5 minutes, all of the women who received CSE reported adequate analgesia compared with 41.2% women in the epidural group (*P* < 0.05). This difference remained significant at 10 and 15 minutes, by which time the proportion of women reporting adequate analgesia in the epidural group had risen to 60.8%. By 30 minutes all women in each group reported adequate analgesia. No significant differences were found for degree of ambulation, mode of birth, duration of first stage, duration of second stage or women's satisfaction with pain relief, which was high for both groups with approximately 80% women in each group reporting their overall pain relief to be 'excellent' and the remainder reporting it as 'satisfactory'. Significantly more women in the CSE group reported pruritus as a side effect (38% versus 14%, *P* < 0.05). No other differences were noted regarding side effects or complications. The authors stated that neonatal outcomes were similar for the two groups, although figures were not reported for these.

A summary report was reviewed which gave brief details of the main findings for a UK RCT with a prospective matched cohort study for long-term outcomes, the COMET trial.[209] [EL = 2+] Short-term findings from this trial are included in the meta-analysis for the systematic review described above.[207] The primary long-term outcome was backache, for duration of over 6 weeks, occurring within 3 months of giving birth. No significant differences were found in the incidence of long-term backache between women in the three different epidural groups involved in the RCT, namely CSE, traditional (bolus injection) epidural and low-dose infusion epidural. The non-epidural group of women (recruited prospectively as a matched cohort group, *n* = 351) reported significantly less backache than the traditional epidural group (OR 1.46 [95% CI 1.02 to 2.09]). Women's long-term satisfaction with their overall childbirth experience did not differ between the epidural groups (findings from non-epidural group not reported). A much greater proportion of women who received a CSE would choose the same method again, compared with the proportion of women in the traditional epidural group who would choose a traditional epidural again (figures not given).

Evidence statement
There is high-level evidence that:

- CSE provides a more rapid onset of analgesia than epidural analgesia alone
- once analgesia is established, both techniques are equally effective
- CSE is associated with a higher incidence of pruritus where opioids are used.

6.7.2 Intrathecal opioids with or without local anaesthetic versus no intrathecal opioids

Description of included studies
There was one systematic review[185] and two relatively new trials[210,211] identified for this intervention. The systematic review included 3513 women in 24 trials.[185] [EL = 1+] Three intrathecal opioids were tested (sufentanil, fentanyl and morphine), with or without various doses of intrathecal or epidural bupivacaine. A trial conducted in the USA in 2003 included 108 women.[210] [EL = 1+] This trial compared six different doses (0, 5, 10, 15, 20, 25 microgram) of intrathecal fentanyl, combined with 2.5 mg of bupivacaine. The other trial was conducted in Singapore in 2004, and included 40 women.[211] [EL = 1+] This trial combined intrathecal 25 micrograms of fentanyl with placebo, combined with 2.5 mg of levobupivacaine, followed by a 10 ml/hour epidural infusion of 0.125% levobupivacaine and 2 micrograms/ml fentanyl.

Review findings

Analgesia outcomes
Meta-analyses of the included trials showed that women with intrathecal opioid had a higher incidence of fetal bradycardia within 1 hour of analgesia than the control group, although there was no evidence of a difference in incidence of other fetal heart abnormalities.[185,210,211] There was strong evidence that women with intrathecal opioid experienced more pruritus than the control group who had received no intrathecal opioid. The first trial showed that all women who received 15 microgram or more of fentanyl had a VAS score of less than 20 mm (on a VAS from 0 to 100 mm), while those who received less than 15 micrograms did not.[210] There was no evidence of a difference in the incidence of nausea and vomiting, or fetal heart abnormalities, although there was higher incidence of pruritus in those women who were given intrathecal fentanyl. The other trial showed a significantly longer effect of analgesia for those with 25 micrograms fentanyl than 2.5 mg levobupivacaine alone.[211] The study was underpowered to allow evaluation of adverse events.

Women's outcomes
No evidence of a difference in mode of birth or use of oxytocin was reported in the systematic review.[185] No other outcomes were reported in any study above.

Newborn outcomes
There was no evidence of a difference in incidence of a low Apgar score at 5 minutes. No other fetal outcomes were reported.

Women's satisfaction
Satisfaction was not reported in the above studies.

Evidence statement
A moderate level of evidence showed that intrathecal opioid might increase fetal bradycardia and the incidence of pruritus. Intrathecal local anaesthesia with fentanyl is more efficacious than fentanyl alone.

6.7.3 Intrathecal opioids versus epidural local anaesthetics

Description of included studies
There was one systematic review identified for this comparison.[212] [EL = 1+] The study included seven trials. Three opioids (morphine, sufentanil and fentanyl) were compared with bupivacaine or lidocaine.

Review findings
A meta-analysis showed comparable analgesic efficacy 15–20 minutes after intrathecal opioid administration, although there was evidence that intrathecal opioids seemed to be associated with increased incidence of pruritus. There was no evidence of a difference in nausea or mode of birth.

Evidence statement
An intrathecal opioid appeared to have comparable analgesic efficacy at 15 minutes of administration, although there is increased incidence of pruritus, compared with local anaesthetics.

6.7.4 Different doses for initiation of combined spinal–epidural analgesia

Description of included studies
There were six randomised controlled trials identified that compared different doses for initiation of CSE analgesia.[213–218] Due to heterogeneity in the study designs, the results are summarised by the study with the description.

Review findings

0 mg versus 1.25 mg versus 2.5 mg bupivacaine combined with 25 micrograms fentanyl
One trial conducted in the USA was published in 1999 and included 90 women.[217] [EL = 1+] The trial compared three different doses (0 mg, 1.25 mg or 2.5 mg) of bupivacaine combined with 25 micrograms fentanyl for CSE analgesia. There was evidence that women with 2.5 mg bupivacaine had analgesia of a longer duration than those without bupivacaine, and women with bupivacaine had faster onset of analgesia than those without bupivacaine. There was no evidence of differences in other outcomes.

2.5 mg/25 micrograms versus 1.25 mg/12.5 micrograms levobupivacaine/fentanyl
One trial conducted in Singapore was published in 2004 and included 40 women.[213] [EL = 1+] The trial compared 2.5 mg/25 micrograms and 1.25 mg/12.5 micrograms of intrathecal levobupivacaine/fentanyl for CSE analgesia. There was evidence that women with a lower dose experienced less motor block than the other groups, although there was no evidence of differences in onset/duration of analgesia or adverse events such as hypotension, shivering, pruritus, nausea and vomiting.

1.25 mg versus 2.5 mg bupivacaine
One trial conducted in Hong Kong was published in 1999 and included 49 women.[214] [EL = 1+] The trial compared 1.25 mg and 2.5 mg of bupivacaine combined with 25 micrograms of fentanyl for initiation of CSE analgesia. There was evidence that women with the larger dose of bupivacaine had a longer duration of analgesia but higher level of sensory block and more incidence of motor block. There was no evidence of differences in other outcomes.

5, 10, 15, 20, 25, 35 or 45 micrograms fentanyl
Another trial conducted in the USA was published in 1998 and included 84 women.[215] [EL = 1+] The trial compared seven different doses (5 to 45 micrograms) of intrathecal fentanyl for initiation of CSE analgesia. A dose–response curve indicated that the median effective dose of intrathecal fentanyl was 14 micrograms [13–15 micrograms].

0, 5, 15 or 25 micrograms fentanyl
One trial, conducted in the UK, was published in 2001 and included 124 women.[216] [EL = 1+] The trial compared three different doses (0, 5, 15 or 25 micrograms) of intrathecal fentanyl for

CSE analgesia. There was evidence of dose-dependent increases in both pruritus and duration of spinal analgesia with increasing doses of fentanyl. There was no evidence of differences among different doses of fentanyl in other outcomes.

25, 37.5 or 50 micrograms fentanyl
Another trial conducted in the USA was published in 1999 and included 60 women.[218] [EL = 1+] The trial compared 25 micrograms, 37.5 micrograms or 50 micrograms of intrathecal fentanyl for initiation of CSE analgesia during labour. There was no evidence of differences in duration of analgesia or adverse events.

Evidence statement
There was limited evidence that showed starting CSE with a larger dose of local anaesthetics and/or opioid had longer analgesia effects, more incidence of motor block and higher sensory block, than a smaller dose. A dose-finding study suggested that the optimum dose of intrathecal fentanyl is approximately 15 micrograms.

6.7.5 Different doses for initiation of epidural analgesia

Description of included studies
Trials including opioids other than fentanyl were excluded from this review as they are regarded as not relevant to the UK setting. Three trials were identified that compared different doses for the initiation of epidural analgesia.[219–221] Owing to heterogeneity in the study designs, the results are summarised by the study with the description.

Review findings

15 mg versus 25 mg bupivacaine combined with 50 micrograms fentanyl
One trial conducted in the UK was published in 1996 and included 60 women.[221] [EL = 1+] The trial compared 15 mg and 25 mg bupivacaine (both in 15 ml) combined with 50 micrograms of fentanyl for establishing epidural analgesia. There was evidence that women who received the lower dose of bupivacaine had less motor block than the other group. There was no evidence of differences in other outcomes.

0.5% versus 0.2% versus 0.1% bupivacaine
A trial conducted in Belgium was published in 1998 and included 58 women.[220] [EL = 1+] The trial compared bupivacaine 20 mg administered as 0.5% (4 ml), 0.2% (10 ml) or 0.1% (20 ml) for establishing epidural analgesia. There was evidence that women with 0.2% or 0.1% bupivacaine experienced less pain, and women with 0.1% bupivacaine had a quicker onset of analgesia than the 0.2% group. There was no evidence of differences in other outcomes.

0.2% versus 0.15% versus 0.1% ropivacaine
A study conducted in the USA was published in 1999 and included 68 women.[219] [EL = 1+] The trial compared 13 ml of either 0.2%, 0.15% or 0.1% ropivacaine solution for establishing epidural analgesia during labour. There was evidence that women with 0.2% ropivacaine were more likely to have adequate analgesia (measured by the pain score) than the other groups. There was no evidence of differences in adverse events.

Evidence statement
There is limited evidence from one trial that establishing epidural analgesia with larger volumes of more dilute solution of local anaesthetics achieves quicker and more effective analgesia than smaller volumes of more concentrated solution. There is also limited evidence that establishing epidural analgesia with larger doses of local anaesthetics causes a higher incidence of motor block than a smaller dose.

6.8   Maintenance of regional analgesia

6.8.1   Traditional versus modern regimen of epidural infusion

Introduction
Traditional epidural analgesia without opioid (e.g. bolus doses of bupivacaine 0.25%) was compared with epidural infusion with opioid (e.g. 0.0625–0.1% bupivacaine with 2 micrograms/ml fentanyl) administered as a continuous infusion).

Description of included studies
An RCT conducted in the UK compared (a) 10 ml bolus doses of bupivacaine 0.25% (traditional regimen) with (b) analgesia established with (i) 15 ml of 0.1% bupivacaine with fentanyl 2 micrograms/ml or (ii) intrathecal bupivacaine 0.25% (1 ml) and fentanyl 25 micrograms (modern regimen). Analgesia in group (a) was maintained with further boluses of bupivacaine 0.25% while in groups (i) and (ii) analgesia was maintained with a continuous infusion of bupivacaine 0.1% with fentanyl 2 micrograms/ml.[222,223] The trial comparing these methods was published in 2001 and included 703 women (traditional $n = 353$; modern $n = 350$). The trial was of reasonable quality. [EL = 1+]

Review findings

Analgesia outcomes
There was no evidence of differences in median visual analogue scores, of the severity of labour pain after the epidural was inserted (traditional $n = 14$; modern $n = 12$) or women's ability to push during labour (RR 1.04, $P = 0.77$). There was also no evidence of a difference in the mean amount of bupivacaine used throughout labour, excluding top-ups for operative procedures (traditional = 103.8 (SD 56.1) mg; continuous = 101.1 (SD 55.1) mg).

Obstetric outcomes
There was evidence that women in the modern regimen group had more spontaneous vaginal births (RR 1.39 [95% CI 1.02 to 1.88]) and a shorter length of second stage ($\leq$ 60 minutes RR 1.36 [95% CI 1.01 to 1.84]) than the traditional regimen group. There was no evidence of a difference in the incidence of CS (RR 1.07 [95% CI 0.77 to 1.49]).

Newborn outcomes
There was evidence that newborn babies in the modern regimen group were more likely to have a low Apgar score at 1 minute ($\leq$ 7 RR 1.64, $P = 0.01$) and require high-level resuscitation (one or more mask and bag and/or intubation (intubation or naloxone) RR 5.00, $P = 0.02$), although there was no evidence of a difference in the 5 minute Apgar score (RR 3.00, $P = 0.09$) for admission to neonatal unit (RR 0.80, $P = 0.72$).

Women's satisfaction
Women's long-term satisfaction with their overall childbirth experience did not differ between the two groups

Long-term outcomes
There was no evidence of a difference in long-term backache, headache or neckache or paraesthesiae between the two groups, although women in the continuous group had less stress incontinence and bowel control problems compared with the traditional group.

Evidence statement
High-level evidence from one trial showed that the modern epidural regimen (maintained with a continuous infusion of bupivacaine 0.1% with fentanyl 2 micrograms/ml) not only increased rate of spontaneous vaginal birth and shortened duration of the second stage of labour, but also increased the number of babies who had a low Apgar score and required high-level resuscitation, than the traditional regimen (maintained with boluses of bupivacaine 0.25%).

6.8.2 Local anaesthetic with opioid versus local anaesthetic without opioid

Introduction
Addition of opioids to a local anaesthetic, for an epidural analgesia during labour, was tested with the comparisons between bupivacaine versus bupivacaine with fentanyl. There were two comparisons: 0.125% bupivacaine versus 0.125% bupivacaine plus 2–3 micrograms fentanyl, and 0.125% bupivacaine versus 0.0625% bupivacaine plus 2–3 micrograms fentanyl.

0.125% bupivacaine versus 0.125% bupivacaine plus 2–3 micrograms fentanyl

Description of included studies
There are two trials identified for this comparison.[224,225] The first trial included 42 women and was conducted in the UK in 1991. The second trial included 60 women and was conducted in Canada in 1991. Both showed reasonable quality and homogeneity; hence meta-analyses were conducted to summarise the results. A total of 93 women were included in this review. [EL = 1++]

Review findings

Analgesia outcomes
The analysis was underpowered, such that there was no evidence of differences in the onset of analgesia, total dose of bupivacaine or incidence of adverse events including hypotension, pruritus, urinary retention, vomiting/nausea and motor block.

Women's outcomes
There was no evidence of a difference in the mode of birth and duration of second stage. No other outcomes were reported.

Newborn outcomes
There was no evidence of a difference in the Apgar score of the newborn babies. No other neonatal outcomes were reported.

Women's satisfaction
Only the second trial reported the satisfaction of the women with their analgesia. There was borderline evidence to suggest that the women who received fentanyl were more satisfied with their pain relief in the first stage of labour, although there was no evidence of a difference in the second stage.

Evidence statement
There was no strong evidence of any differences between 0.125% bupivacaine and 0.125% bupivacaine plus 2–3 micrograms fentanyl.

0.125% bupivacaine versus 0.0625% bupivacaine plus 2–3 micrograms fentanyl

Description of included studies
Five articles studied this comparison.[226–230] These trials showed reasonable quality and homogeneity, such that meta-analyses were conducted to summarise the results. A total of 667 women were included in the analysis. The three trials[226–229] were conducted in the UK in 1995–98. Another trial was conducted in the USA in 1988.[230] [EL = 1++]

Review findings

Analgesia outcomes
The analyses showed significant evidence that the women with fentanyl had a lower total dose of bupivacaine and less motor block, with a longer duration of analgesia and more pruritus than the other group. There was no evidence of a difference in the incidence of hypotension, urinary retention and nausea/vomiting.

Women's outcomes
There was no evidence of a difference in the mode of birth and duration of second stage.

Newborn outcomes
There was no evidence of differences in the Apgar scores, cord arterial pH or neurological and adaptive capacity score (NACS) of newborn babies.

Women's satisfaction
There was no evidence of a difference in women's satisfaction with their pain relief.

Evidence statement
There is high-level evidence that the women with fentanyl had a lower total dose of bupivacaine and less motor block, with longer duration of analgesia and more pruritus than the other group. There was no strong evidence of other differences between these two groups.

Different drugs for epidural analgesia

Bupivacaine versus levobupivacaine

Description of included studies
There were six trials identified for this comparison.[231–236] Among the included trials, three were initiated with CSE analgesia,[232,234,236] and the rest with epidural analgesia. All the trials were of reasonable quality. Meta-analyses were conducted to summarise the results. [EL = 1+]

Review findings

All regional analgesia
There was evidence that women with levobupivacaine had a shorter duration of analgesia, although there was no evidence of a difference in incidence of hypotension, nausea/vomiting, motor block and abnormal fetal heart trace.

There was no evidence of differences in mode of birth, duration of second stage, in Apgar scores or NACS. Women's satisfaction was not reported in a relevant form.

Epidural analgesia only
When subgroup analysis was conducted only including trials examining epidural analgesia, there was no evidence of differences in the mode of birth (spontaneous vaginal birth one trial RR 1.39 [95% CI 0.58 to 3.37], and CS one trial RR 1.33 [95% CI 0.59 to 2.97]), duration and onset of analgesia (onset of analgesia one trial WMD −1.00 minutes [95% CI −4.93 to 2.93 minutes], and duration of analgesia WMD −1.77 minutes [95% CI −4.00 to 0.47 minutes]), adverse events (hypotension five trials RR 1.61 [95% CI 0.79 to 3.27], nausea/vomiting five trials RR 0.58 [95% CI 0.31 to 1.08], Bromage score = 0 six trials RR 0.99 [95% CI 0.89 to 1.10], abnormal or non-reassuring fetal heart trace three trials RR 0.86 [95% CI 0.30 to 2.42]) or neonatal outcome (umbilical arterial pH one trial WMD 0.01 [95% CI −0.03 to 0.05]).

Evidence statement
There is no strong evidence on differences between bupivacaine and levobupivacaine for maintenance of epidural analgesia.

Levobupivacaine versus ropivacaine

Description of included studies
There were seven trials identified for this comparison.[232,234,237–241] Among included trials, three were initiated with CSE analgesia,[232,234,239,240] and the rest with epidural analgesia. One trial was with PCEA.[239] All the trials were of reasonable quality. Meta-analyses were conducted to summarise the results. [EL = 1+]

Review findings

All regional analgesia
There was no evidence of differences in the onset of analgesia, duration of analgesia, incidence of hypotension, motor block or abnormal fetal heart trace, except incidence of vomiting, which were higher in the ropivacaine group than the levobupivacaine group. There was no evidence of differences in the mode of birth or in NACS for newborn babies. There was also no evidence of difference in women's satisfaction.

Epidural analgesia only
When subgroup analysis was conducted only including trials examining epidural analgesia, there was no evidence of differences in the mode of birth (spontaneous vaginal birth one trial RR 1.39 [95% CI 0.58 to 3.37] and CS one trial RR 1.33 [95% CI 0.59 to 2.97]), onset of analgesia (one trial WMD −1.00 minutes [95% CI −4.93 to 2.93 minutes]) or neonatal outcome (umbilical arterial pH one trial WMD 0.01 [95% CI −0.03 to 0.05]), although there was a significant reduction in duration of analgesia (two trials WMD −12.14 minutes [95% CI −21.23 to 3.05 minutes]), as well as incidence of nausea and/or vomiting (two trials RR 0.41 [95% CI 0.20 to 0.84]), by levobupivacaine. There was no evidence of differences in other adverse outcomes including hypotension (two trials RR 2.09 [95% CI 0.73 to 5.97]) and motor block (Bromage score = 0 three trials RR 1.05 [95% CI 0.81 to 1.36]).

Evidence statement
There is no strong evidence of a difference between ropivacaine and levobupivacaine for epidural analgesia.

Bupivacaine versus ropivacaine

Description of included studies
There were 29 trials identified for this comparison.[232,234,242–266] Among included trials, four were initiated with CSE analgesia[232,234,252,264] five were with PCEA[244,247,251,260,263] and the rest with epidural analgesia.[242,243,245,246,248–250,253–259,261,262,265,266] All the trials were of reasonable quality. Meta-analyses were conducted to summarise the results. [EL = 1+]

Review findings

All regional analgesia
There was evidence that women with ropivacaine had a shorter duration of analgesia and less motor block, although there was no evidence of a difference in the onset of analgesia, incidence of hypotension, nausea/vomiting or abnormal fetal heart trace. There was evidence that women with bupivacaine had a shorter duration of their second stage of labour, although there was no evidence of a difference in mode of birth. There was evidence that more newborn babies born with ropivacaine had more than 35 NACS at 2 hours after birth than those with bupivacaine, although there was no evidence of differences in Apgar scores at 1 and 5 minutes, cord arterial pH or NACS at 24 hours. There was no evidence of a difference in women's satisfaction with their pain relief.

Epidural only
When subgroup analysis was performed only including trials of epidural analgesia, there was no evidence of a difference in onset of analgesia (four trials WMD −0.32 minutes [95% CI −1.09 to 0.44 minutes]) or duration of analgesia (seven trials WMD 3.20 minutes [95% CI −3.03 to 9.43 minutes]). There was also no evidence of a difference in the mode of birth (spontaneous vaginal birth 22 trials RR 1.03 [95% CI 0.96 to 1.10], and CS 21 trials RR 0.95 [95% CI 0.80 to 1.12]), although prolonged duration second stage (nine trials WMD 3.22 minutes [95% CI 1.08 to 5.36 minutes]) was observed in women in the ropivacaine group, compared with the bupivacaine group. There was evidence that fewer women experienced motor block in the ropivacaine group (18 trials RR 1.21 [95% CI 1.04 to 1.39]), although there was no evidence of differences in other adverse outcomes including hypotension (12 trials RR 0.98 [95% CI 0.69 to 1.40]) and nausea and/or vomiting (eight trials RR 1.04 [95% CI 0.50 to 2.15]). There was evidence that more babies were alert at 2 hours (NACS more than 35 at 2 hours three trials RR 1.25 [95% CI 1.06 to 1.46]) in the ropivacaine group compared with the bupivacaine group, although there was no evidence of differences in other fetal and neonatal outcomes including NACS score at 24 hours (> 35 four trials RR 1.02 [95% CI 0.96 to 1.07]), abnormal/non-reassuring fetal heart trace (three trials RR 1.29 [95% CI 0.59 to 2.82]), Apgar scores (Apgar score less than 7 at 1 minute ten trials RR 0.85 [95% CI 0.63 to 1.14]; Apgar score less than 7 at 5 minutes 13 trials RR 1.39 [95% CI 0.69 to 2.82]) and umbilical arterial blood pH (five trials WMD 0.01 [95% CI −0.02 to 0.03]). There was also no evidence of a difference in women's satisfaction score (rated as excellent or good six trials RR 1.03 [95% CI 0.99 to 1.06]).

Evidence statement
The available evidence is insufficient to allow interpretable comparisons of low-dose local anaesthetic doses for regional analgesia.

Different doses/rates for maintaining epidural analgesia

Description of included studies
There were 11 trials identified that compared different doses or rates of continuous infusion/ injection for epidural or CSE analgesia.[258,267-276] Owing to heterogeneity in the study designs, the results are summarised by the study with the description.

Review findings

0.125% versus 0.0625% versus 0.04% bupivacaine
The first trial was conducted in the USA, published in 2002 and included 89 women.[267] [EL = 1+] The trial compared epidural infusion of saline (*n* = 23), 0.125% bupivacaine (*n* = 22), 0.0625% bupivacaine (*n* = 22), and 0.04% bupivacaine plus 1 : 600 000 epinephrine (*n* = 22), after subarachnoid fentanyl 25 microgram and total 4 ml of 0.25% bupivacaine. The study was underpowered in that there were no significant findings that compared the three bupivacaine groups, in any of the results, including duration of analgesia, and adverse events.

0.08% versus 0.25% bupivacaine
The second trial was conducted in the UK, published in 1986 and included 53 women.[271] [EL = 1+] The trial compared between 0.08% (*n* = 25) and 0.25% (*n* = 28) of bupivacaine infusion with the same amount of drug dose per hour (20 mg/hour of bupivacaine) for epidural analgesia during labour, following a test dose of 3 ml of 0.5% bupivacaine plain being administered. There was evidence that the 0.08% group had longer intervention-free intervals or fewer top-ups than the other group.

0.0625% versus 0.125% bupivacaine
The third trial was conducted in the UK, published in 1985 and included 98 women.[272] [EL = 1+] The trial compared five different rates and concentrations of bupivacaine infusion for epidural analgesia: (i) no bupivacaine; (ii) 0.0625%, 6.25 mg/hour; (iii) 0.125%, 6.25 mg/hour; (iv) 0.125%, 12.5 mg/hour; and (v) 0.125%, 18.75 mg/hour. Although there were no statistically significant different results among bupivacaine groups ii–v, the 0.125%, 12.5 mg/hour (10 ml/hour) group seemed to have the smallest dose used with less motor block.

0.031% versus 0.062% versus 0.125% bupivacaine
The fourth trial was conducted in the UK, published in 1991 and included 56 women.[273] [EL = 1+] The trial compared infusion of 0.125%, 0.062% or 0.032% bupivacaine combined with 0.0002% fentanyl with the same rate (at 7.5 ml/hour) following an initial 0.5% 8 ml dose of bupivacaine. There was evidence that women with 0.032% bupivacaine had less analgesic drug than the other groups. However, there was no evidence of difference in pain scores. The study was underpowered to show any evidence of differences in other outcomes including mode of birth and neonatal outcomes.

0.0625% versus 0.125% bupivacaine
The fifth trial was conducted in the UK, published in 1994 and included 98 women.[274] [EL = 1+] The trial compared 0.0625% and 0.125% bupivacaine (both at 10 ml/hour) for epidural analgesia during labour. There was evidence that women with 0.0625% bupivacaine were more likely to have Kielland rotational forceps but less likely to have Neville–Barnes forceps than the other group.

0.5% 6–8 ml versus 0.25% 10–14 ml versus 0.25% 6–8 ml bupivacaine
The sixth trial was conducted in the UK, published in 1981 and included 517 women.[275] [EL = 1+] The trial compared three different doses (0.5% 6–8 ml, 0.25% 10–14 ml or 0.25% 6–8 ml) of bupivacaine, for initial and top-up injection for epidural analgesia. There was evidence that women with the 0.25%/6–8 ml dose had more spontaneous vaginal births but rated analgesia pain relief as lower than the other groups. Women with higher concentration or volume of bupivacaine injection were more likely to have motor block and urinary retention, although there was no evidence of differences in other outcomes.

0.25% versus 0.125%, bupivacaine versus ropivacaine
The seventh trial was conducted in Sweden, published in 2001 and included 68 women.[258] [EL = 1+] The trial compared two different doses and two different drugs (0.25% bupivacaine,

0.25% ropivacaine, 0.125% bupivacaine, 0.125% ropivacaine) for epidural analgesia during labour. There was evidence that women with 0.25% of either drug were more likely to have motor block than the other groups and, among the 0.25% groups, women with bupivacaine were more likely to have motor block than those with ropivacaine. There was no evidence of a difference in the mode of birth, Apgar score and incidence of hypotension.

4, 6, 8 and 10 ml/hour of ropivacaine
The eighth study was conducted in France, published in 1997 and included 133 women.[268] [EL = 1+] The trial compared four different rates (4, 6, 8 and 10 ml/hour) of 2 mg/ml ropivacaine for epidural analgesia during labour. There was evidence that the 4 ml/hour group required more bolus doses than the other groups and that the 10 ml/hour group had higher total dose of ropivacaine than the other groups. There was no evidence of differences in the pain score, sensory block, motor block, mode of birth or Apgar scores of the newborn babies.

4, 6, 8 and 10 ml/hour of ropivacaine
The ninth study was conducted in the USA, published in 1998 and included 127 women.[270] [EL = 1+] The trial compared different infusion rates (4, 6, 8 and 10 ml/hour) of 2 mg/ml ropivacaine for epidural analgesia during labour.[270] There was evidence that the women in the 4 ml/hour group required more additional top-up injections than the other groups, although the 4 ml/hour group had less motor block than the other group. There was no evidence of differences in Apgar scores or NACS for newborn babies.

0.2% versus 0.125% ropivacaine
The tenth trial was conducted in Singapore, published in 1999 and included 50 women.[276] [EL = 1+] The trial compared 0.2% and 0.125% ropivacaine for PCEA. There was evidence that women in the 0.125% group had less motor block, although there was no evidence of differences in other outcomes.

12, 16 and 20 ml of 0.1% ropivacaine plus 0.5 micrograms fentanyl and 4, 6 and 8 ml of 0.2% ropivacaine plus 0.5 micrograms fentanyl
The eleventh study was conducted in France, published in 2003 and included 150 women (25 for each).[269] [EL = 1+] The trial compared six different doses (0.1% ropivacaine plus 0.5 micrograms fentanyl (i) 12 ml, (ii) 16 ml and (iii) 20 ml, 0.2% ropivacaine plus 0.5 micrograms fentanyl (iv) 6 ml, (v) 8 ml and (vi) 10 ml) of ropivacaine plus fentanyl for PCEA during labour. The results showed that effectiveness of analgesia is dependent upon drug mass rather than volume or concentration.

Evidence statement
A reduced dose of local anaesthetic seems as effective as a higher dose, although there is no strong evidence to confirm appropriate dosage during epidural analgesia.

GDG interpretation of the evidence (how to maintain regional analgesia: drug and dosage)
High concentrations of local anaesthetic (0.25% or above of bupivacaine or equivalent) for epidural analgesia resulted in less mobility for women (more motor block), increased instrumental birth and increased incidence of maternal hypotension. In the longer term (12 months), women in the high-dose group appear to have more stress incontinence and bowel control problems. The addition of opioids (e.g. 2 micrograms/ml fentanyl) to low-concentration local anaesthetics (less than 0.125% bupivacaine or equivalent) provides effective analgesia with less motor block and less instrumental birth. In terms of analgesic efficacy and obstetric outcomes, there is little to separate the various low-concentration (0.0625% to 0.1% bupivacaine or equivalent) local anaesthetic/opioid solutions.

There is limited evidence to suggest that the addition of opioids may result in increased requirement for high-level neonatal resuscitation.

Recommendations on establishing and maintaining regional analgesia

Either epidural or combined spinal–epidural analgesia is recommended for establishing regional analgesia in labour.

If rapid analgesia is required, combined spinal–epidural analgesia is recommended.

It is recommended that combined spinal–epidural analgesia is established with bupivacaine and fentanyl.

It is recommended that epidural analgesia is established with a low-concentration local anaesthetic and opioid solution with, for example, 10–15 ml of 0.0625–0.1% bupivacaine with 1–2 micrograms per ml fentanyl. The initial dose of local anaesthetic plus opioid is essentially a test dose and as such should be administered cautiously to ensure that inadvertent intrathecal injection has not occurred.

Low-concentration local anaesthetic and opioid solutions (0.0625–0.1% bupivacaine or equivalent combined with 2.0 micrograms per ml fentanyl) are recommended for maintaining epidural analgesia in labour.

High concentrations of local anaesthetic solutions (0.25% or above of bupivacaine or equivalent) should not be used routinely for either establishing or maintaining epidural analgesia.

7 Normal labour: first stage

7.1 Introduction

Care during labour should be aimed towards achieving the best possible physical, emotional and psychological outcome for the woman and baby.

The onset of labour is a complex physiological process and therefore it cannot be easily defined by a single event. Although labour is a continuous process, it is convenient to divide it into stages. Definitions of the stages of labour need to be clear in order to ensure that women and the staff providing their care have an accurate and shared understanding of the concepts involved, enabling them to communicate effectively. In order to facilitate this, the guideline aims to provide practical definitions of the stages of labour.

Recommendations on normal labour

Clinical intervention should not be offered or advised where labour is progressing normally and the woman and baby are well.

In all stages of labour, women who have left the normal care pathway due to the development of complications can return to it if/when the complication is resolved.

7.2 Definition of the first stage of labour

Clinical question
What are the appropriate definitions of the latent and active phases of the first stage, the second stage, and the third stage of labour?

Previous guideline
No previous guideline has considered definitions of the stages of labour.

Description of included studies
No relevant study was identified that investigated outcomes of different definitions of labour.

The GDG explored various definitions that have been used in practice and research. Definitions of stages of labour used in six descriptive studies, investigating duration of labour, were used to inform the discussion on definitions of labour.

Review findings
Definitions of the onset of labour may involve the onset of contractions,[277–280] evidence of cervical change[281] or both.[277] While the consideration of contractions alone in defining the onset of labour enables this decision to be reached by women themselves, the inclusion of cervical change means that the onset of labour requires professional confirmation. Within the literature, and in clinical practice, an early or 'latent' phase of labour is recognised. This has been defined as 0–2 cm cervical dilatation[279] and 0–4 cm dilatation,[282–284] and is characterised by a slow rate of cervical dilatation and effacement and contractions that may be irregular in strength and frequency. This is followed by an active first stage of labour. Again, this can be defined solely in terms of cervical dilatation, e.g. 2–10 cm dilatation[279] or 4–10 cm dilatation[282–284] or in a way which includes the experience of the labouring woman, e.g. the onset of regular contractions as perceived by the woman until the commencement of pushing at full dilatation.[280]

GDG interpretation of the evidence
The GDG have adopted the following definition of normal birth for the purpose of this guideline – it is the WHO definition: 'Labour is normal when it is spontaneous in onset, low risk at the

start and remaining so throughout labour and birth. The baby is born spontaneously and in the vertex position between 37–42 completed weeks of pregnancy. After birth woman and baby are in good condition'. [285]

Where labour is progressing normally and both woman and baby are well the midwife's role is to offer support (physical and psychological) and to observe the woman and baby. Should it be necessary to offer an intervention it should one that is known, as far as is possible, to be of benefit.

Recommendations on definitions of the first stage of labour

For the purposes of this guideline, the following definitions of labour are recommended:

- Latent first stage of labour – a period of time, not necessarily continuous, when:
  - there are painful contractions, and
  - there is some cervical change, including cervical effacement and dilatation up to 4 cm.
- Established first stage of labour – when:
  - there are regular painful contractions, and
  - there is progressive cervical dilatation from 4 cm.

For definitions of second and third stages of labour, refer to Sections 8.1 and 9.1.1, respectively.

7.3   Duration of the first stage of labour

Introduction

In considering 'normal' labour, it is important to define the boundaries that distinguish what is normal from what is abnormal. These limits can then be used to inform women and their carers about what to expect, and when it is appropriate for midwives to refer women for an obstetric opinion.

Clinical question

Do duration and progress of the first and second stages of labour affect outcomes?

Previous guideline

Duration of labour has not been considered in any previous guideline.

Description of included studies

One large ($n = 10\,979$) US cross-sectional study examined duration of the early first stage of labour (unestablished labour) and its effect on outcomes.[278] [EL = 3] A second, much smaller study ($n = 30$) investigated the effect of duration of the first stage of labour on maternal anxiety.[286] [EL = 3] A further three studies were identified that investigated the total duration of labour and its impact on clinical outcomes.[287–289] In addition, six observational studies were reviewed that described lengths of the first stage of labour and some factors associated with length of the first stage.[277,279,280,282–284] One descriptive study described progress of labour in multiparous women with uncomplicated pregnancies and labours.[290]

Review findings

One US cross-sectional study ($n = 10\,979$) investigated prolonged latent phase of labour and intrapartum outcomes.[278] [EL = 3] Logistic regression analysis controlling for confounding factors showed some evidence of associations of prolonged latent phase of labour (defined as over 12 hours for nulliparous women and over 6 hours for multiparous women) with higher CS rates (RR 1.65 [95% CI 1.32 to 2.06]), increased need for newborn resuscitation (RR 1.37 [95% CI 1.15 to 1.64]) and more babies with an Apgar score less than 7 at 5 minutes (RR 1.97 [95% CI 1.23 to 3.16]).

A second US cross-sectional study ($n = 30$) found no evidence of an association between the duration of first stage of labour (cervical dilatation 3–10 cm) and maternal anxiety score.[286] [EL = 3]

There are three studies that did not specify stages of labour. A small matched case–control study ($n = 34$) conducted in the UK showed some evidence of a longer duration of labour being associated with puerperal psychosis (MD 4.6 hours, $P < 0.05$).[287] [EL = 2–] One US cross-sectional study (*n* = 198) using controls matched for age, parity and birthweight (*n* = 198) demonstrated that short labour (less than 3 hours of first and second stage of labour) was not associated with major (defined as those of the external anal sphincter or of the rectal mucosa) perineal lacerations (RR 0.5, *P* = NS), PPH (RR 0.72, *P* = NS) or Apgar scores less than 7 at 5 minutes (RR 1.5, *P* = NS).[288] [EL = 3]

One nested case–control study performed in the USA demonstrated that prolonged labour was associated with maternal intrapartum complications (women having vaginal birth RR 12.5 [95% CI 4.94 to 23.38]; women having CS RR 28.89 [95% CI 20.00 to 39.43]).[289] [EL = 2–]

Six observational studies were identified that described the total duration of labour. [EL = 3] In some cases, factors associated with length of labour were also investigated.

A large (*n* = 932), prospective study carried out in Germany in 1994–95 aimed to describe factors associated with the duration of normal labour.[280] Labours and births occurred in a midwife-led maternity unit or at home. The mean duration of the first stage of labour, excluding women defined as having 'prolonged' labour by their upper limits, was found to be 7.3 hours for nulliparous women [range 1.0 to 17.0 hours] and 3.9 hours [range 0.5 to 12.0 hours] for multiparous women. Regression analysis showed that multiparous women had shorter first stages than nulliparous women but no other demographic variables were found to be associated with duration of the first stage of labour (ethnicity was not considered). A short interval between onset of labour and start of midwifery care was associated with a shorter duration of the first stage of labour, the effect more pronounced, especially in multiparous women, if membranes ruptured prior to the onset of midwifery care.

A large US study described spontaneous term labour lasting more than 3 hours in 1162 nulliparous women.[284] The median duration of the first stage of labour was 7.3 hours (10th and 90th percentiles: 3.3 and 13.7 hours, respectively).

A second US study aimed to describe the duration of the active stages of labour and the clinical factors associated with longer labours.[283] Data were collected from 2511 women from nine midwifery practices during 1996, in spontaneous labour at term, at low risk of developing complications during labour and who did not receive oxytocin or epidural analgesia. The mean length and upper limits (two standard deviations) of the active first stage of labour was 7.7 hours and 17.5 hours for nulliparous women, and 5.6 hours and 13.8 hours for multiparous women. Multivariate analysis by logistic regression showed that continuous electronic fetal monitoring and ambulation in labour were significantly associated with longer labour. The use of narcotic analgesia was significantly associated with longer labours in multiparous women. These are associations only and do not imply causality.

Earlier work undertaken in the USA (1991–1994) examined length of labour in 1473 low-risk women by ethnicity (non-Hispanic white, Hispanic and American Indian women).[282] The overall mean length and upper limit (defined as two standard deviations) of the first stage of labour was 7.7 hours and 19.4 hours for nulliparous women, and 5.7 hours and 13.7 hours for multiparous women. There were no statistically different findings between the ethnic groups.

A secondary analysis of US birth data collected from 1976 – 1987 described lengths of labour for 6991 term women giving birth normally. Oxytocin was not used and analysis included parity and conduction analgesia (95% epidural analgesia). The mean lengths and upper limits (95th percentile) of the active first stage of labour were as follows: nulliparous women – no conduction anaesthesia 8.1 hours (16.6 hours); with regional anaesthesia 10.2 hours (19.0 hours); multiparous women – no conduction anaesthesia 5.7 hours (12.5 hours); with conduction anaesthesia 7.4 hours (14.9 hours).

A smaller, older US study described the length of the latent and first stages of 100 first labours.[279] The sample was very mixed and included one breech birth, one set of twins, four induced labours and only 29 spontaneous births. The latent period of labour was found to range from 1.7 to 15.0 hours, with a mean of 7.3 hours (SD = 5.5 hours). The length of the active first stage of labour was found to range from 1.8 to 9.5 hours, with a mean of 4.4 hours (SD = 1.9 hours).

A recent UK observational study described progress in labour for multiparous women giving birth in a midwife-led unit.[290] [EL = 3] Based on findings from 2 hourly vaginal examinations for 403 women in established labour, a simple regression model showed the mean rate of cervical dilatation to be 2.9 cm/hour; median 1.9 cm/hour (10th centile 0.7 cm/hour; 5th centile 0.5 cm/hour). For women who entered the trial at a cervical dilatation of less than 4 cm, rates of cervical dilatation tended to increase over time. Several individual profiles showed periods of no progress followed by progress. Taking a cervical dilatation of 4 cm as the beginning of the active phase of labour and using the median rate of dilatation, this would give a median duration of the active first stage of labour of 3 hours 9 minutes. Using the 10th centile as the upper limit, this would extrapolate to duration of active first stage of labour of 13 hours.

Pooling findings from the descriptive studies summarised above, the range of upper limits for the duration of normal labour are as follows: women giving birth to their first baby 8.2–19.4 hours; women giving birth to second or subsequent babies 12.5–14.9 hours (Table 7.1). These figures are flawed, however, since they include some calculations based on standard deviations, which assumes a normal distribution, which is not the case when considering duration of labour.

Table 7.1 Summary table showing ranges for duration of stages of labour

	Lower value	Upper value
Nulliparous		
Latent phase	1.7 hours	15.0 hours
Active first stage	1.0 hour	19.4 hours
Parous		
Latent phase	Not studied	Not studied
Active first stage	0.5 hour	14.9 hours

n = 6 descriptive studies; includes women with epidural analgesia.

Evidence statement
The duration of established labour varies from woman to woman, and is influenced by parity. Progress is not necessarily linear.

In established labour, most women in their first labour will reach the second stage within 18 hours without intervention. In their second and subsequent labours, most women will reach the second stage within 12 hours without intervention.

Recommendation on duration of the first stage of labour

Women should be informed that, while the length of established first stage of labour varies between women, first labours last on average 8 hours and are unlikely to last over 18 hours. Second and subsequent labours last on average 5 hours and are unlikely to last over 12 hours.

Research recommendation on duration of labour

A prospective cohort study on impact of length of labour on outcomes is needed.

For duration of second and third stages of labour, refer to Sections 8.2 and 9.1.2, respectively.

7.4   Observations on presentation in suspected labour

Introduction
It is traditional to carry out a number of routine observations of the woman and the baby. These are aimed at assessing maternal and fetal health, determining the stage and progress of labour, evaluating the woman's needs, determining whether admission to her chosen place of birth is required, and, if not, what follow-up observation and advice is required.

Clinical questions

Is there evidence that the timing of admission to maternity units, and of cervical dilatation, affects outcomes?

- Subgroups include nulliparous women and multiparous women.

Is there evidence that midwife assessment at home affects outcomes?

- Subgroups include nulliparous women and multiparous women.

Is there evidence that the assessment of the following on admission, and throughout labour and the immediate postnatal period, affect outcomes?

- observation of vital signs
- bladder care
- palpation and presentation/position of baby
- frequency and duration of contractions
- membrane and liquor assessment/placental examination
- maternal behaviour
- vaginal examination
- length, strength and frequency of contractions
- assessment of cervical effacement, dilatation and position
- presentation and descent of the presenting part
- assessment of liquor if membranes ruptured.

7.4.1 Women's observations (including women's behaviour)

No relevant study was identified.

7.4.2 Palpation and presentation/position of baby

No relevant study was identified.

7.4.3 Presentation and descent of the presenting part

No relevant study was identified.

7.4.4 Membrane and liquor assessment and assessment of liquor if membranes ruptured

No relevant study was identified.

7.4.5 Contractions

No outcome-related studies were identified for inclusion in this section of the review. However, a small (*n* = 24 women) US study of low quality [EL = 2–] was found which compared transabdominal electromyography (EMG) with transabdominal pressure transducers (TOCO) for differentiating between 'true' and 'false' labour.[291] While transabdominal tocography was found to be unable to distinguish between 'true' and 'false' labours, EMG-recorded (electrical) energy levels of contractions were found to be significantly predictive of birth before 48 hours (*P* < 0.0001), with positive and negative predictive values of 94% and 88%, respectively.

7.4.6 Vaginal examinations

Introduction

The intimate nature of any vaginal examination should never be forgotten and, as with any procedure, consent obtained. While they may be useful in assessing progress in labour, to many women who may already be in pain, frightened and in an unfamiliar environment, they can be very distressing. The adverse effect on the woman may be reduced by having due regard for the woman's privacy, dignity and comfort. Good communication, as in all aspects of care, is vital and caregivers should explain the reason for the examination and what will be involved. Caregivers should also be sure that the vaginal examination is really necessary and will add important information to the decision-making process. The findings, and their impact, should also be explained sensitively to the woman – using the word 'only' when referring to the amount of dilatation may not be a good start and could easily dishearten or even frighten her.

Overview of available evidence
No relevant studies were identified that investigated vaginal examinations on initial contact with healthcare professionals.

7.4.7 Assessment of cervical effacement, dilatation and position

No relevant study was identified.

7.4.8 Admission CTG

Admission CTG versus auscultation at admission

Description of included studies
One systematic review including three randomised controlled trials and 11 observational studies was identified.[292] The systematic review, assessing prognostic value of labour admission test (admission CTG) and its effectiveness compared with auscultation only, was published in December 2005 and is of good quality. All trials targeted low-risk women. Two trials were conducted in Scotland, and the other in Ireland.

Review findings
Meta-analyses of the three trials included showed evidence that women with admission CTG were more likely to have epidural analgesia (RR 1.2 [95% CI 1.1 to 1.4]), continuous EFM (RR 1.3 [95% CI 1.2 to 1.5]) and fetal blood sampling (RR 1.3 [95% CI 1.1 to 1.5]). There was also borderline evidence that women with continuous EFM were more likely to have an instrumental birth (RR 1.1 [95% CI 1.0 to 1.3]) and CS (RR 1.2 [95% CI 1.0 to 1.4]), compared with the auscultation group, although there was no evidence of differences in augmentation (RR 1.1 [95% CI 0.9 to 1.2]), perinatal mortality (RR 1.1 [95% CI 0.2 to 7.1]) or other neonatal morbidities.

7.4.9 Timing of admission to place of birth

Description of included studies
One Canadian RCT was identified that investigated timing of admission to maternity hospital.[293] [EL = 1–] The study was identified from a systematic review. The study population comprised 209 low-risk pregnant women. Three observational studies also identified for review, relating to cervical dilatation and timing of admission, consisted of two poor-quality cohort studies conducted in Canada[294,295] [both EL = 2–] and one cross-sectional study conducted in the USA.[296] [EL = 3] One poor-quality RCT (*n* = 237) conducted in Canada was identified that considered the impact of the first contact being at home.[297] [EL = 1–] The study investigated intrapartum outcomes of women in early labour who received a home visit by an obstetric nurse (*n* = 117), compared with women who received telephone triage (*n* = 120).

Review findings
A Canadian RCT allocated women to one of two groups: early assessment of labour status (active phase or latent phase) or direct hospital admission.[293] [EL = 1–] Those not in active labour were given encouragement and advice and told to return home or walk outside until labour became more active. Women in the early assessment group had significantly reduced medical interventions including use of oxytocin (OR 0.44 [95% CI 0.24 to 0.80]) and use of any anaesthesia/analgesia (OR 0.36 [95% CI 0.16 to 0.78]). Women in the early labour assessment group reported being more satisfied with their care (Labour Agentry Scale, *P* = 0.001). There was no evidence of differences in neonatal outcomes owing to the small sample size.

One Canadian cohort study (*n* = 3220) reported intrapartum outcomes of women whose cervix was dilated by 3 cm or less at initial presentation, compared with women with cervical dilatation of 4 cm or more.[294] [EL = 2–] Women presenting early had a longer length of labour (MD 3.10 hours, *P* < 0.001), higher rate of oxytocin use (RR 1.58, *P* < 0.001) and higher CS rate (RR 2.45, *P* = 0.001). A second Canadian cohort study (*n* = 3485) compared intrapartum outcomes for two groups of low-risk pregnant women. The first group were booked under the care of family physicians who had 50% or more of their patients admitted to maternity units early (defined as a cervical dilatation of less than 3 cm). The second group were booked under family physicians who had fewer than 50% of their patients admitted early.[295] [EL = 2–] Adjusted logistic regression analysis showed women under care of physicians who admitted their patients early had higher rates of epidural (OR 1.34 [95% CI 1.15 to 1.55]), CS (OR 1.33 [95% CI 1.00 to 1.65]) and EFM (OR 1.55 [95% CI 1.27 to 1.89]). A US cross-sectional study (*n* = 8818) also compared intrapartum outcomes of women presenting in the active phase in labour with those presenting in the latent phase.[296] [EL = 3] Women presenting in the latent phase of labour had more active phase arrest (OR 2.2 [95% CI 1.6 to 2.6]), use of oxytocin (OR 2.3 [95% CI 2.1 to 2.6]) and epidural anaesthesia (OR 2.2 [95% CI 2.0 to 2.4]). There were more newborns who were intubated after birth (OR 1.2 [95% CI 1.0 to 1.4]), women with amnionitis (OR 2.7 [95% CI 1.5 to 4.7]) and maternal postpartum infection (OR 1.7 [95% CI 1.0 to 2.9]) in the latent phase admission group.

One RCT investigated intrapartum outcomes of women in early labour who received a home visit by an obstetric nurse (*n* = 117) compared with women who received telephone triage (*n* = 120).[297] [EL = 1–] Women who received a home visit had less opiate analgesia (OR 0.55 [95% CI 0.32 to 0.96]) and fewer babies admitted to neonatal units (OR 0.13 [95% CI 0.03 to 0.60]). There were no other significant differences, including costs.

Evidence statement
There is little evidence for the use of routine observations or examinations on first presentation to healthcare professionals of women in suspected labour.

There is high-level evidence that women who had routine admission CTGs were more likely to have interventions during labour, although there were no statistical differences in neonatal outcomes.

There was no good-quality evidence for timing of admission. Limited quality of evidence showed that early assessment by a midwife, compared with early admission to maternity units, appeared to reduce medical intervention rates and increase women's satisfaction. There was insufficient evidence on morbidity and mortality of both women and their babies.

There was little evidence for the effect on outcome of a home visit by a midwife in early labour.

Recommendations on initial observations

The initial assessment of a woman by a midwife should include:

- listening to her story, considering her emotional and psychological needs, and reviewing her clinical records
- physical observation – temperature, pulse, blood pressure, urinalysis
- length, strength and frequency of contractions
- abdominal palpation – fundal height, lie, presentation, position and station
- vaginal loss – show, liquor, blood
- assessment of the woman's pain, including her wishes for coping with labour along with the range of options for pain relief.

In addition:

- The FHR should be auscultated for a minimum of 1 minute immediately after a contraction. The maternal pulse should be palpated to differentiate between maternal and FHR.
- If the woman does not appear to be in established labour, after a period of assessment it may be helpful to offer a vaginal examination.
- If the woman appears to be in established labour, a vaginal examination should be offered.

Healthcare professionals who conduct vaginal examinations should :

- be sure that the vaginal examination is really necessary and will add important information to the decision-making process
- be aware that for many women who may already be in pain, highly anxious and in an unfamiliar environment, vaginal examinations can be very distressing
- ensure the woman's consent, privacy, dignity and comfort
- explain the reason for the examination and what will be involved, and
- explain the findings and their impact sensitively to the woman.

Some women have pain without cervical change. Although these women are described as not being in labour, they may well consider themselves 'in labour' by their own definition. Women who seek advice or attend hospital with painful contractions but who are not in established labour should be offered individualised support and occasionally analgesia, and encouraged to remain at or return home.

The use of admission cardiotocography (CTG) in low-risk pregnancy is not recommended in any birth setting.

Research recommendation on initial observation

Studies to examine the clinical efficacy of the initial contact observations/examination.

7.5 Observations on term PRoM while awaiting onset of labour

For observations on term PRoM while awaiting onset of labour, refer to Chapter 11.

7.6 Observations during the established first stage of labour

Introduction

It is usual practice to carry out a number of maternal and fetal observations during the first stage of labour, to detect changes in maternal or fetal health. These provide an important overview of how the woman is progressing during her labour and what her needs are over time. These observations can be recorded in the woman's records or on a pre-designed chart (partogram).

Clinical question

Is there evidence that the assessment of the following on admission, and throughout labour and the immediate postnatal period, affect outcomes?

- observation of vital signs
- bladder care
- palpation and presentation/position of baby
- frequency and duration of contractions
- membrane and liquor assessment/placental examination
- maternal behaviour
- vaginal examination
- length, strength and frequency of contractions
- assessment of cervical effacement, dilatation and position
- presentation and descent of the presenting part
- assessment of liquor if membranes ruptured.

7.6.1 Women's observation (including women's behaviour)

No relevant study was identified.

7.6.2 Palpation and presentation/position of the baby

No relevant study was identified.

7.6.3 Contractions

No relevant study was identified.

7.6.4 Membrane and liquor assessment

No relevant study was identified.

7.6.5 Bladder care

No relevant study was identified.

Evidence statement

There was no evidence found concerning the impact upon outcomes of performing maternal observations during the first stage of labour.

7.6.6 Vaginal examinations

Introduction

A vaginal examination during labour often raises anxiety and interrupts the woman's focus in labour.

Description of included studies

One UK RCT was identified which compared 2 hourly and 4 hourly vaginal examinations (VEs) and their effect on the duration of labour (n = 109).[298] [EL = 1–] A small Swedish case–control study (n = 68) also investigated number of vaginal examinations as a possible predictor of neonatal sepsis.[299] [EL = 2–]

Review findings

A UK RCT (1996) involving 109 nulliparous women in spontaneous labour at term, compared 2 hourly and 4 hourly VEs and found that there was no significant difference in duration of labour between the two groups.[298] [EL = 1–] However, the study also found there was no difference in the number of VEs performed between the two groups. A case–control study (1988) was also found which sought to determine predictive factors in neonatal sepsis.[299] The study samples comprised 26 neonates with sepsis, compared with 42 controls. The study is of low quality (including inappropriate statistical analysis). [EL = 2–] The authors considered seven intrapartum variables as possible predictive factors of sepsis, including VEs. No predictive factors of neonatal sepsis were confirmed. However, where there is term prelabour rupture of membranes (PRoM), increasing numbers of VEs have been found to be associated with neonatal sepsis (refer to Section 11.1.4 in Chapter 11).[300] [EL = 2++]

Evidence statement

There is low-quality evidence on the frequency of vaginal examinations during labour, with some evidence that the number of digital vaginal examinations is associated with neonatal and maternal sepsis, where the membranes rupture prior to the onset of labour.

7.6.7 Charting of observations

Introduction

Most UK labour wards use some form of formal charting of observations during established labour. These are usually referred to as partograms. A partogram usually contains up to three charts or graphs onto which the midwife records a woman's physical observations, frequency and strength of contractions, descent of the fetal head as felt on abdominal palpation, and cervical dilatation. A number of different partograms have evolved for use, some of which contain lines drawn to guide interventions, usually referred to as alert or action lines. These action lines are drawn to the right of the line which denotes progress by cervical dilatation at a rate of 1 cm/hour. A 2 hour action line would be displaced 2 hours to the right of the progress line and if progress then slows so as to cross the action line interventions for delay in the first stage of labour would be considered. For a 4 hourly action line this line is drawn 4 hours to the right of the progress line, i.e. more time is given before interventions would be considered.

Clinical question

What is the effectiveness of the following interventions or techniques in labour on outcomes?
• formal charting of fetal and maternal observations.

Previous guideline

The NICE clinical guideline on *Caesarean Section* reviewed this intervention.[6] Three RCTs were included.[301–303] The guideline recommended: A partogram with a 4-hour action line should be used to monitor progress of labour of women in spontaneous labour with an uncomplicated singleton pregnancy at term, because it reduces the likelihood of CS.

Description of included studies

A cluster RCT conducted in South-East Asia (n = 8 hospitals; 35 484 women) compared the use of the WHO partogram (a partogram that has an action line) with no use of a partogram.[301] [EL = 1+]

Review findings
The trial presented the results for nulliparous and parous women separately. For all nulliparous women, use of the partogram seemed to reduce the proportion of women with prolonged labour (women whose labour lasted > 18 hours, RR 0.56 [95% CI 0.47 to 0.67]), use of augmentation (RR 0.43 [95% CI 0.39 to 0.47]), rate of postpartum sepsis (RR 0.09 [95% CI 0.03–0.31]), and rate of CS (RR 0.70 [95% CI 0.61 to 0.81]), whereas it increased rate of spontaneous cephalic birth (RR 1.05 [95% CI 1.03 to 1.08], when compared with no use of a partogram. For all parous normal women, the findings were similar.

No studies have been identified that examine outcomes using partograms without action or alert lines.

Evidence statement
Evidence from low income settings show that the use of pictorial representations of progress in labour (partograms), that have an action line, increases vaginal birth and reduces maternal morbidity. A 4 hour action line is associated with fewer intrapartum interventions than a 2 hour action line with the same outcomes.

There is no current evidence on the efficacy or otherwise of partograms without action or alert lines.

GDG interpretation of the evidence
The benefits offered by use of the partogram which provides a pictorial summary of labour were felt to be applicable to the UK, even though the evidence was drawn from low income countries.

Research recommendation on charting of observations

Studies looking at the efficacy of the use of the partogram, and the comparison of a partogram with an action line and one without, should be carried out.

For further advice on partogram line placement, refer to Section 7.7.2

7.6.8 Monitoring of fetal wellbeing

Refer to Chapter 13 (monitoring babies in labour).

7.6.9 Pain assessment during labour

Use of pain scales during labour

Introduction
This systematic review was undertaken to answer the clinical question: does the use of pain scales during labour affect outcomes? In addition, the impact of pain scales on women's experience of labour, validity and reliability of pain scales used during labour, predictive value of pain scores, acceptability of using pain scales during labour, observer ratings versus self-ratings and comparison of pain scales were also investigated.

Previous guidelines
The use of pain scales has not been considered in any previous guideline.

Description of included studies
The review included 13 papers providing evidence of a fair to poor quality regarding the use of pain scales during labour. This low level of evidence can be explained by the fact that the impact of pain scales on labour outcome is not the main focus of the studies under review, many of which are descriptive in nature.

Review findings

Impact on women's experience of labour
A large-scale prospective survey of women's expectations and experiences of labour conducted in Finland included women's experiences of pain and pain relief (*n* = 1091; 33% nulliparous

women).[123] [EL = 3] Pain was measured using an 11-point box scale (BS-11) and a 5-point verbal rating scale (VRS) (anchor points 'no pain' and 'intolerable pain'). Despite the regular use of pain scales (every 30 minutes), after administration of pain relief 50% of multiparous women still reported pain scores of 8–10 on the BS-11 (this figure was 19% for nulliparous women). 18% of women rated their pain relief as poor, 37% rated it as moderate, and 45% as good. Views of pain relief were not related to parity. Ratings of overall satisfaction were not related to parity, level of pain experienced or pain relief received.

A small US study (n = 23) of women giving birth with no pharmacological analgesia asked women to rate labour pain sensation intensity and pain affect (unpleasantness).[304] [EL = 2−] Women were asked to state what they had been thinking about in the few minutes prior to pain assessment: the pain/avoiding pain or having the baby. Women who focused on having the baby had significantly lower pain affect scores than those who focused on the pain of labour or avoiding pain in all stages of labour.

Validity and reliability of pain scales used during labour
Research conducted in France compared observer ratings of pain intensity with women's self-ratings on a 5-point numerical scale, the Present Pain Intensity (PPI) scale.[305] [EL = III] The study involved 100 nulliparous women asked to rate their labour pain at 30 minute intervals from the onset of labour (defined as 3 cm cervical dilatation) until full dilatation was confirmed. Mean PPI ratings increased significantly with increasing cervical dilatation.

A US descriptive correlational study was undertaken to investigate the sensory and emotional aspects of labour pain.[306] [EL = 3] The study involved a convenience sample of 79 women in established labour. Pain was assessed by each woman using four methods: a 10 cm visual analogue scale (VAS); the question 'What does your pain feel like?'; the question 'How strong is your pain?'; and by an observer (research assistant) using the Behavioural Index of Pain (BIP). All four measures of pain showed a significant difference between early and late established labour.

A recent German study examined women's experience of pain and feeling of 'fitness' (mental and physical energy) during labour.[307] [EL = 3] Fifty women were asked to complete a VAS every 45 minutes during both stages of labour. The mean pain score increased steadily as labour progressed. The administration of pharmacological analgesia had the effect of reducing pain scores. This was more marked for epidural analgesia than intramuscular analgesia.

Secondary analysis of data obtained from three RCTs compared pain scores reported before and after the administration of epidural analgesia (n = 311).[308] [EL = III] Pain was measured using a 10-point verbal numeric scale. Findings showed that 2% of women with a pain score of 0 or 1 wanted additional analgesia, 51% of women with a score of 2 or 3 wanted additional analgesia and 93% of women with a score of > 3 wanted additional analgesia.

A small US study of 33 adolescent women measured pain using a small plastic hand-held tool incorporating pain descriptors (e.g. cramping, agonising) and a 10 cm numerical scale.[309] [EL = 3] Scores obtained using the numeric visual analogue scale (VAS) increased with cervical dilatation. There were significant increases in VAS scores for pain sensation intensity from early to active labour and from first stage of labour to transition. This increase in score was not seen from transition to pushing.

The effect of pethidine on women's ability to use the VAS reliably has been investigated as part of a small UK study.[310] [EL = III] Two subgroups of women in labour were asked ten times to judge one-fifth of the length of a 15 cm VAS line. They were also asked to rate their current pain level on two occasions, 5 minutes apart. Group One (n = 10) conducted the test approximately half an hour after the administration of 150 mg of pethidine, Group Two (n = 10) did so without pethidine. There were no significant differences between the mean error nor variance of women's ratings of one-fifth along the 15 cm line, whether the woman had pethidine or not. Women's assessment of current pain made 5 minutes apart also showed no significant differences.

Predictive value of pain scores
A Canadian study of 115 low-risk women from a single institution examined the relationship between pain scores obtained in the latent phase of labour and labour outcomes, including length of labour and mode of birth.[311] [EL = II] Pain intensity assessed during the early phase of

labour ($\leq$ 3 cm cervical dilatation) was positively correlated with the duration of the latent phase ($r = 0.58$, $P < 0.0001$) and the duration of active labour ($r = 0.50$, $P < 0.0001$). Analysis of variance showed that latent labour pain was prognostic of the dilatation levels at which analgesia was requested, the number of requests for analgesia and the mode of birth. The incidence of spontaneous birth declined with each increase in pain category recorded during the latent phase ($\chi^2 = 12.09$, df = 4, $P = 0.01$).

Acceptability of using pain scales during labour
The recent German study described above also asked for women's opinions regarding using the pain assessment scale during labour.[307] [EL = 3] Written evaluations ($n = 28$, response rate 56%) suggested that most women ($n = 21$) felt positive about their participation in the research. However, three women felt it had interfered with their own needs and six expressed negative views regarding the timing of the assessments (too frequent/at the wrong time).

A small-scale study ($n = 13$ women and nine midwives) carried out in Australia compared the perceptions of pain of labouring women with those of their attendant midwife.[312] [EL = III] Women were asked to rate their labour pain at 15 minute intervals throughout the first and second stages of labour using three pain scales. While most women were able to complete the pain scales during the first stage of labour, 12 of the 13 women were not able to complete the scales towards the end of the first stage. Unfortunately, women were not asked their views of completing the scales so frequently during labour.

A US study which investigated the congruence between intrapartum and postnatal labour pain scores also reported briefly on women's responses to being asked to complete the pain scales during the first stage of labour.[313] [EL = 3] Fifty women were asked to complete a 6-point PPI (anchors 'no pain' and 'excruciating') and a scale involving scoring of 20 adjectives. The authors reported that the women 'responded favourably' to administration of the tool and were usually able to complete both scales between contractions until late into the first stage of labour.

A small-scale study conducted in Scotland also used a list of 20 pain descriptors.[314] [EL = 3] In this case, the words were presented verbally and women ($n = 23$) were asked to choose words which best described their current experience of pain. Women were reported as having 'little difficulty' in selecting and reporting words that described their pain.

Observer ratings versus self-ratings
A descriptive cohort study carried out in Israel investigated the effect of ethnic differences between labouring women and their care provider on the carers' perceptions of pain.[315] [EL = 2−] Two groups of women in early established labour (4–5 cm cervical dilatation) at term were compared, one group included Jewish women ($n = 255$), the other comprised Bedouin women ($n = 192$). Despite marked differences in demographic variables and pregnancy education, self-assessments of pain were found to be similar for the two groups of women. Clinical staff (Jewish doctors and/or midwives) rated Bedouin women's experience of labour pain as lower than that of Jewish women (6.89 versus 8.52, $P < 0.001$). For Jewish women, 60% of self-assessments of labour pain agreed with assessments made by carers, this agreement was just 30% for Bedouin women.

The French study described above, conducted to validate an observer-rated behavioural pain index, compared observer ratings (midwife or obstetrician) of pain intensity with women's self-ratings on a 5-point numerical scale.[305] [EL = 3] Significant positive correlations were obtained between self-ratings and observer ratings for each phase of labour. However, self-ratings were significantly higher than observer ratings for all phases of labour, F values obtained from analysis of variance being 354.62, 348.34, 360.95 and 396.78, respectively, $P < 0.0005$ for all values. These findings suggest staff were underestimating the woman's experience of pain throughout the first stage of labour.

The US study discussed in the validity of pain scales subsection above compared different pain scales used during labour.[306] [EL = 3] It was found that observer ratings of pain using the BIP, although closely correlated with self-rated pain scores, were consistently lower, suggesting that carers may underestimate the pain a woman is experiencing.

A small-scale but detailed study carried out in Australia compared the perception of pain of labouring women with those of their attendant midwife.[312] [EL = 2−] There was a significant positive correlation between women's and midwives' assessments of pain on all three pain scales used. However, for two of the scales, although there was no significant difference between women's and midwives' scores for mild–moderate pain, there was a significant difference between the two sets of scores when pain intensity was severe, with midwives consistently giving lower ratings of pain intensity (VAS: $t(30) = 2.157$, $P < 0.05$; PPI: $t(25) = 2.301$, $P < 0.05$).

Evidence statement
Evidence is drawn from mostly descriptive studies of variable methodological quality. There is some evidence that pain scales provide a valid measurement of women's pain during labour. No study evaluated their effect on clinical outcomes.

There is also evidence that caregivers tend to underestimate women's level of pain during labour.

Focusing on pain and pain relief has a negative impact on some women's experience of labour.

There is some support for the use of a verbal scale over a pencil and paper scale for use by women during labour.

There may be some correlation between high pain scores in early labour and prolonged labour and instrumental birth.

GDG interpretation of the evidence
The evidence for the use of formal pain scores as a routine method of assessing a woman's needs in managing her pain is not convincing, even allowing for some evidence that healthcare professionals may underestimate the severity of a woman's pain.

Recommendation on verbal assessment of pain

Verbal assessment using a numerical pain score is not recommended routinely.

Research recommendation on assessment of pain

Further studies are required to investigate methods of assessing pain relief, attitudes to pain, effects of labour pain, and long-term outcomes.

For pain-relieving strategies, refer to Chapters 5 and 6 on choosing pain relief in labour.

Recommendations on observations during the established first stage of labour

A pictorial record of labour (partogram) should be used once labour is established.

Where the partogram includes an action line, the World Health Organization recommendation of a 4 hour action line should be used.* [repeated from Section 7.7.2]

Observations by a midwife during the first stage of labour include:

- 4 hourly temperature and blood pressure
- hourly pulse
- half-hourly documentation of frequency of contractions
- frequency of emptying the bladder
- vaginal examination offered 4 hourly, or where there is concern about progress or in response to the woman's wishes (after abdominal palpation and assessment of vaginal loss).

In addition:

- Intermittent auscultation of the fetal heart after a contraction should occur for at least 1 minute, at least every 15 minutes, and the rate should be recorded as an average. The maternal pulse should be palpated if an FHR abnormality is detected to differentiate the two heart rates. (See recommendations in Section 7.8 for reasons to transfer to continuous EFM.)

---

* Anonymous. World Health Organization partograph in management of labour. World Health Organization Maternal Health and Safe Motherhood Programme. *Lancet* 1994;343(8910):1399–404. See also www.who.int/reproductive-health/impac/Clinical_Principles/ Normal_labour_C57_C76.html.

Ongoing consideration should be given to the woman's emotional and psychological needs, including her desire for pain relief.

Women should be encouraged to communicate their need for analgesia at any point during labour.

7.7 Possible routine interventions in the first stage of labour

Introduction
Although most would not intervene in normal labour, a number of policies have been examined in attempts to reduce unnecessary interventions, particularly in nulliparous women.

Clinical question
What is the effectiveness of the following interventions or techniques in labour on outcomes?

- active management
- amniotomy
- oxytocin.

7.7.1 Active management of the first stage of labour

Introduction
Active management includes:

- one-to-one continuous support
- strict definition of established labour
- early routine amniotomy
- routine 2 hourly cervical examination
- oxytocin if labour becomes slow.

Description of included studies
There were four trials identified: a US trial[316] involved 1934 nulliparous women in labour (intervention $n = 1017$; control $n = 917$) with mixed ethnicity; a Mexican trial[317] involved 405 nulliparous women (intervention $n = 200$; control $n = 205$) also with mixed ethnicity; a New Zealand trial[318] involved 651 nulliparous women (intervention $n = 320$; control $n = 331$) with mixed ethnicity; and a Nigerian trial[319] that involved 448 nulliparous women (intervention $n = 221$; control $n = 227$) in labour with a black population.

Review findings
Based on reasonable homogeneity of the trials, a series of meta-analyses were conducted. The analyses showed that active management does not reduce the rate of CS (four trials, RR 0.83 [95% CI 0.67 to 1.03]) or increase spontaneous vaginal birth (four trials, RR 1.04 [95% CI 0.99 to 1.08]). The analyses also showed that active management of labour shortens the length of first stage (two trials, WMD –121.93 minutes [95% CI –134.54 to –109.31 minutes]), but not the second stage (two trials, WMD –2.11 minutes [95% CI–4.49 to 0.26 minutes]. There was no evidence of difference in use of epidural (three trials, RR 1.03 [95% CI 0.92 to 1.16]) or neonatal outcome (admission to neonatal unit two trials, RR 0.93 [95% CI 0.89 to 1.73]). One trial reported maternal satisfaction, although there was no evidence of differences (satisfied with labour and birth care RR 1.04 [95% CI 0.94 to 1.15]; would choose the same management plan RR 1.05 [95% CI 0.94 to 1.18]).[318]

Evidence statement
The package known as active management of labour (one-to-one continuous support, diagnosis of labour, early amniotomy, 2 hourly vaginal examinations and oxytocin if labour becomes slow) appears to reduce the duration of the first stage of labour but has no effect on the incidence of CS. There was no assessment of pain for women, nor of neonatal outcomes. Overall, there is no evidence of any other effect from 'the package' to either woman or baby.

GDG interpretation of the evidence
It is the view of the GDG that the component of the package known as the active management of labour that most influenced outcomes was one-to-one care. Other components of the package have not been shown to be of benefit. The high level of routine interventions associated with active management of labour do not justify its use.

Recommendation on active management of the first stage of labour

The package known as active management of labour (one-to-one continuous support; strict definition of established labour; early routine amniotomy; routine 2 hourly vaginal examination; oxytocin if labour becomes slow) should not be offered routinely.

7.7.2 Partogram line placement

Description of included studies
Two RCTs were identified that compared different action line placements. The first trial was conducted in Liverpool (UK) and comprised 928 women in labour.[302] [EL = 1++] The study compared use of 2 hour and 3 hour action lines with a 4 hour action line. A second trial conducted in South Africa (*n* = 694) compared a single action line at 2 hours with the WHO partogram (4 hour action line).[303] An additional recent UK RCT compared a partogram with a 2 hour action line with one using a 4 hour action line.[320] [EL = 1+] The trial involved 2975 nulliparous women and compared outcomes of labour following use of a partogram with an action line 2 or 4 hours to the right of the alert line. If progress crossed the action line a diagnosis of prolonged labour was made and labour managed according to a standard protocol. Primary outcome measures were caesarean section rate and women's satisfaction. Postal questionnaires were completed 2–10 days postnatally by 1929 women (65%).

Review findings
Findings from the UK RCT suggested that use of the 2 hour action line, compared with the 3 hour line, seemed to increase women's satisfaction (satisfaction score MD 3.5 [95% CI 1.7 to 5.3]), but there is no evidence of a difference in interventions, e.g. amniotomy: OR 0.9 [95% CI 0.6 to 1.3]; epidural OR 1.3 [95% CI 0.9 to 1.8]; CS for failure to progress OR 0.7 [95% CI 0.4 to 1.3]; or instrumental birth OR 0.9 [95% CI 0.6 to 1.4]).[302] [EL = 1++] There was no evidence of differences in neonatal outcomes between use of the 2 and 3 hour action line. Use of the 3 hour action line compared with the 4 hour action line seemed to increase the rate of CS (OR 1.8 [95% CI 1.1 to 3.2]), but not rates for CS for fetal distress (OR 1.8 [95% CI 0.6 to 5.5]) or for failure to progress (OR 1.8 [95% CI 0.9 to 3.4]). There is no evidence of a difference in other interventions, women's satisfaction or neonatal outcome. Use of a 2 hour action line compared with a 4 hour action line seemed to increase women's satisfaction (satisfaction score MD 5.2 [95% CI 3.4 to 7.0]). There was no evidence of a difference in rate of interventions or neonatal outcome.

A second trial conducted in South Africa showed that use of a single action line reduced the rate of CS (RR 0.68 [95% CI 0.50 to 0.93]), and instrumental births (RR 0.73 [95% CI 0.56 to 0.96]), and increased use of oxytocin (RR 1.51 [95% CI 1.10 to 2.07]).[303] There was no evidence of differences in use of analgesia (RR 1.01 [95% CI 0.93 to 1.11]) or neonatal outcomes (Apgar < 8 at 1 minute (RR 1.24 [95% CI 0.93 to 1.65]); perinatal death RR 7.12 [95% CI 0.37 to 137.37]).

For the UK RCT,[320] there was no evidence of difference for either of the primary outcomes between the 2 and 4 hour action line trial groups: caesarean birth RR 1.0 (CI 0.80 to 1.26); women dissatisfied with labour experience RR 0.89 [95% CI 0.66 to 1.21]. More women in the 2 hour action line group crossed the partogram action line (854/1490 versus 673/1485; RR 1.27 [95% CI 1.18 to 1.37]) and therefore received more interventions to augment labour (772/1490 versus 624/1486; RR 1.23 [95% CI 1.14 to 1.33]). There were no significant differences between groups for instrumental birth, cord pH < 7.1, Apgar score < 7 at 5 minutes or admission to SCBU.

Evidence statement
There are no studies which involve the use of a partogram with no action line. Placing an action line earlier than that recommended by the WHO (at 4 hours) increases interventions without any benefit in outcomes to either woman or baby.

Recommendation on partogram line placement

Where the partogram includes an action line, the World Health Organization recommendation of a 4 hour action line should be used.*

7.7.3 Routine amniotomy

Early routine amniotomy with selective oxytocin versus conservative management

Introduction
For this review, the intervention was defined as routine early amniotomy, with oxytocin if labour becomes slow compared with conservative management (no routine amniotomy).

Description of included studies
Two trials were identified for inclusion in this review: a Belgian study[321] involving 306 nulliparous women (intervention $n = 152$; control $n = 154$) and a US trial[322] involving 705 nulliparous women in labour (intervention $n = 351$; control $n = 354$). Based on reasonable homogeneity in study designs, a series of meta-analyses were conducted.

Review findings
The meta-analyses showed that there was no evidence of differences in mode of birth (CS (two trials): RR 0.80 [95% CI 0.55 to 1.17]; spontaneous vaginal birth (two trials): RR 1.06 [95% CI 0.97 to 1.16]; use of epidural (two trials): RR 1.02 [95% CI 0.92 to 1.12]; length of first stage of labour (two trials): WMD −65.06 minutes [95% CI −134.83 to 4.71 minutes]; length of second stage of labour (two trials): WMD 1.80 minutes [95% CI −1.83 to 5.44 minutes]; or neonatal outcomes (Apgar score less than 7 at 5 minutes: (two trials): RR 1.22 [95% CI 0.38 to 3.93]; admission to neonatal unit (two trials): RR 0.90 [95% CI 0.47 to 1.72]). No other findings relating to major outcomes were available.

Evidence statement
There is no evidence of differences in mode of birth, use of epidural, length of labour or neonatal outcomes between early routine amniotomy plus selective use of oxytocin, and more conservative management.

Recommendation on routine amniotomy

In normally progressing labour, amniotomy should not be performed routinely.

7.7.4 Routine 'amniotomy and oxytocin'

Early routine amniotomy and oxytocin

Introduction
Early routine amniotomy and oxytocin was defined as routine use of oxytocin, in addition to early routine amniotomy for normal healthy women at the beginning of labour.

Description of included studies
One US RCT was identified.[323] The study population involved 150 (intervention $n = 75$; control $n = 75$) nulliparous women in labour with mixed ethnicity.

Review findings
The results showed no evidence of a difference in mode of birth (spontaneous vaginal birth RR 0.97 [95% CI 0.82 to 1.14]; CS RR 0.91 [95% CI 0.41 to 2.01]). There was no strong evidence on duration of labour (latent phase MD −0.73 hours [95% CI −0.84 to −0.62 hours]; active phase MD 0.24 hours [95% CI 0.12 to 0.36 hours]; deceleration phase MD 0.00 hours [−0.02 to 0.02 hours]) and Apgar score (at 1 minute MD 0.35 [95% CI 0.30 to 0.40]; at 5 minutes MD 0.02 [95% CI 0.00 to 0.04]). There was no other outcome available.

---

* Anonymous. World Health Organization partograph in management of labour. World Health Organization Maternal Health and Safe Motherhood Programme. *Lancet* 1994;343(8910):1399–404. See also www.who.int/reproductive-health/impac/Clinical_Principles/Normal_labour_C57_C76.html.

Evidence statement
Limited evidence showed no substantial benefit for early amniotomy and routine use of oxytocin compared with conservative management of labour.

> **Recommendation on routine 'amniotomy and oxytocin'**
>
> Combined early amniotomy with use of oxytocin should not be used routinely.

7.8 Fetal heart assessment and reasons for transfer to continuous EFM

Introduction
The monitoring of the fetal heart rate (FHR) in labour aims to identify hypoxia before it is sufficient to lead to long-term poor neurological outcome for babies.

7.8.1 Admission test

For use of continuous EFM for admission test, refer to Section 7.4.8.

7.8.2 Continuous EFM versus intermittent auscultation

Clinical question
Do the following methods of fetal monitoring affect outcomes?

* admission CTG
* intermittent auscultation (Pinard, Doppler)
* intermittent electronic monitoring
* continuous electronic monitoring.

Description of included studies
One systematic review, including 12 trials, was identified.[324] The systematic review compared effectiveness of continuous EFM for fetal assessment during labour with intermittent auscultation or EFM. Among the 12 trials, only three targeted low-risk women in the USA, Ireland and Australia. The studies were of moderate to good quality.

Review findings

All women (including low- and high-risk pregnancies)
There was evidence that women with continuous EFM were more likely to have CS (RR 1.70 [95% CI 1.32 to 2.20]), CS for abnormal FHR (RR 2.45 [95% CI 1.94 to 3.09]), instrumental vaginal birth (RR 1.26 [95% CI 1.05 to 1.50]) and need for analgesia (RR 1.09 [95% CI 1.02 to 1.15]), and less likely to have spontaneous vaginal birth (RR 1.28 [95% CI 1.20 to 1.36]), compared with those in the intermittent auscultation group, although there was no evidence of a difference in the use of epidural analgesia (RR 1.00 [95% CI 0.90 to 1.11]).

Although there was no evidence of a difference in perinatal mortality (RR 0.88 [95% CI 0.61 to 1.27]), there was evidence that fewer infants developed neonatal seizures from women with continuous EFM (RR 0.50 [95% CI 0.31 to 0.80]).

Only women with low-risk pregnancies
There was evidence that women with continuous EFM were more likely to have CS for abnormal FHR pattern (RR 2.31 [95% CI 1.49 to 3.59]), instrumental vaginal birth (RR 1.29 [95% CI 1.02 to 1.62]) and all instrumental birth (including CS and instrumental vaginal birth; RR 1.35 [95% CI 1.09 to 1.67]), compared with those with intermittent auscultation. There was also evidence that women with continuous EFM were less likely to have babies with neonatal seizures (RR 0.36 [95% CI 0.16 to 0.81]) and more likely to have babies admitted to neonatal units (RR 1.37 [95% CI 1.01 to 1.87]), compared with those with intermittent auscultation, with no evidence of difference in perinatal mortality (RR 1.02 [95% CI 0.31 to 3.31]).

Doppler ultrasound versus Pinard stethoscope

Description of included studies
One trial conducted in Zimbabwe compared the hand-held Doppler ultrasound and the Pinard stethoscope, used by the research midwife or attending midwife for monitoring of FHR during labour.[325] The women were a mix of low and high risk. The trial was of a moderate quality.

Review findings
Although women monitored using a hand-held Doppler device had less spontaneous vaginal birth (RR 0.83 [95% CI 0.76 to 0.91]) and more CS (RR 1.95 [95% CI 1.47 to 2.60]), there was evidence that women monitored by Doppler were less likely to have babies with admissions to neonatal units (RR 0.65 [95% CI 0.46 to 0.94]), neonatal seizures (RR 0.06 [95% CI 0.00 to 1.07]), and hypoxic encephalopathy (RR 0.12 [95% CI 0.02 to 0.88]) than those monitored using a Pinard stethoscope. There was no evidence of differences in perinatal mortality (RR 0.29 [95% CI 0.07 to 1.25]) or low Apgar scores (Apgar score less than 6 at 5 minutes RR 0.37 [95% CI 0.11 to 1.24]).

Evidence statement
There is high-level evidence that continuous EFM reduces the rate of neonatal seizures but has no impact on rates of cerebral palsy. There is high-level evidence that continuous EFM increases the rates of instrumental and caesarean birth.

There is no high-level evidence about the value of auscultation of the fetal heart rate when women are in early labour.

There is moderate-level evidence from a single small study in a low income country, of both low- and high-risk women, which showed that assessing the fetal heart rate by hand-held Doppler is more effective than by Pinard stethoscope. In the opinion of the GDG this evidence was not robust enough to differentiate between the two techniques.

Recommendations on fetal heart assessment and reasons for transfer to continuous EFM

Intermittent auscultation of the FHR is recommended for low-risk women in established labour in any birth setting.

Initial auscultation of the fetal heart is recommended at first contact in early labour and at each further assessment undertaken to determine whether labour has become established.

Once a woman is in established labour, intermittent auscultation of the fetal heart after a contraction should be continued as detailed in Section 7.6.

Intermittent auscultation can be undertaken by either Doppler ultrasound or Pinard stethoscope.

Changing from intermittent auscultation to continuous EFM in low-risk women should be advised for the following reasons:

* significant meconium-stained liquor, and this change should also be considered for light meconium-stained liquor (see recommendations in Section 12.1)
* abnormal FHR detected by intermittent auscultation (less than 110 beats per minute [bpm]; greater than 160 bpm; any decelerations after a contraction)
* maternal pyrexia (defined as 38.0 °C once or 37.5 °C on two occasions 2 hours apart)
* fresh bleeding developing in labour
* oxytocin use for augmentation
* the woman's request.

8 Normal labour: second stage

8.1 Definition of the second stage of labour

Introduction

Definitions of the stages of labour need to be clear in order to ensure that women and the staff providing their care have an accurate and shared understanding of the concepts involved and can communicate effectively. In order to facilitate this, the guideline aims to provide practical definitions of the stages of labour.

Clinical question

What are the appropriate definitions of the latent and active phases of the first stage, the second stage, and the third stage of labour?

Previous guideline

No previous guideline has considered definitions of the stages of labour.

Description of included studies

No relevant study was identified that investigated outcomes of different definitions of labour. The GDG explored various definitions that have been used in practice and research. Definitions of stages of labour, used in six descriptive studies investigating duration of labour, were used to inform the discussion on definitions of labour.

Review findings

Definitions of the second stage of labour may commence with a fully dilated cervix, e.g. from full dilatation of the cervix to the birth of the baby.[277] Alternatively, they may take into account maternal effort e.g. from the commencement of maternal pushing and full dilatation of the cervix to the birth of the baby.[280] The latter differentiates an active second stage from an early or passive second stage. This may be useful when a woman enters the second stage with the baby's head still relatively high in the pelvis, i.e. with no urge to push, or with epidural analgesia.

> **Recommendations on definitions of the second stage of labour**
>
> For the purposes of this guideline, the following definitions of labour are recommended:
> * Passive second stage of labour:
>   o the finding of full dilatation of the cervix prior to or in the absence of involuntary expulsive contractions.
> * Onset of the active second stage of labour:
>   o the baby is visible
>   o expulsive contractions with a finding of full dilatation of the cervix or other signs of full dilatation of the cervix
>   o active maternal effort following confirmation of full dilatation of the cervix in the absence of expulsive contractions.

For definitions of the first and third stages of labour, refer to Sections 7.2 and 9.1.1, respectively.

8.2   Duration and definition of delay in the second stage of labour

Introduction
In considering labour, it is important to define the boundaries that distinguish what is normal from what is abnormal. These boundaries can then be used to inform women and their carers about what to expect, and when it is appropriate for midwives to refer women to obstetricians for advice and support regarding the management of labour.

Clinical question
Do duration and progress of the first and second stages of labour affect outcomes?

Previous guideline
Duration of labour has not been considered in any previous guideline.

Description of included studies
Ten observational studies that investigated the association between the duration of the second stage of labour and the defined outcomes were identified. The quality of the studies varied.

Review findings
A large US cross-sectional study (*n* = 15 759) investigated prolonged duration of the second stage (more than 4 hours) and the defined outcomes.[326] [EL = 3] Logistic regression analysis, controlling for various confounders, showed that there was moderate evidence of an association between a prolonged second stage and chorioamnionitis (OR 1.79 [95% CI 1.44 to 2.22]), third- or fourth-degree lacerations (OR 1.33 [95% CI 1.07 to 1.67]), CS (OR 5.65 [95% CI 4.46 to 7.16]), instrumental vaginal birth (OR 2.83 [95% CI 2.38 to 3.36]), and low Apgar score (< 7 at 5 minutes OR 0.45 [95% CI 0.25 to 0.84]). There was no evidence of an association between prolonged second stage of labour and endomyometritis (OR 0.79 [95% CI 0.49 to 1.26]), PPH (OR 1.05 [95% CI 0.84 to 1.31]), meconium-stained liquor (OR 1.11 [95% CI 0.93 to 1.33]), or admission to the neonatal unit (OR 0.59 [95% CI 0.35 to 1.03]).

A large US cross-sectional study (*n* = 7818) compared prolonged second stage of labour (121+ minutes) with normal duration (1–120 minutes) on the defined outcomes. The associations between two levels of prolonged second stage (121–240 minutes versus 241+ minutes) on the defined outcomes were also compared.[327] [EL = 3] The analysis, which did not control for confounding variables, showed some evidence that a longer second stage of labour (more than 120 minutes) is associated with various medical interventions. For prolonged duration of second stage, the analysis (again without controlling for confounding factors) showed some evidence that duration of more than 240 minutes is associated with various medical interventions.

A German cross-sectional study (*n* = 1200) investigated prolonged second stage of labour (more than 2 hours) and intrapartum outcomes.[328] [EL = 3] The results showed evidence of an association of prolonged second stage with a low Apgar score at 1 minute, PPH, perineal tears and postpartum fever, although the analyses did not control for confounding factors.

A cross-sectional study conducted in Taiwan (*n* = 1915) investigated prolonged second stage of labour and intrapartum outcomes.[329] [EL = 3] The results showed no evidence of an association between a prolonged second stage and neonatal and maternal intrapartum outcomes, although the analyses did not control for any confounding factors.

One retrospective case–control study (*n* = 173) found no evidence of an association between stress urinary incontinence and the duration of the second stage of a woman's first labour, when followed up 7–8 years following the birth (OR 1.07 [95% CI 0.9 to 1.3]).[330] [EL = 2+] It is notable that the study was unable to evaluate parity as an independent risk factor for urinary incontinence.

A large Canadian cross-sectional study (*n* = 6041) investigated the duration of the second stage of labour and perinatal outcomes.[331] [EL = 2+] There was no evidence of associations between the duration of second stage and low Apgar scores at 5 minutes, neonatal seizures or admission to neonatal units.

One large UK cross-sectional study (n = 25 069) investigated prolonged second stage of labour and perinatal outcomes.[332,333] [EL = 2+] Logistic regression analysis showed that there was evidence of association between a longer duration and a higher rate of PPH (durations: 120–179 minutes OR 1.6 [95% CI 1.3 to 1.9]; 180–239 minutes 1.7 [95% CI 1.3 to 2.3]; 240+ minutes OR 1.9 [95% CI 1.2 to 2.8]), but there was no evidence of an association with postpartum infection (120–179 minutes OR 1.1 [95% CI 0.9 to 1.4]; 180–239 minutes OR 1.1 [95% CI 0.7 to 1.6]; 240+ minutes OR 1.2 [95% CI 0.7 to 2.0]), or an Apgar score less than 7 at 5 minutes (120–179 minutes OR 1.3 [95% CI 0.8 to 2.0]; 180–239 minutes OR 0.9 [95% CI 0.3 to 2.3]; 240+ minutes OR 1.9 [95% CI 0.8 to 4.7]).

A US population-based study (n = 1432) investigated prolonged second stage of labour (more than 120 minutes) and intrapartum outcomes.[334] [EL = 2+] Analysis, without controlling for confounding factors, showed evidence of association with increased rates of CS and instrumental vaginal birth. There was no association with any adverse neonatal outcomes.

A small US longitudinal descriptive study (n = 30) investigated the association between the duration of the second stage of labour (cervical dilatation 10 cm to birth) and anxiety scores.[286] [EL = 2–] The study found no significant association between the duration of the second stage of labour and anxiety scores (inter-correlation –0.24).

A large cross-sectional study conducted in the USA (n = 4403) investigated different lengths of the second stage of labour and their association with intrapartum outcomes.[335] [EL = 2–] The analyses, without controlling for confounding factors, showed no evidence of an association between the duration of the second stage and neonatal outcomes, apart from low Apgar scores at 1 minute (P < 0.03). Both puerperal haemorrhage and febrile morbidity showed evidence of an association with length of labour (P < 0.001 for both).

There are three studies that did not specify stages of labour.

A small, matched case–control study (n = 34) conducted in the UK investigated the association between length of labour and puerperal psychosis.[287] [EL = 2–] It showed some evidence of a longer duration of labour being associated with puerperal psychosis (MD 4.6 hours, P < 0.05).

One US cross-sectional study (n = 198) investigated the impact of short labour (less than 3 hours of first and second stage of labour) upon perinatal outcomes, with matched controls (matched for maternal age, parity and birthweight).[288] [EL = 3] There was no evidence of associations between short labour and major (defined as those of the external anal sphincter or of the rectal mucosa) perineal lacerations, PPH or Apgar scores less than 7 at 5 minutes.

One nested case–control study, performed in the USA, investigated the effects of prolonged labour on maternal complications in the intrapartum period.[289] [EL = 2–] Both For women who had a vaginal birth or CS, prolonged labour was associated with maternal complications (women with vaginal birth RR 12.5 [95% CI 4.94 to 23.38]; women with CS RR 28.89 [95% CI 20.00 to 39.43]).

Descriptive studies
Three studies were identified for review that described the duration of the second stage of labour. In some cases, factors associated with the duration of labour were also investigated. By definition, all studies in this subsection are evidence level 3.

A US study aimed to describe the duration of the active stages of labour and the clinical factors associated with longer labours.[283] Data were collected from 2511 women, in spontaneous labour at term, at low risk of developing complications during labour and who did not receive oxytocin or epidurals. The data were collected from nine US midwifery practices in 1996. The mean length of the second stage was 54 minutes for nulliparous women and 18 minutes for parous women (upper limits: 146 and 64 minutes, respectively). It should be noted, for this and other studies, that the use of means and SDs is inappropriate as data for the duration of labour is not normally distributed (it has a long right hand tail). Multivariate analysis by logistic regression showed that continuous electronic fetal monitoring and ambulation in labour were significantly associated with longer labour. The use of narcotic analgesia was significantly associated with longer labours in parous women. Maternal age over 30 years was associated with a longer second stage, particularly in women giving birth to a first baby. It should be remembered that these are associations only and do not imply causality.

Earlier work undertaken in the USA (1991–94) examined the duration of labour in 1473 low-risk women in an attempt to identify differences between ethnic groups.[282] The three ethnic groups were non-Hispanic white, Hispanic and American Indian women. The mean duration of the second stage of labour was 53 minutes for nulliparous women and 17 minutes for parous women (upper limits: 147 and 57 minutes, respectively). American Indian women having their first baby had significantly shorter second stages than non-Hispanic white women giving birth for the first time ($P < 0.05$).

A secondary analysis carried out in the USA using birth data collected from 1976 to 1987 described lengths of labour for 6991 women.[277] All included labours were at term, did not involve the use of oxytocin and babies were born spontaneously. Four subgroups were analysed, comprising nulliparous and parous women with or without conduction anaesthesia (95% of which was epidural anaesthesia). The mean lengths and upper limits (95th percentile) of the second stage were as follows: nulliparous women – no conduction anaesthesia 54 minutes (132 minutes), with conduction anaesthesia 79 minutes (185 minutes); parous women – no conduction anaesthesia 19 minutes (61 minutes), with conduction anaesthesia 45 minutes (131 minutes).

A summary showing mean duration and upper limits for the duration of the second stage of labour for women without epidural analgesia calculated using data from all three decriptive studies discussed above is given in Table 8.1

Table 8.1 Summary table showing duration of the second stage of labour

	Mean (SD) (minutes)	Upper limit (mean + 2SDs) (minutes)
Nulliparous women ($n = 3664$)	54 (44)	142
Parous women ($n = 6389$)	18 (21)	60

$n = 3$ descriptive studies. Excludes women with epidural analgesia and/or oxytocin.

Evidence statement
Limited quality of evidence makes it difficult to assess the significance of a prolonged second stage of labour on perinatal outcomes for both woman and baby. The woman's position and whether pushing was directed or not are unclear from the studies.

GDG interpretation of the evidence (duration and definition of delay in the second stage of labour)
Pooling findings from the descriptive studies summarised above, the range of upper limits for the normal duration of the active second stage of labour are as follows:

• women giving birth to their first baby – about 0.5–2.5 hours for women without epidural, and 1–3 hours for women with epidural
• women giving birth to second or subsequent babies – up to about 1 hour for women without epidural, and 2 hours for women with epidural.

Unfortunately, these figures are flawed since they are calculated using SDs, the use of which assumes a normal distribution, which is not the case when considering the duration of labour.

Recommendations on duration and definition of delay in the second stage of labour

Nulliparous women:
• Birth would be expected to take place within 3 hours of the start of the active second stage in most women.
• A diagnosis of delay in the active second stage should be made when it has lasted 2 hours and women should be referred to a healthcare professional trained to undertake an operative vaginal birth if birth is not imminent.

Parous women:
• Birth would be expected to take place within 2 hours of the start of the active second stage in most women.
• A diagnosis of delay in the active second stage should be made when it has lasted 1 hour and women should be referred to a healthcare professional trained to undertake an operative vaginal birth if birth is not imminent.

If full dilatation of the cervix has been diagnosed in a woman without epidural analgesia, but she does not get an urge to push, further assessment should take place after 1 hour.

For durations of the first and third stages of labour, refer to Sections 7.3 and 9.1.2, respectively.

8.3 Observations for women and babies in the second stage of labour

Introduction
For many women, the physical demands and the psychological challenge of labour are increased during the second stage. For this reason, combined with the increased vulnerability of the baby, the second stage of labour has traditionally been associated with increased surveillance of the fetal condition and intensive support and encouragement for the labouring woman.

Clinical question
Is there evidence that the assessment of the following on admission, and throughout labour and the immediate postnatal period, affect outcomes?

- observation of vital signs
- bladder care
- palpation and presentation/position of baby
- frequency and duration of contractions
- membrane and liquor assessment/placental examination
- maternal behaviour
- vaginal examination
- length, strength and frequency of contractions
- assessment of cervical effacement, dilatation and position
- presentation and descent of the presenting part
- assessment of liquor if membranes ruptured.

8.3.1 Women's observations (including women's behaviour)

No relevant study was identified.

8.3.2 Palpation and presentation/position of baby

No relevant study was identified.

8.3.3 Contractions

No relevant study was identified.

8.3.4 Membrane and liquor assessment and assessment of liquor if membranes ruptured

No relevant study was identified.

8.3.5 Bladder care

No relevant study was identified.

8.3.6 Wellbeing of babies

No relevant good-quality study was identified.

Recommendations on observations during the second stage of labour

All observations should be documented on the partogram. Observations by a midwife of a woman in the second stage of labour include:

- hourly blood pressure and pulse
- continued 4 hourly temperature
- vaginal examination offered hourly in the active second stage or in response to the woman's wishes (after abdominal palpation and assessment of vaginal loss)
- half-hourly documentation of the frequency of contractions
- frequency of emptying the bladder
- ongoing consideration of the woman's emotional and psychological needs.

In addition:

- Assessment of progress should include maternal behaviour, effectiveness of pushing and fetal wellbeing, taking into account fetal position and station at the onset of the second stage. These factors will assist in deciding the timing of further vaginal examination and the need for obstetric review.
- Intermittent auscultation of the fetal heart should occur after a contraction for at least 1 minute, at least every 5 minutes. The maternal pulse should be palpated if there is suspected fetal bradycardia or any other FHR anomaly to differentiate the two heart rates.
- Ongoing consideration should be given to the woman's position, hydration, coping strategies and pain relief throughout the second stage.

8.4 Women's position and pushing in the second stage of labour

Clinical question
What is the effectiveness of the following interventions or techniques in labour on outcomes?

- pushing techniques in the second stage (including not pushing).

8.4.1 Position in the second stage of labour

Previous guideline
Position in the second stage of labour was reviewed in the NICE *Caesarean Section* guideline.[6] One systematic review (including 18 RCTs) was reviewed. The guideline recommended that women should be informed that adopting a non-supine position during the second stage of labour has not been shown to influence the likelihood of CS .

Description of included studies and review findings
Evidence for the effect of different positions and mobilisation during the second stage of labour on labour outcomes is drawn from one systematic review of 19 RCTs.[336] One large (*n* = 2595) observational cohort study also informs this subsection regarding the use of the lateral position for birth.[337] [EL = 2+] An important confounder may be the way the woman pushes and this information was not available.

A systematic review has been recently updated which assesses the benefits and risks of the use of different positions during the second stage of labour.[336] [EL = 1+] The review included 19 trials involving 5764 women. Caution is advised in interpreting the findings, since the quality of the included trials is variable. Sources of potential bias include non-random allocation (three trials), random allocation on admission to the labour ward rather than late in the first stage of labour (seven trials) and the exclusion of subjects following randomisation in some trials. In addition, the data from most trials were not normally distributed, further contributing to possibly unreliable findings. Upright positions included: sitting (including birthing chair/stool); semi-recumbent (trunk tilted backward 30 degrees to the vertical); squatting (unaided or using bars); squatting (using birthing cushion). For the purpose of this review, upright positions were combined with the lateral position for comparison with supine or lithotomy positions. The use of any upright or lateral position compared with supine or lithotomy was associated with: reduced duration of second stage of labour (ten trials): weighted mean reduction 4.29 minutes [95% CI 2.95 to 5.64 minutes] (this reduction was mainly attributable to the large reduction associated with use of the birthing cushion (two trials): weighted mean reduction in duration 16.9 minutes [95% CI 14.3 to 19.5 minutes]); a reduction in assisted births (18 trials): RR 0.84 [95% CI 0.73 to 0.98]; a reduction in episiotomies (12 trials): RR 0.84 [95% CI 0.79 to 0.91]; an increase in second-degree tears (11 trials): RR 1.23 [95% CI 1.09 to 1.39]; increased estimated blood loss greater than 500 ml (11 trials): RR 1.68 [95% CI 1.32 to 2.15]; reduced reporting of severe pain during the second stage (one trial): RR 0.73 [95% CI 0.60 to 0.90] and fewer abnormal FHR patterns (one trial): RR 0.31 [95% CI 0.08 to 0.98]. No significant differences were demonstrated for: analgesia or anaesthesia used during the second stage of labour (seven trials); third- or fourth-degree perineal tears (four trials); need for blood transfusion (two trials); manual removal of placenta (three trials); unpleasant birth experience (one trial); dissatisfaction with the second stage of labour (one trial); feeling out of control (one trial); admission to NICU (two trials); birth injuries (one trial); or and neonatal death (three trials).

A prospective cohort study undertaken in the USA, collected data for women cared for intrapartum at three nurse-midwifery services (all clinical teaching sites) during a 12 month period (n = 3049).[337] [EL = 2+] Data collection was carried out using a standardised, validated tool. Multivariate analysis by logistic regression was used to identify predictors of episiotomy and spontaneous tears. Forty-four percent of women were having their first baby. Episiotomy was performed in 11.2% of births and tears occurred in 43.4%. Findings suggested that the lateral position for giving birth was associated with a lower incidence of spontaneous tears among nulliparous women (n = 919) (OR 0.6 [95% CI 0.2 to 1.0]). This trend towards a protective value was not found for multiparous women (findings from statistical analysis not reported).

A multicentre RCT investigated the effects of a hands-and-knees position during the second stage of labour for nulliparous women with a baby in the occipitoposterior position in labour.[338] [EL = 1+] Women allocated to the hands-and-knees position (n = 70) were asked to maintain this position for at least 30 minutes during a study period of 1 hour during the second stage of labour. The control group (n = 77) were actively discouraged from adopting this position during the 1 hour study period, and could adopt any other position they wished. The primary outcome was a baby in the occipitoanterior position (as determined by ultrasound) following the 1 hour study period. There was no significant difference between the two trial groups with respect to this main outcome (17% in intervention group versus 7% in control group; RR 2.4 [95% CI 0.88 to 6.62]). The secondary outcome of persistent back pain during the second stage was measured using three pain scores, all of which were lower for women allocated to the hands-and-knees group (VAS: mean difference −0.85 [95% CI −1.47 to −0.22], P = 0.0083; PPI score: mean difference −0.50 [95% CI −0.89 to −0.10], P = 0.014; SF-MPQ score: mean difference −2.60 [95% CI −4.91 to −0.28], P = 0.028). There were no significant differences seen in any other maternal or neonatal outcomes.

A recent RCT undertaken in Sweden investigated the effects of a hands-and-knees position, compared with a sitting position, on the duration of the second stage of labour.[339] [EL = 1+] Women were required to maintain their allocated position throughout the second stage, until the baby was crowning (hands-and-knees n = 138; sitting n = 133). There was no significant difference in the length of the second stage of labour between the two trial groups (kneeling 48.5 minutes [SD 27.6 minutes]; sitting 41 minutes [SD 23.4 minutes]). However, a number of positive outcomes were noted for the hands-and knees position regarding women's experience of the second stage. Women allocated to the hands-and-knees position were more likely to report that they found the position comfortable for giving birth (OR 0.5 [95% CI 0.1 to 0.9], P = 0.030); were less likely to report their second stage as being long (despite there being no significant difference in the actual length of second stage between the two groups) (OR 1.4 [95% CI 0.8 to 0.9], P = 0.002); reported the second stage as less painful (OR 1.3 [95% CI 1.1 to 1.9], P = 0.01); and reported less postpartum perineal pain in first 3 days following birth (OR 1.9 [95% CI 1.3 to 2.9], P = 0.001) compared with women in the control group. There were no significant differences in clinical outcomes for either women (including degree of perineal trauma) or their babies.

Evidence statement
There is high-level evidence that remaining supine in the second stage of labour increases vaginal instrumental birth, increases pain and may increase the incidence of fetal heart rate abnormalities although there is no information on how women pushed. There is no difference in the proportion of women who give birth with an intact perineum. There is also some high-level evidence that using the hands-and-knees position in the second stage of labour, reduces women's reported pain and has no adverse effects on maternal or neonatal outcomes. The use of a rigid birthing chair or stool, but not upright positions *per se*, is associated with recorded blood loss greater than 500 ml.

Recommendation on position in the second stage of labour

Women should be discouraged from lying supine or semi-supine in the second stage of labour and should be encouraged to adopt any other position that they find most comfortable.

For advice on position of women with regional analgesia, refer to Section 6.4.3.

8.4.2 Pushing in the second stage

Introduction
These studies considered women without epidural.

Description of included studies
Two US RCTs of good quality compared coached with uncoached pushing in the second stage of labour.[340,341] [both EL = 1+] Three further RCTs were also identified that investigated pushing in the second stage of labour.[342–344] However, the methodological quality of these studies was poor [all EL = 1–].

Review findings
A recent US RCT compared coached and uncoached pushing in the second stage of labour.[340] [EL = 1+] Nulliparous women who were allocated to the coached pushing group ($n = 163$) received standardised closed glottis coached pushing instructions during contractions and were encouraged to breathe normally between contractions. The uncoached group of women ($n = 157$) were attended by the same group of midwives who gave no instructions on pushing, and were encouraged to do 'what comes naturally'. The mean duration of the second stage of labour was significantly shorter for women in the coached group compared with the uncoached group (46 minutes versus 59 minutes, $P = 0.014$). There were no differences noted in any other maternal or neonatal outcomes.

A US RCT was conducted to determine whether refraining from coaching second stage pushing affects postpartum urogynaecological measures of pelvic floor structure and function ($n = 128$).[341] [EL = 1+] Women were randomised when they were found to be fully dilated, to receive either coached or uncoached pushing during the second stage of labour. Pelvic floor assessment was carried out 3 months postpartum by nurses blinded to the second stage management. There were no significant differences between the two groups regarding demographic factors, incidence of prolonged second stage of labour (> 2 hours), episiotomy, tears involving the anal sphincter, second stage epidural, forceps birth, oxytocin augmentation of the second stage or babies weighing over 4.0 kg. Urodynamic testing revealed decreased bladder capacity ($P = 0.051$) and decreased first urge to void ($P = 0.025$) in the coached group. No other significant differences were found.

A Danish RCT compared spontaneous pushing ($n = 151$) with a 'forced' breath-holding technique ($n = 155$) in the late second stage of labour, in women giving birth vaginally for the first time (this sample included women who had had a previous caesarean section but the numbers involved were not given).[342] [EL = 1–] The allocated method of pushing was not encouraged until the baby's head was visible. Up until that point, women were able to push as they wished without direction or encouragement from the midwife. Recruitment into the study was difficult, with only 350 of the 1413 women eligible to join taking part. Reasons given for this include women's reluctance to be allocated to the spontaneous pushing group with its perceived lack of midwifery guidance/encouragement, and midwives' lack of support for the trial. A further 44 women were lost to follow-up, following randomisation, mainly because they gave birth by caesarean section. These difficulties undermine the reliability of the findings. The two study groups were well matched for maternal and baby characteristics. No significant differences were found between the two groups in length of labour, length of second stage, length of expulsive second stage (from vertex visible to birth of the baby), mode of birth, perineal trauma, Apgar scores, umbilical arterial pH or arterial standard base excess. The authors explain these similarities in terms of non-compliance with the allocated pushing technique. The frequent use of oxytocin (40.1% in the spontaneous group and 45.8% in the forced group) and episiotomy (36% in the spontaneous group and 30% in the forced group) may have also contributed to these findings.

A small UK RCT also investigated the effects of spontaneous ($n = 15$) versus directed, breath-holding pushing ($n = 17$).[343] [EL = 1–] The two groups were well matched for a number of maternal and baby characteristics, but these did not include fetal position or station. The duration of the first stage of labour was significantly longer in the spontaneous pushing group (means [SD]: 12.32 hours [5.13 hours] versus 7.88 hours [2.62 hours], $P = 0.005$). There were no other significant differences noted regarding the first stage of labour including use of Entonox, use of pethidine or the need for an intravenous infusion. No mention is made of the use of oxytocin augmentation. A researcher was present throughout the second stage in order to ensure trial allocation was adhered to by the midwife providing care. Analysis was carried out on an intention-to-treat basis. There was no difference in outcome between the two groups for type of birth, perineal trauma, estimated maternal blood loss, resuscitation of baby at birth, cord venous blood as levels and cord blood pH. Women's views of the second stage of labour (e.g. 'What was the pushing part of your labour like?', 'How satisfied do you feel with the way you coped during the pushing part of your labour?'), as expressed using a 10 cm visual analogue scale, were also similar for the two groups. The second stage of labour was significantly longer in the spontaneous pushing group (means [SD]: 121.4 minutes [58.4 minutes] versus 58 minutes [42 minutes], $P = 0.002$). This may have been contributed to by differences which also led to significantly longer first stages of labour in this group, rather than be attributable to the different pushing techniques employed.

A small US randomised trial compared women encouraged to use a breath-holding pushing technique ($n = 10$) with those encouraged to use an exhalation pushing technique ($n = 17$).[344] [EL = 1−] All women gave birth sitting on a birthing chair. This final sample of women represents a fairly small proportion of the 94 women who originally agreed to participate in the study. It is not clear from the paper when randomisation was carried out, but it appears that a number of women were dropped from the analysis after randomisation for not complying with the study protocol, e.g. for not using the birthing chair for the second stage ($n = 20$) or not using the designated style of pushing ($n = 9$). No significant differences were found in the length of the second stage of labour between the two groups (mean = 45.6 minutes for both groups). Some differences were described in FHR patterns between the two groups, e.g. an increase in variable decelerations being noted in the breath-holding pushing group (30% versus 17.6%, no P value given). However, the clinical significance of this is not discussed and no clinical outcomes were examined, e.g. Apgar scores, need for resuscitation, admission to NICU.

Evidence statement
There is no high-level evidence that directed pushing affects outcomes.

> **Recommendations on pushing in the second stage of labour**
>
> Women should be informed that in the second stage they should be guided by their own urge to push.
>
> If pushing is ineffective or if requested by the woman, strategies to assist birth can be used, such as support, change of position, emptying of the bladder and encouragement.

For advice on pushing of women with regional analgesia, refer to Section 6.4.4.

8.5 Intrapartum interventions to reduce perineal trauma

Clinical question
What is the effectiveness on perineal or genital trauma (including previous third- or fourth-degree trauma or female genital mutilation) of the following techniques?

- perineal massage
- hand position
- heat
- cold
- maternal position
- analgesia
- episiotomy
- operative vaginal delivery.

Previous guideline
No previous guidelines have considered interventions related to perineal care during childbirth.

8.5.1 Intrapartum perineal massage

Description of included studies
One RCT was identified which investigated the effects of perineal massage in the second stage of labour upon perineal outcomes.[345] [EL = 1+] This Australian study enrolled 1340 women across three trial sites. For women allocated to the experimental group (*n* = 708), perineal massage was performed by the attending midwife during each contraction of the second stage of labour, unless this was uncomfortable for the woman in which case the massage would not be performed. Midwives at each hospital were instructed on perineal massage through use of verbal instruction, a specially made video and an illustrated pamphlet. Compliance with trial group allocation is not detailed.

Review findings
There were no significant differences between groups for most perineal outcomes (massage group versus control group): intact perineum: 198/708 versus 171/632, RR 1.03 [95% CI 0.87 to 1.23]; first-degree tear: 122/708 versus 106/632, RR 1.03 [95% CI 0.81 to 1.30]; second-degree tear: 190/708 versus 164/632, RR 1.03 [95% CI 0.86 to 1.24]; episiotomy: 176/708 versus 170/632, RR 0.92 [95% CI 0.77 to 1.11]. There was a difference in incidence of third-degree tears, with these being less frequent in the massage group: 12/708 versus 23/632; RR 0.47 [95% CI 0.23 to 0.93], although the trial was underpowered to detect a statistically significant difference in this rare outcome. No significant differences were found between pain outcomes at 3 days, 10 days or 3 months postpartum: at 3 days: vaginal pain: 416/597 versus 359/499, RR 0.97 [95% CI 0.90 to 1.05]; at 10 days: vaginal pain: 184/632 versus 187/555, RR 0.86 [95% CI 0.73 to 1.02]; at 3 months: vaginal pain: 58/503 versus 54/436, RR 0.93 [95% CI 0.66 to 1.32]; dyspareunia: 78/503 versus 68/436; RR 0.9 [95% CI 0.74 to 1.34]; intercourse not resumed: 49/503 versus 60/436; RR 0.71 (0.50 to 1.01). There were also no significant differences regarding urinary and bowel control.

> **Recommendation on perineal massage**
>
> Perineal massage should not be performed by healthcare professionals in the second stage of labour.

8.5.2 Heat/cold

Description of included studies
A large observational cohort study conducted in the USA investigated perineal care measures that were associated with perineal trauma during childbirth.[337] [EL = 2+] Statistical analysis was performed on a subset of births that included all spontaneous vaginal term births (*n* = 2595).

Review findings
Data were collected for women cared for intrapartum, at three nurse-midwifery services (all clinical teaching sites) during a 12 month period. Multivariate analysis by logistic regression was used to identify predictors of episiotomy and spontaneous tears. Findings suggested (at borderline level of significance) that application of warm compresses to the perineum during the second stage of labour was protective against spontaneous tears in women who did not have an episiotomy (*n* = 2363), for both nulliparous women (OR 0.7 [95% CI 0.4 to 1.0]) and multiparous women (OR 0.6 [0.3 to 0.9]). Application of warm compresses was also found to be protective against episiotomy for nulliparous women (OR 0.3 [95% CI 0.0 to 0.8]). For multiparous women, the findings are of borderline significance (OR 0.3 [95% CI 0.0 to 1.0]).

8.5.3 Hand position during birth of baby

Description of included studies
A large UK RCT (*n* = 5471) compared two methods of perineal management used during spontaneous vaginal birth – a 'hands on' method whereby the midwife's hands were used to put pressure on the baby's head (to flex the head) and support ('guard') the perineum; and a 'hands poised' method where the midwife keeps her hands poised but not touching the head or perineum.[346]

[EL = 1+] A similar quasi-randomised trial conducted in Austria also investigated the effects of the hands on versus hands poised techniques of perineal care during birth (n = 1076).[347] [EL = 1+]

An RCT conducted in the USA compared three perineal care measures undertaken during the second stage of labour: warm compresses to the perineal area; massage with lubricant; and no touching of the perineal area until the baby's head was crowned.[348] [EL = 1+] The study involved 1211 women allocated to midwife care during labour. Forty percent of participants were nulliparous women. Warm compresses or massage with lubricant were applied as continuously as possible until crowning of the baby's head, unless the woman requested that they be stopped or the technique changed. Data collection included details of allocated technique, what was actually done and for how long, also whether the woman asked for the technique to be stopped or changed.

Review findings
The large UK RCT compared hands on with hands poised methods for midwife care during the birth of the baby.[346] [EL = 1+] Compliance with the allocated trial group was very good for the hands on group (95.3%) and somewhat lower in the hands poised group (70.1%), reflecting the greater number of midwives who expressed a preference for the hands on technique. The main outcome measure for the trial was perineal pain in the previous 24 hours reported by the woman at 10 days. This was found to be significantly lower in the hands on group compared with the hands poised group: 910/2669 versus 823/2647, RR 1.10 [95% CI 1.01 to 1.18]. This represents an absolute difference of 3% [95% CI 0.5% to 5.0%]. The difference resides predominantly in the category of mild pain (23.5% versus 20.9%; moderate pain: 9.2% versus 8.8%; severe pain: 1.4% versus 1.4%). There were no other significant differences in pain outcomes, e.g. at 2 days: pain felt in previous 24 hours: some pain: 70.0% versus 71.3%, NS; mild: 27.5% versus 28.8%, NS; moderate: 37.0% versus 37.4%, NS; severe: 5.2% versus 5.1%, NS. Incidences of reported pain were also very similar at 3 months postpartum. Stratified analyses showed that more of the differences between groups for reported pain at 10 days were apparent for women having their first vaginal birth, for women without epidural analgesia in the second stage of labour and in the latter part of the trial (after the first 6 months). There was also evidence of an effect of midwives' practice preferences biasing the findings to favour the expressed preference, with the hands on technique only being significantly better (in terms of reported pain at 10 days) when the midwife favoured this technique (heterogeneity test $P = 0.03$).

While the rates of second-degree trauma (including episiotomy) were similar between the two groups (36.9% versus 36.6%), the episiotomy rate was higher in the hands on group (10.2% versus 12.9%, RR 0.79 [99% CI 1.02 to 2.78]). The rates of third-degree trauma were similar for the two groups (1.5% versus 1.2%), as were incidences of vaginal and anterior genital trauma. The manual removal of the placenta was performed significantly more frequently for women in the hands poised group: n = 71 (2.6%) versus 42 (1.5%), RR 1.69 (99% CI 1.02 to 2.78). While this result is difficult to explain, the authors point out that the difference was evident in both trial centres, supporting its validity as a 'true' finding. A large number of other outcomes were investigated with no differences found between study groups. These included neonatal outcomes (Apgar scores, need for resuscitation at birth, additional neonatal care, breastfeeding at 2 days, 10 days and 3 months) and women's outcomes at 3 months (dyspareunia, urinary problems, bowel problems, treatment for perineal trauma; postnatal depression).

A quasi-randomised trial conducted in Austria has also investigated this intervention (n = 1076).[347] [EL = 1+] Only midwives who agreed with the aims of the trial participated in the study. Quasi-randomisation was carried out by alternating hands on and hands poised policies according to the date the woman entered the second stage of labour. Compliance with trial group allocation was high (92% and 94%). The rate of first- and second-degree perineal trauma was similar for the two trial groups (hands on 29.8%; hands poised 33.7%, NS), although there was a higher rate of third-degree trauma in the hands on group (n = 16 (2.7%) versus n = 5 (0.9%)). The study was underpowered to detect the statistical significance of this rare event. Women in the hands on group were more likely to have an episiotomy performed than women in the hands poised group: 17.9% versus 10.1%, $P < 0.01$. No difference was observed between groups regarding labial and vaginal trauma, length of the second stage of labour or manual removal of placenta (hands on n = 10 (1.7%) versus hands poised n = 7 (1.3%)). Neonatal outcomes were very similar between the two groups with only one baby in each group having an Apgar score < 7 at 5 minutes.

Findings from the US RCT comparing warm compresses, massage with lubricant and no touching of the perineal area showed that overall compliance with the allocated technique was very high, 94.5% by self-report and 95.5% in an observed group (25% of whole study sample). In 5.8% of all births the midwife was asked by the woman to stop using the allocated technique; 75% of these requests were made by women allocated to the perineal massage with lubricant technique. The overall episiotomy rate was very low in the study (0.8%). Twenty-three percent of women (n = 278) had no genital trauma, and the genital tract trauma profiles were the same across all three study groups. Twenty percent of women (n = 242) experienced more severe levels of trauma (defined as second-, third- or fourth-degree perineal tear, a tear of the mid or inner vaginal vault, or a cervical tear), and 57% (n = 691) had minor trauma (defined as a first-degree perineal tear, outer vaginal or external genitalia tear). No differences were found when comparing warm compresses with the hands off technique: RR 1.04 [95% CI 0.81 to 1.35] or massage versus hands off technique: RR 1.05 [95% CI 0.81 to 1.35]. Stratified analysis and adjusted relative risks controlling for parity, epidural usage, infant birthweight or first year versus later years of the study also showed no differences between study groups. For the warm compress group the mean time the technique was used was 17.8 minutes (SD 19.5 minutes) among women with trauma compared with 13.4 minutes (SD 16.1 minutes) for women without trauma (P = 0.06). For the massage group the mean time this technique was used was 11.6 minutes (SD 14.0 minutes) for women with trauma compared with 5.8 minutes (SD 6.8 minutes) among women without trauma (P < 0.01). A final regression model demonstrated two care measures that were protective for perineal trauma, a sitting position for birth and birth of the fetal head between (rather than during) contractions.

Evidence statement

There is high-level evidence that intrapartum perineal massage or application of warm compresses in the second stage of labour does not improve perineal outcomes.

There is limited high-level evidence that women allocated to a 'hands on' perineal management group reported less mild pain at 10 days, compared with those allocated to a 'hands poised' group. The rates of reported perineal trauma (including episiotomy) were similar between the two groups but episiotomy was higher in the 'hands on' group.

Recommendation on hand position

Either the 'hands on' (guarding the perineum and flexing the baby's head) or the 'hands poised' (with hands off the perineum and baby's head but in readiness) technique can be used to facilitate spontaneous birth.

8.5.4   **Local anaesthetic spray**

Description of included studies and review findings

One RCT was reviewed which evaluated the effectiveness and acceptability of lidocaine spray in reducing perineal pain during spontaneous vaginal birth.[349] [EL = 1+] Women were randomised to receive either an application (five sprays) of lidocaine spray to the perineum and inside aspect of the labia when birth was thought to be imminent (n = 93), or application of a placebo spray, identical in appearance to the treatment spray (n = 92).

The primary outcome for the trial was reported pain during birth, as measured using a 0–100 numeric scale.[349] Trial groups were comparable for most obstetric and sociodemographic variables considered, although some differences did arise, namely parity, smoking, augmentation, induction, use of pethidine prior to randomisation and birthweight. These differences were adjusted for in the secondary analyses. In both trial groups, the mean number of sprays received was 4.8 and approximately two-thirds of women in each group received the intervention as intended. No difference was found between groups for the main outcome, pain during birth (mean [SD]: lidocaine: 76.9 [21.6] versus placebo 72.1 [22.2], difference between means 4.8 [95% CI −1.7 to 11.2], P = 0.14). A slightly larger difference between means is seen if adjustments are made for the differences between trial groups, but this still fails to reach statistical significance: 6.3 [95% CI −0.8 to 13.3], P = 0.081. Most secondary outcomes were similar between groups, including vaginal trauma, neonatal resuscitation, feelings during birth, overall rating of birth experience, sutured after birth and perineal pain 1 week after birth. There was, however, a significantly lower incidence of second-degree perineal trauma in the lidocaine group: 28.0% versus 44.6%, RR 0.63 [95% CI 0.42 to 0.93], $P = 0.019$. Women in the lidocaine spray group were also less likely to report dyspareunia on resumption of sexual intercourse: 27.1% versus 52.7%, RR 0.52 [95% CI 0.35 to 0.76], $P = 0.0004$. The authors, however, pointed out that the large number of secondary analyses undertaken means these differences could be chance findings.

Evidence statement
There is a small amount of high-level evidence that the use of lidocaine spray during the second stage of labour is not associated with a reduction in perineal pain, but may be associated with a reduction in perineal trauma during birth.

> **Recommendation on local anaesthetic spray**
>
> Lidocaine spray should not be used to reduce pain in the second stage of labour.

8.5.5 Routine versus restricted use of episiotomy

Description of included studies
One systematic review including seven RCTs and eight cohort studies, plus an additional RCT, inform this subsection. The findings from the systematic review supersede an earlier (1999) previous systematic review including six of the seven RCTs.[350]

A recent systematic review has been published which considers maternal outcomes following routine, compared with restrictive, use of episiotomy.[351] [EL = 1+] The review included evidence from seven RCTs involving a total of 5001 women and eight cohort studies involving 6463 women. Six of the trials studied mediolateral episiotomy and only one used midline episiotomy. Three trials included only women having their first baby. All studies focused on spontaneous vaginal births, although a small proportion of instrumental vaginal births were included in most trials (0–5% in four trials and 5–15% in three trials).

Review findings
Evidence from the trials is usually summarised descriptively rather than meta-analysed. All trials achieved a wide difference in episiotomy use, between the trial aims in the direction expected, ranging from 7.6% in the restrictive group to 93.7% in the routine group. In the trial judged by the authors to be the strongest (best quality) ($n = 1000$), the incidence of intact perineum was 33.9% in the restrictive group versus 24% in the routine group. In the largest trial ($n = 2606$), the need for surgical repair was reported as 63% in the restrictive group compared with 88% in the routine group. In the other five trials, the need for perineal repair was less frequent in the restrictive group: RR 0.46 [95% CI 0.30 to 0.70]. The need for any suturing was 26% higher in routine groups (three trials): RR 1.26 [95% CI 1.08 to 1.48].

All trials were underpowered to detect any differences in third- or fourth-degree tears, with an incidence of 105/5001 (seven trials).

Women's experiences of pain were considered in five trials. In the largest trial, pain outcomes were found to be very similar between the two groups. Routine use group: mild pain 14.6%, moderate pain 7.8% and severe pain 0.2% versus restrictive use group: 14.1%, 7.5% and 0.9%, respectively ($n = 885$ and $n = 1000$, respectively). The use of oral analgesia and pain ratings at 3 months were also similar. Three other trials reported pain as higher in the routine use groups, each trial using a different pain outcome measure. The largest trial ($n = 2422$ and $n = 2606$, respectively) reported 'pain on the day of discharge'. In the routine use of episiotomy group, this was found to be 42.5% of women reporting pain, compared with 30.7% in the restrictive group. A second trial assessed pain using a VAS for four activities (day 1 to 5 postpartum) as follows: bed rest: routine 39 mm (SD 28 mm) versus restrictive 22 mm (SD 21 mm); sitting down: 69 mm (SD 23 mm) versus 51 mm (SD 25 mm); walking: 56 mm (SD 24 mm) versus 37 mm (SD 24 mm); opening bowels: 36 mm (SD 30 mm) versus 21 mm (SD 21 mm). Across all activities, the restrictive use group experienced less perineal pain than the routine use group ($P = 0.005$ to 0.048).

Urinary incontinence was investigated by two RCTs. The largest trial ($n = 895$ and $n = 1000$, respectively) reported involuntary loss of urine at 3 months and use of a pad for incontinence. Both outcomes had very similar findings for the two study groups (involuntary loss of urine: routine 19.0% versus restrictive 18.9%). Meta-analysis of findings from the two trials shows no difference in incidence of urinary incontinence between routine versus restrictive use of episiotomy: RR 1.02 [95% CI 0.83 to 1.26].

Five prospective cohort studies also examined self-reported urinary incontinence. No difference was found between groups of women who had an episiotomy versus those who had a spontaneous tear (five studies): RR 0.88 [95% CI 0.72 to 1.07]. Four cohort studies asked women about rectal incontinence. None found episiotomy to be associated with a statistically significant reduced risk of incontinence of stool or flatus. Pooling of data from the two cohort studies with comparable outcome measures indicates an increase in risk associated with use of episiotomy: RR 1.91 [95% CI 1.03 to 3.56].

Two trials reported sexual function on an intention-to-treat basis. The largest trial ($n = 895$ and $n = 1000$, respectively) found that women allocated to the restrictive use of episiotomy group were more likely to have resumed sexual intercourse at 1 month compared with women allocated to the routine group: routine 27% versus restrictive 37%, $P < 0.01$. No differences were found between groups regarding resumption of sexual intercourse by 3 months, dyspareunia at 3 months, or 'ever suffering painful intercourse' at 3 years. Five prospective cohort studies found no differences in sexual function between women who had had an episiotomy and women with spontaneous tears. Dyspareunia at 3 months was also found to be similar between the two groups of women (two trials): RR 1.53 [95% CI 0.93 to 2.51].

A recent RCT conducted in Germany compared restrictive use of episiotomy (fetal indications only) ($n = 49$) with more liberal use (fetal indications and if a tear was deemed imminent) ($n = 60$).[352] [EL = 1+] Episiotomy rates were 41% in the restrictive group and 77% in the liberal group (RR 0.47 [95% CI 0.3 to 0.7]. The incidences of intact perinea and 'minor' perineal trauma (defined as intact perinea or first-degree tears) were more frequent in the restrictive policy group: intact perineum: 14/49 versus 6/60, RR 2.9 [95% CI 1.2 to 6.9]; intact perineum or first-degree tear: 19/49 versus 8/60, RR 2.9 [95% CI 1.6 to 10.5]. There was no significant difference regarding anterior trauma: 27/49 versus 25/60, RR 1.1 [95% CI 0.8 to 1.8]. Pain was found to be significantly lower for women allocated to the restrictive episiotomy group: sitting (mean): 51 mm [SD 25 mm] versus 69 mm [SD 23 mm]; mean difference 18 mm [95% CI 5 to 31 mm], $P = 0.009$; walking (mean): 37 mm [SD 24 mm] versus 56 mm [SD24 mm]; mean difference 19 mm [95% CI 6 to 33 mm], $P = 0.005$. No difference was noted between groups for babies' Apgar scores or umbilical artery pH.

Owing to similarities between studies and outcome measures, it was possible to pool some of the findings from the single RCT[352] and the 1999 systematic review[350] and perform a meta-analysis. The meta-analysis was performed using a random effects model owing to the significant heterogeneity between study outcome measures and uncertainty regarding reliability of classification of outcome measures, e.g. diagnosis of third-degree tears and ratings made on a pain VAS. Findings are as follows:

- severe perineal trauma (third- and fourth-degree tears): RR 0.74 [95% CI 0.42 to 1.28] (six trials, one with no incidents)
- any posterior perineal trauma: RR 0.87 [95% CI 0.83 to 0.91] (five trials)
- anterior trauma: RR 1.75 [95% CI 1.52 to 2.01] (five trials)
- Apgar score < 7 at 1 minute: RR 1.05 [95% CI 0.76 to 1.45].

Owing to differences in outcome measures, data relating to perineal pain could not be pooled.

Angle of episiotomy

Description of included studies
One prospective observational study was identified which aimed to identify risk factors associated with third- and fourth-degree perineal tears following childbirth.[353] [EL = 3] The study involved 241 women giving birth vaginally for the first time. Following birth an experienced researcher performed a perineal and rectal examination in order to identify and classify perineal trauma. Dimensions and direction of episiotomy was noted and obstetric variables recorded prospectively.

Review findings
Of the 241 women included in the study, 59 (25%) sustained anal sphincter injury. Multiple logistic regression identified higher birthweight (*P* = 0.021) and mediolateral episiotomy (OR 4.04 [range 1.71 to 9.56] as independent risk factors for sphincter injury. Further investigation revealed that episiotomies angled closer to the midline were significantly associated with anal sphincter injuries (26 versus 37 degrees, *P* = 0.01). No midwife and only 22% of obstetricians performed 'true' mediolateral episiotomies (defined as being at least 40 degrees from the midline).

Evidence statement
There is considerable high-level evidence that the routine use of episiotomy (trial mean 71.6%; range 44.9% to 93.7%) is not of benefit to women either in the short or longer term, compared with restricted use (trial mean 29.1%; range 7.6% to 53.0%).

Recommendations on episiotomy

A routine episiotomy should not be carried out during spontaneous vaginal birth.

Where an episiotomy is performed, the recommended technique is a mediolateral episiotomy originating at the vaginal fourchette and usually directed to the right side. The angle to the vertical axis should be between 45 and 60 degrees at the time of the episiotomy.

An episiotomy should be performed if there is a clinical need such as instrumental birth or suspected fetal compromise.

Tested effective analgesia should be provided prior to carrying out an episiotomy, except in an emergency due to acute fetal compromise.

8.5.6 Vaginal birth following previous third- or fourth-degree perineal trauma

Description of included studies
No studies were found assessing care of women with genital mutilation.

Two descriptive studies were identified that investigated the incidence of repeat third- and fourth-degree perineal tears following previous severe trauma. A third retrospective cohort study examined the incidence of anal incontinence following previous third- or fourth-degree tears.

Review findings
A retrospective US population study described the incidence of recurrence of third- and fourth-degree perineal tears, in subsequent births, following a previous third- or fourth-degree tear.[354] [EL = 3] All cases of third- and fourth-degree lacerations (termed 'severe' lacerations) for the 2 year period 1990–91 were identified (*n* = 18 888; 7.31% incidence rate). These women were then traced over the following 10 years, which included a further 16 152 births. Of these, 14 990 were vaginal births with an incidence rate of repeat severe laceration of 5.67% (*n* = 864), this being significantly lower than the original incidence rate (OR 1.29 [95% CI 1.2 to 1.4]). It should be noted, however, that all women in the second group were multiparous and over the same time period there was a 69% fall in the forceps birth rate (from 7.75% to 2.4%), a 28% fall in the rate of use of vacuum extraction, and a 24% reduction in the episiotomy rate. Women with a prior fourth-degree tear had a higher incidence of recurrent severe laceration than women with a previous third-degree tear (410/5306 (7.73%) versus 454/9684 (4.69%)). The association between a number of risk factors and recurrent severe perineal laceration was calculated. A number of significant associations were found: episiotomy (global): OR 2.6 [95% CI 2.25 to 3.04]; episiotomy alone without instruments: OR 1.7 [95% CI 1.46 to 1.92]; all forceps: OR 3.0 [95% CI 2.2 to 4.0]; forceps + episiotomy: OR 3.6 [95% CI 2.6 to 5.1]; all vacuum: OR 2.2 [95% CI 1.76 to 2.69]; vacuum + episiotomy: OR 2.7 [95% CI 2.14 to 3.39]. The use of forceps or vacuum extraction without episiotomy was not found to be significantly associated with recurrent severe laceration: forceps, no episiotomy: OR 1.4 [95% CI 0.7 to 2.9]; vacuum, no episiotomy: OR 1.0 [95% CI 0.6 to 1.7]. Multivariate logistic regression was used to estimate the association of the use of forceps, vacuum extraction, episiotomy, woman's age and year of birth as independent risk factors for recurrent laceration. All were found to be significant independent risk factors. The authors pointed out that some other important confounders were not included in the model, e.g. parity, birthweight and indication for instrumental vaginal birth.

A second prospective descriptive study has also investigated the risk of subsequent anal sphincter disruption following a previous severe laceration.[355] [EL = 3] This study, conducted in Ireland, did not distinguish between third- and/or fourth-degree perineal trauma. From 20 111 consecutive vaginal births, 342 (1.7%) women were identified as having sustained a third-degree tear. Each of these women underwent a series of investigations at 3 months postpartum to ascertain perineal functioning (e.g. continence scoring and manometry) and identify anal defects (using ultrasound imaging). Fifty-six of these women gave birth to a subsequent child during the following 3 years and formed the study sample. Forty-two (75%) women had sustained the initial trauma during birth of their first child, 34 cases following extended mediolateral episiotomy. All of these 56 women underwent continence symptom scoring, anal manometry and endosonography during the last trimester of their subsequent pregnancy. Nine were identified as having an anal defect of greater than one quadrant of the external sphincter (deemed large), five had resting manometric pressures ≤ 25 mmHg and two had squeeze pressures ≤ 40 mmHg. Six of these 56 women had significant symptoms of faecal incontinence (scores of 5 or more on the continence scoring system). How symptoms related to manometric pressures and/or evidence of anal sphincter defect is not described. Four of these women gave birth by elective caesarean section, along with three other women who wished to avoid perineal trauma. Of this group of 45 women who gave birth vaginally, following previous third-degree trauma, the scores for faecal incontinence following previous birth versus following subsequent birth were as follows: score 0–2: 39 versus 33; score 3–4: 3 versus 4; score 5–6: 1 versus 0; score 6–10: 2 versus 3; not assessed: 0 versus 5. The episiotomy rate among this group was 62% (n = 28), 7% (n = 4) had an instrumental birth and 27% (n = 12) sustained a perineal tear of which two were third-degree tears (an incidence of 4.4%), both associated with spontaneous vaginal births. The authors reported that, following repair of a subsequent third-degree tear, the outcome for both women was 'excellent' in terms of faecal continence. Two women who had reported severe symptoms of faecal incontinence antenatally, and went on to give birth to the subsequent child vaginally, remained symptomatic (scoring in the 6–10 range). The one extra case of severe faecal incontinence following a subsequent birth was due to the development of irritable bowel syndrome rather than as a consequence of perineal trauma.

A retrospective cohort study conducted in Switzerland investigated the incidence of anal incontinence in women who had had a vaginal birth following a previous third- or fourth-degree tear.[356] [EL = 3] Women were identified using the computer records of one hospital, and eligible women were contacted by telephone to request their participation in the study. Of the 448 women identified, 208 (46%) were contacted. Of these, 177 agreed to participate (response rate = 86%). The mean age of the respondents was 40.7 years [range 32 to 54 years] and ten women considered themselves as menopausal. Of this sample, 114 had had subsequent vaginal births. Findings suggest that, while subsequent births are not associated with increased incidence of anal incontinence in women with previous third-degree perineal tears, there is a trend towards an increased incidence following previous fourth-degree tears. While 17/49 (34.7%) women with no subsequent births had symptoms of anal incontinence (incontinence or urgency), this was true of 12/80 (15%) women who went on to have more babies (P = 0.02). For women following a fourth-degree tear, the reverse was seen. Symptoms of anal incontinence or urgency were reported by 2/14 (14.3%) women who had not given birth subsequently, compared with 16/34 (47.1%) who had had subsequent births (NS, P = 0.07). The authors noted that the majority of third- and fourth-degree tears in this study were extensions of midline episiotomies (third: 101/129; fourth: 45/48). They suggested that these tears might carry a different functional prognosis to sphincter tears, complicating a spontaneous tear or mediolateral episiotomy. They also pointed out that the questionnaire asked only for information regarding anal incontinence, and therefore mode of subsequent vaginal birth or any related perineal trauma is not known. It is also very surprising that only 15% women who sustained a third-degree tear and 21% who sustained a fourth-degree tear could remember this, suggesting little was done at the time of the trauma or postnatally to ensure the women had adequate knowledge of this fact.

Evidence statement
For women with previous severe perineal trauma, the rate of repeat severe trauma is similar to the original incidence.

There is no evidence about the use of episiotomy for birth following third- or fourth-degree trauma.

There is low-level evidence that in asymptomatic women a vaginal birth following previous severe perineal trauma does not increase the risk of subsequent urgency or continence symptoms.

There is low-level evidence that in symptomatic women vaginal birth following previous severe perineal trauma does increase the risk of subsequent urgency or continence symptoms.

Recommendations on vaginal birth following previous third- or fourth-degree perineal trauma

Women with a history of severe perineal trauma should be informed that their risk of repeat severe perineal trauma is not increased in a subsequent birth, compared with women having their first baby.

Episiotomy should not be offered routinely at vaginal birth following previous third- or fourth-degree trauma.

In order for a woman who has had previous third- or fourth-degree trauma to make an informed choice, discussion with her about the future mode of birth should encompass:

* current urgency or incontinence symptoms
* the degree of previous trauma
* risk of recurrence
* the success of the repair undertaken
* the psychological effect of the previous trauma
* management of her labour.

Women with infibulated genital mutilation should be informed of the risks of difficulty with vaginal examination, catheterisation and application of fetal scalp electrodes. They should also be informed of the risks of delay in the second stage and spontaneous laceration together with the need for an anterior episiotomy and the possible need for defibulation in labour.

Research recommendation on prevention of perineal trauma

Studies are needed to investigate strategies to reduce the chance of having perineal trauma.

8.6   Water birth

Introduction
While the Winterton report recommended that all maternity units should provide women with the option to labour and give birth in water, the number of women in England and Wales who choose to actually give birth in water is not known.[95] A survey between April 1994 and March 1996 identified 0.6% of births in England and Wales occurring in water, 9% of which were home births.[126] It is known, however, that in some birth settings this proportion is much higher, with one birth centre reporting up to 79% of women giving birth in water.[127]

Clinical question
What is the effectiveness of the following interventions or techniques in labour on outcomes?

* water (including temperature regulation).

Description of included studies
There was one systematic review, one RCT and one cross-sectional study identified for inclusion in the review. The systematic review included eight trials.[128] [EL = 1+] Out of the eight trials, six examined immersion in water in the first stage of labour, one examined immersion in water in the second stage of labour and one investigated the timing of the use of water in the first stage of labour. Another RCT was conducted since the systematic review was updated.[357] [EL = 1+] The RCT examined effectiveness of water birth in the second stage of labour. A population-based cross-sectional study in England and Wales investigated perinatal mortality and morbidity of babies, who were born in water, using a postal survey.[126] [EL = 3]

Review findings

Two trials evaluated immersion in water during the second stage of labour.[128,357] In the latter trial, only 23 women out of 60 received the allocation to be immersed in water. There is no evidence of differences in interventions or complications for either women or their babies during labour.

The cross-sectional study reported a perinatal mortality of 1.2 [95% CI 0.4 to 2.9] per 1000 and an admission rate to the neonatal unit of 8.4 [95% CI 5.8 to 11.8] per 1000 for babies born in water, compared with three previously reported perinatal mortalities (from 0.8 to 4.6 per 1000) and an admission rate of (9.2 to 64 per 1000) from other studies of low-risk populations.[126]

Evidence statement

There is insufficient evidence on the use of water in the second stage of labour, particularly its effect on neonatal outcomes.

Recommendation on water birth

Women should be informed that there is insufficient high-quality evidence to either support or discourage giving birth in water.

9 Normal labour: third stage

9.1 Definition and duration of the third stage of labour

9.1.1 Definition of the third stage

Introduction
Definitions of the stages of labour need to be clear in order to ensure that women and the staff providing their care have an accurate and shared understanding of the concepts involved and can communicate effectively. In order to facilitate this, the guideline aims to provide practical definitions of the stages of labour.

Clinical question
What are the appropriate definitions of the latent and active phases of the first stage, the second stage, and the third stage of labour?

Previous guideline
No previous guideline has considered definitions of the stages of labour.

Description of included studies
No relevant study was identified that investigated outcomes of different definitions of the third stage of labour.

Evidence statement
There is no high-level evidence to suggest any particular definition of the third stage of labour

GDG interpretation of the evidence (definition of the third stage of labour)
The GDG explored various definitions that have been used in practice and research. Definitions of stages of labour used in the three descriptive studies investigating duration of labour were used to inform the discussion on definitions of labour.[277,282,283] (Refer to Sections 7.2 and 8.1.)

No definitions were found in the literature for the third stage of labour, but a consensus of opinion of the GDG members was reached easily as this is a simple and easily recognisable stage of labour.

> **Recommendation on definition of the third stage of labour**
>
> For the purposes of this guideline, the following definition of the third stage of labour is recommended:
>
> • The third stage of labour is the time from the birth of the baby to the expulsion of the placenta and membranes.

For definitions of the first and second stages of labour, refer to Sections 7.2 and 8.1, respectively.

9.1.2 Duration of the third stage of labour

Clinical question
What is the appropriate definition of retained placenta?

Description of included studies
There were two observational studies identified (one cohort study[358] and one cross-sectional study[359]) describing active management. Data from one systematic review [360] was also extracted for duration of the third stage for women with physiological management.

Review findings
The cohort study was conducted in Australia between 2000 and 2002 (*n* = 6588).[358] [EL = 2+] The study investigated the association between the duration of the third stage and risk of post-partum haemorrhage (PPH). All the study population was actively managed in the third stage of labour. The median duration of the third stage was similar in women with and without PPH. The risk of PPH, however, became significant at 10 minutes (at 10 minutes OR 2.1 [95% CI 1.6 to 2.6]; at 20 minutes OR 4.3 [95% CI 3.3 to 5.5]; at 30 minutes OR 6.2 [95% CI 4.6 to 8.2]). The best predictor for developing PPH from the receiver operating characteristic (ROC) curve was 18 minutes.

The cross-sectional study was conducted in the USA between 1975 and 1986, and included 12 979 singleton vaginal births.[359] [EL = 3] The study investigated prolonged third stage and outcomes. The incidence of PPH and other complications remained constant in third stages less than 30 minutes, then rose progressively, reaching a plateau at 75 minutes. The increase in these complications was observed with both spontaneously delivered and manually extracted placentas.

There was one systematic review of the active management of the third stage.[360] The review compared various outcomes between women with active management and those with physiological management of the third stage. Mean duration of third stage for women with expectant management were reported from three included trials. [EL = 3] One trial conducted in Abu Dhabi reported mean duration of physiologically managed third stage (*n* = 821) as 14.0 minutes with SD of 2.5 minutes. The second trial of low-risk women conducted in Dublin reported mean duration of physiologically managed third stage (*n* = 724) as 11.56 minutes with SD of 8.41 minutes. The third trial of low-risk women conducted in the UK reported mean duration of expectantly managed third stage (*n* = 764) as 20.81 minutes with SD of 20.46 minutes.

Evidence statement
There is a moderate level of evidence that an actively managed third stage of 30 minutes or longer is associated with increased incidence of PPH.

A physiological third stage has duration of less than 60 minutes in 95% of women.

> **Recommendations on duration of the third stage**
>
> For the purposes of this guideline, the following definitions are recommended:
>
> * Active management of the third stage involves a package of care which includes all of these three components:
>   * routine use of uterotonic drugs
>   * early clamping and cutting of the cord
>   * controlled cord traction.
> * Physiological management of the third stage involves a package of care which includes all of these three components:
>   * no routine use of uterotonic drugs
>   * no clamping of the cord until pulsation has ceased
>   * delivery of the placenta by maternal effort.
>
> The third stage of labour is diagnosed as prolonged if not completed within 30 minutes of the birth of the baby with active management and 60 minutes with physiological management.

For durations of the first and second stages of labour, refer to Sections 7.3 and 8.2, respectively.

9.2 Observations in the third stage of labour

Clinical question
Is there evidence that the assessment of the following on admission, and throughout labour and the immediate postnatal period, affect outcomes?

- observation of vital signs
- bladder care
- palpation and presentation/position of baby
- frequency and duration of contractions
- membrane and liquor assessment/placental examination
- maternal behaviour
- vaginal examination
- length, strength and frequency of contractions
- assessment of cervical effacement, dilatation and position
- presentation and descent of the presenting part
- assessment of liquor if membranes ruptured.

9.2.1 Observations (including maternal behaviour)

No relevant study was identified.

9.2.2 Bladder care

No relevant study was identified.

Evidence statement
There is no high-level evidence on maternal observations in the third stage of labour.

Recommendation on observations in the third stage of labour

Observations by a midwife of a woman in the third stage of labour include:

- her general physical condition, as shown by her colour, respiration and her own report of how she feels
- vaginal blood loss.

In addition, in the presence of haemorrhage, retained placenta or maternal collapse, frequent observations to assess the need for resuscitation are required.

9.3 Physiological and active management of the third stage

Introduction
The interventions below, targeting normal healthy women in the third stage of labour, were reviewed.

- physiological versus a package of active management of the third stage
- timing of cord clamping
- comparison of uterotonics for management of the third stage:
  - ergot-alkaloids (ergometrine)
  - oxytocin plus ergot-alkaloids (Syntometrine®)
  - intramuscular or intravenous injection of oxytocin
  - umbilical injection of oxytocin
  - prostaglandin.

Clinical question
Does the method of management of the third stage of labour affect outcomes?

- physiological management
- active management
- cord clamping.

Previous guideline
No previous NICE clinical guideline has reviewed third stage management.

9.3.1 **Physiological versus active management of the third stage of labour**

Introduction
Active management of the third stage of labour comprises three components of care, as outlined below:

- use of uterotonics
- early cord clamping/cutting
- controlled cord traction.

Only trials that included all of the three components have been included.

Description of included studies
There was one systematic review of this intervention identified.[360] [EL = 1+] The systematic review was published in 2000, and included five trials with reasonable quality. Meta-analyses were conducted using data from all women in the included trials, as well as subgroup analysis of women at low risk of PPH.

Review findings

All women
Meta-analysis of the included trials showed that there was evidence that active management of the third stage of labour reduced the risk of PPH (clinically estimated blood loss greater than or equal to 500 ml, four trials, 6284 women, RR 0.38 [95% CI 0.32 to 0.46]; severe PPH, clinically estimated blood loss greater than or equal to 1000 ml, four trials, 6284 women, RR 0.33 [95% CI 0.21 to 0.51]; mean blood loss, two trials, 2941 women, WMD −79.33 ml [95% CI −94.29 to −64.37 ml]; maternal haemoglobin less than 9 g/dl 24–48 hours postpartum, four trials, 4255 women, RR 0.40 [95% CI 0.29 to 0.55]; blood transfusion, five trials, 6477 women, RR 0.34 [95% CI 0.22 to 0.53]; iron tablets during the puerperium, one trial, 1447 women, RR 0.60 [95% CI 0.49 to 0.74]). The analysis also showed evidence that active management of the third stage reduced the need for therapeutic oxytocics (five trials, 6477 women, RR 0.20 [95% CI 0.17 to 0.25]) and shortened the length of the third stage of labour (third stage longer than 20 minutes, three trials, 4637 women, RR 0.15 [95% CI 0.12 to 0.19]; third stage longer than 40 minutes, three trials, 4636 women, RR 0.18 [95% CI 0.14 to 0.24]; mean length of third stage, three trials, 4589 women, WMD −9.77 minutes [95% CI −10.00 to −9.53 minutes]), but there is no evidence of difference in rate of manual removal of placenta. However, it also showed evidence of increased maternal complications such as diastolic blood pressure higher than 100 mmHg between birth of the baby and discharge from the labour ward (three trials, 4636 women, RR 3.46 [95% CI 1.68 to 7.09]), vomiting between birth of the baby and discharge from the labour ward (three trials, 3407 women, RR 2.19 [95% CI 1.68 to 2.86]), nausea between birth of the baby and discharge from the labour ward (three trials, 3407 women, RR 1.83 [95% CI 1.51 to 2.23]) and headache between birth of the baby and discharge from the labour ward (three trials, 3405 women, RR 1.97 [95% CI 1.01 to 3.82]). There was no evidence of differences in other complications including maternal pain during third stage of labour, secondary PPH, bleeding needing readmission or antibiotics, or maternal fatigue at 6 weeks. Women with the active management seemed to be less dissatisfied with the management than the expectant management (maternal dissatisfaction with third stage management, one trial, 1466 women, RR 0.56 [95% CI 0.35 to 0.90]). There was no evidence of differences in neonatal outcomes.

Women at a low risk of PPH
The analyses were repeated including only women at a low risk of PPH. There was evidence that the active management of the third stage significantly reduced the rate of PPH (PPH clinically estimated blood loss greater than or equal to 500 ml, three trials, 3616 women, RR 0.34 [95% CI 0.27 to 0.43]; severe PPH, clinically estimated blood loss greater than or equal to 1000 ml, three trials, 3616 women, RR 0.47 [95% CI 0.27 to 0.82]; mean blood loss, two trials, 2941 women, WMD −79.33 minutes [95% CI −94.29 to −64.37 minutes]; maternal haemoglobin lower than

9 g/dl 24–48 hours postpartum, four trials, 3417 women, RR 0.29 [95% CI 0.19 to 0.44]; need for blood transfusion, four trials, 3809 women, RR 0.27 [95% CI 0.13 to 0.55]; iron tablets during the puerperium, one trial, 1447 women, RR 0.60 [95% CI 0.49 to 0.74]). It also showed that active management of the third stage reduced use of therapeutic oxytocics (four trials, 3809 women, RR 0.16 [95% CI 0.12 to 0.21]), and shortened duration of the third stage (third stage longer than 20 minutes, three trials, 3617 women, RR 0.18 [95% CI 0.14 to 0.23]; third stage longer than 40 minutes, three trials, 3616 women, RR 0.20 [95% CI 0.14 to 0.28]; mean length of third stage, two trials, 2941 women, WMD −3.39 minutes [95% CI −4.66 to −2.13 minutes]), but required more manual removal of placenta (four trials, 3809 women, RR 2.05 [95% CI 1.20 to 3.51]) and increased the rate of hypertension (diastolic blood pressure higher than 100 mmHg between birth of the baby and discharge from the labour ward, three trials, 3616 women, RR 9.65 [95% CI 2.25 to 41.30]). There was no evidence of a significant difference in need for subsequent surgical evacuation of retained products of conception (three trials, 3616 women, RR 0.73 [95% CI 0.36 to 1.49]). The analysis showed that women with the active management had more vomiting, nausea and headache (vomiting between birth of baby and discharge from labour ward, three trials, 2387 women, RR 2.21 [95% CI 1.50 to 3.27]; nausea between birth of baby and discharge from labour ward, three trials, 2387 women, RR 1.88 [95% CI 1.44 to 2.45]; headache between birth of baby and discharge from labour ward, three trials, 2385 women, RR 2.37 [95% CI 0.98 to 5.72]) although headache did not reach statistical significance. There was no evidence of differences in maternal pain during the third stage of labour (one trial, 200 women, RR 3.53 [95% CI 0.97 to 12.93]), secondary PPH (after 24 hours and before 6 weeks: two trials, 2104 women, RR 1.17 [95% CI 0.56 to 2.44]), bleeding needing readmission or antibiotics (one trial, 1429 women, RR 11.30 [95% CI 0.63 to 203.92]) or maternal fatigue at 6 weeks (one trial, 1507 women, RR 0.95 [95% CI 0.74 to 1.22]). Women with the active management seemed to be less dissatisfied with the management than the expectant management (maternal dissatisfaction with third stage management, one trial, 1466 women, RR 0.56 [95% CI 0.35 to 0.90]). There was no evidence of differences in neonatal outcomes.

Evidence statement
Active management of the third stage of labour reduces rates of PPH (blood loss over 1000 ml), mean blood loss, the length of the third stage, postnatal maternal anaemia and the need for blood transfusions, and decreases maternal dissatisfaction. There are associated maternal side effects (nausea, vomiting and headache). There is no evidence of differences in neonatal outcomes.

9.3.2   Timing of cord clamping

Introduction
The effect of delayed cord clamping (DCC), compared with early cord clamping (ECC), on wellbeing of women and babies was evaluated. The purpose of this review is to establish whether or not interfering with placental transfusion has any benefits or harms for the woman and baby. It is plausible that early cord clamping contributes to iron deficiency anaemia in babies.[361] As part of this review, levels of maternal anaemia need also to be considered and may be different between the low to middle income countries and high income countries.

Description of included studies
One systematic review[361] and three trials conducted in low to middle income countries[362–364] were included for this review. The systematic review contained four trials[365–368] from high income countries and four from low to middle income countries.[369–372] Since there was only one RCT from high income countries, three non-randomised controlled trials were also included in the review. A total of seven trials from low to middle income countries (five RCTs and one quasi-randomised trial) and four trials from high income countries (three controlled trials and one randomised trial) were included in the meta-analysis conducted by the NCC-WCH. Studies from low to middle income countries were analysed and interpreted separately because of the high level of anaemia in these countries. All trials compared ECC with DCC and showed reasonable homogeneity but the timing and description of DCC varied enormously. None of the trials was conducted in the UK.

Review findings

Trials in high income countries
Infant haematocrit level 24 hours after birth in two trials in high income countries[365, 366] was significantly raised in the DCC group as compared with the ECC group: (WMD 14.19% [95% CI 11.27% to 17.12%]).

In four trials in high income countries,[365–368] haematocrit at 2–4 hours after birth was significantly increased in the DCC group (WMD 13.12% [95% CI 11.21% to 15.03%]).

In three trials from high income countries,[365–367] haematocrit at 120 hours after birth was significantly increased in the DCC group (WMD 10.46% [95% CI 8.31% to 12.61%]).

Table 9.1 Description and results of included studies on timing of cord clamping

Study, country	Timing of DCC	Infant haemoglobin (g/l) (mean [SD])	Infant haematocrit (%) (mean [SD])	
			2–4 hours after delivery	6 hours after delivery
Geethanath et al. (1997)[369] India	After placental descent into vagina	ECC: 89 [16] DCC: 83 [21] (at 3 months) NS		
Grajeda et al. (1997)[370] Guatemala	When cord stopped pulsating	ECC: 100 [9] DCC-1: 108 [11] DCC-2: 106 [9] (at 2 months) ECC vs DCC-1: $P = 0.03$		
Gupta et al. (2002)[371] India	After placental descent into vagina	ECC: 88 [8] DCC: 99 [9] (at 3 months) $P < 0.001$		
Lanzkowsky (1960)[372] South Africa	After signs of placental separation and after cord stripping 4–5 times	ECC: 111 [10] DCC: 111 [9] NS		
Jose et al. (2006)[362] Argentina	1 and 3 minutes after delivery			ECC: 53.5 [7.0] DCC-1: 57.0 [5.8] DCC-2: 59.4 [6.1]
Chaparro et al. (2006)[363] Mexico	2 minutes after delivery	ECC: 127 [9] DCC: 126 [11] $P = 0.61$		
Emhamed et al. (2004)[364] Libya	After cord stopped pulsating	ECC: 17.1 [1.9] DCC: 18.5 [2.1] $P = 0.0005$		
Linderkamp et al. (1992)[365] Germany	3 minutes after delivery		ECC: 47 [5] DCC: 63 [5] $P < 0.005$	
Nelle et al. (1993)[366] Germany	3 minutes after delivery		ECC: 48 [6] DCC: 58 [6] $P < 0.05$	
Nelle et al. (1995/1996)[367] Germany	3 minutes after delivery		ECC: 53 [7] DCC: 61 [6] $P < 0.05$	
Saigal et al. (1972)[368] Canada	1 and 5 minutes after delivery		ECC: 50 [4] DCC-1: 63 [5] DCC-2: 65 [5] $P < 0.005$	

DCC = delayed cord clamping; ECC = early cord clamping.

Three trials from high income countries[365-367] showed a significant increase in proportion of infants with bilirubin > 15 mg/dl (OR 8.68 [95% CI 1.49 to 50.48]).

Trials in low to middle income countries
Infant haematocrit level 24 hours after birth in two trials from low to middle income countries[362,364] was significantly raised in the DCC group as compared with the ECC group (WMD 4.56% [95% CI 3.01% to 6.10%]).

In six trials from low to middle income countries,[363,364,369-372] infant mean haemoglobin measured was shown to be significantly increased (WMD 0.96 g/l [95% CI 0.29 to 1.64 g/l]) in the DCC group as compared with the ECC group.

In two trials from low to middle income countries,[370,371] the proportions of infants with anaemia at follow-up were significantly reduced (OR 0.14 [95% CI 0.05 to 0.40]) in the DCC group.

One trial from a low to middle income country[362] showed that there was a significant decrease in neonatal anaemia (haematocrit < 45%) at 6 hours (OR 0.05 [95% CI 0.00 to 0.92]) and at 24 hours (OR 0.17 [95% CI 0.05 to 0.61]) in the DCC group. The same trial showed an increase in neonatal polycythaemia at 6 hours and 24 hours of life (haematocrit > 65% at 6 hours of life: ECC group 4/93, delayed clamping for 1 minute group 5/91, delayed clamping for 3 minutes group 13/92; haematocrit > 65% at 24 hours of life: ECC group 2/93, delayed clamping for 1 minute group 3/91, delayed clamping for 3 minutes group 7/92).

There were no significant results for other outcomes: cord mean haemoglobin, infant mean ferritin, cord mean haematocrit or mean serum bilirubin.

Evidence statement
There is limited medium-level evidence from trials in high income countries that showed delayed cord clamping reduced the incidence of anaemia and increases in hyperbilirubinaemia in the baby. Other longer term outcomes are reported variably. There is high-level evidence from low to middle income countries that delayed cord clamping reduces the incidence of anaemia in the baby. Once again, other outcomes are reported variably.

GDG interpretation of the evidence
Most of the evidence is from low income countries where anaemia in babies is more prevalent, and studies from high income countries are, with one exception, not randomised trials. The highly variable descriptions of the timing of cord clamping further confuse the issue.

The impact on babies in high income countries where anaemia is less prevalent is not known.

9.3.3 Comparison of uterotonics in the management of the third stage of labour

Introduction
The following comparisons of drugs and mode of routine uterotonics were evaluated:

- oxytocin versus no other uterotonics
- umbilical oxytocin versus umbilical placebo
- oxytocin versus ergot-alkaloids
- oxytocin plus ergot-alkaloids versus ergot-alkaloids alone
- oxytocin plus ergot-alkaloids versus oxytocin alone
- prostaglandin versus other uterotonics
- umbilical oxytocin versus intravenous oxytocin.

Description of included studies
One systematic review was identified comparing the prophylactic use of oxytocin and no use of uterotonics for the active management of the third stage targeting normal healthy women.[373] [EL = 1+] The study was published in 2001, included seven studies, and evaluated routine use of oxytocin for third stage management, compared with no use of uterotonics and ergot-alkaloids. Another systematic review was identified comparing routine use of ergot-alkaloids plus oxytocin with oxytocin.[374] [EL = 1+] The study was published in 2004, and included six trials and 9332 women. Subgroup analysis was conducted by dose of oxytocin. There were six trials identified

evaluating umbilical injection of oxytocin.[375–380] The included trials were of reasonable quality with similar study designs. Meta-analyses were conducted according to the two comparisons umbilical oxytocin versus intravenous oxytocin and umbilical oxytocin versus umbilical placebo. There were two systematic reviews[381,382] and four trials[383–386] identified for routine administration of prostaglandin, compared with another uterotonic (ergometrine and/or oxytocin), in the third stage of labour. The systematic reviews were of good quality and all the trials were reasonable quality with a reasonable level of homogeneity; hence a new meta-analysis of all included studies was performed to obtain results.[387–412] [EL = 1+]

Review findings

Oxytocin versus no uterotonics
The meta-analysis[373] including all trials showed less blood loss with oxytocin (PPH (clinically estimated blood loss 500 ml or greater), six trials, 3193 women, RR 0.50 [95% CI 0.43 to 0.59]; severe PPH (clinically estimated blood loss 1000 ml or greater), four trials, 2243 women, RR 0.61 [95% CI 0.44 to 0.87]) and less use of therapeutic uterotonics (five women, 2327 trials, RR 0.50 [95% CI 0.39 to 0.64]), but no evidence of a difference in mean length of the third stage (one trial, 52 women, WMD −1.80 minutes [95% CI −5.55 to 1.95 minutes]), need for manual removal of the placenta (four trials, 2243 women, RR 1.17 [95% CI 0.79 to 1.73]) or nausea between birth of the baby and discharge from the labour ward (one trial, 52 women, RR 0.29 [95% CI 0.01 to 6.74]).

When including randomised trials only, the analysis showed evidence that oxytocin seemed to reduce incidence of PPH defined as clinically estimated blood loss 500 ml or greater (four trials, 2213 women, RR 0.61 [95% CI 0.51 to 0.72]), but no evidence of difference in severe PPH (clinically estimated blood loss 1000 ml or greater, three trials, 1273 women, RR 0.72 [95% CI 0.49 to 1.05]).

One included trial compared active management of third stage with oxytocin versus only other two components of active management without oxytocin. The findings from the trial on blood loss showed an even higher significance level (PPH (clinically estimated blood loss 500 ml or greater), one trial, 970 women, RR 0.29 [95% CI 0.21 to 0.41]; severe PPH (clinically estimated blood loss 1000 ml or greater), one trial, 970 women, RR 0.33 [95% CI 0.14 to 0.77]), but there was no evidence of a difference in manual removal of the placenta (one trial, 970 women, RR 0.99 [95% CI 0.62 to 1.59]). However, analysis only including trials of women without any other components of active management of third stage and comparing routine use of oxytocin with no use of oxytocin showed evidence of significant reduction in incidence of PPH (defined as clinically estimated blood loss 500 ml or greater, two trials, 1221 women, RR 0.61 [95% CI 0.51 to 0.73], but no evidence of difference in severe PPH (clinically estimated blood loss 1000 ml or greater, two trials, 1221 women, RR 0.73 [95% CI 0.49 to 1.07].

When analysed including women who had been given oxytocin before placental birth only, the analysis also showed reduction in incidence of PPH of both definitions (clinically estimated blood loss 500 ml or greater, five trials, 2253 women, RR 0.50 [95% CI 0.42 and 0.58]; severe PPH (clinically estimated blood loss 1000 ml or greater, four trials, 2243 women, RR 0.61 [95% CI 0.44 to 0.87]) and use of therapeutic uterotonics (three trials, 1273 women, RR 0.64 [95% CI 0.47 to 0.87]). However, when analysed only including women who had been given oxytocin after placental birth, there was no significant difference in incidence of PPH defined as clinically estimated blood loss 500 ml or greater (one trial, 940 women, RR 0.60 [95% CI 0.32 to 1.12])

Umbilical oxytocin versus umbilical placebo
There were three trials included. One trial was conducted in Thailand, published in 1998.[378] [EL = 1+] The study population included 50 normal healthy women in the third stage of labour. The intervention was oxytocin (20 IU) intra-umbilical injection, compared with intra-umbilical placebo injection. One trial was conducted in Turkey, published in 1996.[379] [EL = 1+] The study population included 47 normal healthy women in the third stage of labour. The intervention was intra-umbilical injection of oxytocin (20 IU), compared with placebo. One trial was conducted in the USA, published in 1987.[413] The study population included 50 normal healthy women in the third stage of labour. The intervention was oxytocin (10 IU) intra-umbilical injection, compared with umbilical placebo injection. The meta-analyses of the trials showed that there was

no evidence of difference in blood loss (pre-/postpartum haematocrit level difference, one trial, WMD −0.20% [−1.40% to 1.00%]; estimated blood loss, two trials, WMD −16.06 ml [−66.63 to 34.50 ml]) or duration of third stage (WMD −1.95 minutes [−5.54 to 1.64 minutes].

Oxytocin versus ergot-alkaloids
The analysis including all trials showed there was no evidence of a difference in PPH (clinically estimated blood loss 500 ml or greater, five trials, 2719 women, RR 0.90 [95% CI 0.70 to 1.16]), severe PPH (clinically estimated blood loss 1000 ml or greater, three trials, 1746 women, RR 0.99 [95% CI 0.56 to 1.74]), use of therapeutic uterotonics (two trials, 1208 women, RR 1.02 [95% CI 0.67 to 1.55]), mean length of the third stage (one trial, 1049 women, WMD −0.80 minutes [95% CI −1.65 to 0.05 minutes]), but there was a reduction in need for manual removal of the placenta (three trials, 1746 women, RR 0.57 [95% CI 0.41 to 0.79]).

Neither an analysis including only randomised trials, nor including women with expectant management, showed evidence of a difference in any of the outcomes above.

When analysed only including women who had been given oxytocics before placental delivery, there was also no evidence of a difference in blood loss, but there was a reduction in need for manual removal of the placenta (three trials, 1746 women, RR 0.57 [95% CI 0.41 to 0.79]). However, when analysed only including women who had been given oxytocics after placental delivery, there was no evidence of a difference in PPH.

Oxytocin plus ergot-alkaloids versus ergot-alkaloids alone

Oxytocin plus ergot alkaloids (Syntometrine) versus ergot alkaloids alone
When analysed including all trials, there was no evidence of a difference in blood loss (PPH (clinically estimated blood loss 500 ml or greater), five trials, 2891 women, RR 1.29 [95% CI 0.90 to 1.84]; severe PPH (clinically estimated blood loss 1000 ml or greater), one trial, 1120 women, RR 1.67 [95% CI 0.40 to 6.94]), duration of the third stage (longer than 20 minutes), three trials, 2281 women, RR 0.89 [95% CI 0.67 to 1.19]), but there was a reduction in the need for manual removal of the placenta with oxytocin plus ergot alkaloids, compared with ergot alkaloids only (two trials, 1927 women, RR 1.02 [95% CI 0.48 to 2.20]).

When analysed only including randomised trials, the intervention showed significant reduction in blood loss (PPH (clinically estimated blood loss 500 ml or greater), two trials, 1161 women, RR 0.44 [95% CI 0.20 to 0.94]) but no evidence of a difference in duration of the third stage (longer than 20 minutes, one trial, 354 women, RR 3.21 [95% CI 0.34 to 30.57]), compared with ergot alkaloids only.

Oxytocin plus ergot-alkaloids versus oxytocin alone
The meta-analyses including all trials showed evidence of reduction of blood loss with ergometrine-oxytocin compared with oxytocin (blood loss 500 ml or greater, six trials, 9332 women, OR 0.82 [95% CI 0.71 to 0.95]) and need for therapeutic oxytocics (three trials, 5465 women, OR 0.83 [95% CI 0.72 to 0.96]). However, there was also evidence of maternal complications such as elevation of diastolic blood pressure (four trials, 7486 women, OR 2.40 [95% CI 1.58 to 3.64]), vomiting (three trials, 5458 women, OR 4.92 [95% CI 4.03 to 6.00]), nausea (nausea, three trials, 5458 women, OR 4.07 [95% CI 3.43 to 4.84]; vomiting and/or nausea, four trials, 7486 women, OR 5.71 [95% CI 4.97 to 6.57]). There was no evidence of other complications such as blood loss 1000 ml or greater, rate of blood transfusion, manual removal of the placenta or duration of the third stage. There was no evidence of differences in neonatal outcomes. Subgroup analysis by oxytocin dose (5 IU or 10 IU) showed that the analysis for both doses showed significant reduction by use of ergometrine-oxytocin in incidence of PPH defined as blood loss of 500 ml or greater, compared with use of oxytocin, although the effect was found to be greater when compared with 5 IU of oxytocin dose. Neither dose showed significant difference in incidence of PPH defined as blood loss 1000 ml or greater.

Prostaglandin versus other uterotonics
The meta-analysis showed that use of prostaglandin was less effective in reducing risk of PPH (16 trials, severe PPH, OR 1.31 [95% CI 1.14 to 1.50]; 21 trials, moderate PPH, OR 1.49 [95% CI 1.39 to 1.59]) than use of other uterotonics, although women in the prostaglandin group experi-

enced more side effects than the control group (nausea, 12 trials, OR 0.86 [95% CI 0.74 to 1.06]; vomiting, 19 trials, OR 1.27 [95% CI 1.04 to 1.55]; diarrhoea, 15 trials, OR 1.97 [95% CI 1.44 to 2.70]; pyrexia, 12 trials, OR 6.67 [95% CI 5.57 to 7.99]; and shivering, 19 trials, OR 3.51 [95% CI 3.25 to 3.80]).

Umbilical oxytocin versus IV oxytocin
There are three trials included. One trial was conducted in India, published in 1995.[376] [EL = 1+] The study population included 100 normal healthy women in the third stage of labour. The intervention was intra-umbilical oxytocin (10 IU) infusion compared with IV oxytocin (10 IU) infusion. One trial was conducted in the USA, published in 1991.[377] [EL = 1+] The study population included 104 normal healthy women in the third stage of labour. The intervention was intra-umbilical oxytocin (20 IU) infusion compared with IV oxytocin infusion (20 IU). Another trial was conducted in the USA and published in 1989.[375] [EL = 1+] The study population included 50 normal healthy women in the third stage of labour. The intervention was intra-umbilical oxytocin (20 IU) infusion, compared with IV oxytocin (20 IU) infusion. The Indian trial[376] and Reddy trial[375] showed a similar direction of results, and the Porter trial[377] showed an opposite direction of results, although no particular difference in study design was found. The meta-analyses of the trials showed that there was no evidence of difference in blood loss (pre-/postpartum haematocrit level difference, three trials, WMD −1.24% [95% CI −5.16% to 2.67%]; pre-/postpartum haemoglobin level difference, three trials, WMD −0.08 g/dl [95% CI −1.41 to 1.26 g/dl]; estimated blood, loss two trials, WMD −134.92 ml [95% CI −255.01 to −14.83 ml]) or duration of third stage (three trials WMD −1.78 minutes [95% CI −4.68 to 1.11 minutes].

Evidence statement
Use of oxytocin alone seemed to reduce the incidence of PPH, compared with no use of uterotonics, with no evidence of difference in incidence of nausea. When oxytocin alone was compared with ergot-alkaloid, there were no significant differences in incidence of PPH, although significant reduction in the need for manual removal of placenta was found in the oxytocin group. There was no evidence of difference between ergot-alkaloids plus oxytocin and single use of ergot-alkaloids. However, ergot-alkaloids plus oxytocin seemed to reduce incidence of PPH with increased incidences of vomiting and nausea, compared with use of single oxytocin. Single use of oxytocin 10 IU showed closer effect to ergot-alkaloids plus oxytocin on reduction in PPH than single use of oxytocin 5 IU. Use of prostaglandin, compared with other uterotonics, resulted in higher incidence of both PPH and adverse events. Routine umbilical injection of oxytocin, compared with intravenous oxytocin, showed significant reduction in estimated blood loss, although there was not enough information on adverse events.

GDG interpretation of the evidence (physiological and active management of the third stage of labour)
Many of the studies do not fulfil the formal criteria of active management of third stage. In view of this, the evidence summarised above, and the side effects of ergometrine plus oxytocin, the GDG concluded that this is sufficient to warrant the recommendations below.

Recommendations on physiological and active management of the third stage of labour

Active management of the third stage is recommended, which includes the use of oxytocin (10 international units [IU] by intramuscular injection), followed by early clamping and cutting of the cord and controlled cord traction.*

Women should be informed that active management of the third stage reduces the risk of maternal haemorrhage and shortens the third stage.

Women at low risk of postpartum haemorrhage who request physiological management of the third stage should be supported in their choice.

---

* At the time of publication (September 2007), oxytocin did not have UK marketing authorisation for this indication. Informed consent should be obtained and documented.

Changing from physiological management to active management of the third stage is indicated in the case of:

- haemorrhage
- failure to deliver the placenta within 1 hour
- the woman's desire to artificially shorten the third stage.

Pulling the cord or palpating the uterus should only be carried out after administration of oxytocin as part of active management.

In the third stage of labour neither umbilical oxytocin infusion nor prostaglandin should be used routinely.

Research recommendation on cord clamping

Studies should be carried out to investigate the timing of cord clamping and balance of risk/benefit to both mother and baby.

Table 9.2 Summary of findings on management of the third stage of labour

Intervention	Comparator	Blood loss at least 500 ml	Blood loss at least 1000 ml	Adverse events	Other outcomes
Active management of third stage (prophylactic uterotonics, early cord clamping/cutting and controlled cord traction)	Physiological management of third stage	*Women with high and low risk* RR 0.38 [95% CI 0.32 to 0.46]	RR 0.33 [95% CI 0.21 to 0.51]	Hypertension RR 3.46 [95% CI 1.68 to 7.09] Vomiting RR 2.19 [95% CI 1.68 to 2.86] Nausea RR 1.83 [95% CI 1.51 to 2.23] Headache RR 1.97 [95% CI 1.01 to 3.82]	Maternal dissatisfaction with third stage management RR 0.56 [95% CI 0.35 to 0.90]
		Women with low risk RR 0.34 [95% CI 0.27 to 0.43]	RR 0.47 [95% CI 0.27 to 0.82]	Hypertension RR 9.65 [95% CI 2.25 to 41.30] Vomiting RR 2.21 [95% CI 1.50 to 3.27] Nausea RR 1.88 [95% CI 1.44 to 2.45] Headache RR 2.37 [95% CI 0.98 to 5.72]	Maternal dissatisfaction with third stage management RR 0.56 [95% CI 0.35 to 0.90]
Delayed cord clamping	Early cord clamping	No evidence of difference	No evidence of difference	Increase in incidences of jaundice and polycythaemia	Reduction in anaemia in babies in developing countries
Comparison of uterotonics					
Oxytocin	No uterotonics	RR 0.50 [95% CI 0.43 to 0.59]	RR 0.61 [95% CI 0.44 to 0.87]	Nausea RR 0.29 [95% CI 0.01 to 6.74]	
Umbilical oxytocin	No uterotonics	No information	No information	No information	Blood loss WMD –16.06 ml [95% CI –66.63 to 34.50 ml]
Oxytocin	Ergot-alkaloids	RR 0.90 [95% CI 0.70 to 1.16]	RR 0.99 [95% CI 0.56 to 1.74]	No information	Need for manual removal of the placenta RR 0.57 [95% CI 0.41 to 0.79]
Ergot-alkaloids plus oxytocin	Ergot-alkaloids alone	RR 1.29 [95% CI 0.90 to 1.84]	RR 1.67 [95% CI 0.40 to 6.94]	No information	
Ergot-alkaloids plus oxytocin	Oxytocin alone	OR 0.82 [95% CI 0.71 to 0.95]	OR 0.78 [95% CI 0.58 to 1.03]	Vomiting OR 4.92 [95% CI 4.03 to 6.00] Nausea OR 4.07 [95% CI 3.43 to 4.84] Vomiting and/or nausea OR 5.71 [95% CI 4.97 to 6.57])	
	Oxytocin 5 IU only	OR 0.43 [0.23 to 0.83]	OR 0.14 [0.00 to 6.85]	No information	
	Oxytocin 10 IU only	OR 0.85 [0.73 to 0.98]	OR 0.78 [0.59 to 1.04]	Vomiting OR 4.92 [4.03 to 6.00] Nausea OR 4.07 [3.43 to 4.84] Vomiting and/or nausea OR 5.71 [4.97 to 6.57]	
Prostaglandin	Other uterotonics	OR 1.49 [95% CI 1.39 to 1.59]	OR 1.31 [95% CI 1.14 to 1.50]	Nausea OR 0.86 [95% CI 0.74 to 1.06] Vomiting OR 1.27 [95% CI 1.04 to 1.55]	
Umbilical oxytocin	Intravenous oxytocin	No information	No information	No information	Estimated blood loss WMD –134.92 ml [95% CI –255.01 to –14.83]

10 Normal labour: care of the baby and woman immediately after birth

10.1 Introduction

Birth is an immensely important, often life-changing, event. Not only does the process of labour and birth present challenges to the baby but there are also major rapid physiological changes that take place to enable the baby to adapt to life after birth. These include the establishment of respirations, changes to the cardiovascular system, the regulation of body temperature, digestion and absorption and the development of a resistance to infections.

The vast majority of babies make this transition uneventfully but vigilance on the part of healthcare professionals, and timely intervention when necessary, can influence the baby's longer term health and development.

Care of the baby immediately after birth in the intrapartum period is discussed in this chapter. Further care thereafter is discussed in the NICE clinical guideline on *Postnatal Care*,[414] including promotion of breastfeeding, infant and mother bonding, and vitamin K supplementation for newborn babies.

Care of the woman immediately after birth includes assessment of her physical and emotional condition, as well as assessment (and possible repair) of trauma sustained during birth. It is also crucially important that appropriate assessment and treatment of any complications is undertaken, as failure to do so can have long-term consequences for the woman's physical, emotional and psychological wellbeing. As with the immediate care of the newborn baby, this should be balanced between assessing the woman's physical needs (and intervening should that be required) and giving the new mother/parents the opportunity to savour and enjoy this momentous and life-changing event.

10.2 Initial assessment of the newborn baby and mother–infant bonding

10.2.1 Apgar score

Introduction
The Apgar score was developed in 1953 and has been widely adopted to assess the baby at the time of birth.[415] It was first planned as an indicator for the need for resuscitation. It was not originally intended to predict longer term prognosis and includes assessment of colour, heart rate, tone, respiratory rate and reflex irritability.[415–417]

Clinical question
What is the evidence that different methods of initial neonatal assessment and examination influence outcomes?

- Including cardiovascular-respiratory and abnormalities assessment.

Description of included studies
A total of five cohort studies and one systematic review (containing 16 cohort studies) were identified.[418–423] Only studies comparing the Apgar score with neonatal death and diagnosis were considered homogeneous enough to provide a new meta-analysis of the data. [EL = 2+]

Review findings

The results of meta-analyses on neonatal mortality and diagnosis of cerebral palsy are shown in Tables 10.1 and 10.2. Overall, the Apgar score appeared to be a moderate level predictor for neonatal deaths and the development of cerebral palsy, with the Apgar at 5 minutes having better predictive value than at 1 minute. Surprisingly, only one study was identified that examined predictive values of the Apgar score on longer term neurological development of the infants. There was no high-level study that examined the correlation between Apgar score and immediate neonatal outcomes.

Table 10.1   Meta-analysis on predictive value of Apgar score (neonatal mortality)

Cut-off of Apgar score	Sensitivity (%) [95% CI]	Specificity (%) [95% CI]	Diagnostic OR [95% CI]	Number of studies
1 minute Apgar				
0–3 vs 4–10	46.0 [43.7 to 48.3]	95.4 [95.3 to 95.5]	17.71 [16.07 to 19.51]	11
0–6 vs 7–10	66.9 [64.7 to 69.1]	84.2 [83.9 to 84.4]	10.73 [9.72 to 11.85]	11
5 minute Apgar				
0–3 vs 4–10	36.2 [34.9 to 37.5]	99.7 [99.7 to 99.8]	218.42 [203.09 to 234.90]	11
0–6 vs 7–10	55.5 [54.1 to 56.8]	98.7 [98.7 to 98.8]	97.16 [91.58 to 103.07]	11

Table 10.2   Meta-analysis on predictive value of Apgar score (cerebral palsy)

Cut-off of Apgar score	Sensitivity (%) [95% CI]	Specificity (%) [95% CI]	Diagnostic OR [95% CI]	Number of studies
1 minute Apgar				
0–3 vs 4–10	24.8 [18.1 to 31.6]	95.3 [95.1 to 95.5]	6.67 [4.63 to 9.61]	1
0–6 vs 7–10	42.7 [34.9 to 50.4]	81.9 [81.5 to 82.2]	3.36 [2.44 to 4.61]	1
5 minute Apgar				
0–3 vs 4–10	8.5 [5.9 to 11.1]	99.8 [99.8 to 99.8]	39.90 [28.37 to 56.11]	2
0–6 vs 7–10	25.0 [21.0 to 29.0]	98.9 [98.9 to 98.9]	29.59 [23.80 to 36.78]	3

Evidence statement

There is low-level evidence that the Apgar score at 5 minutes is moderately accurate at predicting neonatal death and cerebral palsy with reasonable specificity but low sensitivity. No high-level evidence could be found on immediate or longer term neonatal outcomes.

10.2.2   Mother–infant bonding and promoting breastfeeding

Introduction

Immediate skin-to-skin contact of mothers and babies to promote bonding and breastfeeding was reviewed in the NICE *Postnatal Care* guideline.[414] For ease the relevant recommendations from that guideline are reproduced.

Clinical question

Are there effective ways of encouraging mother–infant bonding following birth?

• Including skin to skin contact with mothers, breastfeeding.

Description of included studies

There was one systematic review identified that considered intrapartum interventions for promoting the initiation of breastfeeding, although there was no relevant intervention that this guideline covers.[424]

Recommendations on initial assessment of the baby and mother–infant bonding

The Apgar score at 1 and 5 minutes should be recorded routinely for all births.

If the baby is born in poor condition (the Apgar score at 1 minute is 5 or less), then the time to the onset of regular respirations should be recorded and the cord double-clamped to allow paired cord blood gases to be taken. The Apgar score should continue to be recorded until the baby's condition is stable.

Women should be encouraged to have skin-to-skin contact with their babies as soon as possible after the birth.*

In order to keep the baby warm, he or she should be dried and covered with a warm, dry blanket or towel while maintaining skin-to-skin contact with the woman.

Separation of a woman and her baby within the first hour of the birth for routine postnatal procedures, for example weighing, measuring and bathing, should be avoided unless these measures are requested by the woman, or are necessary for the immediate care of the baby.*

Initiation of breastfeeding should be encouraged as soon as possible after the birth, ideally within 1 hour.*

Head circumference, body temperature and birthweight should be recorded soon after the first hour following birth.

An initial examination should be undertaken by a healthcare professional to detect any major physical abnormality and to identify any problems that require referral.

Any examination or treatment of the baby should be undertaken with the consent and in the presence of the parents or, if this is not possible, with their knowledge.

10.3 Initial assessment of the mother following birth

Introduction
Appropriate maternal observations immediately after birth are discussed in this section. Advice on further appropriate maternal observations thereafter in the postnatal period are discussed in the NICE *Postnatal Care* guideline.[414]

Clinical question
Is there evidence that the assessment of the following, on admission, and throughout labour and the immediate postnatal period, affect outcomes?

- observation of vital signs.

Description of included studies
There was no relevant study identified to investigate effectiveness of each component of maternal observations immediately following birth.

Evidence statement
There is no high-level study investigating appropriate maternal observations immediately after birth.

Recommendation on initial assessment of the mother

Observations taken following the birth of the baby should include:

- maternal observation – temperature, pulse, blood pressure, uterine contraction, lochia
- examination of placenta and membranes – assessment of their condition, structure, cord vessels and completeness
- early assessment of maternal emotional/psychological condition in response to labour and birth
- successful voiding of the woman's bladder.

---

* Recommendations relating to immediate postnatal care (within 2 hours of birth) have been extracted from 'Postnatal care: routine postnatal care of women and their babies' (NICE clinical guideline 37). Please see NICE clinical guideline 37 for further guidance on care after birth.

10.4   Perineal care

Previous guideline
No previous guidelines have considered interventions related to perineal or genital care immediately following childbirth.

10.4.1   Definition of perineal or genital trauma

Clinical question
What is the appropriate definition of perineal or genital trauma?

Overview of available evidence and evidence statement
The GDG discussed this and reached consensus to use the following recommendation for the definition of perineal or genital trauma, taken from the Green Top Guideline by the Royal College of Obstetricians and Gynaecologists on methods and materials used in perineal repair.[425]

Recommendation on definition of perineal/genital trauma

Perineal or genital trauma caused by either tearing or episiotomy should be defined as follows:

- first degree – injury to skin only
- second degree – injury to the perineal muscles but not the anal sphincter
- third degree – injury to the perineum involving the anal sphincter complex:
  - 3a – less than 50% of external anal sphincter thickness torn
  - 3b – more than 50% of external anal sphincter thickness torn
  - 3c – internal anal sphincter torn.
- fourth degree – injury to the perineum involving the anal sphincter complex (external and internal anal sphincter) and anal epithelium.

10.4.2   Assessment of perineal trauma

Clinical question
Is there evidence that the type of assessment used to identify perineal or genital trauma affects outcomes?

Description of available evidence
Three studies are reviewed in this subsection. The first is an evaluation of a perineal assessment and repair course. The other two prospective intervention studies examine the incidence of third- and fourth-degree perineal trauma and highlight under-diagnosis as a problem in this aspect of care.

Review findings
A recent UK before and after study evaluated the effectiveness of a perineal repair course.[426] [EL = 2+] The one-day course included lectures, video demonstrations and hands-on teaching of rectal examination and suturing skills using foam pads and models. Participants completed a self-assessment questionnaire prior to the course and 8 weeks afterwards. Findings for the evaluation are based on responses to 147 pairs of pre- and post-course questionnaires (response rate = 71%). Most respondents were midwives (95%), 68% of whom had been qualified for more than 5 years. Seven junior doctors and three students also attended the courses. Following attendance at the course, self-assessed responses showed an improvement in the correct classification of tears depending upon degree of anal sphincter injury: external anal sphincter (EAS) partially torn: 77% versus 85%, $P = 0.049$; EAS completely torn: 70% versus 85%, $P = 0.001$; internal anal sphincter (IAS) exposed but not torn: 63% versus 82%, $P < 0.001$; IAS torn: 45% versus 67%, $P < 0.001$; anal sphincter and mucosa torn: 80% versus 89%, $P = 0.031$. There was also a significant change in practice reported with more respondents performing a rectal examination prior to repairing perineal trauma after attending the course: 28% versus 89%, $P < 0.001$, McNemar's test). There was also a significant shift in favour of a continuous suture to the perineal muscle and skin: continuous suture to muscle: 32% versus 84%, $P < 0.001$; continuous suture to skin 39% versus 81%, $P < 0.001$. The paper does not mention two-stage perineal repair as an option.

A prospective intervention study recently conducted in the UK involved re-examination by an experienced research fellow of nulliparous women who sustained perineal trauma in order to ascertain the prevalence of clinically recognisable and true occult anal sphincter injuries.[427] [EL = 2+] Women were initially assessed by the attending clinician. Where obstetric anal sphincter injuries (OASIS) were identified, this was confirmed by a specialist registrar or consultant. All participating women (n = 241; response rate = 95%) had an endoanal ultrasound scan performed immediately following birth (prior to suturing). Most of these women (n = 208 (86%)) attended for a repeat ultrasound scan at 7 weeks postpartum. One hundred and seventy-three of the 241 births were attended by midwives, 75% of these births being attended by midwives with at least 5 years of experience. Of the 68 births attended by obstetricians, 63 were instrumental births. The prevalence of OASIS increased significantly from 11% to 24.5% when women were re-examined by the research fellow. Of the 173 births attended by midwives, eight women were diagnosed as having sustained an OASIS. Only four of these were confirmed by the research fellow. Of the remaining 26 women who sustained OASIS, the midwife made a diagnosis of second-degree tear in 25 cases and first-degree tear in one case. All 30 incidents of OASIS were confirmed by the specialist registrar/consultant. Of the 68 births attended by obstetricians, 22 women (32%) had OASIS diagnosed and confirmed by the research fellow. A further seven cases of OASIS were identified by the research fellow, three of these cases had been missed by the duty specialist registrar but were subsequently confirmed by the specialist consultant. Of the 68 births attended by an obstetrician, the midwife caring for the woman was also asked to perform an examination. Only one of the 29 OASIS was identified by a midwife and no midwife performed a rectal examination. All women with OASIS had a defect detected by endoanal ultrasound performed immediately after birth. In addition, there were three defects seen on ultrasound that were not seen clinically. No additional defects were seen at the 7 week follow-up.

A UK prospective observational study was undertaken to assess whether clinical diagnosis of third-degree tears could be improved by increased vigilance in perineal assessment.[428] [EL = 3] The study involved assessment of perineal trauma sustained by women having their first vaginal birth at one large teaching hospital. A group of 121 women were assessed initially by the obstetrician or midwife attending the birth and then again by a single independent assessor (a clinical research fellow). Findings from this group were compared with all other women giving birth over the same 6 month period who were assessed by the attending clinician only (i.e. usual care) (n = 362). Both groups were similar for a number of key characteristics, including gestation, mode of birth, analgesia used, duration of labour, birthweight, and head circumference. Episiotomies which extended to involve the anal sphincter were classified as third-degree tears. There were significantly more third-degree tears identified in the assessed group, 14.9%, compared with 7.5% in the control group. The study was underpowered to show statistical significance. In the assessed group, only 11 of the 18 third-degree tears were identified by the clinician attending the birth. Once the diagnosis was made there was no disagreement between attending clinician and research fellow. Third-degree tears were most often associated with instrumental births, especially forceps births. The percentages of women sustaining a third-degree tear for each mode of birth was spontaneous vaginal birth 3.2%, ventouse 14.9% and forceps 22%. Comparing study data with findings for a similar group of women during the 6 months before and after the study period, the overall rates of third-degree tears were before 2.5%, during 9.3%, and after 4.6%, again suggesting that many third-degree tears go undiagnosed.

Evidence statement
There is low-level evidence that suggests the systematic assessment of the vagina, perineum and rectum is required to adequately assess the extent of perineal trauma.

There is low-level evidence that current training is inadequate regarding assessment of perineal trauma.

Practitioners who are appropriately trained are more likely to provide a consistent, high standard of perineal care.

Recommendations on assessment of perineal trauma

Before assessing for genital trauma, healthcare professionals should:

- explain to the woman what they plan to do and why
- offer inhalational analgesia
- ensure good lighting
- position the woman so that she is comfortable and so that the genital structures can be seen clearly.

The initial examination should be performed gently and with sensitivity and may be done in the immediate period following birth.

If genital trauma is identified following birth, further systematic assessment should be carried out, including a rectal examination.

Systematic assessment of genital trauma should include:

- further explanation of what the healthcare professional plans to do and why
- confirmation by the woman that tested effective local or regional analgesia is in place
- visual assessment of the extent of perineal trauma to include the structures involved, the apex of the injury and assessment of bleeding
- a rectal examination to assess whether there has been any damage to the external or internal anal sphincter if there is any suspicion that the perineal muscles are damaged.

The timing of this systematic assessment should not interfere with mother–infant bonding unless the woman has bleeding that requires urgent attention.

The woman should usually be in lithotomy to allow adequate visual assessment of the degree of the trauma and for the repair. This position should only be maintained for as long as is necessary for the systematic assessment and repair.

The woman should be referred to a more experienced healthcare professional if uncertainty exists as to the nature or extent of trauma sustained.

The systematic assessment and its results should be fully documented, possibly pictorially.

All relevant healthcare professionals should attend training in perineal/genital assessment and repair, and ensure that they maintain these skills.

10.4.3 Perineal repair

Clinical question
Is there evidence that undertaking repair, the timing, analgesia and method and material of perineal repair affect outcomes?

Previous guideline
No previous guideline has considered performing perineal repair following childbirth.

Undertaking repair

Description of included studies
Two studies are reviewed under this heading. One RCT compared suturing of first- and second-degree perineal tears with non-suturing, and one qualitative study explored women's experiences of perineal repair.

Review findings
One UK RCT compared suturing with non-suturing of first- and second-degree perineal tears (SUNS trial).[429] [EL = 1+] Randomisation was carried out across two hospital labour wards with stratification for degree of tear to produce a group of nulliparous women who had perineal tears sutured (*n* = 33) and nulliparous women whose perineal trauma was not sutured (*n* = 41). Suturing was conducted in accordance with the hospital protocols, which included continuous subcutaneous sutures to the perineal skin. No differences were apparent between trial groups at any time point postnatally regarding level of pain as measured using the McGill Pain Questionnaire. The

median total pain scores and point difference in medians for sutured versus unsutured groups were: day 1: 11 [range 0 to 33] versus 10 [range 0 to 44]; 1 [95% CI −2 to 4.999]; day 10: 0 [range 0 to 18] versus 0 [range 0 to 33]; 0 [95% CI 0 to 0.001]; 6 weeks: 0 [range 0 to 28] versus 0 [range 0 to 7]; 0 [95% CI 0 to 0]. Scores obtained using a 10 cm VAS also showed no differences between groups. Healing was measured using a standardised and validated tool, the REEDA scale. Findings showed significantly better wound edge approximation for women in the sutured group (again expressed in terms of median for scores): day 1: 1 [range 0 to 3] versus 2 [range 1 to 3]; −1 [95% CI −1.0001 to 0], $P < 0.001$; day 10: 1 [range 0 to 2] versus 2 [range 0 to 3]; −1 [95% CI −1.0001 to −0.0003], $P = 0.003$; 6 weeks: 1 [range 0 to 1] versus 1 [range 0 to 3]; 0 [95% CI −0.9999 to 0.0001], $P = 0.001$. Total healing scores suggested a tendency towards better wound healing in the sutured group at days 1 and 10: day 1: [range 0 to 9] versus 5 [range 1 to 10]; −1 [95% CI −2 to 0], NS; day 10: 1 [range 0 to 6] versus 2 [range 0 to 8]; 0 [95% CI −1 to 0], NS. At 6 weeks women in the sutured group had significantly better healing scores than those in the unsutured group: 0 [range 0 to 3] versus 1 [range 0 to 3]; 0 [95% CI −1.0001 to −0.0003], $P = 0.003$. The authors conclude that, despite the small sample size for this trial, the findings show significantly improved healing following perineal suturing compared with non-suturing.

One qualitative study was identified which explored women's experiences of perineal trauma both during its repair and in the immediate postnatal period.[430] [EL = 3] This small ($n = 6$), in-depth, unstructured interview-based study is limited by its reliance on the snowballing technique, which tends to result in a sample of people with similar experiences and/or views. It does, however, highlight the intense and far-reaching effects of bad experiences of care. The importance of interpersonal relationships between women and their carers was illustrated through four emergent themes:

- the importance of communication between women and health professional
- the importance of good pain relief during suturing
- women feeling 'being patched up'
- women having to endure a procedure that had to be 'got through'.

Postnatally, women described the feelings associated with coming to terms with perineal trauma. The themes here comprised:

- the severity of negative emotions (anger, upset, frustration)
- concerns about the degree of skill of practitioners
- failing to be heard and taken seriously when there were problems with perineal healing.

Evidence statement
There is limited high-level evidence that not suturing first- or second-degree perineal trauma is associated with poorer wound healing at 6 weeks.

There is no evidence as to long-term outcomes.

Recommendations on perineal repair

Women should be advised that in the case of first-degree trauma, the wound should be sutured in order to improve healing, unless the skin edges are well opposed.

Women should be advised that in the case of second-degree trauma, the muscle should be sutured in order to improve healing.

Timing of repair

Description of included studies
No study was identified which considered the timing of perineal repair following childbirth.

Evidence statement
There is no high-level evidence on timing of perineal repair following childbirth.

Recommendations on timing of repair

Repair of the perineum should be undertaken as soon as possible to minimise the risk of infection and blood loss.

Analgesia used during perineal repair

Description of included studies
There is no evidence regarding the use of analgesia during perineal repair.

Evidence statement
There is no high-level evidence on use of analgesia during perineal repair.

Recommendations on analgesia for perineal repair

Perineal repair should only be undertaken with tested effective analgesia in place using infiltration with up to 20 ml of 1% lidocaine or equivalent, or topping up the epidural (spinal anaesthesia may be necessary).

If the woman reports inadequate pain relief at any point this should immediately be addressed.

Method of perineal repair

Description of included studies
A systematic review of four RCTs plus an additional RCT investigated the effects of continuous subcuticular with interrupted transcutaneous sutures for perineal repair. Two further RCTs compared a two-layer repair technique (leaving the skin unsutured) with a three-layer repair technique.

Review findings
One systematic review (1998) was identified which compared the effects of continuous subcuticular with interrupted trancutaneous sutures for perineal repair.[431] [EL = 1+] Four RCTs were included in the review involving a total of 1864 women. The continuous subcuticular method was found to be associated with less short-term pain (up to day 10 postpartum) compared with interrupted sutures (three trials): 160/789 versus 218/799, OR 0.68 [95% CI 0.53 to 0.86]. No other differences were apparent between the two trials groups for the outcomes tested: analgesia up to day 10 (two trials): 56/527 versus 65/541, OR 0.86 [95% CI 0.58 to 1.26]; reported pain at 3 months (one trial): 58/465 versus 51/451, OR 1.12 [95% CI 0.75 to 1.67]; removal of suture material (up to 3 months) (one trial): 121/465 versus 16/451, OR 0.61 [95% CI 0.46 to 0.80]; failure to resume pain-free intercourse (up to 3 months) (one trial): 157/465 versus 144/451, OR 1.09 [95% CI 0.82 to 1.43]; resuturing (up to 3 months) (two trials, one with no incidents): 3/487 versus 3/531, OR 1.11 [95% CI 0.22 to 5.53]; dyspareunia (up to 3 months) (three trials): 172/775 versus 184/749, OR 0.88 [95% 0.69 to 1.12]. The authors concluded that the continuous subcuticular technique of perineal repair may be associated with less pain in the immediate postpartum period than the interrupted suture technique. The long-term effects are less clear. It is also noted that, while three studies used the same suture material (Dexon) throughout the repair, one trial compared repair using chromic catgut with repair using Dexon. Also, there was considerable heterogeneity between studies regarding skill and training of persons carrying out the repair. The single trial that demonstrated a statistically significant reduction in short-term pain for women in the continuous subcuticular repair group was the trial that also ensured staff were trained and practised in this technique prior to the trial.

A recent UK RCT compared continuous versus interrupted perineal repair with standard or rapidly absorbed sutures.[432] [EL = 1+] The study was a 2 × 2 factorial design to allow both comparisons to be made. Findings from the trial relating to method of repair will be reported here (see the next subsection for findings from the materials arm of the trial). A continuous suturing technique for perineal repair (vaginal wall, perineal muscle and skin repaired with one continuous suture) (n = 771) was compared with interrupted sutures (continuous suture to vaginal wall, interrupted sutures to perineal muscle and skin) (n = 771). The trial included women with first- or second-degree tears or an episiotomy following a spontaneous birth. Continuous subcuticular sutures were associated with significantly less short-term perineal pain compared with interrupted sutures: pain at 2 days: 530/770 versus 609/770, OR 0.59 [95% CI 0.44 to 0.79]; pain at 10 days: 204/770 versus 338/769, OR 0.47 [95% CI 0.35 to 0.61]. This reduction in pain at 10 days was noted while sitting, walking, passing urine and opening bowels. No difference was noted between groups regarding long-term pain measures, for example: pain at 3 months: 70/751 versus 96/741, OR 0.70 [95% CI 0.46 to 1.07]; pain at 12 months: 31/700 versus 47/689, OR 0.64 [95% CI 0.35 to 1.16]; dyspareunia at 3 months: 98/581 versus 102/593, OR 0.98 [95% CI 0.72 to 1.33]; dyspareunia at 12 months: 94/658 versus 91/667, OR 1.05 [95% CI 0.77 to 1.43]. Fewer women with continuous sutures reported that the sutures were uncomfortable 2 days post-repair: 273/770 versus 318/770, OR 0.78 [95% CI 0.64 to 0.96]. This difference was slightly more marked at 10 days (OR 0.58 [95% CI 0.46 to 0.74]). Significantly more women in the interrupted group reported tight sutures both at 2 and 10 days, although the numbers were quite small. The need for suture removal was significantly higher in the interrupted group: suture removal between 10 days and 3 months: 22/751 versus 63/741, OR 0.36 [95% CI 0.23 to 0.55]. Wound gaping was more frequent following repair using the continuous technique, although again the numbers were quite small (wound gaping at 10 days: 23/770 versus 50/769, OR 0.46 [95% CI 0.29 to 0.74]). Significantly more women were satisfied with their perineal repair following repair using a continuous suture technique both at 3 months: 628/751 versus 560/741, OR 1.64 [95% CI 1.28 to 2.11] and 12 months: 603/700 versus 542/689, OR 1.68 [95%1.27 to 2.21]. Women in the continuous repair group were also more likely to report that they felt 'back to normal' at 3 months postpartum: 414/700 versus 332/689, OR 1.55 [95% CI 1.26 to 1.92]. It is noted that senior midwives (Grade G) were significantly more likely to use the continuous suturing technique compared with Grade E and F midwives. Subsequent analyses were undertaken taking this into consideration.

A UK RCT published in 1998 compared a two-stage perineal repair (n = 890) with the more usual three-stage repair (n = 890).[433] [EL = 1+] This trial also employed a 2 × 2 factorial design comparing both the method of repair and suture material used (findings regarding the latter are reported in the following subsection). At 2 days no differences were noted between the trial groups for any of the pain measures investigated: any pain in last 24 hours: 545/885 (62%) versus 569/889 (64%); analgesia in last 24 hours: 400/885 (45%) versus 392/889 (44%); tight stitches:162/885 (18%) versus 196/889 (22%). Significantly more women in the two-stage repair group had a gaping perineal wound: 203/885 (23%) versus 40/889 (4%), P < 0.00001. At 10 days, while there were no significant differences in reported pain and analgesia use (reported pain in last 24 hours: 221/886 (25%) versus 244/885 (28%); analgesia in last 24 hours: 73/886 (8%) versus 69/885 (8%)), significantly more women in the three-stage repair group reported tight stitches: 126/886 (14%) versus 163/885 (18%), RR 0.77 [95% CI 0.62 to 0.96], P = 0.02. Incidence of perineal gaping was still higher in the two-stage repair group at 10 days: 227/886 (26%) versus 145/885 (16%), P < 0.00001. Women in the two-stage repair group were also significantly less likely to have had suture material removed: 26/886 (3%) versus 67/885 (8%), P < 0.0001. Incidences of repair breakdown were very low and similar for the two groups (n = 5 versus n = 7). At 3 months postpartum there were no differences in most pain measures, for example: any pain in last week: 64/828 (8%) versus 87/836 (10%); resumption of sexual intercourse: 704/828 (85%) versus 712/836 (85%); resumption of pain-free intercourse: 576/828 (70%) versus 551/836 (66%). There was, however, a difference in reported dyspareunia: 128/890 (14.3%) versus 162/890 (18.2%), RR 0.80 [95% CI 0.65 to 0.99], P = 0.04. The difference for removal of suture material was still apparent at 3 months in favour of the continuous method group: 59/828 (7%) versus 98/836 (11%), RR 0.61 [95% CI 0.45 to 0.83]. There was little resuturing required and no difference between groups (n = 4 versus n = 9).

A 1 year postal questionnaire follow-up study was carried out for the above trial, involving 793 women.[434] [EL = 1+] The follow-up sample was deliberately biased to include 31% women who had had an instrumental birth (compared with 17% in the original sample). There was no difference between groups regarding persistent pain at 1 year: 28/396 versus 26/396. Women who had undergone the three-stage perineal repair were significantly more likely to report that the perineal area 'felt different' than women who had undergone two-stage repair: 17/395 versus 157/396, RR 0.75 [95% CI 0.61 to 0.91]. Subgroup analyses showed this difference to be more marked following spontaneous births compared with instrumental births: instrumental: 45/123 versus 55/124, RR 0.82 [95% CI 0.61 to 1.12]; spontaneous: 72/272 versus 102/272, RR 0.71 [95% CI 0.55 to 0.91]; and more marked following repair using interrupted sutures compared with mixed technique or subcuticular technique: interrupted technique: 57/209 versus 87/202, RR 0.63 [95% CI 0.48 to 0.83]; mixed technique: 46/133 versus 55/136, RR 0.86 [95% CI 0.63 to 1.17]; subcuticular: 14/53 versus 15/58, RR 1.02 [95% CI 0.55 to 1.91]. There were no significant differences between groups for dyspareunia, failure to resume pain-free intercourse or need for resuturing.

A second RCT conducted in Nigeria (2003) also compared two-stage repair with three-stage repair.[435] [EL = 1+] The trial was conducted across four sites and recruited 1077 women, 823 of whom were followed up to 3 months postnatally (response rate = 76.4%). As with the UK trial, midwives and labour ward obstetricians were trained in the two-stage repair technique prior to the study. Where skin repair was undertaken, a continuous technique was taught and encouraged. Most repairs were undertaken using chromic catgut. Postnatal assessments of wound healing were carried out by a researcher blinded to the trial allocation of the woman. Compared with three-stage repair, two-stage repair was associated with less pain and fewer reports of tight sutures at 48 hours postnatally (perineal pain: 57% versus 65%, RR 0.87 [95% CI 0.78 to 0.97); tight sutures: 25% versus 38%, RR 0.67 [95% CI 0.54 to 0.82)). Analgesia use and degree of inflammation and bruising were also significantly less in the two-stage group (analgesia use: 34% versus 49%, RR 0.71 [95% CI 0.60 to 0.83]; inflammation/bruising: 7% versus 14%, RR 0.50 [95% CI 0.33 to 0.77]). Wound gaping (skin edges > 0.5 cm apart) was more prevalent in the two-stage repair group: 26% versus 5%, RR 4.96 [95% CI 3.17 to 7.76]. The differences regarding perineal pain and analgesia were still apparent at 14 days and 6 weeks postpartum in favour of the two-stage repair group. The difference in wound gaping was much smaller by 14 days: 21% versus 17%, RR 1.25 [95% CI 0.94 to 1.67]. There was no difference in wound breakdown: 3% versus 2%, RR 1.27 [95% CI 0.56 to 2.85]. At 3 months postpartum, women in the two-stage repair group reported a lower incidence of dyspareunia compared with women in the three-stage repair group: 10% versus 17%, RR 0.61 [95% CI 0.43 to 0.87]. The authors pointed out that the differences in short-term pain found in this study may be due to the fact they used catgut for most of the perineal repairs rather than a synthetic absorbable suture material.

Evidence statement
There is high-level evidence that a continuous non-locked suturing technique for repair of perineal muscle is associated with less short-term pain More women who were repaired with a continuous non-locked technique were also satisfied with their perineal repair and felt back to normal at 3 months.

A two-stage repair (where the skin is opposed but not sutured) is associated with no differences in the incidence of repair breakdown but is associated with less dyspareunia at 3 months. There is some evidence that it is also associated with less short-term perineal pain when compared with skin repair undertaken using chromic catgut sutures.

Continuous subcuticular skin repair is associated with less short-term pain when compared with interrupted skin repair.

Recommendations on methods of perineal repair

If the skin is opposed following suturing of the muscle in second-degree trauma, there is no need to suture it.

Where the skin does require suturing, this should be undertaken using a continuous subcuticular technique.

Perineal repair should be undertaken using a continuous non-locked suturing technique for the vaginal wall and muscle layer.

Materials for perineal repair

Description of included studies
One systematic review and two additional RCTs have compared the effects of absorbable synthetic suture material with catgut or chromic catgut. An additional UK RCT compared rapidly absorbed synthetic suture material with standard synthetic suture material.

Review findings
One systematic review (1999) has been conducted to assess the effects of absorbable synthetic suture material compared with catgut on short- and long-term pain experienced by women following perineal repair.[436] [EL = 1+] The review included eight trials involving 3642 women. Seven trials used polyglycolic acid (Dexon) and one trial used polyglactin (Vicryl). Women allocated to groups using absorbable synthetic suture material reported significantly less short-

term pain compared with those sutured using catgut: day 3 or before: OR 0.62 [95% CI 0.54 to 0.71], eight trials; days 4–10: OR 0.71 [95% CI 0.58 to 0.87], three trials; analgesia use up to day 10: OR 0.63 [95% CI 0.52 to 0.77], five trials. Women allocated to perineal repair using absorbable synthetic suture material also reported less suture dehiscence up to day 10: OR 0.45 [95% CI 0.29 to 0.70], five trials; and need for resuturing of the perineal wound up to 3 months: OR 0.26 [95% CI 0.10 to 0.66], four trials. However, the need for removal of suture material up to 3 months was greater in the absorbable synthetic group: OR 2.01 [95% CI 1.56 to 2.58], two trials. There was no difference reported for long-term pain: OR 0.81 [95% CI 0.61 to 1.08], two trials. The authors of the review noted that the skill level of clinicians may be very different between trials, e.g. suture dehiscence in one trial was 37/71 for the control group and 12/77 for the experimental group, while in another trial there were no incidents of suture dehiscence.

One additional RCT has been conducted in Australia comparing absorbable synthetic suture material (polyglactin) (n = 194) with chromic catgut (n = 197).[437] [EL = 1+] Women with a third-degree tear or an instrumental birth were excluded from the trial. Owing to chance imbalance in the proportion of nulliparous women between the two trial groups, parity-adjusted odds ratios were calculated. There was a tendency towards reduced short-term pain in women allocated to the polyglactin group, but differences did not reach statistical significance: perineal pain at 1 day: adjusted OR 0.64 [95% CI 0.39 to 1.06]; perineal pain at 3 days: adjusted OR 0.70 [95% CI 0.46 to 1.08]. No significant differences were seen between groups for any of the longer-term pain outcomes (any perineal pain, resumed intercourse, dyspareunia) at 6 weeks, 3 months or 6 months. At 6 weeks postpartum, eight women repaired with polyglactin reported problems with their sutures compared with three women in the catgut group (one woman in each group reported infection at wound site, the remainder reported tight sutures that required removal) (adjusted OR 2.61 [95% CI 0.59 to 12.41]).

A recent US RCT compared the healing characteristics of chromic catgut with fast-absorbing polyglactin 910.[438] [EL = 1+] Although women were recruited and randomised into trial groups during labour, analysis was only performed for those women requiring perineal repair (polyglactin 910: 459/684; chromic catgut: 49/677). This study is unusual in that pain outcomes were measured both for the perineal area (referred to as 'vaginal' pain) and uterine cramping. No differences were found between groups for vaginal pain at 24–48 hours, 10–14 days or 6–8 weeks. There were, however, some differences in uterine pain, with significantly more women in the chromic catgut group reporting moderate/severe uterine pain at 24–48 hours: no pain: n = 81 (18%) versus n = 63 (14%), NS; a little/some pain: n = 264 (58%) versus n = 232 (52%), NS; moderate/severe pain: n = 114 (25%) versus n = 154 (34%), P = 0.006. This significant difference was also evident at 6–8 weeks. No differences in uterine pain were noted at 10–14 days. The authors have no explanation for the observed differences in uterine cramping between groups based on suture material used. Given that this difference was only seen at one of the two study sites they conclude that it may simply be an anomaly of the data. At 6–8 weeks no difference was found between groups for persistent suture material (n = 2 women in each group) or perineal wound breakdown (n = 4 versus n = 3).

A UK RCT compared rapidly absorbed synthetic suture material (n = 772) with a standard form of the synthetic suture material (n = 770) within a 2 × 2 factorial study design also comparing suture method.[432] [EL = 1+] The study involved women who had sustained either a second-degree tear or an episiotomy. There was no significant difference between the two groups for the primary outcome of pain at 10 days postnatally, although findings favoured the rapidly absorbed suture material: OR 0.84 [95% CI 0.68 to 1.04]. There was, however, a significant reduction in analgesia used in the previous 24 hours reported at 10 days for women in the rapidly absorbed suture material group: OR 0.55 [95% CI 0.36 to 0.83]; and a significant reduction in pain on walking for this group: OR 0.74 [95% CI 0.56 to 0.97]. The need for removal of sutures in the 3 months following birth was also less for women sutured with the rapidly absorbed suture material: OR 0.26 [95% CI 0.18 to 0.37].

Evidence statement
There is high-level evidence that a rapidly absorbable synthetic suture material is associated with less short-term pain, less suture dehiscence and less need for resuturing of the perineum up to 3 months postpartum.

Recommendations on materials for perineal repair

An absorbable synthetic suture material should be used to suture the perineum.

The following basic principles should be observed when performing perineal repairs:

- Perineal trauma should be repaired using aseptic techniques.
- Equipment should be checked and swabs and needles counted before and after the procedure.
- Good lighting is essential to see and identify the structures involved.
- Difficult trauma should be repaired by an experienced practitioner in theatre under regional or general anaesthesia. An indwelling catheter should be inserted for 24 hours to prevent urinary retention.
- Good anatomical alignment of the wound should be achieved, and consideration given to the cosmetic results.
- Rectal examination should be carried out after completing the repair to ensure that suture material has not been accidentally inserted through the rectal mucosa.
- Following completion of the repair, an accurate detailed account should be documented covering the extent of the trauma, the method of repair and the materials used.
- Information should be given to the woman regarding the extent of the trauma, pain relief, diet, hygiene and the importance of pelvic-floor exercises.

Research recommendation on analgesia during perineal repair

Research is needed into the optimum analgesia required during perineal repair.

Analgesia for perineal pain following perineal repair

Description of included studies
A systematic review of three RCTs and one additional RCT were identified which assessed the effectiveness of analgesic rectal suppositories for pain from perineal trauma following childbirth.

Review findings
A systematic review including 249 women assessed the effectiveness of analgesic rectal suppositories for pain from perineal trauma following childbirth.[439] [EL = 1+] All trials used nonsteroidal anti-inflammatory analgesia suppositories, one trial (Saudi Arabia) compared indometacin with a placebo, while the other two trials (UK) compared diclofenac (Voltarol) with a placebo. All trials administered a suppository immediately after perineal repair was complete. In one UK trial, a single dose of 100 mg was given, in the second (Saudi) trial, 2 × 100 mg suppositories were inserted together immediately following perineal repair, and in the third trial (UK), one suppository was given immediately after suturing and another 12 hours later. Findings suggest that nonsteroidal anti-inflammatory drugs (NSAIDs) administered as rectal suppositories provide effective pain relief following perineal repair (two trials). For indometacin the incidence of perineal pain in the first 24 hours was 6/30 versus 30/30, RR 0.20 [95% CI 0.10 to 0.41]; for diclofenac: RR 0.65 [95% CI 0.50 to 0.85]. The meta-analysis of these two findings produces a wide confidence interval that crosses 1 (RR 0.37 [95% CI 0.10 to 1.38] (two trials)). Findings from the other trial are reported as median scores obtained using a VAS. Women in the diclofenac group reported significantly less pain at 24 hours than women in the placebo group (diclofenac: median 1 [range 0 to 2.5], placebo: median 1 [range 0 to 3], $P < 0.05$ using Mann–Whitney U test). Only one trial included the outcome of any pain experienced 24–72 hours after perineal repair, with the effect of treatment just failing to reach statistical significance: RR 0.73 [95% CI 0.53 to 1.02]. Findings from a stratified analysis for level of pain experienced within the first 24 hours following perineal repair suggest that NSAIDs have their best level of effect for moderate pain compared with mild or severe pain: mild: RR 1.12 [95% CI 0.70 to 1.80] (two trials); moderate: RR 0.13 [95% CI 0.02 to 0.76] (two trials); severe: RR 0.21 [95% CI 0.01 to 4.12] (two trials). Use of additional analgesia was also measured as an outcome in two trials, although not in a way that allows pooling of data. Both trials showed a significant reduction in use of additional analgesia up to 48 hours postpartum. None of the trials reported longer term outcomes such as breastfeeding, effects on mother–infant interactions, postnatal depression or return to pain-free intercourse. All three trials

reported that there were no side effects associated with the treatment, although none investigated this as an identified outcome.

An RCT conducted in Australia (2004) also evaluated the effectiveness of rectal diclofenac compared with a placebo.[440] [EL = 1+] Women in the treatment group (n = 67) received a diclofenac suppository immediately after perineal repair (of a second-degree tear, third-degree tear or episiotomy). Women randomised to the control group received a placebo (Anusol) suppository. Both groups received a second suppository 12–24 hours later. Pain was measured in three ways – using the Short-form McGill Pain Questionnaire (SF-MPQ), using a 10 cm VAS and using the Present Pain Inventory (PPI). At 24 hours postnatally, women's pain scores were significantly lower for the treatment group compared with the control group, although this was not evident across all measurement scales: at rest: SF-MPQ total score: median 6 [IQR 3 to 11] versus 7 [IQR 3 to 12], NS; VAS: mean 2.8 [SD 0.3] versus 3.9 [SD 0.3]: RR −1.1 [95% CI −1.9 to −0.3], $P = 0.01$; PPI: mean 31 [SD 53.4] versus 32 [57.1]; RR 0.9 [95% CI 0.7 to 1.3], $P = 0.69$. For pain scores with movement at 24 hours both the VAS and the PPI score were significantly lower in the treatment group, although this difference was not evident for total SF-MPQ scores. By 48 hours there were no differences in reported pain between the two groups for any of the pain outcome measures. There was also no difference between groups regarding the use of additional analgesia prior to discharge: 81% versus 86%, RR 0.9 [95% CI 0.8 to 1.1] or time from birth to first analgesia (hours): median 6.4 [IQR 3.5 to 10.5] versus 5.8 [IQR 2.9 to 10.2]. Pain outcomes during activities at 10 days and 6 weeks postnatally were also similar for the two groups.

Evidence statement
There is high-level evidence that rectal NSAIDs reduce immediate perineal pain following repair.

Recommendation on analgesia for perineal pain following perineal repair

Rectal nonsteroidal anti-inflammatory drugs should be offered routinely following perineal repair of first- and second-degree trauma provided these drugs are not contraindicated.

11 Prelabour rupture of membranes at term

11.1 Prelabour rupture of membranes at term

Introduction

Little guidance exists on what advice women should be given following prelabour rupture of membranes (PRoM) at term, including how long it is safe to await the onset of labour, the potential role of prophylactic antibiotics and what observations should be carried out during this period. This section seeks to determine what should happen after contact with healthcare professionals when a diagnosis of term PRoM has been made.

For guidance relating to method of induction following ProM, please refer to the NICE clinical guideline on *Induction of Labour* (2001).[441] (Note that the update for this guideline is expected to be published in 2008.)

Clinical question

Is there evidence of factors or interventions that affect outcomes in term prelabour rupture of the membranes?

- Including septic screen for mother and baby.

Is there evidence that, following prelabour rupture of the membranes at term, the length of time from prelabour rupture of membranes (before onset of labour and total), digital vaginal examination, electronic fetal heart-rate monitoring, or frequency and type of maternal surveillance influence outcomes?

Following the birth of a healthy infant where there has been prelabour rupture of the membranes, is there evidence that the length of time from prelabour rupture of membranes (before onset and total), presence of pyrexia during or before labour, routine admission to neonatal units, frequency and type of neonatal observations, or frequency and type of neonatal investigations (including invasive tests) influence outcomes?

Is there evidence that the use of antibiotics before delivery in asymptomatic or symptomatic women with prelabour rupture of membranes influences outcomes?

What are the criteria for the use of antibiotics in healthy babies born following prelabour rupture of membranes?

Previous guideline

(PRoM has been considered in the guideline *Induction of Labour*.[441] Four systematic reviews were included. The summary of evidence concluded that there was no difference in instrumental birth rates (no distinction is made between vaginal instrumental births and caesarean sections) between induction versus a more conservative approach in women with term or near-term PRoM. Furthermore, a policy of induction of labour is associated with a reduction in infective sequelae for woman and baby. Two practice recommendations were made:

'Women with prelabour rupture of membranes at term (over 37 weeks) should be offered a choice of immediate induction of labour or expectant management.'

'Expectant management of labour of women with prelabour rupture of membranes at term should not exceed 96 hours following membrane rupture.'

11.1.1 Surveillance following term PRoM

Description of included studies
No evidence was found regarding the effect of carrying out electronic fetal heart rate (FHR) monitoring, checking of maternal temperature and pulse, or carrying out infection screening on women following PRoM.

11.1.2 Length of waiting period following term PRoM with no additional complications

Description of included studies
One systematic review (2006) of 12 trials involving 6814 women[442] plus secondary analyses of findings from an international, multicentre trial involving 72 institutions in six countries (*n* = 5041 women)[300] [EL = 2++] provides the evidence for this section.

Review findings
A systematic review has compared the effects of planned early birth (immediate induction of labour or induction within 24 hours) with expectant management (no planned intervention within 24 hours).[442] [EL = 1+] All trials involved only healthy women with an uncomplicated pregnancy of at least 37 completed weeks. Meta-analysis of findings showed that women in the planned early birth groups had a significantly shorter period of time from rupture of membranes to birth compared with women in the expectant management groups (five trials): WMD −9.53 hours [95% CI −12.96 to −6.10 hours]. Women in the planned early birth groups were less likely to develop chorioamnionitis than women in the expectant management group: 226/3300 versus 327/3311; RR 0.74 [95% CI 0.56 to 0.97]. Endometritis was less common in women allocated to the planned early birth groups: 5/217 versus 19/228; RR 0.30 [95% CI 0.12 to 0.74], although there was no significant difference between groups regarding incidence of postpartum fever: 82/2747 versus 117/2774; RR 0.69 [95% CI 0.41 to 1.17]. There was no difference between groups regarding mode of birth: caesarean section (CS): 333/3401 versus 360/3413; RR 0.94 [95% CI 0.82 to 1.08]; instrumental vaginal birth: 487/2786 versus 502/2825; RR 0.98 [95% CI 0.84 to 1.16]. The largest trial in the review (*n* = 5041) also investigated women's satisfaction with care. Women in the planned early birth group were significantly less likely to report that there was 'nothing liked' about the management of their care: 138/2517 versus 320/2524; RR 0.43 [95% CI 0.36 to 0.52]. Women in the planned early birth group were also more likely to say there was 'nothing disliked': 821/2517 versus 688/2524; RR 1.20 [95% CI 1.10 to 1.30]. It should be noted, however, that the comparison groups here were immediate induction of labour versus expectant management up to 96 hours. Babies born to women in the planned early birth groups were less likely to be admitted to neonatal intensive care unit (NICU) or special care baby unit (SCBU): 356/2825 versus 484/2854; RR 0.73 [95% CI 0.58 to 0.91]. However, this difference in admission rate may well reflect hospital policies rather than clinical need. No significant differences were found for any other investigated neonatal outcomes, including: fetal/perinatal mortality: 3/2946 versus 7/2924; RR 0.46 [95% CI 0.13 to 1.66]; Apgar score less than 7 at 5 minutes: 335/3000 versus 366/3005; RR 0.93 [95% CI 0.81 to 1.07]; mechanical ventilation: 25/2566 versus 28/2592; RR 0.99 [95% CI 0.46 to 2.12]; neonatal infection: 74/3210 versus 93/3196; RR 0.83 [95% CI 0.61 to 1.12].

Secondary analyses of data from an international, multicentre trial were performed to identify predictors of neonatal infection following term PRoM. Findings showed that longer periods of time from rupture of membranes to active labour were associated with a higher incidence of neonatal infection: 48 hours or longer versus 12 hours: OR 2.25 [95% CI 1.21 to 4.18]; 24 to 48 hours versus 12 hours: OR 1.97 [95% CI 1.11 to 3.48].

11.1.3 Place of care for women with term PRoM

Description of included studies
Secondary analyses of data from a large, international trial (*n* = 1670 women),[443] one small UK RCT (*n* = 56)[444] and a Danish prospective observational study (*n* = 276)[445] provide the evidence for this section.

Review findings

The term ProM study data set was also analysed to determine whether adverse effects of expectant management of term PRoM and women's satisfaction were greater if women were cared for at home rather than in hospital.[443] [EL = 2+] The analysis involved 653 women managed at home compared with 1017 managed as hospital inpatients. Multiple logistic regression analyses showed that women having their first baby were more likely to have antibiotics if they were cared for at home, compared with women having their first baby cared for in hospital: OR 1.52 [95% CI 1.04 to 2.24]. Women who were not colonised with group B streptococcus (GBS) were more likely to have CS if they were cared for at home rather than in hospital: OR 1.48 [95% CI 1.03 to 2.14]. Multiparous women were more likely to say they 'would participate in the study again' if they were cared for at home rather than in hospital: OR 1.80 [95% CI 1.27 to 2.54]. The risk of neonatal infection was higher if women were cared for at home compared with in hospital: OR 1.97 [95% CI 1.00 to 3.90].

An RCT (2002) compared expectant management at home ($n = 29$) with expectant management in hospital ($n = 27$) for women with term PRoM.[444] [EL = 1−] Women in both groups were induced if labour had not started by the time 24 hours had elapsed. There was no difference between groups regarding time from rupture of membranes to birth (home: 31.39 hours (SD 12.70 hours); hospital: 26.99 hours (SD 11.78 hours), t value = 1.34, $P = 0.18$). No differences were found between groups for: maternal infection on first admission (high vaginal swab on admission): 7/28 versus 9/27, $\chi^2 = 0.46$, $P = 0.49$; maternal infection at the onset of labour (high vaginal swab at onset of labour): 14/24 versus 11/23, $\chi^2 = 0.521$ $P = 0.47$, or neonatal infection (neonatal infection screen negative): 12/17 (12 not screened) versus 11/12 (15 not screened), $\chi^2 = 2.98$, $P = 0.23$. The authors acknowledge, however, that the trial is underpowered to detect a significant difference in these outcomes.

A prospective observational study compared outcomes for women managed at home with outpatient check-ups to await spontaneous onset of labour following term PRoM ($n = 176$) with a historical group of women managed as hospital inpatients with induction of labour between 6–12 hours ($n = 100$).[445] [EL = 2−] Women managed at home were asked to check their temperature twice daily and attend the antenatal clinic every other day for electronic FHR monitoring and to check for signs of infection. The range of time intervals from rupture of membranes to birth for women in the intervention group (10th–90th centile) was 14–85 hours. Although maternal infectious morbidity, fetal distress during labour and instrumental vaginal birth due to failure to progress were higher in the intervention group where there was longer elapsed time from rupture of membranes to birth, this did not reach statistical significance. The incidence of neonatal infectious morbidity was 2% in each study group. There were two neonatal deaths in the expectant management at home group; however, neither baby had positive cultures for infection.

11.1.4 Risk factors associated with maternal infection following term PRoM

Description of included studies

Evidence for this section is drawn from subgroup analyses carried out as part of the systematic review of 12 trials described above[442] [EL = 1+] plus secondary analyses of findings from the international, multicentre trial.[443,446] [EL = 2++] One small quasi-RCT,[447] [EL = 1−] one prospective observational study[449] [EL = 2+] and a retrospective case–control study[448] [EL = 2+] are also included.

Review findings

Parity

Subgroup analyses of findings from the systematic review described above investigated the effects of parity on maternal and neonatal outcome following term PRoM.[442] [EL = 1+] No significant differences were found between outcomes for nulliparous and multiparous women.

A retrospective case–control study of women with PRoM at 37 weeks of pregnancy or more has been conducted in Israel (2004) ($n = 132$ cases and $n = 279$ controls).[448] [EL = 2+] The study compared three groups of women: those who had had labour induced immediately; women who had been managed expectantly up to 24 hours and then induced; and women who had been managed expectantly for over 24 hours. The primary outcome was chosen as all infection, no distinction being made between maternal and neonatal infection, although it is noted that the rate of neonatal infection overall was very low (less than 1%). Multivariate analysis by stepwise logistic regression revealed that nulliparity was independently associated with infections in the woman and the baby (maternal and neonatal): OR 1.92 [95% CI 1.19 to 3.00].

Unfavourable/favourable cervix

The systematic review also undertook a subgroup analysis to investigate the effects of an unfavourable versus a mixed state or unstated state of cervix.[442] [EL = 1+] No significant differences were found between outcomes when comparing these two subgroups.

A small US quasi-randomised RCT compared immediate induction of labour (n = 32) with expectant management (n = 35) for women with PRoM between 38 and 41 weeks of pregnancy.[447] [EL = 1–] All women included in the study had a cervix which was deemed unfavourable for induction of labour (2 cm or less dilated and no more than 50% effaced). The incidence of endometritis was higher in the immediate induction group: 4/35 versus 10/32, P = 0.04 (Fisher's Exact Test). This may be partly explained by the longer labours observed for women in this group: (mean) 10.44 hours (SD 5.5 hours) versus 14.1 hours (SD 6.0 hours); and the higher number of vaginal examinations performed during labour for women in this group: (mean) 3.9 versus 5.7. There were no incidents of neonatal sepsis in either group.

Vaginal examinations

The international, multicentre trial of term PRoM also investigated predictors of clinical chorioamnionitis and postpartum fever.[443,446] [EL = 2++] The predictors were calculated using secondary analysis of trial data which compared immediate with expectant management for up to 4 days following term PRoM. Clinical chorioamnionitis was defined as one or more of the following: maternal fever greater than 37.5 °C on two or more occasions 1 hour or more apart, or a single temperature greater than 38 °C before giving birth; maternal white blood cell count greater than 20 000 cells/mm³ or foul-smelling amniotic fluid.[446] [EL = 2++] Clinical chorioamnionitis occurred in 6.7% women (n = 335). The number of vaginal examinations (VEs) was found to be the most important independent predictor, the risk of infection rising as the number of VEs increases. For example: less than 3 VEs versus 3–4 VEs: OR 2.06 [95% CI 1.07 to 3.97]; while less than 3 VEs versus 7–8 VEs: OR 3.80 [95% CI 1.92 to 7.53], and the incidence of chorioamnionitis increased from 2% to 13%.

The retrospective case–control study conducted in Israel also found number of vaginal examinations to be an independent predictor of infection (maternal and/or neonatal).[448] [EL = III] Women who had undergone seven or more vaginal examinations during labour were found to be at increased risk of infection (themselves or their baby) compared with women who had been examined vaginally less than seven times (OR 2.70 [95% CI 1.66 to 4.34]).

Duration of labour

Secondary analysis of data from the large, international multicentre trial of term PRoM also found that the effect of duration of active labour became very significant once labour duration exceeded 9 hours, with the incidence of chorioamnionitis being 12% compared with 2% where labour lasted less than 3 hours (OR 2.94 [95% CI 1.75 to 4.94]).[446] [EL = 2++] The effect of the length of the latent interval becomes statistically significant for durations over 12 hours: 12 to less than 24 hours versus less than 12 hours, incidence of infection 10% (n = 115) OR 1.77 [95% CI 1.27 to 2.47]; greater than and equal to 48 hours versus less than 12 hours, incidence of infection 10% (n = 68) OR 1.76 [95% CI 1.21 to 2.55]. Postpartum fever occurred in 3% of the study participants (n = 146).[446] [EL = 2++] The most significant independent predictor of postpartum fever was clinical chorioamnionitis (OR 5.37 [95% CI 3.60 to 8.00]). Duration of labour was also an important predictor, with the incidence rising from 2% for labour 3 hours to less than 6 hours (OR 3.04 [95% CI 1.30 to 7.09]) to 8% for labour 12 hours or longer (OR 4.86 [95% CI 2.07 to 11.4]).

Bathing

A prospective observational study conducted in Sweden compared rates of maternal and neonatal infection between women who chose to bathe following PRoM (n = 538) and those who chose not to bathe (n = 847).[449] [EL = 2+] All women in the study had PRoM at or after 34 weeks of gestation: mean gestational age in each group 39 weeks (SD 1.5 and 1.6). Women were advised not to have a bath if there was meconium-stained liquor, fetal distress or any signs of infection (not defined). There were a significantly higher proportion of nulliparous women in the bathing group (78% versus 53%). There was a low frequency of maternal and neonatal infections. Chorioamnionitis during labour occurred in 1.1% (n = 6) women in the bath group and 0.2% (n = 2) in the no-bath group, P = 0.06. There were three incidents of endometritis in each group, 0.6% and 0.4%, respectively, P = 0.68. The frequency of neonates receiving antibiotics was 3.7% and 4.8%, respectively (P = 0.43).

Risk factors associated with neonatal infection
Secondary analyses of the findings from the international, multicentre trial of term PRoM trial were performed in order to identify independent predictors of neonatal infection.[300] [EL = 2++] Neonatal infection was defined as either definite or probable based upon clinical signs supported by at least one of an extensive range of well-recognised laboratory tests. Definite or probable infection occurred in 2.6% of neonates (n = 133). The strongest predictor of neonatal infection following term PRoM was clinical chorioamnionitis (OR 5.89 [95% CI 2.02 to 4.68]). Other independent predictors identified included positive maternal GBS status (compared with unknown or negative) (OR 3.08 [95% CI 1 2.02 to 4.68]); 7 or 8 VEs (compared with 0 to 2) (OR 2.37 [95% CI 1.03 to 5.43]); and maternal antibiotics administered before birth (OR 1.63 [95% CI 1.01 to 2.62]).

11.1.5 Use of intrapartum prophylactic antibiotics

Description of included studies
A systematic review of two RCTs[450] (n = 838 women) [EL = 1+] and subgroup analysis from a systematic review of 12 RCTs[442] [EL = 1+] provide the evidence for this section.

Review findings
A systematic review has been conducted to assess the effects of antibiotics administered prophylactically to women with PRoM at 36 weeks or beyond.[450] [EL = 1+] Two trials were included in the review, involving a total of 838 women. Both trials used management policies involving the administration of IV antibiotics and delayed induction of labour with oxytocin (up to 24 hours). The use of antibiotics resulted in a statistically significant reduction in: endometritis, RR 0.09 [95% CI 0.01 to 0.73]; chorioamnionitis and/or endometritis (3% versus 7%), RR 0.43 [95% CI 0.23 to 0.82]; and a reduction in the neonatal length of hospital stay (reported by one trial), mean difference −0.90 days [95% CI −1.34 to −0.46 days]. No other significant differences were found, including no significant differences in outcomes for neonatal morbidity.

Subgroup analysis from a second systematic review including 12 RCTs also examined the effects of administering prophylactic antibiotics.[442] [EL = 1+] Because of the limitations of the included trials, the comparison groups were not usefully defined, with the resultant comparison being between trials where all women had received antibiotics versus trials where some women had received antibiotics. No differences were found between the two sets of trials for incidence of maternal or neonatal infection.

Evidence statement
There is high-level evidence that shows an increase in neonatal infection when membranes rupture at term before labour starts. This risk increases with the duration of membrane rupture and while neonatal infection is rare, it is potentially serious and can result in death or disability. Expectant management up to 24 hours shows no evidence of a significant increase in neonatal infection rates. There is absence of evidence on long-term outcomes.

For other neonatal outcomes or instrumental vaginal birth or CS rates, there are no differences between immediate induction and expectant management up to 96 hours after membrane rupture. There is significant increase in the risk of chorioamnionitis and endometritis in the mother with expectant management over 24 hours. There is no evidence for expectant management over 96 hours after membrane rupture, as the vast majority of women have given birth by then.

There is limited high-level evidence of the effect of routine maternal antibiotic prophylaxis for term PRoM on infection rates, but results are conflicting.

Recommendations
See the end of this chapter for all recommendations relating to prelabour rupture of membranes.

11.1.6 Prolonged rupture of membranes and intrapartum fever as risk factors of neonatal infection

Description of included studies
There was one cohort study within a randomised controlled trial[300] and six observational studies that were identified.[451–456] Among them, two were conducted in the UK.[453,455] All the studies, except for one,[456] investigated GBS-related disease as an outcome.

Review findings
Babies of women with PRoM, who enrolled in the international, multicentre RCT comparing induction of labour and expectant management, were observed to investigate various risk factors for developing neonatal infection.[300] [EL = 2+] Multivariate analysis showed the following as risk factors for neonatal infection: clinical chorioamnionitis (OR 5.89, $P < 0.001$); positive maternal GBS status (versus negative or unknown, OR 3.08, $P < 0.001$); seven to eight vaginal digital examinations (versus 0 to 2, OR 2.37, $P = 0.04$); 24 to less than 48 hours from membrane rupture to active labour (versus less than 12 hours, OR 1.97, $P = 0.02$); 48 hours or less from membrane rupture to active labour (versus less than 12 hours, OR 2.25, $P = 0.01$); and maternal antibiotics before birth (OR 1.63, $P = 0.05$).

A UK cross-sectional study was conducted in 2000/2001 involving all babies with GBS disease in the UK and Ireland, younger than 90 days.[453] [EL = 3] Among the total of 568 babies, incidence of GBS disease was assumed to be 0.72 per 1000 live births [95% CI 0.66 to 0.78]. Mothers of 140 babies (44%) had prolonged rupture of membranes.

A UK case–control study was conducted between 1998 and 2000.[455] [EL = 2+] A total of 37 cases of early onset neonatal GBS sepsis were compared with 147 hospital controls. A logistic regression analysis showed that risk of developing early onset neonatal GBS sepsis for babies from women with prolonged rupture of membranes longer than 18 hours was RR 4.8 [95% CI 0.98 to 23.1], and with rupture of membranes before onset of labour: RR 3.6 [95% CI 0.7 to 17.6].

A Danish cross-sectional study was conducted between 1992 and 2001.[454] [EL = 3] A total of 61 babies with blood-culture-positive GBS sepsis/meningitis were investigated (incidence 0.76 per 1000 live births [95% CI 0.0 to 1.91]). Nineteen percent of the babies had a mother with prolonged rupture of membranes (longer than 18 hours) and 16% of those had maternal pyrexia (higher than 38 °C).

A Dutch case–control study was conducted between 1988 and 1995.[451] [EL = 2+] A total of 41 neonatal early onset GBS-related cases were compared with 123 hospital controls. A multivariate analysis showed that there was an increased risk of developing early onset GBS-related disease when maternal temperature increased by 0.1 above 37.4 °C (OR 2.0 [95% CI 1.4 to 2.8]), but there was no evidence of association between interval from rupture of membranes to birth (OR per hour between 8 and 24 hours 1.0 [95% CI 0.92 to 1.1]) and prolonged rupture of membranes (OR 2.0 [95% CI 0.47 to 9.6]).

A US cohort study was conducted in 1987/88.[456] [EL = 2–] Babies of 205 women with a history of prolonged rupture of membranes were compared with 8586 babies of women without a history of prolonged rupture of membranes. Among 175 out of 205 babies following prolonged rupture of membranes of 24 hours or more, 8.2% yielded positive blood culture. In comparison, 0.1% had positive blood culture from the remaining 8586 babies of women without prolonged rupture of membranes.

A US case–control study was conducted between 1991 and 1992.[452] [EL = 2+] Ninety-nine cases of early onset GBS disease were compared with 253 matched hospital controls. A multivariate logistic regression analysis showed strong evidence of association between increased risk of developing early onset GBS disease and prolonged rupture of membranes (OR 8.7, $P < 0.001$) and intrapartum fever (OR 4.3, $P < 0.05$).

Evidence statement

There is medium-level evidence that risk of developing early onset GBS-related disease, for babies born to women with prolonged rupture of membranes, ranges between 2.0 and 8.7 times higher than those born to women without. The risk of developing fever is about four-fold higher in babies born to women with PRoM when compared with babies born to women without. Up to 40% of babies with early onset GBS-related disease were born to women with prolonged rupture of membranes in the UK.

11.1.7 Clinical manifestation of babies

Description of included studies

One cohort study and two case series were identified, all of which were conducted in the USA.[456-458] One study compared laboratory test results between symptomatic and asymptomatic babies.[456] The other two studies investigated time of onset of symptoms for neonatal infection.

Review findings

Symptoms and laboratory tests

One cohort study was conducted in the USA.[456] [EL = 2+] In the 175 babies born to women with prolonged rupture of membranes, using blood culture and complete blood counts results, six symptomatic infants were compared with nine asymptomatic babies. Out of the six symptomatic babies, all had abnormal complete blood counts (two with abnormal white blood cell counts; five with abnormal neutrophil count; four with high band/metamyelocyte count; four with increased immature to total neutrophil ratio). Of the nine asymptomatic babies, seven had abnormal complete blood counts, five with a high white blood cell count, five with a high neutrophil count, two had a high band/metamyelocyte count and one with a high immature to total neutrophil ratio. The sensitivity of the complete blood count was 86% and specificity 66%.

Onset of symptoms

The other two studies investigated time of onset of symptoms for early onset neonatal GBS disease. The first study was conducted between 1995 and 1996, targeting babies with 2000 g birthweight or more.[458] [EL = 3] The study reported that 75.8% of babies with sepsis were first noted to be at risk for sepsis before or at the moment of birth, and 91.2% were identified by 12 hours of age. The second study specifically investigated early onset GBS disease.[457] [EL = 3] The population included 37% of preterm babies. The study reported that the median age at onset was 20 minutes ranging from 0 to 77 hours. Sixty-three percent of the babies showed clinical signs within 1 hour of age and 90% were symptomatic within 12 hours.

Evidence statement

There is low-level evidence that over 90% of neonatal sepsis presents within 12 hours of age. The majority of babies with sepsis were first noted to be at risk before or at the moment of birth. There is insufficient evidence on the diagnostic value of tests for neonatal sepsis.

11.1.8 Postnatal prophylactic antibiotics for babies

Description of included studies

One systematic review with two trials[459] and one observational study[458] were identified. One of the trials included assessed effectiveness of prophylactic antibiotics on babies born to women with GBS colonisation, hence excluded from this review. The other trial investigated effectiveness of prophylactic antibiotics (intramuscular penicillin and kanamycin for 7 days, $n = 24$), compared with no prophylactics ($n = 25$).[459] [EL = 1−] The second study, a population-based cohort study in the USA, investigated the relationship between predictors and neonatal bacterial infection.[458] [EL = 2+]

Review findings

The trial that investigated the effectiveness of prophylactic antibiotics compared with no antibiotics reported no neonatal mortality. It was underpowered to show any differences in incidence of neonatal sepsis (RR 0.12 [95% CI 0.01 to 2.04]).

The US cohort study evaluated 2785 out of 18 299 newborns of 2000 g or more, without major abnormalities for sepsis, with a complete blood count and/or blood culture. Multivariate analysis showed that among 1568 babies whose mothers did not receive antibiotics, initial asymptomatic status was associated with decreased risk of infection (OR 0.27 [95% CI 0.11 to 0.65]). However, there was evidence of an increased risk of neonatal sepsis by antepartum fever (highest antepartum temperature 101.5 °F (38.6 °C) or higher (OR 5.78 [95% CI 1.57 to 21.29]), rupture of membranes for 12 hours or longer (OR 2.05 [95% CI 1.06 to 3.96]), low absolute neutrophil count for age (OR 2.82 [95% CI 1.50 to 5.34]), and meconium in amniotic fluid (OR 2.24 [95% CI 1.19 to 4.22]).

Evidence statement
There is no high-level evidence from trials on prophylactic antibiotics for babies born to women with prolonged rupture of membranes at term.

There is medium-level evidence that, if the baby is asymptomatic at birth, there is a significantly lower risk of it developing neonatal sepsis.

Recommendations on prelabour rupture of membranes

There is no reason to carry out a speculum examination with a certain history of rupture of the membranes at term.

Women with an uncertain history of prelabour rupture of the membranes should be offered a speculum examination to determine whether their membranes have ruptured. Digital vaginal examination in the absence of contractions should be avoided.

Women presenting with prelabour rupture of the membranes at term should be advised that:

- the risk of serious neonatal infection is 1% rather than 0.5% for women with intact membranes
- 60% of women with prelabour rupture of the membranes will go into labour within 24 hours
- induction of labour* is appropriate approximately 24 hours after rupture of the membranes.

Until the induction is commenced or if expectant management beyond 24 hours is chosen by the woman:

- lower vaginal swabs and maternal C-reactive protein should not be offered
- to detect any infection that may be developing women should be advised to record their temperature every 4 hours during waking hours and to report immediately any change in the colour or smell of their vaginal loss
- women should be informed that bathing or showering are not associated with an increase in infection, but that having sexual intercourse may be.

Fetal movement and heart rate should be assessed at initial contact and then every 24 hours following rupture of the membranes while the woman is not in labour, and the woman should be advised to report immediately any decrease in fetal movements.

If labour has not started 24 hours after rupture of the membranes, women should be advised to give birth where there is access to neonatal services and advised to stay in hospital for at least 12 hours following the birth.

If there are no signs of infection in the woman, antibiotics should not be given to either the woman or the baby, even if the membranes have been ruptured for over 24 hours.

If there is evidence of infection in the woman, a full course of broad-spectrum intravenous antibiotics should be prescribed.

Women with prelabour rupture of the membranes should be asked to inform their healthcare professionals immediately of any concerns they have about their baby's wellbeing in the first 5 days following birth, particularly in the first 12 hours when the risk of infection is greatest.

---

* Care of women who have their labour induced is covered by 'Induction of labour' (inherited clinical guideline D).

Blood, cerebrospinal fluid and/or surface culture tests should not be performed in an asymptomatic baby.

Asymptomatic term babies born to women with prelabour rupture of the membranes (more than 24 hours before labour) should be closely observed for the first 12 hours of life (at 1 hour, 2 hours and then 2 hourly for 10 hours). These observations should include:

- general wellbeing
- chest movements and nasal flare
- skin colour including perfusion, by testing capillary refill
- feeding
- muscle tone
- temperature
- heart rate and respiration.

A baby with any symptom of possible sepsis, or born to a woman who has evidence of chorio-amnionitis, should immediately be referred to a neonatal care specialist.

Research recommendations on routine antibiotics for women with prelabour rupture of membranes

A randomised controlled trial to evaluate the effect of routine administration of prophylactic antibiotics on neonatal infection, in women with term prelabour rupture of membranes, over 24 hours.

The investigation and management of babies born with risk factors for infection requires further evaluation.

For further advice on newborn care immediately after birth, refer to Chapters 10 and 16.

12 Meconium-stained liquor

12.1 Monitoring and treatment of women with meconium-stained liquor

Introduction
Between 15% and 20% of term pregnancies are associated with meconium-stained liquor (MSL), which, in the vast majority of labours, is not a cause of concern. However, in some circumstances, the passage of meconium *in utero* is associated with significant increases in perinatal morbidity and mortality. The aspiration of meconium into the lungs during intrauterine gasping, or when the baby takes its first breath, can result in a life-threatening disorder known as meconium aspiration syndrome (MAS) and this accounts for 2% of perinatal deaths.

Four main types of intervention were found in the literature that may influence outcomes of labour where there is MSL, namely: use of a scoring system for MSL; amnioinfusion; prophylactic intrapartum antibiotics; and suctioning of the baby at birth (oropharyngeal, nasopharyngeal and endotracheal). The first three of these will be addressed in turn below, following review of a small study that was undertaken to determine the risk factors associated with MAS.

Clinical question
Is there any evidence that identification and management of meconium-stained liquor affect outcomes?

Previous guideline
Meconium-stained liquor has been considered in the guideline *Use of Electronic Fetal Monitoring*.[460] It states: 'Meconium-stained liquor was found to be associated with an increased risk of cerebral palsy and death in one case–control study but not with cerebral palsy in a large cohort study. Meconium-stained liquor is a significant risk factor for neonatal encephalopathy'.

12.1.1 Grading of meconium-stained liquor

Description of included studies and review findings
A retrospective cohort study has examined the use of a meconium scoring system and its impact on neonatal outcomes.[461] [EL = 2+] Eighty meconium-stained babies were scored for: presence of fetal distress; meconium quality/thickness; performance of nasopharyngeal suctioning before first breath; and clinical condition in first minute of life. A low score (0 or 1) indicated the need for oropharyngeal suctioning only, while a score of 2 or more indicated that intubation and endotracheal suctioning should be performed. Outcomes for these babies were compared with a randomly selected sample from the previous year. Protocol for the comparison group was laryngoscopy to allow visualisation of the vocal cords followed by endotracheal intubation and suctioning if meconium was present at the cords. Outcomes investigated included Apgar scores, intubation and MAS. The comparison group comprised women who were significantly older and of a significantly higher parity than the intervention group. There was a significantly higher proportion of baby girls in the intervention group. Mode of birth, presence of fetal distress, Apgar scores, mean gestation and mean birthweight did not differ significantly between the two groups. While the use of the scoring system reduced the rate of endotracheal intubation (22.5% versus 30%), this difference is not statistically significant. No significant differences were noted for any of the outcomes studied.

A cross-sectional study assessed inter- and intra-observer agreement of grading of MSL in Australia.[462] Four samples, each of clear, lightly (thin), moderately, and heavily (thick) meconium-stained amniotic fluid were divided in two portions, which were assessed by 20 midwives (a total of 320 samples). Although there was a good agreement in defining a clear sample, there is not a good agreement between midwives' assessment and the standard agreed for the study. Mean kappa values for inter-observer agreement were 0.52 [range 0.13 to 0.79] at the first assessment and 0.57 [range 0.21 to 0.75] at the second assessment, and that intra-observer agreement was 0.64 [range 0.24 to 0.91] and 0.63 [range 0.42 to 0.91], respectively.

A cross-sectional study of 106 women evaluated the diagnostic value of 'meconiumcrit' (percentage by volume of the solid component of meconium) on umbilical artery pH and Apgar score in the USA.[463] A 10 ml sample of amniotic fluid was collected by an intrauterine pressure catheter. The sample was centrifuged in a glass tube. The meconiumcrit was measured by diving the solid volume by the total volume, as with haematocrit, and the samples were graded as thin, moderate, and thick according to the solid component by volume (< 10%, 10% to 30%, and 30%, respectively). Meconium was also graded by physicians. There was good correlation between physicians' subjective assessment and meconiumcrit (Spearman's rho = 1.00, Pearson's r = 0.997, P = 0.05). There was no correlation between the grading of meconium and umbilical artery pH < 7.20 (13%, 19% and 11%, respectively). There was no evidence of good correlation between the grading and Apgar score (less than 6 at 1 minute, 5%, 14% and 22%, P > 0.05; less than 6 at 5 minutes, 2%, 3% and 11%, respectively, P > 0.05). None of the babies with thin or moderate meconium had MAS, although there were two babies with MAS from thick meconium.

Evidence statement
There is limited poor-quality evidence of the use of grading for meconium-stained liquor and its impact on neonatal outcomes.

There is no evidence that shows good correlation of grading of meconium-stained liquor in relation to inter/intra observer agreement.

12.1.2 Meconium-stained liquor, continuous EFM and babies' outcomes

Description of included studies
No studies were identified that looked at the effect on outcomes of using continuous EFM for women in labour with MSL. Seven observational studies were found that examined the relationship between MSL and abnormal fetal heart rate (FHR) tracings for women in labour with no medical or obstetric complications. The overall quality of reporting of the included studies is quite poor, making it difficult to determine the rigour with which they have been conducted. Where information is missing, it has been assumed that the underlying method was lacking in rigour.

Review findings
A UK cross-sectional study (data collected during 1984) was carried out to investigate the relationships between FHR patterns, MSL, umbilical cord artery pH and Apgar score.[464] [EL = 2+] Over a 6-month period, a study group was defined retrospectively including all women who experienced labour and who had a complete data set recorded (i.e. FHR trace, cord artery pH, presence or absence of meconium and Apgar scores) (n = 698). Associations between all four variables were explored. MSL was present in 115/698 (16%). The MSL was not graded. No relationship was found between MSL and either cord artery pH or base deficit (figures not given). There was a significantly greater incidence of Apgar scores less than 7 at 1 minute for babies born through MSL compared with babies with clear amniotic fluid (41/115 (36%) versus 78/583 (13%), P = 0.0005). This difference was also evident for Apgar scores less than 7 at 5 minutes (7/115 (6%) versus 9/583 (1.5%), P < 0.005). When combining MSL and FHR tracings, if the FHR tracing was abnormal during the first stage of labour, the mean cord artery pH was significantly lower for babies with MSL than for those with clear liquor (pH 7.17 (SD 0.12) versus pH 7.22 (SD 0.10), P < 0.02). The association between MSL and low Apgar scores existed regardless of FHR tracing classification. Stepwise multiple regression analysis revealed that the major contributor to cord artery pH was an abnormal FHR tracing (r = 0.345). MSL did not correlate significantly (r = 0.039). Adding MSL to FHR tracing did not significantly improve the correlation. Of all the other variables considered for the model (woman's age, parity, marital status, gestational age, mode of birth, length of labour and birthweight), only gestational age (pH falling with increasing gestational age, r = 0.13) and mode of birth (r = 0.14) correlated significantly with pH. For low Apgar scores at 1 minute, the major correlation was mode of birth (r = 0.25) and MSL (r = 0.224). FHR tracing classification was the next most important (r = 0.186). Adding MSL to the FHR tracing significantly increased the r value to 0.274, and adding mode of birth further improved it to 0.41.

A cross-sectional US study compared measurements of wellbeing of 128 babies with late MSL (i.e. meconium observed in labour after an initial intrapartum period of clear liquor).[465] [EL = 2+] The sample represents women with a complete data set drawn from a population of 166 women in labour with late MSL. The women next to labour and give birth without MSL formed a comparison group. One hundred and thirty-four women had a complete data set and were included in the final sample. Intrapartum and postpartum details were collected prospectively. FHR tracings were interpreted by an investigator blinded to study group allocation and classified according to predetermined criteria. No significant difference was noted between women with late MSL and those with clear liquor for the following FHR and neonatal variables: periodic accelerations (> 10 bpm), non-periodic accelerations, good baseline variability, early decelerations, variable decelerations, late decelerations, repeated (> 20) late decelerations, Apgar score 7 or less at 1 minute, and Apgar score 7 or less at 5 minutes. Two variables were found to be associated with the presence of meconium: repeated early decelerations (17.2% versus 7.5%, $P = 0.27$) and repeated variable decelerations (28.9% versus 15.7%, $P = 0.015$). In babies born to women with late MSL, the absence of non-periodic accelerations increased the likelihood of an Apgar score 7 or less at 1 minute (53.8% versus 32.4%, $P = 0.45$), but not at 5 minutes (12.1% versus 0%, $P > 0.05$). The absence of good baseline variability increased the likelihood of an Apgar score 7 or less at 5 minutes (19.4% versus 2.5%, $P = 0.007$), but not at 1 minute (61.3% versus 39.5%, $P > 0.05$). The presence of repeated variable decelerations increased the chance of an Apgar score 7 or less at 5 minutes (18.9% versus 4.4%, $P = 0.02$) but not at 1 minute (56.8% versus 44.0%, $P > 0.05$).

A UK prospective observational study (1992) investigated the validity of MSL as an indicator for fetal blood sampling (FBS).[466] [EL = 3] Details were collected by obstetricians performing the FBS, who were asked to record the indication for the blood sampling and whether they felt the FHR tracing was normal or abnormal. The FHR tracing was also classified retrospectively by a senior obstetrician and classified as normal, abnormal or severely abnormal using a predetermined classification system. It is not stated whether or not this second classification process was blinded. No distinction was made between thin and thick meconium. At the time of FBS, meconium was present in 165 of the 401 women who took part in the study. In 77 of the 165 women, the FHR tracing was classified as normal both by the attending obstetrician and at second assessment by the senior obstetrician (group A). In 31 of the 165 women, the FHR tracing was recoded as normal by the attending obstetrician but was later classified as abnormal or severely abnormal by the senior obstetrician (group B). In 18 women, the reverse was true, where an FHR tracing identified as abnormal by the attending obstetrician was later classified as normal by the senior obstetrician (group C). For the remaining 39 women, both obstetricians classified the FHR tracing as abnormal or severely abnormal (group D). The fetal blood sample pH was significantly higher in group A compared with group D (median [IQR] 7.36 [7.33 to 7.39] versus 7.31 [7.27 to 7.35], $P < 0.01$). Fetal blood base excess was significantly greater in group D compared with group A [−4.5 (−6.4 to −1.5] versus −2.3 [−6.0 to −0.8], $P = 0.01$). Apgar scores at 1 minute were also significantly lower in group D as compared with babies in group A (8 [7 to 9] versus 9 [8 to 9], $P = 0.01$). No significant difference was found in cord artery pH values between the two groups. It should be noted, however, that only a small subsample of women had cord artery pH values measured ($n = 15$ in group A; $n = 17$ in group D).

A cross-sectional study collected details of all women with uncomplicated pregnancies who gave birth at one hospital in Jordan, during a 6-month period in 1997.[467] [EL = 2+] Of the total sample of 4068 births, 344 (8.5%) had MSL and, of these, 90.4% had particulate meconium. Birth by caesarean section (CS) was significantly more frequent in women with MSL (36/344 (10.5%) versus 31/3288 (0.94%)). Comparisons are made between babies who developed MAS ($n = 19$) and those who did not develop MAS but were born with MSL ($n = 325$). The incidence of FHR abnormality during labour was significantly higher in babies who developed MAS than in those who did not (10/19 (57.9%) versus 79/325 (24.3%), $P = 0.002$). Length of labour was also found to be significantly longer in those babies who developed MAS (7.2 hours (SD 9.2 hours) versus 4.1 hours (SD 3.1 hours), $P = 0.0004$).

A cohort study (described as prospective) conducted in Jordan (2000) compared neonatal outcomes of 390 babies with MSL with 400 babies in a matched comparison group with clear amniotic fluid.[468] [EL = 2−] These study groups were identified from a study sample of 3850 live births undertaken at a single hospital in an 8-month period. Matching was not undertaken in a comprehensive way, but both groups included women in labour at term with a single baby in a cephalic presentation. Women with diabetes and pregnancy-induced hypertension were excluded. Inclusion criteria also included umbilical cord gas analysis, birthweight heavier than 2500 g and absence of congenital abnormalities, which suggests a number of exclusions were made retrospectively, although the reporting of this is unclear. Indeed, few methodological details are given. Of the 390 babies with MSL, 215 were identified as having thick meconium. Moderate or thick meconium was associated with: a significantly greater risk of abnormal FHR tracing: in each stage of labour (64/215 (30%) versus $n = 52/400$ (13%), $P = 0.01$); umbilical artery pH less than 7.2 (45/215 (21%) versus 36/400 (9%)); and SCBU admission (28/215 (13%) versus 12/400 (3%)). No further analyses were undertaken to examine FHR tracings in relation to fetal intrapartum wellbeing or neonatal outcomes.

A cohort study conducted in Hong Kong between 1996 and 1999 was included.[469] The study population was 9542 singleton pregnant women who had babies at a tertiary hospital. Birth attendants recorded the appearance of the liquor at artificial or spontaneous rupture of membranes, during vaginal examinations and at birth. Thin MSL was defined as green- or yellow-tinged fluid. Moderate MSL contained particulate matter in a thin green or yellow base. Thick MSL had 'pea soup' characteristics and was usually darker green or brown in colour. This information was collected prospectively. Thin to thick MSL was identified in 20.4% women. Continuous FHR monitoring was performed in 96% of the study women. Fetal distress was defined according to the abnormal CTG findings as defined in the guideline on FHR monitoring by the International Federation of Obstetrics and Gynecology (FIGO). There was no evidence of difference in incidence of fetal distress between all MSL and clear liquor up to 38 weeks of gestation (< 37 weeks, OR 1.00; 37 weeks, OR 0.54; 38 weeks, OR 0.30; all P values < 0.05), but there is strong evidence that babies with MSL were more likely to experience fetal distress compared with babies with clear liquor after 38 weeks of gestation (39 weeks, OR 1.8 [95% CI 2.6 to 12.0]; 40 weeks, OR 1.9 [95% CI 1.4 to 2.7]; 41 weeks, OR 1.7 [95% CI 1.1 to 2.6]).

A cohort study in Zimbabwe was identified.[628] This study was to evaluate the role of meconium staining of the liquor in the low-risk obstetric population in terms of fetal distress and perinatal morbidity and mortality. Low-risk women with a singleton term gestation were included. Women in the study comprised those with meconium staining of the liquor and controls comprised similar women but with clear liquor. Meconium staining of the liquor was associated with poor outcome in all the outcome measures assessed. FHR abnormality was more closely associated with adverse outcome than meconium staining, and thin MSL alone was not associated with any adverse outcome except respiratory distress.

There are no good-quality studies that report the long-term consequences of newborn babies with MSL.

Evidence statement
There is limited quality evidence of an association between significant MSL and poor neonatal outcome.

GDG interpretation of the evidence (meconium-stained liquor)
The unpredictable consequences of any degree of meconium-stained liquor are such that the GDG felt transfer for continuous fetal monitoring and specific neonatal care (see below) should be considered.

Recommendations on management of meconium-stained liquor before birth

Continuous EFM should be advised for women with significant meconium-stained liquor, which is defined as either dark green or black amniotic fluid that is thick or tenacious, or any meconium-stained amniotic fluid containing lumps of meconium.

Continuous EFM should be considered for women with light meconium-stained liquor depending on a risk assessment which should include as a minimum their stage of labour, volume of liquor, parity, the FHR and, where applicable, transfer pathway.

> ### Research recommendation on a scoring system for degree of meconium staining
>
> There is a need for development of a standardised scoring system for degree of meconium staining and association with neonatal outcomes.

12.1.3   Amnioinfusion

Amnioinfusion versus standard care

Description of included studies and review findings
One systematic review was identified which considered the effects of amnioinfusion for MSL on perinatal outcome.[470] [EL = 1+] The review includes 12 RCTs involving a total of 1807 women (number of participants in 11 of the 12 studies). Most studies involved 100 women or less. All studies used saline for amnioinfusion, although the rates of infusion varied. Most infusion protocols included an initial bolus of e.g. 500–600 ml over the first hour followed by a maintenance dose of, for example, 150–180 ml/hour. Trials were divided into two subgroups: those conducted with standard peripartum surveillance (continuous FHR monitoring, facilities for fetal blood sampling, paediatrician available for birth) ($n = 11$); and one larger study with limited peripartum surveillance ($n = 652$). Findings from meta-analysis of the 11 studies conducted under standard peripartum surveillance showed that amnioinfusion for MSL was associated with a reduction in: heavy meconium staining of the liquor (RR 0.03 [95% CI 0.01 to 0.15]); variable FHR decelerations (RR 0.65 [95% CI 0.49 to 0.88]); overall rate of CS (RR 0.82 [95% CI 0.69 to 0.97]); and CS for fetal distress (RR 0.34 [95% CI 0.21 to 0.55]). Measures of the neonatal outcome at birth tended to favour the amnioinfusion groups, although individual trial results often varied considerably. No perinatal deaths were reported. Under limited perinatal surveillance, the following reductions were noted: MAS (RR 0.24 [95% CI 0.12 to 0.48]); neonatal hypoxic ischaemic encephalopathy (RR 0.07 [95% CI 0.01 to 0.056]); and neonatal ventilation or NICU admission (RR 0.56 [95% CI 0.39 to 0.79]). There was a trend towards reduced perinatal mortality in this subgroup (RR 0.34 [95% CI 0.11 to 1.06]).

Three additional RCTs were identified that addressed the effectiveness of amnioinfusion for improving outcome when there is MSL. The first of these was an international, multicentre trial involving 56 centres in 11 countries (South Africa, Canada, Argentina, Uruguay, USA, France, UK, Tunisia, Belgium, Switzerland and Eire).[471] [EL 1++] The trial enrolled 1998 women with thick MSL in labour at 36 weeks or later. Women were randomly assigned to receive amnioinfusion or standard care. Randomisation was stratified according to the study centre and according to the presence or absence of variable decelerations (three or more in the 30 minutes prior to randomisation). Block randomisation was carried out, with block size varying randomly between two and four women. A total of 1975 women were included in the analysis (986 in the amnioinfusion group, 989 in the control group). Both groups were well matched, although women in the amnioinfusion group were more likely to undergo continuous electronic fetal heart monitoring (95.0% versus 92.4%, $P = 0.02$). Compliance with random allocation was also good, with analysis undertaken on an intention-to-treat basis. The composite primary outcome (perinatal death, moderate or severe MAS, or both) occurred in 44 infants in the amnioinfusion group (4.5%) and 35 infants in the control group (3.5%) (RR 1.26 [95% CI 0.82 to 1.95]). Moderate or severe MAS assessed on the basis of clinical criteria occurred in 43 infants in the amnioinfusion group (4.4%) and 31 in the control group (3.1%) (RR 1.39 [95% CI 0.88 to 2.19]). There were five perinatal deaths in each group (0.5%). The frequency of mild respiratory distress did not differ significantly between the two groups (2.9% amnioinfusion group versus 2.7% control group). A stratified analysis showed no significant effect of amnioinfusion on the rate of primary outcome regardless of whether decelerations in FHR pattern were present (3.4% amnioinfusion group versus 3.2% control group; RR 1.05 [95% CI 0.84 to 3.99]). There were no differences between groups regarding rates of oropharyngeal suctioning, laryngoscopy and intubation immediately following birth, or proportions of infants with meconium seen below the vocal cords. Fetal umbilical artery pH was assessed in approximately half of the infants in each group. Again, no significant difference was found between groups. Abnormal pH (less than 7.15) occurred in 69 cases (13.5%) in the amnioinfusion group and 57 (12.1) in the control group (RR 1.11 [95% CI 0.80 to 1.55]). Frequency of abnormal FHR patterns was also similar between the two groups, occurring in 14.1% ($n = 111$) of women in the amnioinfusion group and 13.9% ($n = 107$) of women in the control group (RR 1.02 [95% CI 0.79 to 1.30]). Outcomes relating to maternal complications were also similar between the two groups. There were no significant differences in the rates of CS overall, CS for fetal distress, peripartum fever, maternal death or serious maternal morbidity (incidences of which were very low, n = 15 (1.5%) in each group).

An RCT conducted in Spain investigated the effect of amnioinfusion for moderate to very thick MSL.[472] [EL = 1+] One hundred and three women were assigned to each study group, amnio-infusion and control. Groups were similar regarding maternal and labour characteristics, with over half the labours in each group being induced (57.3% versus 55.3%, respectively). The concentration of meconium in the liquor was also tested objectively and found to be similar in the two groups. Two-thirds of women in each group were nulliparous, and a similar proportion used epidural analgesia. A number of significant differences were reported between the two groups, favouring amnioinfusion. The overall rate of CS was lower in the amnioinfusion group, 12% versus 23% (RR 0.50 [95% CI 0.26 to 0.95], P = 0.043); as was the rate of CS for fetal distress, 2.9% versus 13% (RR 0.23 [95% CI 0.07 to 0.79], P = 0.019). There were also fewer abnormal FHR patterns noted in the amnioinfusion group: variable decelerations, 52.4% versus 70.9% (RR 0.74 [95% CI 0.59 to 0.92], P = 0.009); variable late decelerations, 12.6% versus 33.9% (RR 0.37 [95% CI 0.21 to 0.66], P < 0.001). There were also fewer incidents of low umbilical arterial pH (less than 7.2), 17.5% versus 30.1% (RR 0.58 [95% CI 0.35 to 0.97]); and meconium below the vocal cords, 10.7% versus 29.1% (RR 0.37 [95% CI 0.19 to 0.69], P = 0.001). It is noted that the high rates of abnormal FHR patterns may have been caused by the high proportion of umbilical cord complications present: 32% of the babies had the cord around their neck and 27.2% had a true knot in the cord (unusually high). Distribution of these complications across the two study groups is not described. No complications were observed, e.g. iatrogenic polyhydramnios or uterine hypertonicity, following amnioinfusion.

Further subgroup analysis of the trial data was undertaken in order to ascertain whether there was any difference in the usefulness of amnioinfusion in relation to the degree of meconium staining.[473] [EL = 2+] The amount of meconium present in the liquor was measured following centrifugation and findings used to divide participants into two groups: less than or equal to 15% meconium (moderate meconium) and greater than 15% meconium (thick meconium). The frequency of variable, late and atypical variable decelerations were similar with or without amnioinfusion for babies with moderate and heavy MSL. Differences were found regarding late variable decelerations, where the effects of amnioinfusion, although significantly beneficial for both groups, were greater where there was heavy meconium staining. In women with moderate MSL, the frequency of variable decelerations was 12.7% in the amnioinfusion group versus 29.3% in the control group (P < 0.05). For women with heavy MSL, the figures were 12.5% and 40.0%, respectively (P < 0.01). The reduction in CS rate following amnioinfusion was significantly greater for women with heavy MSL compared with those with moderate MSL. For women with moderate MSL the CS rate in the amnioinfusion group was 14.3% versus 19.0% in the control group (NS), and for women with heavy MSL, the CS rates were 7.5% and 28.9%, respectively (P < 0.05). In contrast, there was a significant reduction in the incidence of meconium below the cords for babies born through moderate MSL following amnioinfusion (6.4% versus 25.9%, P < 0.01), but this reduction was not statistically significant in the group with heavy MSL (17.5% versus 33.3%, respectively, NS). The authors concluded that there were benefits of amnioinfusion to be gained for both moderate and heavy MSL. However, because the subgroups were fairly small for these analyses, the reliability of the findings was undermined.

A third RCT again investigated the effectiveness of amnioinfusion for moderate or thick MSL.[474] [EL = 1+] This trial involved 200 women (100 in each arm) and was carried out in India where there were no facilities for continuous FHR monitoring, FBS or the attendance of a paediatrician at birth. The amnioinfusion group and control group were well matched for maternal and labour characteristics. The overall CS rate was significantly lower for women in the amnioinfusion group compared with those in the control group, 21% versus 36% (RR 0.47 [95% CI 0.24 to 0.93]). CS for fetal distress was also significantly lower for women in the amnioinfusion group, 12% compared with 26% in the control group (RR 0.39 [95% CI 0.17 to 0.87]). The presence of meconium at the vocal cords was also lower in babies born to mothers in the amnioinfusion group, 10% versus 24% (RR 0.35 [95% CI 0.15 to 0.83]). Neonatal outcomes were also improved for babies born to women in the amnioinfusion group, although the numbers involved are small. There were three admissions to NICU from the amnioinfusion group compared with 11 from the control group (RR 0.25 [95% CI 0.05 to 1.01]) and respiratory distress was diagnosed for one baby in the amnioinfusion group compared with 12 in the control group (RR 0.07 [95% CI 0.00 to 0.57]). Only one infant (in the control group) developed MAS. No maternal complications associated with amnioinfusion are reported.

A meta-analysis was conducted to include all identified RCTs in where it is likely that there are facilities for EFM, FBS and advanced life support. Eleven of the RCTs under standard peripartum surveillance that were included in the systematic review[470] and two additional RCTs,[471,472] a total of 13 RCTs, were included in the analysis. The analysis shows that there is a trend of reduction in overall CS rate (12 trials, RR 0.81 [95% CI 0.65 to 1.01]), but the reduction became significant in the rate of CS due to fetal distress (10 trials, RR 0.40 [95% CI 0.21 to 0.77]) by amnioinfusion, compared with standard care. There was no evidence of difference in incidences of MAS and admission to neonatal units between the two groups (MAS, 13 trials, RR 0.86 [95% CI 0.61 to 1.21]); admission to neonatal units, four trials, RR 0.70 [95% CI 0.44 to 1.10])

Methods of amnioinfusion

Description of included studies
Two additional trials comparing different solutions for amnioinfusion and one non-systematic review investigating use of infusion pumps and solution warmer were identified.

Review findings
One RCT has been carried out to investigate whether amnioinfusion with an antibiotic solution decreased the rate of clinical chorioamnionitis and puerperal endometritis in women with MSL.[475] [EL = 1+] The trial, conducted in the USA, involved 183 women in labour, at 36 weeks or more of gestation. Women in the intervention group received amnioinfusion with 1 g of cefazolin per litre of saline. Women in the control group received amnioinfusion using saline only. The incidence of suspected or proven neonatal infection was also examined. Clinical chorioamnionitis was diagnosed based on the presence of one or more of the following: maternal temperature 38 °C or higher, maternal or fetal tachycardia, uterine tenderness, and foul-smelling amniotic fluid. The diagnosis of puerperal endometritis was also made clinically, based on a maternal temperature of 38 °C or higher on two occasions postpartum, uterine tenderness or foul-smelling lochia. No statistically significant differences were found between study groups for any of the outcome variables investigated. Incidences of chorioamnionitis were 7.8% for women in the antibiotic group and 8.6% for women in the control group; endometritis 10.0% versus 11.8%, respectively; suspected neonatal infection 17.8% versus 21.5%, respectively and proven neonatal infection 0.0% versus 2.2%, respectively.

A small prospective RCT was identified that was carried out to determine whether the use of normal saline or lactated Ringer's solution for amnioinfusion in cases of MSL was associated with significant changes in neonatal plasma electrolyte concentrations or pH.[476] [EL = 1+] Two intervention groups of women in labour at term with particulate (thick) MSL were allocated to receive amnioinfusion using lactated Ringer's solution (n = 20) or normal saline (n = 20). A control group received no amnioinfusion (n = 21). Immediately after birth, cord blood arterial samples were taken for laboratory analysis to determine pH, sodium chloride and potassium plasma concentrations. No significant differences were found between the three study groups for neonatal plasma pH or electrolyte concentrations.

One non-systematic review was identified which was undertaken to determine whether infusion pumps or solution warmers were beneficial during amnioinfusion.[477,478] [EL = 1−] The review included 14 studies (13 RCTs and one prospective cohort study) involving 1543 women. Studies were excluded if they involved less than 40 participants or did not have a comparison group. None of the studies were designed to investigate outcomes associated with warmers and/or infusion pumps as their primary objective. Seven of the trials had MSL as the indication for amnioinfusion. There was a significant lack of homogeneity between studies. No benefits were demonstrated for the use of infusion pumps or solution warmers. In multiple regression analysis, pumps were associated with a significantly increased risk of fetal distress ($R = 0.83$, $P = 0.01$).

Evidence statement
Where there are facilities for EFM, FBS and advanced life support, there is no evidence that amnioinfusion for moderate to thick meconium staining improves neonatal outcomes or reduces CS, although there is high-level evidence that it reduces the rate of CS due to fetal distress.

GDG interpretation of the evidence (amnioinfusion)
Although there was reduction in CS due to fetal distress, there was no statistically significant difference in overall CS rate, and no improvement in neonatal outcomes.

> **Recommendation on amnioinfusion**
>
> Amnioinfusion should not be used for the treatment of women with meconium-stained liquor.

12.2 Resuscitation of babies with meconium-stained liquor

Description of included studies
A systematic review has been undertaken to determine whether endotracheal intubation and suction of the airways at birth, in vigorous term babies with meconium staining, is more beneficial than routine resuscitation including aspiration of the oropharynx.[479] RCTs were included in the review if they compared routine versus no, or selective, endotracheal intubation and aspiration in the immediate care of vigorous babies born through MSL. [EL = 1+] Four RCTs were identified and included 2884 babies (most from one large multicentre trial, $n = 2094$). Clinical outcomes included: mortality, MAS, respiratory symptoms, pneumothorax, need for oxygen, stride, hypoxic ischaemic encephalopathy and convulsions.

Review findings
Meta-analysis of the four trials provided no evidence that endotracheal intubation at birth had an effect on any of the outcomes studied: mortality (RR 1.73 [95% CI 0.37 to 8.1]); (intubated group $n = 4$, control group $n = 2$); MAS (RR 1.29 [95% CI 0.80 to 2.08]); other respiratory symptoms or disorders (two studies RR 0.87 [95% CI 0.58 to 1.31], $n = 2763$); need for oxygen (three studies RR 1.49 [95% CI 0.86 to 2.60], $n = 790$).[479] For all other outcome variables, the number of cases was too low to provide a reliable estimate of treatment effect. In the large multicentre trial, complications of intubation were also recorded. Of the 1098 successfully intubated infants, the total number of complications was 42 (3.8%), the most common being bradycardia, larygospasm and hoarseness. Most complications were transient, lasting 15 to 60 seconds.

A multicentre RCT conducted predominantly in Argentina (11 centres, 1 US centre) enrolled 2514 women in labour at term with MSL (of any consistency) to one of two groups: an intervention group where the baby would receive suctioning of the oropharynx and nasopharynx before the birth of the shoulders and trunk ($n = 1263$), or a control group where no suctioning was carried out ($n = 1251$).[480] 14 [EL = 1+] The primary outcome was MAS. No significant difference was found between the suctioning and no-suctioning groups regarding incidence of MAS, it being 4% in each group ($n = 52$ and 47, respectively) (RR 0.9 [95% CI 0.6 to 1.3]) or the need for mechanical ventilation for MAS, 2% ($n = 24$) versus 1% ($n = 18$), respectively (RR 0.8 [95% CI 0.4 to 1.4]). Nine babies died in the suction group versus four in the no-suction group (RR 0.4 [95% CI 0.1 to 1.5]). Duration of oxygen treatment, duration of mechanical ventilation and duration of hospital stay were also similar for the two groups.

Evidence statement
There is insufficient high-level evidence that the use of routine endotracheal intubation and aspiration, for babies that are vigorous and have meconium staining, improves neonatal outcomes.

There is no evidence to support suctioning of the nasopharynx before the birth of the baby's shoulders and trunk.

Recommendations on resuscitation of babies with meconium-stained liquor

If significant meconium-stained liquor is identified, healthcare professionals trained in FBS should be available in labour and healthcare professionals trained in advanced neonatal life support should be readily available for the birth.

Suctioning of the nasopharynx and oropharynx prior to birth of the shoulders and trunk should not be carried out.

The upper airways should only be suctioned if the baby has thick or tenacious meconium present in the oropharynx.

If the baby has depressed vital signs, laryngoscopy and suction under direct vision should be carried out by a healthcare professional trained in advanced neonatal life support.

If there has been significant meconium staining and the baby is in good condition, the baby should be closely observed for signs of respiratory distress. These observations should be performed at 1 and 2 hours of age and then 2 hourly until 12 hours of age, and should include:

- general wellbeing
- chest movements and nasal flare
- skin colour including perfusion, by testing capillary refill
- feeding
- muscle tone
- temperature
- heart rate and respiration.

If there has been light meconium staining, the baby should be similarly observed by the healthcare professional at 1 and 2 hours and should be reviewed by a neonatologist if the baby's condition causes concern at any time.

13 Complicated labour: monitoring babies in labour

13.1 Introduction

The monitoring of babies in labour aims to identify hypoxia before it is sufficient to lead to damaging acidosis and long-term neurological adverse outcome for the baby. The limitations of the tests of wellbeing of babies mean that, in order to avoid significant hypoxia, other interventions such as caesarean section are undertaken when there is concern. This leads to higher rates of intervention. Whichever method of monitoring is undertaken, there needs to be a balance between correctly identifying the babies who have given rise to an appropriate cause for concern, and over-identifying babies as having problems when they do not, leading to higher rates of intervention.

This chapter will consider what is the appropriate monitoring method of babies in labour for low-risk women, when to use electronic fetal monitoring (EFM), how to interpret electronic monitoring and when to intervene on the basis of EFM.

Clinical question
Do the following methods of fetal monitoring affect outcomes?

- none
- intermittent auscultation (Pinard, Doppler)
- intermittent electronic monitoring
- continuous electronic monitoring (including method of interpretation)
- ST analysis
- fetal blood sampling
- fetal blood gas analysis
- fetal lactate.

13.2 Women's views on fetal monitoring and mobility

Introduction
It is important to understand and take into consideration women's views on monitoring fetal wellbeing.

Description of included studies
There were two trials identified, which assessed women's views and attitudes to continuous fetal monitoring compared with intermittent auscultation.[481,482] The Danish trial included 385 women, and investigated women's views by interviewing them before and after their labour.[481] The Irish trial included 200 women, and investigated women's views by semi-structured interviews after their labour.[482] No other relevant studies were identified.

Review findings

EFM and auscultation

The Danish trial
Women who preferred auscultation before labour but had EFM became more positive towards the method and a significant number were positively influenced by the EFM signal/trace and found the method promoted their partner's involvement in labour. Enforced immobility, however, was a major disadvantage, as was the technical milieu.

The Irish trial
More women allocated to EFM reported that they felt restricted in their movements than those allocated to intermittent auscultation. On the other hand, there was no evidence that the method of monitoring influenced the support the women had. There was a suggestion that women monitored with EFM were more likely to be left alone for short periods.

Evidence statement
There is qualitative evidence from two trials that shows women's concern about restricted movement with continuous fetal monitoring.

GDG interpretation of the evidence
The GDG considered the above evidence, as well as other evidence from this chapter and developed an example of information for women regarding fetal wellbeing.

Recommendation on women's view on fetal monitoring and mobility

Women should be informed that continuous fetal monitoring will restrict their mobility.

13.3 Indications for continuous EFM

Introduction
When risk factors develop in labour, continuous EFM is generally considered and discussed. Reviews were undertaken to consider the evidence for this with specific risk factors. The lack of high-level evidence meant that reviews of each separate risk factor were undertaken.

13.3.1 The use of continuous EFM for meconium-stained liquor

For continuous EFM and meconium-stained liquor, refer to Section 12.1.2.

13.3.2 The use of continuous EFM with augmentation of labour

For continuous EFM and augmentation of labour, refer to Section 14.2.5 in the chapter on the first stage of labour.

13.4 EFM and record-keeping

This guideline updates and replaces *The Use of Electronic Fetal Monitoring: the Use and Interpretation of Cardiotocography in Intrapartum Fetal Surveillance* (inherited clinical guideline C),[460] issued in 2001.

Recommendations on EFM and record-keeping

In order to ensure accurate record-keeping regarding EFM:

- The date and time clocks on the EFM machine should be correctly set.
- Traces should be labelled with the mother's name, date and hospital number.
- Any intrapartum events that may affect the FHR should be noted at the time on the FHR trace, which should be signed and the date and time noted (for example, vaginal examination, FBS or siting of an epidural).
- Any member of staff who is asked to provide an opinion on a trace should note their findings on both the trace and the woman's medical records along with the date, time and signature.
- Following birth, the healthcare professional should sign and note the date, time and mode of birth on the FHR trace.
- The FHR trace should be stored securely with the woman's medical records at the end of the monitoring process.

13.5   Interpretation of FHR traces

Introduction

The interpretation of a fetal heart rate (FHR) trace should take into consideration the stage of labour, progress in labour, maternal and fetal condition, and prior or additional risk factors present as well as the features of the FHR trace and the availability of extra tests or assessments.

13.5.1   Specific features and categorisation of FHR patterns and outcome

Introduction

The specific features and classification of FHR abnormalities were reviewed in the EFM guideline, and no new studies have been added.[460] The detail is available in this guideline.[460] The evidence summaries detailed the following.

Description of included studies and review findings

Most FHR features in isolation, with the exception of late decelerations, are poor at predicting poor neonatal outcome. Uncomplicated baseline tachycardia (161–180 bpm) or bradycardia (100–109 bpm) does not appear to be associated with poor neonatal outcome. The predictive value of reduced baseline variability alone is unclear. The presence of FHR accelerations is associated with a good outcome. Repeated late decelerations are associated with an increased risk of cerebral palsy, umbilical artery acidosis and an Apgar score of less than 7 at 5 minutes. Reduced baseline variability, together with late or variable decelerations, is associated with an increased risk of cerebral palsy. Atypical variable decelerations alone are associated with an increased risk of umbilical artery acidosis and an Apgar score of less than 7 at 5 minutes. Prolonged decelerations are associated with poor neonatal outcome. When all abnormal FHR patterns are combined, those traces classified as 'abnormal', by whichever system, appear to be associated with an increase in neonatal encephalopathy, cerebral palsy rates, neonatal acidosis and Apgar scores of less than 7 at 5 minutes.

GDG interpretation of the evidence (specific features and categorisation of FHR patterns)

The intrapartum care GDG felt that the categorisation of the FHR trace as defined in the EFM guideline has been invaluable in improving the interpretation of monitoring. However, clarification of some areas of the classification was thought to add value, so extra recommendations and clarification has been made.

Recommendations on specific features and categorisation of FHR patterns

The recommended definitions and classifications of the FHR trace/cardiotocograph produced during EFM are shown in Tables 13.1 and 13.2.

Table 13.1   Definition of normal, suspicious and pathological FHR traces

Category	Definition
Normal	An FHR trace in which all four features are classified as reassuring
Suspicious	An FHR trace with one feature classified as non-reassuring and the remaining features classified as reassuring
Pathological	An FHR trace with two or more features classified as non-reassuring or one or more classified as abnormal

---

Table 13.2   Classification of FHR trace features

Feature	Baseline (bpm)	Variability (bpm)	Decelerations	Accelerations
Reassuring	110–160	≥ 5	None	Present
Non-reassuring	100–109 161–180	< 5 for 40–90 minutes	Typical variable decelerations with over 50% of contractions, occurring for over 90 minutes Single prolonged deceleration for up to 3 minutes	The absence of accelerations with otherwise normal trace is of uncertain significance
Abnormal	< 100 > 180 Sinusoidal pattern ≥ 10 minutes	< 5 for 90 minutes	Either atypical variable decelerations with over 50% of contractions or late decelerations, both for over 30 minutes Single prolonged deceleration for more than 3 minutes	

Further information about classifying FHR traces is given below.

- If repeated accelerations are present with reduced variability, the FHR trace should be regarded as reassuring.
- True early uniform decelerations are rare and benign, and therefore they are not significant.
- Most decelerations in labour are variable.
- If a bradycardia occurs in the baby for more than 3 minutes, urgent medical aid should be sought and preparations should be made to urgently expedite the birth of the baby, classified as a category 1 birth. This could include moving the woman to theatre if the fetal heart has not recovered by 9 minutes. If the fetal heart recovers within 9 minutes the decision to deliver should be reconsidered in conjunction with the woman if reasonable.
- A tachycardia in the baby of 160–180 bpm, where accelerations are present and no other adverse features appear, should not be regarded as suspicious. However, an increase in the baseline heart rate, even within the normal range, with other non-reassuring or abnormal features should increase concern.

For women having continuous EFM, a documented systematic assessment based on these definitions and classifications should be undertaken every hour.

During episodes of abnormal FHR patterns when the woman is lying supine she should be advised to adopt the left-lateral position.

Prolonged use of maternal facial oxygen therapy may be harmful to the baby and should be avoided. There is no research evidence evaluating the benefits or risks associated with the short-term use of maternal facial oxygen therapy in cases of suspected fetal compromise.

In the presence of abnormal FHR patterns and uterine hypercontractility not secondary to oxytocin infusion, tocolysis should be considered. A suggested regimen is subcutaneous terbutaline 0.25 mg.*

In cases of suspected or confirmed acute fetal compromise, delivery should be accomplished within a time appropriate for the clinical condition.

Continuous EFM in the presence of oxytocin:

- If the FHR trace is normal, oxytocin may be continued until the woman is experiencing 4 or 5 contractions every 10 minutes. Oxytocin should be reduced if contractions occur more frequently than 5 contractions in 10 minutes.

---

* At the time of publication (September 2007), terbutaline did not have UK marketing authorisation for this indication. Informed consent should be obtained and documented.

- If the FHR trace is classified as suspicious, this should be reviewed by an obstetrician and the oxytocin dose should only continue to increase to achieve 4 or 5 contractions every 10 minutes.
- If the FHR trace is classified as pathological, oxytocin should be stopped and a full assessment of the fetal condition undertaken by an obstetrician before oxytocin is recommenced.

13.6 Adjuncts to the use of continuous EFM including FBS

Introduction
EFM alone considers the patterns of FHR but other tests can be used alongside EFM. This section considers whether these adjuncts can improve outcomes in addition to EFM.

13.6.1 Fetal cardiogram with continuous EFM

Introduction
Recently combined assessment of the standard FHR tracing with an automated analysis of the fetal electrocardiogram have been developed. The analyses included ST analysis, and PR interval analysis. These are computerised methods to analyse the ST and PR segments of fetal electrocardiogram (ECG) , respectively.

Description of included studies
There was one systematic review published in 2003.[483] One new RCT was published in 2006.[484] The systematic review compared the effectiveness of analysing the fetal electrocardiogram with alternative methods of fetal monitoring during labour. The three trials in the systematic review, which was of a good quality, were conducted in Sweden, the UK, Hong Kong, the Netherlands and Singapore. All the trials included high-risk women and assessed the use of fetal ECG as an adjunct to continuous EFM. Two assessed ST analysis[485-491] and the other, PR interval analysis.[492,493] The new trial in Finland examined effectiveness of ST analysis and included a high-risk population.[484] The two trials included in the above systematic reviews[485-487,491] and the new trial had reasonable homogeneity.[484] Therefore, a new meta-analysis was conducted including these three trials to examine the effectiveness of ST analysis. [EL = 1+] A cost-analysis (Appendix F) was also conducted to examine cost minimisation effect of the ST analysis.

Review findings

ST analysis
The new meta-analysis showed evidence that ST analysis significantly reduced the rate of: instrumental vaginal birth (RR 0.87 [95% CI 0.78 to 0.96]); all instrumental birth (RR 0.89 [95% CI 0.82 to 0.96]); and the need for fetal blood sampling (FBS) (RR 0.69 [95% CI 0.48 to 1.00]). There was no evidence of a difference in the caesarean section (CS) rate and fetal acid–base status. There is evidence that ST analysis reduced the number of babies who developed neonatal encephalopathy (RR 0.33 [95% CI 0.11 to 0.95]) and the number of babies with cord blood acidosis (pH less than 7.05, base excess less than −12 mmol/l, RR 0.53 [95% CI 0.33 to 0.85]), although there was no evidence of differences in other neonatal outcomes (perinatal deaths, RR 2.16 [95% CI 0.48 to 9.58]; Apgar score less than 7 at 5 minutes, RR 0.80 [95% CI 0.56 to 1.14]; admission to neonatal unit, RR 0.90 [95% CI 0.75 to 1.08]). When perinatal deaths and neonatal encephalopathy are combined, there is no evidence of difference (RR 0.60 [95% CI 0.27 to 1.34]).

Details of perinatal death
Details of perinatal deaths were also reviewed (Table 13.3).

PR analysis
The study was underpowered to show statistical differences in women's and babies' outcomes, although there was a trend showing women with PR analysis were less likely to have an instrumental birth (RR 0.87 [95% CI 0.76 to 1.01]).

Table 13.3 Details of perinatal deaths in included trials of ST analysis

Study	ECG + EFM	EFM only
Westgate 1993[485,486]	2 perinatal deaths	0 perinatal deaths
	1 neonatal encephalopathy	4 neonatal encephalopathy
	Details not given	Details not given
Amer-Wahlin 2001[488–491]	3 perinatal deaths	2 perinatal deaths
	3 neonatal encephalopathy (excluding perinatal death cases)	8 had neonatal encephalopathy (excluding perinatal death cases)
	1) Congenital malformation	1) Congenital malformation
	2) Metabolic acidosis at birth. Maternal fever occurred during labour, and EFM showed a pre-terminal pattern without ST waveform changes. CS was done after an undue delay, and the baby died 36 hours after birth with clinical signs of neonatal encephalopathy and sepsis.	2) The recorder disconnected for unknown reasons 2 hours and 11 minutes before an operative vaginal birth for non-reassuring FHR. The baby was severely asphyxiated at birth and died after 24 hours.
	3) Metabolic acidosis at birth. Second-stage FHR and ST changes were not recognised; the scalp electrode was disconnected during ventouse extraction for failure to progress, and a severely asphyxiated baby was delivered.	
Ojala 2006[484]	0 perinatal deaths	0 perinatal deaths
	0 neonatal encephalopathy	1 neonatal encephalopathy
		Details not given

CS = caesarean section; ECG = electrocardiogram; EFM = electronic fetal monitoring; FHR = fetal heart rate.

Evidence statement
There was high-level evidence from three trials of high-risk women that ST analysis reduces instrumental vaginal birth and neonatal encephalopathy, although there was no difference in fetal acid–base.

There was no high-level evidence on PR analysis.

Economic evidence
Using baseline assumptions, the net cost of ST analysis is approximately £3.45 million per annum. This result is sensitive to the relative risk of CS and instrumental vaginal birth with ST analysis, and ST analysis produces net cost savings in a 'best case' sensitivity analysis (Appendix F).

GDG interpretation of the evidence (ST analysis)
ST analysis seems to add value to the use of EFM and reduce intervention. While associated with a lower neonatal encephalopathy rate in surviving infants, when combined with perinatal deaths, there is no significant difference in outcome. It comes at added cost and also requires the use of fetal scalp electrodes and extra staff training. If used when fetal heart rate abnormalities are present, it may be necessary to perform a fetal blood sample before using ST analysis.

Research recommendation on ST analysis

A further randomised controlled trial of ST segment analysis should be undertaken.

13.6.2   Intrapartum fetal stimulation tests

Introduction
The use of intrapartum fetal stimulation tests as an adjunct to EFM is evaluated in this section. These include fetal scalp puncture and digital stimulation of the fetal scalp. Fetal scalp puncture is incidental to obtaining fetal scalp pH. Digital scalp stimulation is performed by gentle digital stroking of the fetal scalp. For any of the methods of scalp stimulation, a reassuring response is defined as acceleration in the FHR. However, the absence of acceleration is not always associated with fetal acidosis.

Description of included studies
One systematic review published in 2002 was identified.[494] The review assessed predictive values of four intrapartum fetal stimulation tests including fetal scalp puncture (six studies) and digital stimulation of the fetal scalp (two studies). The primary outcome was babies' acidaemia. The study was of a moderate quality. [EL = III]

Review findings

Fetal scalp puncture
There were six studies included. The pooled likelihood ratio of acidosis for a negative test was 0.12 [95% CI 0.02 to 0.78], and for a positive test, it was 8.54 [95% CI 1.28 to 56.96].

Digital stimulation of the fetal scalp
There were two studies included. The pooled likelihood ratio for acidosis of a negative test was 0.06 [95% CI 0.01 to 0.31], and for a positive test, it was 15.68 [95% CI 3.22 to 76.24].

Evidence statement
There is observational evidence that response to digital stimulation of the fetal scalp is a good predictive test, and response to fetal scalp puncture during FBS is a moderately predictive test for fetal acidaemia.

Recommendation on intrapartum fetal stimulation tests

Digital stimulation of the fetal scalp by the healthcare professional during a vaginal examination should be considered as an adjunct to continuous EFM.

13.6.3   **Computerised systems versus human interpretation**

Introduction
A new review of computerised systems in FHR trace interpretation was undertaken.

Previous guideline
The *Use of Electronic Fetal Monitoring* guideline includes computerised interpretation of FHR tracings.[460] The same six studies are included as are reviewed here. The summary of evidence concludes that: The use of computerised systems for FHR analysis improves consistency of interpretation. A research recommendation was for further evaluation of the effectiveness of computerised analysis, or decision analysis programs, in the interpretation of the CTG.

Description of included studies
Six studies were identified for review in this section. Five of these studies compared computerised interpretation of FHR tracings with expert interpretation. All studies included women with pregnancy and/or intrapartum complications.

Review findings
A rigorous multicentre comparative study undertaken in the UK investigated whether a computerised system could obtain a performance in labour management comparable with experts when using FHR tracings, obstetric information and FBS. It also investigated the degree of agreement between experts.[495] [EL = II] Seventeen peer-nominated experts were selected from 16 UK maternity units to review 50 complete intrapartum FHR tracings. The 50 tracings were selected to represent a range of possible variables and outcomes and all were obtained from women with high-risk labours. The expert reviewers were also given clinical information pertaining to the progress of labour, and could request findings from FBS to supplement this information. Each expert performed the assessments twice (in a different order), with an interim period of 1 month in order to assess intra-rater reliability. Consistency (intra-rater reliability) of ratings for each reviewer was high, ranging from 73.18% to 89.04% (kappa 0.43 to 0.77). Consistency of ratings for the computerised system was 99.16%. Agreement between reviewers (inter-rater reliability) ranged from 58.17% to 74.27% (kappa 0.12 to 0.46). Agreement between the computerised system and the obstetricians was 67.33% (kappa 0.31). In the 11 cases where the computerised system recommended CS, on average 18/34 (52.9%) of the expert reviews also recommended CS within 15 minutes of the system. An average of 23/34

(67.6%) did so within 30 minutes of the system. Only two reviewers and the computerised system consistently recommended no unnecessary intervention. Twelve examples of poor outcome were included in the sample. Poor outcome fell into one of three categories as follows: birth asphyxia (cord arterial pH < 7.05 and base deficit ≥ 12, Apgar score at 5 minutes ≤ 7 with neonatal morbidity); metabolic acidosis (cord arterial pH < 7.05 and base deficit ≥ 12, Apgar score at 5 minutes > 7 with no neonatal morbidity); acidosis (cord arterial pH < 7.05 and base deficit < 12 with neonatal morbidity). The system detected two of the three incidents of birth asphyxia, two of the four incidents of metabolic acidosis and two of the five incidents of acidosis with no significant metabolic component. This was as good as the majority of experts for birth asphyxia, but fewer than for all reviewers for metabolic acidosis, and fewer than all but one of the reviewers for acidosis.

A small prospective observational study (UK, 2000) compared computerised interpretation of 24 intrapartum FHR tracings with expert ratings.[496] [EL = II] Analysis was performed on 25 minute sections of tracing.

Inter-rater reliability between the seven experts was good for baseline FHR ($r = 0.93$), number of decelerations ($r = 0.93$) and type of decelerations ($r = 0.93$). Inter-rater reliability for baseline variability was poor (kappa = 0.27), as it was for accelerations ($r = 0.27$). Computerised interpretation of the tracings showed good agreement with the experts regarding baseline FHR ($r = 0.91$ to 0.98) and the number of decelerations ($r = 0.82$ to 0.91). Intra-class correlations were lower for the number of late decelerations ($r = 0.68$ to 0.85) and the number of accelerations ($r = 0.06$ to 0.80). There was no agreement between computerised interpretation and expert interpretation for baseline variability (kappa = 0.00 to 0.34).

A similar observational study conducted in Italy (1996) compared interpretations of 63 FHR tracings made by two experts (obstetric consultants), two non-experts (obstetricians with 1 year of experience) and a computerised system.[497] [EL = III] The study population included women with pregnancy complications and preterm labour. 'Randomly' selected 25 minute sections of tracing were used for analysis. Reliability between expert and non-expert observers for FHR, baseline variability, number of accelerations and number of decelerations was fair to good (kappa ratings ranging from 0.38 to 0.67). Only 17 tracings included decelerations. Agreement regarding type of deceleration was poor (kappa = 0.05). Agreement between computerised interpretation and observers was fair to good for most ratings of variability (kappa = 0.16 to 0.74), number of accelerations (0.37 to 0.64) and number of decelerations (0.41 to 0.54). Agreement for FHR baseline and type of decelerations was poor (kappa = 0.18 to 0.48 and kappa = 0.01 to 0.25, respectively).

A UK retrospective observational study assessed the ability of a computerised system for FHR tracing analysis to predict fetal acidosis at birth.[498] [EL = III] Analysis was undertaken of 73 complete FHR tracings for labours lasting more than 3 hours. An umbilical artery pH of < 7.15 was used to define acidosis at birth. Using this definition, 8/73 babies (11%) were found to have acidosis and 65 (89%) were classified as normal. The computer system classified 50 babies (69%) as normal, of whom 49 (98%) had an umbilical artery pH > 7.15. Of the 23 babies (31%) identified by the computer system as having acidosis, 7 (30%) had a pH < 7.15. The overall accuracy of the computer system was 77%, with a sensitivity of 88% and a specificity of 75%. Similar calculations were performed for base excess, with < −8 mmol/l as the cut-off point. Fifty-six of the 73 babies (77%) had a normal base excess and 17 (23%) were classified as abnormal. The computer system identified 50 (69%) babies as normal, 46 (92%) of whom had a base excess of ≥ −8 mmol/l. Of the 23 babies (31%) classified by the computer system as abnormal, 13 (57%) had a base excess < −8 mmol/l. The overall accuracy was 81% with a sensitivity of 76% and a specificity of 82%.

A retrospective observational study (Denmark, 1988) compared interpretations of FHR tracings made by four experienced obstetricians with those made by a computerised system.[499] [EL = III] 50 FHR tracings of the last 30 minutes of the first stage of labour were used for the study. These were classified as either normal or abnormal. The obstetricians were informed of the number of compromised babies within the sample ($n = 16$), the criterion by which a baby was judged to be compromised and the length of the pregnancies. Babies were considered to be compromised if the 1 minute Apgar score was < 7, the umbilical artery pH was < 7.15 or the standard base excess was < −10 mEq/l, or primary resuscitation was needed. Based on the 30 minute segment of FHR tracing, the computer system was able to indicate whether a baby would be born in a healthy state or compromised with 86% accuracy. However, while the system has a high specificity (94%), positive predictive value (85%) and negative predictive value (86%), its sensitivity is quite low (69%), i.e. it did not identify five of the 16 compromised babies. This was higher than that obtained from the four obstetricians, the best of whom achieved the same degree of sensitivity but only 59% specificity, i.e. correctly identifying 20 of the 34 healthy babies from their FHR tracing.

A retrospective observational study compared FHR tracing interpretations of 12 clinical experts with computerised interpretation (UK/Hong Kong, 1997).[500] [EL = III] Sixty 40 minute sections were classified to determine the baseline FHR. There was high concordance between expert ratings and between computer interpretation and that of experts ($r > 0.9$). The 95% confidence interval for the difference between computer and expert ratings was −12 to 15 bpm compared with −10 to 10 bpm for the difference between experts.

Evidence statement
Computerised systems have not been demonstrated to be superior to expert interpretation of the FHR trace and no comparisons have been undertaken with routine care.

> **Research recommendation on computerised system**
>
> Further study investigating computerised expert systems should be undertaken.

13.6.4 Fetal blood sampling

Predictive value of fetal scalp pH

Description of included studies
There were 28 observational studies that assessed predictive values of fetal scalp pH during labour for the Apgar score.[501–515] Among them, 12 studies assessed predictive value of fetal scalp pH below 7.20 for the Apgar score, four studies did that for pH below 7.25, and the remaining 12 did studies of both pH values. The studies used Apgar score of below 4 and below 8 as cut-off points. All studies were of reasonable quality. The studies showed reasonable heterogeneity. Thresholds of above 10 for positive likelihood ratio and 0.1 for negative likelihood ratio were used. [EL = II]

Review findings
Meta-analysis of 24 studies for pH below 7.20 showed summary likelihood ratios of 4.51 [95% CI 3.66 to 5.56] for positive and 0.58 [95% CI 0.46 to 0.73] for negative. Meta-analysis of 16 studies for pH below 7.25 showed summary likelihood ratios of 2.46 [95% CI 1.95 to 3.12] for positive and 0.66 [95% CI 0.55 to 0.79] for negative.

Evidence statement
There was no available evidence of a correlation between fetal scalp pH and improved longer term outcomes.

Predictive values of fetal acid–base, fetal–maternal pH difference and fetal–maternal base deficit difference

Description of included studies
There are two observational studies that reported predictive values of fetal acid–base,[516] fetal–maternal pH difference and fetal–maternal base deficit difference[517] during labour for Apgar score. Both studies showed reasonable quality. [EL = II]

Review findings

Fetal acid–base
Linear regression analysis showed that there is some evidence that fetal acid–base status correlated with a high Apgar score at 1 minute ($r = -0.15$, $P < 0.05$), although there was no evidence to show the correlation between low Apgar score at 1 minute and fetal acid–base status ($r = 0.039$, $P > 0.05$). There was some evidence that there was correlation of fetal acid–base with a high Apgar score at 5 minutes ($r = -0.092$, $P < 0.05$) and a low Apgar score at 5 minutes ($r = -0.32$, $P < 0.05$).

Fetal–maternal pH difference
Linear regression analysis showed that there is some evidence that fetal–maternal arterial pH difference correlated with a low Apgar score at 1 minute ($r = 0.5503$, $P < 0.005$), although there was no evidence to show the correlation between a high Apgar score at 1 minute and fetal base ($r = 0.0029$, $P > 0.05$). There was also some evidence that there was correlation of fetal–maternal arterial pH difference with a low Apgar score at 5 minutes ($r = 0.4959$, $P < 0.05$), although not with a high Apgar score at 5 minutes ($r = -0.1282$, $P > 0.05$).

Fetal–maternal base deficit difference
Linear regression analysis showed that there was some evidence that fetal–maternal acid–base difference correlated with a low Apgar score at 1 minute ($r = -0.4274$, $P < 0.05$), although with no evidence of correlation with a high Apgar score at 1 minute ($r = -0.0993$, $P > 0.05$). There were similar findings on Apgar scores at 5 minutes (fetal–maternal base deficit difference and high Apgar score at 5 minute, $r = -0.0647$, $P > 0.05$; fetal–maternal base deficit difference and low Apgar score at 5 minute, $r = -0.7313$, $P < 0.05$)

Evidence statement
There was limited evidence of a correlation between fetal base deficit and longer-term outcomes. There was no evidence of an advantage of calculating fetal–maternal pH or base deficit differences.

Continuous EFM versus continuous EFM plus FBS

Description of included studies
There was one systematic review, which compared continuous EFM with intermittent auscultation and assessed the effect of FBS on continuous EFM by subgroup analysis.[324] [EL = 2+] There was one observational study with historical controls that compared the effectiveness of FBS plus continuous EFM with continuous EFM.[518] [EL = 2+] Both showed reasonable quality, although there was no statistical analysis or subgroup analysis in the systematic review and therefore, the findings from the study are only suggestive.

Review findings
The systematic review, including all low- and high-risk women, showed a difference in effects on incidence of instrumental vaginal birth (continuous EFM plus FBS versus intermittent auscultation, RR 1.47 [95% CI 1.11 to 1.93]; continuous EFM without FBS versus intermittent auscultation, RR 1.10 [95% CI 0.87 to 1.40]) and neonatal seizures (continuous EFM plus FBS versus intermittent auscultation, RR 0.49 [95% CI 0.29 to 0.83]; continuous EFM without FBS versus intermittent auscultation, RR 0.54 [95% CI 0.20 to 1.44]).[324] A meta-analysis only including low-risk women, showed a difference in only neonatal seizures (continuous EFM plus FBS versus intermittent auscultation, RR 0.37 [95% CI 0.15 to 0.87]; continuous EFM without FBS versus intermittent auscultation, RR 0.54 [95% CI 0.03 to 3.22]). There was no evidence of a difference in effects, on other outcomes.

The cohort study[518] compared continuous EFM with continuous EFM plus FBS and showed evidence that the use of FBS reduced the incidence of instrumental birth for fetal distress (RR 0.33, $P = 0.007$), although there was no evidence of a difference in CS for fetal distress (RR 0.5, $P = 0.5$), an Apgar score less than 8 at 1 minute (RR 0.50, $P = 0.15$) and an Apgar score less than 8 at 5 minutes (with = 0/72, without = 2/70, $P = 0.25$).

Evidence statement
There was only low-level evidence on the use of FBS for continuous EFM. This showed that the use of FBS with continuous EFM may reduce the rate of instrumental vaginal birth, but there was no evidence of differences in other outcomes.

ST analysis versus fetal scalp pH monitoring

Description of included studies
There was one cohort study identified.[519] [EL = II] The study assessed diagnostic value of ST analysis compared with FBS. The study was of reasonable quality.

Review findings
There was evidence of a relationship between lag time ST event and scalp pH $(r = -0.73,$ $P = 0.004)$.

Evidence statement
There was low-level evidence of the diagnostic value of ST analysis compared with FBS. The evidence showed a good correlation between lag time ST event and scalp pH.

Lactate versus fetal scalp blood sampling

Description of included studies
There was one RCT comparing lactate and pH analysis at fetal scalp blood sampling during labour.[520] [EL = 1+] The study was of reasonable quality, although the study is underpowered to show a difference in effectiveness. The comparison was made between lactate measurement using a lactate card requiring 5 microlitres of blood and pH analysis performed by an analyser using 35 microlitres of blood.

Review findings
There was evidence that unsuccessful FBS was more frequent with pH analysis (OR 16.1 [95% CI 5.8 to 44.7]), than the lactate measurement, although there was no evidence of a difference in mode of birth and an Apgar score less than 7 at 1 minute and 5 minutes.

Evidence statement
There was a lack of evidence to show a correlation between lactate values and longer-term outcomes.

Time from decision to obtain fetal scalp pH sampling

Description of included studies
There was one case series identified.[521] The study measured the time interval from the decision made to the performance of obtaining a fetal scalp pH sample from 100 consecutive cases.

Review findings
The median time was 18 minutes (IQR 12 to 25 minutes). The result took longer than 30 minutes in 9% of women.

Evidence statement
There is limited evidence that FBS takes around 18 minutes to carry out.

GDG interpretation of the evidence (fetal blood sampling)
There is limited evidence from randomised trials that FBS with continuous fetal monitoring may reduce instrumental birth and CS. The research evidence does not support the use of FBS because of the lack of direct comparison, but clinical experience and evidence from indirect comparisons suggests that FBS avoids some instrumental births and CS.

Recommendation on fetal blood sampling

If fetal death is suspected despite the presence of an apparently recorded FHR, then fetal viability should be confirmed with real-time ultrasound assessment.

FBS should be advised in the presence of a pathological FHR trace, unless there is clear evidence of acute compromise.

Where assisted birth is contemplated because of an abnormal FHR pattern, in cases of suspected fetal acidosis FBS should be undertaken in the absence of technical difficulties or any contraindications.

Where there is clear evidence of acute fetal compromise (for example, prolonged deceleration greater than 3 minutes), FBS should not be undertaken and urgent preparations to expedite birth should be made.

Fetal blood samples should be taken with the woman in the left-lateral position.

The classification of FBS results shown in Table 13.4 is recommended.

Table 13.4 The classification of fetal blood sample results

Fetal blood sample result (pH)	Interpretation of the results
≥ 7.25	Normal FBS result
7.21–7.24	Borderline FBS result
≤ 7.20	Abnormal FBS result

These results should be interpreted taking into account the previous pH measurement, the rate of progress in labour and the clinical features of the woman and baby.

After an abnormal FBS result, consultant obstetric advice should be sought.

After a normal FBS result, sampling should be repeated no more than 1 hour later if the FHR trace remains pathological, or sooner if there are further abnormalities.

After a borderline FBS result, sampling should be repeated no more than 30 minutes later if the FHR trace remains pathological or sooner if there are further abnormalities.

The time taken to take a fetal blood sample needs to be considered when planning repeat samples.

If the FHR trace remains unchanged and the FBS result is stable after the second test, a third/ further sample may be deferred unless additional abnormalities develop on the trace.

Where a third FBS is considered necessary, consultant obstetric opinion should be sought.

Contraindications to FBS include:

- maternal infection (for example, HIV, hepatitis viruses and herpes simplex virus)
- fetal bleeding disorders (for example, haemophilia)
- prematurity (less than 34 weeks).

13.7 Other monitoring methods

Other methods of fetal monitoring were considered in the EFM guideline but these are not in use in the UK, and were considered outside the scope of the guideline. These include fetal pulse oximetry, near infrared spectroscopy and intrapartum umbilical artery Doppler.

13.8 Risk management when using continuous EFM in labour

13.8.1 Decision to intervene to the birth interval

Introduction
The purpose of fetal monitoring is to establish when there is concern about fetal wellbeing so that intervention, often birth, can be achieved before harm develops. It has to be recognised that when problems are identified, and a decision is made to intervene, that all interventions take some time to achieve birth.

Previous guideline
The EFM guideline reviewed one cohort study.[522] This study investigated the association between abnormal second-stage fetal heart tracings and umbilical acid–base balance. The study found a trend that prolonged abnormal second stage fetal heart tracing is associated with poor neonatal outcomes.

Description of included studies
There is no relevant study other than the study identified above, to answer this question.

Evidence statement
There is no high-quality evidence of association between duration of abnormal fetal heart trace and neonatal outcomes.

Decision to instrumental vaginal birth

Description of included studies
Two UK studies were identified, investigating the interval of decision to birth for instrumental vaginal birth.[523,524] [EL = 3] The study by Okunwobi was published in 2000, and 225 women were included.[523] The study by Eldridge was published in 2004, and 49 women were included.[524]

Review findings
The Okunwobi study showed averages of decision to birth interval as a mean of 34.4 minutes (SD 28.3 minutes), ranging from 5 to 101 minutes, and that for fetal distress as a mean of 26.5 minutes (SD 14.0 minutes); while without fetal distress, the mean was 39.5 minutes (SD 19.0 minutes). The study also showed a mean decision to birth interval with ventouse of 29.2 minutes (SD 13.2 minutes) and with forceps of 23.3 minutes (SD 14.3 minutes). The Eldridge study showed a median decision to birth interval of 19.0 minutes [range 6 to 85 minutes] and a mean of 26.0 minutes [95% CI 20 to 31 minutes], while for fetal distress, the median was 16.0 minutes [range 6 to 61 minutes], with a mean of 22.0 minutes [95% CI 16 to 25 minutes].

Evidence statement
The average interval between decision and childbirth for instrumental vaginal birth due to presumed fetal compromise in the UK, in the study context, seems to range between 20 and 30 minutes.

Decision to caesarean section

Description of included studies
Three UK studies[525–527] and one US study[528] were identified.

The UK national audit of caesarean sections published in October 2001, collected data from all maternity hospitals in England and Wales between May and July 2000.[527] This was estimated to represent 99% of all CS in the defined area/population. [EL = 3]

The second UK study assessed interval of decision to birth by CS in a large district hospital.[525] [EL = 3] The third UK study assessed interval of decision to CS birth with or without fetal distress.[526] Both studies are cross-sectional surveys. [EL = 3] In the US study, CS performed due to non-reassuring EFM was classified as emergent or urgent based on EFM findings and compared decision to birth intervals and other outcomes between the two groups.[528] [EL = 3]

Review findings
The national audit of 29 488 CS showed a median interval of decision to birth by CS for England and Wales as: 26 minutes (IQR 20 to 36 minutes) for cases with fetal blood pH less than 7.20 ($n = 424$); 26 minutes (IQR 17 to 40 minutes) for cases with severely abnormal FHR trace ($n = 1530$); 17 minutes (IQR 12 to 26 minutes) for cases with cord prolapse ($n = 147$); 29 minutes (IQR 20 to 44 minutes) for cases with placenta abruption ($n = 253$); and 27 minutes (IQR 18 to 40 minutes) for urgency cases ($n = 1$) and any of the indications above ($n = 2385$).[527]

In the second UK study, 66.3% women had an interval of less than 30 minutes from decision to CS birth, 88.3% with an interval less than 40 minutes and 4.0% with more than 50 minutes. There was no evidence of a difference in the incidence of babies who were admitted to neonatal units.

The third UK study showed a significant reduction of the interval for women with fetal distress, compared with those without (time interval for fetal distress, mean 42.9 minutes (SD 24.1 minutes); time interval without fetal distress, mean 71.1 minutes (SD 42.3 minutes), $P < 0.0001$).

The US study showed a significant difference in decision to birth interval between emergent CS (mean 23.0 minutes (SD 15.3 minutes)) and urgent CS (mean 36.7 minutes (SD 14.9 minutes)) ($P < 0.001$). There was a significant association between the interval and umbilical arterial pH (linear regression $r = 0.22$, $P = 0.02$) and between the interval and umbilical base excess (linear regression $r = 0.33$, $P < 0.001$). Although there was evidence of a difference between emergent and urgent groups in umbilical arterial pH (emergent = 7.12 (SD 0.16), urgent = 7.22 (SD 0.08), $P < 0.001$); umbilical arterial base excess (emergent = −8.8 mmol/l (SD 4.3 mmol/l), urgent = −3.9 mmol/l (SD 2.4 mmol/l), $P < 0.001$); cord arterial pH < 7.1 (emergent = 6/34, urgent = 2/83, $P = 0.007$); and cord base excess < −12.0 mmol/l (emergent = 8/34, urgent = 1/83, $P < 0.001$); there was no evidence of differences in neonatal outcomes: 1 minute Apgar less than 7 (emergent = 15/34, urgent = 27/83, $P = 0.24$); 5 minute Apgar less than 7 (emergent = 3/34, urgent = 8/83, $P = 1.00$); intra-ventricular haemorrhage (emergent = 2/34, urgent = 5/83, $P = 1.0$); and neonatal death (emergent = 1/34, urgent = 0/83, $P = 0.64$).

Evidence statement
The average interval between decision and childbirth for CS for fetal concern in the UK, in the study context, seems to range between 30 and 40 minutes.

Recommendation on decision to intervene to the birth interval

Clinicians should take into account the time that it will take to achieve birth by both instrumental vaginal birth and caesarean section when making decisions regarding concern over fetal wellbeing during labour.

13.8.2 Risk management in monitoring babies in labour

Introduction
Obstetric litigation is expensive because of the number of cases and the costs of each case. The majority of obstetric litigation claims revolve around FHR trace abnormalities and interpretation. Litigation can ensue many years after alleged harm has been suffered. In order to provide a fair assessment of a case for all parties, FHR traces need to be available and as much information as possible obtained about the causes of poor outcome.

Storage of FHR traces

Description of included studies
This was reviewed in the EFM guideline.[460] No new studies were identified.

Evidence statement (from the NICE EFM guideline)
Storage of FHR traces is complicated due to issues of security, retrieval, space and conservation. FHR traces related to an adverse outcome for mother or baby are more likely to go missing. The quality of some FHR traces deteriorates over time. This could be due to a number of factors including poor quality storage, paper, intense heat, light or moisture.

Recommendations on risk management in monitoring babies in labour

FHR traces should be kept for 25 years and, where possible, stored electronically.

In cases where there is concern that the baby may suffer developmental delay, FHR traces should be photocopied and stored indefinitely in case of possible adverse outcomes.

Tracer systems should be available for all FHR traces if stored separately from women's records.

Tracer systems should be developed to ensure that FHR traces removed for any purpose (such as risk management or for teaching purposes) can always be located.

13.8.3 Cord blood gas analysis

Clinical question
Is there evidence that routine taking of cord blood gases influences outcomes?

Description of included studies
A total of eight cohort studies and one systematic review that examined predictive values of cord blood gas were identified.[418,529–536] The systematic review included 12 cohort studies. Studies on

neonatal mortality and diagnosis of developing cerebral palsy were considered homogeneous enough to consider meta-analyses. [EL = III]

Review findings
The results of the meta-analyses are shown in Table 13.5. Cord arterial gas was not regarded as a good predictor of either neonatal death or developing cerebral palsy, even compared with Apgar scores. Meta-analysis of four studies showed that cord arterial pH seems to be a good positive predictor for the Apgar score, although the negative predictive value seemed to be poor. There are two studies comparing neonatal immediate outcomes and cord arterial gas. Although there is moderate level of accuracy found in these comparisons, sensitivity tends to be low.

Table 13.5   Summary likelihood ratios of predictive values of cord gas

	LR (positive)	95% CI	LR (negative)	95% CI
Low Apgar scores	14.8	13.3 to 16.4	0.43	0.41 to 0.46
Cerebral palsy	1.46	1.10 to 1.93	0.94	0.89 to 0.99
Neonatal deaths	2.87	2.36 to 3.49	0.77	0.71 to 0.84

LR = likelihood ratio.

Evidence statement
There is limited evidence that cord pH is a predictor of neonatal death or cerebral palsy. The highly negative predictive value of a normal paired cord blood gas for the exclusion of intrapartum-related hypoxic ischemic brain damage justifies the use of paired cord gas analysis.

GDG interpretation of the evidence (cord gas)
The highly negative predictive value of a normal paired cord blood gas for the exclusion of intrapartum-related hypoxic ischemic brain damage, justifies the use of paired cord gas analysis where necessary.

> **Recommendations on cord blood gas analysis**
>
> Paired cord blood gases do not need to be taken routinely. They should be taken when there has been concern about the baby either in labour or immediately following birth.
>
> An additional clamp to facilitate double-clamping of the cord should be available at all birth settings.

14 Complicated labour: first stage

14.1 Definition of delay in the first stage of labour

Introduction
Delay in the first stage of labour has been defined in a number of ways and there is no universal consensus. It has been traditional to define delay largely by the rate of cervical progress without taking into account either maternal uterine activity or descent or rotation of the fetal head during labour. Although it is acknowledged that the duration of labour is dependent on parity, clinical practice and local labour guidelines rarely make that distinction.

Clinical question
Do duration and progress of the first and second stages of labour affect outcomes?

Discussion
The GDG discussed the definition of delay in the first stage of labour, based on the evidence presented in Chapter 7 and made the following recommendation.

Recommendation on definition of delay in the first stage of labour

A diagnosis of delay in the established first stage of labour needs to take into consideration all aspects of progress in labour and should include:

- cervical dilatation of less than 2 cm in 4 hours for first labours
- cervical dilatation of less than 2 cm in 4 hours or a slowing in the progress of labour for second or subsequent labours
- descent and rotation of the fetal head
- changes in the strength, duration and frequency of uterine contractions.

14.2 Interventions for perceived delay in the first stage of labour

Clinical question
What is the effectiveness of the following interventions or techniques in labour on outcomes?

- amniotomy
- oxytocin.

Previous guideline
The NICE clinical guideline *Caesarean Section*[6] reviewed evidence from one RCT and two observational studies on oxytocin, as well as one systematic review on amniotomy. The guideline recommended that the following aspects of intrapartum care have not been shown to influence the likelihood of caesarean section (CS) for 'failure to progress' and should not be offered for this reason, although they may affect other outcomes which are outside the scope of this guideline: early amniotomy. A research recommendation was also developed as more RCTs are required to determine the effect of oxytocin augmentation as single interventions or as part of a package of interventions (such as 'active management of labour') on the likelihood of CS and other outcomes including women's satisfaction with care. Further research on the short- and longer-term health impacts of CS during the second stage, compared with instrumental vaginal birth, is needed.

14.2.1   Amniotomy versus expectant management

Description of included studies
One systematic review including nine trials, published in 1999, was identified. The review was of good quality.[537] The results were stratified by parity of the women. The intervention was amniotomy targeting women in labour who required augmentation, compared with expectant management.

Review findings

Nulliparous women
Meta-analysis of included trials showed strong evidence that amniotomy significantly reduced the time to birth: randomisation and birth interval (two trials, $n = 117$ women): MD −53.67 minutes [95% CI −66.50 to −40.83 minutes]; randomisation and full dilatation interval (three trials, $n = 298$ women): MD −39.45 minutes [95% CI −50.10 to −28.80 minutes]; rate of dystocia (one trial, $n = 925$ women): OR 0.63 [95% CI 0.48 to 0.82]); rate of cord prolapse (one trial, $n = 925$ women): OR 0.14 [95% CI 0.00 to 6.84]); and the proportion of women whose labour pain was unbearable (three trials, $n = 1283$ women): OR 0.76 [95% CI 0.60, 0.97]. There was no evidence of differences in any other maternal variable: oxytocin use, use of analgesia, CS rate, instrumental birth rate, incidence of abnormal or suspect fetal heart rate (FHR), maternal febrile morbidity, maternal blood transfusion, or maternal satisfaction (see evidence tables). For the babies, there was no evidence of differences in: malrotation of the fetal head (one trial, $n = 32$ women): OR 0.47 [95% CI 0.12 to 1.89]; Apgar score less than 7 at 5 minutes (five trials, $n = 2518$ women): OR 0.94 [95% CI 0.67 to 1.33]; neonatal jaundice (three trials, $n = 2383$ women): OR 1.05 [95% CI 0.70 to 1.58]; rate of admission to special care nursery (four trials, $n = 1996$ women): OR 1.13 [95% CI 0.78 to 1.62]; incidence of cephalhaematoma (two trials, $n = 1022$ women): OR 1.66 [95% CI 0.86 to 3.21]; and neonatal infective morbidity (two trials, $n = 1353$ women): OR 1.43 [95% CI 0.85 to 2.41].

Parous women
The evidence for multiparous women is limited, although it showed significant reduction in the interval between randomisation and full dilatation (one trial, $n = 269$ women): MD −54.00 minutes [95% CI −101.37, −6.63 minutes]. Otherwise, there was no evidence of differences in the: use of oxytocin (one trial, $n = 940$ women): OR 1.22 [95% CI 0.67 to 2.21]; use of analgesia (epidural/narcotics) (one trial, 940 women): OR 1.14 [95% CI 0.80 to 1.63]; rate of CS (one trial 940 women): OR 2.65 [95% CI 0.75 to 9.29]; rate of instrumental vaginal birth (one trial 940 women): OR 1.20 [95% CI 0.65 to 2.21]; or incidence of neonatal jaundice (one trial 531 women): OR 3.61 [95% CI 0.89 to 14.75].

Evidence statement
When there is delay in the established first stage of labour, there is high-level evidence that the duration is shortened by amniotomy.

14.2.2   Amniotomy and oxytocin versus oxytocin

Description of included studies
One RCT conducted in the USA was identified ($n = 118$: amniotomy = 58; control = 60).[538] The study population involved both nulliparous and parous women with active phase arrest. The intervention of routine amniotomy followed by oxytocin was compared with oxytocin followed by selective amniotomy.

Review findings
There is no evidence of a difference in the interval between randomisation and birth (MD −0.70 hours [−1.55 to 0.15 hours]); rate of CS (RR 1.21 [95% CI 0.34 to 4.28]) and neonatal infection (RR 4.83 [95% CI 0.58 to 40.13]), although there was significantly more women with postpartum infection in the intervention group than in the control group (amniotomy = 7/60; control = 0/58, $P = 0.01$).

14.2.3 Amniotomy versus amniotomy plus oxytocin

Description of included studies
Three UK trials were identified. The first study involved 926 nulliparous and parous women requiring augmentation (oxytocin = 465; control = 461).[539] The second trial involved 61 nulliparous women progressing slowly (amniotomy + high-dose oxytocin = 19; amniotomy + low-dose oxytocin = 21; control = 20).[540] The third trial involved nulliparous and multiparous women requiring augmentation (oxytocin + amniotomy = 21; amniotomy only = 20).[541]

Review findings
Meta-analysis of the trials showed no evidence of differences in the rate of CS (three trials, RR 0.82 [95% CI 0.47 to 1.40]); use of epidural (two trials, RR 1.01 [95% CI 0.79 to 1.30]); proportion of the babies with an Apgar score less than 7 at 5 minutes (two trials, RR 0.95 [95% CI 0.13 to 7.09]); admissions to the neonatal unit (one trial, RR 3.00 [95% CI 0.12 to 78.04]); and maternal satisfaction score (one trial, MD 9.00 [95% CI −6.73 to 24.73]).

14.2.4 Amniotomy and oxytocin versus delayed amniotomy and oxytocin

Description of included studies
The UK trial included in the above review also investigated this comparison.[541] The population comprised 61 nulliparous and multiparous women requiring augmentation (oxytocin and amniotomy = 21; expectant = 19).

Review findings
The trial showed a significant reduction in the interval between randomisation and giving birth (intervention = 266 minutes (SD 166), control = 463 minutes (SD 164 minutes), $P < 0.001$) and an increase in maternal satisfaction (satisfaction score intervention = 149 (SD 23), control = 118 (SD 33), $P = 0.002$), although there was no evidence of differences in the use of epidural (RR 0.55 [95% CI 0.12 to 2.4]), rate of CS (RR 2.6 [95% CI 0.4 to 30.9]) and neonatal outcomes (Apgar < 7 at 5 minutes intervention = 1/21, control = 0/19; admission to SCBU, intervention = 1/21, control = 0/19).

Evidence statement
There is evidence that where labour is delayed, amniotomy followed by an oxytocin infusion with a low-dose regimen (0–3 mU per minute) shortens the duration of the first stage of labour but it does not appear to improve the chance of vaginal birth or any other outcome. Where ruptured membranes have occurred, there is no evidence that giving oxytocin in the first 8 hours after this alters anything except the duration of labour.

14.2.5 Effect of augmentation on electronic FHR abnormalities

Amniotomy for delay in labour

Description of included studies
There is one systematic review including nine trials identified.[537] The systematic review was of good quality. [EL = 1+] Among the included studies, three trials assessed effect of amniotomy for shortening labour on FHR tracing.

Review findings
There was no evidence of a difference in incidence of abnormal or suspect FHR trace (all women including nulliparous and multiparous RR 1.06 [95% CI 0.80 to 1.42]; only nulliparous women RR 0.93 [95% CI 0.67 to 1.31]).

Evidence statement
There is no evidence of a difference in abnormal FHR tracing following amniotomy for delay in the first stage of labour.

Oxytocin

Description of included studies
No trial was found that assessed directly the effect of oxytocin augmentation on FHR. There were two trials identified that assessed the effect of oxytocin augmentation on CS rate for fetal distress.[539,541] The first trial was conducted in the UK and published in 1998 (*n* = 41).[541] The second trial was also conducted in the UK, and published in 1990 (*n* = 926).[539] Both trials showed good quality. [EL = 1+]

Review findings
There was no evidence of a difference in incidence of CS for fetal distress in either trial (first trial, RR 2.86 [95% CI 0.32 to 25.24]; second trial, nulliparous RR 0.40 [95% CI 0.45 to 1.03]; the second trial, multiparous women only RR 0.66 [95% CI 0.20 to 2.13]).

Evidence statement
There is no direct evidence of abnormal FHR tracing with the use of oxytocin augmentation. There is no evidence of differences on rate of CS for fetal distress by oxytocin augmentation.

GDG interpretation of the evidence (augmentation by oxytocin and fetal monitoring)
This lack of evidence does not detract from the clinical need to continuously monitor the fetal heart when oxytocin is being used for augmentation.

14.2.6 Oxytocin administration

High- versus low-dose oxytocin for augmentation

Introduction
For this review, amount of oxytocin was defined as below:

- high dose defined as starting dose and increment of equal to or more than 4 mU per minute
- low dose defined as starting dose and an increment of up to 2 mU per minute
- the increase interval should be between 15 and 40 minutes.

Description of included studies
There were four RCTs identified that compared high versus low doses of oxytocin infusion for augmentation of labour.[540,542–544] Table 14.1 summarises the dosages employed.

Review findings

Women's outcomes
Meta-analysis of the trials showed no evidence of difference in oxytocin to birth interval (two trials, MD −98.45 minutes [95% CI −269.71 to 72.82 minutes]), but a higher maximum oxytocin dose for the higher-dose group than the lower-dose group (three trials, MD 7.49 mU/minute [95% CI 7.06 to 7.91 mU/minute]). There was a reduction in incidence of CS, especially CS for dystocia, and an increase in spontaneous vaginal birth with the higher dose: total CS (four trials):

Table 14.1 Low- and high-dose oxytocin protocols used for augmentation of labour in included studies

Study	Low dose	High dose
Jamal (2004)[544]	Start at 1.5 mU/minute	Start at 4.5 mU/minute
	Increase by 1.5 mU/30 minutes	Increase by 4.5 mU/30 minutes
Merrill (1999)[542]	Start at 1.5 mU/minute	Start at 4.5 mU/minute
	Increase by 1.5 mU/30 minutes	Increase by 4.5 mU/30 minutes
Xenakis (1995)[543]	Start at 1.5 mU/minute	Start at 4.5 mU/minute
	Increase by 1.5 mU/30 minutes until 4 mU/minute	Increase by 4.5 mU/15 minutes
	Wait for 120 minutes	
	Increase by 1.5 mU/30 minutes	
Bidgood (1987)[540]	Start at 2 mU/minute	Start at 7 mU/minute
	Increase by 2 mU/15 minutes	Increase by 7 mU/15 minutes

RR 0.76 [95% CI 0.62 to 0.92]; CS for dystocia (three trials): RR 0.72 [95% CI 0.57 to 0.91]; CS for fetal distress (three trials): RR 0.91 [95% CI 0.58 to 1.40]; and spontaneous vaginal birth (two trials): RR 1.13 [95% CI 1.07 to 1.20]). There were more women with hyperstimulation (four trials): RR 1.35 [95% CI 1.21 to 1.50]) but less women with chorioamnionitis (three trials): RR 0.71 [95% CI 0.56 to 0.90]) with the higher dose, while there was no evidence of a difference in incidence of shoulder dystocia (two trials): RR 1.36 [95% CI 0.63 to 2.95]).

Newborn outcomes
There was no evidence of differences in the proportion of: babies who were admitted to neonatal units (two trials, RR 0.95 [95% CI 0.68 to 1.32]); babies with Apgar scores less than 7 at 5 minutes (four trials, RR 0.98 [95% CI 0.42 to 2.28]); and perinatal deaths (four trials, RR 1.45 [95% CI 0.37 to 5.74]).

Women's satisfaction and other psychological outcomes
No identified study investigated these outcomes.

Evidence statement
There is reasonable quality evidence on high- or low- doses of oxytocin. Women with high dose of oxytocin for augmentation complete their labours quicker but had higher maximum oxytocin dose than those with the lower dose.

Women with high-dose oxytocin for augmentation had less CS, most of which contributed by CS for dystocia, more spontaneous vaginal birth, and less chorioamnionitis, but had more hyperstimulation than those with the lower dose. The studies are underpowered to examine serious neonatal morbidity or mortality.

There is no evidence on women's satisfaction and long-term outcomes.

GDG interpretation of evidence (high- versus low-dose of oxytocin for augmentation)
There is evidence on high- versus low-dose oxytocin, but studies are heterogeneous. Women whose labours are augmented with high-dose oxytocin may have shorter labours, less CS and more spontaneous vaginal birth than those receiving a low dose. However, the GDG remain cautious about the use of higher doses of oxytocin because there is insufficient evidence on neonatal outcomes and none on pain for women receiving high-dose oxytocin (4 mU/minute or greater) for augmentation.

Comparing different oxytocin dosage regimens

Description of included studies
There are five RCTs identified investigating different oxytocin dosages apart from the above studies.[545–549] Because of the heterogeneity of the studies, it was not possible to conduct a meta-analysis, hence a descriptive summary is presented.

Review findings
A trial conducted in Zimbabwe (2001) involved 258 nulliparous women who required augmentation in labour, and compared different high doses of oxytocin use.[545] [EL = 1–] The lower dose started at 4 mU/minute, doubled every 30 minutes until 16 mU/minute, and then 64 mU/minute, while the higher dose started at 10 mU/minute and doubled every 60 minutes until 40 mU/minute. The trial showed a significant reduction in the proportion of women with more than 6 hours from augmentation to giving birth (RR 0.36 [95% CI 0.21 to 0.62]). No difference was found for CS rate (RR 0.95 [95% CI 0.42 to 2.15]) or neonatal outcomes.

A US RCT (1994) involving 1167 women who required augmentation in labour, compared women's and babies' outcomes for different increment times of oxytocin: 20 minute dose (start at 6 mU/minute, increase by 6 mU/20 minutes until 42 mU/minute) versus 40 minute dose (start at 6 mU/minute, increase by 6 mU/40 minutes until 42 mU/minute).[546] [EL = 1+] The findings showed a reduction in incidence of CS for dystocia with quicker dosage than slower dosage (OR 0.65 [95% CI 0.43 to 0.97]), and there was borderline evidence of more uterine hyperstimulation with faster rates (OR 1.3 [95% CI 0.98 to 1.7]), but there is no evidence of difference in chorioamnionitis (OR 0.97 [95% CI 0.66 to 1.4]) and babies admitted to the neonatal unit (OR 1.3 [95% CI 0.77 to 2.4])

A second US RCT involving 487 women who required augmentation in labour, compared a 15 minute dose (start at 1 mU/minute, increase 1 mU/15 minutes until 5 mU/minute, increase by 1–2 mU/15 minutes) and a 40 minute dose (start at 1 mU/minute, increase 1.5 mU/40 minutes until 7 mU/minute, then increase by 1.5–3.0 mU/40 minutes).[547] [EL = 1+]

The results showed more women reached higher maximum dose of oxytocin (mean 15 minutes = 8.2 mU/minute; 40 minutes = 6.5 mU/minute, $P < 0.001$), and experienced fetal distress (RR 1.68, $P < 0.005$) and uterine hyperstimulation (RR 1.69, $P < 0.001$) with the 15 minute dose, compared with the 40 minute dose.

A third RCT conducted in the USA ($n = 94$) compared continuous infusion of oxytocin (start at 1 mU/minute, increase by 1 mU/20 minutes) and repeated pulsatile injection of oxytocin (start at 1 mU per pulse (10 seconds every 8 minutes), doubled every 24 minutes).[548] [EL = 1+] Women with the pulsatile regimen required less amount of oxytocin: average level of oxytocin pulsatile = 2.1 mU/minute (SD 0.4 mU/minute), continuous = 4.1 mU/minute (SD 0.4 mU/minute), $P < 0.001$; total amount of oxytocin pulsatile = 1300 mU (SD 332 mU), continuous = 1803 mU (SD 302 mU), $P < 0.001$); compared with the continuous regimen, with no differences in dysfunctional contractions (RR 1.04, NS).

There was one RCT in the UK identified.[549] [EL = 1–] The study population consisted of 68 nulliparous women who required augmentation in labour. The oxytocin was started at 2.5 mU/minute, and increased by 2.5 mU/30 minutes for both arms. The comparison was made as the oxytocin was increased either until uterine contraction was 6 in 15 minutes or until uterine activity was 1750 kPas/15 minute measured by an intrauterine catheter. The study was underpowered and found no difference in: maximum oxytocin dose frequency = 8.3 mU/minute (SD 3.7 mU/minute); uterine activity = 8.0 mU/minute (SD 3.1 mU/minute); hyperstimulation (RR 0.54, NS); rate of CS (RR 2.00, NS); and Apgar score < 5 at 1 minute (RR 0.33, NS).

Evidence statement
The evidence on different oxytocin dosage regimens for augmentation is limited as the studies tended to be underpowered and use too many different regimens. Women with quicker increments of oxytocin dose for augmentation appeared to have more hyperstimulation, compared with those with slower increments. Women with quicker increments of a high dose of oxytocin seemed to have less CS for dystocia than those with a slower dose, but there is no evidence of a difference in this comparison for low dose. Women with quicker increments of low doses of oxytocin seemed to experience fetal distress, compared with those with the slower increments. There was limited evidence on pulsatile oxytocin compared with continuous infusion. The limited evidence showed a smaller amount of oxytocin was required with pulsatile injections, but there was no evidence of differences in other outcomes. There was insufficient evidence on other outcomes including neonatal outcomes and women's satisfaction on different oxytocin regimens.

GDG interpretation of the evidence (different doses of oxytocin for augmentation)
The evidence on dose regimens for augmentation is limited as the studies are underpowered and use different comparisons. Increasing the rate more frequently than every 20 minutes may be associated with more uterine hyperstimulation and more non-reassuring fetal heart rate patterns.

Recommendations on interventions for perceived delay in first stage of labour

Where delay in the established first stage is suspected the following should be considered:

- parity
- cervical dilatation and rate of change
- uterine contractions
- station and position of presenting part
- the woman's emotional state
- referral to the appropriate healthcare professional,

and women should be offered support, hydration, and appropriate and effective pain relief.

If delay in the established first stage of labour is suspected, amniotomy should be considered for all women with intact membranes, following explanation of the procedure and advice that it will shorten her labour by about an hour and may increase the strength and pain of her contractions.

Whether or not a woman has agreed to an amniotomy, all women with suspected delay in the established first stage of labour should be advised to have a vaginal examination 2 hours later, and if progress is less than 1 cm a diagnosis of delay is made.

In women with intact membranes in whom delay in the established first stage of labour is confirmed, amniotomy should be advised to the woman, and she should be advised to have a repeat vaginal examination 2 hours later whether her membranes are ruptured or intact.

When delay in the established first stage of labour is confirmed in nulliparous women, advice should be sought from an obstetrician and the use of oxytocin should be considered. The woman should be informed that the use of oxytocin following spontaneous or artificial rupture of the membranes will bring forward her time of birth but will not influence the mode of birth or other outcomes.

Multiparous women with confirmed delay in the first stage should be seen by an obstetrician who should make a full assessment, including an abdominal palpation and vaginal examination, before making a decision about the use of oxytocin.

All women with delay in the established first stage of labour should be offered support and effective pain relief.

Women should be informed that oxytocin will increase the frequency and strength of their contractions and that its use will mean their baby should be monitored continuously. Women should be offered an epidural before oxytocin is started.

Where oxytocin is used, the time between increments of the dose should be no more frequent than every 30 minutes. Oxytocin should be increased until there are 4–5 contractions in 10 minutes. (See also Chapter 13 on monitoring babies in labour.)

The woman should be advised to have a vaginal examination 4 hours after commencing oxytocin in established labour. If there is less than 2 cm progress after 4 hours of oxytocin, further obstetric review is required to consider caesarean section. If there is 2 cm or more progress, vaginal examinations should be advised 4 hourly.

Amniotomy alone for suspected delay in the established first stage of labour is not an indication to commence continuous EFM.

Where a diagnosis of delay in the established first stage of labour is made, continuous EFM should be offered.

Continuous EFM should be used when oxytocin is administered for augmentation.

Research recommendation on oxytocin for augmentation of labour

The start dose of oxytocin for augmentation, and the increments, should be the subject of further research.

Studies are needed that investigate the effectiveness of any strategies to increase spontaneous vaginal birth where diagnosis is made of delay in the first stage of labour.

15 Complicated labour: second stage

15.1 Delay in the second stage of labour

Introduction

Delay in the second stage of labour has been defined in a number of ways and there is no universal consensus. This is discussed in Chapter 8.

The definition of the onset of the active second stage of labour: (from Chapter 8)

- the baby is visible
- expulsive contractions with a finding of full dilatation of the cervix, or other signs of full dilatation of the cervix
- there is active maternal effort, following confirmation of full dilatation of the cervix, in the absence of expulsive contractions.

Clinical question

Do duration and progress of the first and second stages of labour affect outcomes?

Discussion

The GDG discussed the definition of delay in the first stage of labour based on the evidence presented in Chapter 8 and made the following recommendations.

> **Recommendations on duration and definition of delay in the second stage of labour**
>
> Nulliparous women:
>
> - Birth would be expected to take place within 3 hours of the start of the active second stage in most women.
> - A diagnosis of delay in the active second stage should be made when it has lasted 2 hours and women should be referred to a healthcare professional trained to undertake an operative vaginal birth if birth is not imminent. [repeated from Section 8.2]
>
> Parous women:
>
> - Birth would be expected to take place within 2 hours of the start of the active second stage in most women.
> - A diagnosis of delay in the active second stage should be made when it has lasted 1 hour and women should be referred to a healthcare professional trained to undertake an operative vaginal birth if birth is not imminent. [repeated from Section 8.2]

15.1.1 Indication for instrument-assisted vaginal birth

Overview of available evidence

No randomised controlled trial was identified.

Evidence statement

There is no high-quality evidence to compare indications for assisted vaginal birth.

15.1.2 Interventions for delay in the second stage

Introduction
The review refers to women without epidural analgesia, and who have not had a previous caesarean section.

Oxytocin versus expectant management

Description of included studies
There is no study identified comparing oxytocin infusion with expectant management, for management of women without epidural analgesia who have a delayed second stage of labour.

Evidence statement
There are no high-quality studies looking at the use of oxytocin for delay in the second stage of labour, for women without epidural analgesia.

Oxytocin versus instrumental births

Description of included studies
There is no study identified comparing these two interventions.

Evidence statement
There is no high-level evidence on effectiveness and safety of oxytocin infusion for management of the second stage of labour, compared with instrumental vaginal birth.

GDG interpretation of the evidence
While there is no evidence on starting oxytocin in the second stage of labour for parous women, the GDG consider the potential risks of uterine rupture are such that we cannot recommend it.

Recommendations on interventions for delay in the second stage of labour

Where there is delay in the second stage of labour, or if the woman is excessively distressed, support and sensitive encouragement and the woman's need for analgesia/anaesthesia are particularly important.

Consideration should be given to the use of oxytocin, with the offer of regional analgesia, for nulliparous women if contractions are inadequate at the onset of the second stage

In nulliparous women, if after 1 hour of active second stage progress is inadequate, delay is suspected. Following vaginal examination, amniotomy should be offered if the membranes are intact.

Women with confirmed delay in the second stage should be assessed by an obstetrician but oxytocin should not be started.

Following initial obstetric assessment for women with delay in the second stage of labour, ongoing obstetric review should be maintained every 15–30 minutes.

15.1.3 Instrument to be used

Clinical question
What are the indications for the use of ventouse or forceps?

Ventouse versus forceps

Description of included studies
The evidence for this subsection was drawn from a good quality systematic review[550] including ten trials, plus three additional recent trials.[551–553] [EL = 1+] The systematic review was published in April 1999, and the last search was performed in February 1999. The trials included in the systematic review were conducted in USA, Denmark, Sweden, UK, South Africa and Greece. The recent trials were conducted in Sri Lanka,[551] Pakistan[552] and Ireland.[553] There are two follow-up studies of trials using the same population that were included in the systematic review, which investigated long-term outcomes of mothers and their children. These studies were conducted in the UK (published in 1999 and 1998).[554,555]

Review findings

Labour events
Meta-analysis of nine trials showed that ventouse-assisted birth was more likely to be associated with failed birth with selected instruments compared with forceps-assisted birth (n = 2849, OR 1.69 [95% CI 1.31, 2.19]).[556] Another recent trial in Pakistan showed the same association (n = 442, RR 2.04 [95% CI 1.14, 3.70]).[552] There was no evidence of differences in rates of CS (meta-analysis of seven trials, n = 1662, OR 0.56 [95% CI 0.31, 1.02]). Meta-analysis of 12 trials showed a significant reduction of the use of anaesthesia with ventouse-assisted birth (n = 5051, OR 0.59 [95% CI 0.51, 0.68]).

Women's complications
Meta-analysis of trials in the systematic review showed that ventouse-assisted birth significantly reduced significant maternal injury (seven trials, n = 2582): OR 0.41 [95% CI 0.33 to 0.50] and severe perineal pain at 24 hours (two trials, n = 495): OR 0.54 [95% CI 0.31 to 0.93]. The Pakistani trial showed that ventouse-assisted birth significantly reduced cervical tears (n = 442: RR 0.19 [95% CI 0.04 to 0.86]) and third-degree perineal trauma (n = 442): RR 0.58 [95% CI 0.04 to 0.86]) compared with forceps-assisted birth.

Newborn outcomes
Meta-analysis of trials in the systematic reviews showed that ventouse-assisted birth increased incidence of cephalhaematoma (six trials, n = 1966): OR 2.38 [95% CI 1.68 to 3.37] and retinal haemorrhage (five trials, n = 445): OR 1.99 [95% CI 1.35 to 2.96]. The Pakistani trial also showed an increase in the incidence of cephalhaematoma with the use of ventouse (n = 442): RR 7.14 [95% CI 1.59 to 33.33]. There was a non-significant increase in the number of babies whose birth was assisted with ventouse who had a lower Apgar score at 5 minutes (five trials, n = 1545): OR 1.67 [95% CI 0.99 to 2.81]. Meta-analysis of trials showed that there was no evidence of a difference in Apgar score less than 7 at 1 minute (meta-analysis of three trials, n = 822): OR 1.13 [95% CI 0.76 to 1.68]; and the Sri Lanka trial (n = 50): RR 0.85 [95% CI 0.24 to 3.03]; scalp or face injuries (not cephalhaematoma) (six trials, n = 2330): OR 0.89 [95% CI 0.70 to 1.13]; use of phototherapy (four trials, n = 1648): OR 1.08 [95% CI 0.66 to 1.77]; perinatal death (seven trials, n = 1800): OR 0.80 [95% CI 0.18 to 3.52]; follow-up/re-admission by hospital (one trial,[557] n = 232): OR 1.33 [95% CI 0.58 to 3.05]; hearing abnormal (confirmed/suspected) (one trial,[557] n = 232):OR 1.66 [95% CI 0.54 to 5.06]; and strabismus or vision abnormality suspected (one trial,[557] n = 232): OR 1.38 [95% CI 0.47 to 4.05]. The Sri Lanka study also showed no evidence of differences in neonatal complications (n = 50): RR 1.00 [95% CI 0.72 to 1.39].

Mental and psychological outcomes and women's satisfaction
Meta-analysis of three trials showed that maternal worries about the baby, significantly increased with ventouse-assisted birth (n = 561): OR 2.17 [95% CI 1.19 to 3.94]. The Irish study investigated women's satisfaction and showed no evidence of a difference (would choose CS for next birth): RR 0.53 [95% CI 0.23 to 1.27]. In the systematic review, only two trials included women's assessment of pain during birth.[558,559] One trial comparing methods of instrumental birth contained a substudy of the views of women and obstetric and midwifery staff.[559] A subsample of 66 of the 304 women participating in the trial were interviewed between the first and eighth day postpartum. Women scored the pain of the birth itself on a 4-point scale ranging from 'not painful at all' to 'extremely painful'. Despite receiving more analgesia, 12 of the 33 women who had undergone a forceps birth considered the birth had been 'very' or 'extremely' painful compared with seven of the 33 who had undergone a vacuum extraction. Similar findings were reported by another study, which found 27% (n = 28) of women considered their forceps birth to have been 'unbearable' compared with 18% (n = 19) of women who had undergone vacuum extraction: OR 1.5 [95% CI 0.5 to 4.2].[558]

A third study concluded that there were significantly fewer women in the vacuum extractor group requiring epidural or spinal anaesthesia (25.4% versus 32.7%) or general anaesthetics (1% versus 4%) compared with the forceps group.[560] The authors concluded that less analgesia is required for vacuum extraction compared with the use of forceps. However, the results reflect the choice of analgesia made prior to the start of the procedure by the attending anaesthetist and obstetrician rather than that requested or desired by the women themselves. No assessment was made of the pain experienced during the procedure and the women's views on the type of analgesia provided were not recorded.

Medium- and long-term outcome
The UK follow-up study of the trial showed a significantly lower incidence with use of ventouse of anal sphincter defects (RR 0.58 [95% CI 0.32 to 0.92]); and higher maximum anal squeeze pressure (ventouse mean = 38, forceps mean = 53, $P = 0.02$); but no evidence of difference in anal incontinence (RR 1.47 [95% CI 0.44 to 4.92]); and maximum anal resting pressure (ventouse mean = 55, forceps mean = 60, $P = 0.32$) at the end of the 5-year follow-up period.[555] Another study using the same population showed no evidence of differences in both bowel and urinary habits of the women after 5 years.[554] This study also investigated long-term outcome of the babies, and showed no evidence of differences in visual problems among the children (OR 0.9 [95% CI 0.38 to 2.5]) or child development.

The Irish long-term study (follow-up = 3 months) showed that there was a significant reduction in altered continence (RR 0.35 [95% CI 0.17 to 0.71]) and a tendency of higher anal pressure among women who had given birth assisted by ventouse compared with forceps-assisted birth: resting pressure (mmHg) (ventouse median = 63, forceps median = 54, $P = 0.05$); squeeze pressure (mmHg) (ventouse median = 96, forceps median = 86, $P = 0.11$); squeeze increment (mmHg) (ventouse median = 25, forceps median = 27, $P = 0.12$); vector symmetry index (RR 0.77 [95% CI 0.39 to 1.54]). There was no evidence of differences in continence score (ventouse mean = 3, forceps mean = 3, $P = 0.17$); faecal urgency less than 5 minutes (RR 0.72 [95% CI 0.34 to 1.54]); and perineal discomfort (RR 0.78 [95% CI 0.37 to 1.64]).

Soft ventouse versus hard ventouse

Description of included studies
One good quality systematic review including nine trials and 1375 women was identified.[561] [EL = 1+] This was published in February 2000 and the last search was performed in February 2000. The included trials were conducted in Saudi Arabia, Nepal, the UK, Sweden, South Africa, the Netherlands, Malaysia, Greece and Thailand.

Review findings

Labour events
Meta-analysis of nine trials showed there was a significant increase of failure to deliver when the instrument chosen was with the soft cups, as oppose to the hard cups ($n = 1368$ women): OR 1.65 [95% CI 1.19 to 2.29]. No other outcome was reported.

Women's outcomes
Meta-analysis of six trials showed there was no evidence of a difference in significant maternal injury ($n = 1137$ women): OR 0.85 [95% CI 0.57 to 1.27].

Newborn outcomes
Meta-analysis of eight trials showed that use of soft cups significantly reduced significant scalp trauma ($n = 1337$): OR 0.45 [95% CI 0.34 to 0.60]. Otherwise, meta-analysis showed no evidence of a difference in Apgar score less than 7 at 1 minute (four trials, $n = 866$): OR 1.21 [95% CI 0.80 to 1.83]; less than 7 at 5 minutes (five trials, $n = 765$): OR 0.68 [95% CI 0.35 to 1.33]; incidence of cephalhaematoma (four trials, $n = 538$): OR 0.70 [95% CI 0.34 to 1.44]; incidence of phototherapy or jaundice (six trials, $n = 1137$): OR 0.73 [95% CI 0.50 to 1.07]; severe retinal/intracranial haemorrhage (two trials, $n = 218$): OR 0.84 [95% CI 0.27 to 2.64]; and neonatal death (one trial, $n = 72$): OR 1.26 [95% CI 0.08 to 20.85].

Evidence statement
There is high-quality evidence comparing ventouse- and forceps-assisted birth. Ventouse is associated with a lower incidence of success, less perineal/genital injury, less perineal pain in the short- and long-term, but with more cephalhaematoma and retinal haemorrhage in babies. When there is failure to achieve birth with the first instrument, there is an increased risk of trauma to the baby with the use of sequential instruments.

There is no evidence of differences between ventouse and forceps in CS rate, long-term babies' outcomes and women's satisfaction and psychological outcomes.

There is moderate level of evidence on soft versus hard ventouse-assisted birth. Soft cup ventouse seems to be associated with higher failure to achieve vaginal birth, but with lower significant scalp trauma on babies. There is no evidence of differences in other major outcomes including long-term outcomes.

Failed/successful instrumental vaginal birth and CS

Description of included studies
One UK cohort study compared women with successful instrumental vaginal birth (*n* = 184), immediate CS (*n* = 102) and attempted instrumental vaginal birth and then CS (*n* = 107).[562] [EL = 2+]

Review findings

CS versus assisted vaginal birth
The UK study showed that women with CS had more blood loss (blood loss more than 1 litre) (OR 2.82 [95% CI 1.10 to 7.62]); more opiates required (OR 10.93 [95% CI 6.44 to 18.91]); more incidents of urinary catheter required for longer than 24 hours (OR 3.09 [95% CI 1.39 to 6.88]); and a longer hospital stay (6 days or more) (OR 3.47 [95% CI 1.58 to 7.62]); compared with instrumental birth, controlling for various confounders. More babies born via CS were admitted to a neonatal unit (OR 2.64 [95% CI 1.16 to 6.02]); but less babies with CS had trauma from the birth (OR 0.37 [95% CI 0.20 to 0.70]; or serious trauma OR 0.34 [95% CI 0.08 to 1.42]), compared with babies who had had an instrumental birth. There is no evidence of a difference in Apgar score < 7 at 5 minutes (OR 2.81 [95% CI 0.48 to 16.74]).

Evidence statement
There is limited evidence on assisted vaginal birth on women's and babies' outcomes, compared with CS. Limited evidence showed women with CS were more likely to lose more blood, and stay in hospital longer, while babies born with CS were more likely to be admitted to a neonatal unit, but less likely to have trauma, compared with assisted vaginal birth.

Recommendations on instruments used for delay in the second stage of labour

Instrumental birth should be considered if there is concern about fetal wellbeing, or for prolonged second stage.

On rare occasions, the woman's need for help in the second stage may be an indication to assist by offering instrumental birth when supportive care has not helped.

The choice of instrument depends on a balance of clinical circumstance and practitioner experience.

Instrumental birth is an operative procedure that should be undertaken with tested effective anaesthesia.

If a woman declines anaesthesia, a pudendal block combined with local anaesthetic to the perineum can be used during instrumental birth.

Where there is concern about fetal compromise, either tested effective anaesthesia or, if time does not allow this, a pudendal block combined with local anaesthetic to the perineum can be used during instrumental birth.

Caesarean section should be advised if vaginal birth is not possible.*

---

* See 'Caesarean section' (NICE clinical guideline 13).

16 Complicated labour: immediate care of newborn

16.1 Basic neonatal resuscitation

Clinical question
What is the evidence that different methods of neonatal resuscitation influence outcomes?

- Including use of oxygen at the time of birth?

Use of 100% oxygen or room air

Description of included studies
There was one systematic review found involving five trials and 1302 babies[563] and one recently conducted quasi-randomised trial[564] identified. [EL = 2+] A new meta-analysis including all six trials was conducted. Among included studies, three trials included low birthweight babies in their populations. Only two trials successfully blinded interventions. Four trials were conducted in low income countries.

Review findings
Meta-analysis of the six trials showed that there was a 25% reduction in neonatal mortality by use of room air (five trials, RR 0.74 [95% CI 0.57 to 0.95]). Use of room air also showed a short-ened time to onset of spontaneous respiration (one trial, $n = 106$): WMD −1.50 minutes [95% CI −2.02 to −0.98 minutes]; time to first breath more than 3 minutes (one trial, $n = 605$): RR 0.53 [95% CI 0.35 to 0.80]; and borderline evidence of less babies with a 5 minute Apgar score < 7 (one trial, $n = 609$): RR 0.78 [95% CI 0.60 to 1.00]. There was no evidence of a difference in: incidence of hypoxic ischemic encephalopathy (Grade 2 or 3, four trials): RR 0.90 [95% CI 0.69 to 1.16]: heart rate at 5 minutes (two trials): WMD 0.06 bpm [95% CI −0.09 to 0.22 bpm]; and failure of resuscitation (five trials): RR 0.96 [95% CI 0.81 to 1.14]. There was also no evidence of differences in adverse neurodevelopmental outcomes, although there was more than 30% of loss of follow-up. In the six trials, 23.7% of 700 babies allocated to room air group received extra oxygen.

Other aspects of basic neonatal resuscitation

Description of included studies
There is no other high-level evidence on other aspects of basic neonatal resuscitation.

Evidence statement
Mortality of the babies at 1 month seems to be reduced by use of room air, compared with 100% oxygen, without evidence of differences in other adverse outcomes, although there are some methodological flaws in the included studies.

There is no high-level evidence on other components, in basic neonatal resuscitation.

Recommendations on basic neonatal resuscitation

All relevant healthcare professionals caring for women during birth should attend a course in neonatal resuscitation at least annually, which is consistent with the algorithm adopted in the 'Newborn life support course' developed by the Resuscitation Council (UK).*

Basic resuscitation of newborn babies should be initiated with air.

Oxygen should be available for babies who do not respond once adequate ventilation has been established.

Emergency referral pathways for both the woman and the baby should be developed and implemented for all birth settings.

---

* Available from www.resus.org.uk/siteindx.htm.

17 Complicated labour: third stage

17.1 Definition of delay in the third stage of labour

Introduction
Delay in the third stage of labour has been defined in a number of ways and there is no universal consensus. This is discussed in Chapter 9.

Definition
Third stage of labour: (from Chapter 9)

- from the birth of the baby to the expulsion of the membranes and placenta.

Clinical question
What is the appropriate definition of retained placenta?

Discussion
The GDG discussed the definition of delay in the third stage of labour and made the following recommendations.

> **Recommendation on definition of delay in the third stage of labour**
>
> Prolonged third stage:
>
> The third stage of labour is diagnosed as prolonged if not completed within 30 minutes of the birth of the baby with active management and 60 minutes with physiological management. [repeated from Section 9.1]

17.2 Treatment of women with a retained placenta

Introduction
Placenta is defined as retained when it has not been delivered within 30 minutes of birth when the third stage is actively managed, and longer than 1 hour when physiologically managed, without signs of postpartum haemorrhage (PPH) or maternal collapse.

Clinical question
What is the effective management of delay in the third stage?

17.2.1 Manual removal of placenta

Description of included studies
There was no relevant study comparing manual removal of placenta with any alternative method on effectiveness of management of retained placenta.

Evidence statement
There is no high-level evidence on the effectiveness of manual removal of placenta for the management of retained placenta compared with other forms of management.

17.2.2 Oxytocin infusion

Overview of available evidence
No relevant study was identified.

Evidence statement
There is no study identified which considers oxytocin intravenous infusion to reduce the need for manual removal of placenta.

17.2.3 Nitro-glycerine for retained placenta

Description of included studies
There was one RCT identified investigating the effectiveness of nitro-glycerine for management of retained placenta compared with placebo.[565] The trial was conducted in Sweden, involving 24 low-risk women diagnosed with retained placenta following active management of the third stage by 10 IU oxytocin. If the placenta still remained undelivered 30 minutes after birth, an additional dose of 10 IU oxytocin was given intravenously, and 5 minutes of cord traction was carried out after 5 minutes of the second administration of oxytocin. Diagnosis of retained placenta was made and either nitro-glycerine tablets or placebo was given, if the placenta remained undelivered within approximately 50 minutes of procedure above. If the placenta remained undelivered after 5 minutes of observation and another 5 minutes of cord traction, operative manual removal was conducted. The primary outcome was need for manual removal of placenta. The trial was good quality. [EL = 1+]

Review findings
Women in the treatment group had more successful delivery of the placenta by controlled cord traction (RR 12.0, $P < 0.001$) and reduced total blood loss (treatment group, 400 ml (SD 108.71 ml), control group, 662.50 ml (SD 144.80 ml) ($P < 0.001$). Although there was no evidence of difference in systolic blood pressure between the two groups before and after administration of the trial drug, diastolic blood pressure in women in the treatment group was reduced more than in the placebo group (treatment, −5.00 mmHg (SD 3.69 mmHg), placebo, −1.25 mmHg (SD 3.11 mmHg) ($P = 0.01$).

Evidence statement
There is high-level evidence from one small study that nitro-glycerine is effective in treating retained placenta, although the risk of reduction in diastolic blood pressure is more, compared with placebo, and this treatment is not used in the UK

17.2.4 Umbilical injection for retained placenta

Description of included studies
There were one systematic review[566] and one RCT[567] identified. These studies investigated effectiveness of umbilical injection as a treatment of retained placenta, compared with expectant management or placebo between the two groups. The systematic review included 12 trials. Both showed good quality. [EL = 1+] The RCT was compared saline solution plus oxytocin versus saline solution.

Review findings

Saline solution versus expectant management
A total of four trials were included.[566] There was no evidence of difference in effectiveness or adverse events between the two groups (manual removal of placenta, RR 0.97 [95% CI 0.83 to 1.14]; PPH, RR 0.37 [95% CI 0.02 to 8.71]; blood loss 500 ml or greater, RR 1.04 [95% CI 0.55 to 1.96]; blood loss 1000 ml or greater, RR 0.73 [95% CI 0.17 to 3.11]; curettage, RR 0.79 [95% CI 0.51 to 1.22]; infection, RR 0.48 [95% CI 0.09 to 2.54]; and stay at hospital more than 2 days, RR 1.19 [95% CI 0.66 to 2.15]).

Saline solution plus oxytocin versus expectant management
A total of five trials were included.[566] There was no evidence of difference in effectiveness or adverse events between the two groups (manual removal of placenta, RR 0.86 [95% CI 0.72

to 1.01]; PPH, RR 1.12 [95% CI 0.07 to 16.95]; blood loss 500 ml or greater, RR 1.53 [95% CI 0.88 to 2.67]; blood loss 1000 ml or greater, RR 1.29 [95% CI 0.38 to 4.34]; curettage, RR 0.69 [95% CI 0.44 to 1.09]; infection, RR 1.16 [95% CI 0.32 to 4.16]; and stay at hospital more than 2 days, RR 1.09 [95% CI 0.60 to 1.97]).

Saline solution plus oxytocin versus saline solution
A total of ten trials were included in the systematic review.[566] The meta-analysis in the systematic review showed that there was significant reduction in the rate of manual removal of placenta with saline plus oxytocin compared with placebo, although there was no evidence of difference in effectiveness as well as adverse events between the two groups (manual removal of placenta, RR 0.79 [95% CI 0.69 to 0.91]; PPH, RR 3.00 [95% CI 0.13 to 70.42]; blood loss 500 ml or greater, RR 1.43 [95% CI 0.83 to 2.45]; blood loss 1000 ml or greater, RR 1.71 [95% CI 0.45 to 6.56]; curettage, RR 0.88 [95% CI 0.54 to 1.43]; infection, RR 2.42 [95% CI 0.48 to 12.15]; and stay at hospital more than 2 days, RR 0.91 [95% CI 0.52 to 1.59]). The recent trial[567] that was not included in the meta-analysis also showed reduction in the need for manual removal of placenta by the use of saline plus oxytocin compared with placebo (RR 0.76 [95% CI 0.41 to 1.39]).

Saline solution plus oxytocin versus plasma expander
Only one trial investigated this comparison. The study is underpowered to show any difference in need for manual removal of placenta (RR 1.34 [95% CI 0.97 to 1.85]) and incidence of PPH (blood loss more than 500 ml, RR 0.88 [95% CI 0.52 to 1.50] and blood loss more than 1000 ml, RR 0.96 [95% CI 0.34 to 2.75]) between the two groups.

Saline solution plus prostaglandin versus saline solution
Only one small trial (*n* = 17) investigated this comparison. Saline plus prostaglandin showed a significant reduction in need for manual removal of placenta (RR 0.05 [95% CI 0.00 to 0.73]) compared with placebo, while there was no evidence of difference in blood loss (WMD −21.00 ml [95% CI −120.18 to 78.18 ml]) and other adverse events (fever, RR 2.18 [95% CI 0.10 to 46.92], and abdominal pain, RR 5.09 [95% CI 0.30 to 85.39]) between the two groups.

Saline solution plus prostaglandin versus saline solution plus oxytocin
Only one small trial (*n* = 21) investigated this comparison. There was significant reduction by use of prostaglandin in duration from injection to delivery of the placenta (WMD −6.00 minutes [95% CI −8.78 to −3.22 minutes]) compared with oxytocin, while there was no evidence of difference in need for manual removal placenta (RR 0.10 [95% CI 0.01 to 1.59]), blood loss (WMD −19.00 ml [95% CI −118.19 to −80.19 ml]) and other adverse events (fever, RR 1.10 [95% CI 0.08 to 15.36], and abdominal pain, RR 3.30 [95% CI 0.58 to 3.00]) between the two groups.

Evidence statement
There was a limited amount of high-level evidence regarding umbilical injection for the treatment of retained placenta. There was no evidence of effectiveness of saline solution versus expectant management, saline solution plus oxytocin versus expectant management, saline solution plus oxytocin versus plasma expander, saline solution plus prostaglandin versus saline solution or saline solution plus prostaglandin versus saline solution plus oxytocin.

High-level evidence from a variety of settings shows that umbilical injection of saline solution plus oxytocin is effective at reducing the need for manual removal of placenta compared with saline alone, although there is limited evidence on other relevant outcomes including effect on incidence of PPH. However, the optimal regimen was not clear in the included studies.

Recommendations on treatment for retained placenta

Intravenous access should always be secured in women with a retained placenta.

Intravenous infusion of oxytocin should not be used to assist the delivery of the placenta.

For women with a retained placenta oxytocin injection into the umbilical vein with 20 IU of oxytocin in 20 ml of saline is recommended, followed by proximal clamping of the cord.

If the placenta is still retained 30 minutes after oxytocin injection, or sooner if there is concern about the woman's condition, women should be offered an assessment of the need to remove the placenta. Women should be informed that this assessment can be painful and they should be advised to have analgesia or even anaesthesia for this assessment.

Research recommendation on use of nitro-glycerine for retained placenta

Further randomised controlled trials investigating the effectiveness of the use of nitro-glycerine in the treatment of retained placenta should be conducted.

17.2.5 Analgesia for retained placenta

Description of included studies
No relevant study was identified.

Evidence statement
There is no evidence as to the most effective analgesia for assessment of delayed in the third stage.

Recommendations on analgesia during interventions for retained placenta

If a woman reports inadequate pain relief during the assessment, the healthcare professional must immediately stop the examination and address this need.

If manual removal of the placenta is required, this must be carried out under effective regional anaesthesia (or general anaesthesia when necessary).

17.3 Risk factors for postpartum haemorrhage

Introduction
Risk factors for developing PPH were reviewed.

Clinical question
Are there effective ways of identifying women at increased risk of postpartum haemorrhage antenatally and during labour?

What is the effective management of women at increased risk of postpartum haemorrhage to minimise this risk?

17.3.1 Multiple factors study

Description of included studies
There were seven studies (two case–control studies[571,572] and five cross-sectional studies[573–577]) looking at multiple risk factors for PPH in high income countries, although three of them were inconclusive.

Review findings
A population based cross-sectional study was conducted in the Netherlands including 3464 nulliparous women between 1990 and 1994.[573] [EL = 3] The study investigated risk factors for standard (more than or equal to 500 ml of blood loss) and severe (more than or equal to 1000 ml of blood loss) PPH. Multivariate logistic regression analyses showed significant risk factors for standard PPH as: retained placenta (adjusted OR 7.83 [95% CI 3.78 to 16.22]); prolonged third stage (longer than 30 minutes) (adjusted OR 2.61 [95% CI 1.83 to 3.72]); multiple pregnancy (adjusted OR 2.60 [95% CI 1.06 to 6.39]); episiotomy (adjusted OR 2.18 [95% CI 1.68 to 2.81]); macrosomia (weight more than or equal to 4 kg) (adjusted OR 2.11 [95% CI 1.62 to 2.76]); perineal trauma (laceration severer than or equal to first-degree) (adjusted OR 1.40 [95% CI 1.04 to 1.87]); and West European race (adjusted OR 1.32 [95% CI 1.00 to 1.73]). Risk factors for severe PPH were reported as: retained placenta (adjusted OR 11.73 [95% CI 5.67 to 24.1]); prolonged third stage (longer than or equal to 30 minutes) (adjusted OR 4.90 [95% CI 2.89 to 8.32]); macrosomia (adjusted OR 2.55 [95% CI 1.57 to 4.18]); and perineal trauma (laceration severer than or equal to first-degree) (adjusted OR 1.82 [95% CI 1.01 to 3.28]). When stratified by background risk of the women, a multiple regression model showed risk factors of severe PPH for low-risk women were: retained placenta (adjusted OR 21.6 [95% CI 5.99 to 78.00]);

and prolonged third stage (longer than 30 minutes) (adjusted OR 3.59 [95% CI 1.60 to 8.03]); while those for high-risk women were reported as retained placenta (adjusted OR 9.29 [95% CI 3.69 to 23.4]); prolonged third stage (longer than 30 minutes) (adjusted OR 6.11 [95% CI 2.94 to 12.7]); macrosomia (adjusted OR 2.75 [95% CI 1.52 to 4.97]); induction (adjusted OR 1.74 [95% CI 1.06 to 2.87]); and prolonged second stage (more than or equal to 30 minutes) (adjusted OR 2.74 [95% CI 1.37 to 5.49]).

A cross-sectional study was conducted in the USA including 763 pregnancy related deaths from haemorrhage associated with intrauterine pregnancies between 1979 and 1992.[574] [EL = 3] Although the study found black race and increased age were related to risk of death from haemorrhage, analysis did not control confounding factors and hence this study was inconclusive.

A case–control study was conducted in the UK including 86 PPH cases and 351 non-PPH controls.[571] [EL = 2–] Although the study suggested significant risk factors were nulliparous, labour induction, forceps birth, prolonged first and second stages, and oxytocin compared with oxytocin with ergometrine as significant risk factors, the analysis did not properly control confounding factors with unmatched controls and hence was inconclusive.

A cross-sectional study was conducted in the UK including 36 312 women between 1967 and 1981.[575] [EL = 3] The study investigated complications of the third stage. Although the study reported nulliparous and induction of labour as risk factors for PPH, the analysis did not control confounding factors and hence was inconclusive.

A case–control study was conducted in Australia including 125 PPH cases versus 125 controls in 2003.[572] [EL = 2+] Multivariate logistic regression analyses showed risk factors for developing PPH (blood loss 500 ml or greater) were: past history of PPH (adjusted OR 14.11 [95% CI 1.62 to 123.06]); prolonged second stage (longer than or equal to 60 minutes) (adjusted OR 2.68 [95% CI 1.27 to 5.64]); forceps birth (adjusted OR 3.47 [95% CI 1.35 to 8.91]); and incomplete/ragged membranes (adjusted OR 3.56 [95% CI 1.52 to 8.36]).

A cross-sectional study was conducted in Australia including 13 868 women between 1998 and 2002.[576] [EL = 3] The study investigated risk factors for developing PPH (blood loss 1000 ml or greater and/or need for a transfusion). Multivariate logistic regression analyses showed risk factors as: Asian race (adjusted OR 1.8 [95% CI 1.4 to 2.2]); maternal blood disorders (adjusted OR 1.3 [95% CI 1.1 to 1.6]); prior PPH (adjusted OR 1.8 [95% CI 1.4 to 2.2]); history of retained placenta (adjusted OR 6.2 [95% CI 4.6 to 8.2]); multiple pregnancy (adjusted OR 2.2 [95% CI 1.5 to 3.2]); antepartum haemorrhage (adjusted OR 1.8 [95% CI 1.3 to 2.3]); genital tract lacerations (adjusted OR 1.7 [95% CI 1.4 to 2.1]); macrosomia (4 kg or greater) (adjusted OR 1.8 [95% CI 1.4 to 2.3]); induction of labour (adjusted OR 1.8 [95% CI 1.4 to 2.2]); chorioamnionitis (adjusted OR 1.3 [95% CI 1.1 to 1.7]); intrapartum haemorrhage (adjusted OR 1.5 [95% CI 1.0 to 2.3]); intrauterine fetal deaths (adjusted OR 2.6 [95% CI 1.1 to 5.7]); compound fetal presentation (adjusted OR 3.0 [95% CI 1.1 to 7.3]); epidural anaesthesia (adjusted OR 1.3 [95% CI 1.0 to 1.6]); prolonged first/second stage of labour (first stage) (adjusted OR 1.6 [95% CI 1.0 to 1.6]); second stage (adjusted OR 1.6 [95% CI 1.1 to 2.1]); and forceps birth after failed vacuum-assisted birth (adjusted OR 1.9 [95% CI 1.1 to 3.2]).

A cross-sectional study was conducted in the UK including 37 497 women in 1988, investigating risk factors for PPH (blood loss 1000 ml or greater).[577] [EL = 3] Although the study reported placental abruption, placenta praevia, multiple pregnancy, retained placenta, labour induction, episiotomy and macrosomia, the analysis did not control confounding factors and hence was inconclusive.

17.3.2 Anaemia

Description of included studies and review findings
A cohort study was conducted in New Zealand in 1996 comparing haemoglobin levels at 4 weeks prior to birth on PPH (blood loss 600 ml or greater within 24 hours of birth).[578] [EL = 2–] Although the study reported no difference, the analysis did not control confounding factors and hence was inconclusive.

17.3.3 Low-lying placenta

Description of included studies and review findings
A cross-sectional study was conducted in Canada between 1997 and 1999 investigating obstetric implications of low-lying placentas diagnosed in the second trimester.[579] [EL = 3] Multivariate logistic regression analysis showed significant increased risk of PPH (blood loss 500 ml or greater for vaginal birth, 100 ml or greater) for caesarean section (adjusted OR 1.72 [95% CI 1.12 to 2.66], adjusted for maternal age and birthweight).

17.3.4 Smoking

Description of included studies and review findings
A cohort study was conducted in the UK comparing obstetric outcomes of 400 smoking women with 400 non-smoking women.[580] [EL = 2–] Although the study reported higher incidence of PPH for smoking women, the analysis did not control for major confounding factors and hence was inconclusive.

17.3.5 Prolonged second stage of labour

Description of included studies
There were five observational studies identified (five cross-sectional studies)[327,328,332,333,335] on duration of second stage of labour on the defined outcomes with various quality.

Review findings
A cross-sectional study (*n* = 15 759) in the USA investigated prolonged duration of second stage (more than 4 hours) on the defined outcomes.[326] [EL = 3] Logistic regression analysis controlling various confounders showed there was no evidence of associations of prolonged second stage of labour with PPH (RR 1.05 [95% CI 0.84 to 1.31]).

One cross-sectional study in the Germany (*n* = 1200) investigated prolonged second stage of labour (more than 2 hours) on intrapartum outcomes.[328] [EL = 3] The results showed evidence of association of prolonged second stage with low Apgar score at 1 minute, PPH, perineal tears and postpartum fever, although the analyses did not control confounding factors.

One cross-sectional study (*n* = 25 069) in the UK investigated prolonged second stage of labour on perinatal outcomes.[332,333] [EL = 3] Logistic regression analysis showed that there was evidence of association between longer duration and higher rate of PPH (duration: 120–179 minutes, OR 1.6 [95% CI 1.3 to 1.9]; 180–239 minutes, 1.7 [95% CI 1.3 to 2.3]; 240 or more minutes, OR 1.9 [95% CI 1.2 to 2.8]).

One cross-sectional study in the USA (*n* = 4403) investigated different length of labour on intrapartum outcomes.[335] [EL = 3] The analyses without controlling confounding factors showed no evidence of association of length of second stage with neonatal outcomes apart from low Apgar score at 1 minute (*P* < 0.03). Both puerperal haemorrhage and febrile morbidity showed evidence of association with length of labour (*P* < 0.001 for both), but analysis did not consider confounding effects.

One cross-sectional study was conducted in the USA (*n* = 7818) investigated maternal and neonatal outcomes in women with prolonged second stage of labour.[327] [EL = 3] Although the analysis of women with longer than 120 minutes of second stage had higher incidence of PPH (RR 2.70, *P* < 0.001), the analysis did not control confounding factors and hence was inconclusive.

17.3.6 Prolonged third stage of labour

Refer to Section 9.1.2 on duration of the third stage of labour.

17.3.7 Body mass index and body weight

Description of included studies
There were four cross-sectional studies (three studies investigated overweight women[581–583] and one study investigated underweight women[584]) identified.

Review findings
One cross-sectional study was conducted in the UK between 1990 and 1999 including 60 167 childbirths.[582] [EL = 3] The study investigated outcome of pregnancy in a woman with an increased body mass index (BMI) (greater than 30 kg/m²). The study reported significant increased risk of developing PPH (blood loss greater than 500 ml) with BMI over 30 kg/m² (OR 1.5 [95% CI 1.2 to 1.8]), although the analysis did not control any confounding.

One cross-sectional study was conducted in Canada between 1988 and 2002, including 142 404 women.[583] [EL = 3] Multivariate logistic regression analyses showed that moderately overweight women (90 – 120 kg) had increased risk of PPH (adjusted OR 1.12 [95% CI 1.02 to 1.22]), but there is no evidence of difference in incidence of PPH by severely overweight women (heavier than 120 kg) (adjusted OR 1.07 [95% CI 0.80 to 1.42]).

One cross-sectional study was conducted in the UK between 1989 and 1997, including 325 395 pregnancies.[581] [EL = 3] Multivariate logistic regression analyses showed increased risk of PPH (greater than 1000 ml) with increased BMI: BMI 25–30 kg/m², adjusted OR 1.16 [99% CI 1.12 to 1.21]; BMI more than 30 kg/m², adjusted OR 1.39 [99% CI 1.32 to 1.46], controlling for other factors including ethnicity, parity, age and history of hypertension.

Another cross-sectional study was conducted in the UK between 1988 and 1997 by using the same population as the study above[581] including 215 105 women.[584] [EL = 3] Multivariate logistic regression analysis showed that women with low BMI (BMI 20–25 kg/m²) have less PPH (PPH, adjusted OR 0.85 [99% CI 0.80 to 0.90]; severe PPH, adjusted OR 0.83 [99% CI 0.72 to 0.95]).

17.3.8 Post-term birth

Description of included studies and review findings
One cross-sectional study was identified.[585] [EL = 3] The data were collected between 1978 and 1993 to investigate association between post-term birth and maternal complication. Multivariate logistic regression analysis showed significantly higher risk of developing PPH in post-term pregnancy (adjusted OR 1.37 [95% CI 1.28 to 1.46]).

17.3.9 Macrosomia

Description of included studies
There were four observational studies identified.[586–589]

Review findings
One cross-sectional study was conducted in the UK.[586] [EL = 3] The study investigated risk factors and clinical consequences of macrosomia, involving 350 311 pregnancies, between 1988 and 1997. Multivariate logistic regression analysis showed that women with babies whose birthweight were more than 4 kg had higher risk of developing PPH (adjusted OR 2.01 [99% CI 1.93 to 2.10]), and the analysis also showed that women with babies whose birthweight was more than the 90th centile had higher risk of developing PPH (adjusted OR 1.63 [99% CI 1.56 to 1.71]) compared with women whose babies were of normal weight.

One cross-sectional study conducted in the UK was identified.[587] [EL = 3] The study investigated clinical consequences of oversized babies, involving 7992 births between 1963 and 1964. Although the study reported double the risk of developing PPH for women with oversized babies than normal sized ones, the analysis did not control confounding factors and hence was inconclusive.

One US cross-sectional study was identified.[588] [EL = 3] The study investigated obstetric complications associated with macrosomia, including 146 526 live births. Multivariate logistic regression analysis showed higher risk of developing PPH by increased birthweight of babies (4000–4499 g birthweight, adjusted OR 1.69 [95% CI 1.58 to 2.10]; 4500–4999 g birthweight, adjusted OR 2.15 [95% CI 1.86 to 2.48]; 5000 g or greater birthweight, adjusted OR 2.03 [95% CI 1.33 to 3.09]).

One cross-sectional study conducted in Germany was identified.[589] [EL = 3] The study described maternal complications of fetal macrosomia, involving 956 between 1990 and 1997. Although the study reported association between macrosomia and PPH, the analysis did not control any confounding and hence was inconclusive.

17.3.10 Age

Description of included studies
There were two cross-sectional studies identified.[590,591] Both studies showed moderate quality. [EL = 3] One study was conducted in the UK[590] and the other study was conducted in Japan.[591]

Review findings
The UK study[590] investigated obstetric risk of women aged 35 years or greater, including 385 120 pregnancies. Multivariate logistic regression analysis showed significant positive association of women's age and risk of developing PPH (age 35–40 years and moderate PPH, adjusted OR 1.14 [99% CI 1.09 to 1.19]; age greater than 40 years and moderate PPH, adjusted OR 1.27 [99% CI 1.15 to 1.39]; age 35–40 years and severe PPH, adjusted OR 1.28 [99% CI 1.16 to 1.41]; age greater than 40 years and severe PPH, adjusted OR 1.55 [99% CI 1.29 to 1.88]).

The Japanese study[591] also investigated effect of maternal age on blood loss, involving 10 053 women. Multivariate regression analysis showed that women of 35 years or more had higher risk of developing: PPH (vaginal birth, adjusted OR 1.5 [95% CI 1.2 to 1.9]; CS, adjusted OR 1.8 [95% CI 1.2 to 2.7]) compared with women under 30 years.

17.3.11 Parity

Description of included studies
There were eight cross-sectional studies identified.[592–599] [EL = 3] Three of them were conducted in the UK,[593,595,597] three were in the USA,[592,598,599] and two in Australia.[594,596]

Review findings
One US study[592] investigated effect of parity on obstetric risk factors in 133 great-grandparous (defined as parity more than ten), 314 grandparous and 2195 parous women. Although the study reported significant increased incidence of PPH in grandparous than parous women, the analysis did not control important confounding factors such as age and hence is inconclusive.

One control-matched study in the UK was identified,[593] which compared 397 grandparous women with 397 age-matched parous women to investigate effect of parity on obstetric risk factors. The study reported that there was no evidence of difference in incidence of PPH between these two groups (OR 1.18 [95% CI 0.6 to 2.4]).

One Australian study was conducted between 1974 and 1975 to investigate obstetric performance of grand multiparous women.[594] Although the study reported no evidence of difference in incidence of PPH by parity, the analysis did not control confounding factors and hence is inconclusive.

One UK study was published in 1987, compared 216 grandparous women with lesser parity matched for age and ethnicity.[595] There was a higher incidence of developing PPH (blood loss greater than 500 ml) for grandparous women compared with parous women (*P* < 0.01), although there was significant difference in gestational age at booking.

One Australian study was conducted between 1992 and 2001.[596] The study investigated obstetric risk of 653 grand multiparous women, compared with 15 255 women with lower parity. Multivariate logistic regression analyses showed borderline increased risk of developing PPH by high parity (OR 1.36 [95% CI 0.99 to 1.87]).

One UK study investigated obstetric risk of 229 grand multiparous women with controls matched for age with one parity, between 1990 and 1991.[597] The study reported no evidence of difference in incidence of PPH, although the proportion of women who had oxytocin administration in the third stage was different and hence the analysis was inconclusive.

One US study investigated obstetric outcomes of 382 grandparous women, compared with age-matched controls with parity of between two and four, between 1989 and 1991.[598] There was no evidence of difference in incidence of PPH between these two groups (OR 0.97 [95% CI 0.57 to 1.63]).

A third US study investigated perinatal outcomes of 25 512 grandparous women, compared with 265 060 parous women aged 30 years or greater between 1997 and 1998.[599] Multivariate logistic regression analysis showed increased risk of developing PPH by grand multiparity, compared with multiparity (adjusted OR 1.2 [1.1 to 1.3]).

A second UK study investigated complications of the third stage of vaginal birth among 36 312 women between 1967 and 1981. There was evidence that higher incidence of PPH in nulliparous women and after induced labour. Analysis of the risks of 6615 women with two or three live births between 1967 and 1980 showed women with a history of PPH and/or retained placenta had higher risks of PPH in a subsequent birth, by between two and four times as much, compared with women without such a history.

Evidence statement (all risk factors for postpartum haemorrhage)
The following conditions are associated with increased risk of postpartum haemorrhage. The list is not exhaustive.

Antenatal: previous retained placenta, or PPH, maternal haemoglobin less than 8.5 g/dl at onset of labour; increased BMI; grand multiparity (parity four or more); antepartum haemorrhage; overextension of the uterus (e.g. multiple pregnancy, polyhydramnios, macrosomia), existing uterine abnormalities; low-lying placenta; and age (35 years or older).

In labour: induction, prolonged first, second or third stage of labour, oxytocin use, precipitate labour, operative birth or caesarean section.

Recommendations on risk factors for postpartum haemorrhage

Women with risk factors for postpartum haemorrhage should be advised to give birth in an obstetric unit where more emergency treatment options are available.

- Antenatal risk factors:
  - previous retained placenta or postpartum haemorrhage
  - maternal haemoglobin level below 8.5 g/dl at onset of labour
  - body mass index greater than 35 kg/m²
  - grand multiparity (parity 4 or more)
  - antepartum haemorrhage
  - overdistention of the uterus (for example, multiple pregnancy, polyhydramnios or macrosomia)
  - existing uterine abnormalities
  - low-lying placenta
  - maternal age (35 years or older).
- Risk factors in labour:
  - induction
  - prolonged first, second or third stage of labour
  - oxytocin use
  - precipitate labour
  - operative birth or caesarean section.

If a woman has risk factors for postpartum haemorrhage, these should be highlighted in her notes and a care plan covering the third stage of labour should be made and discussed with the woman.

The unit should have strategies in place in order to respond quickly and appropriately should a postpartum haemorrhage occur.

17.4 Management of postpartum haemorrhage

Introduction
The interventions below were considered:

- uterotonics
- uterine packing

- vessel ligation
- hysterectomy
- uterine compression
- radiological embolisation.

Any trials or studies to compare two of the above interventions were considered.

Clinical question
What is the most effective way of managing postpartum haemorrhage?

17.4.1   Uterotonics

Description of included studies
There was one systematic review investigating effectiveness of treatment for primary PPH.[568] The review identified two trials investigating use of prostaglandin (misoprostol) for treatment of PPH, compared with placebo or oxytocin/ergometrine after treatment with conventional uterotonics. [EL = 1+]

Review findings

Misoprostol versus oxytocin/ergometrine
There was one included trial that investigated this comparison. A total of 64 women were included. There was significant reduction by misoprostol in persistent haemorrhage (RR 0.18 [95% CI 0.04 to 0.76]) and need for additional uterotonics (RR 0.18 [95% CI 0.04 to 0.76]), while there was no evidence of difference in incidence of hysterectomy (RR 0.33 [95% CI 0.01 to 7.89]) and surgical co-intervention excluding hysterectomy (RR 1.00 [95% CI 0.15 to 6.67]).

Misoprostol versus placebo
There were two trials included. A total of 398 women were included. There was significant reduction in incidence of blood loss 500 ml or greater (RR 0.51 [95% CI 0.28 to 0.94]) by misoprostol, although there was an increased number of women with shivering (RR 3.56 [95% CI 2.23 to 5.69]) and maternal pyrexia (RR 6.93 [95% CI 1.79 to 26.83]), compared with placebo. There was no evidence of difference in incidence of hysterectomy (RR 1.38 [95% CI 0.31 to 6.18]), additional uterotonics (RR 0.96 [95% CI 0.58 to 1.57]), blood loss 1000 ml or greater (RR 0.64 [95% CI 0.17 to 2.50], nausea (RR 0.60 [95% CI 0.14 to 2.60]), headache (RR 0.62 [95% CI 0.23 to 1.69]), manual removal of placenta (7.43 [95% CI 0.38 to 145.39]), and blood transfusion (RR 1.40 [95% CI 0.79 to 2.48]).

Evidence statement
There was high-level evidence from a systematic review that included three studies evaluating misoprostol for the treatment of PPH in the developing world. Two studies were placebo-controlled and the third compared misoprostol with a combination of oxytocin and/or ergometrine.

The review showed misoprostol is associated with a reduced measured blood loss and increased maternal pyrexia but not with decreases in maternal mortality, hysterectomy rates, the additional use of uterotonics and blood transfusion.

There was no high-level evidence identified evaluating other drugs or drug combinations for the treatment of primary PPH.

Recommendations on management of postpartum haemorrhage

Immediate treatment for postpartum haemorrhage should include:

- calling for appropriate help
- uterine massage
- intravenous fluids
- uterotonics.

No particular uterotonic drug can be recommended over another for the treatment of postpartum haemorrhage.

Treatment combinations for postpartum haemorrhage might include repeat bolus of oxytocin (intravenous), ergometrine (intramuscular, or cautiously intravenously), intramuscular oxytocin with ergometrine (Syntometrine), misoprostol,* oxytocin infusion (Syntocinon) or carboprost (intramuscular).

Additional therapeutic options for the treatment of postpartum haemorrhage include tranexamic acid (intravenous) and rarely, in the presence of otherwise normal clotting factors, rFactor VIIa, after seeking advice from a haematologist.*

If possible, a member of the healthcare team should be allocated to remain with the woman and her partner during postpartum haemorrhage to ensure communication and offer support throughout the emergency situation.

Research recommendation on management of postpartum haemorrhage

Further research should identify the best drug combinations, route and dose for the treatment of postpartum haemorrhage

17.4.2 Other procedures

Description of included studies
There were two observational studies included.[569,570] Both were of poor quality. One study was conducted in the USA with cross-sectional study design.[569] [EL = 3] The other was conducted in Saudi Arabia with also cross-sectional design.[570] [EL = 3] There was no other relevant study identified that investigated other procedures.

Review findings

Vessel ligation versus hysterectomy
In the US study, 19 women underwent bilateral hypogastric artery ligation for the control of otherwise intractable obstetric haemorrhage, compared with 59 women undergoing emergency hysterectomy for obstetric haemorrhage without prior ligation of the hypogastric arteries. Hypogastric artery ligation was successful in 42% of the 19 women. The mean blood loss for the unsuccessful ligation group was 5125 ml, while that for the hysterectomy group was 3209 ml ($P > 0.05$). The mean operating time for women undergoing ligation before hysterectomy was 4.2 hours, while that for women without ligation was 3.0 hours ($P < 0.05$). There was increased incidence of both ureteric injury and cardiac arrest secondary to hypovolaemia among the ligation group than the hysterectomy group ($P < 0.05$).

In the Saudi Arabian study, 29 women undergoing bilateral hypogastric artery ligation were compared with 35 women undergoing hysterectomy for severe postpartum haemorrhage (PPH).[570] The ligation failed to control PPH in 34% of the ligation group, while 13.3% of the hysterectomy group required re-exploration. There was a trend that women in the ligation group required shorter operative time (mean 20 minutes versus 55 minutes), estimated blood loss (mean 2230 ml versus 3500 ml) and incidence of intra-operative hypotension (9/19 versus 33/45), although summary statistics were not obtained.

Evidence statement
There was no high-level evidence of the effectiveness of second-line interventions such as uterine packing (including balloons), vessel ligation, hysterectomy, uterine compression or radiological embolisation.

Recommendation on surgical procedures for postpartum haemorrhage

No particular surgical procedure can be recommended above another for the treatment of postpartum haemorrhage.

---

* At the time of publication (September 2007), misoprostol and rFactor VIIa did not have UK marketing authorisation for this indication. Informed consent should be obtained and documented; however, if this is not possible, follow the Department of Health guidelines – 'Reference guide to consent for examination or treatment' (2001) (available from www.dh.gov.uk). It may be appropriate to get consent in the antenatal period.

Appendix A

Declarations of interest

Table A.1 Declarations of interests for GDG members

Tony Ducker	Trial and development of new ventilator, payment to departmental research funds from SLE organisation. Research into the use of KL4 (Surfactant) Protocol 04, payment to departmental research funds by Discovery Laboratories Inc. Trial into the use of Numax RSV antibody, payment to departmental research funds, by PPD/Medimmune. Trial into the use of nitric oxide in pre-term babies for the prevention of chronic lung disease, payment to departmental research funds by Innovo.
Simon Grant	Involved with developing a research protocol around high- and low-dose oxytocin which was submitted to the MRC.
Gill Gyte	No interests declared.
Jayne Jempson	No interests declared.
Sara Kenyon	Involved with developing a research protocol around high- and low-dose oxytocin which was submitted to the MRC.
Carolyn Markham	Works as a breastfeeding specialist at the Baby Café in Northampton a salary is paid from a grant received from Northampton PCT. Involved with developing a research protocol around high- and low-dose oxytocin which was submitted to the MRC.
Geraldine O'Sullivan	No interests declared.
Julia Sanders	No interests declared.
Maureen Treadwell	No interests declared.
Derek Tuffnell	Department has had funding for 20 months from Ferring Pharmaceuticals to support an administrative assistant to audit preterm labour cases in Yorkshire. Ferring Pharmaceuticals have also funded attendance at the European preterm labour meeting in Montreal in 2004 and paid for accommodation and travel. Involved with developing a research protocol around high- and low-dose oxytocin which was submitted to the MRC. Involved with a trial looking at the timing of cord clamping.
Steve Walkinshaw	Involved with developing a research protocol around high and low dose oxytocin which was submitted to the MRC. Involved with a study on partograms at the Liverpool Women's Hospital.
Marina Wells	No interests declared.

Appendix B

Clinical questions

Outcomes:
- labour events (length of labour, interventions, complications)
- birth events (mode or place of birth, complications of birth, perineal trauma)
- newborn events (condition at birth, birth injuries, admission to neonatal units)
- women's satisfaction and women's assessment of birth experience
- women's mental and psychological health
- long-term women's or babies' outcomes (more than 28 days)
- women's and babies' mortality.

1. What are the outcomes (benefits and harms) and costs related to each birth setting?
2. What are the risk factors which should be included in assessment to determine the most appropriate place of birth for women during pregnancy and in labour?
3. What effect does communication have on a woman's perception of her birth experience?
   - Interventions include the effect of control, choice and decision making on psychosocial wellbeing in the medium and long term.
   - Outcomes include postnatal depression and post-traumatic stress disorder.
4. Is there evidence that support in labour for women improves outcomes? Interventions include:
   - any support from partners
   - other birth supporters
   - health professionals
   - continuity of care.
6. What are the indications for the use of ventouse or forceps?
7. Are there effective hygiene strategies for vaginal birth out of water to protect both women and babies, and healthcare professionals?
   - Strategies include vaginal examination and antisepsis.
   - Outcomes include infection control and rates of infection.
8. Are there effective hygiene strategies for vaginal birth in water to protect both women and babies, and healthcare professionals?
   - Strategies include vaginal examination and antisepsis.
   - Outcomes include infection control and rates of infection.
9. What are the appropriate definitions of the latent and active phases of the first stage, the second stage, and the third stage of labour?
10. Do duration and progress of the first and second stages of labour affect outcomes?
11. Is there evidence that the timing of admission to maternity units, and of cervical dilatation, affects outcomes?
    - Subgroups include nulliparous women and multiparous women.
12. Is there evidence that midwife assessment at home affects outcomes?
    - Subgroups include nulliparous women and multiparous women.
13. Is there evidence that the assessment of the following, on admission, and throughout labour and the immediate postnatal period, affects outcomes?
    - observation of vital signs
    - bladder care
    - palpation and presentation/position of baby
    - frequency and duration of contractions
    - membrane and liquor assessment/placental examination
    - maternal behaviour
    - vaginal examination

- length, strength and frequency of contractions
- assessment of cervical effacement, dilatation and position
- presentation and descent of the presenting part
- assessment of liquor if membranes ruptured.

14. Do the following methods of fetal monitoring affect outcomes?
    - none
    - admission CTG
    - intermittent auscultation (Pinard, Doppler)
    - intermittent electronic monitoring
    - continuous electronic monitoring (including method of interpretation)
    - ST analysis
    - fetal blood sampling
    - fetal blood gas analysis
    - fetal lactate.

15. Is there evidence of factors or interventions that affect outcomes in term prelabour rupture of the membranes?
    - Including septic screen for mother and baby.

- Is there evidence that, following prelabour rupture of the membranes at term, the length of time from prelabour rupture of membranes (before onset of labour and total), digital vaginal examination, electronic fetal heart-rate monitoring, or frequency and type of maternal surveillance influence outcomes?

- Following the birth of a healthy infant where there has been prelabour rupture of the membranes, is there evidence that the length of time from prelabour rupture of membranes (before onset and total), presence of pyrexia during or before labour, routine admission to neonatal units, frequency and type of neonatal observations, or frequency and type of neonatal investigations (including invasive tests) influence outcomes?

- Is there evidence that the use of antibiotics before delivery in asymptomatic or symptomatic women with prelabour rupture of membranes influences outcomes?

- What are the criteria for the use of antibiotics in healthy babies born following prelabour rupture of membranes?

16. Is there any evidence that identification and management of meconium-stained liquor affect outcomes?

17. What is the effectiveness of the following interventions or techniques in labour on outcomes?
    - positions including:
      – 'freedom to choose' option
      – standing
      – squatting
      – kneeling
      – semi-recumbent
      – lying on back
      – left lateral
      – birth stool, etc
    - breathing and relaxation
    - massage
    - complementary therapies
    - birth balls
    - injected water papules
    - water (including temperature regulation)
    - mobilisation
    - pushing techniques in the second stage (including not pushing)
    - formal charting of fetal and maternal observations)
    - restricting fluids and nutrition (aspiration vomiting and Mendelson syndrome)
    - active management
    - amniotomy
    - oxytocin.

18. Is there evidence that the type, frequency and mode of administration of the following pharmacological and non-pharmacological pain relief and regional analgesia influence outcomes?
    - pharmacological pain relief:
        - Entonox®
        - PCAs
        - pethidine
        - diamorphine
        - meptazinol (Meptid®)
        - epidural
    - non-pharmacological pain relief:
        - TENS
    - analgesia
        - spinal
        - combined spinal–epidural
        - epidural
        - mobile epidural
19. When is use of each of these methods of regional analgesia appropriate?
20. What observations, above baseline care, should be undertaken on both mother and baby while using regional analgesia?
21. What IV fluids should be used to maintain blood pressure during labour while using regional analgesia?
22. What is the most effective use of regional analgesia to minimise instrumental delivery rates and optimise pain relief in the second stage of labour?
23. Does the method of management of the third stage of labour affect outcomes?:
    - cord clamping
    - active management
    - physiological management.
24. What is the appropriate definition of retained placenta?
25. What is the effective management of delay in the third stage?
26. Are there effective ways of identifying women at increased risk of postpartum haemorrhage antenatally and during labour?
27. What is the effective management of women at increased risk of postpartum haemorrhage to minimise this risk?
28. What is the most effective way of managing postpartum haemorrhage?
29. What is the appropriate definition of perineal or genital trauma?
30. What is the effectiveness on perineal or genital trauma (including previous third- or fourth-degree trauma or female genital mutilation) of the following techniques?
    - perineal massage
    - hand position
    - heat
    - cold
    - maternal position
    - analgesia
    - episiotomy
    - operative vaginal delivery
31. Is there evidence that the type of assessment used to identify perineal or genital trauma affects outcomes?
32. Is there evidence that undertaking repair, the timing, analgesia and method and material of perineal repair affect outcomes?
33. What is the evidence that different methods of initial neonatal assessment and examination influence outcomes?
    - Including cardiovascular-respiratory and abnormalities assessment.
34. What is the evidence that different methods of neonatal resuscitation influence outcomes?
    - Including use of oxygen at the time of birth.

35. Are there effective ways of encouraging mother–infant bonding following birth?
    - Including skin to skin contact with mothers, breastfeeding.
36. Is there evidence that routine taking of cord blood gases influences outcomes?

Appendix C

Selection criteria and validity scores for included and excluded studies for the systematic review comparing planned home birth and planned hospital birth and the systematic review comparing planned standalone midwife-led unit and obstetric unit birth

Method used for this review

The difficulty of conducting a randomised controlled trial (RCT) to evaluate effectiveness and safety of planned home birth and planned standalone midwife-led unit birth, compared with planned obstetric unit birth, is evident from the literature. The paucity of good-quality evidence necessitated the inclusion of studies using a range of methodologies as described in Chapter 1 (methodology section). The details of the search strategies employed are provided on the accompanying CD-ROM.

Inclusion/exclusion criteria

The best study design to address the effectiveness of an intervention is an RCT. However, there is a higher incidence/prevalence of benefits than adverse events, especially serious outcomes, in many clinical contexts, and therefore an RCT will not necessarily be the best method to use to demonstrate safety of an intervention.

Studies that employed an adequate randomised design were regarded as having the highest validity [++]. Any study that considered planned birth populations with an additional adequate study design which controlled for background medical and/or obstetric risks between different places of birth and/or reported relevant outcomes was also included and assigned as having acceptable internal validity [+]. Any study that did not report relevant outcomes or that did not meet the criteria above was considered invalid and excluded ([–]). Use of regression analysis, matched control design, and/or any other means to control the risks of these two groups was regarded as relevant.

Women who planned birth at a place outside hospital settings (e.g. home birth and/or standalone midwife-led unit birth) but had adverse outcomes were more likely to have been transferred to hospital before birth and therefore be considered as an obstetric unit birth. To compensate for this required that any observational study comparing clinical outcomes between births outside and within obstetric units should consider women who *planned* birth outside an obstetric unit with those who *planned* hospital birth. Controlling for risk factors of these two groups is critical.

Transfer rates were obtained from any study where the validity was regarded as [++] or [+].

Applicability to UK setting

Any study conducted in the UK since 1980 was regarded as having the highest applicability to the current UK setting. Clinical practice in the UK was considered to have been significantly different before 1980. Any study conducted in high income countries since 1980 was also considered valid, and therefore included if there was no UK study available or when the included UK studies could not provide enough information to make a conclusion.

Outcome measures

Another important factor is the availability of appropriate outcomes.

For effectiveness, relevant outcomes included mode of birth, incidence of obstetric interventions and any other relevant clinical outcomes as defined in the guideline questions.

Primary outcomes for safety were defined as intrapartum-related perinatal mortality (IPPM), and maternal mortality.

IPPM, defined as death from intrapartum 'asphyxia', 'anoxia' or 'trauma', (Wigglesworth classification 3),[600] was considered to be the most important outcome to assess safety of place of birth. IPPM includes stillbirths and death in the first week but excludes deaths of low birthweight infants or as a result of multiple abnormalities. If there was no relevant single study that reported IPPM, perinatal mortality was used. Similarly, maternal mortality was considered the most important outcome to assess safety of place of birth for mothers (women). If no relevant single study reported this outcome, other important maternal morbidities such as incidence of postpartum haemorrhage (PPH) were reported.

Where there is no single study reported IPPM and/or maternal mortality, perinatal mortality, neonatal morbidities and maternal morbidities were considered as proxy and hence reported.

Note: For further details of included studies, please refer to the evidence tables in the accompanying CD-ROM.

Planned home versus hospital birth

Table C.1 Included studies (planned home birth versus planned hospital birth)

Authors	Year	Country	Study design	Validity
NRPMSCG[45]	1981–1994	UK	Women planned home birth in the Northern Region was compared with all births in the region.	+
Dowswell[26]	1994	UK	A randomised controlled trial including only 11 women to assess feasibility of such a study design.	+
NCC-WCH (Appendix D)	1999–2003	UK	The number of women who booked home birth in all England and Wales was calculated from reported transfer rates with sensitivity. The estimated IPPM rate for booked home birth was compared with overall England and Wales figures.	+
	1994–1998	UK		+
Janssen[29]	1998–1999	Canada	Planned home birth at the onset of labour was compared with planned obstetric unit and planned midwife-led unit birth at the onset of labour in a matched control design.	+
Ackermann-Liebrich[32]	1989–1992	Switzerland	The review only included outcomes that were based on an analysis of matched pairs.	+
Bastian[30]	1985–1990	Australia	Outcomes for women who planned home birth at the onset of labour were compared with outcomes of all births in Australia.	+
Woodcock[35,36]	1981–1987	Australia	Booked home and hospital births were compared.	+

NRPMSCG = Northern Region Perinatal Mortality Survey Coordinating Group.

Table C.2 Excluded studies (planned home birth versus planned hospital birth)

Authors	Year	Country	Reasons for exclusion	Validity
Chamberlain[31]	1994	UK	Although reported as matched by age, lone parent status, parity and hospital, the sizes of the two groups were significantly different. There were over 1000 unmatched planned home birth women, but these women were included in the analysis. Socio-economic status and obstetric backgrounds of these two groups were reported as statistically significantly different; hence, the comparison was invalid. No regression analysis was used. The study reported perinatal mortality, but did not report IPPM.	–
Davies[43]	1993	UK	This was a case series without a control group.	–
Caplan[38]	1980–1981	UK	Women who gave birth at home were compared with a random sample of women who gave birth in hospital. Use of actual place of birth , rather than planned place of birth , and the lack of any controlling for background risk of these two groups made the comparison invalid.	–
Ford[44]	1977–1989	UK	This was a case series without a control group.	–
Shearer[39]	1978–1983	UK	202 women who planned home birth were compared with 185 women who planned hospital birth. No control of background obstetric risks was attempted.	–
Tew[37]	1970	UK	Although regression modelling was used to control some of the confounding factors, these were comparing actual home birth with actual hospital birth. The study was conducted prior to 1980.	–
Johnson[42]	2000	North America	This was a case series without a control group.	–
Wiegers[33]	1990–1993	Netherlands	The study employed matched control design, comparing planned home birth and planned hospital birth women, although the outcome reported was 'perinatal outcome index' defined by the authors, and each relevant clinical outcome was not obtained.	–
Duran[34]	1971–1989	USA	Although regression modelling controlled some of the confounding factors, these were comparing actual home birth with actual hospital birth with completely different backgrounds. The control group was drawn from the 1980 US National Natality/National Fetal Mortality Survey, in which low birthweights and fetal deaths were deliberately oversampled.	–
Mehl[40,41]	1970s	USA	Although regression modelling controlled some of the confounding factors, these were comparing actual home birth with actual hospital birth with significantly different backgrounds. The study was conducted prior to 1980.	–
Olsen[27]	2005	N/A	This systematic review only included the Dowswell study.[26] The included RCT does not report relevant outcomes for the clinical questions.	–
Olsen[28]	1997	N/A	The author conducted meta-analyses of six observational studies, of which five are listed above.[29,32–35] The other study was in a foreign language. The majority of the included studies had significant risk of introducing bias and/or confounding factors as above. In particular, the study by Duran[34] was weighted the most in the meta-analysis owing to the size of the studies. The original study conducted a regression analysis, attempting to control background of these two different populations, although the raw data were used for this Olsen meta-analysis (see above).	–

Planned standalone midwife-led unit versus obstetric unit birth

Table C.3 Included studies (planned standalone midwife-led versus obstetric unit birth)

Authors	Year	Country	Study design	Validity
Saunders[52]	1990s	UK	Booked standalone unit birth was compared with booked home and obstetric unit birth.	+
David[56]	1992–1994	Germany	Planned standalone unit birth at the onset of labour was compared with obstetric unit birth.	+
Feldman[53]	1981	USA	Planned standalone unit birth at the onset of labour was compared with obstetric unit birth.	+
Scupholme[54]	1980s	USA	Planned standalone unit birth at the onset of labour was compared with obstetric unit birth.	+
Stone[55]	1990s	USA	Planned standalone unit birth at the onset of labour was compared with obstetric unit birth.	+

Table C.4 Excluded studies (planned standalone midwife-led versus obstetric unit birth)

Authors	Year	Country	Reasons for exclusion	Validity
Walker[601]	1997	UK	Case series: no control group	–
Fraser[46]	2003	UK	Case series: no control group	–
Eakins[602]	1984	USA	Case series: no control group	–
Rooks[48–51,603]	1985–1987	USA	Case series: no control group	–
Holz[604]	1985–1988	USA	Case series: no control group	–
Waldenstrom[46]	1991–1995	Australia	Case series: no control group	–
Moster[605,606]	1967–1996	Norway	Actual places of birth were compared according to different size of maternity units on perinatal mortality. The definition of standalone midwife-led unit is significantly different from the current UK setting. Although antenatal risk factor was controlled, use of actual place of birth makes the comparison invalid.	–
Bennetts[46]	1972–1979	USA	Case series: no control group	–

Appendix D

NCC-WCH analysis to obtain the best estimate of intrapartum-related perinatal mortality in England and Wales

Background

A systematic review on risks and benefits of home birth showed increased intrapartum-related perinatal mortality (IPPM) in planned home birth groups in one Australian study[30] but no other study has been sufficient to address this issue. The Guideline Development Group was concerned about the lack of UK data and requested the NCC-WCH to conduct an analysis to obtain the best estimate of the IPPM rate in the UK.

Method

Study design

Population-based cross-sectional data were analysed. The primary focus was on booked home births with the outcome established by comparing IPPM rates derived from the Confidential Enquiry into Maternal and Child Health (CEMACH; previously the Confidential Enquiry into Stillbirths and Deaths in Infancy (CESDI)) with overall national IPPM rates. Data about all women who gave birth at home either intentionally or unintentionally in England and Wales between 1994 and 2003 were included. For the purpose of the study, the years were divided into two equal periods: an early period (1994–1998) and a late period (1999–2003). The cut-off, which made both periods equal in length, was arbitrary and not based on any particular clinical implications.

Definitions

Definitions of the terms used in this appendix are as follows:

- **IPPM rate:**
  - The IPPM rate is defined as deaths from intrapartum 'asphyxia', 'anoxia' or 'trauma', derived from the extended Wigglesworth classification 3,[600] which is used by CEMACH.[607,608] This includes stillbirths and death in the first week. The denominator was all births (live births and stillbirths).
- **Booked, unintended and actual home birth:**
  - Booked home birth refers to the intended place of birth at the time of the first antenatal visit (booking). This includes women who intended a home birth at booking but who may have later transferred her care during pregnancy or labour.
  - Unintended home birth refers to women who gave birth at home but at booking had actually intended to give birth elsewhere.
  - Actual home birth refers to all births (intended and unintended) that occurred at home.
- **Unintended home birth rate and transfer rate:**
  - The unintended home birth rate is the proportion of unintended home births among the total of actual home births.
  - The transfer rate is the proportion of all women who intended a home birth at booking but who gave birth in hospital or elsewhere, among the total of women who intended a home birth at booking. The transfer includes those that occurred during pregnancy as well as in labour.
- **Completed home birth group, unintended home birth group and transferred group (subgroups of home birth):**
  - Completed home birth group refers to women who intended to have a home birth at booking and had babies at home.

- Unintended home birth group refers to women who did not intend to have a home birth at booking but had babies at home.
- Transferred group refers to women who intended to have a home birth at booking but had babies in hospital or elsewhere.

Data collection

IPPM

The numbers for the overall IPPM and those for each subgroup of home births in England and Wales, between 1994 and 2003, were obtained from CEMACH, which collects data for all deaths by intended place of birth at booking.[608]

Unintended home birth and transfer rates

Unintended home births and transfer rates were extracted from previous studies identified through a systematic search of medical databases (Medline, The Cochrane Library, EMBASE, BNI, CINAHL and MIDIRS), using keywords such as 'home birth' and reference lists of relevant articles. Inclusion criteria stipulated that studies:

- were conducted in the UK
- were population based, which was defined as a study that reflects women at low risk in a certain defined area
- used the same definition of unintended home birth and transfer as above. Details of the systematic reviews are available from the authors. These rates were used to obtain weighted means and to set ranges for sensitivity analysis to calculate denominators for booked home birth.

Denominators (birth numbers) for all national births and actual home births

The numbers of all births and actual home births between 1994 and 2003 in England and Wales were obtained from the Office for National Statistics.[19,20,609–617]

Denominators (birth numbers) for booked home birth

The number of births from the Office for National Statistics, which relates to the actual place of birth, has been modified by removing the unintended home births and then adding back the likely transfers to provide an estimated number of women who had an intended home birth at booking.

Statistical analysis

IPPM rates were calculated from the data described above. χ^2 tests were performed to test for trends and applied to a comparison of IPPM rates when appropriate. Confidence intervals were also calculated when appropriate. Sensitivity analyses were performed using the pre-set ranges derived from previous studies.

Results

Overall IPPM rate

A total of 4991 intrapartum perinatal deaths occurred in England and Wales between 1994 and 2003 among 6 314 315 births. The IPPM rates improved significantly during this period (test for trend: χ^2 value = 100.92, degrees of freedom = 1, $P < 0.001$). The IPPM rate for the late period (0.68 per 1000 births [95% CI 0.65 to 0.71/1000]) was significantly lower than that for the early period (0.90 per 1000 births [95% CI 0.86 to 0.93/1000]) (χ^2 value = 100.09, degrees of freedom = 1, $P < 0.001$; data not shown).

IPPM rate for actual home births

There were 75 intrapartum-related deaths among the 66 115 home births in England and Wales in the early period, while 50 intrapartum-related deaths occurred in the 64 585 home births in the late period. The IPPM rate of 0.77 per 1000 births [95% CI 0.56 to 0.99/1000] for the later period was significantly better than the rate of 1.13 per 1000 births [95% CI 0.88 to 1.39/1000] (χ^2 value = 4.43, degrees of freedom = 1, P = 0.04) for the early years. The IPPM rate for actual home births in the early period was significantly higher than that for all births (χ^2 value = 4.04, degrees of freedom = 1, P = 0.04), but there was no evidence of difference in IPPM rates between actual home birth and all births in the later period (χ^2 value = 0.90, degrees of freedom = 1, P = 0.34).

Unintended home birth rates from previous studies

Unintended home birth rates were taken from previous studies conducted in England and Wales (Table D.1).

Table D.1   Unintended home birth and transfer rates from previous studies conducted in England and Wales

Author	Period conducted	Region	Unintended rate[a]	Transfer rate[b]
Ford[44]	1977–1989	London	Not reported	18.8%
Shearer[39]	1978–1983	Essex	Not reported	11.9%
NRPMSCG[45]	1983	Northern Region	56.0%	(35.0%)[c]
NRPMSCG[618,619]	1988	Northern Region	47.0%	Not reported
Davies[43]	1993	Northern Region	45.0%	43.0%
Chamberlain[31]	1994	England and Wales	Not reported	16.0%
Weighted mean			50.7%	14.3%
Sensitivity analysis	Lower		45.0%	11.9%
	Upper		56.0%	43.0%

NRPMSCG = Northern Region Perinatal Mortality Survey Coordinating Group.
[a] Proportion of women who did not book a home birth but had babies at home divided by all actual home births.
[b] Proportion of women who booked home births but did not have babies at home divided by all home birth bookings.
[c] No denominator was obtained; hence this was not included to calculate the weighted mean.

The unintended home birth rates ranged from 45.0% to 56.0%. The weighted mean of all the included studies was 50.7%. As a result, ranges for sensitivity analyses were set as 45% to 56%.

Transfer rates from previous studies

Transfer rates were also extracted from previous studies in England and Wales (Table D.1). The transfer rates ranged from 11.9% to 43.0%. The weighted mean of all the included studies was 14.3%. As a result, ranges for sensitivity analyses were arbitrarily set as 11.9% to 43.0%.

Estimation of IPPM rates for home birth

The sensitivity analyses (Table D.2) were used to estimate the number of births occurring in both the early and late periods for women in:

- the completed home birth group
- the transferred group
- the unintended home birth group
- the booked home birth group.

The IPPM rate was calculated using the estimated number of births for each subgroup (Table D.2).

In the early period, the completed home birth group had a lower IPPM rate (0.46 per 1000 births [range 0.41 to 0.52]), while both the unintended home birth group (1.79 per 1000 births [range 1.62 to 2.02/1000]) and the transferred group (5.52 per 1000 births [range 1.92 to 8.67/1000]) had higher rates compared with the overall IPPM rate. In the early period, there was no evidence of a difference in IPPM rate between the booked home birth group (1.18 per 1000 births [range 0.71 to 1.36/1000]) and the overall IPPM rate.

In the late period, a similar pattern was observed, with the completed home birth group having a lower IPPM rate (0.50 per 1000 births [range 0.45 to 0.56/1000]), and both the unintended home birth group (1.04 per 1000 births [range 0.94 to 1.17/1000]) and the transferred group (6.59 per 1000 births [range 1.31 to 9.12/1000]) having higher IPPM rates, compared with the overall IPPM rate. However, in the late period, the IPPM rate of the booked home birth group (1.37 per 1000 births [range 0.82 to 1.58/1000]) seemed to be higher than the overall IPPM rate and this was presumably due to the increased IPPM in the transferred group.

Although improvement was observed in the overall IPPM rates, none was seen when the results for booked home births from the late period were compared with those in the early period. The findings were similar for both the completed home birth group and the transferred group.

Table D.2 IPPM, births and IPPM rates for home birth and for overall births in England and Wales (1994–2003)

	Early period (1994–1998)			Late period (1999–2003)		
	IPPM	Births	IPPM rate per 1000 births	IPPM	Births	IPPM rate per 1000 births
Overall	2925	3 259 153	0.90	2066	3 055 162	0.68
Home birth						
Actual home birth	75	66 115	1.13	50	64 585	0.77
Booked home birth (range)	45	**38 033** **(33 020–63 795)**	**1.18** **(0.71–1.36)**	51	37 153 **(32 255–62 319)**	**1.37** **(0.72–1.78)**
Home birth subgroups (range)						
Completed home birth	15	**32 595** **(29 091–36 363)**	**0.46** **(0.41–0.52)**	16	31 840 **(28 417–35 522)**	**0.50** **(0.45–0.56)**
Transferred group	30	**5439** **(3462–15 636)**	**5.52** **(1.92–8.67)**	35	5313 **(3838–26 797)**	**6.59** **(1.31–9.12)**
Unintended home birth group	60	**33 520** **(29 752–37 024)**	**1.79** **(1.62–2.02)**	34	32 745 **(29 063–36 168)**	**1.04** **(0.94–1.17)**

IPPM = intrapartum-related perinatal mortality.
Numbers in **bold** are estimated values and ranges from the sensitivity analyses.

Discussion

The limitations of this study are considered below.

Measurement errors

The numbers of births occurring overall and at home were derived from national statistics. Miscoding and missing values are therefore considered to have been possible but negligible considering the size of the sample.[19,20]

The numerators (IPPM) were derived from routinely collected data in the CEMACH (previously CESDI) programme, which have been validated against national statistics. There remains the possibility of miscoding, misclassification and missing values, although the data collection system is well established.

Unintended home birth rates and transfer rates were taken from studies previously conducted in England and Wales. The range in these rates is large, and this implies that the studies applied different definitions of transfer and unintended home birth rates. However, the details of the definitions were not available. There were insufficient reports to obtain more precise estimates for these rates, and they were considered the best available. Although the transfer that occurred in the study period was considered as that from home to hospital, there were a few women who booked home birth with unknown consequences of their actual place of birth in the CEMACH data. This may have influenced the high IPPM rates in the transferred group. A sensitivity analysis ranging from less than the lowest obtained rate to greater than the highest obtained rate was used in an attempt to compensate for this uncertainty.

Bias

Selection bias could be introduced because only the 10 year period of 1994–2003 was evaluated. The study years were selected because the CEMACH data were available for these years. There might have been further changes since 2003, as there were changes observed between the early and later years. Otherwise, there was no sampling procedure involved and the data were based on the whole population of England and Wales.

Selection bias could be introduced for the studies that reported both unintended home birth and transfer rates. These were conducted between 1977 and 1994, before the time period in this study. Not all of the studies reported results for all of England and Wales and three of the six included studies were conducted in the Northern Region. However, although there was neither evidence of a temporal trend in rates nor any obvious regional effect, there is still a possibility of selection bias.

Data were collected after birth and the intended place of birth at booking was recorded retrospectively. This means that recall bias may have been introduced.

Confounding

Background obstetric and medical risk is highly likely to have been different between the groups and these confounding factors would be likely to have influenced the outcomes, including IPPM. Current practice in the UK means that women with known risk factors are likely to be advised to book for a hospital birth and previous studies support this.[29,31,32,34,35,39,42] White women, those with multiparity and those in higher socio-economic groups are more likely to book a home birth[29,31,32,34,35,39,42] than those from other ethnicities, with single parity and of lower socio-economic status. This means that a lower IPPM rate would be expected among the women who book home births compared with hospital births.

Data had been anonymised and it was not possible to remove data for women who had had more than one birth in the study period, including multiple births. Some regions may have had higher home birth rates with lower IPPM rates. We considered these as a potential effect modifier, rather than a confounding factor, and unlikely to be relevant to the interpretation of these results.

However, the potential for confounding means that the results of the present study must be interpreted with caution.

Possible explanations

The improvement in overall IPPM rates could have resulted from advances in clinical care, including use of more sophisticated strategies for identifying and acting upon risk, or improvements in staffing levels and training. For example, the fourth CESDI report (1994–1995)[608] reported the poor quality of the interpretation of intrapartum fetal heart rate traces and highlighted the need for better education in this area.

However, the IPPM rate for booked home birth in the late period appeared to be higher than the overall IPPM rate and had not improved from the early period and this seemed to arise from the worsening of the outcome in the transferred group over the two periods. Thus, although those women who had intended to give birth at home and did so had a generally good outcome, those requiring transfer of care appeared to do significantly worse and indeed had IPPM rates well in excess of the overall rate. It is not possible to tell from the available data when transfer occurred, i.e. whether during pregnancy or at labour onset.

Acknowledgments

We appreciate and thank CEMACH for providing us with access to aggregated data for analysis.

We are also grateful to Dr Peter Brocklehurst (National Perinatal Epidemiology Unit), Professor Rona McCandlish (National Perinatal Epidemiology Unit and National Collaborating Centre for Women's and Children's Health Board), Professor Pat Doyle (London School of Hygiene & Tropical Medicine), Dr Paul C Taylor (University of Hertfordshire), Dr Moira Mugglestone (National Collaborating Centre for Women's and Children's Health) and Miss Kate Fleming (CEMACH) who reviewed this paper and provided us with valuable comments.

Appendix E

Decision tree modelling framework to assess cost-effectiveness for place of birth

Introduction

This guideline considers four birth settings:

- home birth
- standalone midwife-led unit
- alongside midwife-led unit
- obstetric unit.

The NHS is publicly funded with finite resources and it is not possible, within this resource constraint, to provide all types of health care that would be clinically effective. Economic evaluation is thus used to try to allocate resources in such a way so as to maximise benefit from scarce resources. In considering recommendations for place of birth, it was thought that a comparison of the cost-effectiveness of the various alternatives for place of birth for low-risk women who live in England and Wales was important to inform a recommendation about their use.

Unfortunately, the poor quality of the UK data on health outcomes by place of birth makes it extremely difficult to make meaningful comparisons across different birth settings at the current time. These limitations in the data mean that good evidence-based conclusions about the relative cost-effectiveness of different birth settings in the UK cannot be made.

Nevertheless, publishing the framework for an economic model as part of the guideline can still fulfil a useful function. In particular, it adds weight to the research recommendations of the guideline by highlighting the need for better data if priorities in this area are to be determined with regard to their economic efficiency.

Ideally, an economic model of place of birth would use a measure of health-related quality of life (such as quality-adjusted life years (QALYs)) as its clinical outcome to capture the multidimensional nature of relevant outcomes – infant/maternal mortality and morbidity – in a single comparable generic measure. However, current data limitations do not allow such a comparison across different place of birth settings and the initial preference of the GDG was to use perinatal mortality as the single clinical outcome in the economic modelling. The reasoning for this was as follows:

- wide availability – perinatal mortality is a commonly used outcome measure of perinatal health worldwide
- avoidance of misclassification of stillbirth[*]
- death is always a primary outcome when it occurs
- frequency of event – perinatal deaths are much more common than maternal deaths
- the study/trial data were based on planned place of birth rather than actual place of birth and thus the whole package of care may affect outcomes that might be missed using intrapartum-related perinatal mortality (IPPM) instead, which only captures what happens in labour.

Nevertheless, it was recognised that, while using IPPM as an outcome might not capture differences in outcome attributable to the whole package of care arising from a certain planned place of birth, IPPM is a better marker than perinatal mortality in measuring attributable differences in outcome due to actual place of birth.

---

[*] Use of neonatal mortality often misses babies who died soon after birth from perinatal asphyxia diagnosed as stillbirth. Perinatal mortality includes stillbirth after 28 weeks of gestation.

In terms of this model, the acceptability of using a single measure of efficacy, such as perinatal-related mortality or intrapartum perinatal-related mortality, depends on the extent to which other important outcomes differ across place of birth settings. Although the answer is not known at this time, it is ultimately an empirical question.

Decision trees were developed to illustrate the various pathways that a woman may follow during labour according to the booked place of birth in each of the models. In decision trees, 'time flows from left to right' with the branches depicting all the possible patient pathways contingent on particular events. These events are defined by **nodes**:

- **Decision nodes** represent a choice for the decision maker, in this case, which is the booked place of birth?
- **Chance nodes** are used to represent uncertain events, with the branches emanating from the node indicating *all* the various possibilities. Each of these chance events has an associated probability and these should sum to 1.0 (100%) for all events associated with a particular chance node.
- **Terminal nodes** represent the endpoint of the model and are assigned a value or pay-off. This pay-off can be the outcomes and/or cost of a particular scenario.

Each pathway in the model is constructed so that the costs and clinical outcome (perinatal mortality or IPMM) associated with it can be estimated. Then, using probability parameters defined within the model, a weighted cost and outcome for each planned place of birth is calculated from the costs and outcomes associated with individual pathways.

An outline of the basic decision tree structure is shown in Figure E.1.

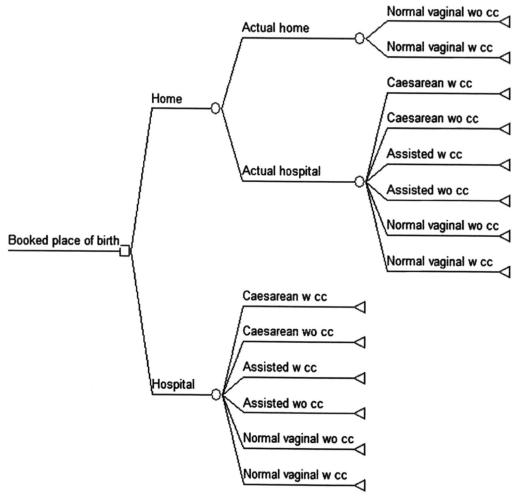

Figure E.1 Decision tree for booked home birth versus booked hospital birth (w = with; wo = without; cc = complications)

Costs

The costs that would be used to populate this model are derived from the Department of Health 2006/07 National Tariff unless otherwise stated. Data on finished consultant episodes from the 2004 NHS Reference Costs are used to obtain a weighted cost according to the proportion of elective and non-elective births.

Table E.1   Costs for each actual birth setting

Actual birth setting	Cost (range)
Normal home birth with complications[a]	£693 (£302–851)
Normal home birth without complications	£467 (£357–734)
Normal birth with complications at standalone or alongside midwife-led unit	£1,484
Normal birth without complications at standalone or alongside midwife-led unit	£774
Normal birth with complications at obstetric unit	£1,413
Normal birth without complications at obstetric unit	£838
Instrumental birth with complications at obstetric unit	£1,705
Instrumental birth without complications at obstetric unit	£1,175
Caesarean section with complications at obstetric unit	£2,638
Caesarean section without complications at obstetric unit	£1,912
Transfer to obstetric unit[b]	£237

[a] Mean value from 2004 NHS Reference Costs (interquartile range).
[b] Unit cost for successfully completed emergency ambulance journey, from Netten and Curtis.[620]

These cost parameters are used to assign a total cost to each terminal node and then a weighted average cost for each place of birth can be calculated according to the probabilities associated with those terminal nodes.

Sensitivity analysis

Even if the structure of the model is well defined in terms of clinical practice, the output can only be as good as the inputs. The confidence in the results of the model will depend on the degree of uncertainty surrounding model parameters and the sensitivity of the model's results to changes in these parameter values. In economic evaluation, the technique of varying parameter values to assess the impact of uncertainty on the model output is known as sensitivity analysis.

However, with the extent of current data uncertainty, it is difficult to adduce plausible ranges for clinical parameters on which to base such a sensitivity analysis.

Discussion

The main conclusion to be drawn is that there is a need for better data. Ideally, more than one dimension of outcome should be factored into the analysis, especially if the differentials in perinatal mortality are subsequently found to be at the lower end of what we consider to be a plausible range. Clearly, as some outcomes will also have 'downstream' cost consequences, this would also ideally be factored into subsequent models. However, it should be borne in mind that the importance of doing this would depend on having good evidence of differentials between different settings and for these differences to be important enough in absolute terms to have a non-trivial impact on the average cost of each birth setting.

Appendix F

Economic evaluation for ST analysis

Meta-analysis of three RCTs of high-risk women that investigated effectiveness of ST analysis showed that it reduces instrumental vaginal birth and neonatal encephalopathy, although there was no difference in fetal acid–base. However, while associated with lower neonatal encephalopathy rate in surviving infants, there is no significant difference in outcome when combined perinatal deaths. It comes at added cost and also requires the use of fetal scalp electrodes and extra staff training. If used when fetal heart rate abnormalities are present it may be necessary to perform a fetal blood sample before using ST analysis.

In the light of this evidence, a costing of ST analysis for intrapartum fetal monitoring using automatic STAN® was undertaken. This was done to assess whether the technology was potentially cost saving from an NHS perspective when 'downstream' resource use is considered.

The purchase of the STAN equipment represents a capital costs, requiring an up-front payment (or investment) before the service can be offered. This payment represents a fixed cost of STAN and does not vary with the quantity of service provided. This capital can then be used over a number of years before it needs to be replaced.

In general, capital costs have two facets:

- Opportunity cost – the money spent on the equipment could have been invested in some other venture yielding positive benefits. This is calculated by applying an interest rate on the sum invested in the equipment.
- Depreciation cost – the equipment has a certain lifespan and depreciates over time. Eventually the equipment has to be replaced. In economic evaluation, the usual practice is to annuitise the initial capital outlay over the expected life of equipment. This gives an 'annual equivalent cost' which can then be divided by the number of patients treated annually to assign a unit cost of using that equipment. Calculating the 'annual equivalent cost' means making allowance for the differential timing of costs which involves discounting.

The formula for calculating the equivalent annual cost is given below.

$$E = \left\{ K - \left[S/(1+r)^n \right] \right\} \Big/ A(n,r)$$

where:

E = equivalent annual cost
K = purchase price of equipment
S = resale value
r = discount (interest rate)
n = equipment lifespan
$A(n,r)$ = annuity factor[*] (n years at interest rate r)

The equipment cost also includes some training and consumables[†] but the analysis does not include any replenishment of consumables needed over the lifespan of the equipment. Nor does the costing include further training costs and the opportunity costs of the time of those being trained.

---

[*] Converts a present value into an annuity, a series of equal annual payments.

[†] The cost of STAN includes the cost of trolley, training, electronic archiving and consumables (fetal scalp electrodes: £231 box of 50).

Table F.1 Source of data populated into the model

		Source
Cost of purchasing STAN	£24,000	Supplier: www.okbemedical.com
Average births per annum per obstetric unit	3500	GDG
Number of STAN machines per obstetric unit	7	GDG
Number of obstetric units	200	GDG

Using the data in Table F.1 we can estimate the average cost of using the ST analysis in all obstetric units in England and Wales:

Total equipment cost of ST analysis = £24,000 × 200 × 7 = £33.6 million

If we assume that STAN has lifespan of 6 years, it is possible to calculate an annual equivalent cost of this equipment using the formula previously described. Using a discount rate of 3.5%, which is recommended by NICE technical manual, this gives an annual equivalent cost of £6.8 million.

However, there is evidence that fetal monitoring by means of STAN can reduce the rates of operative deliveries, which would produce concomitant 'downstream' resource savings. Taking into account that both types of operative deliveries, operative vaginal delivery and CS have a higher cost than normal births, we estimated the potential saving, using NHS Reference cost of ST analysis in terms of reduced operative birth.

Cost savings were calculated as follows:

- averting operative vaginal births = cost of assisted delivery – cost of normal vaginal birth = £1,267* – £862[†] = £405
- averting caesarean section births = cost of CS – cost of normal births = £2,068[‡] – £862[§] = £1,205

Then, using the data from Table F.2, we calculated the annual number of operative births avoided (operative vaginal births and CS) using ST analysis.

Table F.2 Probability of high-risk and operative births

Outcomes	Probability or RR	Source
High-risk births	0.46	NHS maternity statistics, England:2003–2004
High-risk operative vaginal births	0.141	Based on the results of the meta–analysis (Section 8.5.1)
High-risk CS births	0.085	Based on the results of the meta-analysis (Section 8.5.1)
RR of operative vaginal births with ST analysis	0.87	Based on the results of the meta-analysis (Section 8.5.1)
RR of CS births with ST analysis	0.97	Based on the results of the meta-analysis (Section 8.5.1)

Operative vaginal births avoided with ST analysis = 700 000 × 0.46 × 0.141 × (1 – 0.87) = 5897

Caesarean section births avoided with ST analysis =700 000 × 0.46 × 0.085 × (1 – 0.97) = 830

Therefore, the annual cost saving of using ST analysis for the fetal monitoring is:

Annual cost saving = (£405 × 5897) + (£1,205 × 830) = £3,388,603

The crucial point is to compare the average cost of using ST analysis with the equivalent saving due to the lower rates of operative deliveries. In other words, we try to find the net result of using ST analysis.

---

* Weighted average cost of operative vaginal births.
† Weighted average cost of normal births.
‡ Weighted average cost of CS.
§ Weighted average cost of normal births.

So, the net result of ST analysis is:

Cost of ST analysis:	£6.8 million
Saving of averted operating deliveries	£3.4 million
Net cost	**£3.4 million**

Using baseline estimates, it is evident that the cost of purchasing the equipment is higher than the potential cost saving from reduced operative delivery with a net increase in the NHS expenditures of £3.4 million.

To take account of variance and uncertainty in the estimates of some of the cost inputs, a sensitivity analysis was performed. A sensitivity analysis showed that the net result of the model was particularly sensitive to changes in the assumptions about RR of operative vaginal delivery and CS birth. With a 'best case scenario' for ST analysis, using the lower 95% CI RR for both operative vaginal birth (0.78) and CS births (0.84), there was a net saving to the NHS of £2.5 million. Whereas, the sensitivity analysis of the 'worst case scenario', using the upper 95% CI RR for operative vaginal birth (0.96) and CS (1.11), resulted in a net cost of £9.8 million.

The cost analysis presented above can only be considered an indicative estimate of the true cost of routinely using ST analysis for the fetal monitoring in all obstetric units in England and Wales. This analysis does not take into account all consumable and training costs associated with technique. On the other hand, we have assumed that the only source of cost saving is the reduction of operative deliveries. It is possible that ST analysis can reduce other costly interventions e.g. there is evidence that ST analysis can reduce the number of babies who develop neonatal encephalopathy.

Current evidence suggests that ST analysis may be more effective than the alternative. Had there been strong evidence that the technology was also cost saving, that would have suggested that ST analysis was most likely cost-effective. In the absence of strong evidence that the technology is cost saving, a full economic evaluation is required in order to assess cost-effectiveness. A simple costing approach was undertaken because a cost-effectiveness analysis was felt to be difficult within the constraints of this guideline.

References

1. Government Statistical Service and Department of Health. *NHS Maternity Statistics, England: 2002–03*. Statistical Bulletin 2004/10. London: Department of Health; 2004.

2. National Assembly for Wales. *Maternity Statistics, Wales: Methods of Delivery, 1995–2003*. No. SDR 40/2004. Cardiff: National Assembly for Wales; 2004.

3. Royal College of Obstetricians and Gynaecologists: Clinical Effectiveness Support Unit. *The Care of Women Requesting Induced Abortion*. Evidence-based guideline No. 7. London: RCOG; 2000.

4. NHS Executive. *Clinical Guidelines: Using Clinical Guidelines to Improve Patient Care Within the NHS*. London: HMSO; 1996.

5. National Institute for Clinical Excellence. *Induction of Labour*. Clinical guideline D. London: National Institute for Clinical Excellence; 2001.

6. National Collaborating Centre for Women's and Children's Health. *Caesarean Section*. Clinical Guideline. London: RCOG Press; 2004.

7. National Institute for Clinical Excellence. *Infection Control: Prevention of Healthcare-Associated Infection in Primary and Community Care*. London: National Institute for Clinical Excellence; 2003.

8. National Institute for Clinical Excellence. *Antenatal Care: Routine Care for the Healthy Pregnant Woman*. Clinical Guideline 6. London: National Institute for Clinical Excellence; 2003.

9. National Institute for Health and Clinical Excellence. *Guideline Development Methods: Information for National Collaborating Centres and Guideline Developers*. London: National Institute for Health and Clinical Evidence; 2005.

10. Oxman AD, Sackett DL, Guyatt GH. Users' guides to the medical literature. I. How to get started. The Evidence-Based Medicine Working Group. *JAMA: the Journal of the American Medical Association* 1993;270(17):2093–5.

11. Guyatt GH, Sackett DL, Cook DJ. Users' guides to the medical literature. II. How to use an article about therapy or prevention. A. Are the results of the study valid? Evidence-Based Medicine Working Group. *JAMA: the Journal of the American Medical Association* 1993;270(21):2598–601.

12. Guyatt GH, Sackett DL, Cook DJ. Users' guides to the medical literature. II. How to use an article about therapy or prevention. B. What were the results and will they help me in caring for my patients? Evidence-Based Medicine Working Group. *JAMA: the Journal of the American Medical Association* 1994;271(1):59–63.

13. Jaeschke R, Guyatt G, Sackett DL. Users' guides to the medical literature. III. How to use an article about a diagnostic test. A. Are the results of the study valid? Evidence-Based Medicine Working Group. *JAMA: the Journal of the American Medical Association* 1994;271(5):389–91.

14. Jaeschke R, Guyatt GH, Sackett DL. Users' guides to the medical literature. III. How to use an article about a diagnostic test. B. What are the results and will they help me in caring for my patients? The Evidence-Based Medicine Working Group. *JAMA: the Journal of the American Medical Association* 1994;271(9):703–7.

15. Sackett DL, Straus SE, Richardson WS, et al. *Evidence-Based Medicine. How to practice and teach EBM*. 2nd ed. Edinburgh: Churchill Livingstone; 2000.

16. Scottish Intercollegiate Guidelines Network. *SIGN 50: A Guideline Developers' Handbook*. No. 50. Edinburgh: Scottish Intercollegiate Guideline Network; 2001.

17. Drummond MF, O'Brien B, Stoddart GL, Torrance GW. *Methods for the Economic Evaluation of Health Care Programmes*. Oxford University Press; 1997.

18. Resuscitation Council (UK). *Resuscitation Guidelines 2005*. London: Resuscitation Council (UK); 2005.

19. Macfarlane A, Mugford M. *Birth Counts: Statistics of pregnancy & childbirth*. Vol 2. 2nd ed. London: The Stationary Office; 2000.

20. Macfarlane A, Mugford M, Henderson J, et al. Birth Counts: *Statistics of pregnancy & childbirth*. Volume 2. 2nd ed. London: The Stationary Office; 2000.

21. Standing Maternity and Midwifery Advisory Committee. *Domiciliary Midwifery and Maternity Beds Needed*. London: HMSO; 1970.

22. Expert Maternity Group. *Changing Childbirth*. London: HMSO; 1993.

23. Department of Health. *National Service Framework for Children, Young People and Maternity Services – Maternity*. No. 40498. London: Department of Health; 2004.

24. Welsh Assembly Government. *National Service Framework for Children, Young People and Maternity Services in Wales*. Cardiff: Welsh Assembly Government; 2005.

25. National Health Service. *NHS Maternity Statistics, England: 2004–05*. London: National Health Service; 2006.

26. Dowswell T, Thornton JG, Hewison J, et al. Should there be a trial of home versus hospital delivery in the United Kingdom? *British Medical Journal* 1996;312(7033):753–7.

27. Olsen O, Jewell MD. Home versus hospital birth. (Cochrane Review). In: *Cochrane Database of Systematic Reviews*, Issue 1, 2005. Oxford: Update Software.

28. Olsen O. Meta-analysis of the safety of home birth. *Birth* 1997;24(1):4–13.

29. Janssen PA, Lee SK, Ryan EM, et al. Outcomes of planned home births versus planned hospital births after regulation of midwifery in British Columbia. *Canadian Medical Association Journal* 2002;166(3):315–23.

30. Bastian H, Keirse MJ, Lancaster PA. Perinatal death associated with planned home birth in Australia: population based study. *British Medical Journal* 1998;317(7155):384–8.

31. Chamberlain G, Wraight A, Crowley P. *Home Births – The Report of the 1994 Confidential Enquiry by the National Birthday Trust Fund*. Parthenon; 1997.

32. Ackermann-Liebrich U, Voegeli T, Gunter-Witt K, et al. Home versus hospital deliveries: Follow up study of matched pairs for procedures and outcome. *British Medical Journal* 1996;313(7068):1313–18.

33. Wiegers TA, Keirse MJ, van der ZJ, et al. Outcome of planned home and planned hospital births in low risk pregnancies: prospective study in midwifery practices in The Netherlands. *British Medical Journal* 1996;313(7068):1309–13.

34. Duran AM. The safety of home birth: the farm study. *American Journal of Public Health* 1992;82(3):450–3.

35. Woodcock HC, Read AW, Bower C, et al. A matched cohort study of planned home and hospital births in Western Australia 1981–1987. *Midwifery* 1994;10(3):125–35.

36. Woodcock HC, Read AW, Moore DJ, et al. Planned homebirths in Western Australia 1981–1987: a descriptive study. *Medical Journal of Australia* 1990;153(11–12):672–8.

37. Tew M. *Safer Childbirth: A Critical History of Maternity Care.* 3rd ed. London: Free Association Books Ltd; 1998.

38. Caplan M, Madeley RJ. Home deliveries in Nottingham 1980–81. *Public Health* 1985;99(5):307–13.

39. Shearer JM. Five year prospective survey of risk of booking for a home birth in Essex. *British Medical Journal* 1985;291(6507):1478–80.

40. Mehl LE. Research on alternatives in childbirth: what can it tell us about hospital practice? In: Stewart L, Stewart D, eds. *21st Century Obstetrics Now.* Marble Hill, MO: NAPSAC; 1977. p. 171–207.

41. Mehl LE, Peterson GH, Whitt M, et al. Outcomes of elective home births: a series of 1,146 cases. *Journal of Reproductive Medicine* 1977;19(5):281–90.

42. Johnson KC, Daviss BA. Outcomes of planned home births with certified professional midwives: large prospective study in North America. *British Medical Journal* 2005;330(7505):1416–22.

43. Davies J, Hey E, Reid W, et al. Prospective regional study of planned home births. *British Medical Journal* 1996;313(7068):1302–6.

44. Ford C, Iliffe S, Franklin O. Outcome of planned home births in an inner city practice. *British Medical Journal* 1991;303(6816):1517–19.

45. Northern Region Perinatal Mortality Survey Coordinating Group. Collaborative survey of perinatal loss in planned and unplanned home births. *British Medical Journal* 1996;313(7068):1306–9.

46. Stewart M, McCandlish R, Henderson J, Brocklehurst P. *Report of a Structured Review of Birth Centre Outcomes.* Oxford: National Perinatal Epidemiology Unit; 2004.

47. Walsh D, Downe SM. Outcomes of free-standing, midwife-led birth centers: a structured review. *Birth* 2004;31(3):222–9.

48. Rooks JP, Weatherby NL, Ernst EK, et al. Outcomes of care in birth centers. The National Birth Center Study. *New England Journal of Medicine* 1989;321(26):1804–11.

49. Rooks JP, Weatherby NL, Ernst EKM. The National Birth Center Study: Part 1 – methodology and prenatal care and referrals. *Journal of Nurse-Midwifery* 1992;37(4):222–53.

50. Rooks JP, Weatherby NL, Ernst EK. The National Birth Center Study: Part III – Intrapartum and immediate postpartum and neonatal complications and transfers, postpartum and neonatal care, outcomes, and client satisfaction. *Journal of Nurse-Midwifery* 1992;37(6):361–97.

51. Rooks JP, Weatherby NL, Ernst EK. The National Birth Center Study: Part II – Intrapartum and immediate postpartum and neonatal care. *Journal of Nurse-Midwifery* 1992;37(5):301–30.

52. Saunders D, Boulton M, Chapple J, et al. *Evaluation of the Edgware Birth Centre.* London: Barnet Health Authority; 2000.

53. Feldman E, Hurst M. Outcomes and procedures in low risk birth: a comparison of hospital and birth center settings. *Birth* 1987;14(1):18–24.

54. Scupholme A, McLeod AGW, Robertson EG. A birth center affiliated with the tertiary care center: Comparison of outcome. *Obstetrics and Gynecology* 1986;67(4):598–603.

55. Stone PW. Maternity care outcomes: assessing a nursing model of care for low risk pregnancy. *Outcomes Manag Nurs Pract* 1998;2:71–5.

56. David M, von Schwarzenfeld HK, Dimer JA, et al. Perinatal outcome in hospital and birth center obstetric care. *International Journal of Gynaecology and Obstetrics* 1999;65(2):149–56.

57. Hodnett ED. Home-like versus conventional institutional settings for birth. (Cochrane Review). In: *Cochrane Database of Systematic Reviews*, Issue 2, 2003. Oxford: Update Software.

58. MacVicar J, Dobbie G, Owen-Johnstone L, et al. Simulated home delivery in hospital: a randomised controlled trial. *BJOG: an international journal of obstetrics & gynaecology* 1993;100(4):316–23.

59. Hundley VA, Cruickshank FM, Lang GD, et al. Midwife managed delivery unit: a randomized controlled comparison with consultant led care. *British Medical Journal* 1994;309(6966):1400–4.

60. Chapman MG, Jones M, Springs JE. The use of a birthroom: a randomised controlled trial comparing delivery with that in the labour ward. *BJOG: an international journal of obstetrics & gynaecology* 1986;93(2):182–7.

61. Mahmood TA. Evaluation of an experimental midwife-led unit in Scotland. *Journal of Obstetrics and Gynaecology* 2003;23(2):121–9.

62. Gould D, Lupton B, Marks M, et al. Outcomes of an alongside birth centre in a tertiary referral centre. *RCM Midwives* 2004;7(6):252–6.

63. Waldenstrom U, Nilsson CA, Winbladh B. The Stockholm birth centre trial: maternal and infant outcome. *BJOG: an international journal of obstetrics & gynaecology* 1997;104(4):410–18.

64. Waldenstrom U, Nilsson CA. MW vs OBA Randomized controlled study of birth center care versus standard maternity care: effect's on women's health. *Birth* 1997;24(1):17–26.

65. Stone PW, Walker PH. Cost-effectiveness analysis: birth center vs. hospital care. *Nursing Economics* 1995;13(5):299–308.

66. Anderson RE, Anderson DA. The cost-effectiveness of home birth. *Journal of Nurse-Midwifery* 1999;44(1):30–5.

67. Hodnett ED. Pain and women's satisfaction with the experience of childbirth: a systematic review. *American Journal of Obstetrics and Gynecology* 2002;186(5 Suppl Nature):S160–72.

68. Waldenstrom U, Hildingsson I, Rubertsson C. A negative birth experience: prevalence and risk factors in a national sample. *Birth* 2004;31(1):17–27.

69. Green JM, Baston HA. Feeling in control during labor: concepts, correlates, and consequences. *Birth* 2003;30(4):235–47.

70. Lavender T, Stephen A, Walkinshaw SA, et al. A prospective study of women's views of factors contributing to a positive birth experience. *Midwifery* 1999;15:40–6.

71. Waldenstrom U. Experience of labor and birth in 1111 women. *Journal of Psychosomatic Research* 1999;47(5):471–82.

72. Waldenstrom U, Borg IM, Olsson B, *et al*. The childbirth experience: a study of 295 new mothers. *Birth* 1996;23(3):144–53.

73. Brown S, Lumley J. Satisfaction with care in labor and birth: a survey of 790 Australian women. *Birth* 1994;21(1):4–13.

74. Brown S, Lumley J. Changing childbirth: lessons from an Australian survey of 1336 women. *BJOG: an international journal of obstetrics & gynaecology* 1998;105(2):143–55.

75. Creedy DK, Shochet IM, Horsfall J. Childbirth and the development of acute trauma symptoms: incidence and contributing factors. *Birth* 2000;27(2):104–11.

76. Tarkka MT, Paunonen M, Laippala P. Importance of the midwife in the first-time mother's experience of childbirth. *Scandinavian Journal of Caring Sciences* 2000;14(3):184–90.

77. VandeVusse L. Decision making in analyses of women's birth stories. *Birth* 1999;26(1):43–50.

78. Berg M, Lundgren I, Hermansson E, *et al*. Women's experience of the encounter with the midwife during childbirth. *Midwifery* 1996;12(1):11–15.

79. Halldorsdottir S, Karlsdottir SI. Journeying through labour and delivery: perceptions of women who have given birth. *Midwifery* 1996;12(2):48–61.

80. Halldorsdottir S, Karlsdottir SI. Empowerment or discouragement: women's experience of caring and uncaring encounters during childbirth. *Health Care for Women International* 1996;17(4):361–79.

81. McKay S, Smith SY. "What are they talking about? Is something wrong?" Information sharing during the second stage of labor. *Birth* 1993;20(3):142–7.

82. McKay S. Shared power: The essence of humanized childbirth. *Journal of Prenatal and Perinatal Psychology and Health* 1991;5(4):283–95.

83. Adams M. *A Study of Communication in the Labour Ward*. Research and the Midwife Conference Proceedings 1989. Manchester: Research and the Midwife;1990. p. 2–18.

84. Manogin TW, Bechtel GA, Rami JS. Caring behaviors by nurses: women's perceptions during childbirth. *Journal of Obstetric, Gynecologic and Neonatal Nursing* 2000;29(2):153–7.

85. Cheung NF. Choice and control as experienced by Chinese and Scottish childbearing women in Scotland. *Midwifery* 2002;18(3):200–13.

86. Simkin PP, O'Hara M. Nonpharmacologic relief of pain during labor: systematic reviews of five methods. *American Journal of Obstetrics and Gynecology* 2002;186(5 Suppl):S131–59.

87. Bloom SL, McIntire DD, Kelly MA, *et al*. Lack of effect of walking on labor and delivery. *New England Journal of Medicine* 1998;339(2):76–9.

88. MacLennan AH, Crowther C, Derham R. Does the option to ambulate during spontaneous labour confer any advantage or disadvantage? *Journal of Maternal-Fetal Investigation* 1994;3(1):43–8.

89. Flynn AM, Kelly J, Hollins G, *et al*. Ambulation in labour. *British Medical Journal* 1978;2(6137):591–3.

90. Molina FJ, Sola PA, Lopez E, *et al*. Pain in the first stage of labor: relationship with the patient's position. *Journal of Pain and Symptom Management* 1997;13(2):98–103.

91. Andrews CM, Chrzanowski M. Maternal position, labor, and comfort. *Applied Nursing Research* 1990;3(1):7–13.

92. Hodnett ED, Gates S, Hofmeyr GJ, Sakala C. Continuous support for women during childbirth. (Cochrane Review). In: *Cochrane Database of Systematic Reviews*, 2004. Oxford: Update Software.

93. Hodnett ED, Lowe NK, Hannah ME, *et al*. Effectiveness of nurses as providers of birth labor support in North American hospitals: A randomized controlled trial. *JAMA: the Journal of the American Medical Association* 2002;288(11):1373–81.

94. Langer A, Campero L, Garcia C, *et al*. Effects of psychosocial support during labour and childbirth on breastfeeding, medical interventions, and mothers' wellbeing in a Mexican public hospital: a randomised clinical trial. *BJOG: an international journal of obstetrics & gynaecology* 1998;105(10):1056–63.

95. House of Commons Health Committee. *Second Report on Maternity Services* (Winterton Report). London: HMSO; 1992.

96. Department of Health. *Changing Childbirth: Part 1 Report of the Expert Maternity Group*. London: HMSO; 1993.

97. North Staffordshire Changing Childbirth Research Team. A randomised study of midwifery caseload care and traditional 'shared-care'. *Midwifery* 2000;16(4):295–302.

98. Sandall J. Occupational burnout in midwives: new ways of working and the relationship between organisational factors and psychological health and well-being. *Risk, Decision and Policy* 1998;3(3):213–32.

99. National Collaborating Centre for Women's and Children's Health. *Antenatal Care: Routine Care for the Healthy Pregnant Woman*. London: RCOG Press; 2003.

100. Hodnett ED. Continuity of caregivers for care during pregnancy and childbirth. (Cochrane Review). In: *Cochrane Database of Systematic Reviews*, 2004. Oxford: Update Software.

101. Waldenstrom U, Turnbull D. A systematic review comparing continuity of midwifery care with standard maternity services. *BJOG: an international journal of obstetrics & gynaecology* 1998;105(11):1160–70.

102. Hicks C, Spurgeon P, Barwell F. Changing Childbirth: a pilot project. *Journal of Advanced Nursing* 2003;42(6):617–28.

103. Homer CS, Davis GK, Brodie PM, *et al*. Collaboration in maternity care: a randomised controlled trial comparing community-based continuity of care with standard hospital care. *BJOG: an international journal of obstetrics & gynaecology* 2001;108(1):16–22.

104. Homer CS, Davis GK, Cooke M, *et al*. Womens' experiences of continuity of midwifery care in a randomised controlled trial in Australia. *Midwifery* 2002;18(2):102–12.

105. Biro MA, Waldenstrom U. Team midwifery care in a tertiary level obstetric service: a randomized controlled trial. *Birth* 2000;27(3):168–73.

106. Biro MA, Waldenstrom U, Brown S, *et al*. Satisfaction with team midwifery care for low- and high-risk women: a randomized controlled trial. *Birth* 2003;30(1):1–10.

107. Waldenstrom U. Does team midwife care increase satisfaction with antenatal, intrapartum, and postpartum care? A randomized controlled trial. *Birth* 2000;27(3):156–67.

108. Waldenstrom U, McLachlan H, Forster D, *et al*. Team midwife care: maternal and infant outcomes. *Australian and New Zealand Journal of Obstetrics and Gynaecology* 2001;41(3):257–64.

109. Sandall J. Team midwifery and burnout in midwives in the UK: practical lessons from a national study. *MIDIRS Midwifery Digest* 1999;9(2):147–52.

110. Turnbull D, Holmes A, Shields N, *et al.* Randomised, controlled trial of efficacy of midwife-managed care. *Lancet* 1996;348(9022):213–18.

111. Gyte G, Richens Y. Routine prophylactic drugs in normal labour for reducing gastric aspiration and its effects. (Cochrane Review). In: *Cochrane Database of Systematic Reviews*, 2006. Oxford: Update Software.

112. Scrutton MJ, Metcalfe GA, Lowy C. Eating in labour: a randomised controlled trial assessing the risks and benefits. *Anaesthesia* 1999;54(4):329–34.

113. Scheepers HC, de Jong PA, Essed GG, *et al.* Carbohydrate solution intake during labour just before the start of the second stage: a double-blind study on metabolic effects and clinical outcome. *BJOG: an international journal of obstetrics & gynaecology* 2004;111(12):1382–7.

114. Scheepers HC, Thans MC, de Jong PA, *et al.* The effects of oral carbohydrate administration on fetal acid base balance. *Journal of Perinatal Medicine* 2002;30(5):400–4.

115. Scheepers H, Thans MCJ, de Jong PA, *et al.* A double-blind, randomised, placebo controlled study on the influence of carbohydrate solution intake during labour. *BJOG: an international journal of obstetrics & gynaecology* 2002;109(2):178–81.

116. Kubli M, Scrutton MJ, Seed PT, *et al.* An evaluation of isotonic "sport drinks" during labor. *Anesthesia and Analgesia* 2002;94(2):404–8.

117. Lumbiganon P, Thinkhamrop J, Thinkhamrop B, Tolosa JE. Vaginal chlorhexidine during labour for preventing maternal and neonatal infections (excluding Group B Streptococcal and HIV). (Cochrane Review). In: *Cochrane Database of Systematic Reviews*, Issue 1, 2005. Oxford: Update Software.

118. Keane HE, Thornton JG. A trial of cetrimide/chlorhexidine or tap water for perineal cleaning. *British Journal of Midwifery* 1998;6(1):34–7.

119. Kovavisarach E, Jaravechson S. Comparison of perforation between single and double-gloving in perineorrhaphy after vaginal delivery: a randomized controlled trial. *Australian and New Zealand Journal of Obstetrics and Gynaecology* 1998;38(1):58–60.

120. Punyatanasakchai P, Chittacharoen A, Ayudhya NI. Randomized controlled trial of glove perforation in single- and double-gloving in episiotomy repair after vaginal delivery. *Journal of Obstetrics and Gynaecology Research* 2004;30(5):354–7.

121. Kabukoba JJ, Pearce JM. The design, effectiveness and acceptability of the arm sleeve for the prevention of body fluid contamination during obstetric procedures. *BJOG: an international journal of obstetrics & gynaecology* 1993;100(8):714–16.

122. Dickinson JE, Paech MJ, McDonald SJ, *et al.* Maternal satisfaction with childbirth and intrapartum analgesia in nulliparous labour. *Australian and New Zealand Journal of Obstetrics and Gynaecology* 2003;43(6):463–8.

123. Ranta P, Spalding M, Kangas-Saarela T, *et al.* Maternal expectations and experiences of labour pain – options of 1091 Finnish parturients. *Acta Anaesthesiologica Scandinavica* 1995;39(1):60–6.

124. Capogna G, Alahuhta S, Celleno D, *et al.* Maternal expectations and experiences of labour pain and analgesia: A multicentre study of nulliparous women. *International Journal of Obstetric Anesthesia* 1996;5(4):229–35.

125. Huntley AL, Coon JT, Ernst E. Complementary and alternative medicine for labor pain: a systematic review. *American Journal of Obstetrics and Gynecology* 2004;191(1):36–44.

126. Gilbert RE, Tookey PA. Perinatal mortality and morbidity among babies delivered in water: surveillance study and postal survey. *British Medical Journal* 1999;319(7208):483–7.

127. Beech BL. Waterbirth – time to move forward. *Aims Journal* 2000;12(2):1–2.

128. Cluett ER, Nikodem VC, McCandlish RE, Burns EE. Immersion in water in pregnancy, labour and birth. (Cochrane Review). In: *Cochrane Database of Systematic Reviews*, Issue 2, 2004. Oxford: Update Software.

129. Cluett ER, Pickering RM, Getliffe K, *et al.* Randomised controlled trial of labouring in water compared with standard of augmentation for management of dystocia in first stage of labour. *British Medical Journal* 2004;328(7435):314–18.

130. Eriksson M, Mattsson L, Ladfors L. Early or late bath during the first stage of labour: a randomised study of 200 women. *Midwifery* 1997;13(3):146–8.

131. Martensson L, Nyberg K, Wallin G. Subcutaneous versus intracutaneous injections of sterile water for labour analgesia: a comparison of perceived pain during administration. *BJOG: an international journal of obstetrics & gynaecology* 2000;107(10):1248–51.

132. Lee MK, Chang SB, Kang DH. Effects of SP6 acupressure on labor pain and length of delivery time in women during labor. *Journal of Alternative and Complementary Medicine* 2004;10(6):959–65.

133. Ramnero A, Hanson U, Kihlgren M. Acupuncture treatment during labour--a randomised controlled trial. *BJOG: an international journal of obstetrics & gynaecology* 2002;109(6):637–44.

134. Skilnand E, Fossen D, Heiberg E. Acupuncture in the management of pain in labor. *Acta Obstetricia et Gynecologica Scandinavica* 2002;81(10):943–8.

135. Nesheim BI, Kinge R, Berg B, *et al.* Acupuncture during labor can reduce the use of meperidine: a controlled clinical study. *Clinical Journal of Pain* 2003;19(3):187–91.

136. Cyna AM, McAuliffe GL, Andrew MI. Hypnosis for pain relief in labour and childbirth: a systematic review. *British Journal of Anaesthesia* 2004;93(4):505–11.

137. Smith CA, Collins CT, Cyna AM, Crowther CA. Complementary and alternative therapies for pain management in labour. (Cochrane Review). In: *Cochrane Database of Systematic Reviews*, Issue 2, 2005. Oxford: Update Software.

138. Phumdoung S, Good M. Music reduces sensation and distress of labor pain. *Pain Management Nursing* 2003;4(2):54–61.

139. Carroll D, Moore RA, Tramer MR, *et al.* Transcutaneous electrical nerve stimulation does not relieve labor pain: Updated systematic review. *Contemporary Reviews in Obstetrics and Gynaecology* 1997;9(3):195–205.

140. Rosen MA. Nitrous oxide for relief of labor pain: a systematic review. *American Journal of Obstetrics and Gynecology* 2002;186(5 Suppl Nature):S110–26.

141. Bricker L, Lavender T. Parenteral opioids for labor pain relief: a systematic review. *American Journal of Obstetrics and Gynecology* 2002;186(5 Suppl Nature):S94–109.

142. Elbourne D, Wiseman RA. Types of intra-muscular opiods for maternal pain relief in labour. (Cochrane Review). In: *Cochrane Database of Systematic Reviews*, Issue 3, 2000. Oxford: Update Software.

143. Tsui MH, Ngan Kee WD, Ng FF, *et al.* A double blinded randomised placebo-controlled study of intramuscular pethidine for pain relief in the first stage of labour. *BJOG: an international journal of obstetrics & gynaecology* 2004;111(7):648–55.

144. Keskin HL, Keskin EA, Avsar AF, *et al.* Pethidine versus tramadol for pain relief during labor. *International Journal of Gynaecology and Obstetrics* 2003;82(1):11–16.

145. Fairlie FM, Marshall L, Walker JJ, *et al.* Intramuscular opioids for maternal pain relief in labour: a randomised controlled trial comparing pethidine with diamorphine. *BJOG: an international journal of obstetrics & gynaecology* 1999;106(11):1181–7.

146. Sosa CG, Balaguer E, Alonso JG, *et al.* Meperidine for dystocia during the first stage of labor: A randomized controlled trial. *American Journal of Obstetrics and Gynecology* 2004;191(4):1212–18.

147. Soontrapa S, Somboonporn W, Komwilaisak R, *et al.* Effectiveness of intravenous meperidine for pain relief in the first stage of labour. *Journal of the Medical Association of Thailand* 2002;85(11):1169–75.

148. Olofsson C, Ekblom A, Ekman-Ordeberg G, *et al.* Analgesic efficacy of intravenous morphine in labour pain: A reappraisal. *International Journal of Obstetric Anesthesia* 1996;5(3):176–80.

149. Isenor L, Penny-MacGillivray T. Intravenous meperidine infusion for obstetric analgesia. *Journal of Obstetric, Gynecologic and Neonatal Nursing* 1993;22(4):349–56.

150. Nelson KE, Eisenach JC. Intravenous butorphanol, meperidine, and their combination relieve pain and distress in women in labor. *Anesthesiology* 2005;102(5):1008–13.

151. Blair JM, Dobson GT, Hill DA, *et al.* Patient controlled analgesia for labour: a comparison of remifentanil with pethidine. *Anaesthesia* 2005;60(1):22–7.

152. Volikas I, Male D. A comparison of pethidine and remifentanil patient-controlled analgesia in labour. *International Journal of Obstetric Anesthesia* 2001;10(2):86–90.

153. Morley-Forster PK, Reid DW, Vandeberghe H. A comparison of patient-controlled analgesia fentanyl and alfentanil for labour analgesia. *Canadian Journal of Anaesthesia* 2000;47(2):113–19.

154. McInnes RJ, Hillan E, Clark D, *et al.* Diamorphine for pain relief in labour : a randomised controlled trial comparing intramuscular injection and patient-controlled analgesia. *BJOG: an international journal of obstetrics & gynaecology* 2004;111(10):1081–9.

155. Thurlow JA, Laxton CH, Dick A, *et al.* Remifentanil by patient-controlled analgesia compared with intramuscular meperidine for pain relief in labour. *British Journal of Anaesthesia* 2002;88(3):374–8.

156. Anim-Somuah M, Smyth R, Howell C. Epidural versus non-epidural or no analgesia in labour. (Cochrane Review). In: *Cochrane Database of Systematic Reviews*, 2005. Oxford: Update Software.

157. Morgan-Ortiz F, Quintero-Ledezma JC, Perez-Sotelo JA, *et al.* Evolution and quality of care during labor and delivery in primiparous patients who underwent early obstetrical analgesia. [Spanish]. *Ginecologia y Obstetricia de Mexico* 1999;67:522–6.

158. Leighton BL, Halpern SH. The effects of epidural analgesia on labor, maternal, and neonatal outcomes: a systematic review. *American Journal of Obstetrics and Gynecology* 2002;186(5 Suppl Nature):S69–77.

159. Reynolds F, Sharma SK, Seed PT. Analgesia in labour and fetal acid-base balance: a meta-analysis comparing epidural with systemic opioid analgesia. *BJOG: an international journal of obstetrics & gynaecology* 2002;109(12):1344–53.

160. Philip J, Alexander JM, Sharma SK, *et al.* Epidural analgesia during labor and maternal fever. *Anesthesiology* 1999;90(5):1271–5.

161. Lieberman E, Davidson K, Lee-Parritz A, *et al.* Changes in fetal position during labor and their association with epidural analgesia. *Obstetrics and Gynecology* 2005;105(5 I):974–82.

162. Alexander JM, Sharma SK, McIntire DD, *et al.* Epidural analgesia lengthens the Friedman active phase of labor. *Obstetrics and Gynecology* 2002;100(1):46–50.

163. Macarthur A, MacArthur C, Weeks S. Epidural anaesthesia and low back pain after delivery: a prospective cohort study. *British Medical Journal* 1995;311(7016):1336–9.

164. Eriksson SL, Olausson PO, Olofsson C. Use of epidural analgesia and its relation to caesarean and instrumental deliveries-a population-based study of 94,217 primiparae. *European Journal of Obstetrics, Gynecology and Reproductive Biology* 2005; E-print ahead of print.

165. Capogna G, Celleno D, Lyons G, *et al.* Minimum local analgesic concentration of extradural bupivacaine increases with progression of labour. *British Journal of Anaesthesia* 1998;80(1):11–13.

166. Chen L-K, Hsu H-W, Lin C-J, *et al.* Effects of epidural fentanyl on labor pain during the early period of the first stage of induced labor in nulliparous women. *Journal of the Formosan Medical Association* 2000;99(7):549–53.

167. Chestnut DH, Vincent Jr RD, McGrath JM, *et al.* Does early administration of epidural analgesia affect obstetric outcome in nulliparous women who are receiving intravenous oxytocin? *Anesthesiology* 1994;80(6):1193–200.

168. Chestnut DH, McGrath JM, Vincent Jr RD, *et al.* Does early administration of epidural analgesia affect obstetric outcome in nulliparous women who are in spontaneous labor? *Anesthesiology* 1994;80(6):1201–8.

169. Luxman D, Wolman I, Groutz A, *et al.* The effect of early epidural block administration on the progression and outcome of labor. *International Journal of Obstetric Anesthesia* 1998;7(3):161–4.

170. Wong CA, Scavone BM, Peaceman AM, *et al.* The risk of cesarean delivery with neuraxial analgesia given early versus late in labor. *New England Journal of Medicine* 2005;352(7):655–65.

171. Ohel G, Gonen R, Vaida S, *et al.* Early versus late initiation of epidural analgesia in labor: does it increase the risk of cesarean section? A randomized trial. *American Journal of Obstetrics and Gynecology* 2006;194(3):600–5.

172. Hofmeyr GJ. Prophylactic intravenous preloading for regional analgesia in labour. (Cochrane Review). In: *Cochrane Database of Systematic Reviews*, Issue 3, 2000. Oxford: Update Software.

173. Mayberry LJ, Clemmens D, De A. Epidural analgesia side effects, co-interventions, and care of women during childbirth: a systematic review. *American Journal of Obstetrics and Gynecology* 2002;186(5 Suppl Nature):S81–S93.

174. Roberts CL, Algert CS, Olive E. Impact of first-stage ambulation on mode of delivery among women with epidural analgesia. *Australian and New Zealand Journal of Obstetrics and Gynaecology* 2004;44(6):489–94.

175. Roberts CL, Algert CS, Cameron CA. A meta-analysis of upright positions in the second stage to reduce instrumental deliveries in women with epidural analgesia. *Acta Obstetricia et Gynecologica Scandinavica* 2005;84(8):794–8.

176. Downe S, Gerrett D, Renfrew MJ. A prospective randomised trial on the effect of position in the passive second stage of labour on birth outcome in nulliparous women using epidural analgesia. *Midwifery* 2004;20(2):157–68.

177. Torvaldsen S, Roberts CL, Bell JC, Raynes-Greenow CH. Discontinuation of epidural analgesia late in labour for reducing the adverse delivery outcomes associated with epidural analgesia. (Cochrane Review). In: *Cochrane Database of Systematic Reviews*, Issue Oxford, 2005. Oxford: Update Software.

178. Roberts CL, Torvaldsen S, Cameron CA, et al. Delayed versus early pushing in women with epidural analgesia: a systematic review and meta-analysis. *BJOG: an international journal of obstetrics & gynaecology* 2004;111(12):1333–40.

179. Simpson KR, James DC. Effects of immediate versus delayed pushing during second-stage labor on fetal well-being: a randomized clinical trial. *Nursing Research* 2005;54(3):149–57.

180. Gleeson NC, Griffith AP. The management of the second stage of labour in primiparae with epidural analgesia. *British Journal of Clinical Practice* 1991;45(2):90–1.

181. Saunders NJ, Spiby H, Gilbert L, et al. Oxytocin infusion during second stage of labour in primiparous women using epidural analgesia: a randomised double blind placebo controlled trial. *British Medical Journal* 1989;299(6713):1423–6.

182. Hill JB, Alexander JM, Sharma SK, et al. A comparison of the effects of epidural and meperidine analgesia during labor on fetal heart rate. *Obstetrics and Gynecology* 2003;102(2):333–7.

183. Sharma SK, Alexander JM, Messick G, et al. Cesarean delivery: a randomized trial of epidural analgesia versus intravenous meperidine analgesia during labor in nulliparous women. *Anesthesiology* 2002;96(3):546–51.

184. Sharma SK, Sidawi JE, Ramin SM, et al. Cesarean delivery: a randomized trial of epidural versus patient-controlled meperidine analgesia during labor. *Anesthesiology* 1997;87(3):487–94.

185. Mardirosoff C, Dumont L, Boulvain M, et al. Fetal bradycardia due to intrathecal opioids for labour analgesia: a systematic review. *BJOG: an international journal of obstetrics & gynaecology* 2002;109(3):274–81.

186. Beilin Y, Bodian CA, Weiser J, et al. Effect of labor epidural analgesia with and without fentanyl on infant breast-feeding: a prospective, randomized, double-blind study. *Anesthesiology* 2005;103(6):1211–17.

187. Jordan S, Emery S, Bradshaw C, et al. The impact of intrapartum analgesia on infant feeding. *BJOG: an international journal of obstetrics & gynaecology* 2005;112(7):927–34.

188. Chua SM, Sia AT. Automated intermittent epidural boluses improve analgesia induced by intrathecal fentanyl during labour. *Canadian Journal of Anaesthesia* 2004;51(6):581–5.

189. D'Athis F, Macheboeuf M, Thomas H, et al. Epidural analgesia with a bupivacaine-fentanyl mixture in obstetrics: comparison of repeated injections and continuous infusion. *Canadian Journal of Anaesthesia* 1988;35(2):116–22.

190. Eddleston JM, Maresh M, Horsman EL, et al. Comparison of the maternal and fetal effects associated with intermittent or continuous infusion of extradural analgesia. *British Journal of Anaesthesia* 1992;69(2):154–8.

191. Hicks JA, Jenkins JG, Newton MC, et al. Continuous epidural infusion of 0.075% bupivacaine for pain relief in labour. A comparison with intermittent top-ups of 0.5% bupivacaine. *Anaesthesia* 1988;43(4):289–92.

192. Lamont RF, Pinney D, Rodgers P, et al. Continuous versus intermittent epidural analgesia. A randomised trial to observe obstetric outcome. *Anaesthesia* 1989;44(11):893–6.

193. Smedstad KG, Morison DH. A comparative study of continuous and intermittent epidural analgesia for labour and delivery. *Canadian Journal of Anaesthesia* 1988;35(3):234–41.

194. Wong CA, Ratliff JT, Sullivan JT, et al. A randomized comparison of programmed intermittent epidural bolus with continuous epidural infusion for labor analgesia. *Anesthesia and Analgesia* 2006;102(3):904–9.

195. Lim Y, Sia AT, Ocampo C. Automated regular boluses for epidural analgesia: a comparison with continuous infusion. *International Journal of Obstetric Anesthesia* 2005;14(4):305–9.

196. van der Vyver M, Halpern S, Joseph G. Patient-controlled epidural analgesia versus continuous infusion for labour analgesia: a meta-analysis. *British Journal of Anaesthesia* 2002;89(3):459–65.

197. Saito M, Okutomi T, Kanai Y, et al. Patient-controlled epidural analgesia during labor using ropivacaine and fentanyl provides better maternal satisfaction with less local anesthetic requirement. *Journal of Anesthesia* 2005;19(3):208–12.

198. Gambling DR, McMorland GH, Yu P, et al. Comparison of patient-controlled epidural analgesia and conventional intermittent 'top-up' injections during labor. *Anesthesia and Analgesia* 1990;70(3):256–61.

199. Paech MJ. Epidural analgesia in labour: Constant infusion plus patient-controlled boluses. *Anaesthesia and Intensive Care* 1991;19(1):32–9.

200. Paech MJ, Pavy TJG, Sims C, et al. Clinical experience with patient-controlled and staff-administered intermittent bolus epidural analgesia in labour. *Anaesthesia and Intensive Care* 1995;23(4):459–63.

201. Halonen P, Sarvela J, Saisto T, et al. Patient-controlled epidural technique improves analgesia for labor but increases cesarean delivery rate compared with the intermittent bolus technique. *Acta Anaesthesiologica Scandinavica* 2004;48(6):732–7.

202. Gambling DR, Huber CJ, Berkowitz J, et al. Patient-controlled epidural analgesia in labour: varying bolus dose and lockout interval. *Canadian Journal of Anaesthesia* 1993;40(3):211–17.

203. Bernard JM, Le RD, Vizquel L, et al. Patient-controlled epidural analgesia during labor: the effects of the increase in bolus and lockout interval. *Anesthesia and Analgesia* 2000;90(2):328–32.

204. Siddik-Sayyid SM, Aouad MT, Jalbout MI, et al. Comparison of three modes of patient-controlled epidural analgesia during labour. *European Journal of Anaesthesiology* 2005;22(1):30–4.

205. Stratmann G, Gambling DR, Moeller-Bertram T, et al. A randomized comparison of a five-minute versus fifteen-minute lockout interval for PCEA during labor. *International Journal of Obstetric Anesthesia* 2005;14(3):200–7.

206. Anonymous. Review of recommendations for labor and birth care. *American Family Physician* 1992;45(2):927.

207. Hughes D, Simmons SW, Brown J, Cyna AM. Combined spinal-epidural versus epidural analgesia in labour. (Cochrane Review). In: *Cochrane Database of Systematic Reviews*, Issue Oxford, 2005. Oxford: Update Software.

208. Zeidan AZ. Combined spinal-epidural compared with low dose epidural during ambulatory labour analgesia in nulliparous women. *Egyptian Journal of Anaesthesia* 2004;20(3):273–81.

209. MacArthur C. A randomised controlled trial of mobile and non-mobile techniques of regional analgesia for labour, evaluating short and long term outcomes [www.ReFeR.nhs.uk/ViewRecord.asp?ID=1210], 2004.

210. Wong CA, Scavone BM, Slavenas JP, et al. Efficacy and side effect profile of varying doses of intrathecal fentanyl added to bupivacaine for labor analgesia. *International Journal of Obstetric Anesthesia* 2004;13(1):19–24.

211. Lim Y, Sia AT, Ocampo CE. Comparison of intrathecal levobupivacaine with and without fentanyl in combined spinal epidural for labor analgesia. *Medical Science Monitor* 2004;10(7):I87–91.

212. Bucklin BA, Chestnut DH, Hawkins JL. Intrathecal opioids versus epidural local anesthetics for labor analgesia: a meta-analysis. *Regional Anesthesia and Pain Medicine* 2002;27(1):23–30.

213. Chan SY, Chiu JW. Intrathecal labor analgesia using levobupivacaine 2.5 mg with fentanyl 25 microg--would half the dose suffice? *Medical Science Monitor* 2004;10(10):I110–14.

214. Lee BB, Ngan Kee WD, Hung VY, *et al.* Combined spinal-epidural analgesia in labour: comparison of two doses of intrathecal bupivacaine with fentanyl. *British Journal of Anaesthesia* 1999;83(6):868–71.

215. Palmer CM, Cork RC, Hays R, *et al.* The dose-response relation of intrathecal fentanyl for labor analgesia. *Anesthesiology* 1998;88(2):355–61.

216. Stocks GM, Hallworth SP, Fernando R, *et al.* Minimum local analgesic dose of intrathecal bupivacaine in labor and the effect of intrathecal fentanyl. *Anesthesiology* 2001;94(4):593–8.

217. Palmer CM, Van Maren G, Nogami WM, *et al.* Bupivacaine augments intrathecal fentanyl for labor analgesia. *Anesthesiology* 1999;91(1):84–9.

218. Celeski DC, Heindel L, Haas J, *et al.* Effect of intrathecal fentanyl dose on the duration of labor analgesia. *AANA Journal* 1999;67(3):239–44.

219. Beilin Y, Galea M, Zahn J, *et al.* Epidural ropivacaine for the initiation of labor epidural analgesia: a dose finding study. *Anesthesia and Analgesia* 1999;88(6):1340–5.

220. Christiaens F, Verborgh C, Dierick A, *et al.* Effects of diluent volume of a single dose of epidural bupivacaine in parturients during the first stage of labor. *Regional Anesthesia and Pain Medicine* 1998;23(2):134–41.

221. Plaat FS, Royston P, Morgan BM. Comparison of 15 mg and 25 mg of bupivacaine both with 50 mug fentanyl as initial dose for epidural analgesia. *International Journal of Obstetric Anesthesia* 1996;5(4):240–3.

222. Comparative Obstetric Mobile Epidural Trial (COMET) Study Group. Effect of low-dose mobile versus traditional epidural techniques on mode of delivery: a randomised controlled trial. *Lancet* 2001;358(9275):19–23.

223. Huch A, Huch R. Physiological insights based on fetal tcPO2 monitoring. *Journal of Perinatal Medicine* 1981;9(4):184–8.

224. Elliott RD. Continuous infusion epidural analgesia for obstetrics: Bupivacaine versus bupivacaine-fentanyl mixture. *Canadian Journal of Anaesthesia* 1991;38(3):303–10.

225. Enever GR, Noble HA, Kolditz D, *et al.* Epidural infusion of diamorphine with bupivacaine in labour. A comparison with fentanyl and bupivacaine. *Anaesthesia* 1991;46(3):169–73.

226. Russell R, Quinlan J, Reynolds F. Motor block during epidural infusions for nulliparous women in labour. A randomized double-blind study of plain bupivacaine and low dose bupivacaine with fentanyl. *International Journal of Obstetric Anesthesia* 1995;4(2):82–8.

227. Russell R, Reynolds F. Epidural infusion of low-dose bupivacaine and opioid in labour: Does reducing motor block increase the spontaneous delivery rate? *Anaesthesia* 1996;51(3):266–73.

228. Reynolds F, Russell R, Porter J, *et al.* Does the use of low dose bupivacaine/opioid epidural infusion increase the normal delivery rate? *International Journal of Obstetric Anesthesia* 2003;12(3):156–63.

229. Porter J, Bonello E, Reynolds F. Effect of epidural fentanyl on neonatal respiration. [Erratum appears in *Anesthesiology* 1998 Dec;89(6):1615]. *Anesthesiology* 1998;89(1):79–85.

230. Chestnut DH, Owen CL, Bates JN, *et al.* Continuous infusion epidural analgesia during labor. A randomized, double-blind comparison of 0.0625% bupivacaine/0.0002% fentanyl versus 0.125% bupivacaine. *Anesthesiology* 1988;68(5):754–9.

231. Burke D, Henderson DJ, Simpson AM, *et al.* Comparison of 0.25% S(-)-bupivacaine with 0.25% RS-bupivacaine for epidural analgesia in labour. *British Journal of Anaesthesia* 1999;83(5):750–5.

232. Camorcia M, Capogna G, Columb MO. Minimum local analgesic doses of ropivacaine, levobupivacaine, and bupivacaine for intrathecal labor analgesia. *Anesthesiology* 2005;102(3):646–50.

233. El-Moutaz H, El-Said A, Fouad M. Comparative study between 0.25% levobupivacaine and 0.25% racemic bupivacaine for epidural analgesia in labour. *Egyptian Journal of Anaesthesia* 2003;19(4):417–21.

234. Lim Y, Ocampo CE, Sia AT. A comparison of duration of analgesia of intrathecal 2.5 mg of bupivacaine, ropivacaine, and levobupivacaine in combined spinal epidural analgesia for patients in labor. *Anesthesia and Analgesia* 2004;98(1):235–9.

235. Lyons G, Columb M, Wilson RC, *et al.* Epidural pain relief in labour: potencies of levobupivacaine and racemic bupivacaine. [erratum appears in Br J Anaesth 1999;82(3):488]. *British Journal of Anaesthesia* 1998;81(6):899–901.

236. Sah N, Vallejo MC, Ramanathan S, *et al.* Bupivacaine versus L-bupivacaine for labor analgesia via combined spinal-epidural: A randomized, double-blinded study. *Journal of Clinical Anesthesia* 2005;17(2):91–5.

237. Polley LS, Columb MO, Naughton NN, *et al.* Relative analgesic potencies of levobupivacaine and ropivacaine for epidural analgesia in labor. *Anesthesiology* 2003;99(6):1354–8.

238. Benhamou D, Ghosh C, Mercier FJ. A randomized sequential allocation study to determine the minimum effective analgesic concentration of levobupivacaine and ropivacaine in patients receiving epidural analgesia for labor. *Anesthesiology* 2003;99(6):1383–6.

239. Purdie NL, McGrady EM. Comparison of patient-controlled epidural bolus administration of 0.1% ropivacaine and 0.1% levobupivacaine, both with 0.0002% fentanyl, for analgesia during labour. *Anaesthesia* 2004;59(2):133–7.

240. Sia AT, Goy RW, Lim Y, *et al.* A comparison of median effective doses of intrathecal levobupivacaine and ropivacaine for labor analgesia. *Anesthesiology* 2005;102(3):651–6.

241. Supandji M, Sia ATH, Ocampo CE. 0.2% Ropivacaine and levobupivacaine provide equally effective epidural labour analgesia. *Canadian Journal of Anaesthesia* 2004;51(9):918–22.

242. Asik I, Goktug A, Gulay I, *et al.* Comparison of bupivacaine 0.2% and ropivacaine 0.2% combined with fentanyl for epidural analgesia during labour. *European Journal of Anaesthesiology* 2002;19(4):263–70.

243. Campbell DC, Zwack RM, Crone LA, *et al.* Ambulatory labor epidural analgesia: bupivacaine versus ropivacaine. *Anesthesia and Analgesia* 2000;90(6):1384–9.

244. Chua NP, Sia AT, Ocampo CE. Parturient-controlled epidural analgesia during labour: Bupivacaine vs. ropivacaine. *Anaesthesia* 2001;56(12):1169–73.

245. Dresner M, Freeman J, Calow C, *et al.* Ropivacaine 0.2% versus bupivacaine 0.1% with fentanyl: a double blind comparison for analgesia during labour. *British Journal of Anaesthesia* 2000;85(6):826–9.

246. Eddleston JM, Holland JJ, Griffin RP, *et al.* A double-blind comparison of 0.25% ropivacaine and 0.25% bupivacaine for extradural analgesia in labour. *British Journal of Anaesthesia* 1996;76(1):66–71.

247. Evron S, Glezerman M, Sadan O, *et al.* Patient-controlled epidural analgesia for labor pain: Effect on labor, delivery and neonatal outcome of 0.125% bupivacaine vs 0.2% ropivacaine. *International Journal of Obstetric Anesthesia* 2004;13(1):5–10.

248. Fernandez-Guisasola J, Serrano ML, Cobo B, *et al.* A comparison of 0.0625% bupivacaine with fentanyl and 0.1% ropivacaine with fentanyl for continuous epidural labor analgesia. *Anesthesia and Analgesia* 2001;92(5):1261–5.

249. Finegold H, Mandell G, Ramanathan S. Comparison of ropivacaine 0.1%-fentanyl and bupivacaine 0.125%-fentanyl infusions for epidural labour analgesia. *Canadian Journal of Anaesthesia* 2000;47(8):740–5.

250. Gaiser RR, Venkateswaren P, Cheek TG, *et al.* Comparison of 0.25% Ropivacaine and bupivacaine for epidural analgesia for labor and vaginal delivery. *Journal of Clinical Anesthesia* 1997;9(7):564–8.

251. Halpern SH, Breen TW, Campbell DC, *et al.* A multicenter, randomized, controlled trial comparing bupivacaine with ropivacaine for labor analgesia. *Anesthesiology* 2003;98(6):1431–5.

252. Hughes D, Hill D, Fee JP. Intrathecal ropivacaine or bupivacaine with fentanyl for labour. *British Journal of Anaesthesia* 2001;87(5):733–7.

253. Irestedt L, Ekblom A, Olofsson C, *et al.* Pharmacokinetics and clinical effect during continuous epidural infusion with ropivacaine 2.5 mg/ml or bupivacaine 2.5 mg/ml for labour pain relief. *Acta Anaesthesiologica Scandinavica* 1998;42(8):890–6.

254. Lee BB, Ngan Kee WD, Ng FF, *et al.* Epidural Infusions of Ropivacaine and Bupivacanie for Labor Analgesia: A Randomized, Double-Blind Study of Obstetric Outcome. *Anesthesia and Analgesia* 2004;98(4):1145–52.

255. McCrae AF, Jozwiak H, McClure JH. Comparison of ropivacaine and bupivacaine in extradural analgesia for the relief of pain in labour. *British Journal of Anaesthesia* 1995;74(3):261–5.

256. McCrae AF, Westerling P, McClure JH. Pharmacokinetic and clinical study of ropivacaine and bupivacaine in women receiving extradural analgesia in labour. *British Journal of Anaesthesia* 1997;79(5):558–62.

257. Meister GC, D'Angelo R, Owen M, *et al.* A comparison of epidural analgesia with 0.125% ropivacaine with fentanyl versus 0.125% bupivacaine with fentanyl during labor. *Anesthesia and Analgesia* 2000;90(3):632–7.

258. Merson N. A comparison of motor block between ropivacaine and bupivacaine for continuous labor epidural analgesia. *AANA Journal* 2001;69(1):54–8.

259. Muir HA, Writer D, Douglas J, *et al.* Double-blind comparison of epidural ropivacaine 0.25% and bupivacaine 0.25%, for the relief of childbirth pain. *Canadian Journal of Anaesthesia* 1997;44(6):599–604.

260. Owen MD, D'Angelo R, Gerancher JC, *et al.* 0.125% ropivacaine is similar to 0.125% bupivacaine for labor analgesia using patient-controlled epidural infusion. *Anesthesia and Analgesia* 1998;86(3):527–31.

261. Owen MD, Thomas JA, Smith T, *et al.* Ropivacaine 0.075% and Bupivacaine 0.075% with Fentanyl 2 mug/mL are equivalent for labor epidural analgesia. *Anesthesia and Analgesia* 2002;94(1):179–83.

262. Parpaglioni R, Capogna G, Celleno D. A comparison between low-dose ropivacaine and bupivacaine at equianalgesic concentrations for epidural analgesia during the first stage of labor. *International Journal of Obstetric Anesthesia* 2000;9(2):83–6.

263. Pirbudak L, Tuncer S, Kocoglu H, *et al.* Fentanyl added to bupivacaine 0.05% or ropivacaine 0.05% in patient-controlled epidural analgesia in labour. *European Journal of Anaesthesiology* 2002;19(4):271–5.

264. Shah MK, Sia ATH, Chong JL. The effect of the addition of ropivacaine or bupivacaine upon pruritus induced by intrathecal fentanyl in labour. *Anaesthesia* 2000;55(10):1003–13.

265. Stienstra R, Jonker TA, Bourdrez P, *et al.* Ropivacaine 0.25% versus bupivacaine 0.25% for continuous epidural analgesia in labor: A double-blind comparison. *Anesthesia and Analgesia* 1995;80(2):285–9.

266. Bolukbasi D, Sener EB, Sarihasan B, *et al.* Comparison of maternal and neonatal outcomes with epidural bupivacaine plus fentanyl and ropivacaine plus fentanyl for labor analgesia. *International Journal of Obstetric Anesthesia* 2005;14(4):288–93.

267. Beilin Y, Nair A, Arnold I, *et al.* A comparison of epidural infusions in the combined spina epidural technique for labor analgesia. *Anesthesia and Analgesia* 2002;94(4):927–32.

268. Benhamou D, Hamza J, Eledjam J-J, *et al.* Continuous extradural infusion of ropivacaine 2 mg ml-1 for pain relief during labour. *British Journal of Anaesthesia* 1997;78(6):748–50.

269. Bernard JM, Le RD, Frouin J. Ropivacaine and fentanyl concentrations in patient-controlled epidural analgesia during labor: a volume-range study. *Anesthesia and Analgesia* 2003;97(6):1800–7.

270. Cascio MG, Gaiser RR, Camann WR, *et al.* Comparative evaluation of four different infusion rates of ropivacaine (2 mg/mL) for epidural labor analgesia. *Regional Anesthesia and Pain Medicine* 1998;23(6):548–53.

271. Ewen A, McLeod DD, MacLeod DM. Continuous infusion epidural analgesia in obstetrics. A comparison of 0.08% and 0.25% bupivacaine. *Anaesthesia* 1986;41(2):143–7.

272. Li DF, Rees GA, Rosen M. Continuous extradural infusion of 0.0625% or 0.125% bupivacaine for pain relief in primigravid labour. *British Journal of Anaesthesia* 1985;57(3):264–70.

273. Noble HA, Enever GR, Thomas TA. Epidural bupivacaine dilution for labour. A comparison of three concentrations infused with a fixed dose of fentanyl. *Anaesthesia* 1991;46(7):549–52.

274. Stoddart AP, Nicholson KEA, Popham PA. Low dose bupivacaine/fentanyl epidural infusions in labour and mode of delivery. *Anaesthesia* 1994;49(12):1087–90.

275. Thorburn J, Moir DD. Extradural analgesia: The influence of volume and concentration of bupivacaine on the mode of delivery, analgesic efficacy and motor block. *British Journal of Anaesthesia* 1981;53(9):933–9.

276. Sia AT, Ruban P, Chong JL, *et al.* Motor blockade is reduced with ropivacaine 0.125% for parturient-controlled epidural analgesia during labour. *Canadian Journal of Anaesthesia* 1999;46(11):1019–23.

277. Kilpatrick SJ, Laros RK. Characteristics of normal labor. *Obstetrics and Gynecology* 1989;74(1):85–7.

278. Chelmow D, Kilpatrick SJ, Laros RK, Jr. Maternal and neonatal outcomes after prolonged latent phase. *Obstetrics and Gynecology* 1993;81(4):486–91.

279. Friedman EA. The graphic analysis of labor. *American Journal of Obstetrics and Gynecology* 1954;68(6):1568–75.

280. Gross MM, Drobnic S, Keirse MJN. Influence of fixed and time-dependent factors on duration of normal first stage labor. *Birth* 2005;32(1):27–33.

281. Chamberlain G, Steer P. *Turnbull's Obstetrics.* 3rd ed. London: Harcourt; 2001.

282. Albers LL, Schiff M, Gorwoda JG. The length of active labor in normal pregnancies. *Obstetrics and Gynecology* 1996;87(3):355–9.

283. Albers LL. The duration of labor in healthy women. *Journal of Perinatology* 1999;19(2):114–19.

284. Zhang J, Troendle JF, Yancey MK. Reassessing the labor curve in nulliparous women. *American Journal of Obstetrics and Gynecology* 2002;187(4):824–8.

285. World Health Organization and Department of Reproductive Health. *Care in Normal Birth: a practical guide. Report of a technical working group.* Geneva: World Health Organization; 1999.

286. Lederman RP, Lederman E, Work BA Jr. *et al.* The relationship of maternal anxiety, plasma catecholamines, and plasma cortisol to progress in labor. *American Journal of Obstetrics and Gynecology* 1978;132(5):495–500.

287. Sharma V, Smith A, Khan M. The relationship between duration of labour, time of delivery, and puerperal psychosis. *Journal of Affective Disorders* 2004;83(2–3):215–20.

288. Mahon TR, Chazotte C, Cohen WR. Short labor: characteristics and outcome. *Obstetrics and Gynecology* 1994;84(1):47–51.

289. Abitbol MM, Castillo I, Udom-Rice I, *et al.* Maternal complications following prolonged or arrested labor. *Journal of Maternal-Fetal Investigation* 1994;4(1):9–13.

290. Lavender T, Hart A, Walkinshaw S, *et al.* Progress of first stage of labour for multiparous women: an observational study. *BJOG: an international journal of obstetrics & gynaecology* 2005;112(12):1663–5.

291. Maul H, Maner WL, Olson G, *et al.* Non-invasive transabdominal uterine electromyography correlates with the strength of intrauterine pressure and is predictive of labor and delivery. *Journal of Maternal-Fetal and Neonatal Medicine* 2004;15(5):297–301.

292. Blix E, Reiner LM, Klovning A, *et al.* Prognostic value of the labour admission test and its effectiveness compared with auscultation only: a systematic review. *BJOG: an international journal of obstetrics & gynaecology* 2005;112(12):1595–604.

293. McNiven PS, Wiliams JI, Hodnett E, *et al.* An early labour assessment program: a randomised controlled trial. *Birth* 1998;25(1):5–10.

294. Holmes P, Oppenheimer LW, Wen SW. The relationship between cervical dilatation at initial presentation in labour and subsequent intervention. *BJOG: an international journal of obstetrics & gynaecology* 2001;108(11):1120–4.

295. Klein MC, Kelly A, Kaczorowski J, *et al.* The effect of family physician timing of maternal admission on procedures in labour and maternal and infant morbidity. *Journal of Obstetrics and Gynaecology Canada* 2004;26(7):641–5.

296. Bailit JL, Dierker L, Blanchard MH, *et al.* Outcomes of women presenting in active versus latent phase of spontaneous labor. *Obstetrics and Gynecology* 2005;105(1):77–9.

297. Janssen PA, Iker CE, Carty EA. Early labour assessment and support at home: a randomized controlled trial. *Journal of Obstetrics and Gynaecology Canada* 2003;25(9):734–41.

298. Abukhalil IH, Kilby MD, Aiken J, *et al.* Can the frequency of vaginal examinations influence the duration of labour? A prospective randomised study. *Journal of Obstetrics and Gynaecology* 1996;16(1):22–5.

299. Ahlden S, Andersch B, Stigsson L, *et al.* Prediction of sepsis neonatorum following a full-term pregnancy. *Gynecologic and Obstetric Investigation* 1988;25(3):181–5.

300. Seaward PG, Hannah ME, Myhr TL, *et al.* International multicenter term PROM study: evaluation of predictors of neonatal infection in infants born to patients with premature rupture of membranes at term. Premature Rupture of the Membranes. *American Journal of Obstetrics and Gynecology* 1998;179(3 Pt 1):635–9.

301. Anonymous. World Health Organization partograph in management of labour. World Health Organization Maternal Health and Safe Motherhood Programme. *Lancet* 1994;343(8910):1399–404.

302. Lavender T, Alfirevic Z, Walkinshaw S. Partogram action line study: a randomised trial. *BJOG: an international journal of obstetrics & gynaecology* 1998;105(9):976–80.

303. Pattinson RC, Howarth GR, Mdluli W, *et al.* Aggressive or expectant management of labour: a randomised clinical trial. *BJOG: an international journal of obstetrics & gynaecology* 2003;110(5):457–61.

304. Price DD, Harkins SW, Baker C. Sensory-affective relationships among different types of clinical and experimental pain. *Pain* 1987;28(3):297–307.

305. Bonnel AM, Boureau F. Labor pain assessment: Validity of a behavioral index. *Pain* 1985;22(1):81–90.

306. Brown ST, Campbell D, Kurtz A. Characteristics of labor pain at two stages of cervical dilation. *Pain* 1989;38(3):289–95.

307. Gross MM, Hecker H, Keirse MJ. An evaluation of pain and "fitness" during labor and its acceptability to women. *Birth* 2005;32(2):122–8.

308. Beilin Y, Hossain S, Bodian CA. The numeric rating scale and labor epidural analgesia. *Anesthesia and Analgesia* 2003;96(6):1794–8.

309. Sittner B, Hudson DB, Grossman CC, *et al.* Adolescents' perceptions of pain during labor. *Clinical Nursing Research* 1998;7(1):82–93.

310. Revill SI, Robinson JO, Rosen M, *et al.* The reliability of a linear analogue for evaluating pain. *Anaesthesia* 1976;31(9):1191–8.

311. Wuitchik M, Bakal D, Lipshitz J. The clinical significance of pain and cognitive activity in latent labor. *Obstetrics and Gynecology* 1989;73(1):35–42.

312. Baker A, Ferguson SA, Roach GD, *et al.* Perceptions of labour pain by mothers and their attending midwives. *Journal of Advanced Nursing* 2001;35(2):171–9.

313. Lowe NK, Roberts JE. The convergence between in-labor report and postpartum recall of parturition pain. [Erratum appears in *Res Nurs Health* 1988;11(3):following 209]. *Research in Nursing and Health* 1988;11(1):11–21.

314. Niven C, Gijsbers K. A study of labour pain using the McGill Pain Questionnaire. *Social Science and Medicine* 1984;19(12):1347–51.

315. Sheiner EK, Sheiner E, Shoham-Vardi I, *et al.* Ethnic differences influence care giver's estimates of pain during labour. *Pain* 1999;81(3):299–305.

316. Frigoletto FD, Jr., Lieberman E, Lang JM, *et al.* A clinical trial of active management of labor. *New England Journal of Medicine* 1995;333(12):745–50.

317. Rogers R, Gilson GJ, Miller AC, *et al.* Active management of labor: Does it make a difference? *American Journal of Obstetrics and Gynecology* 1997;177(3):599–605.

318. Sadler LC, Davison T, McCowan LM. A randomised controlled trial and meta-analysis of active management of labour. *BJOG: an international journal of obstetrics & gynaecology* 2000;107(7):909–15.

319. Tabowei TO, Oboro VO. Active management of labour in a district hospital setting. *Journal of Obstetrics and Gynaecology* 2003;23(1):9–12.

320. Lavender T, Alfirevic Z, Walkinshaw S. Effect of different partogram action lines on birth outcomes: A randomized controlled trial. *Obstetrics and Gynecology* 2006;108(2):295–302.

321. Cammu H, Van Eeckhout E. A randomised controlled trial of early versus delayed use of amniotomy and oxytocin infusion in nulliparous labour. *BJOG: an international journal of obstetrics & gynaecology* 1996;103(4):313–18.

322. Lopez-Zeno JA, Peaceman AM, Adashek JA, et al. A controlled trial of a program for the active management of labor. *New England Journal of Medicine* 1992;326(7):450–4.

323. Cohen GR, O'Brien WF, Lewis L, et al. A prospective randomized study of the aggressive management of early labor. *American Journal of Obstetrics and Gynecology* 1987;157(5):1174–7.

324. Alfirevic Z, Devane D, Gyte G. Continuous cardiotocography (CTG) monitoring for fetal assessment during labour. (Cochrane Review). In: *Cochrane Database of Systematic Reviews*, 2005. Oxford: Update Software.

325. Mahomed K, Nyoni R, Mulambo T, et al. Randomised controlled trial of intrapartum fetal heart rate monitoring. *British Medical Journal* 1994;308(6927):497–500.

326. Cheng YW, Hopkins LM, Caughey AB. How long is too long: does a prolonged second stage of labor in nulliparous women affect maternal and neonatal outcomes? *American Journal of Obstetrics and Gynecology* 2004;191(3):933–8.

327. Myles TD, Santolaya J. Maternal and neonatal outcomes in patients with a prolonged second stage of labor. *Obstetrics and Gynecology* 2003;102(1):52–8.

328. Janni W, Schiessl B, Peschers U, et al. The prognostic impact of a prolonged second stage of labor on maternal and fetal outcome. *Acta Obstetricia et Gynecologica Scandinavica* 2002;81(3):214–21.

329. Kuo YC, Chen CP, Wang KG. Factors influencing the prolonged second stage and the effects on perinatal and maternal outcomes. *Journal of Obstetrics and Gynaecology Research* 1996;22(3):253–7.

330. van Kessel K, Reed S, Newton K, et al. The second stage of labor and stress urinary incontinence. *American Journal of Obstetrics and Gynecology* 2001;184(7):1571–5.

331. Menticoglou SM, Manning F, Harman C, et al. Perinatal outcome in relation to second-stage duration. *American Journal of Obstetrics and Gynecology* 1995;173(3 Part 1):906–12.

332. Saunders NS, Paterson CM, Wadsworth J. Neonatal and maternal morbidity in relation to the length of the second stage of labour. *BJOG: an international journal of obstetrics & gynaecology* 1992;99(5):381–5.

333. Paterson CM, Saunders NS, Wadsworth J. The characteristics of the second stage of labour in 25,069 singleton deliveries in the North West Thames Health Region, 1988. *BJOG: an international journal of obstetrics & gynaecology* 1992;99(5):377–80.

334. Moon JM, Smith CV, Rayburn WF. Perinatal outcome after a prolonged second stage of labor. *Journal of Reproductive Medicine* 1990;35(3):229–31.

335. Cohen WR. Influence of the duration of second stage labor on perinatal outcome and puerperal morbidity. *Obstetrics and Gynecology* 1977;49(3):266–9.

336. Gupta JK, Hofmeyr GJ. Position in the second stage of labour for women without epidural anaesthesia. (Cochrane Review). In: *Cochrane Database of Systematic Reviews*, 2005. Oxford: Update Software.

337. Albers LL, Anderson D, Cragin L, et al. Factors related to perineal trauma in childbirth. *Journal of Nurse-Midwifery* 1996;41(4):269–76.

338. Stremler R, Hodnett E, Petryshen P, et al. Randomized controlled trial of hands-and-knees positioning for occipitoposterior position in labor. *Birth* 2005;32(4):243–51.

339. Ragnar I, Altman D, Tyden T, et al. Comparison of the maternal experience and duration of labour in two upright delivery positions – A randomised controlled trial. *BJOG: an international journal of obstetrics & gynaecology* 2006;113(2):165–70.

340. Bloom SL, Casey BM, Schaffer JI, et al. A randomized trial of coached versus uncoached maternal pushing during the second stage of labor. *American Journal of Obstetrics and Gynecology* 2006;194(1):10–13.

341. Schaffer JI, Bloom SL, Casey BM, et al. A randomized trial of the effects of coached vs uncoached maternal pushing during the second stage of labor on postpartum pelvic floor structure and function. *American Journal of Obstetrics and Gynecology* 2005;192(5):1692–6.

342. Parnell C, Langhoff-Roos J, Iversen R, et al. Pushing method in the expulsive phase of labor. A randomized trial. *Acta Obstetricia et Gynecologica Scandinavica* 1993;72(1):31–5.

343. Thomson AM. Pushing techniques in the second stage of labour. *Journal of Advanced Nursing* 1993;18(2):171–7.

344. Knauth DG, Haloburdo EP. Effect of pushing techniques in birthing chair on length of second stage of labor. *Nursing Research* 1986;35(1):49–51.

345. Stamp G, Kruzins G, Crowther C. Perineal massage in labour and prevention of perineal trauma: randomised controlled trial. *British Medical Journal* 2001;322(7297):1277–80.

346. McCandlish R, Bowler U, van Asten H, et al. A randomised controlled trial of care of the perineum during second stage of normal labour. *BJOG: an international journal of obstetrics & gynaecology* 1998;105(12):1262–72.

347. Mayerhofer K, Bodner-Adler B, Bodner K, et al. Traditional care of the perineum during birth. A prospective, randomized, multicenter study of 1,076 women. *Journal of Reproductive Medicine* 2002;47(6):477–82.

348. Albers LL, Sedler KD, Bedrick EJ, et al. Midwifery care measures in the second stage of labor and reduction of genital tract trauma at birth: A randomized trial. *Journal of Midwifery and Women's Health* 2005;50(5):365–72.

349. Sanders J, Peters TJ, Campbell R. Does lidocaine spray reduce perineal pain during spontaneous vaginal delivery? A randomised controlled trial. *Current Controlled Trials* 2006 [www.controlled-trials.com/isrctn/trial/ISRCTN99732966/0/99732966.html].

350. Carroli G, Belizan J. Episiotomy for vaginal birth. (Cochrane Review). In: *Cochrane Database of Systematic Reviews*, Issue 3, 1998. Oxford: Update Software.

351. Hartmann K, Viswanathan M, Palmieri R, et al. Outcomes of routine episiotomy: a systematic review. *JAMA: the Journal of the American Medical Association* 2005;293(17):2141–8.

352. Dannecker C, Hillemanns P, Strauss A, et al. Episiotomy and perineal tears presumed to be imminent: randomized controlled trial. *Acta Obstetricia et Gynecologica Scandinavica* 2004;83(4):364–8.

353. Andrews V, Sultan AH, Thakar R, et al. Risk factors for obstetric anal sphincter injury: a prospective study. *Birth* 2006;33(2):117–22.

354. Dandolu V, Gaughan JP, Chatwani AJ, et al. Risk of recurrence of anal sphincter lacerations. *Obstetrics and Gynecology* 2005;105(4):831–5.

355. Harkin R, Fitzpatrick M, O'Connell PR, et al. Anal sphincter disruption at vaginal delivery: Is recurrence predictable? *European Journal of Obstetrics, Gynecology and Reproductive Biology* 2003;109(2):149–52.

356. Sangalli MR, Floris L, Faltin D, et al. Anal incontinence in women with third or fourth degree perineal tears and subsequent vaginal deliveries. *Australian and New Zealand Journal of Obstetrics and Gynaecology* 2000;40(3):244–8.

357. Woodward J, Kelly SM. A pilot study for a randomised controlled trial of waterbirth versus land birth. *BJOG: an international journal of obstetrics & gynaecology* 2004;111(6):537–45.

358. Magann EF, Evans S, Chauhan SP, et al. The length of the third stage of labor and the risk of postpartum hemorrhage. *Obstetrics and Gynecology* 2005;105(2):290–3.

359. Combs CA, Laros Jr RK. Prolonged third stage of labor: Morbidity and risk factors. *Obstetrics and Gynecology* 1991;77(6):863–7.

360. Prendiville WJ, Elbourne D, McDonald S. Active versus expectant management in the third stage of labour. (Cochrane Review). In: *Cochrane Database of Systematic Reviews*, Issue 2, 2005. Oxford: Update Software.

361. Van RP, Brabin BJ. Late umbilical cord-clamping as an intervention for reducing iron deficiency anaemia in term infants in developing and industrialised countries: a systematic review. *Annals of Tropical Paediatrics* 2004;24(1):3–16.

362. Ceriani Cernadas JM, Carroli G, Pellegrini L, et al. The effect of timing of cord clamping on neonatal venous hematocrit values and clinical outcome at term: a randomized, controlled trial. *Pediatrics* 2006;117(4):e779–86.

363. Chaparro CM, Neufeld LM, Tena AG, et al. Effect of timing of umbilical cord clamping on iron status in Mexican infants: a randomised controlled trial.[see comment]. *Lancet* 2006;367(9527):1997–2004.

364. Emhamed MO, Van RP, Brabin BJ. The early effects of delayed cord clamping in term infants born to Libyan mothers. *Tropical Doctor* 2004;34(4):218–22.

365. Linderkamp O, Nelle M, Kraus M, et al. The effect of early and late cord-clamping on blood viscosity and other morheological parameters in full-term neonates. *Acta Paediatrica* 1992;81(10):745–50.

366. Nelle M, Zilow EP, Kraus M, et al. The effect of Leboyer delivery on blood viscosity and other hemorheologic parameters in term neonates. *American Journal of Obstetrics and Gynecology* 1993;169(1):189–93.

367. Nelle M, Zilow EP, Bastert G, et al. Effect of Leboyer childbirth on cardiac output, cerebral and gastrointestinal blood flow velocities in full-term neonates. *American Journal of Perinatology* 1995;12(3):212–16.

368. Saigal S, O'Neill A, Surainder Y, et al. Placental transfusion and hyperbilirubinemia in the premature. *Pediatrics* 1972;49(3):406–19.

369. Geethanath RM, Ramji S, Thirupuram S, et al. Effect of timing of cord clamping on the iron status of infants at 3 months. *Indian Pediatrics* 1997;34(2):103–6.

370. Grajeda R, Perez-Escamilla R, Dewey KG. Delayed clamping of the umbilical cord improves hematologic status of Guatemalan infants at 2 mo of age. *American Journal of Clinical Nutrition* 1997;65(2):425–31.

371. Gupta R, Ramji S. Effect of delayed cord clamping on iron stores in infants born to anemic mothers: a randomized controlled trial. *Indian Pediatrics* 2002;39(2):130–5.

372. Lanzkowsky P. Effects of early and late clamping of umbilical cord on infant's haemoglobin level. *British Medical Journal* 1960;2:1777–82.

373. Elbourne DR, Prendiville WJ, Carroli G, Wood J, McDonald S. Prophylactic use of oxytocin in the third stage of labour. (Cochrane Review). In: *Cochrane Database of Systematic Reviews*, Issue 2, 2005. Oxford: Update Software.

374. McDonald S, Abbott JM, Higgins SP. Prophylactic ergometrine-oxytocin versus oxytocin for the third stage of labour. (Cochrane Review). In: *Cochrane Database of Systematic Reviews*, Issue 2, 2005. Oxford: Update Software.

375. Reddy VV, Carey JC. Effect of umbilical vein oxytocin on puerperal blood loss and length of the third stage of labor. *American Journal of Obstetrics and Gynecology* 1989;160(1):206–8.

376. Dahiya P, Puri M, Rathee S. Influence of intraumbilical oxytocin on the third stage of labour. *Indian Journal of Medical Sciences* 1995;49(2):23–7.

377. Porter KB, O'Brien WF, Collins MK, et al. A randomized comparison of umbilical vein and intravenous oxytocin during the puerperium. *Obstetrics and Gynecology* 1991;78(2):254–6.

378. Kovavisarach E, Rojsangruang S. Effect of umbilical vein oxytocin injection on the third stage of labor: A randomized controlled study. *Journal of the Medical Association of Thailand* 1998;81(9):693–7.

379. Ozcan T, Sahin G, Senoz S. The effect of intraumbilical oxytocin on the third stage of labour. *Australian and New Zealand Journal of Obstetrics and Gynaecology* 1996;36(1):9–11.

380. Young SB, Martelly PD, Greb L, et al. The effect of intraumbilical oxytocin on the third stage of labor. *Obstetrics and Gynecology* 1988;71(5):736–8.

381. Gulmezoglu AM, Forna F, Villar J, Hofmeyr GJ. Prostaglandins for prevention of postpartum haemorrhage. (Cochrane Review). In: *Cochrane Database of Systematic Reviews*, Issue 2, 2005. Oxford: Update Software.

382. Langenbach C. Misoprostol in preventing postpartum hemorrhage: A meta-analysis. *International Journal of Gynecology and Obstetrics* 2006;92(1):10–18.

383. Lam H, Tang OS, Lee CP, et al. A pilot-randomized comparison of sublingual misoprostol with syntometrine on the blood loss in third stage of labor. *Acta Obstetricia et Gynecologica Scandinavica* 2004;83(7):647–50.

384. Vimala N, Mittal S, Kumar S, et al. Sublingual misoprostol versus methylergometrine for active management of the third stage of labor. *International Journal of Gynaecology and Obstetrics* 2004;87(1):1–5.

385. Zachariah ES, Naidu M, Seshadri L. Oral misoprostol in the third stage of labor. *International Journal of Gynecology and Obstetrics* 2006;92(1):23–6.

386. Garg P, Batra S, Gandhi G. Oral misoprostol versus injectable methylergometrine in management of the third stage of labor. *International Journal of Gynaecology and Obstetrics* 2005;91(2):160–1.

387. Cock C-M, Spurrett B, Murray H. A randomized clinical trial comparing oral misoprostol with synthetic oxytocin or syntometrine in the third stage of labour. *Australian and New Zealand Journal of Obstetrics and Gynaecology* 1999;39(4):414–19.

388. Amant F, Spitz B, Timmerman D, et al. Misoprostol compared with methylergometrine for the prevention of postpartum haemorrhage: a double-blind randomised trial. *BJOG: an international journal of obstetrics & gynaecology* 1999;106(10):1066–70.

389. Karkanis SG, Caloia D, Salenieks ME, et al. Randomized controlled trial of rectal misoprostol versus oxytocin in third stage management. *Journal of Obstetrics and Gynaecology Canada* 2002;24(2):149–54.

390. Abdel-Aleem H, bol-Oyoun EM, Moustafa SA, et al. Carboprost trometamol in the management of the third stage of labor. *International Journal of Gynecology and Obstetrics* 1993;42(3):247–50.

391. Walley RL, Wilson JB, Crane JM, et al. A double-blind placebo controlled randomised trial of misoprostol and oxytocin in the management of the third stage of labour. BJOG: an international journal of obstetrics & gynaecology 2000;107(9):1111–15.

392. Poeschmann RP, Doesburg WH, Eskes TKAB. A randomized comparison of oxytocin, sulprostone and placebo in the management of the third stage of labour. BJOG: an international journal of obstetrics & gynaecology 1991;98(6):528–30.

393. Van Selm M, Kanhai HH, Keirse MJ. Preventing the recurrence of atonic postpartum hemorrhage: a double-blind trial. Acta Obstetricia et Gynecologica Scandinavica 1995;74(4):270–4.

394. Ng PS, Chan AS, Sin WK, et al. A multicentre randomized controlled trial of oral misoprostol and i.m. syntometrine in the management of the third stage of labour. Human Reproduction 2001;16(1):31–5.

395. Bhattacharya P, Devi PK, Jain S, et al. Prophylactic use of 15(S)15 methyl PGF(2alpha) by intramuscular route for control of postpartum bleeding – A comparative trial with methylergometrine. Acta Obstetricia et Gynecologica Scandinavica – Supplement 1988;67(145):13–15.

396. Bugalho A, Daniel A, Faundes A, et al. Misoprostol for prevention of postpartum hemorrhage. International Journal of Gynaecology and Obstetrics 2001;73(1):1–6.

397. Oboro VO, Tabowei TO. A randomised controlled trial of misoprostol versus oxytocin in the active management of the third stage of labour. Journal of Obstetrics and Gynaecology 2003;23(1):13–16.

398. Chua S, Chew SL, Yeoh CL, et al. A randomized controlled study of prostaglandin 15-methyl F2 alpha compared with syntometrine for prophylactic use in the third stage of labour. Australian and New Zealand Journal of Obstetrics and Gynaecology 1995;35(4):413–16.

399. Bamigboye AA, Merrell DA, Hofmeyr GJ, et al. Randomized comparison of rectal misoprostol with Syntometrine for management of third stage of labor. Acta Obstetricia et Gynecologica Scandinavica 1998;77(2):178–81.

400. Hofmeyr GJ, Nikodem VC, de Jager M, et al. A randomised placebo controlled trial of oral misoprostol in the third stage of labour. BJOG: an international journal of obstetrics & gynaecology 1998;105(9):971–5.

401. Bamigboye AA, Hofmeyr GJ, Merrell DA. Rectal misoprostol in the prevention of postpartum hemorrhage: a placebo-controlled trial. American Journal of Obstetrics and Gynecology 1998;179(4):1043–6.

402. Hofmeyr GJ, Nikodem VC, de JM, et al. Side-effects of oral misoprostol in the third stage of labour – A randomised placebo-controlled trial. South African Medical Journal 2001;91(5):432–5.

403. Surbek DV, Fehr PM, Hosli I, et al. Oral misoprostol for third stage of labor: A randomized placebo- controlled trial. Obstetrics and Gynecology 1999;94(2):255–8.

404. Caliskan E, Meydanli MM, Dilbaz B, et al. Is rectal misoprostol really effective in the treatment of third stage of labor? A randomized controlled trial. American Journal of Obstetrics and Gynecology 2002;187(4):1038–45.

405. Caliskan E, Dilbaz B, Meydanli MM, et al. Oral misoprostol for the third stage of labor: A randomized controlled trial. Obstetrics and Gynecology 2003;101(5):921–8.

406. El-Refaey H, Nooh R, O'Brien P, et al. The misoprostol third stage of labour study: a randomised controlled comparison between orally administered misoprostol and standard management. BJOG: an international journal of obstetrics & gynaecology 2000;107(9):1104–10.

407. Khan RU, El-Refaey H. Pharmacokinetics and adverse-effect profile of rectally administered misoprostol in the third stage of labor. Obstetrics and Gynecology 2003;101(5 Pt 1):968–74.

408. Gerstenfeld TS, Wing DA. Rectal misoprostol versus intravenous oxytocin for the prevention of postpartum hemorrhage after vaginal delivery. American Journal of Obstetrics and Gynecology 2001;185(4):878–82.

409. Lumbiganon P, Hofmeyr J, Gulmezoglu AM, et al. Misoprostol dose-related shivering and pyrexia in the third stage of labour. WHO Collaborative Trial of Misoprostol in the Management of the Third Stage of Labour. BJOG: an international journal of obstetrics & gynaecology 1999;106(4):304–8.

410. Gulmezoglu AM, Villar J, Ngoc NT, et al. WHO multicentre randomised trial of misoprostol in the management of the third stage of labour. Lancet 2001;358(9283):689–95.

411. Lumbiganon P, Villar J, Piaggio G, et al. Side effects of oral misoprostol during the first 24 hours after administration in the third stage of labour. BJOG: an international journal of obstetrics & gynaecology 2002;109(11):1222–6.

412. Kundodyiwa TW, Majoko F, Rusakaniko S. Misoprostol versus oxytocin in the third stage of labor. International Journal of Gynaecology and Obstetrics 2001;75:235–41.

413. Chestnut DH, Wilcox LL. Influence of umbilical vein administration of oxytocin on the third stage of labor: A randomized, double-blind, placebo-controlled study. American Journal of Obstetrics and Gynecology 1987;157(1):160–2.

414. National Collaborating Centre for Primary Care. Postnatal Care: Routine Postnatal Care of Women and Their Babies. London,: National Institute for Health and Clinical Excellence; 2006.

415. Apgar V. Proposal for new method of evaluation of newborn infant. Anesthesia and Analgesia 1953;32:260–7.

416. Apgar V. Evaluation of the newborn infant – second report. JAMA: the Journal of the American Medical Association 1958;168(15):1985–8.

417. Apgar V, James LS. Further observation on the newborn scoring system. American Journal of Diseases of Children 1962;104:419–28.

418. van de Riet JE, Vandenbussche FP, Le Cessie S, et al. Newborn assessment and long-term adverse outcome: a systematic review. American Journal of Obstetrics and Gynecology 1999;180(4):1024–9.

419. Chong DS, Karlberg J. Refining the Apgar score cut-off point for newborns at risk. Acta Paediatrica 2004;93(1):53–9.

420. Gaffney G, Sellers S, Flavell V, et al. Case-control study of intrapartum care, cerebral palsy, and perinatal death. British Medical Journal 1994;308(6931):743–50.

421. Moster D, Lie RT, Markestad T. Joint association of Apgar scores and early neonatal symptoms with minor disabilities at school age. Archives of Disease in Childhood Fetal and Neonatal Edition 2002;86(1):F16–21.

422. Moster D, Lie RT, Irgens LM, et al. The association of Apgar score with subsequent death and cerebral palsy: A population-based study in term infants. Journal of Pediatrics 2001;138(6):798–803.

423. Casey BM, McIntire DD, Leveno KJ. The continuing value of the Apgar score for the assessment of newborn infants. New England Journal of Medicine 2001;344(7):467–71.

424. Dyson L, McCormick F, Renfrew MJ. Interventions for promoting the initiation of breastfeeding. (Cochrane Review). In: Cochrane Database of Systematic Reviews, Issue 2, 2005. Oxford: Update Software.

425. Royal College of Obstetricians and Gynaecologists. *Peritoneal closure*. Green Top Guideline No. 15. London: RCOG Press; 1998. p. 1–6

426. Andrews V, Thakar R, Sultan AH, *et al*. Clinical issues. Can hands-on perineal repair courses affect clinical practice? *British Journal of Midwifery* 2005;13(9):562–6.

427. Andrews V, Sultan AH, Thakar R, *et al*. Occult anal sphincter injuries—myth or reality? *BJOG: an international journal of obstetrics & gynaecology* 2006;113(2):195–200.

428. Groom KM, Paterson-Brown S. Can we improve on the diagnosis of third degree tears? *European Journal of Obstetrics, Gynecology and Reproductive Biology* 2002;101(1):19–21.

429. Fleming VE, Hagen S, Niven C. Does perineal suturing make a difference? The SUNS trial. *BJOG: an international journal of obstetrics & gynaecology* 2003;110(7):684–9.

430. Salmon D. A feminist analysis of women's experiences of perineal trauma in the immediate post-delivery period. *Midwifery* 1999;15(4):247–56.

431. Kettle C, Johanson RB. Continuous versus interrupted sutures for perineal repair. (Cochrane Review). In: *Cochrane Database of Systematic Reviews*, Issue 1, 2006. Oxford: Update Software.

432. Kettle C, Hills RK, Jones P, *et al*. Continuous versus interrupted perineal repair with standard or rapidly absorbed sutures after spontaneous vaginal birth: a randomised controlled trial. *Lancet* 2002;359(9325):2217–23.

433. Gordon B, Mackrodt C, Fern E, *et al*. The Ipswich Childbirth Study: 1. A randomised evaluation of two stage postpartum perineal repair leaving the skin unsutured. *BJOG: an international journal of obstetrics & gynaecology* 1998;105:435–40.

434. Grant A, Gordon B, Mackrodat C, *et al*. The Ipswich childbirth study: one year follow up of alternative methods used in perineal repair. *BJOG: an international journal of obstetrics & gynaecology* 2001;108(1):34–40.

435. Oboro VO, Tabowei TO, Loto OM, *et al*. A multicentre evaluation of the two-layered repair of postpartum perineal trauma. *Journal of Obstetrics and Gynaecology* 2003;23(1):5–8.

436. Kettle C, Johanson RB. Absorbable synthetic versus catgut suture material for perineal repair. (Cochrane Review). In: *Cochrane Database of Systematic Reviews*, Issue 1, 2006. Oxford: Update Software.

437. Upton A, Roberts CL, Ryan M, *et al*. A randomised trial, conducted by midwives, of perineal repairs comparing a polyglycolic suture material and chromic catgut. *Midwifery* 2002;18(3):223–9.

438. Greenberg JA, Lieberman E, Cohen AP, *et al*. Randomized comparison of chromic versus fast-absorbing polyglactin 910 for postpartum perineal repair. *Obstetrics and Gynecology* 2004;103(6):1308–13.

439. Hedayati H, Parsons J, Crowther CA. Rectal analgesia for pain from perineal trauma following childbirth. (Cochrane Review). In: *Cochrane Database of Systematic Reviews*, Issue 3, 2003. Oxford: Update Software.

440. Dodd JM, Hedayati H, Pearce E, *et al*. Rectal analgesia for the relief of perineal pain after childbirth: a randomised controlled trial of diclofenac suppositories. *BJOG: an international journal of obstetrics & gynaecology* 2004;111(10):1059–64.

441. Royal College of Obstetricians and Gynaecologists: Clinical Effectiveness Support Unit. *Induction of Labour*. No.9. London: RCOG Press; 2001.

442. Dare MR, Middleton P, Crowther CA, Flenady V, Varatharaju B. Planned early birth versus expectant management (waiting) for prelabour rupture of membranes at term (37 weeks or more). (Cochrane Review). In: *Cochrane Database of Systematic Reviews*, Issue 1, 2006. Oxford: Update Software.

443. Hannah ME, Hodnett ED, Willan A, *et al*. Prelabor rupture of the membranes at term: expectant management at home or in hospital? The TermPROM Study Group. *Obstetrics and Gynecology* 2000;96(4):533–8.

444. Jomeen J, Martin CR. The impact of clinical management type on maternal and neo-natal outcome following pre-labour rupture of membranes at term. *Clinical Effectiveness in Nursing* 2002;6(1):3–9.

445. Hagskog K, Nisell H, Sarman I, *et al*. Conservative ambulatory management of prelabor rupture of the membranes at term in nulliparous women. *Acta Obstetricia et Gynecologica Scandinavica* 1994;73(10):765–9.

446. Seaward PG, Hannah ME, Myhr TL, *et al*. International Multicentre Term Prelabor Rupture of Membranes Study: evaluation of predictors of clinical chorioamnionitis and postpartum fever in patients with prelabor rupture of membranes at term. *American Journal of Obstetrics and Gynecology* 1997;177(5):1024–9.

447. Apuzzio JJ, Fenmore B, Ganesh V. Conservative versus aggressive management of premature rupture of membranes at term with an unfavorable cervix. *International Journal of Feto-Maternal Medicine* 1990;3(4):205–8.

448. Ezra Y, Michaelson-Cohen R, Abramov Y, *et al*. Prelabor rupture of the membranes at term: When to induce labor? *European Journal of Obstetrics, Gynecology and Reproductive Biology* 2004;115(1):23–7.

449. Eriksson M, Ladfors L, Mattsson LA, *et al*. Warm tub bath during labor. A study of 1385 women with prelabor rupture of the membranes after 34 weeks of gestation. *Acta Obstetricia et Gynecologica Scandinavica* 1996;75(7):642–4.

450. Flenady V, King J. Antibiotics for prelabour rupture of membranes at or near term. (Cochrane Review). In: *Cochrane Database of Systematic Reviews*, Issue 3, 2002. Oxford: Update Software.

451. Bramer S, Heidy van WF, Mol BWJ, *et al*. Risk indicators for neonatal early-onset GBS-related disease. A case-control study. *Journal of Perinatal Medicine* 1997;25(6):469–75.

452. Schuchat A, aver-Robinson K, Plikaytis BD, *et al*. Multistate case-control study of maternal risk factors for neonatal Group B streptococcal disease. *Pediatric Infectious Disease Journal* 1994;13(7):623–9.

453. Heath PT, Balfour G, Weisner AM, *et al*. Group B streptococcal disease in UK, Irish infants younger than 90 days. *Lancet* 2004;363(9405):292–4.

454. Andersen J, Christensen R, Hertel J. Clinical features and epidemiology of septicaemia and meningitis in neonates due to Streptococcus agalactiae in Copenhagen county, Denmark: A 10 year survey from 1992 to 2001. *Acta Paediatrica* 2004;93(10):1334–9.

455. Oddie S, Embleton ND. Risk factors for early onset neonatal group B streptococcal sepsis: case-control study. *British Medical Journal* 2002;325(7359):308–12.

456. Marlowe SE, Greenwald J, Anwar M, *et al*. Prolonged rupture of membranes in the term newborn. *American Journal of Perinatology* 1997;14(8):483–6.

457. Lin FY, Brenner RA, Johnson YR, *et al*. The effectiveness of risk-based intrapartum chemoprophylaxis for the prevention of early-onset neonatal group B streptococcal disease. *American Journal of Obstetrics and Gynecology* 2001;184(6):1204–10.

458. Escobar GJ, Li DK, Armstrong MA, *et al*. Neonatal sepsis workups in infants >/=2000 grams at birth: A population-based study. *Pediatrics* 2000;106(2 Pt 1):256–63.

459. Ungerer RLS, Lincetto O, McGuire W, Saloojee H, Gulmezoglu AM. Prophylactic versus selective antibiotics for term newborn infants of mothers with risk factors for neonatal infection. (Cochrane Review). In: *Cochrane Database of Systematic Reviews*, Issue 1, 2006. Oxford: Update Software.

460. Royal College of Obstetricians and Gynaecologists. *The Use of Electronic Fetal Monitoring: The Use and Interpretation of Cardiotocography in Intrapartum Fetal Monitoring*. No 8. London: RCOG Press; 2001.

461. Morad Y, Kaplan B, Zangen S, et al. Management of meconium-stained neonates. *Journal of Obstetrics and Gynaecology* 1998;18(3):223–6.

462. van Heijst ML, van RG, Keirse MJ. Classifying meconium-stained liquor: is it feasible? *Birth* 1995;22(4):191–5.

463. Trimmer KJ, Gilstrap LC, III. "Meconiumcrit" and birth asphyxia. *American Journal of Obstetrics and Gynecology* 1991;165(4 Pt 1):1010–13.

464. Steer PJ, Eigbe F, Lissauer TJ, et al. Interrelationships among abnormal cardiotocograms in labor, meconium staining of the amniotic fluid, arterial cord blood pH, Apgar scores. *Obstetrics and Gynecology* 1989;74(5):715–21.

465. Meis PJ, Hobel CJ, Ureda JR. Late meconium passage in labor--a sign of fetal distress? *Obstetrics and Gynecology* 1982;59(3):332–5.

466. Baker PN, Kilby MD, Murray H. An assessment of the use of meconium alone as an indication for fetal blood sampling. *Obstetrics and Gynecology* 1992;80(5):792–6.

467. Alchalabi HA, Abu-Heija AT, El-Sunna E, et al. Meconium-stained amniotic fluid in term pregnancies – A clinical view. *Journal of Obstetrics and Gynaecology* 1999;19(3):262–4.

468. Ziadeh SM, Sunna E. Obstetric and perinatal outcome of pregnancies with term labour and meconium-stained amniotic fluid. *Archives of Gynecology and Obstetrics* 2000;264(2):84–7.

469. Wong SF, Chow KM, Ho LC. The relative risk of 'fetal distress' in pregnancy associated with meconium-stained liquor at different gestation. *Journal of Obstetrics and Gynaecology* 2002;22(6):594–9.

470. Hofmeyr GJ. Amnioinfusion for meconium-stained liquor in labour. (Cochrane Review). In: *Cochrane Database of Systematic Reviews*, Issue 2, 2005. Oxford: Update Software.

471. Fraser WD, Hofmeyr J, Lede R, et al. Amnioinfusion for the prevention of the meconium aspiration syndrome. *New England Journal of Medicine* 2005;353(9):909–17.

472. Puertas A, Paz CM, Molto L, et al. Meconium-stained amniotic fluid in labor: a randomized trial of prophylactic amniofusion. *European Journal of Obstetrics, Gynecology and Reproductive Biology* 2001;99(1):33–7.

473. Puertas A, Carrillo MP, clvarez M, et al. Meconium concentration and amniotic fluid index influence the outcome of amnioinfusion. *Minerva Ginecologica* 2001;53(5):321–30.

474. Rathore AM, Singh R, Ramji S, et al. Randomised trial of amnioinfusion during labour with meconium stained amniotic fluid. *BJOG: an international journal of obstetrics & gynaecology* 2002;109(1):17–20.

475. Edwards RK, Duff P. Prophylactic cefazolin in amnioinfusions administered for meconium-stained amniotic fluid. *Infectious Diseases in Obstetrics and Gynecology* 1999;7(3):153–7.

476. Gonzalez JL, Mooney S, Gardner MO, et al. The effects of amnioinfused solutions for meconium-stained amniotic fluid on neonatal plasma electrolyte concentrations and pH. *Journal of Perinatology* 2002;22(4):279–81.

477. Glantz JC, Letteney DL. Pumps and warmers during amnioinfusion: is either necessary? *Obstetrics and Gynecology* 1996;87(1):150–5.

478. Centre for Reviews and Dissemination. Pumps and warmers during amnioinfusion: is either necessary? (Structured abstract). (Cochrane Review). In: *Database of Abstracts of Reviews of Effects*, 2005. Oxford: Update Software.

479. Halliday HL, Sweet D. Endotracheal intubation at birth for preventing morbidity and mortality in vigorous, meconium-stained infants born at term. (Cochrane Review). In: *Cochrane Database of Systematic Reviews*, 2005. Oxford: Update Software.

480. Vain NE, Szyld EG, Prudent LM, et al. Oropharyngeal and nasopharyngeal suctioning of meconium-stained neonates before delivery of their shoulders: multicentre, randomised controlled trial. *Lancet* 2004;364(9434):597–602.

481. Hansen PK, Smith SF, Nim J, et al. Maternal attitudes to fetal monitoring. *European Journal of Obstetrics, Gynecology and Reproductive Biology* 1985;20(1):43–51.

482. Garcia J, Corry M, MacDonald D, et al. Mothers' views of continuous electronic fetal heart monitoring and intermittent auscultation in a randomized controlled trial. *Birth* 1985;12(2):79–86.

483. Neilson JP. Fetal electrocardiogram (ECG) for fetal monitoring during labour. (Cochrane Review). In: *Cochrane Database of Systematic Reviews*, Issue 4, 2005. Oxford: Update Software.

484. Ojala K, Vaarasmaki M, Makikallio K, et al. A comparison of intrapartum automated fetal electrocardiography and conventional cardiotocography – a randomised controlled study. *BJOG: an international journal of obstetrics & gynaecology* 2006;113(4):419–23.

485. Westgate J, Harris M, Curnow JS, et al. Plymouth randomized trial of cardiotocogram only versus ST waveform plus cardiotocogram for intrapartum monitoring in 2400 cases. *American Journal of Obstetrics and Gynecology* 1993;169(5):1151–60.

486. Westgate J, Harris M, Curnow JS, et al. Randomised trial of cardiotocography alone or with ST waveform analysis for intrapartum monitoring. *Lancet* 1992;340(8813):194–8.

487. Amer-Wahlin I, Hellsten C, Noren H, et al. Cardiotocography only versus cardiotocography plus ST analysis of fetal electrocardiogram for intrapartum fetal monitoring: a Swedish randomised controlled trial. *Lancet* 2001;358(9281):534–8.

488. Ross MG, Devoe LD, Rosen KG. ST-segment analysis of the fetal electrocardiogram improves fetal heart rate tracing interpretation and clinical decision making. *Journal of Maternal-Fetal and Neonatal Medicine* 2004;15(3):181–5.

489. Luzietti R, Erkkola R, Hasbargen U, et al. European Community Multi-Center Trial 'Fetal ECG Analysis During Labor': ST plus CTG analysis. *Journal of Perinatal Medicine* 1999;27(6):431–40.

490. Noren H, mer-Wahlin I, Hagberg H, et al. Fetal electrocardiography in labor and neonatal outcome: data from the Swedish randomized controlled trial on intrapartum fetal monitoring. *American Journal of Obstetrics and Gynecology* 2003;188(1):183–92.

491. Amer-Wahlin I, Ingemarsson I, Marsal K, et al. Fetal heart rate patterns and ECG ST segment changes preceding metabolic acidaemia at birth. *BJOG: an international journal of obstetrics & gynaecology* 2005;112(2):160–5.

492. Strachan BK, van Wijngaarden WJ, Sahota D, et al. Cardiotocography only versus cardiotocography plus PR-interval analysis in intrapartum surveillance: a randomised, multicentre trial. *Lancet* 2000;355(9202):456–9.

493. Luzietti R, Erkkola R, Hasbargen U, *et al.* European Community Multicentre Trial "Fetal ECG Analysis During Labour": the P-R interval. *Journal of Perinatal Medicine* 1997;25(1):27–34.

494. Skupski DW, Rosenberg CR, Eglinton GS. Intrapartum fetal stimulation tests: a meta-analysis. *Obstetrics and Gynecology* 2002;99(1):129–34.

495. Keith RD, Beckley S, Garibaldi JM, *et al.* A multicentre comparative study of 17 experts and an intelligent computer system for managing labour using the cardiotocogram. *BJOG: an international journal of obstetrics & gynaecology* 1995;102(9):688–700.

496. Taylor GM, Mires GJ, Abel EW, *et al.* The development and validation of an algorithm for real-time computerised fetal heart rate monitoring in labour. *BJOG: an international journal of obstetrics & gynaecology* 2000;107(9):1130–7.

497. Todros T, Preve CU, Plazzotta C, *et al.* Fetal heart rate tracings: observers versus computer assessment. *European Journal of Obstetrics, Gynecology and Reproductive Biology* 1996;68(1–2):83–6.

498. Chung TK, Mohajer MP, Yang ZJ, *et al.* The prediction of fetal acidosis at birth by computerised analysis of intrapartum cardiotocography. *BJOG: an international journal of obstetrics & gynaecology* 1995;102(6):454–60.

499. Nielsen PV, Stigsby B, Nickelsen C, *et al.* Computer assessment of the intrapartum cardiotocogram. II. The value of computer assessment compared with visual assessment. *Acta Obstetricia et Gynecologica Scandinavica* 1988;67(5):461–4.

500. Mongelli M, Dawkins R, Chung T, *et al.* Computerised estimation of the baseline fetal heart rate in labour: the low frequency line. *BJOG: an international journal of obstetrics & gynaecology* 1997;104(10):1128–33.

501. Bowen LW, Kochenour NK, Rehm NE, *et al.* Maternal-fetal pH difference and fetal scalp pH as predictors of neonatal outcome. *Obstetrics and Gynecology* 1986;67(4):487–95.

502. Murphy KW, MacDonald D. Fetal blood sampling in Dublin. A year's review. *Journal of Obstetrics and Gynaecology* 1990;10(3):194–8.

503. Suidan JS, Young BK. Outcome of fetuses with lactic acidemia. *American Journal of Obstetrics and Gynecology* 1984;150(1):33–7.

504. Young DC, Gray JH, Luther ER, *et al.* Fetal scalp blood pH sampling: its value in an active obstetric unit. *American Journal of Obstetrics and Gynecology* 1980;136(3):276–81.

505. Weber T. Continuous fetal pH monitoring and neonatal Apgar score. *Journal of Perinatal Medicine* 1980;8(3):158–63.

506. Ayromlooi J, Tobias M, Berg P. Correlation of ominous fetal heart rate pattern and scalp blood pH with one-minute Apgar score. *International Journal of Gynaecology and Obstetrics* 1979;17(2):185–9.

507. Wood C. Diagnostic and therapeutic implications of intrapartum fetal pH measurement. *Acta Obstetricia et Gynecologica Scandinavica* 1978;57(1):13–18.

508. Coltart TM, Trickey NR, Beard RW. Foetal blood sampling. Practical approach to management of foetal distress. *British Medical Journal* 1969;1(640):342–6.

509. McDonald JS. Evaluation of fetal blood pH as a reflection of fetal well-being. *American Journal of Obstetrics and Gynecology* 1967;97(7):912–18.

510. Weber T. The validity of discontinuous pH-measurements on fetal blood and of cardiotocography in predicting neonatal Apgar score. *Danish Medical Bulletin* 1979;26(4):186–91.

511. Hon EH, Khazin AF, Paul RH. Biochemical studies of the fetus. II. Fetal pH and apgar scores. *Obstetrics and Gynecology* 1969;33(2):237–55.

512. Beard RW, Morris ED, Clayton SG. pH of foetal capillary blood as an indicator of the condition of the foetus. *Journal of Obstetrics and Gynaecology of the British Commonwealth* 1967;74(6):812–22.

513. Galloway RK. Clinical experience with fetal blood pH measurement in fetal distress. *Journal of Obstetrics and Gynaecology of the British Commonwealth* 1970;77(7):587–90.

514. De La Rama FE Jr, Merkatz IR. Evaluation of fetal scalp pH with a proposed new clinical assessment of the neonate. *American Journal of Obstetrics and Gynecology* 1970;107(1):93–9.

515. Tejani N, Mann LI, Bhakthavathsalan A. Correlation of fetal heart rate patterns and fetal pH with neonatal outcome. *Obstetrics and Gynecology* 1976;48(4):460–3.

516. Khazin AF, Hon EH, Quilligan EJ. Biochemical studies of the fetus. III. Fetal base and Apgar scores. *Obstetrics and Gynecology* 1969;34(4):592–609.

517. Khazin AF, Hon EH. Biochemical studies of the fetus. IV. Fetal-maternal pH and base deficit difference versus Apgar scores. *Biology of the Neonate* 1971;18(3):225–42.

518. Weber T. Cardiotocography supplemented with continuous fetal pH monitoring during labor. Effect on rate of obstetrical interventions and neonatal condition. *Acta Obstetricia et Gynecologica Scandinavica* 1982;61(4):351–5.

519. Luttkus AK, Noren H, Stupin JH, *et al.* Fetal scalp pH and ST analysis of the fetal ECG as an adjunct to CTG. A multi-center, observational study. *Journal of Perinatal Medicine* 2004;32(6):486–94.

520. Westgren M, Kruger K, Ek S, *et al.* Lactate compared with pH analysis at fetal scalp blood sampling: a prospective randomised study. *BJOG: an international journal of obstetrics & gynaecology* 1998;105(1):29–33.

521. Tuffnell D, Haw W. How long does a fetal scalp blood sample take? *BJOG: an international journal of obstetrics & gynaecology* 2006;113:1–3.

522. Cardoso CG, Graca LM, Clode N. A study on second-stage cardiotocographic patterns and umbilical blood acid-base balance in cases with first-stage normal fetal heart rates. *Journal of Maternal-Fetal Investigation* 1995;5(3):144–7.

523. Okunwobi-Smith Y, Cooke I, MacKenzie IZ. Decision to delivery intervals for assisted vaginal vertex delivery. *BJOG: an international journal of obstetrics & gynaecology* 2000;107:467–71.

524. Eldridge A, Johnson N. How long does it take to perform an operative vaginal delivery? *Journal of Obstetrics and Gynaecology* 2004;24(3):230–2.

525. Tuffnell DJ, Wilkinson K, Beresford N. Interval between decision and delivery by caesarean section-are current standards achievable? Observational case series. *British Medical Journal* 2001;322(7298):1330–3.

526. MacKenzie IZ, Cooke I. Prospective 12 month study of 30 minute decision to delivery intervals for "emergency" caesarean section. *British Medical Journal* 2001;322(7298):1334–5.

527. Thomas J, Paranjothy S, Royal College of Obstetricians and Gynaecologists: Clinical Effectiveness Support Unit. *The National Sentinel Caesarean Section Audit Report.* London: RCOG Press; 2001.

528. Holcroft CJ, Graham EM, ina-Mumuney A, *et al*. Cord gas analysis, decision-to-delivery interval, and the 30-minute rule for emergency cesareans. *Journal of Perinatology* 2005;25(4):229–35.

529. Yudkin PL, Johnson A, Clover LM, *et al*. Clustering of perinatal markers of birth asphyxia and outcome at age five years. *BJOG: an international journal of obstetrics & gynaecology* 1994;101(9):774–81.

530. Valentin L, Ekman G, Isberg P-E, *et al*. Clinical evaluation of the fetus and neonate: Relation between intra-partum cardiotocography, Apgar score, cord blood acid-base status and neonatal morbidity. *Archives of Gynecology and Obstetrics* 1993;253(2):103–15.

531. Melone PJ, Ernest JM, O'Shea MD, Jr, *et al*. Appropriateness of intrapartum fetal heart rate management and risk of cerebral palsy. *American Journal of Obstetrics and Gynecology* 1991;165(2):272–6.

532. Gilstrap LC, III, Leveno KJ, Burris J, *et al*. Diagnosis of birth asphyxia on the basis of fetal pH, Apgar score, and newborn cerebral dysfunction. *American Journal of Obstetrics and Gynecology* 1989;161(3):825–30.

533. Thorp JA, Sampson JE, Parisi VM, *et al*. Routine umbilical cord blood gas determinations? *American Journal of Obstetrics and Gynecology* 1989;161(3):600–5.

534. Ruth VJ, Raivio KO. Perinatal brain damage: predictive value of metabolic acidosis and the Apgar score. *British Medical Journal* 1988;297(6640):24–7.

535. Page FO, Martin JN, Palmer SM, *et al*. Correlation of neonatal acid-base status with Apgar scores and fetal heart rate tracings. *American Journal of Obstetrics and Gynecology* 1986;154(6):1306–11.

536. Sykes GS, Molloy PM, Johnson P, *et al*. Do Apgar scores indicate asphyxia? *Lancet* 1982;1(8270):494–6.

537. Fraser WD, Turcot L, Krauss I, Brisson-Carrol G. Amniotomy for shortening spontaneous labour. (Cochrane Review). In: *Cochrane Database of Systematic Reviews*, Issue 2, 2005. Oxford: Update Software.

538. Rouse DJ, McCullough C, Wren AL, *et al*. Active-phase labor arrest: a randomized trial of chorioamnion management. *Obstetrics and Gynecology* 1994;83(6):937–40.

539. Cardozo L, Pearce JM. Oxytocin in active-phase abnormalities of labor: a randomized study. *Obstetrics and Gynecology* 1990;75(2):152–7.

540. Bidgood KA, Steer PJ. A randomized control study of oxytocin augmentation of labour. 1. Obstetric outcome. *BJOG: an international journal of obstetrics & gynaecology* 1987;94(6):512–17.

541. Blanch G, Lavender T, Walkinshaw S, *et al*. Dysfunctional labour: A randomised trial. *BJOG: an international journal of obstetrics & gynaecology* 1998;105(1):117–20.

542. Merrill DC, Zlatnik FJ. Randomized, double-masked comparison of oxytocin dosage in induction and augmentation of labor. [see comments]. *Obstetrics and Gynecology* 1999;94(3):455–63.

543. Xenakis EM, Langer O, Piper JM, *et al*. Low-dose versus high-dose oxytocin augmentation of labor--a randomized trial. *American Journal of Obstetrics and Gynecology* 1995;173(6):1874–8.

544. Jamal A, Kalantari R. High and low dose oxytocin in augmentation of labor. *International Journal of Gynaecology and Obstetrics* 2004;87(1):6–8.

545. Majoko F. Effectiveness and safety of high dose oxytocin for augmentation of labour in nulliparous women. [Erratum appears in *Cent Afr J Med* 2002;48(5–6):74]. *Central African Journal of Medicine* 2001;47(11–12):247–50.

546. Satin AJ, Leveno KJ, Sherman L, *et al*. High-dose oxytocin: 20- versus 40-minute dosage interval. *Obstetrics and Gynecology* 1994;83(2):234–8.

547. Lazor LZ, Philipson EH, Ingardia CJ, *et al*. A randomized comparison of 15- and 40-minute dosing protocols for labor augmentation and induction. *Obstetrics and Gynecology* 1993;82(6):1009–12.

548. Cummiskey KC, Gall SA, Yusoff DM. Pulsatile administration of oxytocin for augmentation of labor. *Obstetrics and Gynecology* 1989;74(6):869–72.

549. Arulkumaran S, Yang M, Ingemarsson PS, *et al*. Augmentation of labour: does oxytocin titration to achieve preset active contraction area values produce better obstetric outcome? *Asia-Oceania Journal of Obstetrics and Gynaecology* 1989;15(4):333–7.

550. Johanson RB, Menon V. Vacuum extraction versus forceps for assisted vaginal delivery. (Cochrane Review). In: *Cochrane Database of Systematic Reviews*, Issue 2, 2000. Oxford: Update Software.

551. Weerasekera DS, Premaratne S. A randomised prospective trial of the obstetric forceps versus vacuum extraction using defined criteria. *Journal of Obstetrics and Gynaecology* 2002;22(4):344–5.

552. Mustafa R, Mustafa R. Perinatal and maternal outcome in ventouse versus forceps delivery. *Journal of the College of Physicians and Surgeons Pakistan* 2002;12(6):345–8.

553. Fitzpatrick M, Behan M, O'Connell PR, *et al*. Randomised clinical trial to assess anal sphincter function following forceps or vacuum assisted vaginal delivery. *BJOG: an international journal of obstetrics & gynaecology* 2003;110(4):424–9.

554. Johanson RB, Heycock E, Carter J, *et al*. Maternal and child health after assisted vaginal delivery: Five-year follow up of a randomised controlled study comparing forceps and ventouse. *BJOG: an international journal of obstetrics & gynaecology* 1999;106(6):544–9.

555. Sultan AH, Johanson RB, Carter JE. Occult anal sphincter trauma following randomized forceps and vacuum delivery. *International Journal of Gynaecology and Obstetrics* 1998;61(2):113–19.

556. Johanson R, Pusey J, Livera N, *et al*. North Staffordshire/Wigan assisted delivery trial. *BJOG: an international journal of obstetrics & gynaecology* 1989;96(5):537–44.

557. Carmody F, Grant A, Mutch L. Follow up of babies delivered in a randomized controlled comparison of vacuum extraction and forceps delivery. *Acta Obstetricia et Gynecologica Scandinavica* 1986;65(7):763–6.

558. Pusey J, Hodge C, Wilkinson P, *et al*. Maternal impressions of forceps or the Silc-cup. *BJOG: an international journal of obstetrics & gynaecology* 1991;98(5):487–8.

559. Garcia J, Anderson J, Vacca A. Views of women and their medical and midwifery attendants about instrumental delivery using vacuum extraction and forceps. *Journal of Psychosomatic Obstetrics and Gynecology* 1985;4(1):1–9.

560. Johanson RB, Rice C, Doyle M, *et al*. A randomised prospective study comparing the new vacuum extractor policy with forceps delivery. *BJOG: an international journal of obstetrics & gynaecology* 1993;100(6):524–30.

561. Johanson R, Menon V. Soft versus rigid vacuum extractor cups for assisted vaginal delivery. (Cochrane Review). In: *Cochrane Database of Systematic Reviews*, Issue 2, 2000. Oxford: Update Software.

562. Murphy DJ, Liebling RE, Verity L, *et al*. Early maternal and neonatal morbidity associated with operative delivery in second stage of labour: a cohort study. *Lancet* 2001;358(9289):1203–7.

563. Tan A, Schulze A, O'Donnell CPF, Davis PG. Air versus oxygen for resuscitation of infants at birth. (Cochrane Review). In: *Cochrane Database of Systematic Reviews*, Issue Oxford, 2005. Oxford: Update Software.

564. Bajaj N, Udani RH, Nanavati RN. Room air vs. 100 per cent oxygen for neonatal resuscitation: a controlled clinical trial. *Journal of Tropical Pediatrics* 2005;51(4):206–11.

565. Bullarbo M, Tjugum J, Ekerhovd E. Sublingual nitroglycerin for management of retained placenta. *International Journal of Gynecology and Obstetrics* 2005;91(3):228–32.

566. Carroli G, Bergel E. Umbilical vein injection for management of retained placenta. (Cochrane Review). In: *Cochrane Database of Systematic Reviews*, 2006. Oxford: Update Software.

567. Sivalingam N, Surinder S. Is there a place for intra-umbilical oxytocin for the management of retained placenta? *Medical Journal of Malaysia* 2001;56(4):451–9.

568. Mousa HA, Alfirevic Z. Treatment for primary postpartum haemorrhage. (Cochrane Review). In: *Cochrane Database of Systematic Reviews*, 2006. Oxford: Update Software.

569. Clark SL, Phelan JP, Yeh SY, et al. Hypogastric artery ligation for obstetric hemorrhage. *Obstetrics and Gynecology* 1985;66(3):353–6.

570. Chattopadhyay SK, Deb RB, Edrees YB. Surgical control of obstetric hemorrhage: Hypogastric artery ligation or hysterectomy? *International Journal of Gynecology and Obstetrics* 1990;32(4):345–51.

571. Gilbert L, Porter W, Brown VA. Postpartum haemorrhage--a continuing problem. *BJOG: an international journal of obstetrics & gynaecology* 1987;94(1):67–71.

572. Henry A, Birch M-R, Sullivan EA, et al. Primary postpartum haemorrhage in an Australian tertiary hospital: A case-control study. *Australian and New Zealand Journal of Obstetrics and Gynaecology* 2005;45(3):233–6.

573. Bais JMJ, Eskes M, Pel M, et al. Postpartum haemorrhage in nulliparous women: incidence and risk factors in low and high risk women. A Dutch population-based cohort study on standard (> or = 500 ml) and severe (> or = 1000 ml) postpartum haemorrhage. *European Journal of Obstetrics, Gynecology and Reproductive Biology* 2004;115(2):166–72.

574. Chichakli LO, Atrash HK, MacKay AP, et al. Pregnancy-related mortality in the United States due to hemorrhage: 1979–1992. *Obstetrics and Gynecology* 1999;94(5):721–5.

575. Hall MH, Halliwell R, Carr-Hill R. Concomitant and repeated happenings of complications of the third stage of labour. *BJOG: an international journal of obstetrics & gynaecology* 1985;92(7):732–8.

576. Magann EF, Evans S, Hutchinson M, et al. Postpartum hemorrhage after vaginal birth: An analysis of risk factors. *Southern Medical Journal* 2005;98(4):419–22.

577. Stones RW, Paterson CM, Saunders NJ. Risk factors for major obstetric haemorrhage. *European Journal of Obstetrics, Gynecology and Reproductive Biology* 1993;48(1):15–18.

578. Dewar MJ. Antenatal anaemia and postpartum haemorrhage. *Australian and New Zealand Journal of Obstetrics and Gynaecology* 1969;9(1):18–20.

579. Ogueh O, Morin L, Usher RH, et al. Obstetric implications of low-lying placentas diagnosed in the second trimester. *International Journal of Gynaecology and Obstetrics* 2003;83(1):11–17.

580. Guirgis RR, Clark AD, Hogston P, et al. The effects of smoking on labour after uncomplicated pregnancy: A comparison between the progress and outcome of labour in 400 smokers and 400 matched non-smokers. *Journal of Obstetrics and Gynaecology* 1997;17(2):149–52.

581. Sebire NJ, Jolly M, Harris JP, et al. Maternal obesity and pregnancy outcome: A study of 287 213 pregnancies in London. *International Journal of Obesity* 2001;25(8):1175–82.

582. Usha Kiran TS, Hemmadi S, Bethel J, et al. Outcome of pregnancy in a woman with an increased body mass index. *BJOG: an international journal of obstetrics & gynaecology* 2005;112(6):768–72.

583. Robinson HE, O'Connell CM, Joseph KS, et al. Maternal outcomes in pregnancies complicated by obesity. *Obstetrics and Gynecology* 2005;106(6):1357–64.

584. Sebire NJ, Jolly M, Harris J, et al. Is maternal underweight really a risk factor for adverse pregnancy outcome? A population-based study in London. *BJOG: an international journal of obstetrics & gynaecology* 2001;108(1):61–6.

585. Olesen AW, Westergaard JG, Olsen J. Perinatal and maternal complications related to postterm delivery: a national register-based study, 1978–1993. *American Journal of Obstetrics and Gynecology* 2003;189(1):222–7.

586. Jolly MC, Sebire NJ, Harris JP, et al. Risk factors for macrosomia and its clinical consequences: A study of 350,311 pregnancies. *European Journal of Obstetrics, Gynecology and Reproductive Biology* 2003;111(1):9–14.

587. McEwan HP, Murdoch R. The oversized baby. A study of 169 cases. *Journal of Obstetrics and Gynaecology of the British Commonwealth* 1966;73(5):734–41.

588. Stotland NE, Caughey AB, Breed EM, et al. Risk factors and obstetric complications associated with macrosomia. [Erratum appears in *Int J Gynaecol Obstet* 2005;90(1):88]. *International Journal of Gynaecology and Obstetrics* 2004;87(3):220–6.

589. Wollschlaeger K, Nieder J, Koppe I, et al. A study of fetal macrosomia. *Archives of Gynecology and Obstetrics* 1999;263(1–2):51–5.

590. Jolly M, Sebire N, Harris J, et al. The risks associated with pregnancy in women aged 35 years or older. *Human Reproduction* 2000;15(11):2433–7.

591. Ohkuchi A, Onagawa T, Usui R, et al. Effect of maternal age on blood loss during parturition: a retrospective multivariate analysis of 10,053 cases. *Journal of Perinatal Medicine* 2003;31(3):209–15.

592. Babinszki A, Kerenyi T, Torok O, et al. Perinatal outcome in grand and great-grand multiparity: effects of parity on obstetric risk factors. *American Journal of Obstetrics and Gynecology* 1999;181(3):669–74.

593. Bugg GJ, Atwal GS, Maresh M. Grandmultiparae in a modern setting. *BJOG: an international journal of obstetrics & gynaecology* 2002;109(3):249–53.

594. Chang A, Larkin P, Esler EJ, et al. The obstetric performance of the grand multipara. *Medical Journal of Australia* 1977;1(10):330–2.

595. Henson GL, Knott PD, Colley NV. The dangerous multipara: Fact or fiction? *Journal of Obstetrics and Gynaecology* 1987;8(2):130–4.

596. Humphrey MD. Is grand multiparity an independent predictor of pregnancy risk? A retrospective observational study. *Medical Journal of Australia* 2003;179(6):294–6.

597. Irvine LM, Otigbah C, Crawford A, *et al.* Grand multiparity – An obstetric problem in Great Britain in the 90s? *Journal of Obstetrics and Gynaecology* 1996;16(4):217–23.

598. Toohey JS, Keegan Jr KA, Morgan MA, *et al.* The 'dangerous multipara': Fact or fiction? *American Journal of Obstetrics and Gynecology* 1995;172(2 I):683–6.

599. Yasmeen S, Danielsen B, Moshesh M, *et al.* Is grandmultiparity an independent risk factor for adverse perinatal outcomes? *Journal of Maternal-Fetal and Neonatal Medicine* 2005;17(4):277–80.

600. Hey EN, Lloyd DJ, Wigglesworth JS. Classifying perinatal death: fetal and neonatal factors. *BJOG: an international journal of obstetrics & gynaecology* 1986;93(12):1213–23.

601. Walker DS, Koniak-Griffin D. Evaluation of a reduced-frequency prenatal visit schedule for low-risk women at a free-standing birthing center. *Journal of Nurse-Midwifery* 1997;42(4):295–303.

602. Eakins PS. The rise of the free standing birth center: principles and practice. *Women and Health* 1984;9(4):49–64.

603. Rooks JP, Ernst EK. Outcomes of care in Birth Centers. *Birth* 1990;17(4):234.

604. Holz K, Cooney C, Marchese T. Outcomes of mature primiparas in an out-of-hospital birth center. *Journal of Nurse-Midwifery* 1989;34(4):185–9.

605. Moster D, Lie RT, Markestad T. Neonatal mortality rates in communities with small maternity units compared with those having larger maternity units. *BJOG: an international journal of obstetrics & gynaecology* 2001;108(9):904–9.

606. Moster D, Lie RT, Markestad T. Relation between size of delivery unit and neonatal death in low risk deliveries: population based study. *Archives of Disease in Childhood Fetal and Neonatal Edition* 1999;80(3):F221–25.

607. Confidential Enquiry into Maternal and Child Health (CEMACH). *All Wales Perinatal Survey & Confidential Enquiry into Stillbirths and Deaths in Infancy:* Summary of 2002 Annual Report. Cardiff: All Wales Perinatal Survey; 2004.

608. Confidential Enquiry into Stillbirths and Deaths in Infancy (CESDI). *The Confidential Enquiry Into Stillbirths and Deaths in Infancy (CESDI) : 4th Annual Report 1 January – 31 December 1995: Concentrating on Intrapartum Related Deaths 1994–95.* CESDI; 1997.

609. Office for National Statistics. *Birth Statistics: Review of the Registrar General on Births and Patterns of Family Building in England and Wales, 2000.* No. 29. London: Office for National Statistics; 2001.

610. Office for National Statistics. *Birth Statistics: Review of the Registrar General on Births and Patterns of Family Building in England and Wales, 2002.* No. 31. London: Office for National Statistics; 2004.

611. Office for National Statistics. *Birth Statistics: Review of the Registrar General on Births and Patterns of Family Building in England and Wales, 2003.* No. 32. London: 2004.

612. National Statistics. *Mortality Statistics.* Office for National Statistics [online] 2000.

613. National Statistics. *Mortality Statistics.* Office for National Statistics [online] 2001.

614. National Statistics. *Mortality Statistics.* Office for National Statistics [online] 2002.

615. National Statistics. *Mortality Statistics.* Office for National Statistics [online] 2003.

616. National Statistics. *Mortality Statistics.* Office for National Statistics [online] 2004.

617. National Statistics. *Mortality Statistics.* Office for National Statistics [online] 2005.

618. Fergusson DM, Horwood LJ, Shannon FT. Early solid feeding and recurrent childhood eczema: a 10-year longitudinal study. *Pediatrics* 1990;86(4):541–6.

619. Northern Regional Health Authority. *Collaborative Survey of Perinatal, Late Neonatal and Infant Death in the Northern Region, 1990.* Newcastle upon Tyne: Northern Regional Health Authority; 1991.

620. Curtis L, Netten A. *Unit Costs of Health & Social Care 2005.* Canterbury: Personal Social Services Research Unit (PSSRU), University of Kent; 2005.

621. Ratcliffe J. The economic implications of the Edgware birth centre. In: Kirkham M, ed. *Birth Centres: A Social Model for Maternity Care.* London: Books for Midwives; 2003.

622. Chuong CJ, Lee CY, Chuong MC, *et al.* Does 24-hour supervisory staff coverage in the labour and delivery area change the emergency caesarean section rate? *BJOG: an international journal of obstetrics & gynaecology* 1986;93(9):938–42.

623. Meydanli MM, Dilbaz B, Caliskan E, *et al.* Risk factors for meconium aspiration syndrome in infants born through thick meconium. *International Journal of Gynecology and Obstetrics* 2001;72(1):9–15.

624. Adair CD, Ernest JM, Sanchez-Ramos L, *et al.* Meconium-stained amniotic fluid-associated infectious morbidity: a randomized, double-blind trial of ampicillin-sulbactam prophylaxis. *Obstetrics and Gynecology* 1996;88(2):216–20.

625. Department of Health. *Maternity Matters: Choice, Access and Continuity of Care in a Safe Service.* No.278867. London: Department of Health; 2007.

626. Campbell R, Macfarlane AJ, Hempsall V, Hatchard K. Evaluation of midwife-led care provided at the Royal Bournemouth Hospital. *Midwifery* 1999;15(3):183–93.

627. Smith LFP, Smith CP. UK childbirth delivery options: alternatives to consultant unit booking and delivery. *British Journal of General Practice* 2005;55:292–97.

628, Mahomed K, Nyoni R, Masona D. Meconium staining of the liquor in a low risk population. *Paediatric and Perinatal Epidemiology* 1994;8(3):292–300.

Index